D1827763

Modern History of the City of London

Charles Welch F.S.A, Philip Norman F.S.A

BIBLIOLIFE

Copyright © BiblioLife, LLC

This book represents a historical reproduction of a work originally published before 1923 that is part of a unique project which provides opportunities for readers, educators and researchers by bringing hard-to-find original publications back into print at reasonable prices. Because this and other works are culturally important, we have made them available as part of our commitment to protecting, preserving and promoting the world's literature. These books are in the "public domain" and were digitized and made available in cooperation with libraries, archives, and open source initiatives around the world dedicated to this important mission.

We believe that when we undertake the difficult task of re-creating these works as attractive, readable and affordable books, we further the goal of sharing these works with a global audience, and preserving a vanishing wealth of human knowledge.

Many historical books were originally published in small fonts, which can make them very difficult to read. Accordingly, in order to improve the reading experience of these books, we have created "enlarged print" versions of our books. Because of font size variation in the original books, some of these may not technically qualify as "large print" books, as that term is generally defined; however, we believe these versions provide an overall improved reading experience for many.

MODERN HISTORY

OF THE

CITY OF LONDON

A RECORD OF MUNICIPAL AND SOCIAL PROGRESS

FROM 1760 TO THE PRESENT DAY

By CHARLES WELCH F.S.A.

LIBRARIAN TO THE CORPORATION OF LONDON

WITH ILLUSTRATIONS DRAWN AND SELECTED BY

PHILIP NORMAN F.S.A.

LONDON

BLADES EAST & BLADES 23 ABCHURCH LANE E.C.

1896

BLADES, EAST & BLADES,

Printers,

23, ABCHURCH LANE, LONDON, E.C.

government of the City is well shown in the contrast afforded by a picture of the City of London at the close of 1894 as compared with its condition at the beginning of George III's reign.

The story of the Corporation and its work extends to Deptford, the Thames mouth, West Ham, Epping Forest, Burnham Beeches, and many other places beyond the 'one square mile.' With this exception the work is strictly limited to the history of the City of London proper; to have attempted to include outer London would have necessitated at least another volume.

For the assistance of the reader the year is placed at the top of each page, and the mayoralty is indicated by the insertion of the name of the Lord Mayor for each year in the month of November, on the ninth day of which the newly-elected Chief Magistrate commences his year of office.

Every effort has been made to secure accuracy, but the author asks indulgence in this respect on account of the large number of facts recorded and of authorities consulted. For the earlier period, the chief sources of information were the "Gentleman's Magazine" and the "Annual Register." Official publications consulted include the printed minutes and reports of the Common Council and other public bodies, Corporation Addresses, and London's Roll of Fame. For the last forty years, the file of the *City Press* has been chiefly used. Among other valuable authorities the following have been largely consulted:—The "British Almanack and Companion," Timbs' "Curiosities of London," the "Corporation Pocket Book," various Histories of the Livery Companies, etc.

The best thanks of the author are due in the first place to his friend and coadjutor Mr. Philip Norman, F.S.A., whose admirable

List of Illustrations.

Modern History of the City of London.

1760.

KING George II died on 25 Oct., 1760, and a Privy Council immediately assembled at Carlton House to proclaim his successor. The new sovereign, George III, grandson of the late King and son of Frederick, Prince of Wales, who died in 1751, was proclaimed on the following day before Savile House, in Leicester Fields. The ceremony was attended by the great officers of State, the principal Peers, the Lord Mayor, Sheriffs, and Aldermen of the City of London, and other persons of distinction. In accordance with precedent the Lord Mayor, Sir Thomas Chitty, had also been present at the Privy Council. The proclamation was repeated, with the accustomed ceremonies, according to ancient usage, at Charing Cross, and, within the City, at Temple Bar, at the corner of Wood Street, Cheapside, and at the Royal Exchange. On the 28th the Lord Mayor and Aldermen waited on the King at Leicester House, and presented an address of congratulation and condolence, which was read by Sir William Moreton, the Recorder. The Court of Common Council also attended the King, on the 30th, with a similar address.—On the last day of Oct. the first stone of Blackfriars Bridge was laid by the Lord Mayor.—Lord Mayor's Day falling this year on a Sunday, Sir Matthew Blakiston, the Lord Mayor elect, was not sworn into office till the next day. On account of the recent death of the late King, who was not yet interred, the usual ceremonies were omitted, and the Lord Mayor went to Westminster Hall privately in his coach to be sworn.—On 17 Nov. the drawing of a lottery began at Guildhall, and

B

was finished on 13 Dec.—Two important trials took place during this year in the Court of King's Bench, Guildhall. The first was between the citizens of London, plaintiffs, and Edward Smith and Ralph Twyford, salesmen in Newgate Market, defendants. The second was that of the citizens of London against John Cope, salesman, for the sale of provisions in White Hart Street, a passage leading to Newgate. The City were successful in both suits, which were brought to determine their right to tolls, not only in the markets, but in the avenues or passages leading to them.—The number of the principal brewhouses in London this year was fifty-two, and the quantity of beer brewed by them was 975,217 barrels.—At the Dec. Sessions at the old Bailey, two of the convicted prisoners were sentenced to be burned in the hand, and in the following Ap. a prisoner, capitally convicted, was ordered to be hung in chains.

Old London Bridge, from a picture by S. Scott.

In 1757 an Act of Parliament was obtained for repairing London Bridge by taking down all the houses erected on it, removing the great middle pier, and throwing the two adjoining locks into one. To carry out these designs a temporary wooden bridge was constructed. This temporary erection was consumed in the following Ap. by a fire, which also damaged London Bridge, and retarded the progress of the alterations. Within a month, however, a new wooden structure was erected. The removal of the houses was slowly proceeded with. On 3 Feb., 1761, an advertisement announced the sale of six of them by auction at Guildhall, to be put up at £156; and their demolition was begun a week later.—An Act of Parliament empowered the City authorities to remove the gates and carry out other improvements. Under its provisions Cripplegate was sold in July, and Ludgate taken down in November.—Oliver Goldsmith resided from 1758 to 1760 at No. 12, Green Arbour Court, at the corner of Breakneck Steps, in Sea Cole Lane.—During this year 3,539 in-patients were discharged as cured from St. Bartholomew's hospital.

1761.

N 14 Jan., 1761, a carpenter named Blagden, who had purchased several of the City gates, obtained from the City Lands Committee a site, 1,000 feet in length, on the south side of Fore Street, from Moorgate and Cripplegate, at the rate of seven shillings per foot, on his giving £10,000 security to complete the buildings within four years.—On 10 Feb. a fire broke out at a sugar-baker's in Thames Street, which burned Fishmongers' Hall and an adjoining house, besides damaging several other buildings.—A motion made in the Court of Common Council, on 18 Feb., to present the freedom of the City to Sir John Phillips, Bart., and George Cook, Esquire, members for Middlesex, for their services in supporting the City's interests in Parliament, was carried by only a small majority, the proposal having been brought forward without previous notice. The Court resolved that similar motions should in future be made at a Court preceding that on which the question was to be considered.—The poll for the election of Members of Parliament for the City of London closed on 2 Ap., when Aldermen Sir Robert Ladbroke, Sir Richard Glyn, Bart., William Beckford, and the Hon. Thomas Harley were returned, the unsuccessful candidate being Alderman Sir Samuel Fludyer, Bart.—Most of the City offices were obtained by purchase, and on 22 Ap. a Coal Meter's place was sold for £4,430, and a month later the office of Remembrancer for £2,000. Many of these appointments were in the gift of the Lord Mayor, and the emoluments of his year of office depended largely upon the number of vacancies occurring during that period in the principal City offices.—Two more of the City gates were sold, Moorgate for £166, and Aldersgate for £91.—An amusing but alarming accident occurred at the Royal Exchange on 4 May, when a cow from Smithfield Market occasioned great commotion by charging at the south gate of the Exchange. In the panic which ensued many persons were knocked down and severely bruised, while others lost their wigs, hats, shoes, etc. After passing through Sweeting's Alley the cow was secured by a carman in Gracechurch Street. This incident led the Common Council to take action for regulating the driving of horned cattle through the crowded streets of the City.—On 5 May the honorary freedom of the City was granted to the Right Hon. Arthur Onslow, who had been Speaker cf the House of Commons for the past thirty-three years, and during five successive parliaments.—On the 17th the Lord Mayor, Aldermen and Common Council again approached the throne, and conveyed their congratulations upon the

conquest of Belleisle.—More than 300 prisoners from Ludgate, the two Compters, and the Fleet, were released by the Lord Mayor at Guildhall on 24 June under the Insolvent Debtors' Act.—City Road, described as "the finest about London, with a foot-path on each side, and well-lighted," was opened on the 29th from Islington to Old Street, the Doghouse Bar being at the same time demolished.—On 4 July died Samuel Richardson, the printer and novelist, in his house in Salisbury Court. He was buried in the adjoining Church of St. Bride's.—On the 16th the Lord Mayor, at the head of a small deputation of Aldermen and members of the Common Council, went in procession to Savile House, the residence of the Duke of York, accompanied by a committee of the Grocers' Company. The Grocers' Company, being first introduced, presented their Freedom in a gold box with a suitable address to his Royal Highness. Afterwards the Lord Mayor and Corporation tendered the Duke a similar address and the freedom of the City in a gold box which had been voted on 5 June. His Royal Highness made suitable acknowledgments to both.—To allow of the decoration of Ludgate on the approaching Lord Mayor's Day, the prisoners confined there were removed, on 12 Aug., to the London Workhouse in Bishopsgate Street.—The King's marriage with the Princess Charlotte of Mecklenburg-Strelitz was celebrated at the Chapel Royal on 8 Sept., and on the 14th the Corporation presented an address of congratulation to his Majesty upon the auspicious event. On this occasion the Common Council appeared in mazarine blue silk gowns, agreeable to an order of that Court made a short time previously. The King's coronation took place in Westminster Abbey on 22 Sept., and, in accordance with ancient custom, the Lord Mayor officiated as butler.—On 5 Oct. Mr. Pitt resigned office, and the Common Council awarded him their unanimous thanks for the many and important services rendered to his King and country. Much discontent was felt in the country, and particularly in the City, at the measures which led to his resignation, and the Court instructed the four City representatives in Parliament to endeavour to repeal or amend the late Act for the Relief of Insolvent Debtors; to promote economy in the distribution of the national treasure; to oppose all attempts for giving up such places as might tend to lessen the present security, restore the naval power of France, and expose the country to fresh hostilities; to preserve the country's sole and exclusive right to its acquisitions in North America and its fisheries; and, lastly, to concur in prosecuting the war with the utmost vigour so as to obtain a safe and honourable peace.—The punishment of the pillory, which exposed the culprit to the attacks of an exasperated mob, sometimes led to fatal results. A young woollen-draper of Cornhill, who suffered this penalty on 16 Oct. was only rescued from the violence of the mob by the attendance of an unusually large number of peace officers. In returning to Newgate the coach in which he was conveyed was upset, and the officers were compelled to lodge the prisoner in the Compter till the mob dispersed.—Alderman Samuel Fludyer was elected Lord Mayor.—On Lord Mayor's day, (9 Nov.), the King and Queen, according to custom on the accession of a new sovereign, honoured the Lord Mayor, Sir Samuel Fludyer, by their presence at the Guildhall banquet. Their Majesties were attended by the other members of the Royal Family, and, among the distinguished personages who followed in the procession, Mr. Pitt received a remarkable popular ovation. At every pause of the procession the people hung about his carriage, and maintained a continuous applause. At the East end of St. Paul's Churchyard their Majesties were addressed in a speech by the senior scholar of Christ's Hospital. The Royal Family then went to the house of Mr. Barclay, opposite Bow Church, in Cheapside, whence they beheld the City procession, which was in a style of unusual grandeur and magnificence. The pageant of the Armourers' and Brasiers' Company consisted of a youth dressed as an American prince riding in his car, with a bow in his left hand and a quiver and arrows hanging behind his shoulder. The Skinners were represented by seven of their Company dressed in fur, with their skins painted to resemble Indian princes. The Fishmongers' pageant comprised a statue of St. Peter, a dolphin, two mermaids and two sea-horses. These allegorical displays were a revival of the old custom of exhibiting pageants which had fallen into disuse since the early years of George I's reign. The entertainment on this occasion was of an unusually sumptuous character. The contractors were the famous firm of Horton and Birch, of Cornhill, and the bill of fare provided for the Royal Family included the following items :—

FIRST SERVICE :—Dishes of olio, turtle, pottages and soups. Fish, *viz.*, John dories, red mullet, etc. Roast venison. Westphalia hams, richly ornamented. Pullets à la royale. Tongues espagniole. Chickens à la reine. Tondron devaux à la danzie. Harrico. Popiets of veal glassé. Fillets of lamb à la conte. Comports of squabs. Fillets of beef marinate. Fine vegetables.

SECOND SERVICE :—Ortolans, quails, notts, wheat-ears. Goodevau patte. Perrigoa pye. Pea-chicks, woodcocks, pheasants, teal, snipes, partridges. Patty's royal.

THIRD SERVICE :—Ragoût royal. Green morells. Green peas. Asparagus heads. Fat livers. Fine combs. Green truffles. Artichokes à la provençale. Mushrooms au blank. Cardons à la bejamel. Knotts of eggs. Ducks' tongues. Dishes of peths. Truffles in oil. Pallets. Ragoût mille.

FOURTH SERVICE :—Curious ornamental cakes. Blomonges representing different figures. Clear marbrays. Cut pastry. Mille fuelles.

CENTRE OF THE TABLE :—Grand pyramid of demies of shell fish of various sorts. Thirty-two cold things of sorts, *viz.*, temples, shapes, landscapes in jellies, savoury cakes, and almond gothes. Two grand epergnes filled with fine pickles, and garnished round with plates of sorts, as laspicks, rolards, etc.

Total cost of the dishes on the King's table, £374 1s.

A VIEW of CHEAPSIDE, as it appeard on LORD MAYORS DAY last

On 23 Nov. the royal entertainment committee, with the Lord Mayor at their head, waited upon their Majesties, begging them to favour the Corporation by sitting for their portraits, to be placed in the Guildhall together with the statue of the King. The King, in reply, graciously promised to present the City with the portraits.—One of the sights of London at this period was the Tower menagerie, which, during the summer of this year received from India the addition of a previously unknown animal, described by the name of Siyah-ghush, or Black-ear. The animal appears to have been a jackal, and forms the subject of learned and quaintly illustrated papers in the *Gentleman's Magazine* and its rival, the *London Magazine*.

The church of Allhallows Staining fell down, except the tower.—The "Bear at the Bridge Foot," a famous tavern at the Southwark end of London Bridge, was pulled down.—Continuous rain having almost ruined haymakers near the metropolis, a number of them assembled at the Royal Exchange and appealed for charity to the merchants, who subscribed some £16 for their relief.—A satirical writer in the *London Chronicle*, calling himself the "Cobbler of Cripplegate," girds at a number of public nuisances:—"He could wish to see butchers'-boys, who gallop through the streets of London, punished for so doing, or at least their horses seized for the use of the poor of the parish in which they offend. . . A regulation in Smithfield Market, he thinks, ought to take place, because a mad ox may as well gore the lady of a Knight Banneret, as a poor oyster-wench. . . . Ladders, pieces of timber, &c, should by no means be suffered to be carried upon men's shoulders within the posts of this City, because, by a sudden stop, they may as well poke out the eye of a rich man as that of a poor one. . . . Chair-men, as they are a kind of human nags, ought to amble without-side the posts as well as other brutes . . Long swords are a nuisance in the City at Change-time, as the wearer may very well receive a bill without that dangerous weapon. . . . Barbers and Chimney-sweepers have no right by charter to rub against a person well dressed, and then offer him satisfaction by single combat."

1762.

N Feb , 1762, occurred the extraordinary imposture known as the Cock Lane Ghost. The scene of the plot was the house of one Parsons, clerk of St. Sepulchre's parish, in Cock Lane, West Smithfield. Parsons' daughter, a girl ten years old, pretended to be visited by the spirit of Fanny, a young woman who had formerly lived in the house, and had died a year and a half previously. This woman had lived with Mr. Kent, a broker, and the husband of her late sister. Kent was supposed to have offended Parsons by pressing him for the payment of some money he had lent him. The girl Parsons, who had been a favourite of Fanny's, pretended to see her spirit, and was seized with apparent fits and tremblings, and strange noises of knocking, scratching, whispering, fluttering, etc., were heard on these occasions. A woman who lived in the house,

and was an accomplice in the scheme, explained these noises as indications that the deceased Fanny had been poisoned by Kent. The circumstances being repeated with much idle exaggeration, people of all ranks flocked to the scene, and even some dignitaries of the Church lent countenance to the fraud by their presence. Although it was proved by proper certificates that the woman had died of small-pox, and affidavits were produced from the clergyman, physician and apothecary who attended her in her last illness, nothing could remove the popular prejudice against the unfortunate man Kent. As the only means of escape from this dreadful persecution Kent commenced an action for conspiracy against the father and mother of the child, the woman who posed as "interpreter," and a clergyman and a tradesman who had been active in promoting the imposture. The trial took place on 10 July, before Lord Chief Justice Mansfield and a special jury at Guildhall, and resulted in the conviction of all the prisoners. Parsons was sentenced to stand in the pillory three times in one month, and to be imprisoned two years; his wife was imprisoned for one year; the female "interpreter" was committed to Bridewell for six months; the clergyman and tradesman were allowed to compromise their part by paying a large compensation to the prosecutor, and were then dismissed with a severe reprimand.—An Act of Parliament was passed this session for new paving the streets in the City, and removing the posts and signs which had long been felt to be an obstruction in the principal thoroughfares of the metropolis.—An Act was also passed to sanction a project for reducing the price of fish by bringing it to London from distant ports by land carriage. After a few years' trial the expenses were found so greatly to exceed the produce that the experiment was discontinued.—On 6 Ap. the Common Council addressed the King in congratulation upon the conquest of the Island of Martinico.—On 4 June the famous new peal of ten bells at Bow Church, Cheapside, then reckoned the finest in England, were rung for the first time, it being his Majesty's birthday.—An action was brought, on 8 June by a Mr. Isaac Renoux, against the proprietor of Jonathan's Coffee House for ejecting him therefrom, and it was decided in his favour on the ground that the house had been a market for buying and selling Government securities.—Lady Fair, Southwark, was abolished by order of the Common Council on the 17th; and, at the same time, shows, interludes, and "other unlawful pastimes," were prohibited at Bartholomew Fair.—On 5 July the judges finally determined a cause, which had been long pending between the Corporation and the Dissenters, as to the eligibility and obligation of the latter to serve the office of Sheriff. The decision of the judges, afterwards confirmed on appeal by the House of Lords, was that Dissenters were not obliged to serve that office.—On the 14 Aug. the Lord Mayor, Aldermen and Common Council presented to the King an address of congratulation on the birth of a prince, who on the 17th was created Prince of Wales.—On 27 Sept., in a time of complete calm, the Thames suddenly rose to a great height, causing much damage to vessels at various wharves. An earthquake was believed to have caused this phenomenon.—On 4 Oct. an address was presented to the King by the Common Council, congratulating his Majesty on the conquest of Havana and its dependencies.—On 8 Nov. the Lord Mayor received a letter from Lord Egremont, Secretary of State, informing him that preliminaries of peace with France and Spain were signed at Fontainebleau on the 3rd inst., and requesting his Lordship to make an immediate public announcement of the fact.—Alderman William Beckford was elected Lord Mayor.—During this year the great increase both of houses and inhabitants in the metropolis was shown by the amount of coals imported into the Port of London, viz., 570,774 chaldrons, being nearly double the importation of fifty years before.

The stones of Moorgate, which had been sold, were re-purchased by the Corporation, and, on the advice of Smeaton, the Engineer, employed in supporting the middle-arch of London Bridge ; the remaining materials of other gates were also used.—On the decease of the last Lord Hatton, the Hatton estate in Holborn reverted to the Crown—A fire in Newgate Gaol greatly damaged the Chapel, and caused the death of two prisoners.

1763.

THE unpopularity of the Government continued to increase, and the members of the Cabinet were lampooned and assailed with political publications of a violent character. To counteract the effects of these the *Briton*, a periodical pamphlet, was published under the patronage of Government. This was answered by a similar periodical called the *North Briton*, in allusion to the Earl of Bute, who had become Premier in succession to Mr. Pitt. The writers of the *North Briton*, at the head of whom was the celebrated John Wilkes, M.P. for Aylesbury, used every effort to hold up the Government and its measures to ignominy and contempt. The famous Number 45, which appeared in Ap., 1763, contained such severe reflections upon the King's closing speech to Parliament that the Ministry determined upon a prosecution. Wilkes was apprehended on 30 Ap. under an illegal warrant signed by the principal Secretary of State. A writ of *habeas corpus* was obtained from the Court of Common Pleas, in spite of which Wilkes was committed to the Tower, where he continued till 6 May, when, his case having been fully heard before Lord Chief Justice Pratt, the

c

Court ordered him to be discharged. He subsequently brought an action against Robert Wood, Under Secretary of State, for illegally seizing his papers, and obtained £1,000 damages, with full costs. Wilkes emphasised his success by setting up a printing press in his own house, and republishing all the numbers of the obnoxious paper. This exasperated the Ministry so highly that an action was brought against him in the Court of King's Bench in his Majesty's name; and the House of Commons voted the *North Briton*, No. 45, to be "a most seditious and dangerous libel," and ordered it to be burnt by the hands of the Common Hangman. The execution of this order at the Royal Exchange occasioned a riot, during which the mob violently assaulted and dispersed the officials, and the glass of Mr. Sheriff Harley's carriage was broken by one of the billets snatched from the bonfire. Pieces of the "libel" were rescued from the flames, and displayed in triumph in the evening at Temple Bar, where a bonfire was lighted to consume a large Jack-boot, in derision of the Prime Minister. The riot formed the subject of serious debate in both Houses of Parliament, and Mr. Alderman Harley, who had been examined by the Lords, received, with his fellow-sheriff, the thanks of both Houses.—The Lord Mayor entertained the Duke of York, on 4 Feb., at a ball and supper, the guests including two princes of Mecklenburg, many foreign ministers, members of the nobility, and other distinguished persons. —Public proclamation of the peace was made, on 22 Mar., in the usual places within the City, but the citizens were so dissatisfied with the terms that the Common Council refused an address of congratulation. An address was voted by the Court of Aldermen, and its presentation took place on 12 May, when only six Aldermen and the Sheriffs attended, with a *locum tenens* at their head. The people viewed the procession with much disfavour, and, both on its progress and return, the church bells were tolled and rung in muffled peals.—During the month of Mar. the Ministry carried a measure of supply which excited violent opposition in Parliament and in the country, and more especially in the City of London. The Bill received the Royal assent on the 31st, and provided £2,000,000 from the sinking fund, £1,800,000 to be raised by Exchequer bills, £2,800,000 by borrowing on annuities, and two sums of £350,000, each of which was to be raised by a lottery. The interest on these loans was to be met by additional duties on wines, and the imposition of a duty of 4s. a hogshead on cider and perry; the makers of these articles being further subjected to the Excise laws. The Cider Act, as it was called from the latter provisions, was vigorously opposed by the Court of Common Council, who separately petitioned each of the Houses of Parliament against it, and instructed their members to contest the measure "as being inconsistent with those principles of liberty which had hitherto distinguished this nation from arbitrary government." The Act ultimately produced so much disturbance throughout the country that it was first altered, and afterwards repealed.—During the year the two lotteries were held in the Guildhall, this being the first occasion on which more than one had been conducted in one year.   The drawing took place in the Guildhall,

The Representation of the Drawing of the STATE-LOTTERY at Guildhall 1763.

to which the lottery-wheels had been previously conveyed on sledges escorted by troops.   Two scholars of Christ's Hospital were employed to draw out the tickets from the wheels in the presence of the Lord Mayor, the members of the Corporation and the public.   Lotteries were first introduced into England in 1569, and, being found a convenient method of raising revenue, they long continued to receive legal encouragement.   At last, so many private and dishonest enterprises became mixed up with lotteries that they were finally abolished in Feb., 1825.—On 4 Ap. an entertainment of unusual splendour was given by Lord Mayor Beckford.   A large number of guests of the highest distinction were present, and the dinner was followed by a ball, which was prolonged until nearly five the next morning.—On the 7th, James (afterwards Sir James) Eyre was elected Recorder of London, in the place of the late Sir William Moreton.—On the 18th the ambassadors extraordinary from the Republic of Venice made their state entry into London.   They were received with great magnificence, being conveyed and attended from Greenwich to the Tower in State barges, and from the Tower through the Minories, Leadenhall Street, Cornhill, Cheapside, Ludgate Street, Fleet Street and the Strand, to Somerset House, where they were entertained at the King's cost until their audience with his Majesty.—The King's birthday, on 4 June, was celebrated with great rejoicing, a display of fireworks on Tower Hill being unfortunately attended by a serious accident through over-crowding, by which several people lost their lives.—Cornelius Saunders, having been capitally convicted at the Old Bailey, for stealing about £50 from the house of Mrs. White, in Lamb Street, Spitalfields, was executed on 24 Aug., his body being afterwards carried and laid before her door.   A great crowd of people assembled, and proceeded to acts of violence ; and, notwithstanding the arrival of a guard of soldiers, the mob ransacked the house, and, removing the furniture into the street, succeeded in destroying it by fire.—The birth of another prince formed the occasion of an address to the King from the Common Council, which was presented on 25 Aug. —Towards the middle of October a horse patrol, under the direction of Sir John Fielding, and consisting of eight officers well mounted and armed, was established on the roads leading out of the City for the protection of passengers.— Alderman William Bridgen was chosen Lord Mayor.

An allusion to the civic procession of 12 May occurs in Book iv. of Churchill's " Ghost "   The " Asgill " referred to was Sir Charles Asgill, the *locum tenens* for Lord Mayor Beckford .—

" —— To the melancholy knell
Of the dull, deep, and doleful bell,
Such as of late the good Saint Bride
Muffled, to mortify the pride
Of those who (England quite forgot),
Paid their vile homage to the Scot,
Where Asgill held the foremost place,
Whilst my lord figured at a race "

1764.

WILKES having fled to France to avoid the prosecution which threatened him, his conduct was adjudged by the House of Commons to be a contempt of their authority ; and on 16 Jan., 1764, he was expelled the House.   In the following month his trial came on, during his absence, in the King's Bench, before Lord Chief Justice Mansfield.   He was found guilty of republishing his libellous paper, and was subsequently outlawed.—On 21 Feb. the Court of Common Council resolved to present the freedom of the City to Lord Chief Justice Pratt (afterwards Earl Camden) for his constitutional decision upon the warrant in the Wilkes case, which displayed " his duty to the King, his justice to the subject, and his knowledge of the law." His Lordship was also asked to sit for his portrait, for which a suitable inscription was written, it is said, by Dr. Johnson.—On 9 Ap. several thousand silk-weavers who had been brought to distress by importations of French silks went in procession from Spitalfields, through the City, to St. James's Palace, where the King received them with much kindness and promised to lay their grievances before Parliament.—Forty journeymen tailors were taken at the Bull Head, in Bread Street, by a party of master tailors and committed to Wood Street Compter on a charge of unlawful combination. Being brought before the sitting Alderman at Guildhall on the 23rd inst. they were discharged, and the masters and jailers reprimanded for confining them without a warrant.—A severe thunderstorm visited London on 18 Sept. and damaged the spire of St. Bride's, Fleet Street, so much as to necessitate its being rebuilt.—Alderman William Stephenson was elected Lord Mayor.—The value of land in London was now rapidly increasing. A small field in Piccadilly bought a few years before by a brewer for £30 was this year sold for the benefit of his orphan child for the sum of £2,500.—During this year the price of provisions became so high that the Privy Council removed all duty from salt beef, salt pork, and butter from Ireland, and offered a reward of £100 for the discovery of unlawful combinations in the sale of provisions of any kind.

The church of Allhallows-in-the-Wall had fallen into such a dangerous condition that an Act of Parliament was obtained for its demolition   It was rebuilt by the younger Dance, in 1765.—A pedestrian statue of George III, sculptured by Joseph Wilton, was placed in the Royal Exchange.— A satirical pamphlet was issued in allusion to the new pavement and the removal of signboards, with the title " A seasonable alarm to the City of London on the present important Crisis ; shewing, by most convincing arguments, that the new method of paving the streets with Scotch pebbles, and the pulling down of the signs, must be both equally pernicious to the health and morals of the people of England.   By Zachary Zeal, citizen."

1765.

ARLY in 1765 the Corporation petitioned Parliament for relief from the heavy expenditure connected with the improvement of London Bridge, and the charge of rebuilding the temporary bridge after its destruction by fire. They also prayed Parliament for assistance in rebuilding the gaol of Newgate, which was an ancient, inconvenient building, and unfit for the reception of prisoners. Both petitions were referred by the House of Commons for consideration to a Committee.—On 17 Jan. 300 pieces of English cambric were sold by public auction at Garraway's Coffee-house, at thirteen and sixpence per yard. This was at the time looked upon as a hopeful sign of the development of the manufacture in the country.— On the 19th, at the close of a poll for the election of Chamberlain, Alderman Janssen, a past Lord Mayor, obtained a majority of votes. He had only presented himself when the poll was about to open, but was held in great estimation by the citizens for his fearless conduct as a magistrate and for his commercial integrity. He was the first Sheriff to carry out the sentences of the law at Tyburn without the aid of a military force. On his failure, the year after his mayoralty, his relatives settled upon him £600 a year, the greater part of which, with other subsequent sources of income, he honourably assigned to his creditors, although they had given him a full discharge.—During a crowded trial at Guildhall the floor of the court gave way, but the accident was fortunately unattended with any personal injury.—On the 23rd Mr. John Williams, bookseller, was convicted in the King's Bench of republishing the *North Briton*, No. 45, and sentenced to a fine of £100, six months' imprisonment, to stand in the pillory in Old Palace Yard, and give security of £1,000 for his good behaviour for seven years. The sentence of the pillory was carried out on 14 Feb., in New Palace Yard, West-minster, but its purpose was defeated by the acclamations of a crowd of more than 10,000 persons, by whom the Prime Minister was again executed in effigy. —Owing to the sufferings of the poor on account of the high price of bread, the Sheriffs of London presented a petition to the House of Commons, on the 24th, against the continued exportation of corn.—On 23 Mar. the Common Council voted the freedom of the City to the Duke of Gloucester, who was admitted in the usual manner on 6 June following.—Towards the middle of May serious disturb-ances were caused by processions of Spitalfields weavers, thousands of whom had been thrown out of work by the introduction of French manufactured silks. The Duke of Bedford, whom they believed to have obstructed their petition to Parliament, was the chief object of their attack ; and, on the 18th, his house in Bloomsbury Square was much damaged, notwithstanding the protection afforded by the troops. Violent disturbances also took place in Moorfields, where several silk-masters resided, and a special meeting of the Court of Aldermen was summoned. A proclamation was immediately issued, and a party of Guards from the Tower was stationed in Moorfields for some days. These measures, coupled with the personal influence of the Aldermen, were the means of calming the discontent of the people, and of restoring tranquillity.—The price of bread was much reduced at the end of May, chiefly by the importation of Dutch and Flemish wheat. The necessities of the journeymen weavers were also provided for by liberal subscriptions.—At an action brought, on 2 July, at Guildhall, by Messrs. Carr, Ibbetson and Co., silk mercers, on Ludgate Hill, it was decided that Custom House officers had no right to search the premises of merchants for the alleged possession of contraband goods.—The birth of another prince gave occasion to the Common Council to tender to the King a loyal address of congratulation,

Mouth of the River Fleet, from a picture by S. Scott.

which was presented to his Majesty on 28 Aug. As a further mark of their attachment to the throne, the Corporation, on 15 Oct. voted the freedom of the City to H.S.H., the Prince of Brunswick Lunenberg, who was admitted a freeman on 18 Dec.—The scheme for the City approach to the new Blackfriars Bridge, in 1765, involved the covering over of the Fleet from Fleet Street to its mouth, whence it was conveyed some distance into the Thames by a culvert. On 19 Oct. Bridewell arch was taken down, and the brick-work of the new sewer completed from that point to the mouth of the Fleet.

After the Great Fire of London, in 1666, the Fleet Ditch was cleansed and deepened to form a navigable canal up to Holborn Bridge, as part of Wren's plan for rebuilding the City. The cost of this "new canal," including that of the beautiful bridge at Bridewell, was £27,777, but the work proved unprofitable. The stream became choked with Thames mud, and relapsed into a common sewer. As a sanitary necessity the portion of the ditch between Holborn Bridge and Fleet Street was arched over in 1737.

The ancient customs which obliged persons following any trade to become members of the Company having control of that trade, and prohibited tradesmen who were not free of the City from keeping shop within its boundaries, were this month confirmed in two actions brought respectively against offenders by the Farriers' Company and the Chamberlain.—On 7 Nov. a disastrous fire broke out in the house of a peruke-maker, at the corner of Bishopsgate Street and Cornhill. The flames quickly spread to the three houses at the other corners of the thoroughfares. All the houses from Cornhill to the church of St. Martin

Bridewell Bridge, from a water colour drawing.

Outwich were burnt down, and the church and parsonage house greatly damaged, as well as the back part of Merchant Taylors' Hall. Various houses in Thread-needle Street, the White Lion tavern (which had been purchased only the evening before for £3,000), and all the houses in White Lion Court, were entirely consumed, together with fifty-eight houses in Cornhill and several in Leadenhall Street. Many lives were lost, not only by the fire, but by the falling of chimneys and walls, and the damage to property was estimated at £100,000. £3,000 was raised for the relief of the sufferers, to which the King contributed £1,000, the

Grocers' and Ironmongers' Companies £100 each, and the Lord Mayor £50.— In consequence of the death of the King's uncle, the Duke of Cumberland, the usual ceremonies of the procession on Lord Mayor's day were dispensed with, and the new Lord Mayor, Alderman George Nelson, went privately to Westminster,

accompanied only by Sir William Stephenson, the late Lord Mayor, the Aldermen and the Recorder.—The condition of the paving in the roads and foot-paths of the City having long given rise to complaints, the Court of Common Council referred it to the Commissioners of Sewers and Pavements to consider the most effectual means of amending those defects. The Commissioners' report, presented on 15 Nov., gives a graphic picture of the evils complained of, and suggests as a remedy the grant to the Commissioners of more extended powers of control. The pavements, being made

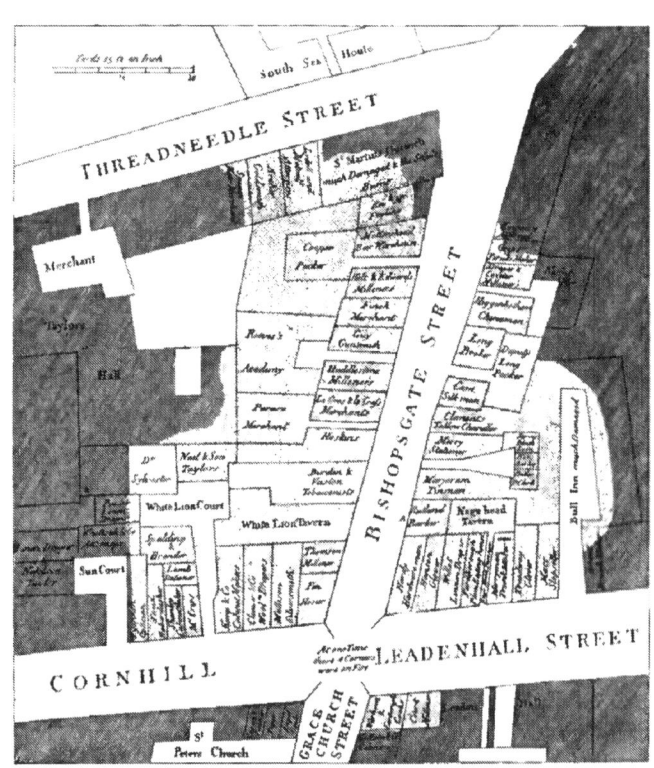

Plan of the great Fire, which began in Cornhill, Nov. 7, 1765.

and repaired by the inhabitants themselves at different times and of different materials, were rough and irregular ; and, being often disturbed by the various water-companies and only slightly repaired, their condition, even in the principal thoroughfares, was most defective. Deep channels existed in the middle of the streets, and, in many cases, cross channels also, rendering the traffic for vehicles highly inconvenient and dangerous. In the less frequented streets the householders or their servants were in the habit of throwing ashes, rubbish, broken glass, offal and other offensive matter into the street ; and even in the more important thoroughfares locomotion was obstructed by the washing of butts, casks and barrels. The footways, not being raised above the level of the road, were covered with mud, and frequently overflowed with water,

The breadth of the paths was confined on the one side by posts, and on the other by the encroachments of shop-windows, show-boards, vaults and cellar doors. The signboards above, which were ever increasing in size and projection, were complained of as being a danger in times of high wind, and as intercepting the light of the lamps at night. The want of proper tablets to distinguish the names of streets and courts, and of regularity in numbering the houses, occasioned great difficulty, especially to strangers. Annexed to the report was an estimate by Mr. George Dance, clerk of the works, of the cost of re-paving the footways and roads, removing posts, etc., in the principal thoroughfares from Temple Bar to Aldgate Church, amounting to £16,860 10s., and an alternative estimate for relaying the old materials at a cost of £10,512 8s. 9d. The representations of the Commissioners resulted in an Act for the better paving, cleansing and lighting of the City of London, etc., passed in the following May, which, amongst other provisions, gave compulsory powers of paving "when, and as often, and in such manner, and with such material, as they shall think fit," and also empowered them to remove all signs and other projections and encroachments within the City, under a penalty of £5 to each offender. Funds were to be provided, partly by a rate, which was not to exceed 1s. 6d. in the pound, and partly by tolls to be taken at nine turnpikes in the north and north-east districts of London.—The injustice caused by the use of false measures had grown to such an extent that the Lord Mayor took special steps to enforce the Act of 11 and 12 William III for stamping weights and measures. Summonses were issued against publicans, milkmen, and other dealers, for selling in vessels not sealed with the City mark ; and by the severe enforcement of the Act the abuses were considerably abated.—During this year there was great activity in building operations both in the City and its suburbs.—Stimulated by the success of the Society for the Encouragement of Arts, Manufactures and Commerce, an association of painters, sculptors, architects and engravers obtained this year a charter of incorporation under the name of "The Society of Artists of Great Britain," with authority to use a common seal and other powers within the City of London and ten miles thereof.

The London Tavern, in Bishopsgate Street, was designed by William Jupp.—Dr. Johnson lived at No. 1, Inner Temple Lane from 1760 to 1765.—The *North Briton, No. 45,* was caught up by tradesmen as an advertising idea, goods being distinguished as "No. 45" in order to catch the public eye. Many years later, the favourite snuff retailed by a Fleet Street dealer was kept in a canister marked "45."

1766.

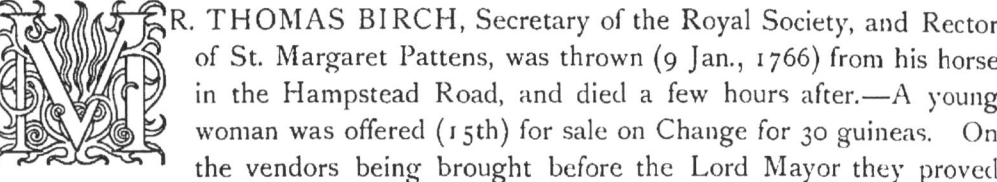

R. THOMAS BIRCH, Secretary of the Royal Society, and Rector of St. Margaret Pattens, was thrown (9 Jan., 1766) from his horse in the Hampstead Road, and died a few hours after.—A young woman was offered (15th) for sale on Change for 30 guineas. On the vendors being brought before the Lord Mayor they proved to be an uncle of the girl and his wife. She had been taken from the workhouse at Bodmin and brought to London at the May assizes. The woman was acquitted, and the man sentenced to six months' imprisonment and a shilling fine. An attempted sale by a workhouse deputy governor was similarly frustrated next year.—Rev. William Romaine was elected (28th) by the parishioners Rector of St. Anne's, Blackfriars —₃¹₆ Share of the New River Company was sold for £4,400 (10 Feb.).—After trial by a special jury of non-freemen a fine of £25 was inflicted (25 Feb.) on one who had acted as a broker without being admitted, under Queen Anne's Act, by the Court of Aldermen. Next year this decision was limited so as to allow a friend to buy or sell for his friend without a licence — The Prince of Wales was appointed Captain-General of the Hon. Artillery Company (8 Mar.)—On the 18th the Act for the repeal of the American Stamp Act received the Royal assent. On its passing the House of Commons (24 Feb.) the city bells were rung from morn till night; those of St. Michael's, Cornhill continued to ring till nearly midnight, and wound up with 45 platoons. Two members of the House of Commons went with the Bill to the House of Lords. On its passing into law the ships in the river displayed their colours; the houses in the city were illuminated, and the Americans then in London celebrated the event by a great banquet (Ap.) in Drapers' Hall, to over 240 guests, among whom were many peers of the realm.—Alderman Trecothick was elected Sheriff (25 Ap.) in place of Mr. Charlewood, deceased.—On the day of the prorogation of Parliament, 14 May, the bill for paving, lighting, &c., the city, received the Royal assent. The highway from Temple Bar to Whitechapel was first put in hand, and the assessment fixed at 1s. 6d. per £, for the streets begun to be paved, and 1s. for the other streets. Sunday tolls were enacted for 21 years from 29 Sept., at all the Middlesex approaches to the city (but not from persons bringing provisions to the London markets), and vested in the Lord Mayor and Commissioners. The paving was to be of Aberdeen granite and the work was begun 14 July.—The silk-weaving trade was very dull; in Feb. 200 weavers were discharged. At the Queen's birthday ball (20 Feb.) only rich silks of Spitalfields manufacture were worn, and the Royal assent was given (14 May) to a Bill prohibiting importation of French-made silks and cambric. Several thousand Spitalfields weavers accompanied the King on this occasion from St. James's to Westminster Hall and back, flying streamers of their own manufacture, and attended by bands of music. On their way home they halted at the Mansion House, their bands playing God Save the King; after three hearty cheers they returned to Spitalfields, where most of the houses were illuminated, bonfires were lighted in the streets, and fireworks displayed in demonstration of their joy.—The Common Council (16 May) recommended the magistrates not to license any assembly or assembly house which should have any tendency to corrupt the morals of the people. They also voted £400 for the sufferers from a fire at Montreal.—Four hundred and forty haymakers assembled at the Royal Exchange (1 June) where a collection was made for their assistance, the heavy rains preventing them from work.—On the King's birthday (4 June) the Mansion House was illuminated, and there was a grand display of fireworks on Tower Hill. At the ball, at St. James's,

Back of Dick's Coffee House, Hare Court, Temple.

there was no article of dress of French manufacture, and the dresses of home manufacture far exceeded in richness the foreign ones usually worn. Severe fines were inflicted on both importers and wearers of foreign silks, and one merchant received £225 as damages against the Custom House for seizing a parcel of silks proved to be of Spitalfields manufacture.— A fine house in Philpot Lane, built by a Mr Ubtorff, at a cost of £7,000, was sold (5th) for £5,340.—The Head Keeper of Wood Street Compter was appointed (14 July) without purchase, a right step in the administration of justice ; formerly this post had been sold for £1,500. On inquiry it was found (30th) that the City of London had a right to import 4,000 chaldrons of coals for the poor at one shilling below the usual Custom duty, a power they resolved to put in force on account of the present distress —The King granted (19 Aug) to the Lord Mayor, Aldermen and Commons of London, the right to hold a market for hops every Wednesday for ever, and on 8 Sept. ninety-three carriages of hops, each upwards of two tons weight, were offered for sale, the largest quantity hitherto known.—The synagogue in Duke's Place was dedicated (31 Aug.) with very great pomp and solemnity.—£500 was voted (19 Sept) for the sufferers from a fire at Barbadoes ; many of the City Companies also made contributions.—A congratulatory address to the King from the Corporation on the birth of a princess (29 Sept.), and the marriage of his youngest sister, Caroline Matilda, by proxy, to Christian VII, King of Denmark (28 Sept.), was presented by the Sheriffs (28 Oct).—The Statue of Queen Elizabeth, which formerly stood over Ludgate, was set (14 Oct.) up at St. Dunstan's-in-the-West.—Alderman Robert Kite was chosen Lord Mayor.—The freedom of the City was voted to His Royal Highness The Duke of Gloucester (11 Dec.), and on the same day the Court of Common Council agreed to petition Parliament for a remedy for great frauds in the measurement of coals.

Riots were frequent all over the country on account of the dearth of bread —From Mar. to the end of June 115,497 quarters of wheat were imported into London, most of which found its way to the country. A City Company, which made a point of having green peas at its feast (29 May), paid sixteen guineas for sixteen quarts, and (17 June) common cherries sold at 4s. a lb, the price three years before being 2d. In Sept apples, which sold last year at 2s. 6d, were selling for 10s. A proclamation was issued against forestalling &c (10 Sept). A bad harvest increased the distress. The Sheriffs prepared a petition (23rd), and were directed by the Common Council to lay it before the King, who ordered them to attend the Privy Council. An embargo was consequently laid by proclamation (26th) on all ships laden with corn for exportation. The price of bread rose in Oct. to 2s. 8d. per peck or 8d per quartern loaf, and 6d for households.—On the assembling of Parliament a further prohibition was ordered (12 Nov.) on barley and malt; the Sheriffs were ordered (30 Nov.) to present a petition to Parliament as to the price of provisions ; and in Dec. exportation was forbidden, and importation free of duty permitted for a limited time   £230,000 were estimated to have been sent out of the country for oats within less than three years.—The acute distress in London was intensified by a severe frost lasting from the middle of Dec. to nearly the end of Jan., 1767.—A high wind and tide spoiled £50,000 worth of goods in the river warehouses. Numbers of larks were found in the hay carts at Smithfield so numbed as to allow themselves to be taken by the hand.   Bread rose to 8½d. per quartern loaf.   Meal barges could not approach the City on the frozen river, either from above or below.   Riots in the country had also limited the supply. In the beginning of 1767 the Court of Common Council voted £1,000 (21 Jan.) for the assistance of the poor who were not in receipt of parish relief.   The Lord Mayor, all the Aldermen, and fifty-two Commoners were appointed as a Relief Committee.   The Lord Mayor subscribed £100, and others gave generously; six days after £1,315 were distributed.—The first of Lloyd's Registers of Shipping (for 1764-66) was published, the vessels registered being classed under the letters A, E, I, O, and U.— Wilson's Loan Charity was founded by the will of Samuel Wilson, of Hatton Garden, who bequeathed £20,000 to the City Chamberlain for the purpose of granting loans at one per cent. for the first year, and two per cent. for the remaining years of the term, to young men who have been in business in the City between one and three years.

1767.

ON 23 Jan., 1767, Deputy Paterson brought forward a scheme for raising £282,000 for paying the deficit on London Bridge, completing Blackfriars Bridge, and redeeming the tolls, making a river embankment from Paul's Wharf to Milford Lane, repairing the Royal Exchange, and rebuilding Newgate.   On the 31st the plan was approved by the Common Council, and ordered to be presented to Parliament by the Sheriffs.   The Royal assent was given in June, and the Common Council ordered (23 June) the freedom of the City, in a gold box, to be conferred on the Right Hon. Charles Townshend, Chancellor of the Exchequer, for the great favour he had shown the City in forwarding the various bills for promoting its embellishment, convenience, and prosperity.   Mr. Townshend did not live long to enjoy the honour, dying on 4 Sept.   Plate to the value of £200 was voted to Deputy Paterson, Chairman of Ways and Means in the House of Commons, for his services generally, but especially for the plan then waiting the Royal assent.—Leave was given to the proprietors of the London Bridge Waterworks to use for their works the fifth arch of the bridge—but should their works interfere with the navigation, the grant would be revoked, and the Common Council refund the expenses of the Company in occupying the said arch.—A report from a Committee, appointed in 1765, to consider in whom was vested the control over the City Hospitals was presented to the Common Council (24 Feb.).   The five Hospitals, St. Bartholomew's, Christ Church, St. Thomas's, Bridewell, and Bethlehem, had been granted by three authentic instruments to the Lord Mayor, Commonalty, and citizens of London.   The management had, however, fallen at an early date into the hands of the Court of Aldermen alone.—The freedom of the City was voted (10 Mar.) to the Duke of Cumberland, the King's brother.—Gresham College and its site in Bishopsgate, was sold to the Government for the Excise Office, for the paltry sum of £500 per annum, and to the lasting injury of this noble Foundation (22 May). The Lectures were to be read in the rooms over the Royal Exchange. The Lecturers, who had hitherto occupied rooms in the College, and, who, in accordance with Gresham's will, were celibates, received compensation for their houses ; and, by an Act of Parliament ratifying this exchange, and passed next year, they were allowed to marry.—In June, a duty of 6d. per chaldron on coals was granted to the City for 46 years, in addition to 35 yet to run of an unexpired grant, to redeem tolls on the bridges, embank the river, and rebuild Newgate.—The rebuilt church of All Hallows-in-the-Wall was consecrated (8 Sept.).—The Gresham Committee resolved (22 Sept.) to pull down the west end of the Exchange and rebuild it after the designs of Mr. Robinson.—The Right Hon. Thomas Harley was elected Lord Mayor (29 Sept.) for the ensuing year. He was brother to the Earl of Oxford , the only instance of a brother of a British peer being Lord Mayor of London. He had only been Alderman for six years, but the resignation of three members, and the indisposition of a fourth, brought him thus early to the Chair.—The Lord Mayor, Aldermen, and Common Council presented (30 Nov.) an address to the King congratulating him on the birth of another prince, and condoling with him on the death of his brother, the Duke of York. They were graciously received. The King expressed his thanks, " for the satisfaction they expressed in the increase of his family, and for the reference to the Duke of York."

A crowd, estimated at 80,000, mostly women, met (19 Jan.) in the centre of Moorfields and was with difficulty restrained from lynching a man who was executed there, near his own residence, for starving and otherwise maltreating his wife.—The Lock-up houses for detaining recruits for the East India Company's service were found to be places of great harshness and cruelty. A man threw himself from the window of one in Chancery Lane (2 Feb.) and was killed. Dead bodies from another in Butcher's Row were carried at night to St. Bride's Churchyard and buried. Young men were decoyed to them under pretence of being engaged as servants, or by executing a warrant against them for some trifling theft. Sailors were seized and locked up. The grand jury of the City presented a memorial (1 Mar.) in reference to these houses, and two of the keepers were sentenced (1 June) to twelve months' imprisonment. Next year (28 Nov.) another agent was sentenced in the Court of King's Bench to eighteen months' imprisonment.—A Jew was charged before the Lord Mayor (26 June) with hawking hats in the City, thereby subjecting himself to a fine of £12, or three months' hard labour in Bridewell. Some years before, a housekeeper in London, a freeman of the City, having a proper hawker's licence, was convicted of a similar offence, and on refusing to pay the fine, committed to Bridewell for three months, on the ground that no person, licensed or unlicensed, might hawk goods within any Corporate town in this Kingdom.—In a dense Nov. fog, two persons lost their lives , one at Billingsgate, by falling into the river ; another by suffocation in the mud of the Fleet Ditch.—Four hundred weavers in Bethnal Green destroyed (11 Dec.)

the looms of a worsted lace maker. The soldiers were sent for and dispersed the mob. Forty ringleaders were seized, and after admonition and reprimand, discharged.—Mr. William Robinson, Surveyor to the City Hospitals, left munificent bequests to several City hospitals and schools — John Newbery, publisher, of St. Paul's Churchyard, died (22 Dec.).—Jacob Tonson, bookseller, in the Strand, died 31 Mar.—Great friction between the Fellows of the College of Physicians and the Licentiates, culminated in a riot, on the occasion of the Fellows dinner on St Luke's Day, the Licentiates forcing the gate of the College in Warwick Lane, and breaking a number of windows with their canes.—During the severe winter of 1767-8 the Lord Mayor had 50 lbs. of beef boiled every day for distribution among the poor, and an unknown person released 26 prisoners from the Poultry, and others from Wood Street, confined for debts between 40s. and £6, and each received a gift of 30s.

<h1 style="text-align:center">1768.</h1>

THE substitution of machine looms for hand looms in weaving, caused serious disturbances among the weavers of Spitalfields and Saffron Hill. Towards the end of 1767, a determined attempt was made at the latter place to destroy the machine looms. Wages at Spitalfields were reduced 4d. per yard. A mob, after breaking machinery there, met in Bishopsgate on 5 Jan., 1768. The Guards were sent for, and after some opposition, dispersed the mob. Further attempts against machinery were made in July and Aug.—Long continued frost bore hard on the watermen and fishermen; 500 of them received 5s. 3d. each from the Archbishop, and £200 was distributed at Almack's.—The free importation of corn was proclaimed (31st), and exportation forbidden till twenty days after Parliament should assemble, the operation of these measures being subsequently prolonged till after the next session of Parliament.—The period of Court mourning was reduced by one half, and for this the manufacturers, traders, and Company of Weavers, formally thanked the King, while a large procession of Spitalfield weavers proceeded through the City to St. James's, for the same purpose. —Two coal merchants were fined (1 Feb.) £100 each and double costs for short measure.—On 8 Mar., Parliament granted additional powers for paving, cleansing, and lighting London, and also for converting Gresham College and its adjoining grounds into an excise office.—The Duke of Monaco (now on a visit to St. James's), at whose court the Duke of York had died, was entertained (18th) at the Mansion House, the Dukes of Gloucester and Cumberland opening the ball with their partners, one of whom was the Lady Mayoress.—In Ap., the coal-heavers on the river struck, and compelled all engaged in the delivery of ships to cease work. A settlement was made before the justices on the 29th, but on 10 May disregarded.—In May, the sailors struck for more wages; the sawyers burnt down Dingley's sawmill, at Limehouse, because machinery had been introduced, for the loss of which Government granted £2,000 in Feb. following ; the glass grinders and journeymen tailors also came out.—The unpopularity of Lord Bute again led to his being burnt in effigy in the City.   On 9 May, a mob assembled in front of the Mansion House carrying, on a gallows, a boot with a petticoat dangling from it, and broke several windows, but dispersed on the seizure of some of the ringleaders.   At the July assizes two were convicted, and, in consideration of their poverty, fined 1s. and ordered a year's imprisonment in Newgate.—The Lord Mayor was admitted (27 May) a member of the Privy Council.—During this month the export of corn was again forbidden, and violent disputes arose between the sailors and the coalheavers arising out of their strikes.—On the recommendation of Sir S. T. Janssen, City Chamberlain, bounties were offered (4 June) encouraging fishermen to bring mackerel and herrings to London.   For delivering three lasts of fish, caught not more than forty-eight hours before landing, the first boat to arrive received £37 10s., the second £30, and

College of Physicians, Warwick Lane, Destroyed 1866.

the third £22 10s.   Meat was thereby reduced one half-penny per lb.   These bounties were afterwards continued till the end of Oct.—In July, London House, in Aldersgate Street, formerly the town residence of the Bishop of London, was burned down, the damage being estimated at £20,000.—Christian VII, King of Denmark, who married Princess Caroline Matilda, the sister of George III, visited England on 11 Aug., and passed through the City on the 19th, on his way to and from the Tower.—On the night of 22 Aug., a stack of chimneys in the centre of the Fleet prison fell down, destroying ten apartments in which forty persons were lodged.   Some were hurt, one dangerously, and most lost their all.   The whole building was in a ruinous condition.   The German chapel, in the Savoy, sent £200 to be divided among the prisoners.—On 23 Sept., the King of Denmark was entertained at the Mansion House, being received by Alderman Sir Robert Ladbroke, in the

E

absence, through illness, of Lord Mayor Harley. The procession by water and road was on a magnificent scale, and on his way the King was entertained at luncheon, in their hall, by the Benchers of the Middle Temple. An address from the City was presented to His Majesty in the Great Parlour, Deputy John Paterson interpreting the King's reply, and dinner was served in the Egyptian Hall. Both the Corporation and the Fishmongers' Company subsequently conferred their Freedom upon the King.—Dr. Newbon, Bishop of Bristol, was installed Dean of St. Paul's (7 Oct.), in place of the former Bishop of Lichfield, now Archbishop of Canterbury.—A coal meter's place for twenty-one years was sold for £6,510, and a corn meter's for £3,300 (18th).—Alderman Samuel Turner was elected Lord Mayor.—An address to His Majesty on the birth of Princess Augusta Sophia was presented (16 Nov.) and graciously received.—On the 18th, the Royal Academy was instituted, with Sir Joshua Reynolds as its first president.— Sir Francis Gosling, banker in Fleet Street, and alderman of Farringdon Without, died on 29 Dec.—An Act for regulating the watch of the City from 25 Dec., 1768, to 25 Dec., 1769, was passed (28 Oct), by the Common Council. The sum to be paid to the watchmen and beadles for the next year amounted to £11,747, and the total assessment to £23,680.

Early in the year, Wilkes again forced himself upon public attention.

After an attempt (1 Nov. 1766), to make terms through the Duke of Grafton, John Wilkes returned from France, and announced himself (10 Mar. 1768) a candidate for the representation of the City in Parliament at the impending general election. Parliament had been dissolved on the 12th. The City election was fixed for the 16th, and at the declaration of the poll (23rd), Wilkes was the lowest of the seven candidates. Two days before, the crowd unloosed the horses from Wilkes's carriage and drew it themselves. Wilkes immediately resolved to contest the representation of Middlesex. He had already determined to surrender to the Court of King's Bench, and in a letter on the 22nd, laid the blame of the proceedings against himself not on the King, but on his ministers. A great crowd attended him to the polling at Brentford (28th), whither he had set out in a coach drawn by six horses. Three candidates were nominated and as a result of the poll Wilkes and George Cooke were elected. A poster with the words "no Blasphemer" was exhibited and roused the anger of the mob. On their way home through the west-end and the City, they insisted upon a general illumination and broke the windows of all who refused. Reaching the Mansion House they broke every window, and the Lord Mayor's private residence in Aldersgate Street only escaped by being out of their reach. Wilkes and Liberty was the cry, and those refusing to shout were knocked down in the street; Wilkes appealed to his friends against disturbance and intimidation. According to promise, he appeared before the Court of King's Bench on 20 Ap., but not being there in due legal form nothing was done. On the 27th, he was brought up with due formality, and bail being refused he was ordered to the King's Bench prison. The coach was stopped on Westminster Bridge by the mob, who drew it to the Two Tuns Tavern at Spitalfields, where, after advising the crowd to retire, he secretly departed on foot and surrendered himself to the marshal of the King's Bench prison. Parliament met on 10 May. A crowd assembled at the King's Bench prison in St. George's Fields, ostensibly to conduct Wilkes to the House of Commons. The crowd became outrageous, the Riot Act was read and several persons, not connected with the mob, were killed. One young man, Allen, was killed in Blackman Street. Wilkes's outlawry was reversed on 8 June ; on the 15th the former verdicts were confirmed ; and on the 18th, sentence was passed of imprisonment for ten months and a fine of £500 for republishing No. 45, and twelve months' imprisonment and a fine of £500 for his *Essay on Woman*, securities for good behaviour for seven years were also required, of himself in £1,000, and two others in £500 each.

Dyers' Hall, in Little Elbow Lane, Dowgate Hill, fell down —Till this year the former mansion of Sir John Frederick, in Frederick Place, Old Jewry, was used as the London Excise Office —For the first time turtle appears by name in the *menu* of civic feasts, the occasion being the banquet to the King of Denmark, at the Mansion House.

1769.

N 27 Jan., 1769, Wilkes was elected alderman of Farringdon Without. His eligibility was disputed, and the Court of Aldermen decided, on 25 Ap, not to send him the customary formal notice of his election. Wilkes had petitioned Parliament (Nov, 1768) on the subject of his public grievances, and on 3 Feb. his petition was refused. On the same day he was expelled the House on account of an "insolent, scandalous, and seditious libel," in which he had referred to the disturbance at St. George's Fields in May as a massacre of the people. On Wilkes's re-election he was declared incapable of sitting in Parliament. He was chosen by the electors a second (16 Mar) and third time (13 Ap.). Enormous processions of his supporters paraded London. His opponent, Luttrel, was declared elected by the House of Commons Excited meetings were held in the City. A number of merchants resolved to demonstrate against Wilkes by an address to the King expressive of their loyalty Six hundred of the signatories proceeded (22 Mar) to St. James's to present the address. A mob attacked them on their way through the City. Some withdrew, some turned back, and some went by bye-ways. In the Strand a hearse, drawn by two black and two white horses, with a representation of the murder of Allen at St. George's Fields, took a place in front of the procession. Those who persevered were so pelted with mud as to be in danger of their lives. Mr. Boehm, who had the address in charge, was obliged to leave his coach and take refuge in a coffee-house. The address, safely lodged under a cushion in the coach, escaped the rioters and was carried home by the coachman. On arriving at St. James's the hearse and mob attempted to enter, and the Riot Act was read. Upon this they turned aside and visited the houses of the more obnoxious members of the administration, while the missing address was obtained, after some delay, and duly presented.

On 27 Ap. thirty Liverymen waited on the Lord Mayor with a request for a Common Hall to take the sense of the Livery on the present state of affairs. The Lord Mayor received them politely and next day replied that he did not feel justified in calling together so numerous a body at the request of so few. On 2 May 500 Liverymen met, signed a request for a Common Hall, and waited on the Lord Mayor, who promised to call a Court of Common Council, lay their request before it, and abide by its decision. A court was held (5th) and the request negatived. On Midsummer-day James Townsend and John Sawbridge were elected Sheriffs, and a humble petition of the Livery of London on the present state of national grievances adopted, which the Lord Mayor, Sheriffs, and City Members were asked to present. They did so at a levee on 5 July. The King made no reply.—On Michaelmas-day Sir Henry Bankes, though next in rotation for Lord Mayor, was rejected on a show of hands, because he had opposed the Common Hall. Alderman Beckford was elected by a poll on 6 Oct., and the choice was ratified, after a warm debate, by the Court of Aldermen.

However, the Recorder reported to the Livery that Beckford, not thinking himself compellable, had, on account of his age, infirmities, and inability to undergo the fatigues of office, declined. A general shout for "Beckford" was raised. Beckford appeared; he had declined, but not in the words of the Recorder. He was willing to serve, but his infirmities were too great. Another shout, "None but Beckford." Mr. Beckford retired, and the Sheriff moved that it be left to the Common Council who would probably prevail on Beckford to serve. The Livery then asked "Had the Lord Mayor received any answer to their petition (5 July) to the King, in which they had made a charge of malversation of public funds against a paymaster, whom they now identified as Lord Holland, and into whose conduct they now demanded a public inquiry. They ordered this to be entered on record as part of their proceedings at their election, and a copy to be sent to each of the City members. At half-past seven the Hall adjourned, after a sitting of nine hours. On the 12th Beckford consented to serve.

Entrance to the Cheshire Cheese Tavern, Wine Office Court.

The Lord Mayor's procession, though accompanied by only five Aldermen, was of a grander character than usual. At the presentation at the Exchequer Court, the only officer of State who met the Lord Mayor was the Lord Chancellor; but Lady Temple graced the occasion by wearing £50,000 worth of jewels. On the return passage by water several of the spectators were drowned through over-crowding of boats.

Blackfriars Bridge was opened for vehicular traffic on Sunday morning, 19 Nov.

A bridle-way was opened in Nov., 1768, and foot-passengers had passed since 1766. The Bridge was designed by Robert Mylne, and was constructed of Portland stone, having nine semi-elliptical arches, the centre one 100 feet wide, with a rise of 41 ft. 6 in.   The total length was 995 ft., and the width 45 ft.   Double Ionic columns, supporting small projecting recesses, stood against the face of each pier.   The structure was at first known as the William Pitt bridge, but this name was soon abandoned. The total cost of the bridge and approaches was £230,000, including £13,000 paid to the Watermen's Company as compensation for the loss of the Sunday ferry.   The bridge itself cost £152,840.   Tolls were levied until 1875.   Mylne, the architect, built himself a handsome residence at the northern end of the bridge.

The constables made a vigorous attempt to prevent the usual barbarous cruelty of throwing at cocks on Shrove Tuesday (7 Feb.)—Foreign point lace to the value of £6,000 was seized (20 Mar.) in the port of London.—In July disturbances at Spitalfields broke out afresh.   A riot took place, in which many were wounded, and 150 looms were damaged.   Two of the rioters were condemned to death, and the execution having been ordered to take place at Bethnal Green, the criminals were brought from Newgate, through the City and Whitechapel, to the gallows at the Cross Road, near the Salmon and Ball (6 Dec.).   Bricks, tiles, and stones were thrown at the men erecting the gallows, and the execution was concluded in haste and confusion.   One of the detachments of soldiers on the way home from guard, at Spitalfields, passed through the City with its band playing.   On the Lord Mayor remonstrating, the military authorities replied "That such a matter had hitherto been left to the discretion of the officer in charge, but that for the future, notice should be given to the Lord Mayor." Other riots occurred (30 Sept. and 7 Oct.), when the soldiers were called out and several cutters were killed and many wounded.—Queen Anne's statue in front of St. Paul's was mutilated by a Lascar, who was caught climbing over the railing (17 Sept.).—On 10 Oct. Wilkes obtained £4,000 damages for illegal outlawry from Lord Halifax, who had been Secretary of State at the time of the judgment.   Two guineas were paid early that day for a seat in court; by ten o'clock the price had fallen to a guinea, and by three in the afternoon to five shillings and three pence.—At the trial at the Old Bailey (20 Oct.) of Baretti, an Italian teacher of languages, who had killed a man in self-defence, Mr. Burke, Mr. Garrick, Mr. Beauclerk, and Dr. Johnson attended to give evidence as to the character of the accused.—The Excise office, designed by William Robinson, was erected on the site of old Gresham College, which extended from Old Broad Street to Bishopsgate Street.

1770.

PARLIAMENT was opened on 9 Feb., 1770, and, on the resignation of the Duke of Grafton, Lord North became Premier.—Lord Mayor Beckford, who was very wealthy, his English estates, as well as those in the West Indies, being extensive and valuable, gave the first of a series of politico-social entertainments at the Mansion House (9 Feb.).   Six dukes and duchesses, two earls, two barons, and many other notables were present.   "Never before," it was said, "had there been such a brilliant gathering at the Mansion House."—Six Liverymen presented a memorial to the Court of Common Council (1 Mar.) asking their concurrence in a request to the Lord Mayor to call a Common Hall.

Great debate ensued.   The Lord Mayor and the two Sheriffs argued in favour, and Aldermen Harley and Turner against the proposal.   On putting the question, three Aldermen and one hundred and nine Commoners voted for, and fifteen Aldermen and sixty-one Commoners against.   From two to three thousand Livery-men assembled on the 6th.   The Lord Mayor said "their principal grievance was the violation of the freedom of election," and sketched out the form which, in his opinion, reform should take. Thrice he exorted them to maintain order, dignity and regularity in their proceedings, so as to shut the mouths of their traducers. In the address to the King, drawn up in Committee and presented to the Hall, complaint was made of the slight put on the Livery by the King making no reply to their address presented on 5 July, 1769; and it concluded "Since therefore the misdeeds of your Majesty's Ministers, in violating the freedom of election and depraving the noble constitution of Parliament, are notorious, as well as subversive of the fundamental laws and liberties of this realm, and since your Majesty, both by honour and justice, is obliged inviolably to preserve them according to your coronation oath, we, your remonstrants, assure ourselves that your Majesty will restore the Constitutional Government and quiet of your people by dissolving this Parliament, and removing those evil Counsellors for ever from your councils." One hand was held up against the remonstrance. Next day (7th) the Sheriffs attended at St. James's to know when the King would be pleased to receive the address. After the levee Lord Denbigh asked the Remembrancer "Was the address signed and sealed, or how was it authenticated?" He replied, "It was no part of his duty, as a City officer, to give an answer." Turning to Sheriff Townsend his Lordship asked, "Was not the proceeding new and singular? Did the City ever present a remonstrance before?" The Sheriff answered, "Did ever a King of England before turn a deaf ear to the petitions of his subjects and his back on those who presented them?" "What made this address a Corporate Act?" "An Act of the Corporation, to be sure," was the reply. On their admission to the King's presence, and on preferring their request, the King said, "As the case is entirely new I will take time to consider it, and send an answer by a principal Secretary of State." Next day (8th) the reply in effect was, "as the case was new, how was the address authenticated, and what was the nature of the assembly by which it was adopted?" Next day, Friday (9th), the Sheriffs went again to St. James's, and, after further parley with the Lords-in-waiting, Lords Rochford and Weymouth, as to putting their requests in writing, they insisted on the right of the Sheriffs of London and Middlesex to a personal interview with His Majesty. The reply was, "The King understanding they came ministerially and authorised, would see them immediately after the levee." On being introduced to His Majesty, who was not as usual alone, but with Lords Gower, Rochford, and Weymouth present, the Sheriffs acknowledged receipt of the Secretary's letter, and announced "that the address was the address of the citizens of London in their greatest court assembled, and ordered by them to be authenticated as their act." The Remembrancer, who had been hindered by a Lord-in-waiting from entering with the Sheriffs, pointed out that, as Remembrancer, it was his right to enter the Royal Closet with the Sheriffs. The Lord-in-waiting pleaded ignorance. On Monday (12th) an answer was received "that His Majesty would receive the address on Wednesday, at two o'clock." On that day (14th) the Lord Mayor, three Aldermen, the two Sheriffs, one hundred and fifty-three Common Council-men, and the Committee of the Livery, in their proper gowns, attended by all the City Officers except the Recorder, arrived at St. James's at two o'clock. On being introduced to His Majesty, who received them according to use and wont seated on his throne, the Common Sergeant began to read the address, but on his getting confused, it was read by Sir James Hodges, the Common Clerk. In reply, His Majesty said "Ready, as I am always, to receive the requests and listen to the complaints of my subjects, it gives me great concern to find that any of them should have been so far misled as to offer me an address and remonstrance the contents of which I cannot but consider as disrespectful to me, injurious to my Parliament, and irreconcilable with the principles of the constitution. It is only by making the law the rule of my conduct, and by executing faithfully the trust reposed in me, so as to avoid the appearance of invading any of those powers which the Constitution has placed in other hands, that I can discharge my duty and secure my subjects in the enjoyment of their lawful rights ; and, while I so act, I have the right to expect, and I am confident I shall continue to receive, the steady and affectionate support of my people." They were graciously received, and retired after having the honour of kissing His Majesty's hand.

On Monday (19 Mar.) the House of Commons resolved that to declare the present Parliament to be illegal and its acts invalid was unwarrantable and indirectly destroyed the public peace, and that to convey such unwarrantable doctrines, under the specious pretence of petition, was a gross and manifold abuse of the undoubted right of the subject to petition the Crown.—On the 22nd, another grand entertainment was given at the Mansion House, to which a number of members of both Houses of Parliament were invited. The Egyptian Hall was illuminated, and persons whose houses were not illuminated had their windows broken.—On the 23rd a joint address of the Lords and Commons in Parliament assembled was presented to the King, expressing their deepest concern at seeing the undoubted right of petition so grossly perverted by being applied to the purpose, not of preserving, but of overthrowing the constitution, and of propagating doctrines which, if generally adopted, must be fatal to the peace of the Kingdom, and lead to the subversion of all lawful authority, at the same time aspersing and caluminating one of the Houses of the Legislature, and denying the legality of the present Parliament and the validity of its proceedings.—The same day the Court of the Goldsmiths' Company characterized the City Remonstrance as most indecent, and resolved "that the wardens do not in future summon the Livery to any Common Hall, except for election purposes, without the express approbation and consent of this court." On the 28th the Court of the Weavers' Company adopted a similar resolution , and, on the 30th, the Court of the Grocers' Company, after expressing their entire disapprobation of the Remonstrance, characterising it as indecent and highly disrespectful to His Majesty, and as an insidious suggestion of ill-designing men, undermining public liberty under pretence of preserving it, adopted a resolution to the same effect as that of the Goldsmiths. On a precept issued by the Lord Mayor, a Common Hall was held on 12 Ap., to receive His Majesty's answer to the address of 14 Mar., the resolutions and address of both Houses of Parliament in reference thereto, and the resolutions of the three Livery Companies. The Lord Mayor delivered a long address, distinguishing between His Majesty and his ministers, and appealing to the law and constitution of the country as their defence.—The same day an order was sent to the King's Bench prison for the discharge of John Wilkes ; and, on the 17th, all his debts having been discharged by the supporters of the Bill of Rights he was discharged and went off privately with his daughter to the country house of Reynolds, his attorney, in Kent. "Never were illuminations so grand and so voluntary," say the reports, "as on this event all over England and, to the praise of the lower order of patriots, no disorders have been complained of." On the 24th the Lord Mayor, attended by four Aldermen, went in procession to the Guildhall to swear in John Wilkes as Alderman of Farringdon Without. The motion was carried without a division, and it was resolved that as Alderman he should take precedence from the time of his election (Jan., 1769).—A Court of Common Council met on Monday, 14 May. It was resolved that a humble address of remonstrance and petition be presented to His Majesty touching the violated right of election, and the applications of the Livery of London with His Majesty's answer thereupon. A committee was appointed to draw up the address, with the assistance of the Recorder and Common Sergeant. The Recorder declared the King's answer could not be considered the act of the ministers, but the personal act of the King. He was over-ruled, and, on report to the Common Council, he protested against the address as a most abominable libel.

The address was approved. On the breaking up of the meeting, the Sheriffs went to the palace to learn when the King would be pleased to receive the address. The King could not be seen, but appointed Wednesday next (16th) to receive the Sheriffs. On Wednesday the Sheriffs attended with the Remembrancer, who, in accordance with immemorial usage, was admitted with them to the audience. His Majesty appointed Wednesday week (23rd). On that day the Lord Mayor, with Aldermen Stephenson and Trecothick, the two Sheriffs, seventy-five Common Councilmen, the City Remembrancer, and the Town Clerk, waited on the King with the Remonstrance and received this reply:—"I should have been wanting to the public as well as to myself, if I had not expressed my dissatisfaction with the late address. My sentiments on that subject continue the same ; and I should ill-deserve to be considered as the father of my people, if I could suffer myself to be prevailed upon to make such a use of my prerogative as I cannot but think inconsistent with the interest, and dangerous to the Constitution of the Kingdom." The Lord Mayor then addressed His Majesty in these words :—

" Most Gracious Sovereign,—Will your Majesty be pleased so far to condescend as to permit the Mayor of your loyal City of London to declare, in your Royal Presence, on behalf of his fellow citizens, how much the bare apprehension of your Majesty's displeasure would, at all times, affect their minds : the declaration of that displeasure has already filled them with inexpressible anxiety, and with the deepest affliction Permit me, Sire, to assure your Majesty, that your Majesty has not in all your Dominions any subjects more faithful, more dutiful, or more affectionate to your Majesty's person and family, or more ready to sacrifice their lives and fortunes in the maintenance of the true honour and dignity of your Crown We do, therefore, with the greatest humility and submission, most earnestly supplicate your Majesty, that you will not dismiss us from your presence without expressing a more favourable opinion of your faithful Citizens, and without some comfort, without some prospect at least of redress. Permit me, Sire, farther to observe, that whoever has already dared, or shall hereafter endeavour, by false insinuations and suggestions, to alienate your Majesty's affections from your loyal subjects in general, and from the City of London in particular, and to withdraw your confidence in and regard for your people, is an enemy to your Majesty's person and family, a violator of the public peace, and a betrayer of our happy Constitution, as it was established at the glorious Revolution."

A special Court of Common Council was held on the 28th to consider an address to the King on the birth of a Princess. Alderman Rossiter complained of the Lord Mayor's speech to His Majesty on the 23rd as not being given to his Lordship in charge by that Court, and was supported by Alderman Harley. Alderman Wilkes and the two Sheriffs defended the Lord Mayor. The Court desired his Lordship to state what he had said , and, on his doing so, voted him, without a division, their thanks for his noble conduct, and ordered the King's answer and the Lord Mayor's reply to be entered on the City records. The address was agreed to.—In addition to the usual congratulations occurred the following expressions —"There are not in your Majesty's Dominions any subjects more faithful, more dutiful, and more affectionate to your Majesty's person and family, or more ready to sacrifice their lives and fortunes in maintaining the true honour and dignity of the Crown."—On their way to present the address (1 June), when the Lord Mayor and senior Aldermen had passed through Temple Bar the gates were suddenly shut against Alderman Harley by a small mob who pelted him with stones and dirt, and pulled him out of his coach, opposite the Swan Tavern, where he had to take refuge. On the arrival at St. James's of the Lord Mayor the Lord Chamberlain addressed to him a request that "As your Lordship thought fit to speak to His Majesty after his answer to the late

remonstrance, I am to acquaint your Lordship that, as it was unusual, His Majesty desires that nothing of the kind may happen in the future." The Lord Mayor desired the paper or a copy. The Lord Chamberlain said "he would acquaint His Majesty and take his directions." After a time he returned with an order for the whole Court to attend with the address. His Majesty expressed his hearty thanks for "the duty and affection to my person and family and for the zeal for the true honour and dignity of the Crown which you express on this occasion."

On 1 June the Committee, appointed by the Common Council, waited on the Earl of Chatham with the City's thanks for his eminent services to his country. On 14 May he had moved in the upper House an address to

Portrait of Lord Mayor Beckford.

the King to dissolve the present Parliament, but was defeated.—Three weeks after (21st) Lord Mayor Beckford died. He had travelled up to London from his Wiltshire estates in one day, while suffering from a cold, and the cold developed into rheumatic fever. On the 30th he was buried at Fonthill, Wilts. Alderman

F

Barlow Trecothick was elected as his successor. On 5 July the Common Council resolved to erect a statue in the Guildhall to the late Lord Mayor, with his speech to the King on 23 May inscribed on the pedestal, the cost not to exceed £1,000.—The Recorder's conduct in not attending the Lord Mayor on 23 May was brought before the Council on 27 Sept.

Though ill he attended the Court and pleaded conscience. He could not read a document couched in such harsh terms—an indignity to his Sovereign and to Parliament. Alderman Wilkes replied that his oath of office covered his conscience; he was only the mouth-piece of the Court, and free from personal responsibility in the matter, and moved that the Recorder in his refusal acted contrary to his oath and the duty of his office, the motion was carried.

On Michaelmas-day Aldermen Brass Crosby, and James Townsend were nominated by the Livery, and the first was elected Lord Mayor. At his request the officers of the Goldsmiths' Company had their gowns trimmed with blue instead of, as formerly, with white. The thanks of the Livery were awarded to the late patriotic Sheriffs for their upright and impartial conduct in the discharge of their office, and ordered to be entered on record.—At a meeting of Common Council (12 Oct.) it was decided that "James Eyre, the present Recorder, be no more advised with, retained or employed in any of the affairs of this Corporation, he being in the opinion of this City unworthy of future trust or confidence;" and that John Glynn, Esq., serjeant-at-law, should, for the future, be retained as counsel for the City. The freedom of the City was voted to John Dunning, Esq., for his defence in Parliament, when Solicitor-General, of the right of the subject to petition and remonstrance—An address was agreed on (15 Nov.), to be presented to the King regarding the violated right of election and praying for a dissolution.—This was presented at St. James's on the 21st. Sir James Hodges, in the absence of the Recorder, read the address, to which His Majesty replied, "As I have seen no reason to alter the opinion already expressed, I cannot comply with it."

A fire broke out in Paternoster Row (8 Jan.) where four houses were burned down, one of them being the Oxford Press warehouse, in which £10,000 worth of Bibles and other books were consumed; another (11 Mar) at Bethlehem Hospital, where the roof had to be broken through to allow the unfortunate patients to escape.—Trade difficulties still continued. The hat-dyers of Southwark seized (19 Feb.) a fellow workman for working overtime without extra pay, mounted him, bearing a label descriptive of his offence, on an ass, visited all the hat works in the Boro' and those in the City, with a band of boys playing rough music, and compelled the men to strike at all the shops visited.—The parishioners of Clerkenwell paying scot and lot were declared (28th) in the Court of Common Pleas to be the electors of the Vicar of the parish.—The Jewish community (7 Ap) offered a reward for the detection of such of their co-religionists as were receivers of stolen goods.—The first stone of the new Prison at Newgate was laid by the Lord Mayor on 31 May; and on 28 June that of the New River Company's offices was laid by the Governor on the site of the Shakespearean playhouse. One 36th part of a King's moiety of this Company was sold (15 Aug) by auction for £6,700.—The first stone of the new Lying-in Hospital, at the corner of City Road and Old Street, was laid by the Lord Mayor and Deputy John Paterson (10th Oct.) amid the acclamations of a vast concourse of people.—A woman, condemned for highway robbery, was driven to Tyburn for execution (10 Oct.), dressed in white, with her coffin on the top of the cart, and two highwaymen, one on her right and the other on her left. She had been tried in three successive sessions for highway robbery and convicted at the third.—The office of one of the Coal Meters of the City was sold (31st) for £5,140.—There being a prospect of a war with Spain about the Falkland Islands, a Royal proclamation was issued (22 Sept.), offering bounties of thirty shillings for able-bodied, and twenty shillings for ordinary seamen ; and the Lord Mayor was requested by the Admiralty to back warrants for impressing seamen within his jurisdiction. This he declined to do. The Common Council, however, offered a bounty of thirty shillings (2 Oct.) for each volunteer enlisting within the City, and afterwards increased the sum to forty shillings over and above the Government bounty (17 Nov.). The City bounty was earned by 482 volunteers Towards the end of December a press-gang on the river impressed upwards of 700 men in one night, having stripped every vessel of all useful hands.— Chatterton poisoned himself in a house in Brooke Street, Holborn, and was buried in the grounds of Shoe Lane Workhouse.—"Lloyd's" was established as a society.—The Dyers' Company erected a new hall.—The last licence to woolwinders was granted this year, under the Woolmen's charter of 1462.— The Royal General Dispensary, 25, Bartholomew Close, was founded.—The King's Printing-house was removed from Printing-house Square to New Street, Gough Square.—During the contest between the City and the House of Commons, "Junius," in his letters to the *Public Advertiser*, sided with the City. —Popular resentment against the King's treatment of civic deputations was displayed in caricatures, such as one printed in the *Oxford Magazine* for April. The cartoon, entitled "The Button-maker," represents the Mayor and Sheriffs tendering their remonstrance, while the King turns away contemptuously and shows two buttons to his lords-in-waiting, and exclaims : " I cannot attend to your remonstrance ; do you not see that I have been employed in business of much more consequence?" One of the courtiers ejaculates : "What a genius ! why, he was a born button-maker."

1771.

ON 4 Jan., 1771, in order to prevent collusion and monopoly of grain, regulations were published in Mark Lane, ordering an exact account of wheat brought in, the prices given, and the names of purchasers.—A press-gang beating their drums in the City was taken before the Lord Mayor in his Court, and reprimanded (15 Jan.). The Common Council ordered (22 Jan.) that " if any one be pressed within the City or liberties under a warrant backed by any justice, the City Solicitor is to prosecute, if the impressed person desire it, the justice who granted and the constable who executed it." The settlement of the differences between Spain and England put an end to this difficulty for a time.—Complaint was made in the House of Commons of certain newspapers reporting, or (as it was termed) misrepresenting the debates in that House. This was held to be a breach of privilege.

Two printers, Wheble and Thompson, were ordered to appear at the bar of the House. They disregarded the order. On an address from the House of Commons, a Royal proclamation was issued (8 Mar.), offering £50 reward for their apprehension. Five other printers were ordered (14th) to appear at the bar of the House. Wheble was arrested by a printer in his employ and brought before Alderman Wilkes (15th) who, after binding him over to prosecute his printer for illegal arrest, discharged him. The Alderman then signed a certificate to the Lords of the Treasury, entitling the printer to the £50 reward. In the evening, Thompson was brought before Alderman Oliver and discharged under the same conditions. Next day Miller, one of the printers in the order of the 14th, was arrested by a messenger of the House of Commons. He refused to go, called in a constable, and charged the messenger with illegal arrest and detention. The constable brought both before the Lord Mayor, and Aldermen Wilkes and Oliver. Miller stated his grievance and was discharged. The messenger was charged with illegally detaining Miller and ordered to prison. Meanwhile, the Serjeant of the House arrived at the Court and demanded the delivery of both Miller and the messenger into his custody. On being asked for a warrant from a magistrate, he could not produce one. The Lord Mayor said that, as guardian of the liberties of his fellow citizens, he could allow no one to arrest a citizen of London without a warrant. The warrant from the House of Commons and the arrest were both illegal. He would, however, take bail for the messenger. The Lord Mayor and Alderman Oliver were ordered to be in their places in the House of Commons on the 19th to answer for what they had done. Wilkes was ordered to attend at the bar, but he insisted on appearing (if he did appear) in his place as the duly elected member for Middlesex. On that morning, an address to the citizens of London was posted on the walls, announcing the Lord Mayor's illness and his determination to be present this day in his place in the House of Commons in support of their rights and privileges, though he should be carried on a litter, and calling on the freemen of London and all friends of freedom to attend and bring the Lord Mayor back in triumph to the Mansion House. Though feeble and infirm the Lord Mayor, attended by Alderman Oliver and his chaplain, set out for Westminster. An immense crowd overflowed into the neighbouring streets, and rending the air with huzzas, followed to the House of Commons, shouting, "the people's friend," "the guardian of the people's rights and the nation's liberties." The Lord Mayor told the House he had only done his duty as chief magistrate of the City of London. By his oath and the City charters he was bound to protect the persons, property and franchise of his fellow citizens. On account of his illness he was allowed to withdraw, and the discussion was put off till Tuesday week. On his return the crowd unloosed the horses from his coach, and drew it from St. Paul's to the Mansion House.

The Lord Mayor's clerk was ordered to attend the House (20th) and bring the book of recognizances. On the motion of the House the recognizance was ordered to be erased, and he erased it accordingly. The Common Council (21st) thanked the Lord Mayor and the two Aldermen for their conduct, ordered this to be signed by the Town Clerk and forwarded to each of the three. Four Aldermen and eight Commoners were appointed a committee of defence. The Lord Mayor and Alderman Oliver attended the House (25th) according to order. A crowd, increasing all the way from the Mansion House, accompanied them to Westminster Hall. At half-past ten the Lord Mayor obtained leave to withdraw. The crowd drew him in his coach home to the Mansion House. At three a.m. Alderman Oliver, by 183 to 83, was ordered to the Tower, whither he was conducted next morning between seven and eight, by the Serjeant-at-arms. Next day (27th) the Lord Mayor went again to the House, attended by crowds as before. The line of carriages extended from St. Paul's to Charing Cross. The justices and constables of Westminster were in readiness, and the Guards also, in case of riots. Being very ill, he was supported to the door of the House by his friends. Great confusion prevailed in the House, and hours elapsed before the orders of the day were reached. The Lord Mayor was ordered to the Tower by 202 to 39. Some proposed to commit him there and then to the custody of the Serjeant-at-arms. He replied he desired no favour, but would gladly follow his brother alderman and friend to the Tower. He returned to the Mansion House about half-past twelve, and at four in the morning went quietly to the Tower in a hackney coach. The mob became very riotous. Lord North lost his hat and was in great danger; Charles James Fox had the windows of his carriage broken; many members were grossly insulted and their carriages broken. The Common Council ordered that the expenses of the two gentlemen in the

Tower should be defrayed from the City purse, and the Easter festivities were put off by the Sheriffs till the Lord Mayor had regained his liberty. On 30 Mar. a number of peers and members of the House of Commons waited on Crosby and Oliver in the Tower, to express their regard for them and their disapprobation of these proceedings. On 1 Ap., two carts, filled with persons intended to represent criminals of rank, and followed by hearses, went through the City to Tower Hill; in the first was a chimney sweep acting as chaplain; the persons in this cart went through a mock process of beheading, were put into the hearses and carried off; while the stuffed figures in the second cart had their heads chopped off and burned, amid the shouts and huzzas of the mob. On the 3rd, the Common Council resolved to apply for a writ of Habeas Corpus. On the 5th, Lord Chief Justice De Grey and Lord Mansfield advised that the two members be re-committed till the prorogation of Parliament; they could not venture to interfere in an affair of this magnitude without the advice of the other judges. The Lord Mayor was brought before the Court of Common Pleas (22nd), which decided that they had no jurisdiction over the House of Commons, who were only acting with respect to their own members. His Lordship's act was not only a contempt of the House of Commons but even of the citizens of London themselves, who, by their representatives, are virtually a part of that House. The Mayor was sent back to the Tower. Alderman Oliver was brought before the Court of Exchequer (27th) and sent back on similar grounds. The Lord Mayor received the freedom of six cities and towns (30th), and most of the City wards by their Common Councilmen, and the Society of the Bill of Rights paid their compliments to the two prisoners in the Tower. The Common Council resolved (3 May) to attend (with the City officers, and the Aldermen wearing their scarlet gowns), the Lord Mayor and Alderman Oliver, in procession from the Tower to the Mansion House, on their release at the prorogation of Parliament. In accordance therewith, they were met (8th) by a train of fifty-three carriages and the Honourable Artillery Company as an honorary guard at the Tower gate, and conducted to the Mansion House, amid the shouts of the populace. At night the City was illuminated. The gates of Serjeants' Inn in Fleet Street, the windows of the Speaker of the House of Commons and of others who did not illuminate, were broken. Meanwhile (8 Ap.), the grand jury found true bills against Whetham, the messenger of the House of Commons, for arresting Miller, and against Carpenter for arresting Wheble. A *nolle prosequi* was entered (13 May) in the case of the messenger, and Carpenter (30 June) was found guilty and ordered to pay one shilling fine, and to be imprisoned for two months in Wood Street Compter. The "Society of the Supporters of the Bill of Rights" voted £100 each to Wheble, Thompson and Miller, for having appealed to the law and not betrayed by subjection the rights of Englishmen.

Wilkes's Middlesex election expenses and numerous debts had been discharged by the "Society of the Supporters of the Bill of Rights." In the spring of 1771 differences occurred between Wilkes and John Horne (known afterwards as Horne Tooke) as to the

Remains of the Bull Inn, Aldgate, now destroyed.

disposal of certain subscriptions, and Horne unsuccessfully endeavoured to bring about a dissolution of the Society. On the evening of 24 June, when Wilkes and Bull were elected Sheriffs, the effigy of Mr. Horne, in a canonical habit, with a pen in one hand, and in the other a salt box (representing the treasury of the Bill of Rights Society), after being carried through the streets, was burnt in front of the Mansion House.

In May, the carver to the Lord Mayor sold his place for £1,600; and, in June, a City Marshal's place was purchased for £2,400.—On 11 June, a congratulatory address was presented to the King from the Court of Common Council on the birth of a prince. The deputation having received a gracious reply, the lord-in-waiting asked if any of them chose to be knighted, but the honour was declined.—A

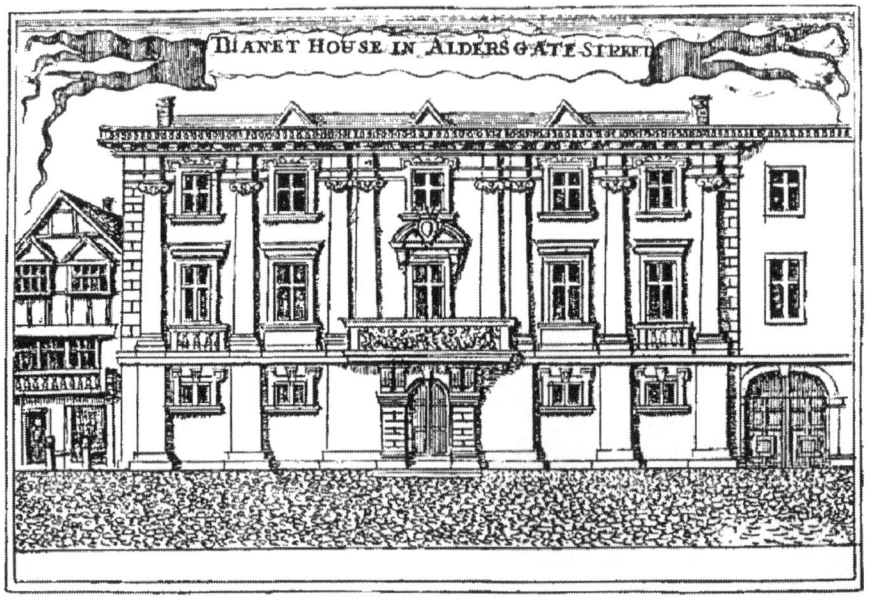

dispute as to the patronage of Bow Church was decided in the Court of Common Pleas (13 June). The right of presentation was shared between the Archbishop of Canterbury and the Grocers' Company; on this occasion the Grocers' claim to present was sustained, and the Rev. Dr. Sclater appointed.—At the Common Hall, for the election of Sheriffs, a committee was appointed to draw up a Remonstrance to His Majesty in reference to the violated right of election, imprisoning their chief magistrate and an alderman, erasing a judicial record, and depriving them of Durham Yard, in the absence from Parliament of two of their representatives, and, asking for a speedy dissolution of Parliament. On 10 July, the Lord Mayor, attended by a numerous company in 50 carriages, waited on His Majesty with the address. The King, in reply, said, " It is with concern that I see a part of my subjects so far misled and deluded as to renew in such reprehensible terms a request with which I have repeatedly declared I cannot comply."—On 26 Sept., the Sheriffs dined in Goldsmiths' Hall. The new Sheriffs, Wilkes and Bull, issued an address to the Livery to the effect that they would not use the soldiers in settling riots, but rely entirely on the civil powers. On the 28th they were sworn into office.—The show of hands for the election of Lord Mayor was in favour of the then Lord Mayor and Alderman Sawbridge. At the ensuing poll, Alderman William Nash was the only candidate who attended the hustings. He was ill-treated by the populace, and carried off by Wilkes in his carriage. On 8 Oct., Nash was duly elected.—On 23 Oct., new regulations were made by the Sheriffs for the conduct of trials at the Old Bailey.

The public were to be admitted, prisoners to be arraigned singly, and without fetters; trials were to come on in rotation as they stood on the list. Next day the public crowded in in such numbers that the business of the court was sometimes stopped. The grand jury claimed their privilege of having a gallery in the court for themselves to hear the trials during the session.—A number of Jews being convicted (6 Dec.) of robbery and housebreaking, the Recorder called attention to the laudable conduct of the principal Jews, and hoped no one would stigmatize a whole nation for the villainies of a few, whom they had done everything in their power to bring to justice.—Cooks' Hall, on the east side of Aldersgate Street, was burned down.—Thanet House, in Aldersgate Street, was utilized as a Lying-in-Hospital, 1750–1771.—The London Coffee House was established in Ludgate Hill. Here met a Club, of which Priestley and Benjamin Franklin were members.—Thavies Inn, Holborn, was sold by the Society of Lincoln's Inn.—"Lloyd's" engaged temporary rooms in Pope's Head Alley.—During the summer the Lord Mayor held a Court of Conservancy at Stratford, and made the customary journey down the river to the boundary stone below Rochester, which marks the limit of the City's conservancy in the Medway. Some letters illegally cut in the stone were erased, and the inscription carved "Brass Crosby, Esq.; Lord Mayor, 1771." The sword of state was laid upon it, and several small pieces of silver distributed among the spectators.—A Court of Escheats was held at Guildhall this year before the Lord Mayor by virtue of a commission issued by the Court of Chancery. No similar court had been held in the City for 150 years.—In opposition to a Board of Works (Scotland Yard) bill for embanking the river at Durham Yard, the Corporation pleaded their rights over the river bed as proved by cases (some 200 years ago) of removal or erection of stairs, the receipt of rents for riverside property, etc.

1772.

ON 21 Jan., 1772, Parliament re-assembled, and on the 24th a presentation of plate to Aldermen Crosby, Wilkes and Oliver, was made by the Common Council; a cup, worth £200, to the Ex-Mayor, and one of £100 value to each of the two Aldermen. The Oliver cup now forms part of the City plate at the Mansion House.—The Carpenters' Company (5 Feb.) ordered to be given to each Liveryman of their Company a silver medal, for admission to the Guildhall on election days.

The example was followed by other Companies.—Alderman Sawbridge had introduced a Bill to the House of Commons for shortening the duration of Parliaments.

One hundred and forty-three Liverymen requested (12 Feb) the Lord Mayor to call a Common Hall, for giving instructions to their representatives to support this Bill which was to be read on the 15th. His Lordship promised to consider the matter, and returned answer, that "At present the right of the Lord Mayor to summon extraordinary Common Halls was disputed, and is now under litigation and waiting for decision. All constitutional questions may be discussed at the Common Council meetings which he is ready to call when necessary." On the receipt of this reply by the Livery a deputation of twenty Common Councilmen waited on his Lordship (15 Feb.), desiring him to call the Common Council together on Tuesday, 18th. He promised (amid marks of disapprobation) to summon it on some convenient day next week. It was carried at this meeting (20th) that the Lord Mayor call together a Common Hall, to which he replied he neither would nor could comply with the requisition. On 4 Mar. Alderman Sawbridge's Bill was lost by 251 to 83.

On 11 Feb. the order for prohibiting exportation of corn was renewed.—On 25 Feb. over £500 were subscribed at the Chapter Coffee House, and by 25 Mar. £8,000 had been raised there and at Lloyd's Coffee House for reducing the price of provisions.

With this money beef was sold from 3½d. to 4d. per lb. ; and mutton for 3½d. to 4¼d. per lb. by the carcase. Coals, which, owing to contrary winds, cost 20d. a bushel (25 Mar.), and £4 a chaldron, fell (8 Ap.) to 31s. a chaldron Waggons, loaded with meat for Leadenhall, were seized by the populace at various places in the eastern counties. On 8 Ap. a petition from the Common Council was presented to the House of Commons for free importation of corn, and the prayer was granted. At this time French beans cost one guinea a hundred, and roses 2s. 6d. each at Covent Garden.—After the Spital sermon at St. Bride's (22 Ap.) the mob broke the windows of the Lord Mayor's Coach, because he had not lowered the price of provisions, and he was, with difficulty, preserved from personal violence.

On 6 Mar. an *émeute* broke out in the Fleet Prison ; a prisoner had died, it was said, from the dampness of the walls. Twenty-two ringleaders were seized and the rest thereupon submitted.—On the 27 Ap. the tailors brought the question of wages forward at the sessions, and were complimented for seeking redress in a legal manner. The sessions advanced wages 6d. per day, and 12d. in time of court mourning.—On 8 May a fire broke out in Throgmorton Street, in which twenty-three houses were consumed. Drapers' Hall was burnt, the furniture, pictures, &c., in the hall and court room were saved, but the grand lantern at the bottom of the stairs, which cost £200, was destroyed. The whole damages from the fire were estimated at £30,000.—The bounties for mackerel and herrings were still continued ; over £540 had been expended, and the Common Council gave the Committee power to draw to the extent of £200 more.—On 11 May the statue of Lord Mayor Beckford, which had been voted immediately after his death, was set up in the Guildhall. He was represented in the attitude he assumed when he made reply to His Majesty.

His speech was inscribed on the pedestal in letters of gold.—On 10 June the banking house of Neale, James, Fordyce, and Down stopped payment. This was brought about by the speculations in Change Alley of Fordyce, one of the partners. News of the disaster was received forty-three hours after in Edinburgh, a distance of 425 miles. The bank had in its coffers £20,000 of the Scottish Land Tax. The failure caused great consternation. Rumours were set afloat that all the banks were failing. The merchants of London and the Bank of England interposed, and restored confidence; and in December a dividend of 4s. in the £ was declared.—On 18 June the Corporation voted £400 for the sufferers from a fire at Grenada.—The Lords of the Treasury purchased Ely House and grounds in Holborn; the house was to be pulled down, and on the site Hackney Coach, Salt, and Stamp Offices were to be erected.—On 23 Oct. James Eyre, recorder, was appointed a Baron of the Exchequer and received the honour of knighthood.—Alderman James Townsend was elected Lord Mayor.

On Lord Mayor's day Wilkes' supporters created a disturbance outside the Guildhall Lord Mayor Townsend tried to induce the gentlemen in the company to sally out with him, sword in hand, against the rioters, but more peaceful counsel prevailed The Hon. Artillery Company sent a party of men to guard the Guildhall, and they remained on duty all night.

On 13 Nov. the Court of Common Council passed resolutions—

"That the late Lord Mayor (Nash) in refusing to call a Common Hall and to call a Court of Common Council on the request of a considerable body of members, to put questions in Common Hall of consequence to the rights of the Livery, and in ordering the sword to be taken up both in a Common Hall and in a Court of Common Council before business was finished, was guilty of violating the rights and privileges of this City;" and "that if any future Recorder accept the office of Judge in any of the Royal Courts at Westminster, or any patent of precedence from the Crown, if appointed Recorder of this City, shall from that time receive only the ancient salary of £120 for him and his deputy." Serjeant John Glynn was elected Recorder on the 17th, by a majority of one vote

On 3 Dec. a vagrant, who had been passed on to his parish and had come back to London, was found begging near the Exchange, and was ordered by the Lord Mayor to be whipped from one end of Cornhill to the other as an incorrigible rogue, and then returned to his parish; and, on the 8th, a special order was issued for the apprehension of hawkers, vagrants, &c., within the City. On the 9th the Lord Mayor caused a number of vagrant boys in the City to be taken and placed in the Compter for security, till the Marine Society could find opportunity to provide for them. On his recommendation the Court of Common Council voted £300 for this Society.

An Act was passed for London by which the turncock who first supplied water on an outbreak of fire was to receive 10s.; the first engine which arrived on the spot 30s., the second 20s., and the third 10s.—The negro, Somerset, who was liberated by the exertions of Sharpe, had been confined in the Poultry Compter.—Punishment by pressure (inflicted on Newgate prisoners who refused to plead at the bar) was abolished.

G

1773.

T HE Lord Mayor gave notice that he did not intend to be present at the service in St. Paul's on 30 Jan., 1773, the anniversary of the execution of Charles I.—On 5 Feb. the Lord Mayor and others waited on the King, and presented an address from the Common Council on the birth of a prince. Aldermen Halifax and Lewes were knighted.—The Court of Aldermen passed a resolution (16th) in favour of shorter Parliaments.—Damage to the extent of £50,000 was done in the river (26th) from a severe hurricane.—A petition was presented to Parliament by the Lord Mayor and Sheriffs (3 Mar.) asking for a bounty of 4s. per quarter on the importation of wheat, from 31 Mar. to 31 July. The request was refused, and on the 16th £2,000 were voted out of the Chamber of London as a bounty of 4s. per quarter for the first 20,000 quarters of wheat imported between the last day of Mar. and the last day of June. —The Livery met in Common Hall (11th) on summons from the Lord Mayor, and agreed to an address to the King requesting redress of grievances, and a dissolution of Parliament. Some opposed it as "being only the second part of the same tune." The King's reply concluded as follows :—"Your petition is so void of foundation, and is, besides, conceived in such disrespectful terms, that I am convinced you do not yourselves seriously imagine it can be complied with."—A petition from the City was presented by Sheriff Lewes (17 Mar.) to the House of Commons against lotteries. "Individuals," it was affirmed, "resort to methods of raising money by dangerous and unwarrantable practices in order to get shares in the lotteries. They involve themselves in difficulties in very distressful consequences, and the ruin of many families result therefrom."—In issuing the Speaker's summonses for the members of Parliament to be present on 26 Ap., the Sheriffs addressed those for Middlesex to Wilkes and Glynn. Wilkes wrote to the Speaker in support of his claim (20th), and presented himself to be sworn a member of the House, but was refused admission (26th).—The first stone of a house for the Marine Society in Bishopsgate was laid by Lord Romney, the president (30th). —The Common Council presented a petition to the House of Commons against the Bill for the East India Company, chiefly on the ground that it permitted Parliament to interfere with individual as well as corporate rights.—Alderman Wilkes proposed (9 June) that an address be presented to the King on the safe delivery of the Duchess of Gloucester. This was negatived, as it was unusual for the City to address except in the case of the issue of the immediate heir to the throne.—£1,000 per annum was granted (16th) to the Recorder during the pleasure of the Court, and £200 to the Common Serjeant.—In 1770 some of the City Companies, offended by the tone of a Remonstrance adopted at a Common Hall, forbade their members to attend Common Halls, except on occasions of elections. Alderman Plumbe, of the Goldsmiths' Company, lost his case in a suit by which the Corporation desired to test the question whether Liverymen were bound to attend a Common Hall on the Lord Mayor's precept (14 July).

In 1775, however, this judgment was reversed, and no Lord Mayor has since been able to compel obedience to a summons for a Common Hall

A gang of freshwater pirates who infested the river was broken up by the arrest of "Black Jemmy," the ringleader, at his lodgings in Milford Lane (Aug.).— Alderman Frederick Bull was elected Mayor for next year (29 Sep.), his opponent, Alderman Wilkes, being only defeated by the Lord Mayor's casting vote.

The election was conducted with much altercation and recrimination, perhaps best described in a print issued at the time, under the heading, "The City Bull-fight." The patriot [Wilkes] with the staff of liberty is pushing his Bull at two opponents, one of whom is making his attack in a suit of Tower armour, and the other with the dagger of Brutus. The parson of Brentford [Horne], in endeavouring to halter the bull, has haltered himself Sir Watkin [Lewes, Sheriff] with a goat's head, is backing the patriot, and at the hustings is Hopping Jimmy [Lord Mayor Townsend] with bags of City savings. One of the court candidates, Haxxy [Alderman Halifax], is in the air, tossed by the bull, and the other, Alderman Esdaile, walking away from the scene.

On 21 Oct., two freshwater pirates were detected in plundering a ship in the river. The crew, instead of prosecuting, bound them neck and heels and tied them up to the shrouds, where they remained for four hours, and every half-hour received fifty lashes with a cat till the time was expired. When taken down, they were almost dead, in which condition the tars put them on shore and there left them to shift for themselves.—On the 31st died Sir Robert Ladbroke, Alderman of Bridge Ward, and one of the City representatives.

A livery was granted to the Wheelwrights' Company.—The new Jonathan's Coffee-house in Change Alley was now known as the "Stock Exchange."

1774.

THE Court of Aldermen refused (24 Jan., 1774) the request of Messrs. Adams to have their lottery tickets for the Adelphi building drawn at Guildhall.—A young woman applied at the Mansion House, before Alderman Wilkes (29th) for a pass to her own parish. The Alderman elicited from her that her husband was a negro, a slave to a merchant in Lothbury, and granted a warrant for his appearance before the Lord Mayor. He had been fourteen years in England as a slave to his master, without wages.   On applying for assistance when his wife was confined his master refused to help him.   His Lordship discharged the negro as he was in a free country, and promised, if he were molested, to see justice done.   A small sum was given to the slave, and an Attorney in the Lord Mayor's Court was instructed to bring an action against the master for fourteen years' wages.— A proposal was made in the House of Commons (25 Feb) for cutting a canal, projected by James Sharp (an ironmonger, of Leadenhall Street, and Common Councilman of Lime Street Ward), from Waltham Abbey along the course of the Lea, through Homerton, the south side of Hackney Road and Shoreditch, to Moorfields.   A goods depôt was to be made between Holywell-mount and the Tabernacle in City Road.   The water was to be brought to a pond, with a spacious gravel walk around it, in Moorfields   Passengers were to be carried at three-pence a head.   The water in the pond was to be available for extinguishing fires and for flushing the common sewers.—A congratulatory address was presented (4 Mar.) to the King on the birth of Prince Adolphus Frederick.   Alderman Walter Rawlinson received the honour of knighthood.—Oliver Goldsmith died at his chambers in the Temple (4 Ap.).—It was determined in the Lord Mayor's Court (12 Ap) that no two-wheeled car, drawn by men, be employed in the streets of London, under penalty of 40s.—In order to avoid confusion at the Common Halls, whether for election or for other purposes, a temporary screen was provided (24th) for erection across the Guildhall Yard, with thirty-five doors, on which were the names of the Companies.   At the several doors, the Companies' beadles were stationed to see that only Liverymen belonging thereto entered, while the doors were so contrived that only one person could enter at a time.—In May a Bill for the reform of prisons was passed, John Howard being greatly instrumental in directing the attention of Parliament to the subject.

According to Dr. Lettsom the Wood Street Compter was, at this period, greatly in need of such reform.   One room was 12 feet high, 33 feet long, and 15 feet broad.   Within, the beds were arranged one over the other in little separate cabins , the uppermost was reached by a pair of steps   In this room forty prisoners were lodged.   Their victuals were dressed at a large fire in the same room, which had only one door and no other opening but the chimney.   No provision was made for sickness—not even an apothecary attended them.   The General Dispensary (established 1770, with 100 subscribers ; in 1773, 600 subscribers), supplied these poor captives with medical attendance, which they could not otherwise have obtained.

The Royal assent was given (14 June) to three Bills affecting London.

The first was a Thames Navigation Bill, against which on 5 May a petition from the Corporation was presented, stating that, being desirous to promote a work of so much public concern as the improvement of the navigation of the river, they were willing, on condition that the present Bill be withdrawn, to apply £10,000 out of their estates, if necessary, to this important object within their liberties westward of London Bridge ; and they believed this sum to be sufficient without toll or duty on any person navigating the river within the said liberties. The second provided for licensing drovers, and for penalties on unlicensed drovers or for cruel and wanton driving within the City. The third was a Building Act which obliged the churchwardens of every parish, under a penalty of £10, to provide three or more ladders of one, two, and three stories high, for fire escape for each parish.

The London booksellers had invested about £200,000 in purchasing copyrights, and had obtained a legal decision in favour of their claim to the literary property. This decision, on appeal, was reversed on 22 Feb. in the House of Lords. A Bill for protection of the London booksellers' property was introduced to the House of Commons, supported by Aldermen Harley and Sawbridge (28 Feb.), read a third time on 27 May, but thrown out by the House of Lords (2 June) by 21 to 11.—The Common Council elected (30 July) a High Bailiff for Southwark. The value of this office was said to be £1,000. The High Bailiff's salary was fixed at £400, payable by the Chamber of London, and all perquisites belonging to the office were to be paid into the Chamber.

Portrait of Wilkes.

Parliament was dissolved on 30 Sept. Wilkes and Glynn were nominated for Middlesex, and entered into an engagement to defend the Revolution settlement, to promote shorter Parliaments, to exclude placemen and pensioners from the House of Commons, to secure the representative rights of Middlesex, and to repeal the last four Acts relating to the American Colonies and the Quebec Act. The election for the City resulted in the return of Lord Mayor Bull and Aldermen John Sawbridge, George Hayley and Richard Oliver   Wilkes and Glynn were elected for Middlesex (20 Oct.) without opposition —On Michaelmas-day Wilkes, Bull, Esdaile, and Kennet were nominated for Lord Mayor.   On the declaration of the poll (6 Oct.) Wilkes and Bull were at the top.   The Court of Aldermen elected Wilkes (7th).

The mob unloosed the horses from his coach, and in the struggle for the honour of drawing the Lord Mayor Elect to the Mansion House a man lost his life   At the Coroner's inquest the jury returned a verdict of accidental death, and as the law exacted the forfeiture of the moving body causing the accident they adjudged it to be the near fore wheel of the Lord Mayor's carriage and valued it at 40s.—On the election of Wilkes to the mayoralty, a medal was struck in his honour ; the obverse bore a figure of Wilkes in his robes, the reverse represented Lord Bute's head springing out of a jack-boot, and threatened by an axe, with the encircling inscription, " Britons strike home "

Sir James Hodges, Knight, Town Clerk of the City of London, died at Highgate (18 Nov.), and William Rix was elected in his place.

Lord Hardwicke's Act declared the irregular Fleet marriages henceforth null and void.   The register-books of the marriages are now preserved at Somerset House.—The Common Council ordered that no person should be permitted to carry on the business of a distiller in the City or Liberties unless he were a member of the Distillers' Company.—The Marine Society's House was built in Bishopsgate Street Within.   This institution, dating from 1756, trained poor boys for service at sea —" Lloyd's " leased from the Gresham Committee apartments at the north-west corner of the Royal Exchange.— Sixteen String Jack, a notorious highwayman, was convicted at the Old Bailey.—Horace Walpole, writing to Mason this year, indulged in prophetic speculations as to the future of America.   " At last," he remarked, " some curious traveller from Lima will visit England, and give a description of the ruins of St. Paul's "—During this year, 94,000 head of black cattle and about 800,000 sheep and lambs were sold in Smithfield Market.

1775.

THE dispute with the American Colonies as to the right of the Home Government to impose taxes on the colonies, had now become acute.

The Court of Common Council voted (10 Feb) thanks to Lord Chatham and those who supported him in his attempt in the House of Lords to put an end to the disputes between the home country and the colonies   Lord Chatham replied that " he deemed himself fortunate to find his efforts for preventing the ruin and horrors of a civil war, appreciated, honoured, and strengthened, by the greatest corporate body of the kingdom."   At a meeting (13th) it was resolved " that it is the duty of this Court to use every possible endeavour to prevent further oppression and to obtain relief for the oppressed colonists, and in the event of a Bill being introduced to restrain the colonists' trade to the home country and the colonies and to prohibit them from the fishery on the Newfoundland coasts," the Lord Mayor was requested to convene a meeting to consider what course they should pursue.   Leave was granted to introduce such a Bill for the Northern States on the 17th, and the Common Council petitioned against it (24th), as being unjust, cruel, partial, and oppressive   The same day, two pamphlets, referring to the present crisis, were ordered to be publicly burnt in front of the Royal Exchange. The Lord Mayor ordered certain constables to attend next day at noon. An immense crowd assembled. The City Marshal and constables were hustled. The faggots collected for the fire were scattered ; more were procured, dipped in turpentine, and the luckless pamphlets consumed in the blaze. On the Bill passing the House of Commons the Sheriffs presented their petition against it to the House of Lords, where it was passed against the protests of the minority, and received the Royal Assent on the 30th. Another Bill was introduced on 9 Mar. to restrain the commerce of the Southern colonies. A Common Hall was held on 5 Ap. to adopt a remonstrance as to these proceedings, and to return thanks to those Members of either House who had voted against these Bills. The Lord Mayor, with the usual number of the Livery, attended on His Majesty with the remonstrance (10th), when the Lord Chamberlain intimated to the Lord Mayor that His Majesty had requested there should be no speeches. He replied he neither expected nor desired that honour. At the audience the Lord Chamberlain delivered His Majesty's answer in writing, in which astonishment was expressed at any of his subjects "encouraging the rebellious disposition which, unhappily, exists in some of my American Colonies," and adding, that the

King "will steadily pursue those measures which Parliament have recommended for the support of the constitutional rights of Great Britain, and the protection of the commercial interests of his Kingdom." Next day, a letter was received from the Lord Chamberlain that His Majesty would not receive on the throne any address except from the Lord Mayor, Aldermen and Commons in their corporate capacity, to which the Lord Mayor sent a long reply as to Common Hall rights (23 June). The Royal Assent was given to the second Bill on 13th. A letter was read from the New York

Lloyd's Underwriters' Room, Royal Exchange. Present day.

Committee, addressed to the Lord Mayor of London, in which they said, "All the horrors of a civil war will never compel America to submit to taxation by authority of Act of Parliament." At the Midsummer Common Hall (24th) an address to the King was prepared, and ordered to be presented in the usual way, the Sheriffs to ascertain when it would be convenient for the King to receive it in the usual mode. They waited on the King (28th) when the King appointed the following Friday, at the Levee, upon which Sheriff Plomer reminded him that the Livery had ordered it to be presented to His Majesty on the throne. "I am ever ready to receive addresses and petitions, but I am the judge where," was the reply. The Common Hall agreed (5 July) that the address, instead of being presented, should be printed. Public thanks were voted to the Earl of Effingham for having, "as a true Englishman, refused to draw that sword which had been employed to the honour of his country against the lives and liberties of his fellow-citizens in America." Instructions were given to the City representatives that as the Ministry had planted popery in Quebec, plunged us into an unnatural war with the colonies, subverted the fundamental principles of English liberty, ruined commerce, and destroyed His Majesty's subjects, they should impeach the authors of these measures. These resolutions were engrossed, and presented to the King by Sheriff Plomer. His Majesty received them without saying a word. The Court of Common Council (7th) resolved, in its corporate capacity, on an address, against imposing laws made in this country on the Americans without their consent; this was presented (14th) to the King, who replied, "While the constitutional authority of this Kingdom is openly resisted by a part of my American subjects I owe it to the rest of my people to continue to enforce those measures by which alone their rights and interests can be asserted and maintained." "The declaration of causes and of the necessity of taking up arms" was made by the Americans (6 July). A motion was made in the Council (21st) to send an answer to the address received from New York (23 June), but negatived by sixty-nine to fifty-six. The Royal proclamation for suppressing rebellion and sedition was read (23 Aug.) at the Royal Exchange, by one of the Lord Mayor's officers, attended by the Common Crier, amid the hisses of the crowd; and the Lord Mayor neither allowed the officers' horses as usual, nor the mace to be carried there. At the Common Hall on Michaelmas day the Lord Mayor announced the receipt of a letter from the Congress of twelve ancient colonies at Philadelphia (8 July). Twelve hands were held up against the proposal to enter it on record. An appeal to the electors of Great Britain on behalf of the Colonists was adopted by the Common Hall, and published in the papers. A petition, signed by 1,171 gentlemen, merchants and traders of the City, was presented to the King (11 Oct.) in favour of the Americans, and on the 14th, another was presented from merchants and traders of the City in support of the Government, signed by 941 persons. Parliament met on the 26th. A petition from the Common Council was presented to the House of Lords, by Lord Camden, for the Sheriffs (27th), while they themselves presented a similar one to the House of Commons, praying that, as the King had resolved to abide by the sense of Parliament, so both Houses might be pleased to adopt speedy, permanent, and honourable measures, for healing the present unhappy disputes. A Bill, prohibiting all trade and intercourse with the American colonies now at war, received the Royal Assent (23 Dec.), and a Royal Proclamation as to division of war prizes was read at the Royal Exchange and Holborn Bars. A curious incident during this agitation was the arrest of Stephen Sayre, Esq., on a charge of conspiring to seize the Tower for the American rebels. Sayre was confined for a short time in the Tower, but was released on the absurdity of the charge becoming evident (Oct.).

Owing to the severe weather the Queen gave £500 to be distributed among the poor of London and Westminster, and the Archbishop and his lady £200, one half to be distributed in bread, meat, and coals, and one half in money.—A mob rescued a prisoner from the watch-house in Moorfields (3 Feb.), and another from Hicks' Hall (29 Ap.); some of the rioters were sentenced to three, some to five, and others to seven years' imprisonment in Newgate.—The Recorder and Common Serjeant reported (21 Feb.) that the places of Head Marshal and Under-Marshals should, according to ancient usage, be given away, for then, on their misconduct, these officers could be dismissed by proper authority. Under present arrangements the appointment was by purchase for life, without any proper security for enforcing discharge of duty. In accordance with this report the Court allowed the four City Marshals, who had purchased their places, £30 a year additional as from 1773, whilst the two others were to continue at their former salary (25 May). For the future, the disposal of these places was to be with the Common Council. The place of one of the fifteen Coal Meters, for twenty-one years, was sold for £6,050 (5 Ap.). "The sale of such places," the papers add, "may be reckoned worth £4,000 a year to the City.—The marshals were ordered (7th) to attend at Smithfield on market days to prevent iniquitous practices, and especially barbarous treatment of cattle.— To encourage dispatch in rescue from fire, several of the London parishes offered rewards for those bringing fire-escape ladders to an outbreak, and special arrangements were made for having the keys of the ladders lodged in one or more convenient places.—University privileges in publishing books for the advancement of learning, were specially restricted (23 May) to the Universities of Great Britain, and the three great public schools : should they grant privilege to any other for printing any book, such book was to come within the Copyright Act.— A recruiting serjeant and drummer were ordered by the Recorder (18 Sept.), to be brought before him for beating a drum in the Old Bailey while the Court was sitting.   They pleaded ignorance and were dismissed on apologising and promising not to repeat the offence.—On Michaelmas-day Lord Mayor Wilkes and Alderman John Sawbridge were nominated for Lord Mayor; Alderman Sawbridge was elected by the Court of Aldermen.—The regulations for the publication of the proceedings at the gaol delivery at Newgate, for London and Middlesex, were revised by the Common Council (17 Nov.).

The obelisk in honour of Wilkes was erected at the foot of Ludgate Hill.—Brush Collins delivered satirical lectures on Modern Oratory in the great room of the Devil Tavern, by Temple Bar.—A Regatta (the term was only just coming into use) was held on the river in the summer   Pleasure-boats crowded the Thames from London Bridge to Millbank ; vessels were moored in the river for the sale of drink.   The boats were marshalled in three divisions, white, blue, and red, according to the colour of the dress worn by the rowers.   Barges of the City Companies were employed to accommodate spectators.   "A City barge," says a journalist of the day, "used to take in ballast, was, on this occasion, filled with the finest ballast in the world—above 100 elegant ladies"   The Lord Mayor's barge was saluted at Westminster Bridge by twenty-one guns.   At the conclusion of the races a procession of boats, witnessed by 200,000 persons, made its way to the Ranelagh Gardens.

1776.

IT was decided in the Court of King's Bench (10 Mar, 1776) that an Alderman of London was not exempted from discharging parish duties, such as those of churchwarden, etc., in the parish where he resided.—Dr. Richard Price, minister at Newington Green, the author of the celebrated *Northampton Mortality Tables*, was granted the freedom of the City, in a gold box of £50 value (14 Mar.) for his "Observations on civil liberty and the justice and policy of the war with America." He was also admitted to the honorary freedom of the Drapers' Company (27th).— The Lord Mayor presented an address (22nd) to the King from the Common Council entreating a policy of forbearance and conciliation towards the American

Colonies, to which His Majesty replied by deploring the miseries they had brought on themselves by their unjustifiable resistance to the constitutional authority of this kingdom, and expressing his happiness and readiness to alleviate those miseries by acts of clemency and mercy as soon as that authority is established, and the existing rebellion at an end, towards this he would pursue the most proper and effectual means.— Sir Stephen Theodore Janssen intimated (4 Feb.) his intention, owing to age and infirmities, to resign the office of City Chamberlain, which he had held for eleven years.

The Common Council voted their thanks (10th) to the late Chamberlain for his services as representative of the City in Parliament, Alderman, Sheriff, Mayor and Chamberlain. Sir Stephen had acquired an honourable name by the singular exertions he had made, after a reverse of fortune, to pay off his creditors. In a letter to the Livery of London when a candidate for the Chamberlainship Sir Stephen wrote as follows : " During the year I had the honour of being Lord Mayor I met with very unexpected disappointments of considerable sums of money : this occasioned my leaving several debts unpaid, contracted during that year. Soon after a commission was issued against me, upon which I laid down my equipage, discharged all my servants except three and retired with my wife and child to a house of £36 per annum in Hertfordshire. My wife died about two years after. I then took a lodging in town of eighteen shillings a week and lived there, as I have ever since, without a servant, although often afflicted with illness. I may also aver that I have spared myself clothes, and that in my diet I have been as sparing as any mechanic. All this while my income has been about £600 per annum, consisting of an annuity of £300 from my late father-in-law and further allowance from my family, out of this I can safely say I have not spent more than £120 per annum, and that all this has been faithfully

Seventeenth Century Houses, Aldgate.

paid among my creditors (though not obliged by law, they having signed my certificate) amounting on the whole to four or five thousand pounds. A list of many of them paid in full is left with the Common Council of Bread Street Ward, of which I am Alderman. I do further declare it is my determined resolution to continue living in the same frugal manner till the last shilling is discharged, and in case any turn of fortune should happen to me, my whole just debts shall be discharged so much the sooner, as I am determined to persevere in preserving the character of an honest man." He not merely discharged the remainder of his debts, but regained an ample and independent provision for the future. He died 7 Ap., 1777.

It was decided that the Chamberlain should, in future, find security for £40,000. Alderman Hopkins was elected successor to Sir S. T. Janssen (26 Feb.),

Wilkes being the defeated candidate. The latter again offered himself for election on Midsummer-day, but was unsuccessful, Hopkins being re-elected. The dispute was now carried to the Court of Aldermen on an old ordinance of 1572, and was carried in favour of Hopkins (5 Oct.).—The Lord Mayor and Corporation presented (3 May) a congratulatory address to the King on the birth of the Princess Mary. In returning thanks the King added "The security of the laws and liberties of my people has always been and ever shall be the object of my constant attention."—A bell was erected in the middle of Smithfield on a high pyramid of four posts, to give notice at twelve on Sunday night for bringing cattle in, and at three on Mondays and Fridays for the market to cease, when all cattle not removed were to be sent to the greenyard.—All interludes and plays were forbidden at Bartholomew Fair (3 Sept.), and the marshals were ordered to keep the market clear of pickpockets and sharpers, and preserve such order among horse dealers as should prevent trampling on passengers.—On Michaelmas-day, Sir Thomas Halifax was elected Lord Mayor. Hitherto the annual allowance for the Lord Mayor from the City had been £4,000, while the expenses averaged over £7,000. It was resolved (1 Nov.) that £1,000 be added to the Lord Mayor's allowance, and that all sums arising from the sale of offices be paid into the Chamber of London.—James Ferguson, F.R.S., a self-taught genius, lecturer on natural philosophy and astronomy, died (16 Sept.) at Bolt Court, Fleet Street.—David Hartley, M.P. for Hull, son of the author of the *Observations on Man*, received (5 Nov.) the freedom of the City for his invention for the protection of houses against fire, the idea being to wall the rooms with thin iron plates, and make the stairs of stone. He was afterwards (1782) plenipotentiary for Great Britain at Paris for concluding peace with the American Colonists.

A register preserved in the library at Lloyd's and dated 1775-76, is the earliest book in which first-class vessels are described as A 1. (See illustration on page 47).

1777.

THE question of the liability of citizens to naval service continued to produce friction between the City and the Admiralty.

The Court of Aldermen, after warm debate, agreed (21 Jan.) that the Lord Mayor be desired to give instructions to the City Marshals to patrol the streets, for the protection of the inhabitants, against the lawless practices of the press-gangs, acting under a pretended authority from the Admiralty. A freeman and Liveryman of London was impressed on 27 Mar. The Admiralty, when appealed to for his discharge, replied that they did not apprehend that his being a freeman and Liveryman exempted him from being impressed or otherwise liable. A committee of the Court of Common Council was appointed to take up this case, with power to take all proper measures, and the City Solicitor was ordered to obey their instructions. Their defence was based on the Charter of Edward III., and on a statute of William and Mary, exempting freemen of London from service out of the City against their inclination. The Admiralty replied they would consult with the Crown lawyers before answer. Meanwhile a constable of Queenhithe ward had also been impressed while on duty. Early in Ap. Lord Mansfield granted a writ of *habeas corpus* for both. The first returned in charge of the City Marshal from the Nore, and the second was discharged by his captain.

The Rev. William Dodd, LL.D., a popular and impressive preacher, founder of the Magdalen Charity, and an active supporter of the Society for the Relief of Imprisoned Debtors, was charged (8 Feb.) with forging a bond for £4,200.

His popularity had led him into extravagant expenses, and finding at the close of 1776 that to meet his tradesmen's bills was beyond his present supply of ready money, he uttered a bill for £4,200, bearing the forged signature of Lord Chesterfield, to whom he had formerly been tutor. His immediate necessity required only about £300. This he could easily have repaid in a short time as his church preferments alone brought him in £800 a year. The large sum in the bond was supposed to have been inserted, in order to support the notion that the bill was really Lord Chesterfield's. On the forgery being discovered by the money-lender's attorney, Dr. Dodd repaid the amount of the bond in the expectation that no prosecution would follow. He was tried, however, and found guilty on 22 Feb., after a trial of seven hours, but, as exception had been taken to the condition under which the bill-broker's evidence was given, sentence was deferred till the opinion of the Judges on that matter had been delivered. When brought up for judgment on 16 May, he delivered an eloquent appeal for sparing his life (written by Dr. Samuel Johnson), and at its close sunk down quite overcome with agony He was sentenced to be executed at the usual place. Petitions for a respite were presented by the Sheriffs, on behalf of the Corporation (written by Dr. Johnson, but altered by the Council), to the King, from the Magdalen Charity to the Queen, and by Lord Percy from Westminster, signed by 20,000 people, based on his former usefulness, and on absence of any intention to defraud. Dr. Johnson and many others interested themselves in different unostentatious ways to procure a respite. All was of no avail. He was carried from Newgate, while all the streets along which he passed were crowded with spectators, to Tyburn, where he was executed (27 June).

Lord North presented (9 Ap.) to the House of Commons a message from the King stating that by reason of the expenses of his household and of his civil government his debts amounted to over £600,000, and expressing his belief in the readiness of that House to concur in enabling him to discharge this debt and to make some further provision for the better support of his household, and of the honour and dignity of the Crown.

On Sir Fletcher Norton, Speaker of the House of Commons, presenting the Bill for this purpose for the Royal Assent (7 May), he added, "In a time of public distress, full of difficulty and dangers, their constituents labouring under burdens almost too heavy to be borne, your faithful Commons have not only granted to your Majesty a large present supply, but also a very great additional revenue (£100,000 per annum), great beyond example, great beyond your Majesty's highest expense. But all this they have done in a well-grounded confidence that you will apply wisely what they have granted liberally; and feeling what every good subject must feel with the greatest satisfaction that, under the direction of your Majesty's wisdom, the affluence and grandeur of the Sovereign will reflect dignity and honour on his people." The Common Council ordered this speech to be entered on their journals

(15 May), and voted the freedom of this City, in a gold box of fifty guineas, to the Speaker for having declared, in manly terms, to His Majesty the real state of the nation. In returning thanks, nearly a year after, Sir Fletcher added, "I cannot wish to have omitted one word of that speech which has attracted the extraordinary notice of the Common Council. My behaviour has been repeatedly approved by the unanimous voice of the House of Commons, who alone by this constitution have the right to call in question and to decide upon the parliamentary conduct of their Speaker." He politely declined the gold box.

The war in America had stopped the outlet for transportation. Some of the convicts were employed in forming an embankment in Woolwich; some at other works on the river. Newgate prison, still unfinished, was crowded. In May, two brothers, Sheffield bricklayers, sentenced to death, found means to escape by digging through the six feet brick walls. In consequence the walls were faced with large stones so as to be rendered as secure as possible The Moorfield rioters (sentenced in Feb., 1774) were the leaders in a general outbreak in the prison against the governor (20 Aug.). Windows were broken, the iron casements were thrown into the Quadrangle, and attempts were made to break down the prison walls. The complaint was that seven years' imprisonment, under existing conditions, was a burden too great to bear, and, on the Lord Mayor promising that he would represent the case of those who conducted themselves properly to the King, with a view to a remission of sentence, the outbreak was subdued.— The Bishop of London issued a pastoral (19 Mar.) on the due observance of Good Friday, and the Court of Aldermen ordered that the Royal Exchange be shut, and recommended the citizens to close their shops and in other ways observe the day; notice was given that the Aldermen would hear a sermon in St Paul's.— Bills received the Royal assent (Ap.), for Improving the Navigation of the River from London Bridge to Staines; and for enabling the City to purchase the tolls of the River westward of London Bridge and within the liberties, and to levy small tolls in lieu thereof.—A white marble statue of Mrs. Catherine Macaulay, who was yet living, was set up (8 Sept.) in the chancel of St. Stephen's, Walbrook, by the Rector, Dr. Thomas Wilson, and ordered by the Vestry to be removed because erected without their consent. On appeal to the Spiritual Court the monument was ordered to be boarded up till after the lady's death. The first volume of her "History of England from the Revolution" contains an engraving of this statue, with St. Stephen's, Walbrook, in the distance.— Sir James Esdaile, alderman of Cripplegate, was elected Lord Mayor (29 Sept.). On his being sworn into office the Lord Chancellor said, "His Majesty highly approves of the choice made by the City of London," and added, for himself, "What pleasure the citizens must feel on a return of that dignity, peace, and tranquillity which had been lost and disturbed for many years past," and hoped " matters would return to the old channel."—The Lord Mayor and Corporation presented (7 Nov.) a congratulatory address on the birth (3rd) of a Princess.— Much scandal was caused by the stealing of dead bodies, for dissection, from several graveyards. The gravedigger of St. George's, Bloomsbury, and his assistant were sentenced to six months' imprisonment and to be publicly and severely whipped twice from Kingsgate Street, Holborn, to Dyott Street, St. Giles, a distance of half a mile. The latter part of the sentence was remitted for fear of violence to the criminals on the part of the mob.—A petition from certain creditors of John Wilkes was presented (23 Oct.) to the Common Council, asking for payment of debts contracted by him during his mayoralty. It was ordered to lie on the table. A motion was made (19 Nov.) for paying £500 a year, during the pleasure of the Court, to Alderman Wilkes for his services in the cause of liberty, but it was decided that such a proceeding would be an improper application of the City's funds and a dangerous precedent.—A committee was appointed, of which the City representatives were members, at the King's Arms, Cornhill (24 Dec.), for relieving the distresses of American prisoners in British jails. Nearly £4,000 was subscribed.

Nelson's earliest extant letter is dated from the Navy Office in Seething Lane, 14 Ap. 1777.—St. Alphage, London Wall, was rebuilt 1774-1777, by Sir William Staines, on the site of the old Priory of St. Mary-the-Virgin.—From Donkin's *Military Collections*, published this year, it would appear that the City recognised the right of the 3rd regiment of foot (the Buffs) to march through London with drums beating and colours flying, as successors of the City Trained Bands.

1778.

THE Lord Mayor laid a plan before the King (15 Jan., 1778) for opening a subscription to raise land and sea forces, but the Common Council (16th) resolved that "to give any countenance, or to be in any way instrumental in continuing the present war with the Colonies will reflect dishonour on humanity." Next day, however, the proposed subscription was opened at the London Tavern, and £14,000 was subscribed for enlisting men for service in the war.—Three petitions were presented (3 Feb.) by the Sheriffs to the House of Commons, one for raising £15,000 for a new Sessions House for Middlesex, with £6,000 for buying up old houses to clear a proper foundation for the same ; another for raising £20,000 for finishing Newgate Prison ; and the third for £20,000 for forming a new street from Bishopsgate to Barbican.—The Government lotteries had aroused a spirit of gambling.

The holders of tickets re-sold shares of the tickets they had bought. The result was that tradesmen of every description advertised as an attraction to customers the chance of a share in a lottery-ticket. The barbers, for instance, where a man on paying three-pence for being shaved obtained a chance of £10 in the lottery. An eating-house in Wych Street, where if you paid for sixpenny-worth of roast or boiled beef you received a note, which if fortunate at the draw might entitle the customer to sixty guineas. An old woman, a sausage seller, in a little alley in Smithfield, put up in chalk "sausages, or 5s. to be gained by a farthing relish." To check this practice, a Bill was passed (27 Mar.) enacting that vendors of lottery-tickets should pay a licence of £50, and that any person selling less than one-sixth of a ticket should incur a penalty of £50.

William Pitt, Earl of Chatham, who had been exhausted by his speech (7 Ap.) against terms of peace with the Colonists, died on 11 May. The House of Commons voted a public funeral, and a monument in Westminster Abbey. The Common Council, through the Sheriffs, petitioned the House of Commons (21 May) and through the Lord Mayor, the King (5 June) that his body might be buried in St. Paul's. They also appointed a committee to consider what mark of respect would most fitly perpetuate the memory of the deceased nobleman. In Dec., 1779, it was agreed to erect a statue in the Guildhall, over the hustings, facing Lord Mayor Beckford's; Mr. Bacon to be the sculptor, and the cost not to exceed £3,000. This monument was completed in 1782, and unveiled on 10 Oct. of that year.— At the Midsummer poll Hopkins was again elected Chamberlain by a large majority over Wilkes. — The Corporation was nonsuited by Lord Mansfield (3 Aug.) in a claim for 1s. 8d as toll upon fruit brought from Kent, Essex and Berkshire, and landed at Blackfriars stairs.—The Custom House officers with some musqueteers entered the Fleet Prison (9 Aug.) to search for contraband goods, and seized 2,491 lbs of tea, 1,874 lbs. of coffee, 1,020 lbs. of chocolate and £1,500 worth of lace. These had been placed in the prison by raising ladders against the outer wall, and dropping the goods inside —Alderman Oliver declined to be nominated as Lord Mayor, and resigned the aldermanic gown (25 Nov.). The critical state of the West India Islands, where his property lay, required his presence there.—Alderman Samuel Plumbe was elected Lord Mayor (29 Sept.). Lord Mayor Esdaile refused to put to the Common Hall a resolution of thanks to the four City members for their opposition to "a weak and wicked administration," recommending them also to continue their best endeavours to prosecute them to shame and punishment.—The Common Council (19 Nov.) gave instructions to their representatives to make strenuous efforts to prevent the loss of our Colonies, and "the shame and distress of this unhappy country."

In this year a Livery was granted to the Gunmakers' Company.

1779.

N 16 Feb., 1779, the body of Dr. William Boyce, musician, was interred in St. Paul's Cathedral.—The news of the acquittal of Admiral Keppel by a court martial, on 11 Feb., was received with much joy in London.

The City and Westminster were illuminated. The Mansion House displayed 300 glass lamps, and the Monument was gaily lighted up. The mob broke un-illuminated windows, and especially those belonging to the Ministers who had issued a commission for the trial. The house of Sir Hugh Palliser, Keppel's accuser, was put under guard, and on the withdrawal of the guard, about one o'clock in the morning, the mob attacked the house, broke open the doors, and destroyed the furniture, and threw it out of the windows. Effigies of Palliser were carried about the City suspended, and then burnt. Next day the Common Council voted the Admiral thanks for the protection he had afforded to trade by his spirited conduct, and accorded him the freedom of the City in a heart-of-oak box. The Corporation went to his house in South Audley Street (22nd) and presented their thanks, with the offer of the freedom of the City, and an invitation to dine with them that night at the London Tavern. The sailors unyoked the horses from the Admiral's carriage and drew it to the Tavern.

Robert Vyner, a descendant of Sir Robert Vyner, Lord Mayor (1675) made request to the Common Council that the celebrated statue erected by his ancestor in Stocks Market, and taken down in 1738 for the purpose of erecting the Mansion House on the site, should be handed over to him. The request was granted (28 May), and the statue subsequently erected in Gautby Park, Lincolnshire.

Pennant says that Sir Robert Vyner, anxious to erect a statue in honour of Charles II "fortunately discovered one, made at Leghorn, of John Sobieski trampling on a Turk. The good Knight caused some alteration to be made, and christened the Polish monarch by the name of Charles, and bestowed on the turbaned Turk that of Oliver Cromwell."

The state of the prisons was still highly unsatisfactory.

In the King's Bench there were 140 rooms and 600 prisoners; one who had been a prisoner for debt for some years had assumed the status of Chief Justice of the King's Bench Prison, and with the aid of his self-appointed marshals dispensed justice among the prisoners. The number of prisoners and the scarcity of beds raised the value of the latter. Seniority in prison seems to have established a claim to a bed as it became vacant. These the "Chief Justice" and his satellites claimed in virtue of their seniority, and having obtained the bed put it up to the highest bidder. The current price for a bed was 24s., of which 1s. went to the governor as rent, the balance into the hands of the mock officers of justice. These self-constituted justices obtained in this way a fair revenue, and when discharge time came, instead of leaving, they got a friend to set up a claim against them for debt, and in virtue of decree, remained in the prison without losing their seniority. To remedy this abuse an order was made by the Court of King's Bench : "that every prisoner who had been supersedable for six months, and who had not been superseded should be immediately discharged unless such prisoner should be freshly charged, and in that case he should lose the benefit of his seniority."

The Common Council petitioned (1 June) the House of Lords, and also addressed the King against the House Tax in its present form.—A special jury affirmed (14 July) the right of the City to a duty of 6d. per load on all hay, the

Stocks Market and the statue of King Charles II, 1738.

1

property of non-freemen, sold at Smithfield Market.—The foundation stone of the new Session House at Clerkenwell was laid (20 Aug.).—The Rev. Charles Plumptre, Dean of Ely, Archdeacon of Ely, Rector of St. Mary, Woolnoth, London, and of Orpington, in Kent, died on 14 Sept.; and John Glynn, Recorder of the City, on the 16th. The salary of the Recorder was now (5 Oct.) fixed at £600, which with other perquisites amounted to about £1,200. Mr. Serjeant Adair was appointed to the vacant office. Since 1680, there had been fifteen Recorders, ten of whom had been appointed Judges in the King's Courts, and five had died while holding the office.—Alderman Brackley Kennet was elected Lord Mayor on Michaelmas-day.—Alderman William Bridgen of Farringdon Within, died at his house at Four Tree Hill, Enfield, 18 Oct. Since his Mayoralty he had attended neither Council nor Wardmote meetings till the last election of Recorder, when he was brought up by Wilkes to vote for Serjeant Adair, in such a state of weakness as to need supporting into the hall.—Benjamin Hopkins, the City Chamberlain, died (9 Nov.). He was elected Feb., 1776, and had since been re-elected four times, each after a contest with Wilkes. The contests are said to have cost him £5,000. On the 30th Wilkes was elected Chamberlain.

1780.

THE Court of Common Council, following the example of York (20 Dec.) and Westminster (2 Feb.), petitioned (10 Feb., 1780) the House of Commons in reference to the increased and increasing expenditure of the country on pensions, &c.—The freedom of the City, in a gold box, was voted (6 Mar.) to Admiral Rodney for his gallant action against the Spaniards off Cape St. Vincent.

This gave rise to a couplet—

> For Rodney, brave, but low in cash, you golden gifts bespoke;
> To Keppel, rich, but not so rash, you gave a heart of oak.

Every publican, within the jurisdiction of the City, was directed (3 Ap.) to appear in person when his licence was renewed, and to enter into recognizances for the good order and proper conduct of his house.—The plan of an Association for pledging candidates for Parliament to check the present profuse expenditure, to shorten Parliaments, and to obtain more equal representation was adopted (13th) by the Common Council.—Mr. Justice Wilmot was fined (26 Ap.) £100 for imprisoning a fellowship porter who had been impressed for His Majesty's service.—An Act for relieving Roman Catholics from certain disabilities imposed in the 11th and 12th of William and Mary was passed in 1778. A similar Bill was proposed for Scotland.

The Anti-Roman zeal in Scotland burst into flame, and societies called Protestant Associations were formed in various places. Roman Catholic chapels were destroyed in Edinburgh and Glasgow. In consequence the Government allowed the proposal to drop. Lord George Gordon, a brother of the Duke of Gordon, and a member of Parliament, was President of those societies in Scotland whose action had deterred the Ministry from proceeding with their proposal. In the end of 1779 he was elected President of a similar association in England. Early in 1780 he had waited with a deputation on Lord North urging a repeal of the obnoxious English Act, but had obtained no satisfactory answer. Other petitions followed with a like result. The leaders of the agitation met in Coachmakers' Hall,

Riot in Broad Street, June 7, 1780; Hon. Artillery Company firing on the mob.

Noble Street (29 May), and made arrangements for presenting on Friday (2 June) a petition to the House of Commons for repeal. Lord George gave notice (30th) in the House of Commons of their intention, and the same day the Court of Common Council resolved to support the petition. The petitioners assembled in St. George's Fields on Friday, 2 June (each man wearing a blue cockade), marched in procession in three divisions, one by London Bridge, another by Blackfriars, a third by Westminster, and arrived at the House of Commons about half-past two. Attempts were made to force the closed doors of the House. Several members of both Houses were attacked and insulted. Lord George addressed the crowd and order was partly restored. The petition, said to be signed by 120,000, was brought in. Lord George, seconded by Alderman Bull, proposed that it be received and immediately considered. This suggestion not being in accordance with the rules of the House, consideration was put off till Tuesday, 6th. Lord George returned to the crowd and advised them to rely on the goodness of their gracious Sovereign who, now that he knew the desires of his people, would be ready to meet their wishes. On the House adjourning, the crowd dispersed, the more quiet and orderly part returning home, while the more violent started in two divisions, one to the Sardinian

Ambassador's in Lincoln's Inn Fields, the other to the Bavarian Ambassador's in Warwick Street, Golden Square   There they pulled down the altars in both chapels, broke the ornaments and furniture, and made a bonfire of them in the street.   The Guards were summoned, but, before their arrival, the destruction was complete.   Thirteen rioters were seized and the mob dispersed.   The rioters were brought before Sir John Fielding next day (3rd), examined and re-committed, amid little or no disturbance, and the rioting was believed to have ceased.   A crowd, however, which met in Moorfields on Sunday afternoon (4th), proceeded to the Roman Catholic chapel in Ropemakers' Alley, gutted the building, demolished the altar and ornaments, and carried the pieces to the street, and set them on fire   The Guards coming on the scene about half-past nine, the mob dispersed   Next day (5th) they met again in Moorfields, returned to the scene of disturbance, wrecked the school-house and the three dwelling houses belonging to the priests, and burned their valuable library.   They destroyed also the Roman Catholic schools in Charles Square, Hoxton   Dividing their forces into three sections, one attacked and destroyed the house of Sir George Saville (who had introduced the obnoxious Act), and the houses of two others who had appeared as witnesses against the rioters.   The other two divisions destroyed all the Roman Catholic chapels, insulted Romanists, plundered their homes, carried out the furniture and set it on fire in the streets   A reward of £500 was offered for the discovery of the leaders of the attacks on the Ambassadors' chapels.   Friday's rioters were re-examined and three committed to Newgate, under an escort of Guards, who, though pelted on their return by the mob, were restrained by the officers from firing.   The associations counselled legal proceedings and peaceable deportment, but their advice was unheeded.   Scouts were stationed at every corner to give notice of the approach of the military, upon which the mobs disappeared.   Magistrates and all in authority seemed panic-struck.   The House of Commons was to take the petition into consideration on Tuesday (6th); the mob re-appeared before the Parliament House, in small parties, from different directions, and, in the early part of the day, was orderly, but apparently resolute.   In the afternoon it became tumultuous.   The House adjourned at six p m. till Thursday.   The crowd unharnessed Lord George's horses and drew his carriage to Alderman Bull's residence in Palace Yard,   Justice Hyde, with a party of Guards, dispersed those who remained.   In revenge the crowd, about seven p m , stripped Hyde's house in St. Martin's Lane of its furniture, which they burned in the street before his door.   The Guards, as before, arrived too late. The house of Sir John Fielding (who had committed the rioters) and the public offices at Bow Street were next broken up and the furniture set on fire.   The mob passed on to Newgate prison to release the imprisoned rioters.   After parley, the Keeper went to consult the Sheriffs, who, with the Aldermen, were at the Guildhall.   During his absence the mob broke open the doors of the Keeper's house, threw his furniture into the street, placed it against the prison doors, and set them on fire.   One hundred constables appeared on the scene.   The rioters made way for them, then surrounded them, maltreated them, took their batons, and used them for stirring up the fire.   From the house the fire spread to the chapel, and from the chapel to the prison.   Three hundred prisoners made their escape, and the building, which had cost £40,000, was reduced to ashes.   The house of Lord Mansfield in Bloomsbury Square was next attacked.   They gutted the house, burned the furniture, and distributed the wines and spirits   Though soldiers were present, no magistrate dared give orders to fire.   Lord Mansfield and his lady, rather than expose the ignorant multitude to the fire of the soldiery, made their escape by a back door.   The house of Lord Justice Cox in Red Lion Square was also destroyed.   The King, in Council, issued a proclamation authorizing the military to act without waiting for directions from the civil authority, and to use force for dispersing the illegal and tumultuous assemblies of the people.   During the day (7th) the other prisons, the King's Bench, the Fleet, the Borough Clink, the Surrey Bridewell, and the City Compters were broken open and the prisoners released   At night they returned and set these, with the toll-house on Blackfriars Bridge, on fire. Dr. Johnson wrote, " I walked with Dr. Scot to look at Newgate, and I found it in ruins with the fire yet glowing.   As I went by, the Protestants were plundering the Sessions House at the Old Bailey There were not, I believe, a hundred, but they did their work at leisure, in full security, without sentinels, without trepidation, as men lawfully employed in full day. Such is the cowardice of a commercial place." The premises of Mr. Langdale, distiller in Holborn, were broken open and set on fire. It is said that twenty different fires were to be seen at one time from one place. The roar of the drunken rioters was heard mingled with the report of the soldiers' guns. Many killed themselves with drinking, others were buried or burnt in the ruins of Langdale's distillery. An attempt was made this night on the Bank of England, the Royal Exchange, the Excise and Paymaster's Offices, but defeated by a party headed by John Wilkes. The Common Council met again this evening and passed resolutions for the repeal of the obnoxious Act and for the defence of the City. On Thursday, the House of Commons adjourned to Monday, 19th. Military guards were placed at different points to secure the people against the rioters. One was posted in St. Paul's Churchyard. The King offered a military guard to the Judges, to which Mr. Justice Gould replied, " However much some might be misled, the people in general loved and respected the law. He would rather die under these than live under the protection of any other." All shops were shut from Tyburn to Whitechapel. On the shutters over the

closed shops was written "No Papist," while the windows were decorated with blue cockades. In Duke's Place and Houndsditch the Jews put up " This house a true Protestant." On Friday (9th) the Courts at West- minster resumed their sittings. A warrant was issued for apprehending Lord George Gordon, who quietly went with the officers, under pro- tection of a strong guard over West- minster Bridge, by St. George's Fields, through the Borough to the Tower. The secretary of the Associations was taken to the Tower, examined, and dismissed. The military were ordered to use their utmost endeavours to restore peace, but every prisoner was to be tried by due course of law. The Lord Mayor was summoned before the Privy Council and dis- missed the same evening. It was arranged (Saturday, 10th) that a

Burning of Newgate by the Rioters, 1780.

Committee of Staff Officers of the six regiments of City Trained Bands should assemble every evening, at eight o'clock, armed, to patrol the streets till four o'clock next morning, and to take into custody all suspicious persons. Addresses to the King for his seasonable interposition were presented from Southwark (12 June) from the Corporation by sixty-five to sixty (28 July), and from the Liverymen, freemen, and inhabitants of London (10 Aug.). Eighty-five persons were tried at the Old Bailey for taking part in the riots, of whom thirty-five were capitally convicted, seven convicted, and forty-three acquitted; at the Surrey Assizes fifty were charged, of whom twenty-four were convicted and twenty-six acquitted. The executions passed off without disturbance. The Court of Aldermen resolved (22 July) that the allowance for soldiers for protection be stopped, the cost having amounted to £100 a day, or £4,000 in all. Lord George Gordon was tried for high treason 5 Feb. next year and acquitted. The City Remembrancer waited (26 June) on Mr. Justice Gould to thank him, in the name of the Corporation, for his reply to the King's offer of a military guard, but the Judge declined the freedom of the City which had been voted to him.

Lord Mayor Kennet was ridiculed for his hesitation and timidity in the following lines :—

The Lord Mayor's dilemma.

The Riot quite confused the Mayor,
But where's the wonder, when it
Was such a critical affair,
His lordship could not Ken—it.

Parliament was dissolved on 1 Sept. Of seven candidates nominated for the City, Hayley, Kirkman, Bull, and Newnham were elected (14th). Wilkes and Byng were elected for Middlesex. On the day of the declaration of the City poll Alderman Kirkman died at Margate. His body was brought privately to the obelisk in St. George's Fields, where it was met by the officers of the Militia and Trained Bands, who escorted it to Blackfriars Bridge. There the Lord Mayor and Aldermen joined them and accompanied the funeral to St. Michael's, Bassishaw, where the interment took place. An immense concourse of people lined the way. —Alderman Sawbridge was chosen member for the City.—Sir Watkin Lewes was elected Lord Mayor.—Langdale, the Holborn distiller, claimed damages (17 Oct.) for the destruction of his property in the riots. The City Solicitor opposed, alleging that the blame lay with the Westminster. authorities who had power to stop the riot in its origin. A special jury awarded £18,725 damages. The loss by the devastations, in general, were estimated at £180,000. The late Lord Mayor did not attend the Show on 9 Nov., his conduct during the disturbances having offended the citizens. He was subsequently brought to trial before Lord Mansfield and a jury, in the Court of King's Bench, Guildhall (10 Mar., 1781), on a charge of "wilful, obstinate, and contemptuous neglect of duty" during the June riots. The jury brought in a verdict of "neglect of duty," but the Clerk of the Court would not receive it.

A Livery was granted to the Gold and Silver Wire Drawers' Company.—Crabbe, the poet, lodged at 119, Bishopsgate Within.

1781.

THE Court of Common Council met (19 Jan., 1781) to consider certain resolutions agreed to at a meeting of merchants at the London Tavern, on Friday (12th), to petition Parliament for a grant in aid of British subjects in the West Indies, who had suffered from a series of bad seasons and severe storms. The House of Commons voted £80,000 for the Barbadoes, and £40,000 for Jamaica. The Common

Council also voted £1,000 (22 Mar.).—The Committee of Correspondence, formed (in April, 1780) under the auspices of the Corporation for the furtherance of political reform, was dissolved (15 Mar.).—Parliament voted £10,000 (16 May) for the re-building of Newgate prison.—Lord Mayor Watkin Lewes was elected member for the City in place of Alderman Hayley, deceased. Previous to this election, the foot-guards were removed from the Bank and the Government offices in the City, and the City militia took their place. While the election was in progress (23 Sept.—1 Oct.), the Recorder gave his opinion that it was absolutely necessary that the present Sheriffs should continue in office till the polling was over, and the Common Council passed an Act to indemnify the Sheriffs-elect for not appearing to be sworn.—Alderman William Plomer was elected Lord Mayor.— The Court of Common Council passed an Act (15 Nov.) for levying a certain sum on the personal estates of the inhabitants of London, for paying the damages sustained in the late riots (June, 1780), and £28,219 was assessed as the sum required.—Parliament met (27 Nov.), and the King in his opening speech announced his determination to prosecute the American War. The Lord Mayor summoned a Common Hall for 6 Dec.

An address to the King—on the present alarming state of affairs, and on His Majesty's intention of persevering in a system of measures which had proved so disastrous to this country, deprecating the plan of reducing the Colonists by force, and requesting the dismissal of all the advisers, both public and secret, of those measures, as a pledge of His Majesty's fixed determination to abandon a system incompatible with the interests of his crown and the happiness of his people—was ordered to be presented to His Majesty on the throne, and the Sheriffs were directed to ascertain when such presentation would be convenient. The King replied to Sheriff Gill, " I shall take time to consider of the manner in which I shall receive [the address], and of the time when, and will let you know " The King subsequently answered, through Lord Hertford, by referring to his reply of 11 Ap., 1775, that he could only receive on the throne an address from the City in its corporate capacity, but consented to receive this address at the levee on Friday (14th). The Lord Mayor, in his reply, referred to the answer of Lord Mayor Wilkes on the former occasion, and added, that as the Common Hall had ordered it to be presented to the King on his throne, that condition could not be dispensed with.

The church of St. Christopher-le-Stocks was demolished, to provide for the enlargement of the Bank of England. The old churchyard still exists as the well-known enclosure within the Bank, ornamented with trees and a fountain.—Wraxall, in his Memoirs, refers to the "coarse invectives of Alderman Sawbridge" when speaking in the House of Commons at this period.—" I remember," writes Strutt, in 1801, in his *Sports and Pastimes*, "about twenty years back, the magistrates caused all the skittle frames in or about the City of London to be taken up, and prohibited the playing at dutch-pins, nine-pins, or in long bowling-alleys; when, in many places, the game of nine-holes was revived as a substitute, with the new name of ' Bubble the Justice.' "

Bank of England and Churches of St. Christopher-le-Stocks and St. Bartholomew by the Exchange, 1781.

1782.

COMMON HALL was summoned for 31 Jan., 1782, to receive a report as to the reception of the address. A formal protest against holding such Common Halls, as not legal and not concerning the City in its corporate capacity, was forwarded (29th), signed by five Liverymen on behalf of a number of the Livery who had met at the Half Moon, Cheapside. The Common Hall disregarded the protest, thanked the Lord Mayor for his spirited conduct, and expressed their opinion that whoever advised the King to depart from his usual mode of receiving the Livery address, sitting on his throne, was an enemy to the rights and privileges of this great capital of the British Empire They also affirmed that unequal representation was the cause of the American War, and appointed a Committee to confer with associations for promoting representative reform.— The attorneys representing the sufferers from the riots claimed the sums due, upon which the Court made order for payment of £27,000.—The Right Rev. Thomas Newton, Bishop of Bristol (1761) and Dean of St. Paul's (1768), editor of Milton, and author of *Dissertations on the Prophecies* (1754–7), died (14 Feb), and was interred under the south aisle of St. Paul's. Thomas Thurton, Bishop of Lincoln and brother of Lord Chancellor Thurton, was appointed (23 Feb.) and installed (23 Mar.) Dean of St. Paul's.—The entry in the House of Commons Register (17 Feb., 1769), that John Wilkes be adjudged incapable of sitting in this Parliament, was expunged (6 May).—Bartholomew Fair was reported to be an encouragement for rogues to meet, and an intolerable nuisance.—Robert Peckham was elected Lord Mayor at Michaelmas, but on account of ill-health declined to serve; Alderman Nathaniel Newnham was elected instead (31 Oct.).—A report was presented to the Court of Aldermen (8 Oct.) that the Company of Shipwrights, being an ancient Company, and tracing an enrolment of an apprentice as far back as Richard II, ought to have a livery. The Court ordered precepts for the future to be issued to this Company.—The resolution to fit up and use the Guildhall Chapel as a Court of Requests was approved (12 Dec.). The last occasion of its use for divine worship was on Michaelmas-day, 1770. Since then it had been used as a repository for Corporation papers and documents.—The Court of Common Council resolved (12 Dec.) that the Lord Mayor and Sheriffs, instead of collecting charitable benefactions for prisoners at Christmas, should draw on the City for £100.

K

Disaster had befallen the British armies in America. France, Spain, and the States of Holland had joined in commercial treaties with the Colonists. Great Britain was being gradually isolated in the struggle.

One hundred millions had been already expended. Three millions of yearly interest had already been incurred for loans The fleet was inferior to that of the enemy, and trade in the Port of London had been reduced by one-half; A motion was made in the House of Commons (22 Feb.) for peace, and lost by one vote. It was renewed (27 Feb.) A petition from the Corporation was read "to interpose in such a manner as to their [the House's] wisdom shall seem most effectual for preventing the continuance of the unfortunate war with America." The motion was carried and, next day, leave was asked to bring in a Bill to enable His Majesty to conclude a peace or truce with the revolted Colonies in America. A warning was sent from the Secretary of State (28th) to the Lord Mayor, to take proper methods for securing the public peace, as there was a probability of riots and tumults in the evening.—Lord North resigned, and a new Ministry, of which Lord Rockingham was chief, entered on office at the end of March. An address of thanks, agreed to 9 Ap., was presented by the Lord Mayor to His Majesty (12th) "for having graciously complied with the wishes of your people in making a change in your Majesty's councils, &c." A favourable answer was returned, and Lord Mayor Plomer received the honour of knighthood.

Admiral Rodney defeated and destroyed the French fleet in the West Indies (12 Ap.), saved Jamaica, and gave a finishing blow to the war by sea. London, on receipt of the news (18 May) was illuminated. The Lord Mayor presented a congratulatory address to His Majesty (5 June) on the late glorious successes in different quarters of the world. The freedom of the City was ordered to be conferred on Lord Hood and Admiral Drake. Lord Rodney was invited to a banquet (23 Nov.) at the London Tavern. Six Aldermen and twelve Commoners went to conduct him from his house in Hatford Street, and the sailors unharnessed the horses and drew him in triumph to the banqueting house.—In answer to a circular letter from the Privy Council (7 May) for organizing Trained Bands, the Light Horse Volunteers of the City of London offered their services. The Commander-in-Chief, in acknowledging this offer, said His Majesty highly applauded the example the City had shown and the readiness it now expressed to distinguish itself by further exertions, whereby the surest means were offered to give security, both at home and against their enemies abroad, at this most important crisis.—The Marquis of Rockingham died on 1 July.—Lord John Cavendish and Mr. Fox resigned their places in the Cabinet (5th), and Lord Shelburne became First Lord of the Treasury (10th).—Parliament was prorogued to December.—In November the Secretary of State promised to give immediate announcement to the Lord Mayor of the result of the pending negotiations at Paris. Notice was accordingly received (3 Dec.) that a provisional article had been signed, on behalf of Great Britain and the American colonies, to be inserted in and constitute a treaty of peace, to be concluded when terms of peace are arranged between Great Britain and France.

Fleet Prison was rebuilt 1781–2.

1783.

N 23 Jan, 1783, notice was sent to the Lord Mayor that peace preliminaries between Great Britain and France and Great Britain and Spain had been signed on the 20th, and on 17 Feb. a proclamation of cessation of arms by sea and by land was made by the Common Crier at the Royal Exchange and Cheapside.   On the 20th a Common Council, very numerously attended, voted an address to His Majesty on the peace, which was presented on the 26th.   A lengthy and sympathetic reply was made by the King, and Robert Taylor, sheriff, received the honour of knighthood.   Provisional articles of peace were arranged (13 Aug.) at Paris between His Majesty's plenipotentiaries and those of the United States of America, and on 3 Sept. definitive treaties of peace were signed between Great Britain and the King of France, Great Britain and the King of Spain, and Great Britain and the United States of America.   On the 6th, C. J. Fox, who in April had become Secretary of State in the coalition ministry, formally announced the settlement to the Lord Mayor.   Peace was formally proclaimed the same day.

After the proclamation had been read at St. James's and Charing Cross, the procession moved on to Temple Bar, the gates of which were shut, and the Junior Officer-of-Arms coming out of the ranks between two trumpeters, preceded by two Horse Grenadiers to clear the way, rode up to the gates, and after the trumpets had sounded thrice, knocked with a cane. He was asked by the City Marshal from within: "Who comes there?" He replied "The Officers-of-Arms, who demand entrance into the City to publish His Majesty's proclamation of peace." The gates being opened, he was admitted alone, and the gates shut again. The City Marshal, preceded by his officers, conducted him to the Lord Mayor, to whom he showed His Majesty's warrant, which his lordship having read returned, and gave direction to the City Marshal to open the gates. The trumpeters and Grenadiers being in waiting conducted the Officer-of-Arms to his place in the procession, which then moved on into the City, the officers of Westminster filing off and retiring as they came to Temple Bar The proclamation was read a third time at Chancery Lane, and a fourth time at the end of Wood Street, where Cheapside Cross formerly stood. The procession moved on to the Royal Exchange, where it was read for the last time. The trumpets sounded thrice previous to, and immediately after, each reading. "God Save the King" was frequently repeated by a military band, and the crowd of people delighted with the return of peace was so dense that Temple Bar was with difficulty opened, and the Lord Mayor's coach was detained almost an hour in returning

Alderman Woolridge, of Bridge Ward, having been removed from office, commenced an action against the City, in the Court of King's Bench.   A mandamus was issued to the Court of Aldermen, to show cause for the dismissal (Nov.).   In Nov. 1784, two points were decided in Woolridge's favour, and a third reserved.—Petitions to Parliament for equal representation were approved by the City and by London freeholders (Mar.).—The Blue Coat School at Hertford, in connection with Christ's Hospital, was reported ready (10 Ap.) and orders were given to take in 150 children.—Two thousand seamen proceeded from Tower Hill (18 Ap.) to the Admiralty to demand arrears of wages and prize-money. Receiving no definite answer they walked to St. James's and scaled the walls, but, after parley with the guard, peaceably dispersed. Guards were placed at Newgate, where the prisoners had lately attempted the life of Sir Robert Taylor, sheriff.—Several leases from the Royal Hospitals being ready for signature (3 June), the acting Governors intimated that the seal ought to be placed in the Court of Aldermen, as was the custom previous to the late dispute between the Corporation and those Governors.

Discussion had taken place in 1767 as to the relation of the Common Council to the City Hospitals. The original deeds were examined. The hospitals were given to the Mayor, Commonalty, and citizens of London, as grantees and governors. The manage-ment had been left to the Court of Aldermen, who had administered the hospitals till the outbreak of the Civil War. In order to obtain additional funds persons who had given a certain donation were added as life governors. The exclusion of Common Councilmen as ex-officio governors resulted. Another agitation occurred in 1772, when Serjeants Glynn, Dunning, and Nugent in a legal opinion suggested compromise between the contending parties. A Committee of the Common Council was appointed (10 Jan., 1780) to inquire into the right of that Court to be the governors of the hospitals, to report the state of the proceedings, and to defend their rights. The living of Enford, Wilts., was in the gift of Christ's Hospital. The Corporation, as Chartered Governors, elected (7 Ap.) an incumbent. The president and the donation governors petitioned (11th) the Lord Chancellor, as visitor of Royal foundations, and on 24th, elected by ballot another in-cumbent, to whose appointment the Court of Aldermen refused to append the Hospital Seal, as the former appointment had been sealed and settled. This dispute was finally settled, on the lines suggested in 1772, by an Act of Parliament passed in 1782. In addition to the Lord Mayor, Aldermen, and life governors, forty-eight Common Councilmen were to be appointed by the Common Council as governors, twelve for St. Bartholomew's, twelve for Christ Church, twelve for St. Thomas's, and twelve for Bridewell and Bethlehem.

Sign of Bear,
Lower Thames Street.

The Recorder (22 July) gave his opinion on a case laid before him that a Jew, renouncing Judaism, and being publicly baptised according to the rules and forms of the Church of England, and conforming himself to the oaths of allegiance, might and ought to be admitted to the freedom of the City.—For several months a dispute was waged between the Common Council and the Livery as to the alleged right of the Livery at large to elect to the offices of City Marshal and Water Bailiff. A Committee of Aldermen reported that the right of election lay with the Corporation; but certain members of the Livery maintained the agitation for some time.—The Lord Mayor presented an address (10 Sept.) to the King and to the Queen (25th), on the birth of a Princess, and on the Prince of Wales attaining his majority.—Alderman Robert Peckham was elected Mayor (29th).—The workshops of Mr. Seddon in Aldersgate Street and thirty houses were burnt (5 Nov.), the damage being estimated at £100,000.—Carrying the prisoners for execution from Newgate to Tyburn in open carts, through streets crowded with spectators, was found to have an effect entirely opposite to what was intended ; the sheriffs, therefore, with whom lay the power of fixing the place of execution, resolved (3 Dec.) that thenceforth all executions should take place in front of Newgate. The first took place on 9 Dec., the last execution at Tyburn having been carried out on 6 Nov.

The theatre in Barber Surgeons' Hall was pulled down. It had been erected in 1637 from the designs of Inigo Jones, and was used (as depicted in Hogarth's well-known engraving) for the dissection of bodies of criminals after execution at Tyburn.—A caricature by James Sayer had an immense vogue at the close of the year. It was aimed at Fox's India Bill, which placed very largely increased powers in the hands of the Imperial Government The cartoon is entitled "Carlo Khan's triumphal entry into Leadenhall Street " Fox, as Carlo Khan, is attired in oriental costume ; he rides on an elephant whose face is a portrait of Lord North ; and Burke, as trumpeter, leads the way to the entrance to the India House.

1784.

 ARLY in 1784 the Lord Mayor presented an address to the King, thanking His Majesty for dismissing Fox, whose Bill for the regulation of the East India Company had proved highly unpopular. Fox had been succeeded by Pitt, to whom the Court of Common Council (10 Feb.) voted their thanks and the freedom of the City.

A committee went (28th) in procession to Berkeley Square to present the resolutions of the Court to Mr. Pitt, Alderman Townsend being spokesman. They returned amid the acclamations of the crowd to Grocers' Hall, where Pitt received the freedom from Chamberlain Wilkes. The crowd drew Pitt's carriage from Berkeley Square to Grocers' Hall, and back in the evening. Windows not illuminated were broken by the crowd.

Parliament was prorogued on the 24th, and dissolved next day. The writs were returnable for 18 May. The City poll closed 6 Ap., when Watson, Lewes, Newnham, and Sawbridge were declared duly elected. Wilkes, in his address to the Middlesex electors, said, "I anxiously supplicate the honour of your suffrages that I may be enabled to strengthen the hands of our present virtuous young minister, in his patriotic plans to retrieve your affairs, to restore public credit, to recover the faded glory of our country!" He and Maynwaring were returned for

Middlesex.—In Ap., Prebendary Wilson was buried at St. Stephen's, Walbrook, with much pomp, two hundred flambeaux being carried in the cortége.—Sir Barnard Turner, Sheriff, and M.P. for Southwark, died in his house at Paul's Wharf. His body was carried down Thames Street into Chatham Square, at the foot of Blackfriars Bridge, where it was met by the Artillery Company and the Foot Associations, and escorted through the City to Shoreditch, on its way to the family burying place, at Therfield, near Royston, Herts. He and his colleague had distinguished their term of office by improvements in prison discipline and in the execution of distraints for debt, and by fixing executions at Newgate instead of Tyburn.—On 7 July, the proclamation of peace between Great Britain, the States of Holland, and the United States of America, was read at the Royal Exchange.—Lunardi made his ascent from Moorfields in a balloon on 15 Sept. The papers were filled with accounts of aërostatic attempts.—Alderman Richard Clark was elected Mayor (29th).—Dr. Samuel Johnson died at his residence in Bolt Court, Fleet Street (13 Dec.), and was buried in Westminster Abbey (20th), in Poets' Corner, close to the grave of his friend David Garrick. A monument to his memory, by Bacon, first proposed to be erected in Westminster Abbey, but afterwards erected in St. Paul's, was unveiled 23 Feb., 1796.

Mirabeau lodged at a house in Hatton Garden.—Sir Joshua Reynolds was presented with the freedom of the Painter-Stainers' Company.—John Palmer introduced coaches for the conveyance of mails.—The Sovereign's head, which forms part of the hall-mark of the Goldsmiths' Company, was added this year.

1785.

THE Insurance offices made attempts to obtain for themselves the damages paid by the City of London to sufferers by fire in the riots of 1780, but failed in the Court of King's Bench (11 Feb., 1785).—Twenty persons were executed in front of Newgate, 2 Feb., and nineteen on 28 Ap.

There were, at this time, in Newgate forty-nine prisoners under sentence of death, and one hundred and eighty under sentence of transportation, with a total of 540. The numerous executions for petty crimes against property were arousing a strong feeling against such a punishment for minor offences.

A proposed tax on retail-shops raised an agitation of protest in the City (May).

Pitt replied to the complaining citizens that they could compensate themselves by raising the prices of their wares. A petition to Parliament dwelt upon the fact that London and Middlesex paid 80 parts out of 513 of the whole Land Tax raised in the Kingdom. The Bill, however, became an Act on 30 May. It was repealed in 1789.

The coal traders entered into combination and refused to land their coals from the river. The Lord Mayor offered a reward of £200 (28 July) to anyone of the combination who would give evidence, and threatened that, unless coals were

Christopher Atkinson, standing in the Pillory, 25 Nov., 1785.

delivered by 1 Aug., the laws would be put in force. This had the desired effect.—The Government victualling department was removed (27 Aug.) from Tower Hill to the victualling yard lately built at Deptford, the clerks being provided for at Somerset House.—Richard Atkinson, alderman of Tower Ward and M.P. for New Romney, died at Brighton (28th). He is said to have come to London without either friends or money, and with no educational advantages beyond reading and writing. He left means amounting to £300,000. —Alderman Thomas Wright was elected Mayor (29 Sept.).—The City Surveyor was ordered (27 Oct.) to prepare a correct plan of all London within the limits, with a general description, with a view to improvements.—Christopher Atkinson, victualling contractor to the Government, had been expelled from the House of Commons on his conviction for perjury (Dec., 1783), and was sentenced to a fine of £2,000, to stand in the pillory, and to twelve months' imprisonment. The conviction was confirmed on appeal to the House of Lords. He was placed in a pillory this year (25 Nov.), erected close to the Corn Exchange, Mark Lane. The pillars were labelled "Christopher Atkinson, Esq., for perjury." A great concourse of people attended, and the Sheriffs were present on horseback, with the two chief City Marshals and 500 constables.—A new Session House was built in the Old Bailey, which, together with the re-building of Newgate, cost the Corporation £90,000.

1786.

THE Lord Mayor, Recorder, and Sheriffs, on going to St. Margaret's Hill, Borough, to hold a Court (13 Jan., 1786) of Quarter Sessions, found a County Justice holding a Court for the County. The Recorder insisted that the Justice (Sir Joseph Mawbey) was infringing the rights of the City. The Justice insisted on the privilege of the County. Sir Joseph, however, quitted the chair, and the Lord Mayor took his place.—A fire occurred (7 Feb.) in the lower apartments of the Chamberlain's house, at Guildhall, by which his office, and in it the registers and books of admission of freemen were destroyed.—The Sheriffs and Remembrancer waited on the King (22 Mar.) with a petition relating to the congested state of Newgate.—A Bill had been introduced to provide for keeping Blackfriars Bridge in repair by levying Sunday tolls on the bridge, and a petition from the City was presented (12 July, 1785) to the House of Lords in its favour. The Bill was put off for three months, but was passed in the present session (26 May). These tolls on the Surrey side of the bridge came into force on Sunday, 25 June.—The Corporation presented an address to the King (11 Aug.) on his escape from assassination (2nd) at the hands of a mad woman, Margaret Nicholson.—Alderman Thomas Sainsbury was elected Lord Mayor (29 Sept.). On Lord Mayor's day there was no procession, owing to the death of the Princess Amelia, only surviving daughter of George III.

Watermen's Hall, 18, St. Mary-at-Hill, Lower Thames Street, was erected. The old Hall was situated in Cold Harbour, Upper Thames Street.—The east and west wings of the Bank of England were added by Sir Robert Taylor, 1766-86.

1787.

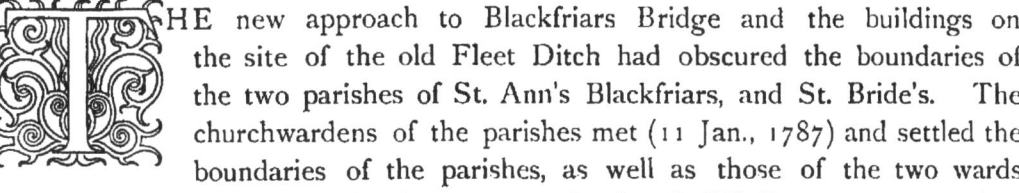

HE new approach to Blackfriars Bridge and the buildings on the site of the old Fleet Ditch had obscured the boundaries of the two parishes of St. Ann's Blackfriars, and St. Bride's. The churchwardens of the parishes met (11 Jan., 1787) and settled the boundaries of the parishes, as well as those of the two wards of Farringdon.—The City shopkeepers met in the Guildhall to protest against the shop-tax.—Sir James Eyre was promoted to be Chief Baron of the Exchequer (27th); the day following witnessed the revival of the old custom of the Judges returning from St. Paul's to luncheon at the Mansion House on the first day of the term.—Newgate prison being so crowded as to be a source of danger to the health, not only of the prisoners, but of the judges and other officials, the Court of Aldermen ordered the Sheriffs to wait on the Secretary of State, with a request that such prisoners as were sentenced to transportation to Botany Bay might be removed to the transport ships. Nine of these, with their convoy, sailed (21 Mar.) from Spithead for Botany Bay. This was the first shipment of convicts for New South Wales.—A long discussion on forestalling took place (29 Mar.) at a meeting of the Common Council.

Buyers met the sellers at Knightsbridge, Islington, Kensington, and Mile End, bought up the animals coming to the markets, and thus (it was alleged) artificially raised the prices. A Committee recommended that licensed salesmen, who were not butchers, should be appointed, that a register of all entries and sales should be kept, and that every salesman should give an account of all animals brought or consigned to him for sale, with the owners' names, and if sold, the prices realised. An additional proposal was made (1 May) that no live stock for the London markets should be sold within eighteen miles of London, except on market days and fairs. This, on the motion of Sir James Sanderson, was sent back to the Committee. The Sheriffs (4 May) presented a petition to the House of Commons to give effect to these recommendations, and a Bill, brought in by Alderman Le Mesurier, was supported by the City members, but vigorously opposed by Alderman Townsend, and ridiculed by Edmund Burke, who moved that the reading be put off till 1 Aug. The Bill was negatived (16th).

An individual (Thomas Davis) known as "Old Simon," who was in the habit of wandering about the City in rags, with clouted shoes on his feet, three hats on his head, and his fingers studded with brass rings, was brought (24 Ap.) on a charge of vagrancy before Alderman Townsend at the Guildhall.

He appeared to be a Greek, residing in East Smithfield, and had some money on his person. The Alderman ordered him to be shaved and washed, committed to Bridewell for a month, whipped as he went in and came out; his money to be restored to him, his rags and beggar's habits to be burned, other apparel being given him instead. He was then to be dispatched to his own country. Simon, on his discharge, preferring London, resumed his former habits, and being again committed to Bridewell died there on 25 Ap. next year.

Five out of twenty-four bookbinders who had combined to demand shorter hours, and on refusal of their request, had left their work, were sentenced (8 May) in the Court of King's Bench, to two years' imprisonment in Newgate.—James Townsend, alderman of Bishopsgate, died (1 July) at Bruce Castle, Tottenham. He had been Sheriff (1769) and Lord Mayor (1772). He was buried privately in the family vault in Tottenham Churchyard. An old custom of breaking a passage through the garden wall into the churchyard, was observed at the funeral.— Press warrants, signed by the Admiralty (at 9 p.m., 21 Sept.), were issued at 1 a.m., and before 9 a.m. 2,000 seamen were impressed in the river.

The Lord Mayor had an interview with Lord Howe at the Admiralty (2 Oct.), as to backing warrants in the City, and expressed doubts as to their legality. On being assured that they were legal, he requested time for consideration as he was doubtful of his power to back them without the concurrence of the citizens. The Common Council agreed (11th) to offer bounties of 40s for able and 20s. for ordinary seamen, to take effect, as requested by the Admiralty, after the 18th. At a Court of Aldermen (23rd) it was reported that warrants had been circulated in the City; all, however, except three, had been returned. The Sheriffs, through whose office these had been circulated, were desired not to issue warrants at all. The amount paid in bounties was reported (4 Dec.) as £500.

Alderman John Burnell was elected Lord Mayor, though in his 84th year.— During this and the next year, Child's Place was erected on the site of the old Devil Tavern, near Temple Bar, the resort of Ben Jonson and the City wits of the Stuart period. In 1751, Dr. Johnson and his friends supped there on a "magnificent hot apple-pie."

The members of the Stock Exchange introduced the plan of exposing on a black-board the names of dealers who did not either pay their deficiencies or name their principals.

1788.

THE first stone of the Cordwainers' Company's new hall in Distaff Lane was laid (1 Jan., 1788).—On New Year's-day was issued the first number of the *Times*, which first appeared in 1785 as the *Daily Universal Register*.—The Common Council resolved (1 Feb.) to petition the House of Commons against the slave trade, and also against the shop tax. Both petitions were presented (4th) by the Sheriffs.

The Sheriffs of London have the privilege of presenting petitions from the City without the usual leave having been previously asked. Notice is given to the Sergeant-at-Arms that the Sheriffs are in attendance and desire to be admitted. This is communicated to the Speaker and by him to the House. When the question that the Sheriffs be called in is put, and passed in the affirmative, they are admitted. The two Sheriffs in their scarlet gowns of office walk up to the bar, and, on being asked what their business is, the senior delivers the Corporation petition. On doing this the Sheriffs retire. There being on this occasion two petitions, the form was gone through twice Both these petitions were ordered to lie on the table. The House, notwithstanding the agitation all over the country against the shop tax, refused (13 Mar.) to repeal it, and the Court of Common Council (25 Ap) recorded a vote of thanks to those members of the House who had supported repeal.

Another motion was carried (1 Feb.) that no person should be eligible to serve on any Corporation committee who should have defrauded in weights or measures, compounded with his creditors, or being a bankrupt had not paid 20s. in the pound.—The City Solicitor, having read a report on the landing of oysters at several wharves on Sunday, was directed (8 Ap.) to take measures to stop such practice.—The Court of King's Bench decided (21st) that a woman is competent to serve the office of Commissioner of Sewers and Overseer of a parish. The qualification is defined by the statute of Elizabeth as "substantial householders," without distinction of sex. Judge Ashurst quoted an instance where a woman was chosen constable.—A woman convicted of forming and uttering base coin was branded (25th) in front of Newgate. Appeals were made to Mr. Pitt not to allow this cruel remnant of savage legislation to longer disgrace the Statute Book.— Thomas Cradock, a baker, committed suicide by throwing himself from the Monument (7 July).—About this time a suggestion was made by J. L. Delolme, author of *The English Constitution*, to remove the live cattle market from Smithfield to St. Pancras or Battlebridge [King's Cross].

He did so on the following grounds : first, such a position would be more accessible to all parts of London, secondly, the existing market was no ornament to the City, thirdly, the streets about Smithfield were among the narrowest and most crowded in London, fourthly, there was no provision for water for cattle on the present site, and this could be easily provided at St. Pancras. He proposed that Parliament should be asked to assist in this matter. The removal of the live stock market to Caledonian Road, did not, however, take place until 1855

Sir Robert Taylor, Knight, architect to the Bank of England, and the holder of other public offices, died (27 Sep.).

He was Sheriff in 1783 He left a considerable sum of money to the Chancellor and scholars of Oxford, for erecting an edifice within the jurisdiction of the University and establishing a foundation for improving the study of European languages. His bequest did not take effect till 1835. It became known as Sir Robert Taylor's Institute, and provided lectures on and instruction in European languages, and an extensive library of foreign literature.

Alderman William Gill was elected Lord Mayor (29th).—At the Common Hall Alderman Pickett's motion for the demolition of Temple Bar found no supporter. —The Court of Aldermen sent (21 Oct.) a request to the Secretary for War that the bank guard be withdrawn.—The King was seized with indisposition (17 Oct.), and in consequence there was neither music nor dancing at the Guildhall Banquet (9 Nov.). Special prayers were ordered (13th) for His Majesty's recovery.—At a meeting of Common Council (16th) it was resolved, "that the thanks of this Court be given to the Right Honourable William Pitt, Chancellor of the Exchequer, and the 267 worthy members of the Honourable House of Commons, for their support of the right of the Lords and Commons of this realm to provide the means of supplying the defect of the personal exercise of the royal authority arising from His Majesty's indisposition." This referred to the resolution of the House on Wednesday (10th), to appoint a Committee to inquire into precedents, &c.—At the beginning of Dec. Newgate held upwards of 700 prisoners, the greatest number ever known to be confined there.

The church of St. Peter-le-Poor, which had long obstructed the passage into Broad Street, was (under Act of Parliament, 1788) taken down and rebuilt farther back on the churchyard and the site of a court. The City granted £400 for this purpose, and the remaining £4,000 was raised by the parish on annuities.

1789.

ERY severe frost attended the opening of the year 1789.

From Putney to Rotherhithe the Thames was frozen over. At Shadwell an ox was roasted whole (9 Jan.), and sold to the skaters, for whom booths had been erected on the frozen river. A young bear was baited (9th) on the ice at Rotherhithe without any accident to interrupt the sport. Pigs and sheep were roasted on the ice and sold to all comers. The river is said to have presented the appearance of Bartle Fair, improved and magnified. But this cold implied want and misery to the poor. Owing to the King's indisposition the royal New Year bounties had been delayed, and the Prince of Wales contributed (6 Jan.) £1,000 for the poor of London and Westminster. A special Court of Common Council ordered £1,500 to be contributed from the Chamber for the assistance of such poor as did not receive parish relief.

The merchants, bankers, and traders of London agreed (7 Jan.) upon a vote of thanks to be presented to William Pitt for his able, spirited, and manly defence of the constitution of the Empire, and to his supporters in the House of Commons. —While the business at a Common Council was proceeding (12th), the Lord Mayor announced a favourable report he had just received as to His Majesty's health.

The letter was read amid much emotion and applause, and led to the breaking up of the meeting as soon as the necessary committees had been appointed. The King was pronounced perfectly recovered (26th), the special form of prayer was discontinued (28th), and a thanksgiving collect ordered instead. The City was illuminated (10 Mar.), the bells were rung, and guns fired. The illuminations at the India House, in Leadenhall Street, the Mansion House, and the public offices were especially grand ; and on the 19th the Lord Mayor, in his coach with six horses, the Sheriffs, in their state coaches, with the proper City Officers, went to Kew to present to the King and Queen the City's congratulatory addresses on His Majesty's recovery. A public thanksgiving for the King's recovery was ordered (2 Ap.) for St. George's day (23rd). A Common Hall adopted a congratulatory address (7th). The King announced his intention of going in state to St. Paul's, accompanied by the Queen, the Royal family, both Houses of Parliament, the great officers of State, and the Corporation of London, to return public thanks for his restoration to health. Along the route, from Pall Mall to the Cathedral, galleries for spectators, surmounted with awnings, were erected against many of the public offices, churches, and private dwellings. On both sides of the steps at the west door of St. Paul's galleries were erected, with a lofty awning overhead, stretching from side to side. Such was the eagerness to welcome the King on his first public appearance, that many took up their position in the galleries on the evening before. All stages, coaches, and horses within a hundred miles of the Metropolis, had been engaged for a week past, in bringing up those who wished to take part in the welcome, and the number of foreigners who came to England was immense. Early in the morning

of the 23rd, the streets leading from St. James's to Temple Bar were lined with the Guards. Within Temple Bar, both sides of Fleet Street and Ludgate Hill were kept by members of the Hon. Artillery Company and the City Trained Bands. The spires of the churches were decorated with flags and streamers; that of St. Bride's attracted much attention from its display of man-of-war flags. The first to arrive at St. Paul's were the children of the different Charity schools, in their various uniforms. Nearly 6,000 of these entered about seven by the north and south doors, and were arranged at the express wish of the Queen in special galleries erected in the north and south transepts. The Common Councilmen assembled at the Guildhall at eight, each bearing a wand of blue and gold and wearing a

Front Entrance to Sieve Inn, Minories.

cockade of purple and gold, and proceeded to the cathedral, in two divisions, with a standard and band of music. The Lord Mayor, with the City delegates, viz.: two Aldermen, the Sheriffs, two Deputies and two Commoners, went on to Temple Bar, where they waited for the King's approach. The House of Commons (167 in number) left Palace Yard in carriages, the Speaker, in his coach of state, bringing up the rear; next the officers of the Courts of Justice with the Judges, then 72 members of the House of Lords, with the Lord Chancellor in his state coach at the close of their procession. After the Lord Chancellor came the Royal Dukes and the Prince of Wales, attended by Oxford Blues, in coaches each with six horses. The departure of the King and Queen from St. James's was announced by a discharge of the Park and Tower guns. As they approached Temple Bar, the Lord Mayor, in a rich gown of crimson velvet, the two Aldermen, in their scarlet gowns, and the four Commoners, in their mazarine gowns, attired in dark blue coats, white waistcoats, and breeches, with large purple roses in their shoes and at their knees, and carrying bouquets, mounted their white palfreys. On the arrival of His Majesty the Lord Mayor dismounted and surrendered the sword to the King, who graciously returned it, adding, "My Lord, the sword cannot be in better hands." The Lord Mayor, carrying the City sword, having remounted, with the Sheriffs and the six delegates, bareheaded, took their place in the procession, immediately in front of their Majesties. The Civic party was preceded by a detachment of the Hon. Artillery Company, and by fifteen of the Toxophilites or Ancient Society of Archers, the latter dressed in green, with bows in their hands and quivers slung at their sides. Within St. Paul's a throne, with a canopy overhead, was erected at the west end of the choir. A platform, leading from the west door to the throne, had been constructed, on the right and left of which were ranged a single line of Yeomen of the

Guard, and a double row of Grenadiers behind. The arrival of their Majesties at St. Paul's, shortly before noon, was announced by another discharge of the Park and Tower guns. When the procession was formed, the members of the Common Council ushered it into the Cathedral, filing off as they approached the choir into their allotted seats, on either side of the platform, in front of the children's galleries. Then followed in order the Archbishop of York, the Lord Chancellor, the Archbishop of Canterbury, fourteen Bishops, the delegates of the Common Council, the Sheriffs, the Lord Mayor, the Earl Marshal with the sword of state, the Royal Dukes, the Prince of Wales, the King, with the Bishops of London and Lincoln on his right and left, followed by his Lord-in-waiting, the Queen, attended by her ladies, the Princesses, and at the close the band of Gentlemen Pensioners, Yeomen of the Guard, etc. The children sang the hundreth psalm. At half-past twelve the service began, and concluded at three. On the return of their Majesties, the Sheriffs preceded them to Temple Bar. Next evening there was a general illumination in London and Westminster. The Bank appeared as in one blaze of lamps. A brilliant transparency, fifteen feet from the ground and about seventeen feet high, depicting Britannia bearing the flag of liberty on a triumphal car, with four iron-grey horses drawing her chariot, and in the foreground a dignified personification of London, with civic sword and charter, and on her head a mural crown, was among the many decorative devices at the Bank.

Ralph Dodd painted a picture of the King delivering the City sword to the Mayor at Temple Bar. The large canvas was employed for many years as a screen in the Mansion House. It is now preserved in the lobby of the Guildhall.

The freemen of London claimed exemption from exchange, tolls, and all other customs on the exportation by them of goods from any seaport in England.

This exemption was refused at Lynn Regis to all freemen of London, except to those actually residing in Lynn. The case was tried (6 May) before the judges of the Court of Common Pleas and a special jury of the county of Norfolk. The Recorder of London undertook to prove by prescription, by charters, by the evidence of witnesses, the existence of this exemption. The jury returned a verdict in favour of London freemen. This decision was reversed by the Court of King's Bench (28 Jan., 1791) on the ground that the declaration did not state that the City of London had received such injury as would maintain such an action. The Corporation of Lynn had demanded, but had neither received, nor distrained for, the port dues in dispute.

The freemen of London in Liverpool presented a petition (13 Sept., 1789) to the Court of Common Council, complaining that actions had been brought against them for port dues contrary to their privileges, and praying that court to interfere. It was referred to the committee of general purposes for inquiry and report. In April, 1799, this Liverpool case came before the Lord Chief Baron and a jury. The jury found for the Corporation of Liverpool on all the issues, adding that the exemption was confined to inhabitant householders and residents within the City. On the ground that this decision limited the exemption to resident freemen in London and not to freemen of London generally, the Court of Common Council (31 May), resolved that it was of no advantage to the City of London to pursue litigation further.

The Royal Assent was given (19 May) to a Bill for the repeal of the much-controverted Shop Tax.—The City having purchased the toll on the City Road, by the Artillery Ground, the tolls at the bar by the "London Apprentice" in Old Street were doubled (24 June).—Mr. Pitt invited the corn factors of London to Downing Street (2 July), to advise how far an application from France for 20,000 sacks of flour might be complied with. In their opinion such a proceeding, though they could supply it at present, was unadvisable till the result of the year's harvest was known.—Alderman William Pickett was elected Lord Mayor.— Mr. Simpson, surgeon of the Newgate Infirmary, reported (2 Oct.) on the illness among the prisoners. The Sheriffs waited on the Home Secretary next day and pointed out the unsatisfactory state of the prison from overcrowding, and in November 222 prisoners were removed on board the vessels for transportation.— On 3 Dec. died John Paterson in his 85th year. He was grandson of Archbishop Paterson of Glasgow, who had been deprived at the Revolution (1689). He was the originator of the plans for raising money for paying off the debt on London Bridge, for erecting Blackfriars Bridge, for rebuilding Newgate, and for widening old streets and opening out new.—The interior of St. Bartholomew's-the-Less was reconstructed by George Dance, R.A.—The old refectory and cloisters of St. Helen's, Bishopsgate (dating from about 1212) were demolished.

1790.

O N 11 Jan., 1790, John Burnell, Lord Mayor in 1787, died in his 86th year.

> He began life as a working stone mason. At a City banquet he showed some awkwardness in cutting and opening a pie, when Wilkes, who was one of the company, shouted, "You had better take a trowel to it."

Alderman Sawbridge presented (25th) a petition to the House of Commons from the manufacturers of tobacco, etc., in London, against Excise Bills in general and that on tobacco in particular.—Mr. Walter, the printer of the *Times* newspaper, who had been convicted (23 Nov., 1789), of printing a libellous reflection in his paper, "that the Royal Dukes were insincere in their professions of joy at the King's recovery," and sentenced to a year's imprisonment in Newgate, a fine of £50, to stand in the pillory at Charing Cross, and to find security for good behaviour for seven years, was again brought up (3 Feb.) to the Court of King's Bench to receive sentence for two other libels on the Prince of Wales and the Duke of York, of which he had been convicted. He was sentenced to pay a fine for each of £100, and to be imprisoned in Newgate for one year after the expiration of his present confinement. Having, at the instance of the Prince of Wales, received the Royal pardon, he was liberated (9 Mar., 1791), after sixteen months' imprisonment instead of two years, with fines and securities.—The Spaniards had seized two British vessels on the north-west coast of America, and claimed exclusive rights to the whole west coast of that continent.

Reparation was demanded by the Government, and in view of hostilities the river was stripped (5 May) of its sailors by a pressgang. Bounties were offered (8th) of £3 for able-bodied, £2 for ordinary seamen, and £1 for landsmen. A City waterman asked the protection of the Common Council (1 June), and complained that a City officer had demanded a large sum of money from him for protection. A Convention was signed (28 Oct.) between Britain and Spain, and on 24 Nov. an address was presented to the King by the Lord Mayor, &c., from the Common Council expressing "their ardent joy at the termination of pending hostilities."

A general election took place in June.—Three of the former representatives of the City were returned, Aldermen Brook Watson, Sawbridge, and Sir Watkin Lewes. Alderman Curtis took the place of Alderman Newnham.—Alderman John Boydell was elected Mayor (29 Sept.).—The Chamberlain sued John Pardoe, who, when chosen Sheriff in 1787, had declined to serve because incapacitated, for £600 as fine for not serving. A special jury in the Sheriffs' Court gave a verdict (21 Oct.) for the defendant, on the ground of his age (69), infirm state of health, and total unfitness to serve that office.—On a report as to the estimated expenditure on the repairs of London Bridge, the Common Council (2 Nov.) ordered them to be carried out. On 4 Mar., 1795, these expenses were reported as £10,478.—Two young men were executed in Aldersgate Street for setting on fire, with a view to plunder during the confusion, premises there and in Long Lane.—The East India Docks, ten acres in extent, were opened for traffic (20th); the depth of water at high tide was seventeen feet.—The Rev. Michael Lort, rector of St. Matthew, Friday Street, and prebendary of St. Paul's, for many years a vice-president of the Society of Antiquaries, and successor to Dr. Ducarel as librarian at Lambeth, died (5 Nov.). The sale of his books and prints in the May following lasted for twenty-seven days; the former were sold for £1,269, and the latter for over £400.

Stow's Monument in the Church of
St. Andrew Undershaft.

The present Ionic front to Skinners' Hall, with the Company's arms in the pediment, was erected by Richard Jupp.—The indecorous disturbance of Milton's grave, in St. Giles's Church, Cripplegate, drew a bitter protest from Cowper.—In 1788 a woman was stabbed by an unknown man in Fleet Street, in 1789 another suffered in a similar manner; in 1790 a number of ladies received wounds in the same mysterious way, until the town was in a ferment; police rewards were offered; allusions to "The Monster" were made on the stage. The crimes were at length brought home to Renwick Williams, who was convicted at the Old Bailey.

1791.

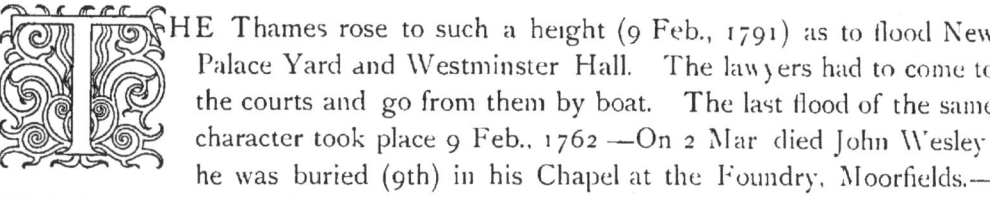

THE Thames rose to such a height (9 Feb., 1791) as to flood New Palace Yard and Westminster Hall. The lawyers had to come to the courts and go from them by boat. The last flood of the same character took place 9 Feb., 1762 —On 2 Mar died John Wesley, he was buried (9th) in his Chapel at the Foundry, Moorfields.— With the concurrence of the Archbishop of Canterbury, the Bishop of London, and the Dean and Chapter of St. Paul's, a Committee was appointed (6 May) by the Royal Academicians to fix on proper subjects and sites for monuments in St. Paul's. Those of John Howard and of Dr. Samuel Johnson were to be the first erected; both statues were the work of John Bacon.—During the year ended July, 49,112,660 gallons of porter are said to have been brewed in London.— On account of a great advance in stocks it was agreed (26 Aug.) in Change Alley, to settle the one day and pay the next, but, as by this arrangement, Jews would have from Friday to Monday, they were to pay on Friday evening, and for that purpose the House was to be kept open —Alderman John Hopkins was elected Mayor.—On 19 Nov. the Lord Mayor and the Sheriffs in state, thirteen Aldermen, the Recorder, and two hundred Councillors, went to St. James's and presented an address to the newly married Frederick, Duke of York, and Princess Frederica of Prussia.—A dispute between Southwark and the City was decided at the Court of King's Bench (19 Nov.).

A meeting of the justices of Surrey had granted licences to publicans. The City magistrates did not attend this meeting, but, a few days later, granted licences to certain publicans who had been refused by the Surrey justices. The question now argued was "whether the City of London had an exclusive jurisdiction to grant licences in the borough of Southwark, or possessed only a concurrent jurisdiction with the justices of Surrey?" The Court determined that the City's jurisdiction was concurrent only, and the recent action in regard to licences was therefore illegal. —A theatre was specially erected for Dr. Abernethy's Lectures in St. Bartholomew's Hospital —Wood Street Compter was removed to Giltspur Street.

1792.

SIR JOSHUA REYNOLDS, president of the Royal Academy, died in his house in Leicester Fields (29 Feb., 1792) and was buried in the crypt under the south aisle of the choir of St. Paul's, next to the grave of Bishop Newton, the late Dean. The funeral procession consisted of forty-two mourning coaches and forty-nine private carriages. On its passing Temple Bar the Lord Mayor ordered the gates to be shut, to prevent interruption. —Robert Adam, architect, head of the firm of Adam Brothers, architects, the designer and builder of the Adelphi Buildings, Strand, died 3 Mar. and was buried (10th) in Westminster Abbey.

In preparing the ground for the construction of these buildings a great bank of rubbish was shot into the river, thus narrowing the channel. The brothers proposed to embank this rubbish and thereby extend their premises. The City offered to allow a quay, at which goods for storage in the new premises might be landed. This was not thought sufficient. The brothers applied to Parliament (in which the elder represented Kinross 1765-92), to embank this ground on the plea of public improvement. The City, as Conservators of the river, opposed the Bill by petition and counsel at every stage, and presented an address to the King requesting him to withhold his sanction on the morning of the day on which it received the Royal assent (8 May, 1771). The citizens were much annoyed and thought, probably not without reason, that, because of the support they had given Wilkes and the favour they had then shown for their magistrates who had defeated the attacks on the printers of Parliamentary reports, Parliament allowed the Bill to pass.

A Frenchman committed to the Fleet for debt escaped by a window through a dwelling-house in Belle Sauvage Yard. The creditors sued the jailor for damages and the judge laid down as the law (22 Mar.) that nothing but irresistible force (such as the riots of 1780) could be pleaded as excuse for the jailor, who is bound to keep his prisoners safe.—The hitherto apparent success of the Revolution in France had led to much restlessness and some rioting in this country. A Royal Proclamation was issued (21 May) against seditious meetings and publications, in response to which the Common Council adopted (25th) and presented to the King (1 June) an address, expressing their thanks for His Majesty's care and attention to the safety and happiness of his subjects in directing the late proclamation to be issued against seditious publications and criminal correspondence. Before Sept., 311 similar addresses had been forwarded to the King.— The number of postal deliveries in London was increased (31 May) from two to seven. A general office was established in Abchurch Lane and numerous receiving offices in other convenient places —Mr. Christopher Atkinson, corn factor in the City, and of Clayhill, Enfield, who had been under sentence for perjury, was honourably restored by letters patent to all his former franchises.—At Michaelmas Sir James Sanderson was elected Lord Mayor.—An address was presented to the King by the Lord Mayor, etc., in state (12 Oct.) on the victories gained, under Lord Cornwallis, in the East Indies. On this occasion Lord Mayor Hopkins and Sheriff Tebbs were knighted.—The new church of St. Peter-le-Poor, designed by Jesse Gibson, was consecrated by Bishop Porteus (19 Nov.).—Mr. Akerman, governor of Newgate, died (19 Nov.). Of him, Dr. Johnson, after relating an instance of his coolness and firmness, said " He who has long had constantly in his view the worst of mankind and is yet eminent for the humanity of his disposition, must have had it originally in a great degree and continued to cultivate it very carefully."—The same day two men were tried for affixing a seditious libel to the gate of the Fleet.—On the 24th the government issued a circular, calling upon the magistrates to enforce the proclamation of 21 May.

The members of some Levelling Societies in the Borough resolved (25th) to go to Kennington Common on Sunday and plant a tree of liberty. As no notice was taken of the proposal, it fell to the ground. The Court of Lieutenancy resolved (27th) that the officers and privates of the London Militia should hold themselves in readiness on a short notice to be under arms, if necessary, for suppressing riots and tumults; and the Common Council passed unanimously three resolutions affirming their duty of loyalty to the King and the laws, and the necessity for suppressing all unlawful and seditious assemblies within the City, and calling on every citizen to assist. Early in December a proclamation was issued for drawing out and embodying the Militia ; the defences of the Tower were repaired ; the Bank was placed under double guard ; soldiers were billeted in the neighbourhood of London ; and the cavalry ordered to be constantly in readiness. The merchants, bankers, and traders of London united (5 Dec.) in a declaration of firm attachment to the Constitution. This was signed in a few days by upwards of 8,000 persons.

Thomas Paine was found guilty of sedition, in publishing the second part of the "Rights of Man." The trial was held at Guildhall before Lord Kenyon and a special jury (19 Dec.). The defendant had left the country, and was subsequently outlawed.

A Livery was granted this year to the Playing Card Makers' Company.

1793.

BOUNTIES of 40s. for able-bodied and of 20s. for ordinary seamen, were ordered (10 Jan., 1793) to be paid for one month to all enlisting for the navy at Guildhall.—Louis XVI, King of France, was executed (21st) at Paris, by order of the National Convention.

An attorney, named Lloyd, who had advertised the Fleet Prison to let, in the first year of English liberty, was set (7 Feb.) for an hour in the pillory, in front of the Royal Exchange. An immense concourse assembled. Two hundred constables were in attendance, but no violence was attempted.— Notice was sent to the Lord Mayor (9th) of the declaration of war by France against Great Britain and Holland with a request that he would take proper measures for making public this intelligence.— An address to the King was agreed to by the Corporation (12th) and presented (16th), thanking him for his paternal care for the preservation of public tranquillity, expressing abhorrence of the late atrocious acts in Paris, and assuring him of their determination and readiness to support the crown and kingdom against the ambitious designs of France.

Brass Crosby, alderman of Bread Street Ward, died (14 Feb). in his 68th year at his house at Chatham Place. He was then Chairman of the four principal City Committees.

A native of Stockton-on-Tees, he came to London and settled as an attorney first in Little Minories, and afterwards in Seething Lane, and by three successive marriages with rich widows became possessed

of a handsome fortune. He entered the Common Council in 1758; bought the office of City Remem-
brancer for £3,600 in 1760 and sold it next year. He was elected Sheriff 1764, Alderman 1765, and
Lord Mayor 1770. His term of office was marked by the disputes as to printing Parliamentary debates.
He was buried at Chelsfield Church, Kent, in which parish his widow had considerable property.

Two men, Pigott and Hudson, were brought (1 Oct.) before Alderman
Anderson for proposing treasonable toasts in a coffee house, on Ludgate Hill;
they were committed to the New Compter, whence they were liberated (5 Oct.)
on a writ of *habeas corpus*, upon bail of £250 each, by Justice Gould.—Lord
George Gordon died in Newgate prison, where he had been confined in default
of obtaining security for good behaviour; he was buried in a vault in St.
James's burying ground, in Hampstead Road.—A man condemned to death
for robbery in Hatton Garden, committed suicide in Newgate. The body,
extended on a plank on the top of an open cart, clothed and fettered, the face
covered with a white cloth, was carried to the brow of Holborn Hill opposite the
end of Hatton Garden, and deposited in a deep pit, with a stake driven through
the chest. The Sheriffs, City Marshals, 500 Constables, and a great crowd of
people were present.—Alderman Paul le Mesurier was elected Mayor, Alderman
Brook Watson, the senior in rotation, being in Holland acting as Commissary-
General of stores, provisions and forage, to the forces serving there.—
£500 were subscribed by the Court towards supplying the British troops in
Holland with comforts, clothes, and other necessaries, during the winter, and a
committee was appointed to receive further subscriptions. The Duke of York
returned public thanks to the Lord Mayor for these seasonable gifts.

A bust of Milton, by the elder Bacon, was placed in the Church of St. Giles, Cripplegate, at the
expense of Samuel Whitbread, founder of the well-known brewery.—Copley's picture of the Siege of
Gibraltar and Elliot's defence of the Rock, was placed in the Council Chamber. It now covers a wall
of the Guildhall Art Gallery.—A dishonest baker in Bishopsgate Ward was fined 5s. per ounce on 16
ounces short weight.—The Post Office letter-carriers were provided with red uniforms, faced with blue,
and marked by numbers.

1794.

AT the end of 1793 a Committee had been appointed to consider
the improvement of the western approaches to the City.

They reported in favour of widening the approach to Temple Bar by pulling
down and setting back the houses on the north side, by setting back the houses on
the south side so as to form a triangular space, with St. Clement's Church in the
centre, or by pulling down the existing church and re-building it on the base of the proposed triangle at
Holborn. They passed in review the plan of the Rev. Mr. Pridden (1790) for erecting a large open
arch over the north end of Fleet Market, and raising a roadway on a level with Newgate to the rise on

Holborn Hill ; and dismissed it on the score of expense. Two plans were proposed instead : one to re-build and set back the houses on the west and south of Snow Hill, and thus form a circular road from the top of Turnagain Lane to the corner of Fleet Market ; and the other, which was specially recommended in the report, to form a new street forty feet wide from the top of Turnagain Lane to the bottom of Holborn Hill. The cost of the Temple Bar improvement was estimated at over £89,000, that of the circular street at £24,000, and that of the new street at £10,590.

The Committee, appointed by the Common Council, waited (5 Ap.) on the Marquis of Cornwallis (who had returned towards the end of the year from the Viceroyaltyship of India) at his house in New Burlington Street to present him with the freedom of the City.

After an address from the Lord Mayor the Marquis accompanied the deputation back to the Mansion House, where the freeman's oath was administered and an address delivered by the City Chamberlain to the newly admitted freeman. In front of the procession were carried the standard of England, the arms of the City of London, and those of the Lord Mayor, followed by a band of music, the City Marshals and the Sheriffs in their state carriages. Crowds lined the streets, testifying their gratitude to Lord Cornwallis for the peace he had established in India. A banquet was given in his honour at the Mansion House, said to be the first of its kind given in the City by a Lord Mayor. A large transparency, representing the Marquis receiving the sons of Tippoo Sahib as hostages, was exhibited in front of the Mansion House.

City of London
Militiaman, 1896.

The spread of the French Revolution and the extreme views urged by some of its supporters in England led to much disquiet. A special Common Council was held (17 Ap.) to consider what steps ought to be taken for defence of the City in case of emergency. All agreed that the Corporation ought to manifest its zeal by the most vigorous exertions in defence of the Constitution.

A proposal was made to raise a regiment of infantry and a troop of cavalry to be called the Loyal London Volunteers. This was met by an amendment, affirming the Militia to be the Constitutional defence and requesting the Court of Lieutenancy to put the same on a sufficient footing for defence. A Corporation Committee was appointed to suggest a plan on which all might agree. Their report was presented (24th), recommending the raising of an infantry regiment, but declaring the Militia the City's proper military defence, and suggesting that the Court of Lieutenancy be requested to formulate a plan for rendering the Militia efficient. The recommendation as to the Militia was carried, and the other proposal postponed till after the report of the Court of Lieutenancy. The Lord Mayor reported (8 May) the wish of the Lieutenancy to put the Militia on a proper footing. A London Militia Bill was brought into the House of Commons by Sir Watkin Lewes (17 June), but opposed by Sheridan as being a breach of the charters and customs of the City of London. It was read a third time (20th), all the City members supporting it, and passed the House of Lords (30th). It enabled the Commissioners of Lieutenancy to raise two regiments of ten Companies, each including grenadiers and light infantry. Every commissioned officer in these was to be a freeman of London. Privates were to be chosen by ballot. Every householder and every corporate body were to find men according to their land tax assessment. £50 to provide one man, £100 two, and £200 three.

Corporate bodies were to find a full complement, according to valuation. Every one valued below £15 land tax was exempt. A list of all persons liable was to be made out by the Alderman and Council of each ward. Substitutes must not have more than one child born in wedlock; must be resident in or within three miles of the City, and, if approved, must serve for five years. The result of the Bill was that London instead of being defended by six regiments of Trained Bands, of nominally 9,000 untrained and undisciplined men, would have at its command two regiments of Militia, each consisting of 1,600 trained and disciplined men, one-half of whom must always be in the City, while the other half could only be sent twelve miles beyond its border. The balloting clauses and other provisions of the Act aroused general dissatisfaction. At the Common Hall there was open expression of dissatisfaction with the City members for their part in the Bill. A special meeting of Farringdon Ward Without passed strong resolutions against the Bill, and requested their representatives to use every endeavour to amend it. [An amended Act was passed next year (1795).] While this discussion was proceeding, the Light Horse Volunteers, who had been originally organised in 1779 on the dread of a French invasion, had been found effective in the riots of 1780, and on the return of quieter times had been disbanded in 1783, were re-organised. They were composed of gentlemen living within ten miles of the Metropolis and serving at their own expense. Slight accidents sometimes form an outlet for expressing dissatisfaction. A young man who had been taken for enlistment to a recruiting house near Charing Cross threw himself (15 Aug.) from a garret window and was killed by the fall, when found his hands were tied behind his back. A mob which assembled pulled the house down. On Monday (18th) a meeting of the Court of Lieutenancy was held in the Guildhall to hear appeals under the Militia Bill. A crowd of several thousands assembled. The cry was raised, "Down with the recruiting houses." The mob gathered at a recruiting house in Shoe Lane (20th). The Lord Mayor in person with constables proceeded to the scene, and seeing the temper of the mob ordered out the Artillery Company and the Light Horse Volunteers, and sent to the Tower for the military. Towards evening the Riot Act was read, on which the mob dispersed, one party to Bride Lane recruiting house and another to Holborn, opposite Castle Street. On the reading of the Act again they set off to other depôts in Long Lane, Golden Lane, Upper Moorfields, St. Mary Axe, and Whitecross Street, where they were either anticipated or dispersed by the military, Artillery, or Light Horse. On Friday a public meeting was called by bills at Founders' Hall, Lothbury, to discuss "an appeal from the Militia Act." The Lord Mayor prohibited the meeting and the crowd dispersed. For ordering the man who had given directions for printing the bills into custody by parole, instead of by warrant, the Lord Mayor was found guilty by a jury, and a farthing damages was awarded the plaintiff. On Saturday, 23rd, the City was again quiet.

On 16 May died John Spiller, of Temple Lane, Blackfriars, a pupil of Bacon the sculptor, and the carver of Charles II's statue in the Royal Exchange.—The freedom of the City was voted (17th) to Lieut.-Gen. Sir William Meadows, K.C.B., who had been second in command under Lord Cornwallis in India, and to General Sir Charles Grey and Admiral Sir John Jarvis (27th) for their conduct in the West Indies.—The colours taken at Martinico were publicly placed in St. Paul's (17th).—The news of Lord Howe's victory over the French fleet at Ushant (1 June) was received in London on the evening of the 13 June and announced in the theatres. London and Westminster were illuminated for three nights. Public thanks were voted to Lord Howe and his sailors (16th). The Common Council (17th) voted an address to the King on his victory, thanks to Lord Howe and his sailors, the freedom of the City to Lord Howe in a gold box, and

£500 to be paid into the hands of the master of Lloyd's Coffee House, as the City's subscription for wounded petty officers, soldiers, and seamen, and for the widows and orphans of those who fell in action.   The address was presented on 20 June. —Alexander Brander (sheriff 1792–3), died on 29 June.   On an outbreak of jail fever in Newgate he paid a visit to the prison in discharge of his duties, resulting in an illness from which he never recovered.—Alderman Skinner was elected Lord Mayor on Michaelmas day.

Emanuel Hospital, Westminster.

Five-pound notes were first issued by the Bank of England.—The following quaint advertisement appeared in the *Times* of 29 Dec. :—"The unfortunate DEBTORS in LUDGATE PRISON beg leave, thus publicly, to return their grateful thanks to LADY TAYLOR, of Spring Gardens, for her munificent Benefaction of 149 lbs. of Beef, 21 half-peck loaves, 21 sacks of coals, and 66 lbs. of cheese, each Article being of the best quality.   At the same time they entreat the LORD MAYOR to accept their unfeigned thanks for his kind present of a Guinea, which was equally divided among the unfortunate Debtors.   N.B. The smallest Benefaction from their fellow Citizens and other liberal minded persons, will at all times be thankfully received, particularly at this inclement season of the year."—An Act was obtained by the Lord Mayor and Aldermen, as governors of Emanuel Hospital, to extend and increase the number and objects of the Charity (founded in 1600).   Ten out-pensioners were elected, and the number of boys on the foundations increased by eight.—A penny post was established in London, the charge covering only letters passing from one part of the metropolis to another.   The public soon had occasion to complain of the carriers extorting 2d. for what were legally penny missives.   An earlier penny post had been established in London by Dockwra in 1680.

1795.

PETITION was presented (15 Jan., 1795) to the House of Commons from the Common Council in favour of a Bill which (26 June) became an Act, for widening the passage beyond Temple Bar by removing Butcher Row, for making a new street between Snow Hill and Holborn, and for removing a shameful nuisance in Bridge Street by making an entirely new sewer.—A petition from a Common Hall was presented to Parliament (26th), praying that the House, while disclaiming all right of interfering with the internal affairs of France, would be pleased to take measures for promoting a speedy peace.

Complaint was made of the increase of the National Debt through subsidies to Powers which had violated public engagements, and rendered no adequate service in return.—An address from the Common Council was presented to the King (28th), praying that he might be pleased to defend this country against its enemies, and to restore to us the blessings of peace whenever it can be done consistently with the honour and dignity of the State and with that permanent security required for maintaining trade, commerce, and prosperity.—The suspension of the Habeas Corpus Act was continued.—Alderman Curtis (2 Feb.) presented a petition, signed by 1,659 Liverymen, stating their readiness to support His Majesty in the prosecution of the war, as the only means of obtaining an honourable peace.

At his house in Gloucester Place, Portman Square, on 20 Feb., in his 63rd year, died Alderman John Sawbridge, of Langbourn Ward.

He was elected member of Parliament for Hythe in 1768, and distinguished himself in the discussions on the Middlesex election of that year. He was in consequence elected, with James Townsend, Sheriff of London (June, 1769), Alderman 1769, and Lord Mayor 1775. He thrice represented the City in Parliament, and was Colonel of the East Battalion of the Kent Militia. For the last few years he had, in consequence of indisposition, lived in retirement. He was buried at Wye, in Kent.

Amendments to the City Militia Bill were discussed in Common Council (27 Feb.).

There had been a discussion on its introduction into the House of Commons between the City members, who asserted it was now satisfactory to the citizens, and Sheridan, who pronounced it an invasion of the City Charters. It passed the third reading, supported by all the City members (20 Mar.). Sir Watkin Lewes, Colonel of the East London Regiments, chose as the uniform of his regiment, scarlet turned up with blue, and Sir James Sanderson, Colonel of the West London Regiment, scarlet and orange (28 June).

The Prince of Wales was married to the Princess Caroline of Brunswick (8 Ap.), and the Common Council resolved (9th) to present addresses to the King and Queen. Those to the King and Queen were presented on the 17th, and those to the Prince and Princess on the 23rd at Carlton House. The Princess had already become popular.   Sheriffs Eamer and Burnett were knighted.—A committee of Common Council was appointed on 17 June, to consider the best means for reducing the high price of provisions, and in what way the poor could be relieved.

Exportation had been forbidden and importation allowed (13 Feb.).   Wheat was now 70s. a quarter and bread 1s. per quartern loaf   The Lord Mayor stated (7 July) that the Privy Council (who had themselves entered into an engagement to use only standard bread till 1 Oct) recommended that public subscriptions be applied towards encouraging the use of meat and vegetables, and such food as may be a substitute for wheat, rather than to cheapen bread which would only produce greater scarcity.   £1,000 was ordered to be paid the Committee for distribution in the several Wards   The Court resolved to discontinue the use of hair powder for a time, and requested the Lord Mayor and City members to submit to the Privy Council the propriety of recommending this generally (an ingenious calculator, in a pamphlet of the time, estimated the value of flour thrown away in hair powder at £2,292,000 of British money annually, at 9d. per quartern loaf), and of giving a premium to such bakers as would undertake to make bread for general use, wholesome and cheaper.   Large sums were subscribed.   The Common Council also resolved that no civic dinners should be given at the expense of the Corporation between 16 July and 1 Oct   By the end of August the price had fallen, as the harvest was abundant, to 2s. 6d. and 2s a stone

In June, some of the Artsmasters' houses at Bridewell were being pulled down to enlarge the prison, when a wall suddenly gave way, burying under the ruins twelve or fifteen men, most of whom were severely hurt and two were killed.

Bridewell Hospital had been established in the reign of Edward VI, as a " House of Occupations ', St Thomas's had been established for the impotent aged and sore, St. Bartholomew's for the sick and suffering, Christ's for the fatherless; and Bethlem for the weak of intellect.   Then Bridewell, the ancient residence of kings, was set apart for training imbeciles, or those whom no one would employ to honest labour, and for setting sturdy and idle vagrants to work   The superintendents or apprentice-trainers were called Artsmasters   In 1597 these were discontinued and an attempt made at farming the labour of the inmates, but this not proving successful, Artsmasters were restored in 1601.   Attempts had been made from time to time to render the institution effective, but without success.   In June 1792, it was resolved to abolish Artsmasters and apprentices, but difficulties arose as to the immediate removal of Artsmasters.   Only two apprentices remained in 1795.

The freedom of the Goldsmiths' Company was conferred (1 July) on General Sir Charles Grey, K.B. (afterwards Viscount Howick and Earl Grey), and on Admiral Sir John Jarvis (afterwards Earl St. Vincent), in approbation of their conduct in the West Indies.   They were entertained at dinner in the Goldsmiths' Hall.   The same day they were admitted to the freedom of the Fishmongers' Company; also to the freedom of the City, by Chamberlain Wilkes, who made a graceful speech to both, in praise of their gallant behaviour in the West Indies, and in the course of it a neat side shot at certain charges made against them in Parliament during June.—At Clapham, Surrey, in his 81st year, died (25 July) the Rev. William Romaine, rector of St. Anne's and St. Andrew's, Blackfriars.

He was buried in a vault in the church, where a monument, by Bacon, was erected to his memory. Romaine was elected rector of St. Anne's in 1764, but, owing to a dispute about the election, was only inducted in 1766. He had first been Lecturer at St. George's, Botolph Lane, then at St. George's, Hanover Square, from which he was driven for overcrowding the church, and afterwards at St. Dunstan's in-the-West, 1749. In 1755 he became Gresham Professor of Astronomy, but preferring Mosaic to Newtonian astronomy, his lectures were deserted, and he resigned. He published in four volumes (1747–9) a new edition of Calasio's *Hebrew Concordance*. He was a devoted student of the Scriptures and an earnest, impressive, and popular preacher.

Alderman Curtis was elected Lord Mayor (29 Sept.).—The freedom of the City was voted (8 Oct.) to Vice-Admiral Lord Bridport for his victory over the French at L'Orient (23 June). Lord Bridport attended at Guildhall and received the freedom on 6 Feb., 1798.—Parliament was opened (29 Oct.), and the King, in his opening speech, expressed hopes of peace through the exhaustion of France.

A great crowd, estimated at 200,000, assembled to see the King pass to the opening. Ministers in passing were hooted and hissed. On the King's return a marble or bullet broke a window of the Royal carriage, and the crowd, from St. James's to Buckingham Palace, shouted, " Peace, Peace, Bread, Bread." Next evening the King, Queen, and Royal Family, attended Covent Garden Theatre, and were received most heartily and loyally.

An address from the Common Council was presented (6 Nov.) expressive of detestation at the recent outrage. At the reception of the address Sheriff Richard Glode was knighted.— Early in the morning the same day (6 Nov.), occurred a most tremendous storm of wind. There had been no such tempest in London since 1703. Houses were unroofed, chimneys blown

Street Cries—" Fine Strawberries "

down, and many lives were lost.—In consequence of the late attempt on the King's person, special legislation was proposed in two Bills for the purpose of safeguarding His Majesty, but was keenly contested on the ground of undue interference with the liberty of the subject. All over the country meetings were held for and against. A petition from the Common Council was presented by the Sheriffs (19th), declaring abhorrence of all those seditious meetings which had lately taken place, and which they conceived led to the outrage of 29 Oct., and praying the House to adopt such measures for a limited time as would prevent similar attempts. A Common Hall was held (21 Nov.) to protest against the Sedition Bill. Both Bills, limited to three years, received the Royal Assent (18 Dec.).

Dr. Andrew Kippis, editor of the *Biographia Britannica*, was buried in Bunhill Fields —The Bank of England Rotunda, 57 feet in diameter, was designed by Sir John Soane, R.A.—Trinity House, on Tower Hill, was built, 1793-5, from the designs of Samuel Wyatt. The front and wings are of the Ionic order, on a rusticated basement. Over the windows are medallions, with portraits of George III and Queen Charlotte The members of the Board for 1794 were portrayed in a painting by Gainsborough Dupont.—The picturesque costumes of the London street criers of this period are admirably shown in a folio volume, engraved and published this year, of drawings by Francis Wheatley, R A

1796.

NE of the last of the bookselling fraternity in Little Britain, Mr Edward Ballard, died (2 Jan., 1796).—On the 7th was born the Princess Charlotte, only child of the Prince and Princess of Wales Congratulatory addresses were presented to the King and Queen (27th) in the usual form. The City Remembrancer received a letter (29th) stating that the Prince of Wales, being under the necessity of dismissing his establishment, was unable to receive the City's compliments in a manner suitable to his rank and with that respect which is due to the City of London.—An entertainment and ball was given at the Mansion House (25 Jan.) in honour of the Lord Mayor's birthday, at which were present the Duke of Clarence, Prince William of Gloucester, the Prince of Orange and his son. —The monuments to John Howard and Samuel Johnson were opened to the public (23 Feb.) in St. Paul's.—At a Common Council, 28 Ap., a debate arose as to whether an Alderman had the right to remove his deputy. The general opinion was that he had such a right and that it was essentially necessary he should possess that right.—The Militia Bill Committee were asked to settle with the Hon. Artillery Company in what manner the ground and armoury house of that Company might

be used by the City Militia and Artillery Company, and to report. In September the Court agreed not to interfere further in this dispute.—The foundation stone of the new church of St. Martin Outwich was laid (4 May).—The Sheriffs of London and Middlesex appeared in the Exchequer Chamber to render into Court their estreats, levies, captions, &c., and to answer an Officer called the Opposer for the Crown. Several of the Sheriffs' Officers had neglected to make the returns, and the Sheriffs were ordered to attend, in person, and answer interrogatories. Such a proceeding had not occurred for many years.—Earl Howe, to whom the City freedom had been voted (17 June, 1794), was admitted (6 May) to the freedom; and an entertainment, in honour of the occasion, was given by the Goldsmiths' Company.—Parliament was prorogued (19 May) and then dissolved. Alderman William Lushington, the Lord Mayor (Curtis), Aldermen Harvey Christian Combe and John William Anderson were elected for the City (1 June).—On 11 June, at Bedwell Park, Herts, in his 76th year, died Samuel Whitbread, the famous brewer of Chiswell Street.—Alderman Brook Watson who, being absent abroad, had been passed by in 1793, was chosen Lord Mayor.—The Lord Mayor presented an address (26 Oct.) expressing the satisfaction of the City at hearing that an envoy was to be sent to Paris to negotiate peace, and promising, if the endeavours should prove unsuccessful, their assistance and support in opposing, with increased vigour, the further efforts with which this country may have to contend. The King conferred the honour of knighthood on Sheriffs Stephen Langston and William Staines.—At Snaresbrook, on 14 Oct., died Sir John Hopkins, Knight, Alderman of Castle Baynard, 1782; Sheriff, 1784; Lord Mayor, 1792.—At the Guildhall Banquet, on Lord Mayor's day, was present, at his own desire, the Tunisian Ambassador. He did not dine in the hall, but drank coffee and smoked tobacco in a room by himself while the company were at dinner.—In Weymouth Street, Portland Place, on 17 Dec., died William Pickett, silversmith, Alderman of Cornhill, 1783, Sheriff, 1784, Lord Mayor, 1789, the chief promoter of the scheme for widening the approach to the City in front of Temple Bar.—The war expenditure had been so heavy and the threats of a French invasion so ominous that Government resolved to appeal to the country for a voluntary loan of eighteen millions. With this in view Mr. Pitt communicated with the Bank of England (30 Nov.).

Every hundred pounds subscribed was to reckon as £112 10s. in the 5 per cents., to be irredeemable, unless with the owner's consent, until three years after the present 5 per cents. shall have been redeemed or reduced, or if the holder wished to be paid at par, at any shorter time, not less than two years after a definite treaty of peace. One million was lent by the Bank of England and £400,000 by the Directors Notice was sent to the Lord Mayor (1 Dec), and a special Common Council was summoned to consider the proposal (5th) Before that time the loan had been subscribed and it was only by special favour that the Council had an opportunity of showing their zeal and loyalty by subscribing £100,000   The chief ally Britain now had against the French was the Emperor of Germany.   A subsidy had been sent to the Emperor without consulting Parliament, at that time sitting, and on this Fox made (8 Dec.) a vehement attack.   A Common Hall was held (14th), which instructed the City representatives to move or to support a motion censuring Ministers for sending British money to the Emperor of Germany, while Parliament was sitting, without its consent.   In the evening Alderman Combe seconded Mr. Fox's motion of censure, while the three other representatives opposed the motion.   The Common Council declared (20th) that the pecuniary aid recently furnished by His Majesty's Ministers to the Emperor of Germany has been productive of great advantage to Great Britain, and enabled the Emperor not only to withstand the desperate attempts of the French armies to over-run Germany, but also has given a decided and favourable turn to the war and opened a fairer prospect of obtaining an honourable peace to Great Britain and her allies.   The same day the Commons, in reply to the King's address, voted half-a-million for the Emperor.   Lord Malmesbury, the British Envoy at Paris, was ordered (29 Dec.) to quit France in forty-eight hours as he was only a passive instrument, constantly waiting for the opinion of the British Court.

A Livery was first granted to the Tin-Plate Workers' Company in 1796 —Lord Mayor Curtis, in order to encourage the public to keep the footway in front of their houses clean, fined himself 5s for a breach of the law in this respect.

1797.

ON 12 Dec., 1796, the King had announced to Parliament that Spain had declared war against Great Britain   An address from the Corporation was presented expressing regret at the failure to keep the peace with Spain (11 Jan).   Alderman Herne was created a Knight.—Joseph Bushman, Comptroller of the Chamber of the City of London and Clerk Comptroller (1785) of the Bridge House Estates, died (17th). —The Rev. John Thomas, rector of St. Peter's, Cornhill, for fifty-three years, and of Moulsey for sixty-four years, died (20th) in his 89th year.—News arrived in London (25 Feb.) that some French frigates had landed on the coast of Pembroke 1200 soldiers, but on being attacked by the country people had retired and left 300 soldiers behind.   Other ships were reported to be attempting to destroy the shipping at Ilfracombe.   Rumours were prevalent also of a descent on the coast of Ireland.

A run on the Bank of England for gold was expected.   The Privy Council met (26 Feb) and ordered suspension of cash payments by the Bank.   The Directors issued a circular explaining the affluent and prosperous condition of the Bank, and stating that business would be carried on as usual except that payment would be made in notes instead of in cash.   The principal London merchants and all the bankers resolved (27th) not to refuse to receive bank notes in payment of any sum of money to be paid to them, and to use their utmost endeavours to make all payments in the same manner, only the fractional parts of drafts were to be paid in specie so that everyone may be on an equality.   Parliament sanctioned (4 Ap.) the issue of £1 bank notes by the Bank of England.

The Spanish fleet was defeated off Cape St. Vincent by Sir John Jarvis.   On the arrival of the news in London the Common Council voted thanks to the officers, seamen, and marines who had been engaged in the fight, and £100 to the fund at Lloyds for relief of widows and orphans of seamen and marines who had been killed.   A sword was voted to Admiral Jarvis, already a freeman of London. The City freedom was voted to Vice-Admirals Thompson and William Waldegrave, to Rear-Admiral Parker, and, Commodore Nelson, officers under Jarvis in the battle (10 Mar.).   Nelson took up his freedom on 28 Nov. and Admiral Sir William Waldegrave on 5 Dec.   Sir John Jarvis was created Earl of St. Vincent (27 Ap.), and the sword, voted by the City, was presented to him 14 Dec., 1799.—A Common Hall was held (23 Mar.) and an address to the King agreed to.   The Sheriffs and City representatives were ordered to present it to the King on the throne.

His Majesty, as on former occasions, declined the request, while expressing his readiness to accept the address at a levee.   At a Common Hall (12 Ap) two resolutions were passed declaratory of the rights of the Livery   When a third resolution " to investigate the real cause of the awful and alarming state of public affairs " was proposed, the Lord Mayor ruled it out of Court as not being in the notice calling the Hall.   A heated discussion followed, which the Lord Mayor terminated by ordering the insignia of office to be taken up.   The Hall was thus dissolved.   Another Hall was held (11 May)   They first passed resolutions declaring the rights of the Livery, asserting that Ministers had plunged the country into an unnecessary and unjust war producing unexampled calamities, increase of public debt, and diminution of trade and manufactures ; had abridged the rights and privileges of the subject; had wasted national wealth by subsidies to allies abroad and by supporting corruption at home to the destruction of public credit; and had shown a disposition to sacrifice the blood, treasure, and liberties of the kingdom in support of measures repugnant to the principles of the Constitution, derogatory to the dignity and safety of the King, and inconsistent with the happiness of the people. They directed their representatives to move for an address to the King to dismiss his present Ministers as the most likely means of obtaining a speedy and permanent peace ; censured the Lord Mayor for dissolving the late Common Hall on a frivolous and unfounded pretence, and for refusing to call another Common Hall for all the purposes specified in the requisition.   These resolutions were carried by a majority and ordered to be published in all the newspapers in Great Britain.   Alderman Combe the same night brought forward a motion in the House of Commons for the dismissal of Ministers, but was opposed by Aldermen Curtis and Anderson.   A counter declaration was drawn up and signed by 2,095 Liverymen expressing dissent from and disapprobation of the violent proceedings at the last three Common Halls.   A meeting of the Livery was held (26 May) at the London Tavern in support of this declaration and commending the Lord Mayor's conduct.   The dispute was continued in the election of Sheriffs.   The Earl of Lauderdale purchased his freedom and became a member of the Needlemakers' Company in order to qualify as a candidate for Sheriff.   With his lordship was associated Mr. F. S. Waddington.   Both were supported by those who had censured the Ministers and the Lord Mayor. Sir William Herne and Mr. Alderman Williams were nominated by the other party, and the show of hands (24 June) was in their favour.   On Lord Lauderdale attempting to address the Hall he was met by a torrent of hisses and groans, and Mr. Waddington, after several attempts to speak, was obliged to desist.   The Sheriffs declared Herne and Williams elected.

At Lambeth (9 Mar.) died George Nelson, Common Cryer of the City of London, only son of Alderman Nelson, Lord Mayor in 1765.—The Princess Royal, Charlotte Augusta, was married (18 May) to Frederick, Prince (afterwards King)

of Wurtemberg, and a congratulatory address thereon was presented from the
Common Council to the King and Queen (26th).—The freedom of the City was
voted (19 May) to Sir Robert Calder, first Captain of the fleet, under Sir John
Jarvis, and he was admitted, 2 May, 1799.—A proclamation was issued (31st),
requiring all subjects to be ready to assist the public magistrates in apprehending
and securing all persons concerned in treasonable and rebellious practices. The
Court of Common Council, after hearing the proclamation, agreed (6 June) to
associations of citizen householders being formed, in defence of the City and their
property, against any incendiaries, in order that the army and militia might have
full scope to defend the coast.—John Quincy Adams, afterwards President of the
United States, was married to Louisa Catherine Johnson at the church of
Allhallows Barking (26 July)—Sir Benjamin Hammet was elected Lord Mayor,
but begged to be excused on account of illness. Some doubts having being
expressed as to the validity of this excuse, he was ordered to pay the fine
(£1,000), which he did, and Alderman John William Anderson was elected in
his stead.—Admiral Duncan defeated the Dutch fleet, under De Winter, off
Camperdown, on the coast of Holland (12 Oct.).

The Corporation voted (19 Oct.) an address to the King on this victory, the freedom of the City
and a sword to the Admiral, now created Viscount Duncan of Camperdown, the freedom of the
City and a sword to Sir Richard Onslow, Vice-Admiral, thanks to the captains, officers, seamen and
marines, and £500 to the subscription at Lloyds' Coffee House for the widows and orphans. The
address was presented at St. James's (25th). Viscount Duncan was present at the Guildhall
Banquet (9 Nov.). He was admitted to the freedom 22 May, 1798; Admiral Onslow on 11 Dec, 1798.

On the 26th died, in his 71st year, John Wilkes, F.R.S., alderman of
Farringdon Without, 1769; Chamberlain of the City, 1779; Sheriff, 1771, and
Lord Mayor, 1774. He was buried in Grosvenor Chapel, South Audley Street.
—A public thanksgiving at St. Paul's for the naval victories over the French,
1794, the Spaniards, 1797, and the Dutch, 1797, was held (19 Dec).

Before daylight the houses overlooking the route from St. James's to St Paul's were filled with
eager spectators. Within the City the two regiments of City Militia, the East India Volunteers, the
Light Horse Association, and the gentlemen of the Artillery Company kept order and regularity
A bright clear winter day added to the brilliancy of the scene. The colours taken in the three chief
engagements off Ushant, Cadiz and Camperdown were, amid martial music, carried into the Cathedral
and arranged in a circle under the centre of the Dome. Seamen and marines were arranged on each
side of the nave, while the members of Common Council, with their friends, filled the temporary
galleries on each side of the Dome. The Commons, with the Speaker in state, the Judges, the Lords,
in due order with the Lord Chancellor, next arrived The Royal procession consisted of the Dukes of
Gloucester, York and Clarence, the Royal Households, the King, Queen and Princesses. The King
was received by the Bishops of London and Lincoln (Dean of St. Paul's) who walked on each side of
His Majesty, preceded by the herald-at-arms and prebendaries, while the Princes and Princesses,
with their suites, followed in order. On reaching the Dome, the colours were lowered, and

the members of the Royal family saluted the audience The salute was received with loud acclamations and congratulations. After the reading of the first lesson the flag officers entered the choir in two divisions, to the right and left of His Majesty, supporting the ends of the flags which were carried to the altar and there deposited as trophies of naval success. The anthem was that sung at the thanksgiving for Marlborough's victories Pitt had a very unpleasant reception from the crowd on his way to St. Paul's. He dined in the City and was escorted home by soldiers.

A proposal was made in the House of Commons to increase the assessed taxes. Strong, but temperate, resolutions against the mode of increase, as pressing unduly on the middle classes, were passed at a meeting of Common Council (12 Dec.), at a ward meeting of Farringdon Without (13th), and at a Common Hall (14th). The Bill was modified and passed the House of Commons.

A butcher was reported to have exposed his wife for sale in Smithfield Market, near the Ram Inn, with a halter about her neck, and one about her waist, which tied her to a railing. A hog-driver bought her for three guineas and a crown.—In the City of London and within the Bills of Mortality there were, in this year, 5,204 licensed public-houses.—The desire to obtain a seat at the Mayoralty banquet is oddly illustrated by an advertisement in the *Times* of 9 Nov. —"Three guineas will be given for a gentleman's ticket to dine this day at Guildhall, by sending it before 12 o'clock, to Mr. Short, Hair Dresser, Bearbinder Lane, near the Mansion House."—The increase in the value of the prebendal estate of Finsbury was remarkable. The manor had been, at various times, leased to the Corporation. From a life interest of £39 13s 4d. the prebendary (Dr. Christopher Wilson), with the aid of the Corporation, had raised the annual income, in 1783, to £4,792. In 1797 the profits of the estate were thus apportioned—to the Corporation, £3,646, to Dr. Wilson's heirs, £2,431; to Dr. Apthorpe, prebendary at this time, £1,215.

1798.

ALDERMAN CLARK was elected Chamberlain (9 Jan., 1798).— A crowded meeting was held (9 Feb.) at the Exchange, to promote voluntary subscriptions to aid in the defence of the country, rendered necessary by the conduct of France.

Amid great enthusiasm, to which Alderman Watson (standing on his one leg, having lost the other in service in the navy) gave vent by proposing "One cheer for old England," 218 individual subscribers promised £46,534, in amounts ranging from a guinea to £3,000; Boyd, Barfield & Co., bankers, £3,000 annually during the war; Peel & Yates, cotton manufacturers, £10,000, and the Court of Common Council £10,000. The gifts exceeded (28 Sept.) Mr. Pitt's estimate of one and a half millions, and were expected to amount to half-a-million more Alderman Brook Watson, who in the expedition to Holland had been Commissary-General and had since retired on half-pay, was appointed (24 Mar.) Commissary-General at home.

At the Treasurer's house, Christ's Hospital (26 March), died Alderman William Gill, aged seventy-eight, formerly wholesale stationer in Abchurch Lane.

He was alderman of Walbrook, and Sheriff, 1781 ; Lord Mayor, 1788 ; and treasurer of Christ's Hospital, 1784. Gill's partner in business for fifty years, was Thomas Wright, alderman of Candlewick (1778), who died suddenly at Dulwich on 7 Ap. They began business together on London Bridge and were said to have left fortunes of £300,000 each

The King sent to Parliament a message "that the most formidable preparations were making by France and her allies to attack this country," and an Act was there and then passed enabling His Majesty to keep in prison all suspected persons.

A committee, appointed (24 Ap.) by the Court of Aldermen, to consider the best course of action, under present circumstances, reported "that each alderman should summon a meeting of the inhabitants of his Ward to form an association for learning the use of arms, or to act as constables on any sudden emergency." Meetings were accordingly held in twenty-three Wards at noon (1 May) "to show our enemies that the nation, and London in particular, had one heart, one spirit, and one strong hand to defend against foreign invaders, or any hostile power on earth, our King and the institutions of our country." It was agreed that every able-bodied householder should learn the use of arms, those incapable of learning should be sworn in as supernumerary constables, every alderman to have the command in his own Ward; a committee to be chosen, under the control of the whole, to form regulations and recommend officers, the central point to be the Mansion House, and in case of need to be united in one body, under the command of the Mayor and Court of Aldermen. The Lord Mayor was created a Baronet (5 May)—Instead of invading England, the French fleet proceeded to Egypt (1 July). News of its arrival there reached England (30 Aug.), but a month before that date the enemy's fleet had been entirely destroyed by Nelson (1 Aug) in Aboukir Bay. News of the Battle of the Nile reached London, 2 Oct An autograph letter (dated 8 Aug.) from Admiral Nelson to the Lord Mayor requested the City to honour him with the acceptance of the French Admiral's sword. The metropolis was illuminated in honour of the victory. The Court resolved (16th) that the sword be placed in the most conspicuous place in the Council Chamber; that the Lord Mayor convey to Lord Nelson the high sense which the Court entertain of the invaluable present of the sword, that the thanks of the Court and a sword be presented to Lord Nelson; also thanks to Captain Berry and the officers and seamen of the Mediterranean fleet, with the freedom of the City to Captain Berry. An address to the King was presented (24th) The freedom of the City was voted to Admiral Sir John Borlase Warren for defeating and dispersing a French fleet (12 Oct) which had been hovering round the Irish coast. Sir John was admitted a freeman, 27 May, 1799.

At Easthill, Wandsworth, died (21 June), Sir James Sanderson, Bart., hop merchant, Fish Street Hill, M.P. for Hastings; alderman of Bridge Within, 1783; Sheriff, 1788; Lord Mayor and Baronet, 1792; for a time Colonel of the West Regiment of the London Militia. He was buried in St. Magnus Church.—On 21 July, at his house in Lincoln's Inn Fields, died suddenly of a paralytic stroke, James Adair, Esq., King's Prime Serjeant-at-Law, M.P. for Higham Ferrers, Chief Justice of Chester, and formerly Recorder (1779-89) of London.

In early life Adair was a keen partizan of Wilkes, and thus incurred the ill-will of Horne Tooke, who said "When Mr. Adair sat down, there was a general cry of 'the question, the question'" Wilkes retorted, "True, but never till he sits down. I have heard 'the question' repeatedly and loudly called for while Mr. Horne was still *standing*, long before *he would sit down*. Mr. Adair possesses his subject so entirely that he often exhausts the matter and when he sits down nothing is left but to decide on the *question*."

A motion was made (27 July) to abolish Bartholomew Fair; after much discussion and a proposal to limit it to one day the matter was referred to a Committee.— The Grocers' Company's Hall was rebuilt from designs by Mr. Leverton, and regret was expressed at the disappearance of an oriel window in the old Hall.—

Grocers' Hall and Garden, 1890, from picture by F. W. W. Topham.

Sir Richard Carr Glyn was elected Lord Mayor (29 Sept.) over Alderman Combe, his senior.—The new church of St. Martin Outwich, was consecrated 26 Nov. —On 16 Dec. died, at Downing, in Wales, Thomas Pennant, zoologist, author of *Tours through England and Scotland, An Account of London*, and many other works.

The river police, afterwards merged with the Metropolitan force, was established this year —Only one coach ran from Paddington to the Bank, and this did not pay.—At the rear of the London Coffee House, near the Old Bailey, was found a sepulchral monument dedicated to Claudia Martina, by her husband, Anencletus, a provincial Roman soldier; also a fragment of a statue of Hercules.— Pinmakers' Hall, in Pinners' Court, Old Broad Street, was demolished. It had been used as an Independent Meeting House for many years, among the pastors being Baxter, Manton, Owen, Bates, Howe, Isaac Watts, and Pope's "modest Foster."—Astley Cooper, the distinguished surgeon, succeeded Mr. Cline in the tenancy of No 3 (New) Broad Street. He was now Professor at St. Thomas's Hospital.—A singular robbery occurred at the Mint; a man, armed with a pistol, entered the building, seized 2,804 guineas and escaped.—The lending of newspapers for hire was regarded as a fraud on the revenue. Several keepers of reading rooms in Fleet Street and Shoe Lane were fined £5 for this offence.—Jenkins, a Bank of England clerk of extraordinary stature, was buried in the ground inside the Bank; some surgeons had offered upwards of 200 guineas for the corpse.

1799.

THE Honourable Mrs. Damer's offer (23 Jan., 1799) to execute and present to the Court a bust of Lord Nelson, either in bronze or marble, was accepted.—Mr. Villette, Chaplain of Newgate Prison for thirty years, died (26th) and was succeeded by the Rev. Brownlow Ford.—At Dedham, Essex, died (17 Ap) Joel Johnson, architect of Wapping Church, the Magdalen and London Hospitals, &c.—A general review of the various Volunteer corps of London and the neighbourhood was held by the King on his birthday (4 June).

Over 8,000 volunteers assembled in Hyde Park. His Majesty promised to inspect each corps, in and near London, on its own training ground. This he did (21st) Crossing Westminster Bridge, from the Palace, he first inspected the Surrey Corps between the Asylum and the Obelisk in St. George's Fields. Passing on, he entered the City by Blackfriars Bridge, where the Lord Mayor and Sheriffs, escorted by the Grenadier company of the East London Militia, under Sir Watkin Lewes, met him, and after, as usual, proffering and receiving back the City sword, rode uncovered before him along Bridge Street, Blackfriars, and St. Paul's Churchyard, on his way to the Bank and Royal Exchange. After visiting the Bank and Royal Exchange, the King proceeded to the India House, Tower Hill, and back to Finsbury Square. Here were arranged on the west side the Hon. Artillery Company, under their Captain the Prince of Wales, while on their right, on the south side, were the centre squadron of the Light Horse, with the three dismounted squadrons of riflemen. In all 12,208 volunteers, belonging to the City and its neighbourhood, were inspected by His Majesty, who afterwards expressed his pleasure at their discipline and soldierly bearing.

The Right Honourable Sir James Eyre, Chief Justice of the Common Pleas, died (6 July) at his residence, Rushcombe, Berks.

He was in early life one of the four Common Pleaders of the City of London, and had acted as deputy Recorder for Sir William Morton, on whose resignation and by whose influence he was elected Recorder of London in his 28th year, 1762. At the election, and during the Mayoralty of Alderman Beckford, he took a stand against the extreme measures then popular.

The freedom was conferred on a series of distinguished officers during the latter half of the year.

The freedom of the City and a sword were voted (13 Sept.) to Vice-Admiral Andrew Mitchell for compelling (30 Aug.) the Dutch fleet, in the Texel, to surrender to the British squadron under his command; and to Sir Ralph Abercromby, who (27 Aug.) landed troops on the coast of Holland

St. Helen's Church and Leathersellers' Hall.   The Cornhill Military
Association being drilled, 1798.

and drove the enemy from their fortified position, thus enabling the British squadron to compel the Dutch fleet to surrender. The first was admitted to the freedom 6 Feb., and the second 2 May, 1800. An address to the King, congratulating him on these victories, was also agreed to, presented (25th), and graciously received. On 11 Oct. the freedom of the City and a sword of 100 guineas were voted to Sir W. Sydney Smith, who had, with the aid of his British sailors and marines, enabled the garrison of S. Jean d'Acre, Palestine, to withstand (18 Mar. to 20 May) the siege and repeated attacks of the French army under Bonaparte. Sir Sydney was admitted, 17 Dec., 1801.

Alderman Harvey Christian Combe was elected Lord Mayor.—Specie, to the weight of forty tons, had been taken from two Spanish frigates. The first six wagons, each drawn by eight horses, arrived at the Bank from Plymouth (4 Dec.).

As they passed the Mansion House, the Lord Mayor and his household appeared on the steps and drank, out of a gold cup, success to the British Navy, the band playing "Rule Britannia." The honest tars, who were riding on the outside of the wagons, were not neglected, and in return saluted his Lordship with three hearty cheers.

The Religious Tract Society was established this year.—The old hall of the Priory of St Helen's (then used as the hall of the Leathersellers' Company) was pulled down (Mar.), and St Helen's Place built on the site.—An Ionic portico and an eastern wing, designed by R Jupp, was added to the East India House.—The house, which was formerly the King's Head Tavern, Fleet Street, was demolished in order to widen Chancery Lane.—A well was discovered near the front gate of the Royal Exchange, which had not been used for 600 years.—In consequence of dissatisfaction with the system of classification of ships practised at Lloyd's, a rival committee started a New Register Book of shipping, their offices being at 22, Change Alley, and afterwards, 3, St. Michael's Alley. The New Register was known as the Shipowners' Register or Red Book, and the old as the Underwriters' Register or Green Book The systems were merged in 1834 —A bread inquest in one of the City wards resulted in the fining of a number of bakers for short weight at the rate of 5s. per ounce, the penalties amounting to £20

1800.

ON Christmas-day, 1799, Napoleon was elected First Consul of France. He immediately despatched a courier with a letter to the King of Great Britain, expressing a desire for peace. The King expressed doubts of the permanency of any treaty made with France while her institutions were so unsettled, and negotiations were broken off.

A Common Hall was held (19 Feb, 1800) and a petition to the House of Commons adopted in favour of immediate negotiations for peace. The City representatives were requested to support this petition, which the Lord Mayor promised to do The other three refused, as the prayer of the petition was contrary to their own decided opinions. On its presentation, Sir J. W. Anderson questioned whether the document truly represented the state of City opinion, especially as it bore only fifty-seven signatures. The Lord Mayor replied that the fifty-seven names were merely appended as a matter of form. Sir J. W. Anderson presented a counter petition, signed by 1690 Liverymen. A motion brought forward (30 July) in the Common Council to address the King to enter into an immediate treaty with France, was lost in favour of the previous question

A handsome pump was erected (30 Ap) by the contributions of the Bank of England, the East India Company, the neighbouring Fire offices, and the bankers and traders of Cornhill, over the deep well which had been laid open by a sinking of the pavement in front of the Royal Exchange (16 Mar., 1799). The case, a lofty and ornamental obelisk of iron, was painted and decorated with emblematical figures, one of a house of correction, in memory of a well being first made and a house of correction built there by Henry Wallis, Lord Mayor 1282.—On the evening of 15 May, when the King had just entered his box at Drury Lane Theatre, and was bowing to the audience, a madman, named Hadfield, fired a pistol shot at His Majesty. A by-stander, seeing the man level his pistol, raised the assassin's arm, so that the shot struck on the top of His Majesty's box.   At a meeting next day, the Common Council expressed their horror of the dastardly attempt, and, on the presentation of the address, Alderman Leighton received the honour of knighthood. —Three London rectors were sued (12 July) in the Court of Common Pleas for non-residence.

One, the rector of St. Margaret Pattens, had, during nine years, never lived for an hour in his parish.   One of his parsonages he had let for a broker's shop, and the other for something similar.   The defence was ill-health which made it impossible for him to reside, to which it was answered he had never resided and even now he was making no provision for residence.   The jury awarded the full penalty of £110. Another, the rector of St. Ethelburga, escaped from a flaw in the declaration. The third, rector of St. Mildred, Bread Street, was discharged on proof that his health did not permit of personal residence.

Sir William Staines was elected Lord Mayor.—The freedom of the City (voted 6 Mar.) was conferred (17 Oct.) on Sir Edward Hamilton, in recognition of his recovery of H.M. ship "Hermione," which had been lost to the British Fleet, and placed by the enemy for repair in the harbour of Porto Cavallo, West Indies, under the protection of 200 guns on the heights around.—Sir R. C.

Cornhill Pump.

Glyn was created a baronet (4 Nov.).—On 4 Nov., the Common Council voted the freedom of the City to Mr. W. Adams, who had, on his own account and risk, vended potatos at prices so reduced as to afford great relief to the industrious poor; he was also permitted to occupy premises in Honey Lane as before, rent free.—On the return of the Lord Mayor's procession (10 Nov.) to Blackfriars pier, the populace took the horses from the carriage of the late Lord Mayor, Alderman Combe, and drew him to the Guildhall. At the banquet in the evening Lord Nelson was a specially invited guest.

After some of the toasts had been given his Lordship was invited to come forward and receive, in presence of the brilliant assembly, the sword publicly voted after the battle of the Nile The sword was richly ornamented, the handle, gold with blue enamel, studded with diamonds; the crocodile appeared on it as emblematical of the scene of the great victory, and the guard was supported with anchors. He took up his position under a triumphal arch erected for the occasion, the Chamberlain made the presentation, and addressed the hero in an appropriate speech, to which he replied : "Sir, it is with pride and satisfaction I receive from the honourable Court this testimony of your approbation of my conduct, and with this sword (holding it up in his left remaining hand) I hope soon to aid in reducing our implacable and inveterate enemy to proper and due limits, without which this country can neither hope for nor expect a solid, honourable, and permanent peace." [This sword was given in 1895 to Greenwich Hospital.]

The closing years of this century were marked by scarcity and dearth.

In 1795 the quartern loaf cost 12¼d. Sums of money had been collected to assist the industrious poor by selling provisions at reduced rates In the winter and spring of 1798 soup kitchens had been established, with great benefit, among the poor in Spitalfields. In the winter and spring of 1799, 40,000 persons had been similarly served with 750,918 meals, at an expense of £3,476 9s. A Committee of thirty-five was appointed at a meeting in the London Tavern (6 Dec., 1799), to raise subscriptions for providing kitchens in greater numbers. During 1799 wheat rose from 53s 9d per quarter to 95s. 6d The House of Lords, on the motion of the Archbishop of Canterbury, agreed (10 Feb, 1800), not to consume nor to permit to be consumed in their respective households, more wheaten flour than one quartern loaf for each person weekly, till 10 Oct. next, and to discontinue all pastry An Act was passed at the same time forbidding bread to be sold or exposed for sale till twenty-four hours after it had been baked under a penalty of £5 for each loaf The bakers reported (17 Mar) a reduction of the sale of bread by one-sixth. In Jan., 1800, wheat cost 104s. a quarter, and gradually rose to 140s. in July. An early harvest reduced the price in August Bread riots were frequent in the country In London inflammatory handbills were posted on the Monument and circulated in the City (Sunday, 14 Sept.), calling on all to attend Mark Lane on Monday, and they would soon cause a fall of 6d per quartern loaf. The Lord Mayor collected the peace officers and received assurances of support from the volunteer corps of the Tower, Langbourn, Billingsgate, and Bridge Wards. The mob assembled on Monday morning, hustling and hissing the dealers as they arrived at the Market. The Lord Mayor recommended them to go quietly home, on which they seemed to retire, but he had scarcely returned to Guildhall when the mob re-assembled. Appearing again on the scene with Sir William Leighton, Sir John Eamer, and Sheriff Flower, his conciliatory words were received with a shower of brickbats and stones. The Riot Act was read and they dispersed In the evening they again assembled and broke the windows of corn dealers, butchers, bakers, and cheesemongers. The house of one Rusby, in Blackfriars Street, who had been convicted (4 July) of regrating (that is, of re-selling in the same market on the same day, at a profit, corn he had bought), was gutted. Next day, the Court of Aldermen issued a notice, that such disturbances only kept prices up, and that without security against loss no corn would be brought to the market at all The Common Hall adopted an address (3 Oct), requesting the King to assemble Parliament to consider the present high price of provisions. The Common Council adopted a similar address (14th) On the re-assembling of Parliament (11 Nov), reports from Committees of both Houses indicated that the stoppage of distilleries, and of the starch manufacture, would set free 250,000 quarters of barley, and 40,000 of wheat for food, and recommended the encouragement of fisheries. A Royal proclamation was issued (3 Dec.), recommending the use of other provisions than flour, reduction of use of flour in every household by one-third, and the restriction of one loaf to each person per week.

1801.

THE first day of the century, and of the union between Great Britain and Ireland was ushered in by the ringing of the City bells.— In 1795, tailors' wages had been fixed by the Court at 25s. a week. The journeymen, on account of the high price of provisions, refused to work for less than 30s. The dispute was brought before the Recorder (26 Jan., 1801).

The Court examined three principal masters and three leading journeymen. The masters pleaded increase of work, but also increase of workmen ; the men, that from the present dearth they could not support their families on less than 30s. Being called on to explain their system of mutual help they said they had different houses of call in London. Each house of call kept three books, in which were entered the names of journeymen according to their length of London residence. Those on the third book could not obtain employment till those on the first and second were served. Each member paid twopence a week at his house of call, for the support of sick and infirm members, and for no other purpose. After consultation, the Recorder gave decision for 27s. a week, and double that sum in case of a general mourning.

For engrossing hops a hop merchant was fined (28 Jan.) £500 and imprisoned one month, and another judgment against him was delivered (11 Feb.) for forestalling, the fine being £500 with three months' imprisonment.—An address on the legislative union of Great Britain and Ireland was adopted by the Corporation (5 Feb.), and presented to the King :—

"The accomplishment of this great measure" (so ran a passage in this address) "founded in wisdom, and demonstrative of your Majesty's paternal regard, affords at this momentous crisis the gratifying prospect of consolidating the joint interests and resources of the Empire, and of confirming, by a mutual participation of the peculiar blessings of each, the prosperity and happiness of both kingdoms." The King's reply referred to the Union "as an event which I trust cannot fail under the blessing of Providence to augment and perpetuate the welfare and happiness of all my people."

Sir Ralph Abercromby landed in Egypt, defeated the French army, but died of wounds received in the fight (28 Mar.). A monument in St. Paul's was voted to his memory by the House of Commons (18 May).—The minor canons of St. Paul's were declared in the Court of Exchequer (18 Ap.) to have the right of levying tithe in the parish of St. Gregory, at the rate of 2s. 9d. per pound on all rack rents, instead of 2½d., thus raising the income from £99 16s. 8d. to over £1,000.—Monuments in St. Paul's were voted by Parliament to Captains Moss and Riou, who fell in the Battle of Copenhagen.—Hitherto business in the public funds had been transacted by the stockbrokers, in a room called the rotunda, on the east-side of the court leading into the Bank of England. The extension of this business by the increase of the National Debt rendered the accommodation too limited. The foundation of a new building was laid (18 May) in Capel Court. James Peacock was the architect.—Threats of a French invasion were still frequent, and a rumour was afloat that Bonaparte at the head of his victorious troops in Germany was preparing to invade this country. A review of the volunteers and associated corps in London and vicinity, to the number of 4,734, enrolled, equipped and disciplined at their own expense, was held in Hyde Park (22 July). The weather was favourable, and the volunteers received great praise.—The East India Company resolved to still further enlarge their premises by the addition of several buildings in Leadenhall Market (30 July).—Sir William Plomer, KnightA, lderman of Bassishaw, 1772 ; Sheriff, 1774 , Lord Mayor, 1781 ; died 20 Aug.—Preliminaries of peace between Great Britain and the French Republic were signed, ratifications were exchanged, and a Royal proclamation was issued, announcing that plenipotentiaries from both sides would repair to Amiens for settling a definite peace. Rejoicings and illuminations, damped by a violent thunderstorm (10 Oct.), were resumed on Monday (12th).—Sir John Eamer was chosen Lord Mayor.

On Lord Mayor's Day the carriages of Sir William Staines, ex-Lord Mayor, and of Alderman Combe (former Mayor) were drawn by the populace from Blackfriars Bridge to the Guildhall, while the crowd again and again stopped Lord Nelson's carriage, in order to enjoy the pleasure of looking at the hero. At the upper end of the hustings was erected a transparency with four figures, emblematical of the four quarters of the world, illuminated with peace inscriptions At the lower end of the hall the word PEACE was especially conspicuous Citizen Otto (Resident Commissary of the French Republic in England), on entering the hall was saluted with outbursts of applause, indicating the popular approval of the peace of which he had been the harbinger.

The freedom of the City was voted to Admiral Lord Keith and to Sir John Hely Hutchinson, Sir Ralph Abercromby's successor, and swords to both, for their conduct in Egypt (19 Nov.).—Sir W. Sydney Smith was admitted to the freedom of the City, and received the sword voted to him (17 Dec.).

The London Penny Post was now discontinued, the postage being raised to 2d —The population of London within the walls was returned at 78,000.—The Marine Society, Bishopsgate, during this year sent out 193 boys as servants to naval officers, apprenticed 368 boys in the Merchant and East India services, and provided clothing for 1,817 volunteers for the Royal Navy.—The vanishing pastime of Jack-in-the-Green was at this period in full vogue. "The chimney-sweepers of London" writes Strutt, in 1801, "have singled out the first of May for their festival ; at which time they parade the streets in companies, disguised in various manners. Their dresses are usually decorated with gilt paper, and other mock fineries ; they have their shovels and brushes in their hands, which they rattle one upon the other; and to this rough music they jump about in imitation of dancing. Some of the larger companies have a fiddler with them, and a Jack-in-the-Green, as well as a Lord and Lady of the May, who follow the minstrel with great stateliness, and dance as occasion requires. The Jack-in-the-Green is a piece of pageantry consisting of a hollow frame of wood or wicker-work, made in the form of a sugar-loaf, but open at the bottom, and sufficiently large and high to receive a man. The frame is covered with green leaves and bunches of flowers interwoven with each other, so that the man within may be completely concealed, who dances with his companions, and the populace are mightily pleased with the oddity of the moving pyramid."

1802.

PAUL VAILLANT, father of the Company of Stationers (Sheriff 1760), died in his 87th year, in Pall Mall (1 Feb., 1802). His ancestor, a Huguenot, opened, in 1686, a bookseller's shop in the Strand, opposite Southampton Street, which was continued by the family till the end of last century.—The Income Tax, imposed as a war tax by Pitt in 1798, now came under discussion; Alderman Combe presented a petition from a Common Hall for its repeal, and the Common Council followed suit in a series of resolutions and a petition to Parliament (30 Mar.). A Bill for its repeal eventually received the Royal assent.—On Easter Monday (19 Ap.) after the Spital sermon at Christ's Church, the Prince of Wales and the Royal Dukes attended the banquet given by the Lord Mayor in the Egyptian Hall.

The hall was adorned with a figure of Britannia holding a shield, on which were inscribed the names of Howe, Duncan, Vincent, Nelson and Warren, with a large transparency representing the four quarters of the world worshipping peace. At the request of the Lord Mayor, the Prince presided, dressed in the uniform of the Honorable Artillery Company. The dance was opened by the Prince and Miss Eamer.

The definitive Treaty of Peace, signed at Amiens (at 4 p.m. 27 Mar.) arrived at London at 9 a.m. on the 29th. A Royal proclamation (issued 26 Ap.) announced the treaty, declared the formal conclusion of the war, and ordered a public thanksgiving.

The proclamation was read (29th) with the usual formalities in the City, at Chancery Lane, on the site of the old Cheapside Cross at the end of Wood Street, at the Royal Exchange, and at Aldgate. The procession passed along Cornhill and Leadenhall Street to Aldgate pump, returning by Fenchurch and Lombard Streets to the Mansion House. London was illuminated in the evening.

An address to the King on the Peace of Amiens, "which inscribes in the archives of Europe your Majesty's Navy more proudly pre-eminent than at the termination of any former war," was agreed to by the Common Council (7 May). —A motion made in the House of Commons (7 May) to thank the King for removing Mr. Pitt from his counsels was lost, on which Sir Robert Peel moved an address of thanks to Pitt, which was carried.

In consequence of these attempts to sully the fame and character of Pitt, "who had resigned with scarcely a competence to exist on," his friends resolved to hold a banquet in his honour, on his birthday (28 May) Nine hundred and four guests assembled at Merchant Taylors' Hall. Mr Pitt, in a letter of apology for his absence, said "that the occasion of the meeting would best point out the delicate propriety of his absence, but that no man could recollect with greater pleasure and respect such a very flattering distinction of his friends."

An appeal for subscriptions towards rebuilding Christ's Hospital was issued (28 May).

The Governors had decided in April, 1794, that it was far more for the interest of the hospital to expend whatever sums might hereafter be voted in a gradual and uniform rebuilding of the hospital than to enter into further repair of the existing buildings, and, in January, 1795, it was decided to apply to Parliament for power to enable the Governors to make purchases to complete such a plan. An Act was obtained and plans for rebuilding prepared, but owing to the dearth their income then was barely sufficient to maintain the children, and up to that time they had not felt justified in proceeding further In response to this appeal the Common Council voted £1,000 (28 Jan, 1803).

A decision was given (12 June) legalising the Cattle, Hay and Straw Market, established at Paddington by the Grand Junction Canal Company, whose canal had been opened to Paddington in July, 1801.—Acts were passed (25 June) for repealing 2 Geo. III in so far as it limits the quantity of fish to be sold by wholesale within the City of London, and for the better regulating the sale of fish by wholesale in the market of Billingsgate, also for removing doubts as to the measurement of coals in the City.—Parliament was dissolved (29 June).—A meeting of the Livery was held to receive report as to repeal of the Income Tax, and to consider the qualifications of candidates for representing the City (5 July).

The claim was again put forward that representatives should obey the instructions of the Common Hall. Alderman Curtis stated that he was glad to follow many of the instructions of his constituents, but would never consider himself bound to obey all without qualification Sir J. W Anderson said he had conscientiously discharged his duty as member, and, if elected, would continue to do the same. Alderman Combe was determined to always obey the instructions of his constituents. Combe, Price, Curtis and Anderson were returned.

On 1 Sept. Major Cookson, commanding the Royal Artillery in Egypt, presented a large antique red granite bowl to the Corporation as a testimony of his respect and a memorial of the British achievements in Egypt. [This bowl, which is apparently an inverted base of a Roman column of the period of Diocletian, is now preserved in the Guildhall crypt].—A set of desperate fellows, numbering upwards of 100, armed with large knives and bludgeons stationed themselves in Moor Fields, near Finsbury Square, and robbed every passenger that passed that way. One man lost £42 in bank-notes and cash (2 Sept.).— During the peace many Englishmen visited Paris, among others Alderman Combe. On his presentation to Napoleon, the First Consul congratulated him "on the firm and paternal conduct he had adopted during the scarcity in London, which had ensured him the esteem and gratitude of all Governments and of all Statesmen."—Alderman Charles Price was chosen Lord Mayor.— The monument in St. Paul's, voted by Parliament, and executed by Mr. Banks, to the memory of Captain Burgess, killed at Camperdown, was uncovered to the public (15 Nov.).—Alderman Curtis, of Cullands Grove, Southgate, was created a Baronet (30th).—In Bloomsbury Place, in his 60th year, died (27 Dec.) Thomas Cadell, Alderman of Walbrook, 1798 ; Sheriff, 1800.

A native of Bristol, he was apprenticed to Andrew Millar, to whose business he succeeded about 1767 He published the works of Robertson, Blackstone, Gibbon, Burns, Henry, and other famous authors of the day. When Sheriff, he attended service every Sunday at some one of the prisons, and in doing so contracted asthma, of which he died. One of his latest acts was the presentation of a stained glass window to the Stationers' Hall. He had been a member of that Company for 37 years.

Joseph Strutt, author of *Sports and Pastimes*, was buried at St. Andrew's, Holborn.—The third Grocers' Hall, in the Poultry, designed by Thomas Leverton, was opened. The garden, already diminished in 1798, was further encroached upon for the purpose of widening Princes Street.— Skinner Street, Holborn, was constructed, and was so named after Alderman Skinner.—The new building for the Stock Exchange was opened.

1803.

AT a meeting at the London Tavern, the Lord Mayor in the chair, was established the Royal Jennerian Society for the extermination of small-pox (19 Jan., 1803).

A central house for gratuitous vaccination was established in Salisbury Square, and twelve other stations in different suitable districts were proposed. The Corporation (7 Mar.) unanimously voted £500 in aid. The cases of small-pox had fallen from 360 in November to 50 in July, and this decrease was attributed to vaccination. The freedom of the City, in a gold box of 100 guineas, was voted to Dr. Jenner "for his skill and perseverance in bringing into general use the inoculation of the cow-pock" (11 Aug). The freedom was received, 4 July, 1805. By the end of the year 4,500 persons had been vaccinated at the central and outlying stations.

A sword and the freedom of the City were presented to Sir James Saumarez (3 Feb.) in honour of the victories won, under his command, over the Spanish and French fleets off Algesiras, Cape Trafalgar.—On 21 Feb. the Sheriffs of London presented a petition to the House of Commons to permit the demolition of Bethlehem Hospital in Moorfields, and the conversion of its site into a square.— Colonel Despard and thirty-two labouring men had been arrested on a charge of conspiring to kill the King and overturn the Constitution.

A commission for their trial was opened. Evidence as to the Colonel's former high character was given by Lord Nelson, Sir A. Clarke and Sir E. Nepean, of the Admiralty, but he and others were condemned to death and executed (21 Feb). The Lord Mayor and Sheriffs presented, on behalf of the Corporation, an address to the King "expressive of their abhorrence of the nefarious machinations deliberately planned to whelm them all by one fatal blow, in horror and distraction" (24th).

A new table of regulations for watermen's fares came in force on 2 May, by which every waterman was obliged to carry in his hat a badge corresponding to the number of his boat.—By the treaty of Amiens the Island of Malta was to be restored to the Knights of St. John, but in the absence of proper guarantees for its independence the British Government refused to cede the territory till such were granted.

The First Consul complained, and requested that restrictions should be laid on the British Press, which had been violently attacking France. An incident of 5 May shows the tension during these negotiations. A letter, purporting to be from Lord Hawkesbury, was delivered at the Mansion House intimating that negotiations had come to a favourable conclusion. The funds immediately rose from 63¾ to 71¼. On enquiry the letter was found to be spurious and the Stock Exchange Committee recommended that all bargains made that morning should be considered null and void. Next morning an attempt was made through the *Times* newspaper to re-affirm the story. The Stock Exchange Committee refused to open the doors of the Exchange till the truth was ascertained. The doors were opened shortly after twelve. The British Ambassador left Paris and met the French Ambassador returning at Dover. The King published a declaration in defence, and war was declared (18 May), after a peace of one year and sixteen days. An address to the King was agreed to (1 June) by the Corporation, stating their resolve " to support His Majesty in the dignified and decisive measures for the security of our glorious constitution and the establishment of substantial peace against the insatiable ambition of the French Republic."

War necessitated the re-imposition of the Income Tax. A Common Hall (29 June) instructed their Parliamentary representatives to oppose a tax on income,

Houses on the south side of London Wall, drawn 1803.

though "they were ready to contribute, in all just and equal imposts, towards the vigorous prosecution of the contest in which the country was engaged." Alderman Combe, on the Bill going into Committee (5 July), objected strongly to its principle, urging the instructions of his constituents. The Lord Mayor was of opinion some such tax was absolutely necessary. Sir J. W. Anderson would not comply with the instructions of his constituents.—The Common Council agreed (30 June) to a request from the Home Secretary to furnish 800 men for the army of reserve, and ordered the Remembrancer (2 July) to prepare a Bill giving effect to this recommendation by fixing the proportion for each Ward and the rates to be paid. The Bill was introduced by the Lord Mayor and received the Royal assent (27 July).—A special Court of Aldermen (11 July) called upon the citizens to enrol as volunteers.

Meetings were held in the different Wards, at which it was resolved to form associations of all inhabitants, from eighteen to forty-five, for drill and discipline, so as to preserve what still remained of the Volunteer associations of 1798. Those above forty-five were to be enrolled as special constables. Subscription lists were opened in aid of these associations, and in Portsoken Ward £1,000 was received from the first twenty subscribers. The merchants, bankers, and subscribers to Lloyd's met (20th) to form a fund for the assistance, comfort, and relief of those who might be wounded, or the relatives of those who might fall in defence, and resolved to set aside £20,000 3% consols for that purpose, then standing to the credit of Lloyd's, and to meet again to appoint a committee for receiving and managing subscriptions. The subscriptions amounted to £36,000 (23rd). The houses of Baring, Goldsmid, Augerstein, and others, subscribed £1,000 each. At the Royal Exchange (26th) four to five thousand leading merchants assembled in support of King and constitution, and the honour and independence of their country. A declaration was put forth, unanimously agreeing to stand or fall with their King and country. "We fight, 'they declared,' for that constitution, that system of society which is at once the noblest monument and firmest bulwark of civilization. We fight for the independence of nations, even of those who are most indifferent to our fate, or most blindly jealous of our prosperity." The Lord Mayor recommended the mobilisation of the different corps of Volunteers in four divisions: The Royal Exchange; The St. Paul's; The North-East, and The South-East. The Corporation resolved (6 Oct.) to present each regiment of Loyal London Volunteers with colours, and the Lord Mayor, as Colonel of the Farringdon Without Volunteers, addressed a letter to his regiment urging on his brother soldiers the necessity of attention to drill, order and discipline. A general fast was appointed for 19 Oct. The Lord Mayor, Sheriffs, Aldermen, and City officials attended St. Paul's with over a thousand of the Honourable Artillery Company, under Alderman Le Mesurier, two troops of the Loyal London Volunteers, under Colonel Anderson and Major Alderman Rowcroft, and the third regiment of Loyal London Volunteers. After service, the oath of allegiance was administered, under the dome, to officers individually and to the privates six at a time. The other regiments attended at various City churches. Those companies which had not as yet taken the oath of allegiance, did so either on their drill ground or in their respective churches, and three hundred Jews took the oath on the Book of Leviticus. The City and East-End Volunteers were reviewed in Hyde Park (26th) when 12,401 effective members assembled on the ground.

An Act was passed (13 July) authorizing the advancement of further sums of money from the consolidated funds for the improvement by the Corporation of the

Port of London, and to empower the Treasury Commissioners to purchase the legal quays between London Bridge and the Tower, and another (27th) for establishing a free market in London for the sale of coals, and for prosecuting fraud in the vending and delivery of coals brought into the port of London within certain places therein mentioned.—At Westminster (1 Aug.), in his 58th year, died William Woodfall, the first who reported in detail the debates in Parliament on the night they took place.

Before his time a sketch was merely given next day and a detailed report appeared subsequently. He had been known after listening to a debate in the gallery to write from memory, without notes, the same night, sixteen columns of a report. His remains were interred at St. Margaret's, Westminster.

On Michaelmas Day, Alderman John Perring was elected Lord Mayor.—On 11 Oct., at Peckham, died suddenly Sir John William Rose, Knight, Recorder.— John Sylvester, Common Serjeant, was chosen Recorder, and Newman Knollys, Common Serjeant.—On Lord Mayor's day, the Chief Baron thus addressed ex-Lord Mayor Price.

"It must be a great satisfaction to you that by your example the City of London is placed in a posture of defence fully equal to the purpose for which it was raised. Such a force was never before exhibited, a band of British freemen embodied and trained to arms, determined to transmit to posterity their rights, their franchises, nay, everything that is dear to man, or nobly perish in defence of such invaluable blessings."

On the return of the procession, the populace took the six horses from the ex-Lord Mayor's carriage in Ludgate Hill, and drew it to the Guildhall amid a thunder of acclamations.—Alderman Brook Watson, Commissary General to His Majesty's forces in Great Britain, was created a Baronet (26 Nov.).— One Redhead, a brandy merchant, convicted of defrauding the revenue, was placed (9 Dec.) at mid-day in the pillory at the Royal Exchange for an hour, and condemned to two years' imprisonment, and to be placed a second time in the pillory before his release.

During the construction of new buildings at the Bank the water of Walbrook was observed still trickling among the foundations.—A capital of £700,000 was now employed in the London coal trade, 2,196 barges were engaged; sometimes 90 colliers, each needing 13 barges, were unloading at once in the Pool.—A curious character, described by Charles Lamb, was a familiar object in the City, his portrait being published this year. He was known as the King of the Beggars. Early in life he had lost both legs through the falling of timber from a house in Bow Lane; and for many years moved about with the aid of crutches and a kind of wooden horse on wheels. His complexion was florid, and he was always hatless.

1804.

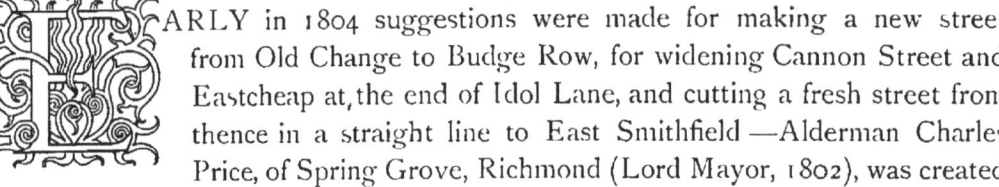

EARLY in 1804 suggestions were made for making a new street from Old Change to Budge Row, for widening Cannon Street and Eastcheap at the end of Idol Lane, and cutting a fresh street from thence in a straight line to East Smithfield —Alderman Charles Price, of Spring Grove, Richmond (Lord Mayor, 1802), was created a Baronet (13 Jan.) —The election of the first officers of the volunteer associations had been left (subject to approval) to the Companies themselves, but when the associations were once formed and officered, it was decided that future appointments should rest with the Lieutenancy (24 Jan.).—The King's health again gave way in Feb., but on the 28th, Mr. Addington announced in the House of Commons that "there is not at this time a necessary suspension of the exercise of the Royal authority." A public thanksgiving for His Majesty's recovery was held, when the volunteers attended Church in the morning, and spent the remainder of the day at drill (25 May).—The British and Foreign Bible Society was instituted (7 Mar.), for promoting the circulation of the Scriptures in the principal living languages.—It was announced (7 May) that Mr. Pitt had received the King's command to submit a plan for a new administration, and he was gazetted Chancellor and Under Treasurer of the Exchequer. He took his seat in the House of Commons the same day that the First Consul was proclaimed Emperor of the French (18th).—The Lord Mayor, on behalf of the Corporation, presented (18 May) on Blackheath, colours to the different regiments of London volunteers, and a standard to the London Loyal Volunteer Cavalry.

The Lord Mayor and Committee, attended by the Duke of York and Lords Harrington and Amherst, embarked at the Tower and proceeded by water to Greenwich. The whole of the troops followed, conveyed in upwards of 100 boats, at distances of about 150 yards. The several regiments on disembarking assembled at the foot of Greenwich Hill, whence they marched to Blackheath. After dedication of the colours the colour ensigns came forward to receive each his regimental colour at the hands of the Lord Mayor, who said : "Powers far superior to mine could pay but an inadequate tribute of applause to those gallant and patriotic bands who, roused by the voice of honour, yield their pleasures and their occupations, a willing sacrifice, at the shrine of their country. Yes, it remained for the present age to prove that the citizens of London inherit the same ardent spirit, glow with the same devotion to the sacred cause of freedom and independence as distinguished their immortal ancestors, who, in the proudest periods of British fame, were still most conspicuous in the career of glory. It was reserved for the present age to prove the falsehood of the imputation that the genius of commerce had subdued the fire of freedom in their breasts and to evince that those who by civilization and industry best learn to acquire wealth, by their intrepidity and actions best know how to preserve it. Gentlemen, in presenting to you the colours, a tribute of the gratitude of your fellow citizens and the best mark of their attachment to their brethren in arms, allow me to say, I rely, with confidence, that you will receive them as the most sacred deposit which can be entrusted to your care, and that as the

City of London is the first in the United Kingdom its citizens will be the first to afford a bright example of devotion in a cause of which they have already shown themselves to be worthy." The ensigns, kneeling, received the colours of their respective regiments.

Mr. Pitt, together with Long, Huskisson, and Sturges Browne, was entertained at dinner by the Grocers' Company (26 July), and five days later the session closed.— Sir Richard Glode, Knight and Sheriff, 1793, died at Orpington, Kent. By his industry and good qualities, he rose from the position of a journeyman bricklayer to the dignity of Sheriff, and left an ample fortune (Oct.).—The Corporation had lately recorded a vote of thanks to the admirals, officers, and men of the fleets, guarding the shores of the country.

Portrait of Alderman Boydell.

Among these Lord Nelson had been included as commander of the fleet blockading Toulon. In reply, he said: "The port of Toulon has never been blockaded by me; every opportunity has been offered for the enemy to put to sea. But I cannot let pass without notice that while the junior flag officers of our other fleets have received the thanks of the Corporation the junior flag officers of the Mediterranean squadron have been omitted, and Rear Admiral Sir Richard Bickerton, the second in command and such an excellent officer too, has been passed over twice: once in the Egyptian expedition, while the first and third were thanked, and now again." It appeared that the vote of thanks to Admiral Cornwallis and Thornborough, proposed by Samuel Dixon, had been amended, with the addition of Lord Nelson's name, by Sir William Curtis, who at the time did not happen to remember the name of the second in command.

Alderman Peter Perchard was elected Lord Mayor.—On Lord Mayor's day, as Mr. Pitt was following the procession in his carriage along Cheapside, a party of the populace took the horses from his carriage and drew it to the Guildhall.—At his seat at Berrington, Leominster, Co. Hereford, died (1 Dec.) the Right Hon. Thomas Harley.

He was Father of the City; Privy Councillor; Alderman of Portsoken, 1761; Sheriff, 1763; Lord Mayor, 1767; M.P. for the City, 1761-74; for Co. Hereford, 1776-1802; Alderman of Bridge Without, 1785. At the commercial crisis of 1797 he gave over his commercial pursuits and

Q

voluntarily resigned all his property, real and personal, for the honourable payment of all his partnership demands These were all with interest honourably discharged. His friends, knowing his means had been diminished, wished to bring him forward for the Chamberlainship on the death of Wilkes. He declined, on the ground that he was already pledged to support the present Chamberlain, and retired to his estate in Hereford Wilkes, his political opponent, said "Harley's political conduct had been at all times manly, uniform, and consistent"

At his house in Cheapside, died (12 Dec.) in his 86th year, John Boydell.

He was elected Alderman of Cheap, 1782; Sheriff, 1785; Lord Mayor, 1790. He began public life as an engraver. With the profits of a book of plates, engraved by himself, he began to employ other and better workmen. Hitherto, prints for the cabinets of the curious had been imported from France. His attention was next directed to engraving works of the best masters The success attending this led to his inviting historical paintings, of which he formed a famous gallery (opened 1789) in illustration of the works of Shakespeare, and of which he published a superbly illustrated edition, 1802. The importation of prints from abroad soon gave way to so great a foreign demand for English engravings that it was stated in the House of Lords that £100,000 yearly revenue accrued from their exportation The wars arising out of the French Revolution destroyed this trade. Boydell applied for an Act of Parliament, in the early part of this year, to enable him to dispose, by lottery, of the paintings and prints he had acquired. In a letter to Sir J. W Anderson, read in the House of Commons, he said "I hope you and every honest man will feel for my anxiety to discharge my debts, but at my advanced age of eighty-five I feel it highly desirable" The Bill received the Royal assent and at the day of his death not a single lottery ticket remained unsold He was buried at St Olave's, Jewry.

NOTE ON THE PORT OF LONDON.

The Port of London extended from North Foreland to London Bridge. The space between London Bridge and the Tower was fixed upon as the legal quays for London in 1558, by the Court of Exchequer, under authority of Parliament. In 1666, these quays numbered twenty-one, one for coasting vessels and the City of London, and twenty for the Crown. All goods paying duty or custom were to be landed at these; other wharves, called sufferance wharves or quays, had been licensed at first for coasting vessels, but these now extended along both sides of the river as far as Blackwall. As trade increased, these sufferance wharves were used for landing goods liable to duty, provided the expenses of the Revenue officer incurred in attending were defrayed. After the close of the American war, the trade at the river increased by leaps and bounds, and when France, in 1793-4, over-ran and annexed Holland, a great part of the carrying trade formerly done by the Dutch was brought by British and neutral ships to the Thames. From 1790 to 1796, the trade in the river increased by one-half. In the latter year, 13,000 vessels are said to have arrived in the Thames. The legal quays could not accommodate one fourth of the traffic of London Port, which was said at this time to amount to three-fifths of the trade of the Empire. Small vessels only could ascend to the

upper pool below the bridge.   To add to the confusion, the East and West
India fleets arrived in great numbers, at the same time under convoy, owing to the
war, and had to be unloaded in the lower pool by lighters.   These lighters served
as warehouses until an opportunity offered for unloading at some wharf, and then goods often lay at the wharves for months before being carried away.   The transfer from the vessels to the lighters, the lying on board the lighters, the transfer from the lighters to the wharves, and the unprotected state of these wharves, afforded ample opportunities for smuggling and for stealing.   Organised bands of ruffians often boarded ships and carried off in their boats whatever they could lay hands on.   From the congested state of the river arose confusion, pillage, fraud and embezzlement.   The coal

Winchester Street, 1804.

distress in 1794 was severely aggravated by the block which thus arose in the
river.   The cost of landing goods at London (7s. 3d.) was double the cost at
Liverpool (3s. 4d.) and Bristol, and merchants said that the outports afforded the
best returns, but London the best price.   The West India merchants alone
estimated their annual loss at £150,000, and the loss to the Revenue at over
£50,000.   The Commissioners of Customs put forward plans in the interest of the
Revenue for improvement.   The London merchants proposed wet docks at Wapping
(1794), in order to keep the pool at all times free for navigation.   Lord Liverpool in

the House of Lords, said the present plunder on the shipping would more than half pay the expense of one of the greatest improvements (the London Docks) that could be suggested for the commerce of the country.   This proposal the Corporation at first opposed on the ground that the river accommodation was not insufficient, but the regulations were defective ; the cost would be excessive, and in the existing state of Europe it would be injudicious to withdraw so much capital from business; the docks, if completed, would destroy the value of the private wharves, and lessen employment for watermen in general.   In 1796, the plans favoured by the Corporation and the Commissioners were nearly identical.   The different proposals were referred to a Committee of the House of Commons.   Next year (1797) the Corporation, to remedy the grievances in the river, brought forward a plan of their own—to excavate one large dock at the Isle of Dogs (102 acres) with a canal across the isthmus, and another dock of similar size at Rotherhithe, for colliers, combustibles, and coasting vessels, with a canal to Vauxhall, along which goods might be transmitted when the tide in the river was unfavourable.   They also proposed to bring forward and embank the old legal quays, so as to have five indented quays; over these, arches would be thrown on which warehouses would be built, and the access to the City by Fish Street and St. Dunstan's Hill opened out and widened.   The West India merchants and the London merchants worked together at first for the Wapping Docks, but owing to the difficulties the scheme met with in the House of Commons, the former, whose trade amounted to one-sixth of the river trade, resolved to provide docks for themselves at the Isle of Dogs, to which all West India shipping should be brought.   The cost of land at Poplar and the Isle of Dogs was less than at Wapping, and the cost of excavation estimated at only one-third. Docks there would still provide employment for lightermen, thus obviating one of the Corporation's objections, and relieve the river of the presence of the large West India merchantmen.   Eight different plans for remedying the block in the River were at this time laid before the House of Commons. In 1798, Sir Frederick Eden Morton suggested the removal of old London Bridge, the construction of a new bridge of wide and higher span farther up the river, together with a new street crossing Cannon Street, by the site of the post office in Abchurch Lane, through Exchange Alley to the front of the Royal Exchange.   The legal quays were then to be extended to the new bridge, and to be used solely for landing high duty commodities, with a range of warehouses erected over the new quays from the bridge to the Tower.   The shoals and sand-banks collected by the old bridge were to be removed in lighters and to form a new embanked terrace from Scotland Yard to Blackfriars bridge, and thus obviate the rising necessity for widening the Strand.

To arrange the differences between the Wet Docks Company at Wapping and the Corporation, a basin from the proposed docks close to the end of the Minories was suggested, which would thus bring the new docks into closer proximity to the City. A Bill for the West India Docks was passed in 1799, as well as an Act for rendering more commodious and for better regulating the Port of London.   Next year, the Bill for the construction of the London Docks passed, and in 1803 the Warehousing Act and an Act for constructing the East India Docks.   In 1804 Commercial Road, 70 feet wide, was formed by another company, from Whitechapel Church to the docks.   £50,000 had already been expended, and another £50,000 was called for.   The power to levy 2s. 6d. in the £ from the ground rents on each side of the road was granted, and at different points of the road the ground had already increased to five times its original value.

1805.

PAIN had declared war against Great Britain (14 Dec), and letters of marque and reprisal were issued (12 Jan., 1805).—The body of Alexander Wedderburn, Earl of Rosslyn, late Lord Chancellor, was buried (11th) in St. Paul's, between the graves of Sir Joshua Reynolds and John Howard.—The question of the right of freemen to carry non-freemen's goods without paying City toll came up for hearing (11th), and it was decided that the freemen were not entitled to full, but only to half, exemption.—The Directors of the West India Docks had been appointed at first without salary.   Towards the end of the previous year salaries had been voted. The interests of the City were represented on this Board by four Aldermen and four Commoners.   A resolution was thereupon passed in the Common Council that any pecuniary emolument for executing a public trust on behalf of the Corporation of London, was unbecoming, and inconsistent with the dignity of the City ; but, as no attention was paid to the resolution, the Council resolved that such as accepted salary should be ineligible for any Commission or Committee of the City, so long as they drew such salary.—The London Docks (Mr. Rennie, Engineer) were opened (30 Jan.) in the presence of a brilliant assembly.—In the House of Commons Mr. Pitt (4 Feb.) stated that the number of volunteers amounted to 325,000, of whom 240,000 had been inspected, and 40,000 were ready for inspection.—Sir J. W. Anderson presented a petition from the master printers in London, stating that their journeymen printers had come out on strike and that work was at a standstill, and praying for a Bill to allow the taking of apprentices for less than seven years   The petition was referred to "a Committee of the Members for London, Westminster, and Middlesex, Counsellors and merchants."—An address was presented (1 May) to the King from the Corporation. "Your Majesty," observed the address, "must have seen with astonishment and indignation that an eminent member of Your Majesty's Government, Lord Viscount Melville, has been guilty of practices which the representatives of the people, in Parliament assembled, have declared to be a gross violation of the law, and a high breach of duty. The virtues which adorn Your Majesty are a pledge to the nation, that in removing Lord Melville from Your Majesty's Councils for ever the punishment of a delinquent, however just, is far less a motive with Your Majesty, than the example held out that no Minister, however powerful, shall presume on Your Majesty's countenance, who shall be found to have trampled on the law, and to have disgraced the functions with which he had been invested. We entertain the fullest assurance that to Your Majesty it will be a source of the profoundest satisfaction that all necessary measures shall be adopted and persevered in towards the correction and punishment of proved malversation."

An Act was passed (1802) appointing five Commissioners to inquire into frauds and irregularities supposed to exist in the several naval departments. Lord Melville, who had been appointed Treasurer to the Navy (Aug., 1782), was charged with malversation of monies under his charge during 1786, in contravention of an Act of Parliament which took effect in July, 1785, and was examined in Nov., 1804, by the Commissioners. On their report coming up for discussion in the following year, a debate took place in the House of Commons, and Lord Melville resigned (10 Ap.). Next year he was tried, and pronounced "not guilty."

Kitchen Range,
No. 23, Great Winchester Street.

A petition from the Common Council against Roman Catholic emancipation was presented to Parliament (3 May).—£60,000 was granted (7 June) from the Consolidated Fund for the improvement of the Port of London, by finishing the canal at the Isle of Dogs.—The thanks of the Corporation were voted (27 June) to Captain Frederick Maitland, of the ship "La Loire," and to Lieutenant James Lucas Yeo, and the other officers and seamen under his command, for taking the Spanish port at Muros, and destroying the shipping, but sparing the town and everything merely commercial.—Reports were current as to an invasion from France.

In July 4,000 vessels were reported as ready to transport from 150,000 to 200,000 men to this country But the fleet which was to guard the invading army had suffered a repulse off Ferrol (24 July) from Sir Robert Calder (who was prevented, by stress of weather, from following up his advantage), and instead of sailing for the English Channel, took refuge in Cadiz, and Napoleon turned his army of invasion towards Germany.

Two aldermen of London, Sir W. Curtis and Sir John Eamer, each lost his second son in the Indian Service, one, aged twenty, in the Civil Service, and the other, aged nineteen, in the Military (Sept.).—Notices appeared in the *Gazette* that an application was to be made to Parliament for enlarging and better regulating Smithfield Market (spoken of in the handbooks of the time as "that detestable nuisance, Smithfield Market, such that on market days it is dangerous to walk in any part of the City"), and for making a new street from the north end of Fleet Market to Clerkenwell Green and thence to the Great North Road near the south end of Islington.—Alderman James Shaw was elected Lord Mayor.—A monument to General Thomas Dundas, by Bacon, junior, was unveiled in St. Paul's (12 Nov.). —The Lord Mayor, on behalf of the Corporation, presented (21 Nov.) to the King an address "expressing their warmest congratulations on the recent most glorious and decisive victory obtained over the combined naval forces of France and Spain, off Trafalgar, by your Majesty's fleet, under the illustrious and ever to be lamented Lord Viscount Nelson."—The Court of Common Council invited (26th) models for a monument in the Guildhall to Lord Nelson, and voted the freedom of the City and a sword of 200 guineas to Lord Collingwood. The freedom of the City and swords of 100 guineas were also voted to Lord Northesk and Sir Robert Strachan ; the former had been second in command to Lord Collingwood at Trafalgar, and the latter had defeated another French fleet off Ferrol on 4 Nov.—Paul Le Mesurier, Alderman of Dowgate, 1784 ; Sheriff, 1787 , Lord Mayor, 1793 ; died (9 Dec.) in his fifty-second year, in his house at Upper Homerton.

Le Mesurier and his partner Le Cras had been prize-agents during the American war He was one of the earliest members of the first volunteers who did good service during the Gordon Riots (1780), and who were afterwards incorporated with the Honourable Artillery Company, of which, at the time of his death, Le Mesurier was Colonel. He was a Director of the East India Company. On the death of Sir Barnard Turner, a few months after the general election of 1784, Le Mesurier was elected Member for Southwark, after a keen contest with Sir Richard Hotham

The monument of Captain G. Blagdon Westcott, of the "Majestic," killed at the battle of the Nile, 1798, was unveiled (9th) in St Paul's. This was the last production of Thomas Banks.—Two men famous in the annals of London publishing and printing, died on the same day (12 Dec.).

One was John Almon, a famous publisher of political pamphlets during the Wilkes agitations , then printer of the *General Advertiser*, and a representative of Farringdon Ward Without , next a prisoner in the King's Bench for libel, and afterwards outlawed. He published (1792) Anecdotes of the life of

William Pitt, Earl of Chatham, and of the principal events of his time, and (1805) The life and letters of John Wilkes. He had retired with the wreck of his fortune to Boxmoor, near Hemel Hempstead, where he died.—The other was Henry Sampson Woodfall of the *Public Advertiser*, in which first appeared the letters of Junius. He used, in after years, to say he had been fined by the House of Lords, confined by the House of Commons, fined and confined by the Court of King's Bench, and indicted at the Old Bailey. He was the third Woodfall printer. The first set up under the auspices of Pope outside Temple Bar, the second, established in Little Britain, was printer of the *Public Advertiser*, in which he was succeeded by the third Woodfall in Paternoster Row, in 1769. On succeeding his father, as printer, he was invited to succeed him as Common Councilman, an honour he declined, saying "his duty was to record, not to perform great actions." On the destruction of his printing office, by fire, in Dec., 1793, he retired from business, having sold his share of the *Public Advertiser* a month before. He was brother of Woodfall, the famous reporter.

The first meeting of the proprietors of the London Institution was held 18 Oct., and on 18 Jan. following, extensive premises in the Old Jewry, erected (1677) by Sir Robert Clayton, were rented for the purposes of the Institution.

Sir Richard Phillips, who published his "Modern London" this year, notes that the "public companies" distributed annually in charity the sum of £75,000.—From the same source we learn that the 25 wards of the City were policed by 765 watchmen and 38 patrols; that, for the protection of property in the river, two fire-engines were maintained below, and two above London Bridge; and that 260 lunatics were confined in Bethlem Hospital.—The following passage from "Modern London" will be of interest as describing the condition of the Tower menagerie in 1805.—The wild beasts "are kept in a yard on the right hand, at the west entrance. A figure of a lion is over the door, and there is a bell at the side to call the keeper. The visitor pays one shilling here, for which the keeper shows him all the wild beasts, explaining their several histories. The principal of these, at present in the Tower, consist of lions, tigers, leopards, panthers, the laughing hyena, the Spanish wolf, the ant-bear, and some mountain cats and racoons. Among them there are, or latterly were, three royal hunting tigers, which are said to have belonged to a pack of the same kind kept by Tippoo Sahib, with which he hunted beasts of prey . . . There were formerly a number of monkeys kept in the yard, but lately they have been removed from this place by his Majesty's orders, one of the largest of them having torn a boy's leg in a dangerous manner. . . . The dens are very commodious; they are about 12 feet in their whole height, being divided into an upper and lower apartment, in the former the animals live in the day, and in the latter sleep at night."—At this period, according to the same authority, the custom prevailed for a beadle, dressed in scarlet gown and gold-laced hat, to silence with a rattle the crowd of stock-jobbers and brokers whenever they conducted their business too noisily in the Rotunda of the Bank of England.—Referring to the Gresham lectures, delivered "twice a day in a room over the east end of the Royal Exchange, during the terms," he says, "they are but ill attended."—Among London street-vendors and criers, Sir Richard enumerates the following:—Women selling hot baked or boiled apples, band-box sellers, bellows-menders, vendors of brick-dust (for knife-cleaning) at 1d. per quart, retailers of "Green-hastens" (peas), of hot spiced ginger-bread, of matches at six bundles a penny, and of sand for cleaning utensils and strewing on floors.—A number of stockbrokers contested the right of the City to require from them a tax of 40s. per annum. The test-case of Mr. Francis Bailey established the City's right.—The Chapter Coffee-house, at the corner of Chapter House Court, on the south side of Paternoster Row, was celebrated as the resort of literary men. Alexander Stevens, who frequented it from 1797 to 1805, enumerates among the company; Dr. Birdmore, the Master of the Charterhouse; Walker, the Dictionary-maker; Robinson, the bookseller; Joseph Johnson (the friend of Priestley, Paine, Cowper and Fuseli); Phillips (of the *Monthly Magazine*); Dr. Busby, the musician; Waithman, the eloquent Common Councillor; &c.

1806.

THE remains of Lord Nelson lay in state in the Painted Hall at Greenwich, from 5 to 8 Jan., 1806.

On the first day over 20,000 were admitted, while three times that number were disappointed. On the two following days the numbers were, it is said, still larger. The body was brought (8th) by water from Greenwich to the Admiralty. The procession consisted of eighteen barges, the third of which carried the remains. In the fourth were the chief mourners, the fifth was the King's barge, in the sixth were the Lords of the Admiralty, in the seventh the Lord Mayor, in the eighth the Corporation Committee, with the tattered colours of the "Victory," borne by seven selected seamen of that vessel, then the barge of the Corporation Committee for Improving the Navigation of the River, followed by the barges of the Drapers, Fishmongers, Goldsmiths, Skinners, Merchant Taylors, Ironmongers, Stationers, and Apothecaries. The procession arrived at Whitehall Stairs a little before three, and at three the body was disembarked and carried to the Admiralty, where it lay in the Captain's room till the funeral (9th); on that day the streets from the Admiralty to St Paul's Churchyard were lined by the Volunteers and Militia, troops who had served in Egypt after the battle of the Nile formed the van of the processsion, led by the Duke of York. The coffin, with the pall removed so as to be seen by the surging crowd of spectators, placed on an open hearse decorated with a carved imitation of the head and stern of the "Victory," was borne on a four-wheeled carriage drawn by six led horses. The funeral was met at Temple Bar by the Lord Mayor, Aldermen, and a deputation of the Common Council. The deputation, in their violet gowns, took their place in front of the physicians of the deceased; the Aldermen, in scarlet gowns, in front of the Masters in Chancery, and the Lord Mayor on horseback, attended by the Sheriffs, rode (by a special sign-manual) between the Prince of Wales and the Herald-at-Arms. St. Paul's was filled at an early hour. The space under the dome was illuminated by a temporary lantern of octagonal shape, bearing about 200 lamps. The coffin was borne by torchlight from the western door to its place within the chancel by twelve men. At the close of the service, the coffin was carried to the grave under the centre of the dome, round which were assembled the private mourners, while the Royal Family, Foreign Ambassadors, and Naval Officers, had seats reserved on the south side of the dome, and the Lord Mayor, Aldermen, and Common Council, on the north. The inner coffin, lined with lead, was made in the hero's lifetime from the mast of the "L'Orient," the French Admiral's flagship at Aboukir.

Four money-lenders, for conspiring to hinder a bankrupt from receiving his discharge, because he would not agree to their presenting a claim for money borrowed at an extravagant rate of interest as a claim for goods received, were sentenced (17 Jan.) to two years' imprisonment, and to be pilloried in Finsbury Square within the first month of their imprisonment.—In Chatham Place, in his 77th year, died (21st) Peter Perchard, Alderman of Candlewick, 1798; Sheriff, 1793; Lord Mayor, 1804.—The Common Council (29th) voted the freedom of the City and a sword of 100 guineas to Captain Masterman Hardy, Captain of Nelson's flag-ship "Victory."—Thomas Skinner, Alderman of Queenhithe 1785, Sheriff 1784, Lord Mayor 1794, died (30 Jan.), aged sixty-nine, at his house in Aldersgate Street.

As Lord Mayor during the trials of Hardy, Tooke and Thelwall, he refused the assistance of the military in case of riots in the City, and preserved the peace by the civil power alone.   He was a keen promoter of the Temple Bar and Snow Hill improvements, and the principal street of the latter was named in his honour.   He began life as an apprentice to an upholsterer, became auctioneer, and had paid £300,000 as auction duty to the Government during the past year.

The Right Hon. William' Pitt, First Lord of the Treasury and Chancellor of the Exchequer, died at Putney (23 Jan.).   The Common Council voted (6 Feb.) a monument in the Guildhall to Pitt's memory.—An address (as to which there had been between the Common Council and the Committee appointed to draw it up, a keen discussion which led to several verbal modifications) was presented to the King (19 Feb.) on the accession of the Grenville Ministry.   The Council contemplated "with the greatest concern, the defeat of the Austrians at Austerlitz, but congratulated his Majesty on the formation of an administration combining men of the highest consideration and talents."—James Barry, the eminent painter, died, and was buried in St. Paul's, between the graves of Sir Christopher Wren and Sir Joshua Reynolds (14 Mar.).—The freedom of the City and a sword of honour were voted (27 Mar.) to Sir Thomas Duckworth for the zeal and alacrity with which he pursued a French fleet to the West Indies, and for a signal attack on that fleet (6 Feb.) off St. Domingo.   To his subordinates, Rear Admirals Lords Cochrane and Louis, were also voted the freedom and swords of honour.   The last died before being admitted, and the Common Council (6 May, 1808) ordered the sword to be presented to his son as a mark of their esteem for his father.—Sir J. W. Anderson obtained leave (22 Ap.), to bring in a Bill to enable the proprietors of the new houses in Skinner Street and Snow Hill to dispose of them by lottery.—It was proposed to remove Bethlehem Hospital from Moorfields, and £10,000 was granted for that purpose by the House of Commons (14 May).—The Royal assent was given (22 July), to a Bill for repealing London's Additional Force Act, which provided for the proportion of the army reserve to be raised by the City.—The Rev. John Brand, Rector of St. Mary-at-Hill and author of "Popular Antiquities," died in his 62nd year (11 Sept.).—Sir William Leighton was chosen Lord Mayor. —The freedom of the City and swords of honour were voted to Major-General Beresford, Commodore Sir Home Popham, Sir John Stuart, K.C.B., and Lieut.- General Sir David Baird (2 Oct.).

Sir John Stuart had gained a victory over the French invaders of Italy at Maida, in Calabria ; Sir David Baird and Sir Home Popham had taken the Dutch Colony at the Cape of Good Hope, and after accomplishing this feat, Sir Home, with Major-General Beresford, in accordance with proposals made by Mr. Pitt before they left England, sailed for Buenos Ayres and took the town.   This was somewhat prematurely hailed as a new outlet for British commerce, for the occupying force was soon obliged to surrender and an attempt next year to re-occupy the city failed.

Parliament was dissolved (25th), and on the 31st, Aldermen Price, Curtis, Combe and Shaw were elected representatives for the City.—Napoleon, having

London Workhouse, Bishopsgate Street.

annihilated the power of Prussia at Jena, published at Berlin his celebrated decrees against British commerce; his hope was to ruin Great Britain by excluding her from every harbour in Europe, proclaiming her in a state of blockade, and declaring all vessels trading to her ports liable to capture by French ships.—The new Parliament met (15 Dec.).

The London Workhouse, in Bishopsgate Street, though sufficient to lodge 500 people, was now only used as an asylum for a few old persons, "and is," remarks a contemporary writer, "a sinecure for Keeper and Officers, who live comfortably as the servants of the community without doing any good."—Theft was, at this period, rife in the Metropolis. Robberies of goods from warehouses in and about Cheapside were incidents of almost daily occurrence, and led to many complaints as to the lack of police vigilance. The City of London, exclusive of Bridge Without, maintained the following police: Marshals, 2; Marshal's-men, 6; beadles, 36; parish constables, 243; extra officers, 32; total 319.—The Courts in the City now numbered seventeen, viz: Court of Husting, Lord Mayor's Court, Court of Requests, Chamberlain's Court, Sheriff's Court, Court of Orphans, Pie Poudre Court, Court of Conservancy, Court of Lord Mayor and Aldermen, Court of Common Council, Court of Common Hall, Court of Wardmote, General and Quarter Sessions of the Peace, daily Petty Sessions, Coroner's Courts, Court of the Tower of London.—Joseph Elkin Daniels, a noted character in Change Alley, defrauded a number of business men of £50,000. He fled to the Isle of Man, was captured, and brought to London; but he had so framed his offences that he was able to escape legal penalty.

1807.

CHARTER of Incorporation was granted to the London Institution (21 Jan., 1807).—In connection with a motion made by Mr. Whitbread for an improvement in the Poor Laws it was stated that the Government, since 1801, had given no attention to the state of the poor in Bethnal Green, Spitalfields, and Mile End, but that within the past twelve months £20,000 had been distributed by Mr. Henry Thornton, in addition to sums granted by Lloyd's Committee. By the existing Poor Law the poor of these quarters, though virtually the poor of the City, were not and could not legally be relieved by the City, and were completely excluded from the benefits originally intended by the legislature simply because the parish boundaries divided them from their more opulent employers.—In one of those huge crowds which assembled to view executions at Newgate a cart had been left standing. Spectators mounted the cart, which broke down under the weight. Thirty persons were killed (23 Feb.) and fifteen injured by the pressure.—Lord Howick, afterwards Earl Grey, proposed to bring forward (4 Mar.), on behalf of Ministers, a Bill to allow Roman Catholics in future to take rank and hold commissions in the army and navy. A motion, made in the Common Council by Deputy Birch to petition against the Bill, was lost (5th).

The King disapproved of the measure as contrary to his Coronation Oath and the constitution. The Ministers offered to withdraw the measure, but insisted on their right to advise His Majesty from time to time as to such measures as circumstances might require in Ireland. The Duke of Portland was called upon to form a new Ministry, and the Grenville party ordered (24 Ap.) to resign. An address from the Corporation was presented (22nd) to the King—"We approach the Throne," said the address, "with our warmest and most unfeigned gratitude for the dignified and decided support and protection recently given by Your Majesty to the Protestant Reformed Religion, as by law established, and for the firm and constitutional exercise of your Royal prerogative to preserve the independence of the crown." The Sheriffs, Jonathan Miles and James Branscombe, were knighted.

Parliament was unexpectedly dissolved (29th). The four former representatives of the City and Alderman Hankey issued addresses to the freemen. Alderman Hankey died on 6 May. The extreme fatigue arising from his active canvas brought on fever. He had the greatest show of hands at the nomination and was third on the poll the day he died. The four former representatives were returned.—John Opie, R.A., died (20 Ap.), aged forty-five, in Berners Street, and was buried (29th) in St. Paul's near the grave of Sir Joshua Reynolds.—At Ramsgate (4 May) died Charles Dilly, the brother and successor of Edward Dilly, bookseller in the Poultry. At his house, in 1776, Johnson and Wilkes met at dinner. The brothers were publishers of the old Presbyterian authors, Doddridge Watts, Lardner, etc.—A country girl had been enticed from Moorfields into a house in Ropemaker Street from which she escaped with difficulty. A crowd from the Fields nearly demolished the house, destroyed the furniture, and pulled out the windows.—The new Parliament met 26 June, and the Royal assent was given to the London Docks Bill, 25 July.—The Duchess of Brunswick, sister of the King and mother of the Princess of Wales, whose husband, the Duke of Brunswick had died of wounds received in defending Prussia against the French, had taken refuge in England (7 July), and was living with the Princess of Wales at Montagu House, Blackheath. Thither the Lord Mayor, four Aldermen, and about eighty Common Councilmen proceeded in state to present the Duchess with an address congratulating her on her safe arrival "in this Imperial country."—Gas lighting was first introduced into London streets in August, the new illuminant being used in Beech and Whitecross Streets, and at the Golden Lane Brewery.—Sir William Staines, Knight, Alderman of Cripplegate; Common Councilman, 1783; Deputy, 1791; Alderman, 1793; Sheriff, 1797, and Lord Mayor, 1800, died at Clapham (11 Sept.). He raised himself by honest industry, from the occupation of a common bricklayer to a position of wealth and influence. He was buried in his family vault in Cripplegate Churchyard.—The freedom of the City and swords of honour were voted (15 Sept.) to Brigadier General Sir Samuel Auchmuty and the Honorable William Lumley for their attack on and capture of Monte Video; and the freedom with a sword of honour to Rear Admiral Stirling for his care in landing the troops previous to the attack.—Alderman John Ansley was elected (29th) Lord Mayor.— In place of the usual vote of thanks to the retiring Sheriffs Sir James Branscombe was thanked for his zealous attention to his duties as Sheriff, while his colleague, Sir Jonathan Miles, was charged with total neglect.—Sir Brooke Watson died at East Sheen, in Surrey (2 Oct.).

He was born at Plymouth 1735, left an orphan 1741, deprived of a leg by a shark, at Havannah, in the naval service, 1749.   He acted as Commissary-General under General Wolfe 1758, and settled in London 1759.   He was one of the first Light Horse Volunteers 1779, and served against the rioters 1780; Member for the City, 1784; Alderman of Cordwainer, and Sheriff 1786; Chairman of the Committee on the Regency Bill, 1788; and Lord Mayor, 1796.   He was buried at Mortlake.

The Rev. John Newton, Rector of St. Mary Woolnoth, for 28 years the friend of William Cowper, the poet, died (21 Dec.) in Coleman Street Buildings, and was buried in the vaults under his church.

From Phillips' "Picture of London," issued this year, we gather that the London Bridge Waterworks, by means of four wheels, raised 40,000 to 50,000 hogsheads of water every 24 hours; that a gallery of Morland's pictures was on view in Fleet Street; that the library of the London Medical Society, in Bolt Court, consisted of 10,000 volumes; and that eight daily morning papers, and six daily evening papers were published in or near the City.   In the "Almanac of Amusements," appended to the "Picture of London," Easter Monday is marked as the day for "the City Hunt at Epping Forest, where the equestrian feats of the cockneys will furnish a rich treat to a stranger;" the Thursday before Whitsunday is the date for the Charity Children's service at St. Paul's, which forms "the grandest and most interesting sight to be seen in the whole world;" on or about 2 Aug. "the State lottery begins drawing at Coopers' Hall, Basinghall Street, instead of Guildhall, as formerly;" and on or about 20 Dec. "the Annual Show of Prize Cattle, sheep, &c., in Barbican, with dinners at the Crown and Anchor."

1808. .

SIR JOHN STUART and Sir Home Popham were received at the Chamberlain's Office and presented with their freedom and their swords (8 Jan., 1808).—Viscount Trafalgar, nephew of Admiral Lord Nelson, was buried by his uncle's grave in St. Paul's (25th). —The Court of Common Council requested (22 Mar.) Mr. William Rogers, late acting Captain of the "Windsor Castle" packet, to accept the thanks of the Court, the freedom of the City, and a purse of 50 guineas for the bravery, personal courage, and great presence of mind displayed by him and his crew, on 1st Oct., 1807, in defending that vessel against a French privateer, and in capturing the enemy.—The Lord Mayor and Corporation waited on the King (30 Mar.) and presented an address in which reference was made to the "influence of France, whereby almost the whole European Continent had been compelled to unite in one vast confederacy against this country.   We view this combination without dread, firmly relying upon the continuance of the Divine protection, upon union amongst all ranks of your people, the extinction of party spirit (most essentially necessary at this very important crisis), upon the goodness of our cause, the valour and skill of your fleets and armies, and on the vigour, firmness and wisdom of Your Majesty's Councils."—Mr. Sheriff Philips was knighted.—Sir Thomas Hardy was, at the Chamberlain's Office, presented (31 May) with his freedom and a sword. In making the presentation the Chamberlain dwelt on the services of Lord Nelson, of whose flagship, the "Victory," at Trafalgar, Sir Thomas had been captain. —The King having completed his 70th year, his birthday (4 June) was made the occasion of illuminations.—The inhabitants of North-West Spain, Gallicia, Asturias and Leon rose against the French invaders and sent deputies to an assembly at Oviedo, which elected two deputies to go to England and invoke assistance.

The deputies arrived in London (9 June), and the Government resolved to assist to their utmost the insurgent patriots. Subscriptions in aid from England were acknowledged at Oviedo (30th) Peace with Spain was proclaimed (4 July), all Spanish prisoners were clothed, set free and sent home (5th).

Parliament was prorogued (5 July), and the King said in his speech, that he would " continue to make every exertion in his power for the support of the Spanish cause." The Court of Common Council voted (14th) an address expressive of their approbation of the decided and magnanimous measures adopted in aid of the patriots of Spain. A dinner was given (4 Aug) to the Spanish deputies at the " City of London Tavern " (Sir Francis Baring in the chair), at which 400 persons were present, Cabinet Ministers, Peers, Bankers, Aldermen, &c., whose united income was estimated at £15,000,000. Meanwhile Sir Arthur Wellesley had landed in Portugal with 10,000 British troops. He was attacked by, and defeated, the main French army, under Junot (21st), at Vimiera. The French asked an armistice, which was signed (22nd), and ended in the Convention of Cintra, by which the French agreed to evacuate Portugal, the British fleet to transport the French occupying army to any French port between Rochefort and L'Orient, and the Russian fleet, then in the Tagus, to be surrendered to the British Admiral Cotton, to be kept in England till six months after peace between Russia and Great Britain.

At this Convention general dissatisfaction was expressed, both in Portugal and Britain. An address and petition from the Corporation was presented to the King (12 Oct.) expressing grief and astonishment at the extraordinary and disgraceful convention by which, after a signal victory gained by the valour of British troops, the laurels so ably acquired were torn from the brows of our brave soldiers, and terms granted to the enemy disgraceful to the British name, and injurious to the best interests of the country. "We therefore humbly pray Your Majesty," continued the address, "in justice to the outraged feelings of a brave, injured and indignant people, whose blood and treasure have been thus expended, as well as to retrieve the wounded honour of the country, and to remove from its character so foul a stain in the eyes of Europe, that Your Majesty will be graciously pleased immediately to institute such an inquiry into this dishonourable and unprecedented transaction as will lead to the discovery and punishment of those by whose misconduct and incapacity the cause of the country and its allies have been so shamefully sacrificed." The King's reply was, in effect, "It is inconsistent with the principles of British justice to pronounce judgment without previous investigation, and the interposition of the City of London could not be necessary for inducing me to direct due enquiry to be made into a transaction which has disappointed the hopes and expectations of the nation." A very large majority of the Common Council ordered (27th) the King's reply to be entered on the City journals, and passed a number of resolutions condemning it in strong terms.

On the formation of the London Institution, the famous Richard Porson, Greek professor at Cambridge, had been appointed principal Librarian. While in residence at the Institution he fell down in the Strand in an epileptic fit and was carried as "unknown" to St. Martin's workhouse, where he lay insensible till six the next morning. He died on 25 Sept.—John Perring, of Membland, Co. Devon, Alderman of London, was created a Baronet (24 Sept.). —Alderman Charles Flower was elected Mayor (29 Sept.), and at the banquet on Lord Mayor's day Mr. Canning and the Spanish deputies were present.—A meeting of merchants, bankers, &c., under the presidency of the Lord Mayor, was held (9 Dec.) at the "City of London Tavern," when a letter from

Mercers' School and Church of St. Michael, College Hill, 1891.

the Chancellor of the Exchequer was read as to the state of the Spanish patriots, and the assistance Government proposed to give. £38,000 were subscribed in aid.—The parishioners of All Hallows, Barking, convened in the parish church, resumed, without litigation, the rights of an open vestry instead of the select vestry which had managed the parish business for the past 140 years.

Mercers' School was removed to its new premises in College Hill, Dowgate.—William Hazlitt married Mary Stoddart, at St. Andrew's, Holborn, Charles Lamb being best man.

1809.

THE House of Commons voted (25 Jan., 1809) a monument in St. Paul's to Sir John Moore, who had fallen at Corunna.—The Duke of York, Commander-in-Chief of the army placed his resignation in His Majesty's hands (18 Mar.). Charges had been brought forward in the House of Commons by Colonel Wardle that promotions in the army had been corruptly bestowed by the Duke, but the House declared its opinion that the charges were wholly without foundation. The Court of Common Council unanimously resolved (6 Ap.) to thank Col. Wardle for the firmness, patriotic spirit and perseverance with which he instituted the late enquiry, and to present him with the freedom of the City. Thanks were voted to the minority in the House of Commons, and a resolution passed that the reform of all abuses was necessary and essential to the safety of the country.—The City of London claimed the exclusive right of gauging in the river under its Charter of 10 Ed. IV. The London Docks being outside the City and liberties, the Company disputed this right.

The emoluments had risen from £7,000 to £70,000. The City pleaded a right exercised for 300 years from Blackwall upwards, and concluded that law and practice were in its favour The Company asserted that the City gauger was employed only for convenience by the merchants, and hence this claim to such extensive jurisdiction. The City was non-suited (17 Ap).

Sir Charles Price brought forward the second reading of the Smithfield Cattle Market Removal Bill (18 Ap.).

Alderman Combe objected that it would be detrimental to the interests of the neighbouring residents in Smithfield, and depreciate property by the Foundling Hospital, near to which it was proposed to remove it. A member stated that the number of cattle had risen from 100,000 to 150,000, and the cattle were so crowded as to injure themselves as well as the buyers and sellers. The Bill was rejected.

The Common Council (1 Aug.) after referring to their votes of thanks and gratitude to Col. G. Lloyd Wardle (6 Ap.), added the following expression of opinion :—

"His conduct seems to have drawn upon him in a high degree the malice and rancour of those who are interested in the continuance of these abuses—that individuals who devote their

Barnard's Inn Hall, occupied since 1893 as part of Mercers' School.

exertions to exposing and correcting public abuses are at all times entitled to the support and protection of the country, particularly at the present moment, when there appears an unabating effort on the part of those not under the influence of government or partakers in the existing frauds, peculations and corruption, to cry down, vilify and traduce every man who has the courage and integrity to denounce such practices, in order to mislead the public, and divert their attention from these great evils."

James Shaw, of the City of London (Lord Mayor 1805) and of Kilmarnock, Co. Ayr, was created a baronet (2 Sept.).—On the motion of Sir William Curtis, the Common Council resolved (15th) to celebrate the 50th anniversary of His Majesty's accession to the throne on 25 Oct.

An attempt made by Mr. Waithman to introduce politics failed. The Corporation went in procession to St. Paul's in the afternoon, the streets being crowded. A dinner was given by the Lord Mayor to the Corporation at the Mansion House, which was decorated with the oak, thistle and shamrock, and a crown in the centre surmounted with G.R. Merchants and bankers met at Merchant Taylors' Hall, where they were joined by several of the nobility. Many of the chief companies met in their respective halls. The Bank, Mansion House, East India House, Lloyds' Coffee House, the Royal Exchange and the Post Office were illuminated.—His Majesty gave £2,000, the London Merchants £2,000, and the City of London £1,000, to the Society for the relief of persons imprisoned for small debts, to be applied for the purposes of the Society. Sheriff Wood proposed instead to build fifty almshouses with the City donation, but was outvoted

An address was presented (1 Nov.) on behalf of the Corporation, to which the Earl of Liverpool read the King's reply: "In the midst of all our unexampled struggles, and, notwithstanding the duration of wars in which for the safety of my people I have been engaged, the commerce and manufactures of my City of London have been carried to an extent unknown at any former period." Lord Mayor Charles Flower, of Lobb, Co Oxford and of Woodford, Co Essex, was created a baronet, and Alderman Plomer was knighted

Alderman Thomas Smith was elected Lord Mayor (29 Sept) At a Common Council (5 Dec.), Mr. Waithman, supported by Aldermen Combe and Wood, moved resolutions characterising the Walcheren expedition as ill-digested, ill-conducted, calamitous and injurious to our army more by privation and disease than by the sword, and urging the necessity of an address to the King praying for enquiry, and for a meeting of Parliament without delay.

Sir William Curtis and others agreed in the propriety of enquiry, and pledged themselves, if Parliament did not on its assembly immediately order one, to support the proposal at a subsequent meeting; Sir William moved the previous question, but the original proposal was carried Sheriff Atkins, at a meeting (13th) called the attention of the Court to the address, and moved that it be read again so that its merits and defects might be fully discussed. An amended address was carried by 114 to 101. Next day (14th) the Livery met in Common Hall and adopted an address, representing that those who complain of abuses in the State were branded as disaffected to His Majesty, that the result of these abuses was seen in the Cintra convention, the retreat to Corunna, in the death of Sir John Moore, in the results attained at Talavera, and last and worst of all in the disastrous expedition to Walcheren.—The Lord Mayor, with the Sheriffs and other officers, presented the Corporation address on 20 Dec. At the levee on the same day the Lord Mayor intimated to the Secretary of State that he had the Livery address with him, and wished then to present it to His Majesty. The Secretary intimated that the King had for the past four years, on account of his failing eyesight, discontinued the receiving of addresses at any levee, but that he would accept the address, and present it to the King in the usual way   To this the Lord Mayor demurred, as the address was for the King and not for the Secretary of State.   The Sheriffs waited on the Secretary (28th), and represented that their order was to present the address to His Majesty, in person   Would he not endeavour to prevail with the King to receive it ?   His Majesty's decision was not to receive in person addresses from any except the Corporation of London and the two Universities ; all other addresses were to be presented through the Secretary of State.

On the 26 Dec., died Nathaniel Newnham, banker in Mansion House Street, Colonel of the West London Militia ; Alderman of Vintry, 1774 ; Sheriff, 1776 ; M.P. for London, 1780–90 ; and Lord Mayor, 1782.

A Livery was granted to the Spectacle-Makers' Company.—The site of Surgeons' Hall was thrown into that of the old Justice Hall, and the Sessions House and Court House constructed on it —The papers were now beginning to publish regularly the price of Consols and other securities, but the lists were signed by stockbrokers, who used the paragraphs as advertisements.

1810.

AFTER the Lord Mayor had reported to a meeting of Common Hall (9 Jan., 1810) the obstacles which had been interposed to his presentation of the address (14 Dec.) to the King, strong resolutions were passed affirming the undoubted right of the Livery to personal audience of the sovereign, and openly suggesting that " interested and corrupt hirelings " had raised a barrier between king and people ; and the Sheriffs were directed to deliver a copy of the resolutions into His Majesty's hand.   At a subsequent meeting, however (24 Jan.), the Sheriffs stated that the Home Secretary had refused both in interview and by letter their request for an opportunity of personal audience, and the Common Hall recorded their solemn protest against "this new and alarming innovation."—The Persian Ambassador was entertained by the East India Company at a banquet at the City of London Tavern (11th).—Lyon Leir, a diamond merchant, whose business affairs had been much embarrassed, flung himself from the top of the Monument and was dashed to pieces (12 Jan.)— Colonel G. L. Wardle took up (31 Jan.) the honorary freedom voted to him by the Common Council on 6 Ap., 1809, for his bold criticism of the late Commander-in-Chief.—Against a measure, now before the House of Commons, for granting Lord Wellington a pension of £2,000 per annum for a term of three lives, the Court of Common Council protested " with grief and concern " (23 Feb.).— Sir Francis Burdett, M.P., lately ordered by the House of Commons to be committed to the Tower on account of an article contributed to Cobbett's *Weekly Register*, was conducted thither on 9 Ap. by a strong civil and military escort.

The soldiers, on their return, were stoned by the mob, and they pursued the rioters up Fenchurch Street, where a stray shot caused the death of a corn-meter. Two days later a builder near Tower Hill applied to the City Finance Committee for £20 compensation for the loss of bricks taken by the mob.—On 4 May the Common Hall resolved upon a remonstrance against the arrest and imprisonment of Sir Francis Burdett and Gale Jones without trial or hearing, reproaching the House with being largely composed of the nominees of peers, and with responsibility for the disastrous Walcheren expedition. A few days afterwards the Sheriffs, followed by a great concourse, proceeded to the Tower and, at the wicket-door, presented to Sir Francis a copy of the Common Hall proceedings. When Parliament was prorogued (21 June), Burdett and Gale Jones were liberated. An immense crowd awaited Burdett's release, but, in order to avoid being the occasion of any regrettable accidents during the public excitement, he had left the Tower by water. The disappointed people, headed by the Sheriffs, formed a procession to Burdett's house in Piccadilly.

Houses, Little Moor-Fields, 1810.

The four hundredth anniversary of the foundation of St. Paul's School was celebrated on 1 May.—On 23 July the Earl of Northesk and Sir Richard Strachan attended at the Mansion House to receive swords voted to them by the City in recognition of their naval services.—The governors of Bethlem Hospital obtained from the City the lease of eleven acres of land in Southwark for the site of a lunatic asylum, in lieu of that at Moorfields. —Six prisoners were led from Newgate, in the custody of the Sheriffs, to a pillory in the Haymarket, and there exposed to a hail of missiles and the execration of the public.—It was decided to increase the financial qualification of Aldermen from £10,000 to £30,000, and to extend the time for election to eight days.—A fire, which threatened St. Bartholomew's Hospital, was extinguished by the aid of the Blue-coat boys (30 Oct.).—A leaden coffin, containing the remains of the notorious Judge Jeffries, was discovered in a vault under the communion-table of St. Mary, Aldermanbury (3 Nov.).—Owing to the indisposition of the King, Lord Mayor's day was not celebrated with the usual state ; Alderman Joshua J. Smith had been elected.—The whole of the silver-gilt communion plate was stolen from St. Paul's on the night of Christmas Eve.

Sir John Collingwood, who commanded a division at Trafalgar, was buried in the crypt of St. Paul's.—The coinage, which had been carried on for hundreds of years in the Tower, was now removed to the Mint on Tower Hill.—Abraham Goldsmid, the eminent financier, and contractor this year for the Ministerial loan of £14,000,000, committed suicide in consequence of embarrassed affairs. His death caused immense excitement in the City, the funds falling three per cent.

1811.

THE Thames was nearly frozen over, only a narrow channel in the centre being clear of ice. Two men walked on the ice from Battersea Bridge to Hungerford Stairs (7 Jan., 1811).—The Common Council voted an address to the Prince Regent, deploring the King's affliction, and taking occasion to allude to the excessive taxation and to the need of reform of the House of Commons (7 Feb.).—The freedom of the City was voted to Lieut–Gen. Sir Thomas Graham and Brigadier W. T. Dilkes for the skill and valour they displayed in the action on the heights of Barrosa ; with the freedom was coupled the gift of swords (4 Ap.).—The Lord Mayor's allowance was increased by £1,500, it having been ascertained that the annual expenses of the Chief Magistrates were £12,000, and their receipts about £6,500.—The Nelson statue was unveiled in Guildhall (27 Ap.). The inscription was written by Sheridan.—The Court of Common Council having resolved (2 May) to present the freedom of the City to the Prince Regent in recognition of "the purity of his constitutional principles," and of his " rare self-denial in refusing to increase the national expenditure by any temporary addition to his state and dignity as Prince Regent," the Lord Mayor waited on His Royal Highness on the 22nd, but was informed, after an expression of the Prince's thanks, that his position debarred him from accepting the proposed honour.—The Court also decided (9 May) to present the freedom, accompanied with a sword, to Viscount Wellington for his late brilliant services in Portugal.—The Census returns published in Sept. showed a population for the City of 57,062 males, and 59,693 females; total, 116,755.—The new street leading northwards from Picket Street was entitled Picket Place (Oct.).

It was now in contemplation to continue this thoroughfare across Holborn to the Foundling Hospital, in order to open up traffic towards Highgate and Hampstead.

The new Lord Mayor was Claudius Stephen Hunter.—Much curiosity was excited by the appearance at Blackfriars of a newly-invented vessel, the "Constellation," from Bristol (22 Nov.).

It was intended to sail against wind and tide, was fifty feet long, had one iron mast, and twelve horizontal sails which could be extended or shortened in an instant.

A sight-seer's arm was dreadfully injured by one of the tigers in the Tower menagerie (23 Nov.).—The Common Council resolved to address the Prince Regent in favour of a restriction of the further distillation of grain, lest corn should rise to famine prices (4 Dec.).

Rogers's Bank was transferred from Freeman's Court, Cornhill, to Clement's Lane, Lombard Street.—The association of underwriters and merchants, known as Lloyd's, had been formally established in 1770. Its organisation was now (1811) thoroughly revised, and the regulations embodied in a Deed of Association.—Robert Mylne, builder of Blackfriars Bridge, was buried in the crypt of St. Paul's.—The nominal value of the forged Bank of England notes for the eleven years, ending 31 Dec., 1811, amounted to £101,661.—An enumeration made in July showed that in one day there passed over Blackfriars Bridge, 61,069 foot passengers, and 2,525 vehicles; over London Bridge, 89,640 foot passengers, and 5,418 vehicles.—Sir C S Hunter, the Lord Mayor, was frequently seen in the streets riding on a white horse. This may have suggested the following epigram :—

> An Emperor of Rome, who was famous for whim,
> A consul his horse did declare,
> The City of London, to imitate him,
> Of a *Hunter* have made a *Lord Mayor*.

1812.

PAYMENT was stopped by the banking-house of Lushington, Boldero and Co.; the effect was felt by many provincial banks (2 Jan., 1812).—Much public sympathy was aroused by the disappearance of the three-year-old son of a Mr. Dellow, of St. Martin's Lane, Cannon Street.

A reward of 100 guineas was offered for recovery of the stolen child, and descriptive bills were circulated. The little boy was at length discovered at Gosport, whither he had been taken by a sailor's wife, who wished to satisfy the often-expressed desire of her husband for a child.

One of the darkest days remembered in the metropolis for many years occurred on 10 Jan.—Frequent recent murders and robberies had created a feeling of uneasiness in London, and a discussion on the subject took place in the House of Commons (18 Jan.).

A Committee was appointed to examine into the state of the nightly watch in the Metropolis and the parishes adjacent. They reported that the police arrangements of London differed in its various quarters, some parishes being largely policed by voluntary zeal. Of the City the Committee spoke in terms of praise, observing that "the system of watch and ward is not a dead letter, but is kept alive and in action by the constant superintendence of the Marshals of the City, with their assistants, who every night visit the different wards and precincts, and take care that the constables, beadles and watchmen, of all descriptions, are alert and do their duty. Morning reports are made to the Lord Mayor; deficiencies are noticed, as well as any disorders or irregularities." The Committee recommended that, when goods had been stolen from the City and removed beyond its boundaries, the warrants of the civic magistrates should operate within a circle of five miles from the Royal Exchange.

The eccentric "Baron Geramb" was ordered to quit the country (April).

He had offered to raise a body of Croat troops for the Government. By dressing in a singular manner, attending public assemblies, and filling the print-sellers' windows with his portraits, he had become the laughing-stock of the Metropolis.

The Court of Common Council voted an address to the Prince Regent (17 Ap.), drawing his attention to the corruption of the public administration, the violation of the freedom of the press, and the unjust restrictions placed on commerce.—On Monday, 11 May, the Right Hon. Spencer Perceval, prime minister, was shot

The old "Charlies," from "Life in London," by Pierce Egan, 1821.

by Bellingham in the lobby of the House of Commons. Addresses were resolved upon to the Prince Regent by the Court of Aldermen (12th) and the Common Council (16th), declaring their horror and detestation of the deed. Bellingham was executed before Newgate on the 18th, persisting to the last in refusing to express contrition.—Daniel Eaton, a bookseller, stood in the pillory at the Old Bailey for publishing the third part of Paine's "Age of Reason" (25th).—The old chapel attached to the east side of Leadenhall, founded by Sir Simon Eyre, and dedicated to the Holy Trinity, was removed in June.—The old-established banking-house of Kensington and Co., Lombard Street, stopped payment on 22 July.—At an influential meeting held at the Mansion House, and addressed by the Chancellor of the Exchequer, an Auxiliary Bible Society was formed for the City (6 Aug.).—London was illuminated for several days (17 Aug., etc.) in celebration of Wellington's victory at Salamanca. Much disorder occurred in the City. An address from the Common Council (passed 3 Sept.) congratulated the Regent on the success of the British arms.—Disgraceful rioting occurred at Bartholomew Fair (5 Sept.). Women were grossly insulted; an infant was suffocated in its mother's arms by the pressure of the crowd, and many persons had their legs or arms broken. The disturbance originated in rough horse-play.—Great activity was displayed at the Tower in preparing arms for foreign service. Ten thousand stand were sent to Port Mahon, 10,000 to Corunna, and 50,000 to the Baltic in Sept.—At the General Election, the City returned Alderman Combe, Sir William Curtis, Sir James Shaw, and Alderman John Atkins (5 Oct.).—Alderman George Scholey was elected Lord Mayor.—The Bank issued new 3s. and 1s. 6d. pieces (Nov.).—A Russian lad, ten years of age, created much astonishment among the members of the Stock Exchange by his facility in calculation (Dec.).

Chapel of Leadenhall.

A question which had taken an hour to prepare was answered by the lad in one minute. He was given a guinea of the reign of William III. and asked the number of years, months, and days since its coinage, and replied correctly and promptly; £50 were collected for him.

Mr. Walter, the founder of the *Times*, died this year.—The number of newspapers printed in London was stated in a Parliamentary return at fifty-four.—The Smithfield Club Cattle Show was held at Sadler's Yard in Goswell Street, the value of the prizes being 210 guineas.

T

1813.

WILLIAM PITT'S monument in the Guildhall was unveiled in the presence of Mr. Canning and Lord G. L. Gower (27 Mar., 1813). J. C. Bubb, who executed the sculptures on the front of the Custom House, was the artist. The inscription was composed by Canning.—A large building in Skinner Street was gutted by fire (4 Ap.). It formed the capital prize in the City lottery, and was valued at £25,000. The firemen fortunately succeeded in staying the progress of the fire.— On Wednesday, 7 Ap., the funding of £12,000,000 of Exchequer Bills occasioned an exciting scene at the office for subscription, a crowd of merchants and others struggling for admission. The amount was subscribed by the first 184 entries. Some of the applicants sustained fractured limbs in the struggle.—Nine waggons, laden with gold dust, bars and silver bullion, arrived at the Bank from the East India Company's possessions in India (21 Ap.).—The wrongs of the Princess Caroline of Wales roused warm sympathy in the City. On 2 Ap., the Common Hall enthusiastically voted an address to Her Royal Highness, expressing indignation at the "foul and detestable conspiracy, which, by perjured and suborned traducers, had been carried on against your Royal Highness's honour and life."

The address was taken by Lord Mayor Scholey, in public procession, to the Princess, on 12 Ap., at Kensington Palace. Immense multitudes lined the streets, and thronged Hyde Park and Kensington Gardens. "I shall not," said the Princess in her reply to the Livery's address, "lose any opportunity I may be permitted to enjoy of encouraging the talents and virtues of my dear daughter, the Princess Charlotte, and I shall impress upon her mind my full sense of the obligation conferred upon me by this spontaneous act of your justice and generosity." The Lord Mayor and Sheriffs kissed hands, after which Her Royal Highness curtsied from the balcony to the crowds outside. A further address of sympathy was passed by the Common Council on 22 May.

Alderman Wood, in the presence of the Dukes of Kent and Sussex, laid the first stone of the Debtors' Prison, in Whitecross Street, opposite Cripplegate Church. —Field Marshal Wellington's great victory at Vittoria formed the subject of an address from the Common Council to the Prince Regent (9 July).—Meetings were held by the Court of Proprietors at the India House, and satisfaction expressed with the provisions of the Bill affecting the East India Company, then pending in Parliament (July).—Several hundred summonses were issued against bakers for pricing flour in official returns as high as 90s. per sack, whereas the average value of wheat was 89s., and City bakers were accustomed to return flour at 15s. less than the average price of wheat. The Lord Mayor intimated his resolve to keep watch upon the matter until the price of flour was reduced to its equitable level.

Several fines were imposed (Sept.).—On St. Matthew's-day (21 Sept.) the Lord Mayor and Sheriffs attended Christ Church, Newgate Street, to hear a sermon preached by Rev. Christopher Wilson, a late scholar of Christ's Hospital.— Dr. Howley's election to the bishopric of London was confirmed, with the accustomed ceremonies, in Bow Church, Cheapside, a very ancient church in the diocese (Oct.).—Alderman William Domville was chosen Lord Mayor.—An address of the Common Council (18 Nov.) to the Prince Regent, declared the exultation of the citizens at the success of the Allies in planting their standard "within the boundaries of ancient France."—Another address (7 Dec.) expressed satisfaction at the recent revolution in Holland, that country having thrown off the rule of the Bonapartes. A distinguished company, presided over by the Duke of Clarence, dined at the City of London Tavern on 14 Dec., to celebrate this event, the chief toast being "The emancipation of Holland."

It was directed by Act of Parliament that all London-made gun-barrels should be marked by the Gunmakers' Company after being tested at their Proof House in the Commercial Road, E— London "within the walls" contained, in 1813, ninety-seven parishes, sixty-seven parish churches, and a population of 55,484.

1814.

DENSE fog over-hung London for several days at the opening of the year. Such darkness had not been experienced since the year of the earthquake of Lisbon, 1755. A remarkable period of frost began on 27 Dec., 1813, and lasted into Feb., 1814.

Floes of ice blocked the river, and were finally united into a solid sheet, across which people walked, on 30 Jan. The unemployed watermen exacted an ice toll of passengers over the Thames, some receiving £6 a day A Frost Fair was celebrated. A street of tents, named the City Road, was erected, and adorned with shop-signs and flags. Music and dancing entertained the crowds of visitors. A sheep was roasted whole, and the "Lapland mutton" sold at a shilling a slice. Among other recreations and attractions were swings, book-stalls, suttling booths, games at skittles, frying sausages, &c Printing presses were set up on the ice, and appropriate broad sheets issued, on one of which appeared the following verse addressed to the frost —

> Amidst the arts which on the Thames appear,
> To tell the wonders of this icy year,
> PRINTING claims prior place, which at one view,
> Erects a monument of THAT and YOU.

On 5 Feb. the ice cracked, and the last piece printed was jestingly dedicated to "Madame Tabitha Thaw"

The Custom House, with adjacent buildings, was destroyed by fire on the early morning of Saturday, 12 Feb.

Several persons were severely burned, two lost their lives   An explosion of gunpowder accelerated the progress of the flames, the concussion being heard as far as Dalston   Many valuable papers, bonds, debentures, &c., were destroyed.   The approaches were guarded during the fire by the East India and Custom House corps of volunteers.

A rumour of the death of Bonaparte was set afloat on the Stock Exchange in order to force up the price of certain stock.   One broker disposed of £650,000 of shares.   After some hours the news was found to lack confirmation.

On the morning of 21 Feb, a person wearing a white cockade rode past the Royal Exchange in a four-horse chaise, the vehicle being decorated with sprigs of laurel   A similar chaise was seen in the West End.   These demonstrations were believed to confirm flying rumours of Bonaparte's defeat and death, and crowds collected near Hyde Park and the Tower awaiting the discharge of the guns   The affair was a hoax arranged to force up the price of certain stock   Lord Cochrane and others were accused of being involved in the conspiracy and condemned to fines and exposure in the pillory.

The abdication of Napoleon shortly afterwards was the occasion for much rejoicing

The City was illuminated for three evenings (11 to 13 Ap.).   The Duke of Sussex spoke on the recent events in France at a Mansion House banquet (11th), which was attended by a very distinguished company.   The Common Council voted an address to the Prince Regent (19 Ap.) upon the brilliant success of the allies, and "the downfall of an individual who had concentrated in his own person power hitherto unparalleled in the annals of history."   The Lord Mayor waited on the restored French King (Louis XVIII) at Grillon's Hotel, Albemarle Street, with an address of congratulation (22nd)

Captain P. B. V. Broke, commander of the "Shannon" in the memorable duel with the American frigate "Chesapeake," attended at the Guildhall on 19 May, to receive the freedom and a sword (voted 12 July, 1813). — The termination of the war was in various ways celebrated by the City.

The Common Council resolved (7 June) on an address to the Regent, declaring their gratification at the success of the British arms under the "immortal Wellington."   The Emperor of Russia and the King of Prussia arrived in London   Illuminations took place three nights running (8th to 10th)   The Czar and the Prussian King were entertained on the 17th by the merchants and bankers of London, at Merchant Taylors' Hall, and, on the 18th, at the Guildhall   At the latter festivity were present the Prince Regent, Marquis Wellesley, Lord Liverpool, Marshal Blucher, Prince Metternich, the Grand Duchess of Oldenburg, &c.   Guildhall was decorated on a scale of unsurpassed splendour.   The Lord Mayor received the honour of a baronetcy —On 8 June the Court of Common Council approved of an address of congratulation to the Emperor and the King of Prussia, and further resolved to present swords of honour to Prince Schwartzenberg, Commander-in-chief of the allied armies, Field-Marshal Blucher, Count Barclay de Tolly (of the Russian army), and to the Hetman Count Platoff.— On 11 June the freedom and a sword were presented to Lieut.-General Sir Rowland Hill for his gallantry at the battle of Vittoria —Peace was proclaimed on 20 June, according to the traditional manner, at the corner of Chancery Lane, Wood Street, and at the Royal Exchange —On 4 July the Court of Common Council protested against the clause in the treaty of peace, which permitted France to continue the slave trade —A thanksgiving service was held in St Paul's on 7 July.   Infantry lined the streets along the Prince Regent's route, from St. James's to Temple Bar, thence to St Paul's the way was kept by the East India Volunteers and the

Honourable Artillery Company. Blucher was loudly cheered on his way to the Cathedral. The Duke of Wellington accompanied the Prince Regent Dr. Law, Bishop of Chester, preached the sermon—On 9 July the Duke of Wellington was entertained at the Guildhall and received the freedom and the gift of a sword. Towards the close of the proceedings all the ladies descended from the galleries and shook hands with the Duke.

The choristers of St. Paul's petitioned the Master of the Rolls with respect to the administration of certain charitable trusts. Judgment was given (5 Aug.) for the Dean and Chapter, coupled with an order for inquiry into the nature and application of the trusts.—Alderman Samuel Birch was elected Mayor.—The *Times* was first printed by steam on 29 Nov., being the first newspaper so produced.—The Navigation Committee of the Court of Common Council reported on the projected improvements of London Bridge.

The first steamboat was seen on the Thames this year —A sceptre was found behind the wainscoting of the old Jewel Office in the Tower—At London House, in Aldersgate Street, a cradle was made, costing £500, for Joanna Southcott's expected "Prince of Peace;" an inscription on it intimated that it was "the free-offering of faith to the promised seed." The baby-linen, &c, cost £550 more Great crowds flocked to see the cradle.—An official return showed that, in 1814, 129,500 London papers were sent to the colonies, and 215,762 to the Continent.—Old Bethlehem Hospital in Moorfields was demolished, the new buildings in Southwark being completed

1815.

PEACE having been concluded with the United States, the Common Council expressed their gratification in an address to the Regent (12 Jan., 1815).—The Corporation strongly opposed the Bill before Parliament, laying restrictions on the importation of corn (12 Mar.)

They pointed out that the late war had produced a rise in the price of land, that the people had expected a diminution of their burdens on the conclusion of peace, and that the proposed measure would benefit landowners at the expense of the labouring and manufacturing classes —Rioting took place in the West End (7-9 Mar.), the houses of supporters of the Bill being attacked.

A silver vase was presented by the scholars of St. Paul's School to the Rev Dr. Roberts, for forty-five years head-master (30 Mar.).—A woman visited the Jewel Room at the Tower, and while being shown the Crown by an attendant, attempted to take it by force. After a struggle she was secured. It was ascertained that she was mentally deranged (31 Mar.).—The first stone of Southwark Bridge was laid by Admiral Keith, attended by Sir John Jackson, chairman of the Committee of Management An inscription was affixed to the stone, and various coins deposited beneath it.—A statue of King George III, voted 31 Oct., 1810, was placed in the Guildhall (3 June); Chantrey was the sculptor.—An expensive litigation between the City authorities and the parish of

St. Mary Woolchurch, resulted in the decision that the Mansion House should be assessed at £1,500 for the poor-rate (10 June).—An address to the Regent on "the recent brilliant victory obtained by the Allied Forces, on the 18th of June instant, over the French army, commanded by Napoleon Bonaparte," was resolved on by the Common Council (27 June), and, at a later meeting, £2,000 was subscribed for the relief of the families of the soldiers killed at Waterloo.—An Act was passed (5 July), abolishing the ancient practice known as the Assize of Bread, and leaving the price of the loaf to be regulated by free competition. The repeal had been opposed by the Bakers' Company.—Acts of Parliament, for enlarging the west end of Cheapside, for providing convenient Courts of Justice for the City, and for building a new prison in the City, were ordered by the Common Council to be carried into effect.—Charles Rossi's monument to Lord Rodney was unveiled in St. Paul's Cathedral (14 Aug.)—Subscriptions were raised by London merchants in aid of the sufferers by the fire at Port Royal.—Alderman Matthew Wood was chosen Lord Mayor.—A fire at the Mint destroyed nearly all the machinery (31 Oct.).—The first stone of the London Institution was laid by Lord Mayor Birch on 4 Nov.—An address from the Common Council to the Prince Regent (14 Dec.) deplored the persecution of Protestants in the south of France, the pillage and destruction of their places of worship, and the sacrifice of innocent lives to the rage of "infuriated bigotry and superstition."

Cloth Fair, West Smithfield, was at this date still occupied chiefly by tailors, clothiers, and piece-brokers, i e, dealers in materials for the use of tailors and remnants for repairs.—William Vincent, the famous master of Westminster School, and rector of Allhallows the Great, died in 1815 —An Act was passed, providing that all apothecaries and their assistants should be examined and certified by the Court of Assistants of the Apothecaries' Company before acting as apothecaries or dispensing medicines —Newgate Prison was now used for felons only, the debtors having been transferred to the new prison in Whitecross Street. The latter building stood on the west side of the street from which it took its name. It was built from the designs of William Montague, Clerk of the City Works, and accommodated 365 prisoners. These were classified as Sheriffs' prisoners, Queen's Bench prisoners, and prisoners committed from the Bankruptcy Courts and County Courts. Such as could maintain themselves were allowed to do so This prison was closed in 1870.

1816.

PEACE with France and the prospect of "a speedy and entire abolition of the African slave trade," inspired the address which the Common Council voted to the Prince Regent on 18 Jan., 1816. —Various poulterers in the City were now selling birds brought in a frozen condition from Sweden by a party of Laplanders. The Laplanders, with their curious reindeer-skin coats, caps and gloves, attracted great crowds whenever they appeared in the streets (Feb.).—Two strongly-worded petitions were presented to the House of Commons from the City, the resolution of the Government to continue the Income-tax having created great discontent (13 Feb.).—A fire took place at the coffee house over the old Stock Exchange, at the corner of St. Swithin's Alley (23 Ap.).—Much satisfaction was expressed in an address to the Regent from the Common Council (3 May) at the recent marriage of the Princess Charlotte with Duke Leopold of Coburg.—The freedom of the

Court of Pie-Powder, Bartholomew Fair.

City was presented (11 July) to the Dukes of Kent, Sussex, and Gloucester, and the Duke of Saxe Coburg. —At a meeting held at the City of London Tavern (29 July) and presided over by the Duke of York, a resolution was proposed by the Duke of York to the effect that the sudden transition from war to peace had resulted in a stagnation of employment and a deplorable

amount of distress among many classes of the community. A dissentient speech by Lord Cochrane was followed by remonstrance from Mr. Wilberforce; and, though the resolution was carried, the meeting was much disturbed.—On the marriage of the Princess Mary, sister of the Prince of Wales, with William, Duke of Gloucester, the Common Council congratulated the Regent and the Queen (30 July).—A meeting of Common Hall passed resolutions of protest at the "unsupportable and frightful" burden of taxes and poor rates, and the excessive size of the standing army; and agreed to an address to the Prince Regent, calling attention to the general depression of trade, and demanding reform of the House of Commons.—A serious riot occurred in Newgate (25, 26 Aug.).

A watch had been stolen from a visitor to the gaol, and the keeper, Mr. Newman, ordered the prisoners to be searched. This they resisted, and, taking possession of the exercise yard, expelled the officers and turnkeys from the four wards. Shots were fired over their heads, and every possible place of escape guarded by constables. The state of siege continued through the night. Next morning the Lord Mayor arrived, and the convicts, to the number of 140, surrendered.

By dint of great exertions the Lord Mayor and City officers succeeded in reducing the customary disorders at Bartholomew Fair (5 Sept.), all the shows and the public houses in the vicinity being closed by midnight.—A singular commotion was caused throughout the City and Westminster, on 21 Sept., by the refusal of tradesmen to accept worn silver.

The proportion of worn to clearly marked coins was said to be thirty to one. Tradesmen had formed an unfounded impression that plain coins would not be received at the Bank. Riots among the common people were feared. The magistrates were beset with excited applications for advice. The Lord Mayor issued notices that the Bank would not refuse worn silver of English minting, and the Bank was thronged with crowds eager to exchange old silver for notes and tokens. Two other notices were published by the Mayor on the same day, and the consternation was at length allayed.

Portrait of Alderman Wood.

Lord Exmouth's naval success at Algiers, and the blow thus dealt at "the horrid system of Christian slavery," occasioned an address from the Common Council to the Regent (26 Sept.). — The "Maria Wood" barge was completed for the Corporation at a cost of £5,000 (Sept.). —Alderman Wood was re-elected Lord Mayor, in recognition of his able conduct during a critical period.—The Surrey side of Blackfriars Bridge was paved with cast-iron blocks overlaid with gravel (Nov.).—Great inconvenience was caused by the influx of destitute foreign and native seamen, who thronged the bridges and streets in a starving condition, many lingering about the Mansion House all night.   The Lord Mayor on one occasion had 200 of these poor seamen brought before him in one day.—Complaints as to wide-spread distress among the masses, and corruption in the Parliamentary system were repeated in an address from the Common Hall (28 Nov.).—Alarming riots occurred in December.

> The disturbances originated at an assemblage in Spa Fields, which was addressed by "Orator" Hunt (2 Dec.).   A procession marched to Snow Hill, where Mr. Platt, a gunsmith, was shot, and his shop looted.   The rioters proceeded to the Royal Exchange, discharging firearms on the way. Many entered the Exchange, where the Lord Mayor awaited the mob   The gates were closed, and several rioters arrested.   Shots were fired from without.   Presently, however, the crowd passed on to the Minories, and at nightfall had all dispersed.   The Bank was guarded by 200 soldiers.

1817.

ON the return of the Prince Regent from the opening of Parliament (28 Jan., 1817) the Life Guards were insulted and gravel was flung at the Royal carriage.   The outrage was condemned in addresses from the Court of Aldermen (30 Jan.) and the Common Council (5 Feb.).—Lord Exmouth and Rear-Admiral Sir David Milne were presented with the freedom and with swords on 31 Jan., in accordance with a resolution of the previous 26 Sept.—The new silver coinage was put into circulation on 19 Feb.—A number of incidents testified to a feeling of unrest and political disaffection.

> Cashman, a sailor, was hanged opposite No. 58, Skinner Street, for being concerned in the plunder of a gunsmith's shop there situated.   A huge concourse assembled to witness the execution.   The Sheriffs were hooted, and Cashman, who displayed great levity in his remarks to the mob, was loudly cheered at his last moments (12 Mar.).—On 14 Feb. Watson senior, Preston, Hooper and Keen, all concerned in the recent disturbances, were committed to the Tower   Warrants were issued for the arrest of Arthur Thistlewood, and Watson the younger, the suspected assailant of Platt, the gunsmith.   On 9 June, Watson the elder, Thistlewood, Preston and Hooper were brought up for State trial, but acquitted.

In the Court of Chancery an injunction to restrain the publication of Robert Southey's "Wat Tyler," on the ground of seditious teaching, was refused.—Two gentlemen applied before the magistrates at the Old Bailey for a licence for an "Academical Society," which proposed to investigate and discuss philosophical, literary, historical, and political subjects.   The society admitted only members of Universities or Inns of Court.   The Lord Mayor and Alderman Perring were ready to sign the licence; the application fell through owing to the opposition of the two other aldermen on the bench, who objected to the improper tendencies of political debate.—Alderman Combe having resigned his position as member for the

City, Sir Matthew Wood was elected (10 June).—An entry in the registers of St. Andrew's, Holborn, runs thus :—" Baptised, July 31, 1817, Benjamin, said to be about twelve years old, son of Isaac and Maria D'Israeli, Viny's Road, Gentleman." A clergyman named Thimbleby performed the ceremony. —The new Custom House, begun in 1814, was finished during the summer. It was designed by David Laing.—Bartholomew Fair (3 to 5 Sept.) passed off quietly each day until nightfall, when the usual riotous scenes were enacted. The Lord Mayor discontinued the old custom of calling on the Keeper of Newgate on the opening day of the fair, to partake of a tankard of wine, nutmeg and sugar.— Alderman Christopher Smith was chosen Lord Mayor.—In consequence of the death of the Princess Charlotte (6 Nov.) the ceremonial of the Lord Mayor's show was omitted.—St. Dunstan's-in-the-East having become dilapidated, the old church

Poultry Compter (interior), 1811.

was pulled down, and the first stone of a new structure was laid on 26 Nov.— Hone, the bookseller, was unsuccessfully prosecuted for publishing blasphemous pamphlets. The Corporation protested against the spirit shown by the Government in such proceedings, and denounced the intrigues of spies and informers, and the imprisonment of men who were brought to trial without knowledge of the charges brought against them (Dec.).

Charles Lamb resided at No. 4, Inner Temple Lane, from 1809 to Oct 1817 He had two rooms on the third floor and five above, for £30 a year. "Hare Court's trees come in at the window" he told Coleridge, "so that it's like living in a garden"—The "Half Moon" in Cheapside had now ceased to be a tavern—The old office of Warden of the Mint was abolished.—The Poultry Compter was taken down, and the prisoners removed to the newly-erected prison in Whitecross Street.—The City of London Gas Light and Coke Company was incorporated for a term of 46 years, but the limit was removed in 1859—One of the six wooden wheels of the London Bridge Waterworks was removed, an iron wheel being substituted at a cost of £6,500   Subsequently another iron wheel was introduced, costing £5,000

1818.

FOR the purpose of raising a fund to assist in the building of churches in London and the kingdom generally, an influential meeting was held at Freemasons' Tavern (6 Feb., 1818), attended by nearly the whole bench of bishops.—Official enquiry established the fact that certain London tea-dealers very frequently adulterated tea with dried ash, sloe and elder leaves ; but the leading merchants published a denial of the statement as applicable to the trade generally (16 Mar).—The Common Council resolved on an address to the Prince Regent on the marriage of his sister, the Princess Eliza, with the Prince of Hesse Homburg (9 Ap.).—Nearly 6,000 children, belonging to the London National Schools, assembled in the Egyptian Hall ; here, in the presence of the Queen, the Lord Mayor and a distinguished company, a portion of them were examined in spelling, arithmetic and reading (29 Ap.). —Flaxman's monument to Nelson was unveiled in St. Paul's (12 May) —The Pitt Club celebrated the anniversary of Pitt's birth at the City of London Tavern, on which occasion Lord Liverpool deprecated the growing profaneness of the age (29th).—The Common Council congratulated the Prince Regent (in an address voted 9 June) on the marriage of the Duke of Cambridge with the Princess of Hesse. A similar address (21 July) related to the marriages of the Duke of Clarence with the Princess of Saxe-Meiningen and of the Duke of Kent with the Princess of Leiningen.—At the General Election, the following members were returned for the City : Matthew Wood, Thomas Wilson, Robert Waithman, and John Thomas Thorp.—During the excavations made for the new Post Office, the foundations of the Collegiate Church of St. Martin-le-Grand were laid bare.

Three inter-communicating vaults were discovered under the foundations of old houses in the rear of St. Leonard's, Foster Lane   They were built chiefly of large square bricks, mixed with

U 2

stone and flint, the interstices being filled with yellow chalky earth The height was 9 feet, depth about 18, breadth 6 or 7.   A stone coffin, pierced with two holes, and measuring 6¾ feet in length, was found.   Short pillars supported intersecting semi-circular arches.   A college was founded here in 700 by Wythred, King of Kent ; it was surrendered in 1548 to Edward VI, and soon afterwards the church was pulled down.

Alderman John Atkins was appointed Lord Mayor.—Much competition took place for the office of the City Sword Bearer, now vacant ; three persons were said to have offered £10,000 for the post.   The Common Council subsequently decided (28 Jan. 1819) that the office should be filled up by election.—Carroll's Lottery office, Cornhill, was destroyed by fire (20 Nov.).—Under the will of the late Rev. W. Hetherington, and from other sources, the governors of Christ's Hospital were able to extend annuities of from £10 to £50 to upwards of 500 blind persons.

This year Mrs. Fry described before the House of Commons Police Committee her reformatory work among the female prisoners of Newgate.

1819.

SIBLEY, a watchman, his wife, and several men and boys, all of them disciples of Joanna Southcott and under the influence of religious mania, marched through Temple Bar, along Fleet Street, to Budge Row, Cannon Street, wearing white cockades and yellow rosettes (14 Jan., 1819).   Sibley sounded a trumpet in Budge Row, and his wife proclaimed " Woe, woe, to the inhabitants of the earth because of the coming of Shiloh ! "   Immense crowds assembled, and Sibley and his companions were pelted.   They were taken into custody, but released the next morning.— Southwark Bridge was opened to traffic at midnight on 24 Mar.

As St. Paul's clock struck twelve the toll of one penny commenced ; the bridge was lighted by thirty gas lamps.   The bridge, designed by Sir John Rennie, comprises three cast-iron arches, the two outer measuring 210 feet in length, and the central 240 feet, the height of the latter above high water at spring-tide being about 42 feet.   The roadway is 42 feet wide, is formed of solid plates of cast-iron, and is supported by stone piers.   The ribs of the arches form a series of hollow voussoirs. In length the bridge is 700 feet, and the weight of the iron-work is 5,700 tons.

An amusing hoax played on Alderman Sir John Eamer resulted in a considerable number of persons calling at his house, under the impression that they were invited to dinner.   The worthy Alderman made the best of the situation and his guests spent an hilarious evening.—The new building of the London Institution, in Finsbury Circus, was opened 21 Ap.

The Institution was founded in 1806, being first established in Sir Robert Clayton's house, in Old Jewry ; it received a Charter of Incorporation, 21 Jan , 1807, and was transferred to King's Arms Yard, Coleman Street, in 1811. The structure in Finsbury Circus was designed by William Brooks. The main body of the building is 108 feet in length, each wing being 16 feet. The centre is adorned with a handsome portico, with four Tuscan pillars which again support four Corinthian columns, the whole being surmounted by a pediment. The great staircase is 97 feet long, and 42 wide. The theatre accommodates 750 persons

The freedom of the Merchant Taylors' Company was presented to Lord Sidmouth on 11 June.—An unusual scene took place at St. Andrew's Church, Holborn, owing to the parish officers refusing to permit an interment in an iron coffin (17 June). The undertaker, who had left the coffin in the churchyard, was arrested, the dispute being subsequently remitted to the King's Bench, which decided that it was a matter for ecclesiastical jurisdiction.—Seditious handbills and placards occasioned the Lord Mayor some apprehension in Aug.

A Radical demonstration, under the leadership of Dr. Watson, Thistlewood and Preston, took place at Smithfield (25th) —A similar meeting at Manchester had been attended with loss of life in consequence of a charge of the Yeomanry. On 9 Sept the Common Council passed a resolution indignantly censuring the action of the Manchester authorities, and drew up an address to the Prince Regent, in which they claimed for all Englishmen the right of public meeting, and affirming that forcible suppression of meetings could only "tend to increase the present discontent, destroy public confidence in the pure and equal administration of justice, excite disaffection, and lead to acts of open violence or secret revenge "—On 13 Sept "Orator" Hunt, accompanied by Watson, Thistlewood and Preston, made a progress through the City, amid a dense concourse of spectators —The Court of Aldermen (5 Oct.) declared their abhorrence of the libellous and seditious publications now inundating the country.—Sheriff Parkins, whose extreme hostility to the Government was not supported by the majority of the Corporation, openly severed himself from his civic colleagues, refused to join the usual procession to Westminster (9 Nov) for the presentation to the barons of the Exchequer (he rode alone on horseback while the Lord Mayor went by water), and had on 8 Oct. declined to accompany the Lord Mayor to the Court of Aldermen, afterwards defending his action in a long statement before the Court of Aldermen.—Richard Carlile, the Fleet Street bookseller, was found guilty (14th) of re-publishing Paine's "Age of Reason."

Alderman George Bridges was elected Mayor.—Several journeymen printers were sentenced at the Guildhall for printing almanacs on unstamped paper (5 Nov.). —Coleridge commenced his course of twelve lectures on Shakespeare in the house held by the Philosophical Society in Crane Court, Fleet Street (8 Nov.).— Considerable friction occurred between the Court of Common Council and the Court of Aldermen, in reference to a threatened prosecution by the latter of Alderman Waithman, for obstructing the election of Mayor.—A meeting of book-sellers and printers deprecated the proposal then before Parliament to inflict penalties of transportation and death for the vending of blasphemous or seditious libels (15 Dec.).

Poultry Chapel (Congregational1st) was erected on the site of the old Compter.—A caricature of the day represents Orator Hunt, with an ass's head, addressing an immense assemblage of cattle, sheep, pigs, etc, in Smithfield "I should be ambitious, indeed," exclaims the Orator, "if I thought my bray would be heard by the immense and respectable multitude I have the honour to address." The audience reply with "Hear, hear!" "Bravo!"

1820.

UCH distress was caused by the severe winter. The Lord Mayor, presiding at a meeting at Mr. Hick's warehouse, London Wall, stated that an almost incredible number of applications for relief had been made to the magistrates. A subscription was opened, and Mr. Hick turned his spacious warehouses into temporary shelters for night-wanderers (13 Jan., 1820).—A fire in Thames Street and Swan Lane wrought damage to the extent of £200,000.—On the death of King George III the Common Council agreed (2 Feb.) upon a loyal address to his successor. A similar address was voted by the Court of Aldermen (20th).—A meeting of merchants at the London Tavern opened a subscription in aid of the sufferers from the extensive floods in the Netherlands.—At the General Election, the following members were chosen for the City: Thomas Wilson, Matthew Wood, Sir William Curtis, and the Lord Mayor (14 Mar.).—The freedom of the City was conferred on the Marquis Camden (23 Mar.), in appreciation of his disinterested conduct in relinquishing a large amount of income derivable from fees as a teller of the Exchequer.—The Roman Catholic chapel, in Moorfields, was opened (22 Ap.).

The structure seated 2,000 persons. The altar was of marble, the ceiling frescoed, the pulpit of marble was presented by Lord Arundel. Behind the columns of the sanctuary was placed a fresco of the Crucifixion.

A thousand school children were regaled with roast beef and plum pudding, in the Coleman Street School, on the occasion of the King's birthday (24 Ap.).—Five of the Cato Street conspirators were executed on 1 May.

They were Thistlewood, Ings, Brunt, Tidd, and Davidson. Thistlewood had escaped from Cato Street when the Bow Street officers broke in upon the meeting of the conspirators, but was taken in bed the next morning at 8, White Street, Little Moorfields. He was committed to the Tower, being the last person immured there as a prisoner. The trial took place at the Old Bailey in Ap. Thistlewood and his companions were the last sufferers of the death penalty for high treason in this country. On the day of their execution at Newgate, Life Guards were stationed in the Old Bailey, Newgate Street, and Ludgate Hill, and six cannon and 100 Artillerymen were placed in the centre of Blackfriars Bridge. When the bodies had been suspended half-an-hour, a masked man decapitated them one by one, each head being lifted up by his assistant, with the thrice-repeated exclamation, "This is the head of a traitor." A large number of women witnessed the scene.

Queen Caroline arrived in London, amid a popular ovation, on 3 June, and for a short time resided at the house of Mr. Alderman Wood in South Audley Street.

The City sided with the Queen in her unhappy dispute with George IV On 16 June the Lord Mayor, in state, with Aldermen Wood, Thorp, Waithman, the Sheriffs, City Officers, and about ninety members of the Common Council, and accompanied by a vast concourse of people, waited on the Queen at her residence in Portman Street, and presented an address expressive of sympathy with her afflictions and asserting her right to a public investigation of the charges brought against her. Similar sentiments were embodied in an address from the Common Hall on the 30th. Queen Caroline's trial lasted from 17 Aug to 10 Nov, when the Government abandoned the Bill of Pains and Penalties. The Queen was received with enthusiasm at all her appearances in public. London was illuminated on 10 Nov. On 21 Nov the Common Council resolved to felicitate Her Majesty on "the triumphant refutation of the foul charges" brought against her character and honour In spite of protests from a section of the Court of Aldermen the Queen attended at St. Paul's on 29 Nov. to join in divine service Enormous crowds filled the streets. Shop doors in the Strand and City were barricaded to guard against the pressure of the multitude The Queen was received at Temple Bar by the Lord Mayor, the Sheriffs, Mr. Alderman Wood, etc. A committee of sixty ladies, arrayed in white satin, received Her Majesty at the Cathedral. No untoward incidents marked the day The Common Hall adopted an address to the Queen (15 Dec.), strongly condemning the attack upon Her Majesty through the Bill of Pains and Penalties In September the Queen had presented to the Corporation portraits of herself and the Princess Charlotte.

A man convicted of perjury stood for an hour in the public pillory opposite Newgate (1 Aug.).—A set of communion plate was presented by the Pope to the Roman Catholic chapel in Moorfields —Alderman John Thomas Thorp was chosen Mayor.—An address of the Common Council to the King (voted 1 Dec.) deplored the exhaustion of the country by excessive public expenditure, and openly reprobated the recent proceedings against Queen Caroline. A different tone animated an address from the Court of Mayor and Aldermen, in which regret was expressed at the propagation of sedition by "infatuated malice and a licentious press" (5 Dec).— At a meeting at the King's Head, Poultry, a society was formed (22nd), under the title of the Constitutional Association, for opposing the progress of disloyal and seditious principles.

George Gwilt rebuilt 42 feet of the spire of St. Mary-le-Bow —Furnival's Inn was rebuilt by William Peto, the contractor, 1818–1820.—Theodore Hook started the *John Bull* newspaper in Johnson's Court, Fleet Street.—The altar-piece, Mary Magdalen anointing the feet of Christ, painted by W. Hilton, R.A., was presented to St. Michael's, College Hill, by the directors of the British Institution.—Benjamin West was buried in the crypt of St. Paul's.—One of the last persons committed to Newgate for a literary offence was Mr. (afterwards Sir John) Hobhouse, who had attacked the House of Commons in a pamphlet entitled " A trifling mistake." He lived in style in the governor's rooms.

1821.

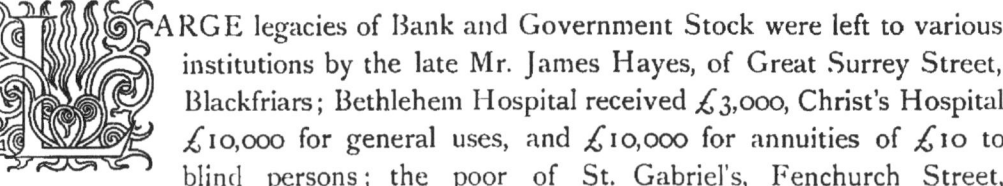

ARGE legacies of Bank and Government Stock were left to various institutions by the late Mr. James Hayes, of Great Surrey Street, Blackfriars; Bethlehem Hospital received £3,000, Christ's Hospital £10,000 for general uses, and £10,000 for annuities of £10 to blind persons; the poor of St. Gabriel's, Fenchurch Street, £1,000, &c.—The new Royal crown, made by Messrs. Randell & Bridge, was deposited in the Tower (Ap., 1820).—The singular case of the iron coffin (*see* 17 June, 1819), was decided by the Consistory Court, the parish authorities of St. Andrew's, Holborn, being permitted to charge an extra fee of £10 for the interment of metal coffins.—The freedom of the City was presented on 2 June to Attorney-General Brougham, Solicitor-General Denman, and Dr. Lushington, for the talent, firmness, and integrity they had displayed in defending the Queen against the Bill of Pains and Penalties.—Interesting facts relating to the river came out in a case heard before the Lord Mayor (11 June) :

A fisherman was charged with working an unlawful net. In defence he complained of the difficulty of procuring a livelihood since the contamination of the stream by discharges from gas-works. Only one salmon had been caught during the past year; shad and smelt had almost disappeared; the water was poisoned as far as Brentford in the one direction, and beyond Rotherhithe in the other; the great mud-bank near the Temple, once frequented by fish in search of red worm, was now deserted. Many fishermen had been driven to seek other occupations. The Lord Mayor expressed sympathy for the defendant, and imposed a very light penalty. Courts of Conservancy were held in the following September at Southwark and Westminster, and testimony heard as to the pollution of the river; the Lord Mayor ordered the prosecution of the offending parties.

The coronation of King George IV was proclaimed in the City in the usual way (14 June), but Wood Street was omitted from the list of halting-places. Loud cries of " The Queen!" greeted the cavalcade during its progress.—The Common Council ordered suitable accommodation to be provided for reporters of their debates (12 July).—At the coronation banquet in Westminster Hall, according to ancient custom, the Lord Mayor, accompanied by twelve citizens, presented the King with wine in a gold cup; and His Majesty, having drunk, returned the cup to the Lord Mayor as his fee (19 July).—The report of the Committee of the

House of Commons on the state of London Bridge recommended the granting of power to erect a new bridge of five arches, and that no toll should be levied, the Bridge House Estates having £112,000 in hand, and a yearly rental of £25,000.—Queen Caroline's funeral procession, on its way to Harwich, was accompanied through the City by the Lord Mayor (14 Aug).—A charge of disturbance at Moorfields Chapel, occasioned by the beadle's demand of threepence for admission, came before the Lord Mayor, (28 Aug.).—Alderman Christopher Magnay was elected Lord Mayor.—Addresses to the King were presented (16 Nov.) from the Court of Mayor and Aldermen and the Common Council, expressing pleasure at His Majesty's safe return from abroad. On the return of the deputation which took charge of the addresses, Mr. Wontner, First City Marshal, was thrown from his horse and sustained a severe fracture of the leg.

The register books of the Fleet marriages, about 1,200 in number, some of them partly relating to marriages performed outside the Liberty of the Fleet, were bought by Government and deposited at Somerset House.—John Rennie, engineer of Waterloo Bridge and designer of new London Bridge, was buried in the crypt of St. Paul's.—Specie payment was fully resumed at the Bank —The population within the walls was returned at 56,174.—A portrait of Lord Mayor Thorp, in Sir George Nayler's work on the Coronation of King George IV, represents the Chief Magistrate as carrying the City Sceptre in the procession.—According to a return made to a Parliamentary Committee this year the annual rental derived from the London Bridge Waterworks was £12,266, the number of houses supplied, 10,417, and the quantity of water, 26,322,705 hogsheads.

1822.

N various accounts the river occupied a considerable share of public attention.

Floods on the Thames, at the close of 1821, formed the subject of a report from the Navigation Committee of the City of London, but it was stated that no delay to shipping had been occasioned (Jan.).—A high south-westerly wind, on 6 Mar, depleted the river of water to such an extent that it was in several places fordable. Valuable articles were found in the river-bed. Ships were seen aground in all parts of the stream below London Bridge. On the return of the tide the water ran with such rapidity as to overturn or injure a number of barges.—An iron steamboat, designed for direct communication between London and Paris, was exhibited between London and Battersea bridges; it was 176 feet long and 17 broad, and was propelled by a 30-horse-power engine.—On 1 Aug. the report of the Bridge House Committee, advising that steps be taken for the erection of a new London Bridge, was agreed to.—A society was organised for the moral and temporal improvement of the watermen, of whom there were stated to be about 9,000.

Thirteen convicts made an attempt at escape from Newgate (29 Jan., 1822). A hole, two feet square, was discovered by the turnkeys in the wall of one of the north wards.—The freedom of the City was presented to Mr. Joseph Hume on account of his exertions in the House of Commons in the interests of public economy (21 Feb.).—On 30, Mar. the Recorder, Sir John Silvester, died.— Mr. Thomas Denman was elected Common Serjeant in the room of Mr. Newman Knowlys, who had been promoted to the Recordership (25 April).— For libels on the late Queen the proprietors of *John Bull* were condemned to fines and imprisonment (20 May).—A young woman, under sentence of transportation for theft, was discovered to be innocent, and released from Newgate (June).

Romantic circumstances attended this case. The young woman's lover, a market salesman, made an appeal to the Home Secretary, and declared his willingness to marry the girl, in the presence of His Majesty's Ministers, if they would be pleased to grant her a pardon In order to keep the salesman to his word, the promise of pardon was at first made conditional on the ceremony taking place. They were married at St Botolph's, Aldgate, and on returning to Newgate, the official pardon was placed in the husband's hands It is said that in one day the governor of Newgate received twenty offers from men to marry female prisoners on similar conditions.

An Act was passed in August for the removal of the London Bridge Waterworks.

On the approaching demolition of the waterworks all the leases derived by the waterworks from the City were transferred to the New River Company for the consideration of £3,750 payable yearly for 260 years. A portion of the area supplied by the old Works was conveyed for the purpose of water-supply to the East London Company on condition of the latter paying an annual sum of £160 to the New River Company for the period of 260 years.

On 16 Oct. died Sir Matthew Bloxam, Knight, aged seventy-nine ; Sheriff in 1787 ; founder of the "Sheriffs' fund" for the relief of debtors ; M.P. for Maidstone, 1790-1806, Alderman of Bridge Ward Within, 1803-1821.—Alderman William Heygate, was elected Lord Mayor.—Mrs. Wright defended herself at the Old Bailey on the charge of selling Carlile's blasphemous publications (14 Nov.).

Carlile, in order to baffle the authorities and prevent identification of the vendor, had erected a partition in his shop, through an aperture there were handed to purchasers such publications as were threatened with prosecution —Waddington, a bookseller, was sentenced to a year's imprisonment in the House of Correction, for selling Palmer's " Principles of Nature "

The Lord Mayor declined to grant an order to the Rector of St. Olave, Hart Street, to compel a parishioner to pay tithe (20 Nov.).

In memory of Emery, the actor, who died in 1822, a tablet was placed in St Andrew's, Holborn.— A new hall (the second) was erected for the Leathersellers' Company, in St. Helen's Place, by

W. F. Pocock, 1820–22.—The present Saddlers' Hall was built by Jesse Gibson.—In 1822, and possibly later, the custom was still observed of presenting two sugar-loaves to the Lord Chief Baron of the Exchequer from the Wardens of the Fleet Prison, as a kind of complimentary acknowledgment, the Wardens receiving the rents and profits of the shops in Westminster Hall.—This is the first year in

Hall of Leathersellers' Company.

which a steam-vessel is entered in Lloyd's Register.—"About thirty years ago," writes a contributor to *Notes and Queries* in 1852, "there might be heard any morning in the smaller streets of the City a cry of 'dolls' bedsteads,' from a lean lame man on a crutch ; he wore an apron, and carried miniature bedsteads for sale. Of this man it was currently reported that he was implicated in the Cato Street conspiracy, and turned King's evidence."

1823.

BUSINESS in foreign stocks was removed from the Royal Exchange to a room in Capel Court (1 Jan., 1823).—The Spanish and Portuguese ambassadors were splendidly entertained at the City of London Tavern, Lord William Bentinck presiding (7 Mar.).—On 29 Mar. died Sir John Eamer, Knight ; Sheriff, 1794 ; Alderman of Langbourn, 1795 ; Knighted, 1795 ; Lord Mayor, 1801 ; Colonel of a London

Militia regiment. His full length portrait is preserved in the Guildhall.—On 18 Apr. died Alderman Thomas Smith, who had represented Farringdon Within Ward since 1803; Sheriff, 1805, Lord Mayor, 1809.—The number of prisoners in Newgate was unusually small, only 101 men and 74 women being returned in the governor's report to the Court of Aldermen (3 June).—The novelty of a female preacher, Mary Brown, attracted great crowds to the chapel in Grub Street.— Mr. Macadam was at this time directing public attention to his schemes for improved paving in London.—The Common Council held frequent discussions during the year on the subject of the proposed new London Bridge, the Act empowering its erection having passed in July.—Alderman Robert Waithman was elected Lord Mayor.—On 26 Dec. died Samuel Thorp, aged eighty-two. For more than fifty years he represented Aldgate Ward in the Common Council. He was the Father of the Court, and three times declined the Alderman's gown.

Vintners' Hall, Upper Thames Street, was rebuilt, 1820-23.—St. Paul's School was built in 1823 from a design by George Smith, this being the third edifice on the old site on the east side of St. Paul's Churchyard.—London was now supplied with 39,504 public gas lamps, furnished by three principal companies, the length of gas-lit streets extending to 215 miles.—The Corporation this year voted sums in aid of the patriotic struggles of the Spaniards and the Greeks.—The church of St Bartholomew-the-Less was restored by Thomas Hardwick.

The following lines on the contemporary Aldermen of London appeared in the *New Monthly Magazine* :—

THE COURT OF ALDERMEN AT FISHMONGERS' HALL.

Is that dace or perch?
Said Alderman Birch.
I take it for herring,
Said Alderman Perring.
This jack's very good
Said Alderman Wood.
But its bones might a man slay,
Said Alderman Ansley
I'll butter what I get,
Said Alderman Heygate
Give me some stewed carp,
Said Alderman Thorp.
The roe's dry as pith,
Said Alderman Smith.
Don't cut so far down,
Said Alderman Brown.
But nearer the fin,
Said Alderman Glynn.
I've finished i'faith, man,
Said Alderman Waithman.
And I, too, i' fatkins,
Said Alderman Atkins.

They've crimped this cod drolly,
Said Alderman Scholey.
'Tis bruised at the ridges,
Said Alderman Brydges.
Was it caught in a drag? Nay,
Said Alderman Magnay.
'Twas brought by two men,
Said Alderman Ven-
Ables Yes, in a box,
Said Alderman Cox.
They care not how *fur 'tis*,
Said Alderman Curtis
From air kept and sun,
Said Alderman Thompson
Packed neatly in straw,
Said Alderman Shaw.
In ice got from Gunter,
Said Alderman Hunter.
This ketchup is sour,
Said Alderman Flower
Then steep it in claret,
Said Alderman Garratt.

1824.

THE first pile of new London Bridge was driven on 15 Mar., 1824. Interesting antiquities were turned up during the excavations, among them being a silver statuette of Harpocrates, now in the British Museum.

Various projects connected with the river were engaging the attention of Parliament. On 25 Mar. the Common Council instructed the Navigation Committee to watch the progress of five Bills dealing with (1) a proposed bridge across the Thames at St. Katherine's, (2) a bridge at Hammersmith, (3) a tunnel under the river, (4) the enlargement of Counter's Creek, Hammersmith, (5) the construction of docks at St. Katherine's.—A meeting of owners of river-side property was held at the Mansion House, the Lord Mayor presiding, to hear an address by Colonel Trench, M.P., on his scheme for an esplanade or terrace, 80 feet wide, and 60 feet high, to extend from London Bridge to Westminster. The top of the structure was to be planted with trees, and used as a promenade, to which people would gain admission by toll. Warehouses were to be built underneath (15 July).—A few days later (20 July) the Court of the Proprietors of the Thames Tunnel Company met at the City of London Tavern. It was stated that Mr. Brunel had been engaged to construct a tunnel from Wapping to Rotherhithe, receiving £10,000 for his patent, and a salary of £1,000 per annum for three years.

New London Bridge from Fenning's Wharf.

The establishment of the Guildhall Library takes its origin from a motion carried by Mr. Richard Lambert Jones, in the Court of Common Council (8 Ap.).—A plan of escape from Newgate was frustrated by the discovery of a rope, made from the prison mats, by which several prisoners had intended to scale the wall. They had been supplied with a brace of pistols, concealed in a parcel of sugar (16 May).—Eight shopmen of Richard Carlile were sentenced to various fines and terms of imprisonment for selling Paine's "Age of Reason," etc. (24 June).—Alderman John Garratt was elected Lord Mayor.

Barclay's brewery was one of the wonders of London. It covered 8 acres of ground, and in 1823 had manufactured 351,474 barrels of beer. The three coppers in which the beer was boiled each held 150 barrels; twenty-five gentlemen once dined in one of these huge vessels, and, after they left, fifty workmen got in and regaled themselves. The fermenting tuns held 1,400 barrels each.—Bread and beer for breakfast were discontinued at Christ's Hospital.—St. Bride's Avenue was formed.—The Corporation contributed (1815–1824) the sum of £80,000 towards the site for the General Post

Office.—A Committee of Inquiry was appointed by the members of Lloyd's Registry, in order to report on reform in the classification of vessels The report was presented in 1826.—Richard Dighton published a series of spirited coloured prints (1817–24), giving portraits of well-known City men, including N M Rothschild, Sir William Curtis, Messrs. Ripley, Gascoigne, Samuel, Charles Grant, Heale, Mellish, Ben Bovill, Richard Thornton, etc

1825.

BRUNEL commenced the Thames Tunnel in Jan., 1825.—The Common Council resolved to petition for the repeal of the House and Window Duties (16 Feb).—The Duke of York laid the foundation stone of the New Hall of Christ's Hospital (28 Ap.).—A meeting at the Crown and Anchor tavern considered a scheme for a London University (subsequently known as University College). Among those present were Mr. Brougham, Lord John Russell, Dr. Birkbeck, Thomas Campbell, the poet, etc.—Dr. Abraham Rees (the editor of the well-known Cyclopædia) was buried at Bunhill Fields (9 June).—The first stone of new London Bridge was laid (15 June).

The cofferdam, the floor of which was 45 feet below high-water mark, was divided into four tiers of galleries, gaily adorned with flags. The Duke of York, accompanied by the Lord Mayor, arrived about four in the afternoon, the children of the schools belonging to Candlewick, Bridge, and Dowgate Wards singing the national anthem In the cavity of the foundation stone, which was laid by the Lord Mayor, were placed coins and an inscription in Latin, engraved on a copper plate. The inscription, written by Dr. Coplestone, runs thus in translation :—"The free course of the river being obstructed by the numerous piers of the ancient bridge, and the passage of boats and vessels through its narrow channels being often attended with danger and loss of life by reason of the force and rapidity of the current, the City of London, desirous of providing a remedy for this evil, and at the same time consulting the convenience of commerce in this vast emporium of all nations, under the sanction and with the liberal aid of Parliament, resolved to erect a bridge upon a foundation altogether new, with arches of a wider span, and of a character corresponding to the dignity and importance of this loyal City, nor does any other time seem to be more suitable for such an undertaking than when in a period of universal peace, the British Empire, flourishing in glory, wealth, population, and domestic union, is governed by a prince, the patron and encourager of the arts, under whose auspices the metropolis has been daily advancing in elegance and splendour. The first stone of this work was laid by John Garratt, Esquire, Lord Mayor, on the 15th day of June, in the sixth year of King George the Fourth, and in the year of our Lord, 1825. John Rennie, F.R.S., architect." The foundation stone weighed 9 tons.

On 30 July died James R. Syms ; he was elected Common Crier and Serjeant-at-Arms of the City in 1797 ; the " London Life Association" was formed at his suggestion.—Henry Woodthorpe, Town Clerk since 1801, died 4 Sept. ; on account of his deafness his son had acted for him since 1818.—A meeting was held at the "Horn" Tavern, Doctors Commons, to ventilate a project for opening up a new street from New Bridge Street to the west front of St. Paul's, the scheme being advocated by Mr. James Elmes.—The subject of tithes agitated the public mind. The Tithes Committee presented to the Court of Common Council a report of their proceedings, from 1811 to the present time (23 Sept.).—Alderman William Venables was chosen Lord Mayor —A financial panic occurred in Dec., several banks stopping payment.

The banking-house of Sir Peter Pole & Co., which was suspended on 5 Dec., had, in the previous week, paid out more than a million and-a-quarter. Lombard Street and other thoroughfares, where banks were situated, were daily besieged by vast crowds A meeting of 150 bankers and merchants at the Mansion House (14 Dec.), under the presidency of the Lord Mayor, deprecated the panic and expressed confidence in the stability of the public credit. A large number of joint-stock, mining and other companies had been floated during the year. Among these companies was one which professed to make gold ; the shares having been all taken up, it was announced that the cost of producing an ounce of gold would be double the value of the precious metal manufactured , the Company was dissolved, and the deposits were retained to pay expenses. A railroad was projected from Dover to Calais. The Chilian Republic borrowed from this country a million at 6 per cent, but paid no interest after 1826. Much money was lost by the mismanagement of the Greek loan At one period of the financial fever of 1825–6, crowds so choked the entrance to the Stock Exchange that fines of £5 were imposed for obstruction.

The livery of the Glass Sellers' Company was increased.—A livery was granted to the Woolmen's Company , and the same privilege was conferred on the Basket Makers.—Henry Fuseli, the painter, was buried in the crypt of St. Paul's.—The old "Cherry Tree" Inn, Wilderness Row, once noted for its tea-gardens, was demolished.—The interior of Bakers' Hall (Harp Lane, Great Tower Street) was restored, under the superintendence of James Elmes.—Mr. Francis Baily, a well-known member of the Stock Exchange, was chosen president of the Royal Astronomical Society

1826.

AT a meeting of Common Council (19 Jan., 1826) the idea of a Guildhall Museum was mooted.

Mr. Hicks moved that a room be set apart for the reception of local antiquities, many valuable relics having been lost to the City for want of accommodation. At the same meeting of the Council it was stated that the Library Committee had purchased, for 250 guineas, a complete set of the *London Gazette*, from its origin in 1665 ; a great number of works relating to the antiquities, history, laws, manners and customs of the City of London and Borough of Southwark had also been collected.

The Court of Proprietors of the Bank acquiesced in the proposal of the Government to remove the limit to the number of partners in country banks beyond 65 miles from London (3 Feb.).—The old South Sea House in Broad Street, which had been occupied as private chambers, was burned down (Ap.).—The Custom House, lately erected, having shown serious signs of dilapidation owing to insecure foundations, an action was entered against Henry Peto, the builder, but failed.—Parliament was dissolved on 31 May A crowded and excited meeting assembled in Guildhall to elect the City members of Parliament by show of hands (9 June). The subsequent poll resulted in the return of Aldermen Thompson and Waithman, Mr. Ward, and Alderman Wood.—The stocks belonging to St. Clement Danes, the last remaining example of that ancient mode of punishment, were removed for the purpose of local improvements.—A bust of Granville Sharp, the philanthropist, was placed in the Council Chamber of the Guildhall (4 July).— Bow steeple gave evidence of instability, part of the stonework falling upon a neighbouring roof (18 Aug.). Mr. Gwilt, the architect, attributed the unsafe condition of the steeple to excessive vibration caused by bell-ringing. The famous peal (cast in 1762) was for a time silenced.—The last State lottery in England was drawn at Coopers' Hall, Basinghall Street, on 18 Oct.—On 26 Oct. died Alderman Magnay, formerly Sheriff (1814), and Lord Mayor (1821). He was a successful stationer, his place of business being situated on College Hill. In 1816 he acted as Master of the Stationers' Company.—Alderman Anthony Brown was elected Lord Mayor.—Farringdon Market for fruit and vegetables, between Farringdon Street and Shoe Lane, was opened on 20 Nov. It was designed by the Clerk of the City's Works, Mr. W. Montagu, and cost £31,186.—The placing of an illuminated dial in the clock of St. Bride's, Fleet Street, was regarded by the citizens as a great novelty (2 Dec.).--At a meeting of the Waterloo Bridge Company, at the "Crown and Anchor" Tavern, a dividend of only one per cent. was declared, and a proposition was raised to dispose of the bridge by lottery.

An Act of Parliament was obtained for the sale of Bangor House, Shoe Lane, to the parish of St. Andrew, Holborn, the proceeds to be devoted to the purchase of a London House for the See of Bangor.—The last vestige of the Grey Friars monastery was removed. The entrance was opposite Warwick Lane, Christ Church, Newgate, was built on part of the site.—The eleven leading breweries of London were as follows: Barclay & Perkins, Truman & Hanbury, Whitbread, Reid, Combe & Delafield, Meux, Calvert, Hoare, Taylor, Elliott, Campbell. In the year ending July, Barclay & Perkins manufactured 380,180 barrels of porter.—The old "Elephant" Tavern, Fenchurch Street, was demolished. It had been built before the Great Fire.

1827.

TRANSPARENT clock-dials were now coming into general use.— Agitation was being directed against the Corporation and Test Acts (1827).

A great meeting, called by the Protestant Society and attended by 3,000 persons, was held at the "City of London" Tavern, Lord Milton presiding. Resolutions were passed against the Acts, which were declared to be a disgrace to the statute book (8 May). On the previous day the Common Council had passed a similar motion.

On Lord Liverpool's death the King placed the administration in the hands of Canning, a step which gave great satisfaction to the Common Council, and an address, commending His Majesty's dignified action "under circumstances of great difficulty," was adopted on 23 May.—An inrush of water on the morning of 18 May checked the operations at the Thames Tunnel.

The aperture was with difficulty stopped by bags of adhesive blue clay. Not till the end of June was the tunnel sufficiently cleared for resumption of work. Enormous thick tarpaulins were also sunk in the river over the spot where the leak had shown itself.

The excavations at London Bridge continued to yield antiquarian relics.

The discoveries included a finely executed leaden horse, Saxon coins, counters, gun-money, a Roman coin inscribed "Plon," many coins of Antoninus Pius, together with spurs, spoons, daggers, crucifixes, chains and manacles. Mr. Newman, Comptroller of the Bridge House Estates, made a considerable collection.

Old Christ Church Hall was now demolished, the materials being sold by public auction ; the oak beams erected in 1672 were found to be thoroughly sound (Aug.).—The Printers' Pension Fund was being formed (Sept.).—At the instance of the City authorities the Rev. Robert Taylor was prosecuted for blasphemous utterances at a meeting held in the Areopagus, Cannon Street. The Attorney-General was counsel for the prosecution. Taylor, who declared himself a Deist, was found guilty (24 Oct.).—Unusual splendour marked the show of the new Lord Mayor, Matthias Prime Lucas, the procession including Waterloo heroes, a detachment of Life Guards wearing cuirasses taken at Waterloo, the figures of Gog and Magog, etc. The Guildhall banquet was marred by the fall of a number of coloured lamps, the Duke of Clarence and the Lord Mayor suffering some inconvenience from the occurrence.—A strike of 400 labourers at St. Katherine's Docks (then in course of construction) was due to a reduction in wages and lasted two days (19, 20 Nov.).

The Clockmakers' Company's Livery was fixed at 250. The present Salters' Hall, St. Swithin's Lane, built in 1823–7, was designed by Henry Carr. The hall is 72 feet by 40 ; the portico is Ionic. Salters' Hall Chapel, removed to afford room for the new hall, had been a notable Dissenting meeting house.—Joseph Gwilt superintended the alterations in Grocers' Hall, Poultry, a new entrance into Princes Street being constructed.—The present Bank of England building was completed under the direction of Sir R. Taylor.—The following nine London Insurance Companies paid duty to the amount of £20,000 or upwards: Sun, Phœnix, County, Royal Exchange, Protector, Guardian, Imperial, Globe, Atlas.

1828.

SIX men were drowned by the renewed flooding of the Thames Tunnel, Mr. Brunel, junr., escaping with difficulty (2 Jan., 1828). —The Rev. Robert Taylor was sentenced at Guildhall to a year's imprisonment (*see* 24 Oct., 1827); in his speech in defence, he had denounced the Lord Mayor as "Persecution sitting in the chair of mayoralty."—The Court of Aldermen decided that persons born of Jewish parents, but baptized as Christians, were eligible for the freedom of the City (4 Mar.).

Y

In 1785, the Court of Aldermen had made a standing order that baptized Jews should not be admitted to the freedom, and all applications from Jewish converts had since been rejected. The point was successfully raised in the present instance on the petition of Messrs. Saul, praying to be allowed to carry on business in the City.

A regatta, attended by the Duke and Duchess of Clarence, Princess Augusta, and other royal personages, was celebrated above Waterloo Bridge.

The City lent its Navigation Barge for the ceremony. Its deck, 146 feet by 19, was covered with an awning; the royal standard was hoisted at the mast head, the City ensign at the stern. Four other City barges took part in the display,— the Lord Mayor's, the Merchant Taylors', the Vintners', and the Drapers', the men being dressed in the uniform of their companies (18 June).

In June the Guildhall Library was opened for the use of members of the Corporation.

Upon the motion of Mr. Richard Lambert Jones, the Court of Common Council (8 Ap., 1824), had referred to a Special Committee the work of inquiring into "the best mode of arranging and carrying into effect, in the Guildhall, a library of all matters relating to this City, the Borough of Southwark, and the County of Middlesex," Mr. Jones being elected chairman. It was decided to expend £500 for outfit and £200 annually for maintenance. The collections were lodged in the rooms lately occupied in the east wing of the Guildhall front, a

Entrance to Great St. Helen's, looking towards Bishopsgate Street.
Destroyed 1892-4.

room of the Exchequer Court being utilized as a temporary store. The books (1,700 vols.) having been arranged by Mr. William Upcott, Librarian of the London Institution, and a catalogue prepared by Mr. Edward Tyrrell, Remembrancer, the post of librarian was bestowed upon Mr. William Herbert.

The election of Dr. Blomfield to the bishopric of London was recognised at Bow Church with the accustomed ceremonies, and the ancient Bow bells were rung (16 Aug.).—The St. Katherine's Docks were opened on 25 Oct.—Alderman William Thompson was elected Lord Mayor.—The new Corn Exchange in Mark Lane, designed by George Smith, was opened.

The building was erected in the Doric style, the façade consisting of a peristyle of six fluted columns, with rectangular wings. Eighty-two stands for factors were placed in the hall. Twelve cast-iron pillars, with wheat-sheaf capitals, supported the roof. The cost was £90,000.—A Parliamentary Committee, reporting on the police of the metropolis, attributed the increase in crime to a rise in population, the low price of gin, the high rate of wages, and the spread of juvenile gambling.—Brunswick Theatre, Wellclose Square, was re-opened (25 Feb.), but fell in three days afterwards, killing ten persons.—William Blake, the poet-painter, was buried in Bunhill Fields.—Brewers' Hall, Addle Street, was repaired by W. F. Pocock.

1829.

EXCITEMENT was caused in the City by the stoppage of the banking house of Remington, Stephenson & Co. The Company suffered largely through the embezzlements of Rowland Stephenson, M.P. for Leominster, and Treasurer of St. Bartholomew's Hospital. He absconded (Jan., 1829).—Dr. Blomfield was installed Bishop of London at St. Paul's, by Dr. Copleston, Bishop of Llandaff (16 Jan.).—Sir William Curtis, Bart., died on 18 Jan.

He was originally a sea biscuit manufacturer, then he launched into the Greenland fisheries, and finally joined the banking house of C. Robarts, Curtis, Were, & Co. The chief steps of his civic career were as follows:—Alderman of Tower Ward, 1785-1821; Alderman of Bridge Ward Without, from 1821 to his death; M.P. for the City, 1790-1818, and 1820-1826; Sheriff, 1789-90; Lord Mayor, 1795. He was created a baronet in 1802. George IV presented his portrait, painted by Lawrence, to "his faithful and loyal subject, Sir William Curtis."

The Common Council resolved to petition for the abolition of the death punishment for forgery, and for the removal of Roman Catholic disabilities (Feb.). —The Right Hon. Sir Robert Peel received the freedom of the City, in recognition of his labours in the abridgment and consolidation of the Criminal Statutes (8 Ap.). —The new hall of Christ's Hospital was publicly opened on 29 May.

It was built in the Tudor style, being 187 feet long, 51½ wide, and 46½ high. The south front was flanked by towers, between which were eight windows separated by buttresses. A gallery was erected at each end of the Hall, and over one of them an organ.

Rioting and collision with police patrols on the part of Bethnal Green silk weavers induced the Corporation to withhold their intended grant of £1,000 towards the relief of the distressed operatives (June).—For the demolition of four houses in Upper Thames Street, in order to make room for the new approach to London Bridge, a tradesman was awarded £14,000, being £30,000 less than the amount claimed.—Shillibeer started the first pair of omnibuses in the Metropolis, from the Bank to the "Yorkshire Stingo," New Road. Each vehicle carried twenty-two passengers inside, only the driver riding outside; the fare was 1s. for the whole journey (4 July).—Thomas Shelton, the much esteemed Registrar of the Lord Mayor's Court, died on 10 July.—The new General Post Office was opened on 23 Sept. at five o'clock in the morning, the Holyhead mail being the first to enter the court-yard.

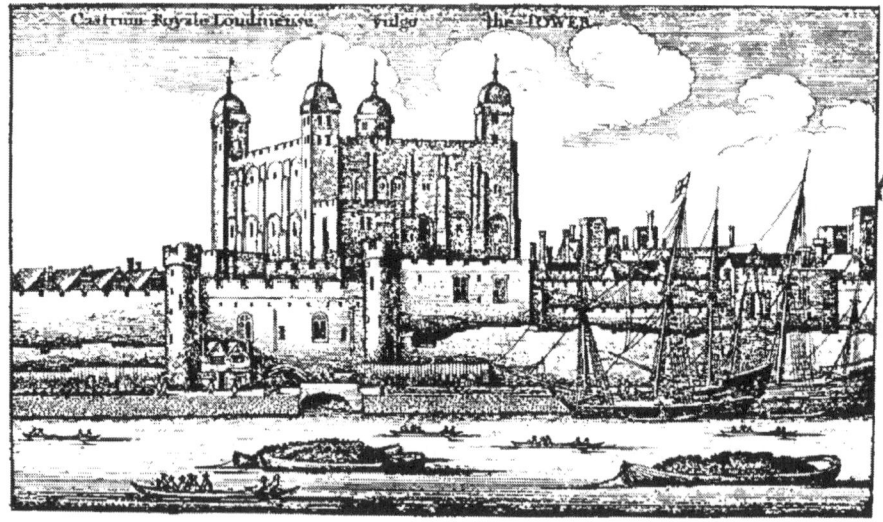

Tower of London, from etching by W. Hollar.

The structure was designed by Sir R. Smirke, R.A.; the material was Portland stone; the order, Ionic; the dimensions, 400 feet long, 130 wide, 64 high. The office stands in the parishes of St. Anne and St. Agnes, St. Leonard, and St. Michael-le-quern; 131 houses were displaced from its site. The chief departments were known as the Inland, Foreign, and Twopenny-post Offices. Letter carriers were conveyed from the General Post Office to various parts of London in vehicles resembling the new omnibuses.

Alderman John Crowder was elected Lord Mayor.—On Lord Mayor's day the tenor bell of St. Sepulchre's, Snow Hill, weighing 3,300 lbs., fell while in the act of ringing.—The new Fleet Market, or Farringdon Market, was opened on 20 Nov.

The market formed a quadrangle of 232 feet by 150. An avenue of shops ran round three sides. In the centre of the roof of the chief avenue a clock turret rose. The cost of the site and erection was £250,000. The street formerly called Fleet Market was now named Farringdon Street. Old Fleet Market had been open ninety-two years.

A new chapel was built on the site of the old Baptist meeting house in Devonshire Square, Bishopsgate, and was opened with a sermon by Rev. Thomas Binney.—St. Augustine's, Watling Street, was restored.—Butchers' Hall, Bartholomew Close, was destroyed by fire.—The old White Hart Inn, Bishopsgate, dating from 1480, was pulled down.—Old Goldsmiths' Hall was demolished.—William Hazlitt resided at No. 3 Bouverie Street.—Old Bethlehem, a thoroughfare running along the north of the former grounds of Bethlehem Hospital, having been rebuilt and widened, took its name of Liverpool Street (Bishopsgate) from Lord Liverpool.—The " City Canal," through the Isle of Dogs, which had been constructed by the Corporation, having proved a failure, it was sold to the West India Dock Company.—Towards the close of this year the Guildhall Library contained 2,800 volumes, and nearly 2,000 prints and 100 drawings, chiefly topographical views and portraits of civic celebrities. —The new police system for the metropolis was introduced.—The standards presented by the Corporation to the Light Horse Volunteers in 1780 were lodged in the Tower. The colours were given in token of the City's appreciation of the aid rendered by the Volunteers at the time of the Gordon Riots.

1830.

MAN was badly injured by one of the leopards in the Tower menagerie (2 Jan., 1830).—The House of Commons passed an Act establishing a horse market at West Smithfield every Thursday (Ap.).—The Common Council decided to petition for mitigation of the laws relating to capital punishment (28 May), and on 17 June further resolved to petition for relief from the "oath of adjuration against the Pretender and his successors," and against "the too common use of oaths generally."—King George IV died 26 June, and on the 28th William IV was proclaimed, with the customary ceremonies at Chancery Lane, Wood Street, Royal Exchange, and Aldgate.

Addresses of the usual loyal character were agreed to by the Court of Mayor and Aldermen and by the Common Council. But a Common Hall, held on 28 July, voted for presentation to His Majesty a lengthy document which reprobated fulsome adulation, and informed the King that "in the year in which your Majesty was born (1765) only eight millions of taxes were imposed upon the people of this country. At the present time at least sixty millions of taxes are annually wrung from the industry of the people." The war with France and America and the increase of poverty and crime were deplored. As the King refused to receive this address upon the throne, the livery declined to present it.

Peter Bossy, condemned for perjury, stood in the pillory at the Old Bailey on 22 June, being the last person so punished in London.—At the General Election, the following members were returned for the City : Aldermen Wood, Waithman, and Thompson, and Mr. W. Ward.—A public meeting at the City of London Tavern congratulated the people of Paris on the recent revolution. The Duke of Wellington ordered the Tower Ditch to be widened four feet, to prepare for the extra water expected to rush up the river on the removal of old London Bridge (Oct.).—Alderman John Key was elected Lord Mayor. Owing to fear of riot the King decided not to carry out his intention of visiting the City on Lord Mayor's day.

The Lord Mayor elect had written a letter on his own initiative to the Duke of Wellington, warning him to provide a guard for his person when proceeding to Guildhall on the 9th, as there were rumours of a design to attack his grace. This letter, coupled with other information, induced the Ministry to advise the King's abstention from the proposed visit, and Sir Robert Peel wrote to that effect to the Lord Mayor elect on Sunday, the 7th. The letter was published on Monday; great alarm spread over the Metropolis, business was suspended, the funds fell three per cent., the Tower moat was flooded by way of precaution, the guards at the Bank were doubled. On Monday

Old church of St. Dunstan-in-the-West.

a mob marched through the City to Westminster, where a conflict with the "new police," as they were called, took place. Tuesday saw a renewal of the disturbances in the West End. Some of the rioters diverted themselves by standing within Temple Bar and pelting the Metropolitan Police, who were stationed outside the City boundary. Shops in St. Paul's Churchyard, Ludgate Hill, and Fleet Street were kept closed. In the Court of Aldermen, held on the 9th (Tuesday), the Lord Mayor expressed regret at his hasty letter to the Duke. On Wednesday confidence was restored, and many people amused themselves by inspecting the magnificent but abortive decorations at the Guildhall. During the disturbances some five or six hundred constables were on duty in the City, including firemen, ticket-porters, and tackle-porters.

The Common Council resolved to petition the House of Commons for repeal of the duty on sea-borne coal (25 Nov.).—The objectionable passage in the inscription on the Monument relating to the alleged Papist connection with the

Fire of London ("sed furor Papisticus qui tam dira patravit nondum restinguitur"), was ordered by the Common Council to be removed (6 Dec.).—An Act was passed for enabling persons to take the oath according to the forms of their own religion (10 Dec.).—The Council were now considering the desirability of making the Gresham lectures more available to the public.

In excavating for the new Goldsmiths' Hall, a stone altar to Diana, 23 inches high, was discovered It is now preserved in Goldsmiths' Hall.—The "City Theatre," opened in Grub Street *circa* 1830, proved a failure. Grub Street now changed its name to Milton Street.—Bartholomew Chapel, used as a Dissenting place of worship, was destroyed by fire. It had once formed part of the old Priory —Sir Thomas Lawrence the distinguished painter, was buried at St. Paul's.—The Sailors' Home in East Smithfield was founded.—Old St Dunstan's, Fleet Street, having been taken down, the materials were put up to auction in 1829 and 1830. The sales included an iron standard, with copper vase, said to be 850 years old, a statue of Queen Elizabeth with crown and sceptre, and a stained glass painting of St Matthew.—Steamboat traffic had largely increased; competition had reduced the fare between London and Calais to 5s. and even 3s.—The number of steam-vessels connected with the Port of London was about fifty.—The City Gas Company maintained about 8,000 lamps, and its mains extended 50 miles.—The average number of oxen sold at Smithfield annually was 156,000; of sheep and lambs, 1,500,000; of calves, 21,000; of hogs, 20,000; the total value being estimated at £8,000,000.

1831.

HE anti-Catholic inscription on the Monument (*see* 6 Dec., 1830), was removed 26 Jan, 1831.—The Reform Bill, introduced in the House of Commons early in the year, re-introduced after the dissolution in April, and rejected by the Lords in October, created great enthusiasm in London.

On 4 Mar. the Common Council, in an address to the King, expressed their entire satisfaction with the measure then before Parliament and with the conduct of Earl Grey's Government. These opinions were confirmed by the Common Hall at a meeting on 7 Mar. Parliament was dissolved on 22 Ap; and on the 27th, at the Lord Mayor's instance, the City and other parts of London were illuminated in token of support of the Bill. At the General Election, the following members were returned for the City:—Aldermen Wood, Waithman, Thompson, and Venables. On 9 July Lord John Russell, who was in charge of the Bill in the House of Commons, received the freedom. "The Bill," said the Chamberlain, "has passed the second reading by a great majority; and in a few days your lordship will have the proud satisfaction of taking it up to the Lords." Lord Russell's reply hinted that the other House was not likely to throw out the Bill. It was, however, rejected by the Lords, an event which was deeply deplored in resolutions and addresses by the Common Hall and Common Council (8 and 10 Oct.).

Service was performed for the last time in the church of St. Michael, Crooked Lane, on 20 Mar., the edifice (built by Wren after the Great Fire) having to make way for the approaches to the new bridge. The bodies were removed from the churchyard.—Letters were now delivered (Ap.) to suburban quarters, within three miles of the General Post Office, without extra charge.—The first stone of the new church of St. Dunstan, Fleet Street, was laid on 7 July.—On 1 Aug. new London Bridge was opened by William IV and his Queen.

Business was suspended throughout the Metropolis. Great crowds cheered the King and Queen, and other royal personages, who attended the inaugural ceremony. The royal pavilion, composed of flags of all nations, was erected near the site of old Fishmongers' Hall, and was equal to the breadth of the bridge. An awning ran from the pavilion part-way across the bridge. Their Majesties journeyed from Somerset House by barge. The Reception Committee were attired in blue coats with white waistcoats and trousers. The bridge was opened by their Majesties walking over it, amid extraordinary enthusiasm. A balloon ascent took place at the same time. A banquet followed in the pavilion, the King drinking out of a gold cup presented by the Lord Mayor, and proposing the toast of "The trade and commerce of the City of London." The return journey was signalized by bell-ringing, discharge of artillery, and immense cheering. A gold medal, commemorative of the opening, was presented to the King.

The bridge, designed by John Rennie, and constructed by his son, Sir John Rennie, consists of five semi-elliptical arches, two of 130 feet, two of 140 feet, and the centre 152 feet 6 inches in span. The roadway has a width of 52 feet. Blue and white granite form the materials of the arches. The piers and abutments rest on timber platforms and piles. Seven years, five months, and thirteen days was the time occupied in the construction. Upwards of 800 workmen were employed; 40 lives were lost. The bridge lies 180 feet west of old London Bridge, which was left standing whilst the new one was in course of building. The total cost of the bridge and approaches was £2,556,170, of which Parliament contributed £192,000. Two medals, engraved by Benjamin Wyon, were struck by the Corporation, thus initiating the series of medals which they have issued in commemoration of public events. The Lord Mayor (the Right Hon. John Key) was created a baronet, and the Sheriffs (Chapman Marshall and William H. Poland) received the honour of knighthood.

Sign of Boar's Head, Eastcheap.

The Lord Mayor attended King William's coronation at Westminster Abbey (8 Sept.).—Sir John Key, Bart., was re-elected Lord Mayor for the ensuing year.—The Irish Society was ordered by the Common Council to present annually a copy of its resolutions, proceedings, receipts, and expenditure (27 Oct.).—Cholera made its appearance in the north of England, the first case occurring at Sunderland, 26 Oct. The disease thence spread in all directions. Special prayers were offered up in the Metropolis on 6 Nov.—New regulations were introduced by the Common Council under the provisions of the recently passed Coal Trade Act.

From 1810 to 1831 Crosby Hall, Bishopsgate, built by Sir John Crosby (died 1475), and once inhabited by Sir Thomas More, was leased to a firm of packers.—The Boar's Head Tavern, immortalised by Shakespeare, was demolished for the purpose of the new London Bridge approaches. The sign of the tavern is preserved in the Guildhall Museum.—Butchers' Hall, in Bartholomew Close, was re-built.

1832.

 PILOT, who was not free of the Watermen and Lightermen's Company, had been convicted by the Lord Mayor for navigating a steam vessel on the Thames, and, on appeal, the conviction was affirmed.——The Common Council awarded £3,000 to tradesmen, whose business had been depreciated by the altered approaches to London Bridge (29 Mar., 1832).——Cholera had now spread to London.

The disease first made its appearance in Rotherhithe, Southwark, and Limehouse. Clergymen were forbidden by the Bishop of London to allow bodies of persons, dying of cholera, to be brought into any church during the funeral service. The Custom House authorities refused clean bills of health to vessels leaving the Thames. The 21 Mar. was observed as a national fast-day. On that day a crowd of nearly 25,000 persons assembled in Finsbury Square, the Political Union having announced their intention of distributing food to the poor, and of conducting processions of distressed working people through different parts of the Metropolis. The demonstration was dispersed, amid much confusion, by the police. On 26 Oct. the Cholera Committee reported to the Common Council the disappearance of the disease from the City.

The City continued to be agitated by the great Reform Bill struggle.

The resignation of Earl Grey's Ministry drew from the Common Hall an address to the King, in which they declared that this step had spread "terror and dismay" amongst His Majesty's subjects.—— On 23 May the freedom of the City was presented to Thomas Attwood, a prominent politician of the Midlands, for his ability in uniting the intelligent and industrious artisans and the inhabitants generally of the Midland districts in their firm but peaceable pursuit of the great national object of Reform. In his reply Mr. Attwood remarked of the City : " It has ever stood in the van of the people in their fight for liberty ; and how proud shall we of Birmingham be to adopt so great a precedent ! " The Reform Bill passed the House of Lords on 4 June. On 11 July the freedom was presented to Earl Grey and Viscount Althorp (afterwards Earl Spencer) for their efforts on behalf of Parliamentary reform. The scene was portrayed in a painting by Benjamin R. Haydon. The Corporation struck a medal in honour of the occasion. A book, containing the signatures of the most distinguished guests at the entertainment which followed, is preserved in the Guildhall Library. On 18 June, the anniversary of Waterloo, the Duke of Wellington, now extremely unpopular on account of his opposition to the Reform Bill, was taunted with abusive epithets, while riding from the Mint through Fenchurch Street and Cheapside ; in Holborn he was even pelted with stones and mud, and had to take shelter in Lincoln's Inn. On 1 Nov. the Common Council granted £1,500 for the erection of almshouses to commemorate the passing of the Reform Bill. The Reform Bill had been so framed as to leave unimpaired the rights of the livery, amendments to that effect having been proposed by the special committee of the Common Council and accepted by the Government.

The King's escape from injury, when struck by a stone thrown by a discontented ex-pensioner, at Ascot races, formed the subject of congratulatory addresses from the Corporation and Common Hall (June).——The Common Council were considering a project for establishing a day and night police in the City (June).

The City police force was remodelled. The day police comprised fourteen officers and eighty-five constables, with some additional men to whom were assigned special duties; the Under Marshal superintended the force, which was under the ultimate control of the Court of Aldermen   The "Nightly Watch" was a distinct body, under the control of the Alderman and Common Council of each Ward

On 13 July the ceremony of commemoration of Sir Thomas Gresham was revived at the church of St. Helen, Bishopsgate, of which Sir Thomas had been a parishioner; the service was musical.—Sir Peter Laurie was chosen Lord Mayor.— The Committee of the House of Commons on the observance of the Sabbath-day, reported that "a systematic and widely-spread violation of the Lord's Day" was prevalent in London.—The Common Council voted an address of congratulation to Sir Thomas Denman, late Common Serjeant, on his becoming Lord Chief Justice.—At the General Election Grote, Wood, Waithman, and Key, were returned for the City (12 Dec.). —The responsibility of the Irish Society to the City Companies was legally tested by the Skinners' Company.

The matter was carried to the House of Lords, and Lord Lyndhurst, in pronouncing judgment in favour of the Irish Society, laid it down that they were not trustees for the private benefit of the Companies. They were liable to the Corporation, and could be restrained, in case of misconduct, by the Corporation or the Crown. In accordance with the provisions of this judgment, the Corporation has always exercised a visitorial power over the Society.

The Newgate Street entrance to Christ's Hospital was opened, and the new Grammar and Mathematical Schools, built by John Shaw, junr.—Thomas Hardy, who was tried with Horne Tooke in 1794 for high treason, was buried in Bunhill Fields, his monument being designed by John W. Papworth.—The Bunhill Fields Burial Ground was closed this year. From 1665 to 1832 the bodies registered as interred here numbered 123,000.—The Bank of England was stated to possess assets of £17,433,000 over and above all its liabilities.

1833.

A PLOT of ground on the east side of the Tower ditch was consecrated for a military burial place (25 Jan, 1833).—Alderman Robert Waithman's death, on 6 Feb., occasioned general and deep regret.

He carried on business first at the south end of Fleet Market, afterwards in New Bridge Street   In 1796 he was elected on the Common Council, on five occasions he was chosen M P. for the City, he was elected Alderman of Farringdon Without in 1818; served as Sheriff in 1820, and Lord Mayor in 1823-4. He figured as a strenuous opponent of free trade. The familiar obelisk in Ludgate Circus was erected to his memory. A critic of the time censured its proportions, and described it as "supremely contemptible."

Another notable City personage, Sir William Domville, Bart., died on 8 Feb., at the age of ninety.

He was Sheriff in 1804; elected Alderman of Queenhithe in 1805; Lord Mayor in 1813-14. His baronetcy was conferred on the occasion of the visit to the City of the Prince Regent, the King of Prussia and the Emperor of Russia. His portrait was painted by William Owen, for the Stationers' Company, of which guild he was Master in 1804 and a Liveryman for nearly seventy years.

On the death of Mr. Waithman, Mr. G. Lyall was elected M.P. in his place (27 Feb.).—The Common Council resolved to petition against the house and window

Portrait of Alderman Waithman.

taxes (21 Mar.) and in favour of abolition of slavery in British Colonies (3 Ap.).—An epidemic of influenza, the severest known for fifty years past, raged in London in April, attacking numerous employés in the Bank of England and other public offices. —The Metropolis was agitated by the demands of the National Union of the Working Classes. A policeman was killed at an open-air meeting in Cold-bath Fields (13 May). —On the occasion of the charity children's anniversary the Queen attended service at St. Paul's, and afterwards accepted hospitality at the Mansion House, where a complimentary address was presented (13 June). The Common Council subsequently affirmed that, whilst they endorsed the loyal sentiments of the address, it was irregular and unauthorised.—A Royal Commission to enquire into Municipal Corporations was appointed on 18 July.

The Court of the Merchant Taylors' Company declined to tender any information to the Commissioners on the grounds that (1) their oath of office precluded them from disclosing detailed particulars as to the disposition of their charitable funds; and that (2) the inquiry was inconsistent with the security of the property and rights of the subject. The Court relied upon the legal authority of Sir James Scarlett.

Sir John Key having retired, Mr. W. Crawford was elected, as one of the City representatives, in his place (12 Aug.).—Much interest was aroused by a case heard before the Lord Mayor on 11 Oct., when, at the instance of the Excise, he ordered a large quantity of "British Leaf," i.e. elm, sloe and willow leaves, to be burned as being an injurious imitation of tea.—Alderman Charles Farebrother was chosen Lord Mayor.—Blackfriars Bridge, though it had been built less than sixty-five years, had been constantly in need of repair. It also suffered from the removal of London Bridge, which served as a barrier against the scour of the tide.

An examination of the structure by Messrs Walker and Burges revealed serious defects, and repairs were ordered, which cost the Corporation £105,000, the foundations being strengthened, the cutwaters re-cased, and the balustrade re-placed by a solid parapet.—Fishmongers' Hall was erected, 1831-33, at the north-west corner of London Bridge, from the designs of Henry Roberts. The splendidly decorated banqueting room is 73 feet long, 38 wide and 33 high.—The City of London Club was built in Old Broad Street after the designs of Philip Hardwick, R.A.—The new edifice of St. Dunstan-in-the-West was consecrated; the tower, 130 feet in height, was copied from that of St. Helen at York.—The expense of the night-watch in the City for this year was £42,077 It had been about that amount for some years past.

1834.

SO crowded had the streets of London become with omnibuses and "cabriolets" that serious complaints were frequent. (1834).

A report laid before the Common Council (30 Jan.) affirmed that much obstruction was thus occasioned, which was extremely detrimental to the interest of traders; it proceeded to recommend application to Parliament for the establishment of stands and a limitation of the number of vehicles plying for hire. It was in December of this year that Joseph Aloysius Hansom took out a patent for his cab.

Considerable protests were raised in various City parishes against a proposed demolition of a number of City churches, the Archbishop of Canterbury and the Bishop of London joining in the remonstrance.—Twelve convicts attempted to escape from Newgate by loosening the masonry of the north wall (24 Mar.).— Captain Ross was accorded the City freedom, in recognition of his bravery in conducting an expedition to discover the north-west passage (27 Mar.).—The Common Council decided to petition Parliament for power to enlarge Smithfield Market, as an alternative to the erection of a Cattle Market at Islington (10 Ap.).—On the same date the Council resolved to approach the King with a request to bestow a charter on the London University [University College], conferring power to grant degrees.—A mass meeting of Trade-Unionists, to protest against the transportation of six Dorsetshire labourers, for administering illegal oaths, took place at Copenhagen Fields on 21 Ap.—The Common Council resolved to petition for the removal of all taxes "which interfere with the diffusion of knowledge" (17 July).—The Queen embarked for Saxe-Meiningen on 5 July, and was accompanied as far as Southend by the Lord Mayor and the different Companies, in their barges. On her return (21 Aug) she was received at Woolwich by the civic representatives Addresses from the Corporation congratulated their Majesties on the Queen's safe return (27 Aug.).—Earl Grey's retirement from office was marked by an appreciative address, which alluded particularly to his exertions on behalf of Parliamentary Reform (resolved 9 Aug.).—On 13 Aug. an Act for establishing the City of London School on the site of Honey Lane Market, and out of funds derived from the John Carpenter estates, received the royal assent.—Alderman Henry Winchester was elected Lord Mayor.—An address to the King (agreed to on 27th) expressed gratitude for His Majesty's hearty co-operation in the passage of the Reform Bill.—The Central Criminal Court was established this year by the Act of Parliament.

The judges of the Court were to be the Lord Mayor, the Lord Chancellor or the Lord Keeper of the Great Seal, all the judges of the High Court, the Dean of Arches, the Aldermen of the City of London, the Recorder, the Common Serjeant, and any retired judges or others whom the Crown might appoint. Precepts for summoning jurors are usually signed by the Lord Mayor and the Recorder. The dates of the Sessions, which are held twelve times a year, are fixed by the judges of the High Court in consultation with the Lord Mayor and Aldermen. The duty of attending the Sessions is borne by the Aldermen in rotation The Sheriffs of London and Middlesex, Essex, and Kent are charged with the execution of all precepts and process as directed by the judges The Corporation bears the larger part of the expense connected with the administration of justice at the Court.— In November the Tower menagerie was removed. It occupied the site of the present refreshment rooms. The collection of animals commenced in 1235, when the Emperor Frederick sent Henry III a gift of three leopards, in token of his regal shield of arms.—In the course of an inquiry before the Corporation Commissioners, in reference to the Dyers' Company, it was stated that this Company kept swans on the Thames, at Richmond, Twickenham, and as far up as Oxford, at a cost of £300 a year.—Thomas Stothard, R.A., was buried in Bunhill Fields Burial Ground.—Lloyd's Register of British and Foreign Shipping was established for the survey and classification of vessels.—The iron gates and railings at the entrance to Christ's Hospital were erected.—An unusually high tide inundated the cellars of riverside houses, and overflowed the underground stores at the Tower.

1835.

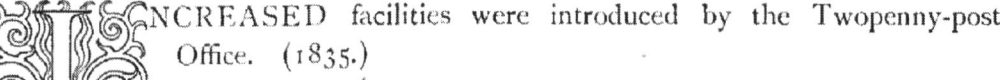

INCREASED facilities were introduced by the Twopenny-post Office. (1835.)

There were now six deliveries and six collections of letters daily in London. The country delivery of the twopenny-post was extended from 9 miles to a circle of 12 miles from the General Post Office. Newspaper packets, open at the ends, passed for a penny within the three-mile radius.

At the General Election, the following members were chosen for the City: Sir Matthew Wood, James Pattison, William Crawford, and George Grote (5 Jan.). —Alderman Sir Charles Flower, Bart. (Alderman of Cornhill 1801, Sheriff 1799, Lord Mayor 1808), died on 15 Feb., aged 72, leaving £550,000. His fortune was accumulated by Government contracts for provisions in time of war; he was buried in Aldgate churchyard.—The Common Council decided that all persons holding corporate offices, or occupying business premises in the City, should be compelled to take up their freedom, the redemption fee being fixed at £5.—A large number of public works, mostly forming part of the scheme of approaches to London Bridge, were in progress.

The new line of street at the western end of Cornhill had been continued; Little Eastcheap and Little Tower Street were being widened; Princes Street was in process of widening; a like improvement was contemplated for Upper Thames Street and Gracechurch Street; a new thoroughfare was planned through the squalid quarter of Saffron Hill.—The work of the Thames Tunnel was being successfully continued.—The London and Birmingham Railway was daily approaching the Metropolis, and a terminus at "Euston Grove" was projected.—New Goldsmiths' Hall, Foster Lane, was opened 15 July; it is 150 feet long by 100 feet broad; of Corinthian style; the exterior of Portland stone, resting on a granite plinth; it was designed by Philip Hardwick, R.A.—The London and Greenwich Railway was nearing completion, 500 arches having been raised by July.

The Common Council resolved that aldermen should be subject to periodical election every seven years (28 Mar.).—A bill-poster was reprimanded by the Lord Mayor for posting a seditious placard on the occasion of a dinner given at Merchant Taylors' Hall to Sir Robert Peel.—Mr. David Salomons was elected Sheriff, being the first Jew ever raised to the office.—The first stone of the City of London School, on the site of Honey Lane Market in Milk Street, was laid by Lord Brougham (21 Oct.).—Alderman William Taylor Copeland was elected Lord Mayor. —On 6 Nov. died Alderman John Thomas Thorp, Governor of the Irish Society (Sheriff 1815, Alderman of Aldgate 1817, Lord Mayor 1820; M.P. for the City in 1818, and for Arundel in 1826, 1830 and 1831).—On 26 Nov. the Common Council passed a severe vote of censure upon the late Lord Mayor Winchester, for his violation of the rules of the Council's procedure, his refusal to call Common Halls and Courts of Common Council on requisition, and for his arrogant conduct in the chair.

119 new companies were started in London this year, having a total capital of over £56,000,000, thirty-four millions being raised for railways.—The Atlas Assurance Office was erected at the corner of King Street and Cheapside.—Much excitement reigned in the money-market, owing to the fall in Spanish and Portuguese funds, and speculation in joint-stock enterprise. The Royal Exchange was, at times, so packed with speculators that the beadle was compelled to drive them away before the merchants could assemble for the transaction of business.

1836.

THE issue of fourpenny-pieces was authorised in the *London Gazette* of 3 Feb., 1836.— The Common Council voted a subscription in relief of the Protestant clergy in Ireland, and censured "one branch of the Legislature" for its refusal to introduce improved methods of tithe-payment in Ireland (17 Feb.).—A number of Aldgate citizens petitioned against the intrusion of railroads.—The Common Council resolved to petition against flogging in the army (17 Mar.).—Samuel Dixon, "Father of the Court" (so termed as being the longest elected member of the Common Council), died on 19 May. In 1833 he had been presented by 209 members and officers of the Corporation with a vase bearing an inscription testifying their high esteem.—The Council indicated their conviction, by a resolution of 31 May, of the value which municipal institutions would have in the case of Ireland, and expressed regret at the rejection by the House of Lords of a

Oriel Window of Crosby Hall.

measure for the improvement of Irish municipal government.—On 22 June the Council signified warm approval of a measure for removing religious disabilities in the case of Jews.—The foundation-stone of the restored Crosby Hall was laid on

27 June.—A Newgate convict, who had scaled the wall of the prison and escaped over the roof of an adjoining house, was re-captured in Hampshire.—A movement, set on foot by the Bishop of London, had for its object increased provision of churches in the Metropolis; large subscriptions were contributed to the fund (July).—The Committee of the whole court of Common Council, appointed in Mar., 1834, to consider the question of Corporate Reform, was dissolved (13 Oct.).—Alderman Thomas Kelly was elected Lord Mayor.—The London and Greenwich Railway was opened by the Lord Mayor on 14 Dec.

The railway was now complete from London Bridge to Deptford. The Lord Mayor and suite rode in a special train, followed by four others, stopping every few minutes to view the line.— The Common Council at this period were frequently occupied with the subject of railways, the following undertakings being reported on by the Committee for Letting the City's Lands: London and Brighton (Stephenson's line); London and Blackwall; Great Western; London and Gravesend; Deptford; Thames Haven and Dock; London and Brighton (Rennie's line); London, Shoreham and Brighton (Cundy's line); London and Cambridge; London and Croydon; London and Dover; London and Norwich; London Grand Junction.

The Common Council voted £500 for the relief of Polish refugees recently arrived.

The privileges of the Copyright Act were taken away from Sion College and other libraries, and a money compensation granted.—The total number of letters transmitted through the twopenny and threepenny posts this year was 13,589,925.

1837.

PARLIAMENTARY Committee was appointed by the Common Council, consisting of the Lord Mayor, the chairmen of the several Committees, three Aldermen, and thirty Common Councilmen, one-fourth part to retire every year. (1837.)—An epidemic of influenza caused much dislocation of work in the public offices, many deaths occurring in the Naval Hospital at Greenwich, the Royal Military College at Chelsea, in workhouses, &c.—The City of London School, Milk Street, was opened on 2 Feb. by the Lord Mayor.

The inaugural address was delivered by the Rev. Dr. Ritchie. Four hundred pupils were registered, the first Head Master being the Rev. Dr. J. A. Giles. The building, which cost the Corporation £20,000, was designed by Mr. J. B. Bunning, who, not long afterwards, was appointed City Surveyor. A commemorative medal was struck by order of the Common Council. The founder of the School was John Carpenter, "Common Clerk" of the City of London in the reign of Henry V, and a man of superior culture for those times. He compiled the *Liber Albus*, and was executor to the famous Richard Whittington. By his will he left books to be chained in the Guildhall "common library" for the use of students. He also bequeathed lands and tenements in Thames Street, Bridge Street, St. Giles-in-the-Fields, Westcheap, and Houndsditch, for the up-bringing of four poor children. This property constituted the original endowment, from which the City of London School was built. The Court of Common Council extended the bequest in 1827. In 1829 an endowment of the obsolete London Workhouse, amounting to about £300 per annum, was made over to the Corporation, who added £2,000, another £1,000 being raised by subscription; the whole to be devoted to endowing a public school. Various difficulties prevented the realisation of this scheme. In May, 1833, the Committee for Letting the City's lands reported that the Carpenter estates yielded £900 yearly, and recommended that the money should be devoted, with the sums just referred to, to the purpose of a new school An Act was passed on 13 Aug., 1834, to this effect, and directed that the site of Honey Lane Market should be utilised The school was to have for its object "the religious and virtuous education of boys, and instructing them in the higher branches of literature and all other useful learning." The first and second masters were to be certified as to proper qualifications by six professors of King's College and University College.

An attempt was made at the East India House to assassinate Mr. Loch, deputy-chairman of the Company (15 Mar.).—The Commissioners of Inquiry into the Municipal Corporations of England and Wales presented a special supplementary report, prepared by their late Chairman, Sir Francis Palgrave, upon the institutions of the City of London (25 Ap.).—A petition was agreed to by the Common Council in favour of a fair and just equalisation of the land tax.—Under the presidency of the Lord Mayor a public meeting was held at the Mansion House to consider means for alleviating the distress among the population of the Western Highlands, the superseding of kelp by barilla in manufactures being a leading cause of the destitution.—King William IV died early in the morning of 20 June. The Lord Mayor and Aldermen attended upon the Princess Victoria at Kensington Palace, and joined in the signature of the declaration of her accession.

The civic dignitaries attended at St. James's Palace on 21 June to hear the Queen proclaimed by Garter King-at-Arms, and then, forming in procession, returned to the City to proclaim the Sovereign's accession in the customary form.—On Friday, 23 June, the Common Council resolved on an address to Her Majesty, acknowledging the mercy of Providence "in prolonging the life of our late beloved Monarch to a period when your Majesty, under the maternal care of your illustrious parent, became qualified to fill the throne of this great Empire." A similar address was presented from the Court of Mayor and Aldermen, and another followed on 5 July from the Common Hall —The Queen was present at the Mayoralty banquet on 9 Nov. Her progress through the City was greeted with deafening cheers and bell-ringing, the house-fronts being decorated with bunting and greenery. At St. Paul's, where booths and stands were erected for the members of City Companies and the boys of Christ's Hospital, the royal carriage halted while the senior scholar of Christ's Hospital delivered an address of congratulation. Her Majesty wore a pink satin dress, shot with silver, her head being adorned with a diamond circlet. On her arrival at Guildhall the Recorder read an address of congratulation. The banquet which followed is represented in the well-known etching by Thomas Deighton. The Corporation struck a commemorative medal.

Mr. Moses Montefiore was chosen Sheriff; Ald. Salomons (1835) and he were the first Jews to serve the office.—The first stone of the Leathersellers' Company's new almshouses at Barnet was laid on 25 July.—At the General Election, the four representatives elected for the City were Grote, Wood, Crawford, and Pattison (22 July). —A meeting was held at the "King's Head," Poultry, in aid of the distressed Paisley weavers.—The Gresham Lectures continued this year to occupy the attention of the Common Council. It was arranged (5 Oct.) that the Music and Astronomy Lectures should be delivered in the Theatre of the City of London School.—The Council resolved on a petition for reduced and equalised postage.—Alderman John

Burning of Second Royal Exchange.

Cowan was elected Lord Mayor. The Common Council voted in favour of the repeal of the duties on fire, life, and marine insurance policies.—St. Paul's Cathedral was opened to the public free of charge (14 Dec.).

A new roof was placed on the church of St. Sepulchre, Old Bailey.

1838.

CONSIDERABLE improvements had recently been made in the gaol of Newgate; the prisoners' quarters enlarged; separate confinement partially introduced; silence enforced; hot and cold baths furnished, etc.—The Royal Exchange was burned down on 10 Jan., 1838.

This was the second Exchange. It was built by Edward Jarman, and was quadrangular in plan. The chief features were, a wooden clock-tower on the south; an inner cloister; a "pawn," or upper floor, above for the sale of gloves, ribbons etc.; statues, in niches, of various sovereigns, from Edward I onwards, mostly executed by Caius Gabriel Cibber; Gresham's statue, carved by Edward Pierce; and Charles II's, by Grinling Gibbons. The fire began in Lloyd's Rooms shortly after 10 p.m. The last air, played by the chimes at midnight, was "There's nae luck about the house." The conflagration was

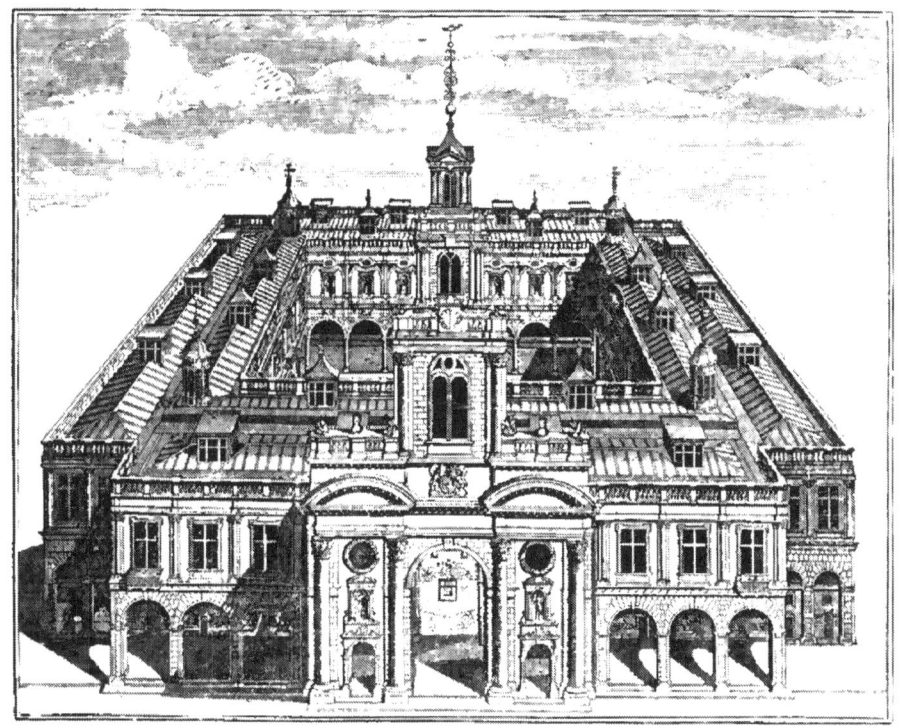

Second Royal Exchange (Exterior).

seen at a distance of 24 miles.—Among the items of the sale of salvage may be noted sixteen statues, the porter's large hand-bell (rung daily before the closing of the Exchange), City griffins, figures of Europe, Asia, Africa, and America, etc. The grasshopper vane was not included in the sale.

Lord Denman's decision in a long-pending case established the right of the Watermen's Company to regulate the speed, of steam vessels between London Bridge and Limehouse Reach; the Company's by-laws laid down a maximum of five miles per hour (16 Jan.).—A severe frost, lasting from 20 Jan. to 6 Feb., produced a block on the Thames; people crossed the frozen river below bridge; skittles were played opposite the Custom House; fires were lighted and refreshments sold on the ice.—The freedom was this year conferred upon two distinguished men.

1. Mr. Andrew Stevenson, the American Minister in London; he intimated, however (22 Feb.), that his position as citizen of the United States precluded him from accepting the honour. 2. Mr. Thomas Clarkson, in recognition of his exertions in securing the suppression of the slave-trade. On account of his advanced age Mr. Clarkson was admitted privately to the freedom at the Mansion House (15 Apr.). A bust of the philanthropist was executed by order of the Corporation.

Arcades of Second Royal Exchange.

London was at this time terrorised by the extraordinary antics of "Spring-heeled Jack," who specially selected women for attack (Feb.).—Sir Richard Carr Glyn, Bart., the well-known banker, died on 27 Ap., aged eighty-three.

He was elected Alderman of Bishopsgate, 1790; Sheriff, 1790; Lord Mayor, 1798-9; M.P. for St. Ives, 1796-1802; created a Baronet, 1820; became Father of the Corporation in 1829 on removing to Bridge Ward Without; President of Bridewell and Bethlehem Hospitals.

Sir Robert Peel was entertained at Merchant Taylors' Hall by 300 Conservative Members of Parliament (12 May).—Queen Victoria's Coronation took place on 28 June. The Corporation gave a banquet, in honour of the event, at the Guildhall on 13 July; the guests including the Ambassadors, the Duke of Wellington and Marshal Soult, the two latter being toasted together.—The

Common Council voted £500 towards the expense of a statue to the Duke of Wellington, in appreciation of his services in obtaining for the citizens the London Bridge Approaches Act (19 July).—The first stone of an extension of Bethlehem Hospital was laid by Sir P. Laurie (26 July).—A new synagogue, erected on the site of warehouses belonging to the East India Company, in Great St. Helen's, was opened by the Chief Rabbi on 13 Sept.—Alderman Atkins died 26 Oct., aged seventy-eight.

He was Alderman of Walbrook, 1808; Sheriff, 1809; Lord Mayor, 1818, M.P for Arundel, 1808, 1826, 1830, 1831, and for the City in 1812. At first a Whig, he subsequently opposed Parliamentary Reform.

Alderman Samuel Wilson was elected Lord Mayor.

Improvements were effected in Eastcheap, Little Tower Street, and Gracechurch Street, Upper Thames Street was widened from Eastcheap to Fish-Street-Hill Smithfield was repaved over an area of six acres, and the rails and pens were re arranged —The husting platform was removed from the east end of Guildhall, and three old figures of Edward VI and Charles I and his Queen were placed there in niches; these figures had formerly adorned the front of the Guildhall Chapel —The London and Westminster Bank was erected in Lothbury, 1837-8, from designs by C R Cockerell, R.A., and Sir W. Tite.—The enforcement of the Act passed by the Common Council with reference to the licensing of carts was entrusted to the General Purposes Committee.

1839.

THE Corporation, desirous of maintaining the control over its own police, made successful efforts to obtain the exemption of the City from the Metropolis Police Act, 1839.

An address of the Common Council to Her Majesty (resolved 12 Mar.) referred to the Charter granted to the City by William I, and confirmed by succeeding sovereigns, and to the reversal, in the reign of William III, of the judgment in a *quo warranto* obtained by Charles II (whereby the privileges of the City had been arbitrarily curtailed); and complained of the proposal to include the City within the operation of the new Police Bill. The brevity of the Queen's reply drew an expression of regret from the Council In the report of the Police Committee on the City Police Act (26 Sept.), it was pointed out that the Council would be required to appoint a Commissioner at a salary of not less than £800. For the purposes of the new Act the Council decided to revise the assessment of City property. On 4 Oct the Committee recommended a salary of £1,000 for the Commissioner, but the Council modified the proposal to £800 per annum, with the provision of "a suitable house, with offices." For the purposes of the Act it was resolved that the precincts of St. Bartholomew the Great and St. Bartholomew the Less should be annexed to the Ward of Farringdon Without; the Liberty of St. James, Duke's Place, to the Ward of Aldgate; the Liberty of Blackfriars to Farringdon Within , and the Liberties of Whitefriars and Bridewell precinct to Farringdon Without. Daniel Whittle Harvey was elected Commissioner on 31 Oct. The Police rate was fixed at 8d. in the pound.

The Common Council resolved to petition the House of Commons in favour of Mr. Rowland Hill's penny postage scheme (11 July).—The Lord Mayor returned, on 27 July, from a six-days' progress "on the business of the conservancy of the Thames."

The diversions included a visit to Windsor Castle, a public dinner at the "White Hart" in the royal borough, and a landing on Magna Charta Island. On this latter occasion the Lady Mayoress was presented with a bouquet, in a cornucopia of white cornelian and gold, by the son of Mr. Harcourt, M P. The ceremony was viewed by crowds of people on the river banks; 120 boys and girls from a charity school stood by the landing-place, dressed in mediæval costume; the state-barge, on its departure, was saluted with guns

The Queen presented her portrait to the Corporation (July).—The Chartist National Convention moved its headquarters from Bolt Court to the Arundel Coffee House, Strand (6 Aug.). On Sunday, 11 Aug., 500 Chartists walked in procession from Smithfield to St. Paul's Cathedral, the majority wearing red ribbons in their button-holes; but they conducted themselves peaceably during divine service.—Sir Robert Peel was entertained by the Goldsmiths' Company at their Hall on 29th Aug.—Margaret Moyes committed suicide by throwing herself from the Monument (11 Sept.), this being the fourth occurrence of the kind; a fifth took place on 18 Oct, when a boy, named Hawes, was killed.—Alderman Scholey died, aged 81, on 4 Oct. (he was 34 years alderman of Dowgate, Sheriff 1804, Mayor 1812).—Alderman Chapman Marshall was chosen Lord Mayor.

Winchester House, Broad Street, was demolished It was the last remnant of a pile of buildings erected by Sir William Powlet, or Paulet (created Marquis of Winchester in 1551), on the site of the Austin Friars' Monastery Winchester House was a picturesque, three-storied structure of red brick with stone dressings, and had been used for some time as warehouses—So flourishing was the condition of Christ's Hospital that 200 presentations, for the admission of children, were made this year.—The Thames Police were now merged with the Metropolitan force —The business of the Clearing-house amounted this year to £954,401,600.

1840.

 DISPUTE occurred in 1840 between the Corporation and the House of Commons, in the course of which the Sheriffs, William Evans and John Wheelton, were imprisoned for an alleged breach of privilege.

Stockdale, a printer, sued Messrs Hansard, printers to the House of Commons, for publishing in the Report of the Commissioners of Prisons certain strictures on books printed by himself Recovering £600 damages, he issued a Fi. fa. to the Sheriff of Middlesex to levy that amount. The Sheriffs complied. Stockdale began another action, but was committed to custody for contempt (17 Jan.)

On 21 Jan. the Sheriffs, who had expressed their regret at having come into collision with the Commons, were also committed to the custody of the Serjeant-at-arms. The Court of Common Council resolutely supported the Sheriffs all through the proceedings, on the ground that they had exercised the "imperative duties of their high and distinguished office, as declared by Her Majesty's Court of Queen's Bench, in a legal and constitutional manner." An address from the Common Hall to the Queen (24 Feb) pointed out that the Sheriffs had been arrested "by the order of a body of men who form only one-third part of the Legislature." On 12 Feb Mr. Sheriff Wheelton was discharged on account of ill-health, but Mr. Evans was not released till 6 May An elaborate report on the whole case of the Sheriffs was laid before the Common Council on 1 June. Each of the Sheriffs was presented by the Corporation with a piece of plate at a public dinner on 12 June, 1841.

Addresses of congratulation on the marriage of the Queen and Prince Albert were presented by the Court of Aldermen, the Common Council, and Common Hall (Feb. and Mar.).—On 2 Ap. died Sir Richard Phillips.

He founded the *Leicester Herald* in 1790; suffered, in 1793, a year's imprisonment in Leicester Gaol for selling Paine's "Rights of Man" With Priestley and other literary men he established the *Monthly Magazine* in 1796. He carried on an extensive publishing business in Bridge Street Sheriff, 1807; Knighted, 1808. He published his "Memoirs" in 1808

The Council granted £100 to the Society for the abolition of the use of children in chimney-sweeping —The freedom of the City was presented to Sir Thomas Phillips, Mayor of Newport, who had displayed much firmness at the time of the Chartist riots (7 Ap); to Lieut.-General Sir John Colborne (Lord Seaton), for his resolute administration when in command of the forces in Canada (21 May); and to the Prince Consort (28 Aug).—An Act of Common Council was passed (8 May) reforming the mode of election of Councilmen.

Four members each were allotted to the Wards of Bassishaw and Lime Street; six each to Dowgate, Candlewick, Cordwainer, Cornhill, Queenhithe, Vintry, and Walbrook, eight each to Bread Street, Bridge, Billingsgate, Broad Street, Cheap, Coleman Street, Cripplegate Within, Cripplegate Without, Tower, Langbourn, Castle Baynard, Aldersgate, Aldgate, and Portsoken; fourteen each to Bishopsgate and Farringdon Within; sixteen to Farringdon Without.

Addresses from the Corporation felicitated the Queen on her escape on the occasion of the outrage by Oxford (11 and 24 June).—A report of the Markets Committee recommending a limitation of the time allowed for Bartholomew Fair was approved by the Council (2 July). The report expressed the hope that before many years had elapsed the Fair would die out without formal suppression.— On 30 July died Alderman William Venables, aged 54, Alderman of Queenhithe, 1821, Sheriff, 1821; Lord Mayor, 1825.—Congratulations on the birth of the Princess Royal were conveyed in addresses from the Corporation (Nov.).— Alderman Thomas Johnson was elected Lord Mayor.—£1,000 were granted by the Council in aid of a new school being erected by the British and Foreign School Society (10 Dec.).

At this period several old-time residences still stood in Leadenhall Street; in Lime Street there existed the 17th century mansion of Sir Thomas Abney, and, near the Church of St Andrew Undershaft, the house in which Stow had lived. Gardens lay at the back of Leadenhall and Lime Streets; the orchards here having been celebrated for their apples.—The Guildhall Library now contained nearly 10,000 volumes; among the additional premises obtained was a room to accommodate a Museum A new edition of the Catalogue was prepared by Mr Herbert, the librarian. An experiment of keeping the library open in the evening did not meet with success —The church of St. Bartholomew, by the Exchange, was pulled down.—Armourers' and Brasiers' Hall, in Coleman Street, was erected from the designs of J. H. Good, Junr., on the site of the old Hall —The "Cock Tavern," behind the Royal Exchange, was demolished.—Dyers' Hall was pulled down and rebuilt. —The Wesleyan Centenary Hall and Mission House, Bishopsgate Street Within, was erected from the designs of W. F. Pocock, 1839–40 —The repairs to Blackfriars Bridge were completed —Courvoisier, the murderer of Lord William Russell, was confined in and executed at Newgate.— Edward Oxford was also imprisoned here for shooting at Her Majesty.—The Penny Postage system came into operation this year.

1841.

SPITALFIELDS and Streatham churches were seriously injured by a violent thunderstorm which broke over the Metropolis (3 Jan., 1841).—The Common Council, being of opinion that the present law was adequate to the City's needs, resolved to make representations to Lord John Russell against including the City in the Poor Law Amendment Bill (25 Feb.).—The Common Council expressed its preference for a viaduct over Farringdon Street rather than a proposed plan for filling up the hollow (21 June).—Parliament having been dissolved on 23 June, Lord John Russell sought the suffrages of the City. The elected members (29 June) were Messrs. John Masterman and George Lyall (Conservatives), and Sir M. Wood and Lord John Russell (Liberals).—*Punch* was first issued on 17 July.—The Court of Common Council were now contemplating the erection of buildings for the Courts of Queen's Bench, Exchequer, and Common Pleas on the east side of Guildhall Yard (17 Sept.).—The freedom was presented to Admiral Sir Robert Stopford and Commodore Sir Charles Napier, in recognition of their gallantry in the recent war off the Syrian Coast (23 Sept.); and, for services on the same occasion, to Sir Charles Felix Smith (25 Nov.).—An unusually high tide occurred, the water being 31 feet deep at the entrance of St. Katharine's Dock (18 Oct.).—The question of the City's jurisdiction in Southwark was considered by the Common Council (28 Oct.).

The General Purposes Committee reported that "the Corporation of London, by various ancient charters, have the jurisdiction and appointment of the office of High Bailiff for the execution of the criminal and civil process of the local Courts within the jurisdiction. The Corporation are likewise Lords of three Manors situate within the Borough, of which the Recorder is High Steward The High Steward holds Courts Leet three times in the year, and presides in the Borough Court of Record,

The Right Hon. the Lord Mayor and the Aldermen who have passed the Chair hold Sessions of the Peace within the Borough. The Aldermen who have passed the Chair are, by charter, Justices of the Peace within the Borough, and have been accustomed for several years past to hold daily sittings at the Town Hall, for the hearing of all cases cognizable by Magistrates." The Committee reported that the Police Act, 2 & 3 Vict., c. 47, had much abridged the City's jurisdiction, and that the Aldermen had ceased to give their attendance in Southwark Counsel's opinion had been given to the effect that this discontinuance would not affect the City's rights and privileges in Southwark. The Council approved the report.

A fire took place at the Tower, in the Grand Storehouse and Small Armoury. It raged for two hours before water could be procured. The regalia were saved. The damage was estimated at £200,000.—Alderman John Pirie was chosen Lord Mayor.—The birth of the Prince of Wales drew forth loyal addresses from the Corporation (10 Nov.).—The number of constables for the City police was fixed at 542 (2 Dec.).—On 10 Dec. died Samuel Birch, aged eighty-four, founder of the well-known firm in Cornhill.

He was elected to the Common Council, for the Ward of Cornhill, in 1781; in 1785 he published "Consilia," in 1788, a poem entitled "The Abbey of Ambresbury," and in 1793, "The Mariners," a play. In 1789 he spoke against the repeal of the Corporation and Test Acts. He proposed the formation of a volunteer force, and, at the Royal review in 1803, commanded the 1st regiment of the City volunteers He received the freedom of Dublin, in 1803, for his opposition to Catholic Emancipation, on which subject he wrote two pamphlets. Elected Alderman of Candlewick, 1807; Sheriff, 1811; Lord Mayor, 1814; resigned the Alderman's gown, 1840.

Excavations for the new Royal Exchange brought to light a large number of Roman relics which had been deposited in a pit. The discoveries included stucco work, Samian ware, an amphora, terra-cotta lamps, wooden tablets for wax, metal styles, sandals, military shoes, a strigil, coins of Vespasian and Domitian, etc. These antiquities formed the foundation of the Museum attached to the Guildhall Library —The widening of Newgate Street and Fetter Lane cost the Corporation £2,000.—The *Times* was sued for libel by Allan Bogle; a verdict of one farthing damages testified the jury's opinion that though legal evidence was incomplete, Bogle had been a party to extensive forgeries of letters of credit. As a testimonial to the *Times* for exposing this conspiracy, the merchants of London subscribed £2,700, which the proprietors asked might be invested in scholarships for boys at Christ's Hospital and the City of London School. Memorial tablets of the event were afterwards placed in the schools, the Royal Exchange, and over the *Times* office door —Coachmakers' Hall was rebuilt.—The Thames Tunnel was completed (but not sufficiently for use).

1842.

IS Royal Highness the Prince Consort laid the foundation stone of the new Royal Exchange (17 Jan., 1842).

A Latin inscription, placed within the stone, after alluding to the burning of two former Exchanges, states that the City of London and the Mercers' Company (as joint administrators of the Gresham estate) undertook to restore the edifice, whilst Parliament provided the cost of the approaches.

Credulous people were alarmed by pretended prophecies of the destruction of London, by earthquake, on the approaching 17 Mar., the prophecies purporting to be derived from ancient documents in the British Museum.—The Common Council negatived a motion that "Upon the office of Alderman of Bridge Without becoming vacant by resignation, death, or otherwise, the same be not filled up, there being no constituency to require the same, or any local duties to perform" (17 Mar)—The City freedom was conferred upon the Duke of Cambridge, son of George III, in recognition of his philanthropic efforts (17 Mar.).—The Council resolved on an address to the Queen regretting the refusal of the House of Commons to sanction free importation of corn, and pointing out the severe distress which prevailed among the labouring classes.—The recent unsuccessful attempt of Francis to shoot the Queen formed the subject of warm congratulatory addresses from the Corporation (31 May).—The Thames Tunnel was opened, some 500 visitors passing through from Wapping to Rotherhithe (1 Aug.).—Jane Cooper committed suicide by throwing herself from the Monument (19 Aug.).—Alderman John Humphery was elected Lord Mayor.—The Common Council passed an emphatic resolution on the subject of the distressed condition of the country (8 Dec.).

The Council resolved "that the continued and increasing depression of the manufacturing, commercial, and agricultural interests of this country and the wide-spreading distress of the working-classes, are most alarming ; manufactures without a market, and shipping without freight, capital without investment, trade without profit, and farmers struggling under a system of high rents, with prices falling as the means of consumption by the people fail ; a working population rapidly increasing and a daily decreasing demand for its labour , Union-houses overflowing as workshops are deserted , corn-laws to restrain importation, and inducing a starving people to regard the laws of their country with a deep sense of their injustice , these facts call for the immediate application of adequate remedies," etc.

A group of the *Deæ Matres*, found at a considerable depth in Hart Street, Crutched Friars, was removed to the Guildhall Museum —Crosby Hall was leased to the Crosby Hall Literary Institute.— The Temple Church was restored 1839-1842.—The Sun Fire and Life Office, at the corner of Bartholomew Lane and Threadneedle Street, was erected from the designs of C. R. Cockerell — Excavations in King Edward Street, Newgate Street, revealed the existence of an old Roman burial-ground.—Field Lane Institution was established by the exertions of Lord Shaftesbury and Mr W C Bevan.—In his annual report upon the City police (presented May, 1843), Commissioner Harvey stated that the annual cost of the day and night watch, under the old system, was above £48,000, under the new, £38,000 Of 5,002 persons charged, 1,871 were summarily convicted, 111 sentenced to transportation, 243 to imprisonment , the value of stolen property amounted to £6,559; the vagrant and destitute cases numbered 2,083. The force numbered 536.

1843.

THAMES Tunnel was opened for public use by foot passengers on 25 Mar., 1843.—The birth of a Princess (Alice) furnished occasion for an address of congratulation from the Common Council (27 Ap.). —An Act of Common Council, passed 1 Aug., reduced the number of persons to be nominated by the Mayor for the Shrievalty, and limited the period of eligibility to serve.—Mr. Cobden, while visiting the Corn Exchange, was insulted and hustled (24 Aug.).—The Common Council showed a lively interest in General Espartero, the exiled Regent of Spain, and voted an address which alluded to his " wise and philanthropic plans for the permanent happiness of Spain." The Lord Mayor entertained Espartero at the Mansion House on 26 Sept., when the address was presented.—On 25 Sept. died Alderman Sir Matthew Wood, aged seventy-six.

> As a young man he was a traveller in drugs at Exeter. He came up to London, and, in 1792, was admitted as a partner into the firm of Adock & Price ; and afterwards established a business in Cross Street, Clerkenwell. In 1804 he set up as hop-merchant   He became Common Councilman for Cripplegate Without in 1802 ; Alderman in 1807 , Sheriff in 1809 ; and Lord Mayor in 1815 and 1816. During his first mayoralty, he quelled riots in Newgate and Spa Fields. He served as Radical M.P. for the City, 1817-1843. He strongly supported Queen Caroline. He promoted City improvements, such as the new London Bridge, the Post Office, etc. His son was Lord Chancellor Hatherley.

On the death of Sir M. Wood a Parliamentary election took place in the City, Mr. Pattison, the Anti-Corn-Law candidate, being returned by a majority of 165 over Mr. Baring (21 Oct.).—On 22 Oct. died Sir James Shaw, Bart., aged seventy-nine. Alderman of Portsoken, 1798 ; Sheriff, 1803 ; Lord Mayor, 1805 ; Conservative M.P. for the City, 1805-1818 ; created a Baronet in 1809 ; Chamberlain, 1841-43. —The new Gresham College in Basinghall Street was opened by the Lord Mayor ; the first lecture (on Astronomy) was delivered, and a musical ode, by Professor Edward Taylor, was performed.—Alderman William Magnay was elected Lord Mayor.—The Common Council signified its assent to a scheme for Thames embankment between Blackfriars and Westminster, proposed in a letter from Lord Lincoln, Chairman of Her Majesty's Commission of Metropolis Improvements.

> The Navigation and London Bridge Approaches Committees jointly reported that "the plan of a proposed embankment between Blackfriars and Westminster Bridges, communicated to the Lord Mayor by Lord Lincoln, appeared to them to coincide so nearly with the line some time since laid down by the engineers employed by the Corporation, that they therefore recommended the Court to signify the willingness of the Corporation, as owners of the soil of the bed of the river, and as Conservators of the said river, to consent to an Embankment in the line proposed, the Government taking upon itself the charges of the terrace, and the responsibility of the measure."

The evidence in a case tried before Sir Peter Laurie, at the Guildhall Police Court, exposed the evils of sweating in the cheap clothing trade in London.—Sir William Heygate, Bart., was this year elected Chamberlain. He entered into a Deed of Covenant with the Corporation, as to the regulation of his office and the disposition of its profits : this being the first instance of such a deed.

> Bagnio Street, Newgate (so called from the establishment in 1679 of a Turkish Bath), was re-named Bath Street. A neighbouring street, Butcher Hall Lane (formerly Stinking Lane, then Chick Lane, then Blow-Bladder Street, then Butcher Hall Lane), changed its name to King Edward Street.—

The Hall of Commerce, Threadneedle Street, built 1840-43, by Edward Moxhay, on the site of the French Protestant Church, was erected to accommodate merchants during the reconstruction of the Exchange. The French Church was removed to St Martin's-le-Grand, the new edifice being designed by T. E. Owen —The Guildhall Library acquired an autograph of Shakespeare at a cost of £145

1844.

FRANCIS HOBLER, for fifty-six years chief clerk at the Mansion House, died on 21 Jan., 1844, aged seventy-eight.—Mr. Thomas Carlyle applied for and received permission to search the City's records (4 Ap.).

The Library Committee reported "upon the application of Mr. Thomas Carlyle for permission to search the City's Records, for the purpose of taking such extracts as may enable him to elucidate the period of English history from 1637 to 1663, and recommending that the same be complied with, with the distinct understanding that the object of the search is purely for historical purposes"

A statue of John Carpenter was placed by the Corporation in the centre of the principal staircase of the City of London School (13 May).—On 17 June died Alderman John Lainson, who for nearly half-a-century carried on business in Bread Street Ward (Alderman of Bread Street, 1835 ; Sheriff, 1838 ; declined the office of Mayor in 1842).—The Wellington statue was unveiled on 18 June; the King of Saxony joining heartily in the cheering of the crowd.—An address (9 Aug.) from the Common Council congratulated Her Majesty on the birth of a Prince (Alfred) —On 28 Aug. died Sir William Heygate, Bart., aged sixty-two (he was Sheriff in 1811 ; Alderman of Coleman Street, 1812 ; Mayor, 1823 ; created a Baronet, 1831 ; Chamberlain of London, 1843).—Burgess, a Bank of England clerk, effected a robbery of £8,000 in gold (3 Sept.) ; he was subsequently captured in the United States and transported for life.—The Lord Mayor and a deputation from the Common Council attended at Windsor Castle to present an address to King Louis Philippe, then on a visit to the Queen (12 Oct.). A picture by M. Alaux, portraying the scene, was afterwards presented by the King to the Corporation.— The new Royal Exchange was opened by the Queen in state (28 Oct.).

The Queen and Prince Consort were met at Temple Bar by the City dignitaries. On alighting at the Exchange the Queen and Prince Albert, preceded by the Lord Mayor bearing his sword of state, made a tour of the building, and then proceeded to the Reading Room at Lloyd's, where, seated on a throne, Her Majesty received the address of the Corporation. Her Majesty signified her pleasure in celebrating "the completion of the work, quickly executed, but grand and perfect in all its parts." The Royal party were present at a *déjeuner* which followed in the Underwriters' Room, and at which 1,300 guests assembled. Commemoration medals were distributed. Lord Mayor Magnay was created a Baronet. The structure was designed by Mr. (subsequently Sir) William Tite. The portico is octo-style and Corinthian, the sculptures of the pediment being the work of Richard Westmacott, R.A

The extreme length of the building is 308 feet; the width of the east end 175, which is 56 more than that of the west end. The Clock Tower is 170 feet high. The inner quadrangle measures 111 feet by 53, and contains statues of the Queen, by Lough, and of Sir Thomas Gresham, Sir Hugh Myddelton, Sir Richard Whittington, and Queen Elizabeth, by Messrs. Behnes, Joseph, Carew, and Watson. The material of the edifice is Portland stone. The cost of the erection amounted to £150,000.

Alderman Michael Gibbs was elected Lord Mayor.—The Common Council resolved to order the removal of the existing passenger steamboats on the river which had been pronounced unsafe. They also ordered that the erection of all new piers should follow a model constructed by Mr. Walker, civil engineer; the model rested on piles, with a rising and falling platform attached to a float.— To Major-General Sir Robert Henry Sale, the heroic defender of Jellalabad, the freedom of the City and a silver cup were voted on 12 Dec.

Church of St. Benet Fink.

It was decided on 17 July, 1845, to forward the cup and a copy of the resolution to Sir Henry Sale, in India. He died in India the same year, and hence his name does not appear in the Admission Book of the Chamberlain. A somewhat similar circumstance attended the vote of the freedom to Major-General Sir William Nott. The honour was accorded in recognition of his services in Afghanistan. He died before the ceremonial of admission, and the silver cup which had been voted was presented to his widow.

St. Benet Fink Church, "commonly called Finke, of Robert Finke the founder" (Stow), was taken down to make room for the new Royal Exchange, 1842-44.—The London Bridge terminus of the London, Brighton and South Coast Railway was designed by Henry Roberts, 1843-44.— Merchant Taylors' Hall, in Threadneedle Street, was reconstructed by Samuel Beechcroft. —The statue of William IV was erected in King William Street; it was executed by Samuel Nixon; the figure is 15 feet 3 inches high, and the weight of the whole structure 20 tons.—The building, known as "The Spanish Ambassador's House," in Gravel Lane, Houndsditch, was demolished.—Water Lane, Fleet Street, had its name changed to Whitefriars Street.—A fire damaged Parish Clerks' Hall, in Silver Street.—By the Bank Act of this year all persons are entitled to obtain from the Bank notes in exchange for gold bullion at the rate of £3 17s. 9d. per ounce.—A robbery of £44,625 was effected at Messrs. Rogers's in Clement's Lane.

1845.

THE merchants of London entered into practical possession of the new Royal Exchange on 1 Jan., 1845.—The Chairman of the City of London Mercantile Committee presented to Mr. Rowland Hill, the author of the penny postage scheme, a cheque for £10,000, being the amount raised by a national testimonial.— The City Lands Committee was authorised to purchase the Fleet Prison for £25,000 (23 Jan.).

The sale of the materials of the old building (erected after the Gordon riots in 1780) began in Ap. this year, but the outer walls were not removed till Feb., 1846. The area formerly occupied by the

Fleet Prison, from drawing by Rowlandson and Pugin.

prison lay waste for the next seventeen years until the commencement of the Holborn Viaduct works; and it was used as a resort for betting-men, gamblers, and doubtful characters generally.

On the occasion of the Queen's visit to Christ's Hospital in March the President and Treasurer took precedence of the Lord Mayor, a proceeding afterwards censured by a resolution of the Common Council, which affirmed that "the Lord Mayor for the time being is the head of all the Royal Hospitals belonging to the

City of London, and entitled to preside there upon all occasions, public or private, when he shall so think fit."—The Rev. R. H. Barham, author of the *Ingoldsby Legends*, died at Amen Corner on 17 June.   He was a Minor Canon and "Elder Cardinal" of St. Paul's, and Rector of St Augustine's, Watling Street.—The Common Council decided to complete improvements at Holborn Hill and Farringdon Street at an expense not exceeding £15,000 (26 June).—Major-General Sir Henry Pottinger, who had successfully negotiated a treaty of peace and commerce between this country and the Chinese Empire, received the freedom on 17 July. — A fire in Aldermanbury did damage to the amount of £250,000.—The Markets Committee were empowered to enlarge the Sheep Market in West Smithfield at a cost of £13,000 (25 Sept.).—It was reported to the Common Council that the Bill to enable Jews to serve municipal offices had become law.—Alderman John Johnson was elected Lord Mayor.—On 11 Dec. the Common Council resolved to address the Queen on the subject of the potato famine, and to suggest that the consequent distress was increased by the erroneous legislation which restricted the importation of food — In the latter part of the year the Common Council considered petitions in favour of the erection of railway termini on the sites of the Farringdon Market and the late Fleet Prison.

St. John's Gatehouse, Clerkenwell, was condemned as unsafe ; funds for its restoration were raised by W. P Griffith, F S A —Lad Lane and Cateaton Street now became Gresham Street, and Maiden Lane was re-named Gresham Street West.—Founders' Hall, St. Swithin's Lane, was re-built — Restrictive regulations were imposed upon the shows and stalls of Bartholomew Fair —At Carpenters' Hall, London Wall, four paintings in distemper were brought to light over the wainscot at the west end , the subjects were Noah building the Ark ; King Josiah ordering the Temple to be repaired ; Joseph at work, our Saviour as a boy assisting ; and Christ teaching in the synagogue.—The monuments from the demolished church of St. Benet Fink were removed to St. Peter-le-Poor, Broad Street.   The almshouses connected with Sion College were removed, their vicinity to the library being regarded as a danger from fire.—On the resignation of Mr. William Herbert, Guildhall librarian, he was succeeded by Mr. William Turner Alchin —Freeman's Place, facing the east front of the Royal Exchange, was erected.—Among City Coffee-houses much frequented by merchants and business-men at this period were the Jerusalem in Cowper's Court, the Jamaica, the Baltic, Tom's, and Garraway's Moxhay's new Hall of Commerce, in Threadneedle Street, was also largely attended ; £70,000 were said to have been laid out upon this imposing building, which possessed a large reading-room, public meeting hall, &c.—The neighbourhood of 'Change swarmed with vagrants, itinerant musicians, flower-girls, &c.—Thirty-two banking firms carried on business in the City.—The discounting-house of Overend, Gurney & Co., Lombard Street, of which Samuel Gurney, the Quaker, was the head, was considered to stand first for reputation and wealth among that class of City firms —The leading men on 'Change at this time were the Rothschilds, Barings, Bates's, Doxats, Salomons, Crawshays, Curries, Wilsons, Goldsmids, Mocattas, Cohens, Raphaels, and Montefiores —Lloyd's Registry was amalgamated with the Liverpool Register.

1846.

TOWARDS the expense of removing the Whiting Shoal at Limehouse, the Common Council contributed £500, making a total of £2,500 given for that purpose (2 Feb., 1846) —A group of distinguished men were voted the freedom of the City on 6 Ap.: Lieutenant-Gen the Right Hon. Sir Henry Hardinge, who had shown great valour at the battle of Sobraon ; Gen. Sir Hugh Gough, also lately engaged in the Sikh war ; Major-Gen. Sir Henry George Wakelyn Smith, who had displayed much bravery and skill at the battle of Aliwal, and Major-Gen. Sir George Pollock, who had served in Afghanistan.—On the 21 Ap., died Thomas Tegg, the Cheapside publisher ; in 1843 he presented a valuable collection of books to the City of London School, together with £100 for a scholarship.—The congratulations of the Court of Common Council on Louis Philippe's escape from an attempt at assassination were conveyed in an address voted 23 Ap.   His Majesty's reply was dated Neuilly, 16 May, and the Council ordered the document to be preserved in a glass case in the Guildhall Library.—It was resolved to proceed with the re-building of the Coal Market and enlargement of the approaches, an Act of Parliament having recently been passed granting the necessary powers (25 June).—Sir Robert Peel's ministry having resigned, and Lord John Russell having been entrusted with the formation of a new Cabinet, the latter statesman issued an address to the City electors (3 June), in which he declared that "great social improvements are required ; public education is lamentably imperfect ; the treatment of criminals is a problem yet undecided ; the sanitary conditions of our towns and villages has been grossly neglected."   He was re-elected, 11 June.—The recently passed Electric Telegraph Act stipulated that no pipes should be laid in the City without the consent of the Commissioners of Sewers.—The improvement of Cannon Street and the widening of Queen Street were decided upon (22 Oct.).—Alderman Sir George Carroll was chosen Lord Mayor.

A *Times* printing machine threw off 6,000 sheets, of eight pages, every hour.—Royal Exchange Buildings, opposite the east front of the Royal Exchange, were designed by Edward I'Anson.—The Corporation expended £1,021,421 on the approaches to London Bridge, 1824–46.   One of the most important of the improvements thus effected was the construction of Moorgate Street.—As instances of the contributions of the Corporation to public and benevolent enterprises, the following objects (among others) to which grants were made during this year may be mentioned : Restoration of St. John's Gate, Clerkenwell, Maiden Lane improvement, Sufferers by fire at St. John's, Newfoundland, Royal Orthopædic Hospital, London Mechanics' Institute, Ragged School Union, City Ward Schools, Whitechapel Schools, Improving the condition of the labouring classes, Protection of life from fire, Elizabeth Fry Refuge. City Kitchen for relief of the Poor.

1847.

FOR the relief of the distress in Ireland and Scotland, £2,000 was voted by the Common Council (21 Jan., 1847).—On 10 Mar., died Alderman Robert Williams, aged 80.

Of the banking-firm of Williams, Deacon and Co., in Birchin Lane; Alderman of Cornhill, 1796; Sheriff, 1797; resigned his gown in 1801; Tory M P. in ten successive Parliaments; Magistrate and Deputy-Lieutenant for Dorsetshire

Proposals for the abolition of Smithfield Market were now before Parliament (the Market was not closed till 1855), and an extensively signed petition against the removal was presented to the Council (11 Mar.).—A Bill for improving the Health of Towns in England being under consideration in the House of Commons, the Committee of Sewers gave reasons for excluding the City from its operation

In their report to the Common Council they stated that, during the last sixteen years, they had built new and capacious sewers at a cost of about £200,000, thus bringing up the City drainage to an extent of forty-eight miles of sewers; and they claimed to have had special success in the paving and sanitation of courts and alleys In the result the City was excluded from the Act.

The Council adopted a motion deploring the deficiency of public education and asserting the necessity for State aid (15 Ap.).—At the General Election, the following members were chosen for the City: Lord John Russell, Mr Pattison, Baron Rothschild, and Mr. Masterman; Mr. Masterman being the only Conservative (July). Baron Rothschild, on account of the difficulty connected with the oath, did not take his seat, though re-elected, until 1858.—At Printing House Square, on 28 July, died John Walter, of Bearwood, proprietor of the *Times*.—The Small Debts Act having authorised the Sheriffs' Court to use, as a prison for the purposes of that Court, any prison within the City of London, the Debtors' Prison in Whitecross Street was fixed upon (21 Oct.).—His Excellency James Brooke, Rajah of Sarawak, received the City Freedom (29 Oct.) which was awarded in testimony of his peaceful government of Borneo and his efforts to promote civilisation and commerce in that region.—Alderman John Kinnersley Hooper was elected Lord Mayor.—Mr. David Salomons was elected Alderman of Cordwainer Ward, being the first Jew who had held this dignity in the City (6 Dec.). On 15 Dec. the Council agreed to petition Parliament for the removal of civil and political disabilities affecting Her Majesty's Jewish subjects.—The foundation stone of the Coal Exchange, in Lower Thames Street, was laid on 14 Dec.

The interior of Ironmongers' Hall, Fenchurch Street, was remodelled.—The Bank Directors were authorised by Government to issue notes in excess of their Parliamentary powers, the step being taken to alleviate panic.—Mr. Philip Salomons (brother of the alderman) presented to the Guildhall Library a valuable collection of about 400 Hebrew books.

1848.

ATTHIAS PRIME LUCAS died on 2 Jan., 1848, aged eighty-six.

A native of London, he served his time to his father as a lighterman. He afterwards realised a large fortune in the shipping trade. Tory in politics, and an English gentleman of the old school, he organised a body of River Fencibles, at the time of Napoleon's projected invasion. Alderman of Tower Ward, 1821; Sheriff, 1822; Lord Mayor, 1827; President of St. Bartholomew's Hospital; Prime Warden of the Watermen's Company; twice Master of the Vintners' Company.

An estimate of £80,000 for building a prison at Holloway was agreed to by the Council (10 Feb.).—The House of Commons was petitioned by the Council on the subject of the proposed continuance and increase of the Income Tax, the inquisitorial nature of the tax rendering it peculiarly obnoxious (25 Feb.).—An address to the Queen on the birth of a Princess (Louise) was voted on 23 Mar.— The great Chartist demonstration assembled on Kennington Common (10 Ap.) and marched with a monster petition-roll to Westminster, contingents joining from various points of rendezvous, such as Whitechapel, Finsbury Square, etc.

Throughout the metropolis 170,000 special constables are said to have been enrolled. The Thames bridges were strongly guarded, and detachments of the military posted at numerous places, including Blackfriars Bridge, Bridewell, and the Rose Inn Yard, at the end of Farringdon Street. Thirty pieces of heavy field ordnance were kept in readiness at the Tower. No disorder of an unusual character occurred. On 12 Ap, Sir George Grey, Home Secretary, wrote a letter of thanks to the Lord Mayor, in recognition of the efforts of the City authorities on behalf of public order.

A resolution of Common Council dealt with the subject of the regulation of costume to be worn on the occasion of presenting addresses.

The mode decided upon was as follows:—Mazarine gown, with Court dress, or black dress coat and waistcoat. White stock or cravat. Black breeches or pantaloons, with silk stockings and shoes, or black trousers with the same, or dress boots. Court or dress hat.

It was resolved to enlarge and improve Billingsgate Market by filling up Billingsgate Dock in a line with the Custom House Wharf, an annual surplus from tolls, estimated at £500, having been devoted to improvement purposes under an Act of 1846.—The Freedom was voted on 25 May to the Rev. G. F. W. Mortimer, Head Master of the City of London School, and to Mr. Robert P. Edkins, the Second Master.—Alderman James Duke was elected Lord Mayor.—On 30 Dec., died Alderman John Johnson (of Dowgate Ward), aged fifty-seven; he served as Sheriff, 1836, and Mayor, 1845.—The "Commissioners of Sewers in the City of London" were constituted under the City of London Sewers' Act, by which it was provided that the Commission consisting of the Lord Mayor, Recorder, Common Serjeant, not more than six aldermen, and eighty-three Commoners, should control the sewers and paving of the City.

In digging the foundations of the new Coal Exchange, portions of a Roman apartment and a hypocaust were discovered. The apartment was laid with red tesseræ, the outer wall being 3 feet thick. The hypocaust (a hollow floor to contain hot air for warming purposes) was of concrete.—St. Stephen's, Walbrook, was restored by John Turner, 1847-8.—The City of London College (now at Moorfields) was established at Crosby Hall as the "Metropolitan Evening Classes for Young Men."—At the Bank of England the breastwork behind the balustrade was erected by C. M. Cockerell.—The Excise Office was removed from Old Broad Street to Somerset House.—The Reform Almshouses at Brixton, founded in 1832 for the reception of householders free of the City, were placed under the control of the Corporation, and have since been known as the London Almshouses.—The Imperial Insurance Office was erected from the designs of J. Gibson

1849.

SMITHFIELD Market still occupied much of the attention of the Common Council. (1849)

On 1 Mar., a motion affirming that "a market for the sale of live cattle in the midst of a City is incompatible with the convenience of persons resorting thither for the purposes of business," and demanding its immediate removal, fell through ; but the subject constantly recurred. On the one hand, petitions were presented for its abolition ; on the other for its enlargement. In October a Committee was appointed to consider the advisability of increasing the area and accommodation of Smithfield, Newgate and Leadenhall Markets.

A petition was agreed to by the Council against all unnecessary oaths required to be taken on admission to municipal offices (3 May), and another petition of 21 June besought the removal of the disabilities of the Jews from sitting in the House of Commons.—On 30 June, died William Ward, aged sixty-two.

Elected a Director of the Bank of England, 1817 ; Tory M P for the City, 1826-1835 ; an eminent merchant, and perhaps the greatest amateur cricketer of his time. He was father of William George Ward, who was connected with the Tractarian movement.

Baron Rothschild, who was still unable to take his seat in the House of Commons in consequence of the religious difficulty, accepted the Chiltern Hundreds, but was re-elected on 4 July, his opponent being Lord John Manners. – An Irish Estates Committee was appointed by the Common Council (5 July) to consider the propriety of purchasing estates and waste lands in Ireland, with a view to their cultivation and the increased employment of the people.—On 14 July, died James Pattison, aged sixty-three ; he was Liberal M.P. for the City, 1837-41, and from 1843 till his decease ; and, for many years, a director of the Bank of England. —In the Health Committee's report on precautions against the Cholera visitation, attention was drawn to the danger caused by the City graveyards and slaughter houses, and the discharge of sewage into Puddle Dock, Whitefriars Dock,

CC 2

Broken Wharf, etc. (26 July). A hospital tent for fifty patients was erected on the site of the late Fleet Prison.—As successor to Mr. Pattison, Sir James Duke was elected member for the City (27 July).—Thomas Johnson (Alderman of Portsoken, 1831-44, and Mayor, 1840-1) died on 8 Sept. He had recently been a pensioner of the Charterhouse.—Mr. Cobden was the chief speaker at a meeting at the London Tavern, convened to deprecate the practice of war loans (8 Oct.).—The City Lands Committee was directed to inquire into the City water supply (16 Oct.).— The new Coal Exchange was opened by Prince Albert (30 Oct.).

Indisposition prevented the Queen's attendance. Prince Albert, who was accompanied by the Prince of Wales and the Princess Royal, came by barge from Whitehall to Custom House Quay. The Royal procession was immediately preceded by the Lord Mayor's Water-Bailiff in his barge, and his Lordship in the City barge. The Lord Mayor presented an address to the Prince. The Royal party returned to Whitehall by water. A baronetcy was conferred on Lord Mayor Duke. The new Exchange, built from the designs of J. B. Bunning, Clerk of the City's works, has two fronts of Portland stone, one in Lower Thames Street, the other in St. Mary-at-Hill. The entrance has Roman-Doric columns; the principal staircase stands in a tower 106 feet high; the public hall is a rotunda, of 60 feet diameter, covered by a glazed dome 74 feet from the floor. On the panels are painted allegorical figures of the chief coal-carrying rivers of England, and other paintings showing views of coal-mines and miners at work, and designs representing Wisdom, Fortitude and other virtues. The chief material of the building is iron. The cost of site and structure amounted to £91,000. A commemorative medal was struck by order of the Corporation.

Alderman Thomas Farncomb was elected Lord Mayor.

Sword-rests, Church of St. Mary-at-Hill.

The interior of the church of St. Mary-at-Hill, Billingsgate, was entirely re-fitted.—The large Drawing Office was constructed at the Bank in place of the Dividend Warrant Office.—The stationary engines, which drew trains by means of wire-rope, were discontinued at Fenchurch Street Station.

1850.

AT a Mansion House Meeting on 25 Jan., 1850, £10,000 was collected in aid of the forthcoming Exhibition of the Industry of all Nations.

On 21 Mar, the Lord Mayor gave a banquet at the Mansion House to the chief magistrates of the boroughs of the United Kingdom, with the aim of exciting interest in the projected Exhibition   The Prince Consort observed, in a speech on the occasion, that "the Exhibition of 1851 is to give us a true test and a living picture of the point of development at which the whole of mankind has arrived in this great task" of industrial production   A similar banquet, attended by the Exhibition Commissioners, took place on 25 Oct

On 18 Feb., died John Mirehouse, aged sixty-one, appointed in 1823 one of the Common Pleaders of the City, and in 1833 Common Serjeant.—Mr. Henry B. H. Beaufoy, F.R.S., of South Lambeth, again evinced his generosity to the City of London School (Mar.).

Mr. Beaufoy, who had already presented three £50 scholarships, now added a fourth of the same value, in memory of his late wife.   He also gave to the Guildhall Library a unique cabinet of London tradesmen's tokens of the 17th century, of which a catalogue was printed by the Corporation. The Council decided to place a bust of the donor in their chamber.

Edward Bullock was elected Common Serjeant (21 Mar.).—An address to Her Majesty (2 May) conveyed the congratulations of the Council on the birth of a prince (Arthur).—Lord Denman, late Lord Chief Justice, returned thanks for an address from the Council expressive of their esteem (2 May).

In his letter of thanks, Lord Denman, who had formerly served as Common Serjeant, expressed the hope that the City would "ever preserve the characteristic qualities which have constituted its unparalleled renown, the splendid and genial hospitality, which harmoniously unites all ranks, all professions, and even all nations, the wise benevolence which provides sustenance for the needy, healing for the sick, education for the poor, the liberal policy which secures and strengthens institutions by timely and temperate reform, the instinctive hatred of oppression and attachment to public order."

Lord Viscount Gough, the distinguished commander in India, and the hero of fifteen victories, received the freedom on 30 May.—Mr. John Simon, the Corporation's Medical Officer of Health, in a report on the prevalent smoke nuisance, mentioned that the total cost of washing in the Metropolis had been estimated at £5,000,000 annually.—A letter to the Lord Mayor from Mr. William Shaw, Chairman of the Islington Cattle Market Company, stated that the Company was prepared to convey the whole of the Islington Market Estate to the Corporation on fair and reasonable terms (11 July).—A meeting was held in the Egyptian Hall, Mansion House, to take steps for the erection of a City memorial to the late Sir Robert Peel (15 July).—Baron Rothschild, M.P. for the City, attended to take his seat at the House of Commons, but withdrew on the refusal of the Speaker to swear him on the Old Testament only (26 July).—On 13 Aug., died the Honourable C. Ewan Law, aged fifty-eight (Common Pleader of the City, 1823; Judge of the Sheriff's Court, 1828; Common Serjeant, 1830; Recorder, 1833; Conservative M.P. for Cambridge since 1835).—Alderman John Musgrove was chosen Lord Mayor.

Old Billingsgate.

The anti-Papal agitation was now raging, "Guy Fawkes' Day" afforded an occasion for many demonstrations against Cardinal Wiseman and the new Catholic bishops. At the Lord Mayor's dinner in Guildhall, Lord John Russell and other Cabinet Ministers made pointed allusions to the insulting action of the Pope in parcelling this country into dioceses. The Common Council had highly approved (7 Nov.) of the letter addressed on this subject by Lord Russell to the Bishop of Durham. Indignant addresses from the Corporation were presented to Her Majesty. The Queen, on 10 Dec., replied that she was resolved "to uphold the pure and Scriptural worship of the Protestant faith, which has long been happily established in this land."

On 17 Nov., died Alexander Raphael, aged seventy-four, a wealthy citizen and Roman Catholic (Sheriff, 1834; M.P. for St. Albans since 1847).—Billingsgate Market was re-built this year.—An Act of Parliament was passed giving authority to the Corporation to erect a school "for the maintenance and the religious and virtuous education of orphans of Freemen of the City of London."

In 1703 the freehold of certain messuages, afterwards known as the London Workhouse, in Bishopsgate was purchased by the governors. The Workhouse was disposed of under an Act of 1829, and the rents and income of the Charity directed to be applied to (1) expenses of management, (2) apprenticeship of poor Freemen's children, (3) support of a school. The governing body was to consist of the Aldermen of the City of London and sixty citizens chosen annually by the Common Council, the Lord Mayor acting as president. The new school at Brixton was by the Act of 1850

The Skinners' Company's Almshouses, Mile End. Destroyed 1893.

placed under the management of a Ward Committee of the Common Council. The school receives the fees paid by new freemen, but its chief source of income is the City's cash. The number of children originally maintained was 100, but in 1863 it was raised to 150. There are now maintained and educated 100 boys and 65 girls.—The Skinners' Company's dining-hall was re-built, under the direction of G. B. Moore, 1847–50.—St. Bartholomew-by-the-Exchange having been removed, a copy of the old tower and church was erected, 1849–50, by C. R. Cockerell, in Moor Lane, Cripplegate. The pulpit and organ, with some masonry and woodwork, were reserved from the old church and placed in the new.—The last vestiges of the cloisters, a former passage from King Street into Smithfield, were demolished.—Cheap waxworks, a very old feature of Fleet Street, were still to be seen near St. Dunstan's.—The new barracks at the Tower were erected.— Hepworth Dixon wrote, this year, strongly condemning the state of Giltspur Street Compter; the building he described as too small, the internal arrangement bad, the discipline worse. It was dark, close, and unhealthy, and never free from foul smells. The cells were narrow, and contained no sanitary conveniences, though numbers of persons were often locked up in them for twelve hours together .Of Bridewell he speaks in milder terms, but, while classing it as fairly well adapted for the imprisonment of refractory City apprentices, asserts it to be unfitted for a House of Correction for criminals, the soil being damp and the air humid.

1851.

EPEAL of the Window Tax formed the subject of a petition from the Common Council, 13 Feb., 1851.—On 26 Feb., died Sir John Pirie, aged seventy (Sheriff, 1831 ; Alderman of Cornhill, 1834 ; Lord Mayor, 1841 ; created a baronet, 1842 ; President of St. Thomas's Hospital) —A further protest against Papal aggression was made by the Council on 13 Mar.—The Smithfield Market Removal Bill still encountered opposition from the City, and petitions were presented against the proposed measure to both Houses of Parliament It was, however, passed in Sept.—The Lord Mayor and a deputation from the Common Council attended the opening of the Great Exhibition on 1 May.

On 9 July, Her Majesty and Prince Albert attended an entertainment, given by the Corporation, in Guildhall An enormous concourse witnessed the Royal procession through the City Among the wines placed on the table was some sherry 105 years old.

On 22 May, the Court affirmed its "deep sympathy with Kossuth and his companions, detained prisoners in the fortress of Kutaiah," and appealed to Lord Palmerston to exert his friendly offices to secure their liberation.

On 30 Oct, Kossuth visited the City amid the acclamations of immense crowds. At the Guildhall he received an address from the Corporation, and replied in English In the course of an eloquent speech he eulogised London as "one of the oldest municipal institutions on the earth ; itself an empire —more than an empire ; itself a nation—more than a nation "

Bridewell was broken into, and several articles of plate stolen (17 Aug.).—It was agreed to appropriate £42,000 Reduced Three per Cents. of the Finsbury Surplus Fund, for the purpose of providing lodging-houses for the labouring poor (23 Oct.).—Alderman William Hunter was elected Lord Mayor.—The plan proposed by Mr. Charles Pearson, for a Central Railway Terminus in the Fleet Valley was referred to a Ward Committee. Mr. Pearson's scheme provided that the Corporation should undertake the work (13 Nov.).—An influential meeting of merchants, held at the London Tavern, urged the necessity for a thorough reform of the Customs Department (3 Dec.).—A Bill for regulating elections in the City of London was approved for submission to Parliament (11 Dec).

St Andrew's, Holborn, was repaired.—The Field Lane Night Refuge was established to afford lodging to thirty destitute men and the same number of women.—J. M. W. Turner, the painter, was buried in St. Paul's crypt.—The London Tavern, Bishopsgate Street, was found too small to accommodate the guests (more than 700) at a banquet in honour of Macready, and the Hall of Commerce was hastily adapted for the occasion At 4 o'clock the merchants were transacting business in the Hall; in two hours, seats, tables, platforms, dinner, and company were all in place.

1852.

 PRIZE medal, awarded to the Corporation in connection with the Great Exhibition, was ordered to be placed in the Library of the Guildhall (27 Jan., 1852) —The Pearson scheme for a City terminus was so far approved that the Common Council referred the matter back to the Committee, with instructions to confer with any company willing to undertake the construction of such a line, ending at the spot proposed (11 Mar.).—The presentation of the Very Rev Monsignor Searle (Catholic Chaplain to Sheriff Swift) at the levee on 26 Feb. was cancelled on the ground that his title was "assumed without the required authority" (23 Mar.). —The duties of the Upper and Under Marshals were detailed in a report laid before the Common Council on 22 Ap.—The Court decided to petition Parliament that "all Her Majesty's British-born subjects may have extended to them the rights of civil and religious liberty, and be qualified to hold all civil offices in any of her dominions without any test of their religious opinions" (27 May).—A petition for the suppression of betting offices was agreed to (17 June).—At the General Election, the following members were returned for the City· Mr. John Masterman, Lord John Russell, Sir James Duke, and Baron Rothschild (6 July). —In July, died John James, aged sixty-eight, for twenty-one years Secondary of the City.—The Court expressed on 7 Oct. its respect for the memory of the late Duke of Wellington, and ordered designs for a monument in Guildhall.

The Duke was buried in St Paul's on 18 Nov. A million and a-half of spectators are said to have lined the route of the funeral procession Prince Albert appeared as a mourner Dean Milman read the service; the titles of the deceased were proclaimed by Garter King-at-Arms; a wand was broken and thrown upon the coffin, and the ceremony closed with the benediction pronounced by the Bishop of London The Corporation were duly represented

The new Holloway Prison was formally handed over to the City Prison Committee on 5 Oct.

It was constructed for the accommodation of 283 male adults, 60 women, and 61 juveniles. Built upon land purchased by the Corporation for a cemetery during the cholera epidemic of 1832, its walls include an area of 10 acres. The building was designed by J. B. Bunning; the gateways are fortified, and the six radiating wings are castellated. Ventilation is obtained by a shaft 146 feet high. Water is supplied by an Artesian well, 319 feet deep. The cost was nearly £100,000.—A contemporary critic speaks slightingly of the general design of the prison and "its extreme whimsicality and phantom-like aspect of unreality, which is probably without a parallel except on the stage or some of Martin's visionary backgrounds."

Holloway Prison.

On 10 Oct., died Thomas Wilson, aged eighty-five, Tory M.P. for the City, 1818–1826.— Alderman Thomas Challis was chosen Lord Mayor.—In petition, the Common Council strongly protested against the proposal of the Chancellor of the Exchequer to double the House Tax (16 Dec.). — The new Billingsgate Market was constructed from the designs of Mr. Bunning. A stone river-wall was erected, and the surface from Thames Street to the wall made level. The lower market was devoted to shell-fish, the upper to the sale and storage of dried fish, etc. The river front comprised a clock tower, and a seven-arched arcade. Red brick, with Portland stone dressings, formed the materials. A view of the old market is given on p. 198.

Wax Chandlers' Hall, in Gresham Street West, was built from the designs of Charles Fowler.— Gerard's Hall Hotel was removed to make way for the new Cannon Street. The Corporation entertained the idea of re-constructing its fine 13th century crypt, but ultimately presented the masonry to the Crystal Palace Company for re-erection at Sydenham, a plan which was never realised.—By the Burials Act the Corporation was empowered to give authority to the Commissioners of Sewers to exercise for the City and its Liberties all the powers vested in Burial Boards. Under the provisions of the Act the City of London Cemetery at Ilford has been laid out and maintained.—By an Act of this year the New River Company, notwithstanding their engagement with the City (in 1824) not to charge more in the district supplied by the old London Bridge Waterworks (which extended to one-third of the City), obtained power to tax the whole of their district according to the annual value of the property supplied.—Under the London City Small Debts Extension Act the business of the Sheriffs' Courts, "holden for the Poultry and Giltspur Street Compters," was transferred to the Court then known as the "Sheriffs' Court," but since 1867 as the "City of London Court."

1853.

ORD JOHN RUSSELL, having been appointed Foreign Secretary, was re-elected on 3 Jan., 1853 —Mr. H. Brown died on 15 Feb., aged eighty-six.

In 1794 he assisted in founding the *Morning Advertiser*, and also in the establishment of the Licensed Victuallers' Schools at Kensington   He was the projector of the Golden Lane Brewery, which was started on the joint-stock principle.   In 1807 Mr Brown was elected Common Councilman for Cripplegate, in 1816, Governor of Newgate, a position which he held for five years; in 1822, Warden of the Fleet Prison, and Keeper of the Old and New Palaces (*i e.* Westminster Hall)   These offices had been held together from the time of the Norman Conquest.   He held the wardenship till its abolition in 1842

Temple Bar occasionally formed the subject of debate at the Common Council.

On the proposal to remove the gate being mooted, the inhabitants of the Parish of St Dunstan-in-the-West petitioned against it (17 Feb.).   The City Lands Committee recommended the restoration of the structure at an expense not exceeding £1,500 (13 Oct); and, later on, further petitions for the preservation of the Bar were sent in to the Council.

A motion to establish "a Free Library and a Free Circulating Library" in the City was unanimously adopted (3 Mar.).

The matter was referred to the Library Committee, in whose report (agreed to 3 Nov) an application for an Act of Parliament was recommended, and the opinion was expressed that "the establishment of a Free Library and a Free Circulating Library would be the means of introducing the works of the most approved authors to the homes and firesides of the inhabitants of this City, give an impulse to diligent and thoughtful reading, and encourage the pursuit of studies, the result of which would extend the boundaries of human knowledge and national civilisation"   Meanwhile, the Guildhall Library was thrown open to students and literary men, each ticket of admission being accompanied by expression of a wish that the holders should make frequent use of them.

An address to the Queen (14 Ap.) congratulated Her Majesty on the birth of a Prince (Leopold).—Lord John Russell having intimated the intention of the Government to appoint a Commission to inquire into the Corporation of London, the Council resolved to offer "every facility and all information to the Commissioners."

A copy of the Commission was laid before the Council on 30 June.   The Commissioners appointed were Sir John Patteson, and Messrs H. Labouchere and G. Cornewall Lewis   They were enjoined to collect information respecting "the rights, privileges, powers, jurisdiction, civil and criminal" of the Corporation; its prisons and police, mode of election of members of the Corporation and of officers, the rights and privileges of Freemen and Liverymen, the nature, amount, and management of the Corporation property and income, and to report whether any measures might be necessary to make better provision for the future government of the City.   The Council again expressed its readiness to afford facilities.

The Jewish Disabilities Bill, which had the warm support of the Corporation, passed the House of Commons by a majority of 288 to 230 (15 Ap).   It was, however, thrown out by the House of Lords on the second reading (29 Ap.).—The Council approved a resolution in favour of the raising of Holborn Valley and

Victoria Street (now Farringdon Road), at an estimated cost of £386,000; the improvement to be undertaken in concurrence with the scheme for a City Terminus in or near Farringdon Street (21 May).—Sir John Key, who had twice served as Lord Mayor, was elected Chamberlain by 3185 votes against 2914 for Mr. Scott, this being the largest vote hitherto recorded by the Livery in such a contest (30 May).—In June died Alderman James Harmer.

Mr. Harmer was the son of a Spitalfields weaver, and was left an orphan at ten years of age. He became an attorney, practising chiefly at the Criminal Court. In 1834 he served the office of Sheriff. His proprietorship of the Radical *Weekly Dispatch* excited a feeling against him sufficiently strong to lose him the vote for the Mayoralty in 1840, whereupon he resigned the gown for Farringdon Without. He resided latterly at Ingress Park, near Greenhithe, a mansion largely erected of stone removed from Old London Bridge.

On 1 Sept., died Mr. George Lyall, Conservative M.P. for the City 1833-5, and 1841-7. —Rules were framed for the City of London Freemen's Orphan School, Brixton (4 Oct.).

The mode of election of children was by application from parent or guardian, recommended by at least one Common Councilman, the election being made (by ballot) by the Common Council. The subjects of instruction included the usual elementary subjects, with Algebra, French, Latin, and Religious Knowledge.

The City of London School was enriched by the establishment of a "Lambert Jones" scholarship, as a memorial of the public services of Mr. R. L. Jones, for many years Common Councilman; a gold medal was presented to Mr. Jones, and his bust ordered to be placed in the Council Chamber (13 Oct.).—Alderman Thomas Sidney was elected Lord Mayor. The Mayoralty Show included allegorical representations of Justice, the Nations and Prosperity.— A great fire in the City destroyed warehouses in Bread Street, Friday Street, Watling Street and Cheapside (31 Dec.).

The Chapter Coffee-house, No. 50, Paternoster Row, was closed as a coffee-house; it had been for many years the resort of booksellers, authors, and politicians.—During the excavations for Cook's warehouse, on the south side of St. Paul's Churchyard, a Danish gravestone was found, inscribed with

Runic characters of the tenth or eleventh century. It is preserved in the Guildhall Museum.—The restoration of the paintings by Sir James Thornhill on the dome of St. Paul's was decided upon —-The Old Excise Office, Old Broad Street, was sold by auction.—Furnival's Inn was sold for £55,000.— The Mayor's Court, hitherto a closed Court, was now opened to all barristers and solicitors.

1854.

THOMAS SAUNDERS, F.S.A., Common Councilman for Bridge Ward, 1814–20, Comptroller of the Chamber of London, 1841, and the leading promoter of the restoration of the " Ladye Chapel," at St. Saviour's, Southwark, died on 25 Jan., 1854, aged sixty-eight.— The Freedom was conferred upon Mr. A. H. Layard, D.C.L., M.P., " as a testimonial of his persevering and zealous exertions in the discovery of the long-lost remains of Eastern antiquity " (9 Feb.).—On 10 Mar. died William Thompson, a wealthy ironmaster, aged sixty-two; he was Liberal M.P. for the City, 1826–32; Alderman of Cheap Ward, 1821; Sheriff, 1823; Lord Mayor, 1828; President of Christ's Hospital; a Director of the Bank of England; and for some years Chairman of the Committee at Lloyd's.—Her Majesty's declaration of war against Russia was read, according to ancient custom, at the Royal Exchange by the Serjeant-at-Arms and Mace Bearer to the Corporation, in the presence of the civic authorities and a large concourse of people (31 Mar.).—The Common Council assured the Queen in a resolution of 6 Ap. of their belief in the justice and necessity of the war "to preserve the balance of power in Europe," and an address to that effect was drawn up.—A public humiliation and fast were observed at St. Paul's (26 Ap.).—On 17 Ap., died John Kinnersley Hooper, aged sixty-three; he was elected Alderman of Queenhithe, 1840; Sheriff, 1842; Lord Mayor, 1847; and was President of St. Bartholomew's Hospital.—The office of Keeper of Bunhill Fields Burial Ground was discontinued (27 Ap.).—The Commission of Inquiry into the Corporation reported on 10 May.

The Commissioners declined to recommend a Municipality for the whole of London on the ground that it would extend the civic authority from an area of 723 acres to one of 78,029 acres, a population of 129,128 to 2,362,236, and an assessment of £953,110 into an assessment of £9,964,348. The creation of a Metropolitan Board of Works was proposed, and it was suggested that the Metropolitan and City police should be amalgamated.

The Common Council protested against the election of any person other than a member of the Court of Aldermen to the Presidentship of Christ's Hospital, as an infringement of the ancient privileges of the Corporation (18 May).—Lord John Russell, on his appointment as President of the Council, was re-elected for the

City (14 June).—The Lord Mayor, on behalf of the Corporation, presented an address of welcome to the King of Portugal, who had come to this country on a visit to the Queen (19 June). In the following Sept. the Lisbon Municipality conveyed their thanks to the Lord Mayor for the attention paid to His Majesty Don Pedro V.—A Committee of the House of Commons appointed to inquire into the want of additional bridge accommodation over the Thames reported in July.

They stated that a great increase of traffic through the streets of London had occurred in four years, 1850-4, the number of railway passengers at the London Bridge termini having risen from 5,000,000 to 10,000,000 a year, while the number of pedestrians and vehicles had also been much augmented. The abolition of tolls was recommended, and it was suggested that the expense of maintaining bridges and roads should be met by a rate levied on the whole Metropolitan District.

The Lord Mayor announced from the Royal Exchange steps at 10 o'clock at night the news of the victory of the Allies at the Alma (30 Sept.).—Alderman Francis Graham Moon was chosen Lord Mayor.—The Common Council ordered a contribution of £2,000 to the Patriotic Fund "now raising for the relief of the widows and orphans of the soldiers, sailors and marines engaged in the present war" (26 Oct.).

Cannon Street was widened and lengthened to St. Paul's Churchyard, at an expense of £200,000 Basing Lane was removed in order to make way for the enlarged thoroughfare.—The interior of the London and Westminster Bank, Lothbury, was reconstructed.—Below the foundations of the old Excise Office, in Old Broad Street, was found a Roman tessellated pavement, 28 feet square, and ornamented with a figure of Ariadne, or a Bacchante, on a panther's back; coins of Hadrian and Constantine were also discovered.—The present Stock Exchange, designed by Thomas Allason, Junr., was opened; the previous edifice had been built in 1802.—In 1853-4 the South Sea Stock, amounting to £10,000,000, was converted or paid off.

1855.

LORD JOHN RUSSELL, on his appointment as Secretary of State, was re-elected for the City (3 Mar., 1855).—A fast day for the supplication of divine aid in the cause of the Allies was appointed (21 Mar.). Services were held in Westminster Abbey, St. Margaret's and St. Paul's, the latter being attended by the civic representatives.—The freedom of the City was voted in Common Council (14 Ap.) to Sir Jamsetjee Jeejeebhoy, of Bombay, testimony of the esteem of the Corporation for his character as a princely benefactor of his country, and a merchant of spotless integrity. The resolution of the Court was forwarded to

Sir Jamsetjee at Bombay.—The Emperor and Empress of the French visited the Queen at Windsor (16 Ap.) and on the 19th they were received with great magnificence at the Guildhall by the Lord Mayor, among whose guests was also included the Prefect of the Seine.

The subject of the war in the Crimea was dealt with in both the Recorder's address and his Imperial Majesty's reply. " Ranged together in a righteous cause," said the Recorder, "and braving like hardships, and shedding their blood side by side in victory, the soldiers of our united armies

Old Smithfield Market.

and the seamen of our combined fleets have learned to regard each other with the love of brave and generous comrades." "The eyes of all who suffer," observed the Emperor, "turn instinctively to the west. Thus our two nations are even more powerful from the opinions they represent than by the armies and fleets they have at their command." The Lord Mayor (the Right Hon. Francis Graham Moon) subsequently received the honour of a baronetcy, and the Sheriffs (Alderman Muggeridge and Mr. Crosley) that of knighthood. By order of the Corporation a commemorative medal was struck.—An exchange of complimentary addresses took place between the Corporation and the Municipality of Paris.—On 3 May the Common Council congratulated the Emperor on his escape from the recent attempted assassination by Pianori in Paris.—On 18 May the Lord Mayor and a deputation from the Corporation visited Paris, and were warmly welcomed by the municipal authorities at the Hôtel de Ville.

Old Smithfield market was closed for the sale of cattle, horses and sheep (11 June), and, on the 13th, the New Smithfield, or Metropolitan Cattle Market was opened in Copenhagen Fields by the Prince Consort.

The new market occupies (1896) about 75 acres, and affords accommodation for 7,190 beasts, 35,946 sheep, 1,920 calves, and 1,440 pigs. As many as 10,100 beasts and 38,500 sheep have been brought to the market in one day The market finds employment for 1,600 persons, and two blocks of model dwellings have been erected in the area, accommodating 124 families The total sum expended on the purchase of the site and the erection of the market has been £504,842 Prior to its removal from Smithfield, the market produced an annual profit of some £6,000, but since 1855, the yearly loss has amounted to about the same sum (£6,000) J B Bunning, the City Surveyor and Clerk of Works, was the architect of the market.

The bronze statue of Sir Robert Peel, at the west end of Cheapside, was unveiled on 21 July. Its height is 11 feet, and the pedestal, of Peterhead granite, is 12 feet high. The statue was executed by William Behnes.—An Act constituting the Metropolitan Board of Works was passed in August.—Bartholomew Fair was proclaimed for the last time on 3 Sept., and was henceforward suppressed as a nuisance.—Alderman Thomas Kelly died, aged eighty (7 Sept.).

He was elected Common Councilman, 1823; Alderman of Farringdon Within, 1830; Sheriff 1825-6; and Lord Mayor, 1836-7. As a publisher he distinguished himself by his enterprise in the issue of popular editions of the Bible, History of England, &c., circulated in numbers by canvassers all over the country

An address to the Queen (voted 11 Oct.) felicitated Her Majesty on the successes of the allied fleets and armies.—The Lord Mayor's offer of a bust of the Queen was accepted by the Court of Common Council (29 Oct.).—At the request of the Common Council the Lord Mayor convened a public meeting to consider the question of adopting the Free Library Act for the City (5 Nov.). The proposition was unfortunately, however, rejected by the ratepayers.—Alderman David Salomons was elected Lord Mayor.—Victor Emmanuel, King of Sardinia, visited the City, and was presented with an address from the Corporation at Guildhall (4 Dec.).

"If," said the King in reply, "I bring to my allies the forces of a kingdom not vast, I bring, however, with me the power of a loyalty which no one has doubted, supported by the valour of an army which follows faithfully, everywhere, the banner of its lawful kings." The Corporation struck a commemorative medal The King gave the Lord Mayor, through the Sardinian Ambassador, a snuff-box as a souvenir of his visit.

The Common Council elected, as their representatives on the newly-formed Metropolitan Board of Works, Messrs. Edward Harrison, Henry L. Taylor and Thomas H. Hall.

Bank of England notes, which had been hitherto printed from copper-plates, were now worked off by McPherson's press from blocks with raised designs.—Giltspur Street Compter was taken down, part of the site being added to the grounds of Christ's Hospital.—Gresham House was built on the site of the old Excise Office in Broad Street, the architect being E N. Clifton.—The South Sea House and the Hall of Commerce were largely reconstructed, and taken by different banking-houses

1856.

THE Metropolitan Board of Works, until suitable premises were provided, met in the Guildhall Council Chamber (1856).—The Library Committee were instructed by the Common Council to consider whether means could be adopted to render the Library more easily available for the use of the Corporation and citizens of London (28 Feb.), and the Library was thrown open to readers, by ticket, in the following Dec.—In petitioning against the Counties and Boroughs Police Bill, which placed in the Home Secretary's hands power to regulate the government, pay, clothing, etc., of municipal forces, the Corporation deprecated the tendency of legislation towards centralisation (3 Mar.).—The Common Council, with the sanction of the Charity Commissioners, resolved to pull down Rogers' Almshouses in Cripplegate, and erect others in lieu thereof at Brixton (13 Mar.).—Congratulations were tendered by the Court to the Emperor and Empress of the French on the birth of the Prince Imperial (24 Mar.).—Michael Prendergast was elected Under-Sheriff of the Poultry and Giltspur Street Compters (3 Ap.).—Sir George Grey's Bill for the Better Regulation of the Corporation of the City of London drew a remonstrance from the Council (11 Ap.)

The measure, said the petition of the Council, might fitly be termed a Bill of Pains and Penalties. It was an essential provision of the Central Criminal Court Act of 1834 that the Lord Mayor should be at the head, and the Aldermen, members of, the Commission: but the present Bill repealed that portion of the Act of 1834. Another privilege of which the citizens were deprived by the Bill was the election of their own magistrates, the composition of the Court of Common Council was to be entirely changed, the election of the Lord Mayor and Sheriffs was to be vested in the Common Council, the Corporation would lose its function as Conservator of the Thames, the rights of the Corporation to Metropolitan markets were threatened, and the metage of 4d. a ton on coal, which rested on an immemorial title, was to be abolished, although, from the proceeds of these coal-dues the Corporation had constructed noble streets, laid out nearly £500,000 on the Metropolitan Cattle Market, and raised nearly £100,000 for the new Holloway prison.

An address to Her Majesty, resolved upon on 2 May, congratulated the Queen on the close of the war in the Crimea. "We proudly rejoice to record," the address ran, "that in no former war has the generous and enduring bravery of the British soldier and sailor, vying with that of their valiant allies, been more brilliantly conspicuous."—Dean Milman preached the sermon in St. Paul's on Thanksgiving-Day before the Lord Mayor and Corporation (4 May).—Admiral Sir Edmund Lyons, Bart., was admitted to the freedom of the City in recognition of his forty-two years of service abroad in diplomacy and the navy, and especially of the ability he had displayed in the disembarkation of the British troops at Varna (19 May).—The Corporation voted £500 in relief of persons suffering through the

EE

recent inundations in France (26 June).—A resolution in favour of the establishment of baths and wash-houses in the City was carried in the Common Council (17 July). —It was decided to accept the gift of a portrait of the Lord Mayor (Salomons) to be placed in Guildhall (24 July).—General Sir William Fenwick Williams, of Kars, Bart, received the freedom of the City (31st) —The Lord Mayor carried out the septennial inspection of the Thames and Medway boundaries.—Alderman William Hunter, Lord Mayor, 1851-2, died, aged seventy-five (22 Sept.).—Thomas Henry Hall died, aged sixty-four (2 Oct).

He was Common Councillor for Coleman Street Ward, 1829–56, and served as a most energetic Chairman of the Improvement Committee, whilst the Cannon Street and new Farringdon Street works were being carried out. A bust of Mr. Hall was ordered to be placed in the Council Chamber.

The fine upon persons nominated and elected but refusing to serve the office of Sheriff, was reduced to £100 (6 Nov.).—Alderman Thomas Quested Finnis was chosen Lord Mayor.—The Common Council passed an Act for the final abolition of Street Tolls (18 Dec.).

The ground was cleared for the construction of Farringdon Road, in continuation of Farringdon Street The new thoroughfare was at first called Victoria Road —Weavers' Hall, in Basinghall Street, was pulled down.—The City Bank was erected in Threadneedle Street from the designs of Messrs. Moseley.

1857.

THOMAS CHAMBERS, M.P., was elected Common Serjeant (29 Jan., 1857).—The action of Lord Palmerston's government at Canton in connection with the *Arrow* having been followed by a defeat in the House of Commons on the motion of Mr. Cobden, the Common Council expressed its regret that the House had not supported Her Majesty's servants in China in their exertions to sustain the honour of the British flag (9 Mar.).—At the General Election which ensued Lord John Russell, and three other Liberals, viz. · Baron Rothschild, Sir James Duke and Mr. R. W. Crawford, were returned (31 Mar).—The birth of a Princess (Beatrice) occasioned a congratulatory address from the Corporation to Her Majesty (23 Ap.).—The great bell of St. Paul's was tolled on the death of the Duchess of Gloucester.—The Court again resolved to petition both Houses of Parliament in favour of the abolition of Jewish disabilities (30th).—Dr. David Livingstone was admitted to the freedom (21 May).

The Chamberlain's address drew a contrast between the recent recipient of the freedom, General Williams, of Kars, and Dr. Livingstone The General had served his country in the "grappling vigour and rough form of war" "Your calling, on the contrary, has led you to seek the honour of your country and the moral elevation of mankind by the peaceful triumph of the missionary, by the expanding influences of scientific discovery, by preparing the way for that intercommunion and commerce between alienated races, the tendency of which is to make a corporate guild of all nations, to unite all the tribes of the earth in a bond of universal brotherhood."

The Bill, introduced by the Government, for admitting Jews into Parliament, was thrown out on the second reading in the House of Lords by 173 votes to 139 (10 July). On the 25th a meeting of the electors of the City of London was

Civic Water Procession, from Picture at Guildhall.

held at the London Tavern when Baron Rothschild, in accordance with his pledge, resigned his seat for the City, but at the same time offered himself again as a candidate. On the 28th the Baron was re-elected for the fifth time, no other candidate having been proposed.—Prince Frederick William of Prussia was presented with the freedom of the City in a gold box (13th).—The first number of the *City Press* appeared (18th). It consisted of four pages and announced itself as a non-party organ.—The Thames Conservancy Act was passed on 17 Aug.

It is described as an Act to provide for the conservation of the river Thames and for the regulation, management, and improvement thereof. The Act recites the suit between the Crown and the Corporation and the agreement of Dec., 1856, for stopping litigation, and vesting the bed and soil of the river in the Corporation on payment of £5,000. The Act vests the said soil in the Conservators.

EE 2

reserving only a small part to the Crown; the powers of the Queen and the Corporation of London were also vested in the Conservators. Twelve Conservators are appointed, viz.: the Lord Mayor, two Aldermen, four members of the Common Council, the Deputy-Master of Trinity House, three members appointed by the Government, and one by the Trinity House Corporation. One Alderman was appointed on the Lea Conservancy Board. These arrangements, however, were subsequently altered, and still further modified by the Act of 1894, to amend the constitution and extend the statutory powers of the Conservators, especially with a view to the prevention of the pollution of the River. The Conservators have now for this purpose jurisdiction over all the tributaries of the river within its catchment area, except a part of the river Lea, the powers as stated in Committee extending from the Cotswold Hills to the Valley of Gravesend, and from Warwick to Winchester. The constitution of the Conservators was the subject of much controversy. The Board now consists of thirty-eight members. The County Councils of Middlesex, Surrey, Kent, Essex, Oxfordshire, Berks, Bucks, and Herts, each appoint one Conservator, the County Boroughs of Oxford, Reading, and West Ham, each appoint one, the Metropolitan Water Companies, one; the Admiralty, two; the Board of Trade, two; Trinity House, two; ship-owners, three; owners of sailing barges, lighters, and steam tugs, two; dock owners, one; wharfingers, one; the Corporation of London, six; and the London County Council, six. The Corporation still has one representative on the Lea Conservancy Board

On the 20th an exhibition of eighty-three competitive designs for the Wellington Monument, to be erected in St. Paul's Cathedral, was thrown open to public inspection in Westminster Hall —A national subscription was opened at the Mansion House for the relief of those suffering through the Indian Mutiny (25th).—Sir Robert Walter Carden, Knight, M.P., was elected Lord Mayor (29 Sep.). —In October the new schools at Hanwell, for pauper children, belonging to the City of London Union, the East London Union, the West London Union, and St. Saviour's and St. Martin's-in-the-Fields Unions were inspected and partially opened. Eleven hundred children were removed from Norwood to the new home, which would accommodate 1,500. The cost of the schools and fittings was under £50,000.—On 29 Oct. a tiger, which was being conveyed from the London Docks, burst out of the van and attacked a boy in the Minories. One of the attendants, armed with a crow-bar, overcame the beast. The boy eventually recovered. —Mr. James Morrison, a wealthy merchant of Fore Street, died at his country seat, Basildon Park, Berkshire (30th).

In 1836 Mr. Morrison commenced the agitation which resulted in the control by the Government, in the interests of the public, of railway and other public works As a result of this the penny a mile regulation was established.

The freedom of the City was bestowed upon the Duke of Cambridge, commander-in-chief of Her Majesty's Forces (4 Nov.). The Corporation also presented the Duke with a sword of the value of 200 guineas, the presentation at the Guildhall being followed by a banquet to His Royal Highness at the Mansion House.—About this time the Presbyterian congregation in London Wall changed its local habitation to Dalston.—Lord Mayor Carden commenced his year of office on 10 Nov. For the first time for many centuries there was no water procession.

The Corporation were no longer the only conservators of the Thames, and it was therefore resolved that the route should be entirely by land. The pageant included twelve knights, mounted on chargers, armed *cap-à-pie*, several juvenile bands, and the boys of the Chelsea Military College in full military array. At the banquet in the evening the Guildhall was decorated in a novel style, the columns on each side of the hall being surrounded with mosaics, intermixed with halberts, bound together with laurel. Lord Palmerston, prime minister, was the chief guest, being accompanied by Earl Granville and the Marquis of Salisbury.

On the same day (10th) there were serious fluctuations in the funds. On the 11th the announcement of the collapse of the house of Sandeman and other great

Rolls House, Chancery Lane, designed by Colin Campbell.

commercial disasters brought consols down to 88½. The Bank Charter Act was suspended on the 12th, it being found that there were in the Bank notes and gold to the value of £1,462,153, while the deposits that might at any time be drawn out amounted to £18,248,003. The prompt action of the Government abated the commercial panic and restored confidence. The Bank Charter Indemnity Act was passed (11 Dec.).—The new City of London Cemetery at Ilford was consecrated by the Bishop of London (16 Nov.). The total area was 89½ acres, of which forty-nine were consecrated and twenty-one reserved for the use of dissenters.—At a special meeting of the Common Council (1 Dec.), the Corporation Enquiry Committee reported that a deputation had waited upon the Home Secretary, and on the 15th they brought up a draft Bill for the better regulation of the Corporation.—The Common Council on the 10th passed a Bill changing the date and mode of returning the names of persons elected to the Common Council. Hitherto the return of elections had been suspended from St. Thomas's day to Plow Monday. Henceforth the return was to be made by the day following the election.—The Court appointed the number of beadles for the different wards of the City, and fixed their wages and allowances, ranging from £25 to £45 each.—Amongst the street improvements of the City was the shop of Messrs. Sarl, silversmiths, on the south side of Cornhill, which was said to be the most costly specimen of shop architecture in London. Weavers' Hall, Basinghall Street, and Dyers' Hall, Dowgate Hill, were completed.—Alterations and improvements at Newgate prison were begun in this year and finished in 1862, at a cost to the Corporation of £25,646.—The new Record Office, Fetter Lane, having been completed, the records of St. John's Chapel, Tower of London, and other depositories, were removed thither.

By the Court of Probate Act, it was provided that all testamentary records of every Court then having jurisdiction to grant probate or administration should be transmitted to the Principal Registry of the Court of Probate The Corporation successfully resisted the provisions of the Act, and the records of the Court of Husting are still preserved at the Guildhall. They commence with the year 1258.—On the passage of the Conservancy Act, which transferred the control of the river to a paid Board, the Corporation and most of the Livery Companies sold their state barges, several of which were afterwards adapted for use as river-side club-rooms at Oxford.

1858.

POSTAL districts were established in London, 1 Jan., 1858.—The Common Council (21st) passed a resolution congratulating the Emperor and Empress of the French on their providential escape "from the recent diabolical attempt at assassination."—At a special meeting of the Common Council (26 Jan.) it was agreed that a dutiful and loyal address should be presented to the Queen and the Prince Consort on the occasion of the marriage of their daughter, H.R.H. Victoria Adelaide Mary Louisa, the Princess Royal of England, with H.R.H. Prince Frederick William of Prussia. At the same time an address was voted to the Duchess of Kent, and compliments to the bride and bridegroom. These were presented, in due course, at Buckingham Palace, whither the Lord Mayor, Sheriffs, and a deputation from the Corporation went in state. Prince Frederick William of Prussia presented the Chamberlain (Sir John Key, Bart.) with a gold snuff box, set in diamonds, he having been the mouthpiece of the congratulations of the Corporation.—On 6 Feb. Sir George Grey introduced a Bill in the House of Commons for the reform of the Corporation of the City of London.

It proposed to divide the City into sixteen wards, instead of twenty-six, each containing, as nearly as possible, an equal population. The Common Council would consist of 112, instead of 232 members. The qualification of a Common Councilman was to be the occupation of a house of not less than £10 annual value, and the electors need no longer be freemen of the City. Any person who possessed the qualification of a Common Councilman would be eligible for the office of Lord Mayor, who would be elected by the Common Council instead of the Livery. The Court of Aldermen was to be abolished as a judicial court, and the Lord Mayor and Aldermen would no longer form part of the Central Criminal Court. The Bill also dealt with the Coal Dues.

The Government shortly afterwards resigned (19th).—Charles Gilpin, a Quaker, on entering the Common Council, made affirmation instead of taking the usual oath (11th).—Alderman Farebrother, who was lord mayor in 1833, died in his 77th year, at his residence at Clapham.—Numerous ward and livery meetings were held to protest against the Bill for the Reform of the Corporation and the proposed interference with its right to the Coal Dues.—In consequence of the passing of the Thames Conservancy Bill, the Common Council (4 Mar.) granted pensions to the water-bailiff and other officials, the consideration of the petitions of the water-bailiff's assistants and the Lord Mayor's thirty-two State bargemen being adjourned.—The Court ordered that a bust of the late Major-General Sir Henry Havelock should be executed and placed within the Guildhall.—On 11 March, some excitement was caused by the publication of a pamphlet, entitled, *L'Empéreur Napoléon III et l'Angleterre*, describing the facilities afforded in England for concocting treasonable schemes. The writer referred to a coffee house near Temple Bar, with a "discussion forum," where the question, "Is regicide permitted under certain circumstances?" had been publicly discussed.—The Common Council (12th) received from the Metropolitan Board of Works, the following resolution —

"That Temple Bar presents an obstruction to the traffic of the Strand and Fleet Street, and that its removal and the widening of the street adjacent, are desirable."

The letter was referred to the City Lands Committee.—On the 18th, a letter was read to the Common Council from the Empress Eugénie (dated 25 Feb.), thanking the Lord Mayor for the medal struck in commemoration of the visit paid by the Emperor of the French and herself to the City, in 1855.— It was referred to the Corporation Enquiry Committee to carry into effect a scheme for reducing the number of wards in the City to twenty (15 Ap.).

On the 26th, a special meeting of the Common Council was held, to consider a report of this Committee, relative to the proceedings in Parliament on the London Corporation Bill.

Meantime, the subject had been referred to a Select Committee of the House of Commons, which, early in May, brought up an amended Bill, ratifying the proposal for a division of the City into sixteen wards, but requiring that the Lord Mayor should be an alderman. On 26 May, the Corporation Enquiry Committee again reported to the Common Council on the London Corporation Bill, stating that the clauses confiscating the metage and other revenues of the Corporation had been allowed to remain unaltered. The committee, moreover, complained that the Corporation had not been permitted to present its case, as promised, before the Select Committee, and recommended that a petition be presented to the House of Commons to re-commit the Bill, and praying that the Corporation might be heard against the confiscating clauses, and generally against the measure. After a spirited discussion, the report was agreed to.

During this month considerable renovations and improvements were carried out at Merchant Taylors' Hall. The ceiling of the dining hall was entirely laid

Temple Bar from West, showing Crockford's Bulk Shop.

in sunk panels of oak, beautifully polished and relieved by arabesque borderings.— Early in June, in accordance with a report of Dr. Letheby, Medical Officer for the City, a beginning was made in the way of beautifying the City graveyards,

which had hitherto been sadly neglected.   Aldgate churchyard and the churchyard of St. Nicholas Olave, in Nicholas Lane, were the first to be planted
with flowers and shrubs.—A meeting, addressed by the Bishop of London and
Dean Milman, was held at the Mansion House, to raise funds for evening
services at St. Paul's.   An appeal was also made for public subscriptions with
the object of adapting the dome area of the Cathedral to purposes of divine
service, in accordance with the original and unfinished plans of Sir Christopher
Wren.   Towards this object, the Corporation subscribed between 1858 and 1861,
£850.—A meeting of the Livery was held at Guildhall, presided over by the Lord
Mayor, for the purpose of considering the provisions of the London Corporation
Reform Bill, which was down for third reading that night (7 June).   The Common
Hall resolved to petition Parliament against the Bill, which, it was stated "struck
at the very roots of their privileges."   The further consideration of the Bill was
postponed to June 24, and meantime, ward meetings were held throughout the City
to protest against it.   The opposition was so strong that Lord John Russell decided
to drop the metage clauses, and proceed with the remainder of the Bill   Eventually,
however, the whole Bill was quietly shelved.—At the Common Council on 10 June,
it was decided to apply for powers to invest the accumulated funds of the Finsbury
Estate, about £140,000, in freehold property.   The lease of the estate would expire
in 1867.   The Special Revenue Committee at the same time made a number of
proposals for reducing the expenditure of the Corporation, which were agreed to
by the Court.   The Chamberlain's Emolument Fund (£1,237 14s. 8d. per annum)
was abolished; the salaries of the sword-bearer and common crier were to be
reduced on the offices falling vacant; the office of train-bearer to the Lord Mayor
was abolished, and it was decided that one marshal instead of two was sufficient.
All extraordinary expenditure was to be avoided, and the fines on renewal of leases
(about £3,800 per annum) were to be carried to the credit of the accumulative
fund.—One-sixth of an entire thirty-sixth share of the New River Company was
sold at a City auction (22nd), for £3,300.—The old controversy about Jewish
disabilities was closed by a virtual surrender of the principle by the House of
Lords (1 July).   The Parliamentary oath having undergone certain modifications,
it was administered to Baron Rothschild, who, at last, took his seat for the City in
the House of Commons.—Sir John Key, Bart., the City Chamberlain, died (14th),
at his residence at Streatham.

He was born in 1785, was elected alderman of Langbourn ward in 1823, sheriff in the ensuing year,
and Lord Mayor in 1830 and 1831, the second time as an expression in favour of reform on the part of
the City.   He was elected Chamberlain with 6,095 votes, a majority of 275 over Mr. Benjamin Scott.

Mr. Benjamin Scott, on the 24th, was unanimously elected to the office of Chamberlain, in Common Hall.—Owing to the almost tropical heat, and the pestilential stench of the Thames, Mr. Disraeli, who was now Chancellor of the Exchequer, on the 15th, moved for leave to bring in a Bill for the main drainage of the Metropolis, a work, which it was calculated, would cost, at least, £3,000,000. (Four years later the actual outlay had risen to £5,000,000.)

It was proposed that Parliament should levy a special rate on the Metropolis for the purpose of purifying the river and completing the main drainage of the Metropolis, the money to be borrowed on the guarantee of the Government, and repaid by a special rate of three-pence in the pound (to be called the sewage rate), in forty years by annual instalments, the work to be completed in five years and a half by the Metropolitan Board of Works. The Bill was passed with some slight alterations, and the Royal Assent given on 2 Aug.

The City Lands Committee reported to the Common Council (29th) the completion of the new Rogers' Almshouses at Brixton. These almshouses, founded by Robert Rogers in the reign of James I, were originally in Hart Street, Cripplegate. —As far back as 1845, Mr. Pearson, the City Solicitor, had proposed a grand scheme for a Central Railway Terminus in the City, and on 29 July the Improvement Committee presented a report to the Common Council urging that the construction of the Metropolitan Railway would be a material advantage to the trade and commerce of the City.—On 16 Aug. the foundation stone was laid of a new Law Library in the grounds of the Middle Temple.—A public meeting of the inhabitants of Middlesex Street (Petticoat Lane), and its vicinity, was held at Sussex Hall, Leadenhall Street, to protest against the "slanderous" statements made against them in certain newspapers (19th) —On the 31st the re-paving of London Bridge was commenced.—The political power of the East India Company was transferred to the Crown on 1 Sept. by Act 21 & 22 Vic. cap. 106, for the better government of India. On the same day the East India proprietors held their last Court as governors of India.—At a meeting of the Commissioners of Sewers (14th) the Medical Officer presented a report on "The mephitic gases of the City," which was ordered to be printed.—Mr. Sergeant Merewether, the town clerk, retired, after 15 years' service, on a pension of £1,000 a year (16th). The emoluments of his office were £2,100.—On the same day a letter was received by the Common Council from the King of Sardinia, presenting a medal which His Majesty had caused to be struck in commemoration of his visit to the City.—About this time a vigorous effort was made by Lord Mayor Carden to clear the City streets of hawkers, a number of whom were fined or sent to prison for obstruction.—Alderman David William Wire was elected Lord Mayor (29th).—On Sunday, 2 Oct., was held the last of a series of open-air services, conducted by the Rev. Thos. Richardson, curate of St. Olave, Old Jewry, in front of the Royal Exchange.—The Common Council (7th) voted the freedom of the City and a sword of the value of 100 guineas to Sir Jas. Outram, K.C.B., in recognition of his signal services in suppressing the Indian Mutiny.—At the same time the freedom of the City, accompanied by a sword of similar value, was voted to Baron Clyde, commander-in-chief of Her Majesty's forces in the East Indies.   These presentations were not made until 20 Dec., 1860.—The City Justices of the Peace (30 Oct.) fixed upon the site at Stone, near Dartford, for the new City of London Lunatic Asylum.   The 32 acres of land were to cost £3,200, and to provide the necessary funds the several unions were to have been assessed.   This decision, however, gave rise to much opposition and eventually the Corporation bore the entire expense of the ground and building.—Mr. Secretary Walpole announced the intention of the Government to legislate for the City in the next session of Parliament, and the Corporation Enquiry Committee obtained permission to confer with Her Majesty's Government.—Sunday evening services were commenced at St. Paul's (28 Nov.), the Lord Mayor attending in state.—Richard Taylor, editor of the *Philosophical Magazine*, Gresham Professor of Music, and Common Council-man, died 1 Dec.—The Commissioners of Sewers (4th) accepted Mr. Samuel Gurney's proposal to erect a drinking fountain in front of the Royal Exchange.— The course determined for the City intercepting sewer, in connection with the main drainage works carried out by the Metropolitan Board of Works, was to enter the City at Temple Bar and pass along Fleet Street to New Bridge Street, where it would intercept the Fleet sewer.   The estimated cost of the sewer was £253,000, its diameter along Fleet Street being 9 feet.—A report was presented to the Common Council (9 Dec.) announcing three gifts to the City of London School.   Baron Rothschild, M.P., gave £2,000 for scholarships to commemorate the passing of the Bill for the admission of Jews into Parliament.   Mr. William Tite, F.R.S., M.P., gave £1,500 for two scholarships, with the condition that a knowledge of German, as well as French, should be requisite.   £1,000 was presented by the Masterman Testimonial Committee for a similar purpose.   The Court ordered that tablets with the armorial bearings of the benefactors should be placed in conspicuous parts of the school —The Common Council resolved to dispose of the state barge, " Maria Wood," it being no longer required for the purposes of the Corporation.—James Chadwick, the City Pavior, who was contractor for paving the entire carriage-way of the City, was buried at Brompton Cemetery (11th).—The Common Council, on the recommendation of the Finance Committee (20th), adopted alterations which it was stated would effect a saving of £7,702 7s. 4d. per annum to the City funds, in addition to an economy of

£132 3s per annum in connection with the Charity and Trust funds.—The General Purposes Committee were authorised to re-purchase one of the Fruit Meters' places, at a sum not exceeding £7,000.—The Church of St. Mildred, Poultry, was re-opened after undergoing considerable repairs.—Mr. Haywood, engineer to the Commission of Sewers, prepared a tabular report showing the number of vehicles passing through fourteen principal thoroughfares of the City on certain days in 1857.

1859.

N January, 1859, owing to the remonstrance of the City Chamberlain and Sheriffs, the ancient custom of presenting the High Officers of the Corporation with venison from the royal parks, which had been discontinued for several years, was resumed.—An ancient hostelry, the Swan-with-Two-Necks, Gresham Street, formerly Lad Lane, was in process of demolition.—The Common Council (10 Feb) voted addresses to the Queen and Prince Consort, on the birth of a prince to the Princess Royal and Prince Frederick William of Prussia.—Mr. Frederick Woodthorpe was elected to the office of Common Clerk or Town Clerk, vacant by the retirement of Mr. Sergeant Merewether. The Court had previously passed a Bill to alter and amend the oath taken by the Town Clerk and for separating the office of Registrar of the Lord Mayor's Court from that of Town Clerk.—The House of Commons (19th) threw out the Bill which had been introduced for the purpose of spreading the deficiencies, arising out of the Paul and Manini frauds, over the ninety-eight City parishes. The creditors had long waited for the payment of their bills and were on the eve of distraining upon the parish goods and chattels. The Sheriff was actually in possession of the City of London Union Workhouse early in March. The action of the Magistrates in granting a distress warrant in this case, against the parish of St. Mary Bothaw, was declared, on appeal, to be illegal (2 July). The Poor Law Board (Ap., 1860) gave their sanction to the payment of bills, which had been owing to tradespeople by the City of London Union since the Paul and Manini frauds of 1857. An order was made for a call upon the different parishes. —The site of Dr. Johnson's house in the Temple, on which a row of new houses had been built, was named Dr. Johnson's Buildings.—A great meeting of citizens was held at the Guildhall to consider the Reform Bill introduced by Mr. Disraeli on the 28th —A letter was read to the Common Council from Messrs. Parker and Sons, stating "that Mr J. A. Froude, whose History of England they are

Inn Yard of the 'Swan-with-Two-Necks,' Lad Lane, about the year 1830.

publishing, is desirous of consulting the City's records for the purpose of his work" (10 Mar.).—The notable collection of books and prints, formed by Samuel Gregory, relating to the City of London, was sold by Messrs. Sotheby and Wilkinson (10th and 11th).—The Common Council (1 Ap.) pledged itself to assist the Metropolitan Railway Company by taking shares to the amount of £200,000. By this means the Corporation secured a purchaser for vacant lands which had for years been an eyesore to the Metropolis.—The old "Rose and Crown," Aldgate, was taken down.—At the General Election (Ap.) Sir James Duke, Lord John Russell, Baron Rothschild, and Mr. Crawford were returned for the City without a poll.—The first drinking fountain in the City, erected by Mr. Samuel Gurney, M.P., was opened at the corner of St. Sepulchre's Churchyard (21st).—A thanksgiving service was held at St. Paul's for the restoration of peace in India (30th).—The Corporation voted 100 guineas to the fund which was being raised for the Neapolitan exiles (5 May). At the same Court Mr. Robert Malcolm Kerr was elected Under-Sheriff or Judge of the Poultry and Giltspur Street Compters.—The Volunteer movement was inaugurated by a letter from General Peel, Secretary of War (11th). —War had broken out between France and Austria, and the Corporation decided on the 20th to present an address to the Queen expressing regret at the occurrence and thanking Her Majesty for the assurance that strict neutrality would be observed by this country. On the same day the Lord Mayor presided over a meeting in the City, addressed by M. Kossuth, Hungarian patriot, in favour of non-intervention.— The freedom of the City was presented to Sir John Lawrence, Bart., G.C.B., chief commissioner of the Punjaub, for the active part he had taken in quelling the Indian Mutiny (3 June).—The remains of General Picton were removed from the cemetery of St. George, Hanover Square, to St. Paul's Cathedral, and placed in the crypt close to Wellington's tomb (8th).—The freedom of the City was voted to the Earl of Elgin and Kincardine, K.T. (10th), for his services in Canada, China, and Japan.—The Home Secretary (Sir George Cornewall Lewis) brought a Bill into the House of Commons "for the better regulation of the City of London" (7 July). —Messages were first sent from the new premises of the Magnetic and Submarine Telegraph Companies in Threadneedle Street (15th).—The London Rifle Brigade was established, and formally inaugurated at a meeting at the Guildhall (21st). The Common Council voted £105 towards the funds of the Brigade. Four hundred representatives of the Corps assembled at Sion College, London Wall (5 Nov.), and proceeded in marching order, headed by their band, to the Mansion House, where they took the oath of allegiance in presence of the Lord Mayor. Alderman William Anderson Rose was the first to take the oath.—Alderman John Carter was elected Lord Mayor.—Charles William Hick, sword bearer, died at the age of ninety-four; Mr. W. H. Sewell who had performed the duties of the office for many years, was elected in his place.—The Commissioners of Sewers obtained the site of the Town Clerk's residence at the Guildhall, in order to enlarge their accommodation.—The Common Council voted £105 for a bust of Mr. Alderman Salomons to be placed in the City of London School.

The City of London Gas Light and Coke Company, by an Act passed this year, was empowered to raise further capital, and was perpetually incorporated. Power was given to the Corporation, on a requisition of not less than five consumers, to appoint a competent person to test the quality of the gas at the Company's works, with power to institute proceedings before the Lord Mayor, or an Alderman, or the Recorder, in case of defective quality.

1860.

ON 7 Jan., 1860, the monument to General Sir Charles Napier was unveiled in St. Paul's Cathedral, the sculptor being Mr. G. G. Adams. The Ancient Society of Cogers celebrated their 104th anniversary by a dinner at their meeting place in Shoe Lane (18th).—The Common Council voted on the 19th the freedom of the City "in a box of British oak," to Captain F. Leopold M'Clintock, R N., for having ascertained the fate of Sir John Franklin and the officers and crew of the *Erebus* and *Terror*, in the Arctic regions. At the same time the Court passed a resolution of condolence with Lady Franklin, deploring the melancholy end of her heroic husband and his brave companions. Captain M'Clintock was presented with the freedom of the City on 19 May, and was afterwards entertained at a banquet at the Mansion House.—The Master of the Rolls decided in favour of the reinstatement of the Rev. G. G. Daugars as pastor of the French Protestant Church, St. Martin's-le-Grand.—The Home Secretary again introduced a Bill (30th) for the reform of the Corporation.

Sir George Cornewall Lewis said, the measure practically embodied the recommendations of the Royal Commission, revised by the Select Committee of the House of Commons. The Bill was limited to the constitution of the Corporation and to certain duties of the officers. It did not include the financial part of the question, viz.: the coal dues, the metage duties, or the brokers' fees. Mr. Ayrton characterised the Bill as a feeble attempt at reform The Common Council discussed the measure on the 27th, and decided that as the total number of Common Councilmen was to be 120, the maximum number for any ward should be eight It was also resolved that the rights of the Livery should be protected as electors, conjointly with the ratepayers, of the Lord Mayor and Sheriffs. The Livery met at Guildhall, and protested against the Bill.

The Common Council, in virtue of their power as shareholders in the Metropolitan Railway Company, appointed three directors and forty members to attend and vote at the meetings of the Company (23 Feb.). At the half-yearly meeting of the Company, at the London Tavern, a complimentary vote was unanimously passed to Mr. Charles Pearson, the City Solicitor, for his exertions in the formation of a Metropolitan Railway.—Extensive alterations were made about this time at the Guildhall Police Court, which had been likened to the Black Hole of Calcutta.—On 18 Feb. a statement was published by the promoters of the Great Northern, Holborn, and City Extension Railway. It mentioned that the extension had been laid out by Mr. Hawkshaw, and that the total estimate for land and works was £1,500,000. As proof of the importance and value of the anticipated passenger traffic, it was stated that 400,000 persons daily, or 124 millions annually, walk into and out of the City ; and that 88,000 persons daily, or twenty-seven millions annually, arrive in or depart from the City by omnibuses.—Mr. Henry Irving read "Virginius," at Crosby Hall, Bishopsgate Street, on the 8th inst   This was the great actor's first public appearance in London. —The Prince Consort visited the Royal Exchange and Lloyd's, and afterwards proceeded to St. Michael's Church, Cornhill, which had just been restored, and Trinity House, where Lord Palmerston was admitted a member of that Corporation. —A motion to confer the freedom of the City upon Richard Cobden was carried in the Common Council (22 Mar.) by seventy-nine votes to thirty-four. The freedom was to be presented in a box, of the value of fifty guineas.—The Prince Consort inaugurated the new hall of the Clothworkers' Company, in Mincing Lane, and was afterwards entertained at a splendid banquet (27th).

The Livery Hall is one of the finest rooms of the kind in the City   The walls are divided by pillars of Peterhead granite, resting on vases of Purbeck marble, with a basement of Italian black marble   Many varieties of the most costly marbles are worked into the details.

Messrs. Pullen & Son submitted to auction, at Westminster Bridge, the Corporation State Barge "Maria Wood" (5 Ap.). It was knocked down for £105. The barge or gondola was built in 1807, costing £2,000.—On the 12th, considerable excitement was created by the sudden and unexpected rise in the rate of discount, first to 4½ per cent, and then to 5 per cent. This was supposed to be due to the withdrawal of £1,550,000 by the Discount House of Overend, Gurney & Co., in resentment at the application of the Bank rule against re-discounting. The amount mentioned was returned to the Bank within a week, and discount was reduced to its former 'rate.—The St. Paul's Cathedral authorities secured for 1,000 guineas, the organ, by Hill, built for the Panopticon, Leicester Square. The original cost was 3,000 guineas.—A great improvement was effected in the vicinity of the Bank by the widening of Lothbury eastward.—George William Pullinger, late Chief Cashier of the Union Bank of London, was convicted of defrauding the Bank of over £260,000, and was sentenced to twenty years' penal servitude (15th).—The Painters' Company held an exhibition of decorative painting, which was opened on 1 June.—A Select Committee of the House of Commons was appointed to consider the proposed new Meat Market at Smithfield (18th).—Judgment was given by the Master of the Rolls, in the matter of Bridewell Hospital, the scheme of the Attorney-General being adopted.—Two eminent City banking establishments were consolidated under the title of Lubbock, Robarts & Co.—The Queen reviewed the volunteers in Hyde Park, being accompanied by Prince Albert and several members of the Royal Family, and the King of the Belgians. The force numbered 21,000 men, including 1,800 from the City of London and 420 from the Inns of Court (23rd).—Public drinking fountains were about this time opened at St. Dunstan's-in-the-West, Fleet Street, and St. Botolph's, Bishopsgate.—The Common Council, on 12 July, instructed the Sheriffs to present a petition to the House of Commons to pass a Bill providing that on the arraignment of any person for felony or misdemeanour, such person shall not be called upon to plead "guilty" or "not guilty," but instead thereof shall be asked whether he wishes to plead guilty or to be tried.—On the 23rd, Mr. Bunning, City Architect and Surveyor, was appointed Inspector of Works, and Mr. Benjamin Scott, the Chamberlain, and Mr. F. Maynard, Accountant, Inspectors of Accounts of the Metropolitan Railway Company.—The new National and Infant Schools of Aldersgate Ward were opened by the Bishop of London on the 31st.—At a meeting convened by the Garibaldi Committee of the City of London Tradesmen's Club at the London Tavern (22 Aug.), a subscription list was opened to aid Garibaldi in his gallant attempt to emancipate the people of Italy from the tyranny of Bourbon rule.—Mr. John Nathaniel Saunders, the last Water Bailiff to the City of London, died on the 30th. He had been pensioned by the Corporation after the passing of the Thames Conservancy Act.—The Remembrancer laid before the Court an Act of Parliament lately passed, entitled "An Act to establish at Smithfield, in the City of London, a Metropolitan Market for meat, poultry, and other provisions, and for other purposes connected therewith."—The Rev. Alex. Fletcher, D.D., Minister of Finsbury Chapel, died on 30 Sept., and was buried at Abney Park Cemetery.—Mr. Serjeant Payne, the High Steward of Southwark, held a Court Leet for the borough. A jury of seventeen inhabitants was sworn. The High Steward explained that the Court-Leets were among the most ancient courts of the Kingdom, having power to prevent nuisances and criminal offences. It was well to preserve this right, in case the Crown ever failed in its duty.—About this time improvements were taking place in public conveyances.

The open "cattle-box," called a third class railway carriage, had, on several railways given way to a much more convenient and civilised arrangement, and in some second class carriages it was even observed that cushions had been placed. A marked improvement was also made in the construction and fitting of omnibuses. The vis-à-vis omnibus was run, for the first time, between Brixton and the City. In the back compartment of the carriage were seats for four persons, two of whom sat face to face on either side, each person having a separate compartment. In the front there was space for seven persons, the seats having springs. In the centre were steps by which the outside of the omnibus was reached, and a light head, which might be easily turned down in fine weather, protected the passengers from wet or wind. There were eight seats in the outer compartment and four box seats. Inside passengers could signal the driver to stop without rising. Arrangements were being made for starting similar vehicles throughout the Metropolis.

The "Rainbow Tavern," Fleet Street, which dated from 1640, and was a resort of Johnson, Reynolds, and Goldsmith, was pulled down about a year previously, and now rebuilt at a cost of £20,000. It was re-opened 30 Oct.—Alderman William Cubitt was elected Lord Mayor.—Mr. Alderman Wire died at Lewisham (9 Nov.). —On the same day, Mr. Gladstone attended the Guildhall banquet and paid a graceful tribute to the vitality and strength of the Corporation. He said :—

"Five centuries had passed over the hall, in which they now were gathered, and it was left still as firm as it was in the day it was founded. In the same way the local institutions yet retained a vigorous life. Whenever reformation was applied, it was always applied to them in the spirit of reverence and caution, and they came out from it, as had been seen on a thousand occasions, fresher and stronger than before."

Lord Brougham on the same occasion spoke of the citizens as having been at all times the constant friends of liberty.—The sudden death of the preacher-poet of St. Stephen, Walbrook, Dr. Croly, took place on 24 Nov., at the age of eighty. The rector was buried in the church.—St. Paul's Cathedral was re-opened after having been closed for five months (2 Dec.). The improvements which had taken place in the meantime included the removal of the screen and organ, at the entrance to the choir, thereby giving an uninterrupted view from east to west of the cathedral.—The Skinners' Company presented its freedom to Lord Clyde, and entertained him at a banquet (6th).—Lord Clyde and Sir James Outram were entertained at a banquet at the Mansion House, after receiving the freedom of the City (20th). The freedom of the Merchant Taylors' Company was also presented to Lord Clyde.—The death of Alderman Sir George Carroll, at the age of seventy-seven, was announced on the 22nd.—A vast pile of Colonial warehouses were put up during the year on the west side of Mincing Lane, while extensive premises at the west end of Cannon Street were rebuilt, partly shutting out the view of St. Paul's. Under the open space in front, the Corporation had formed capacious vaults, to which there is a general entrance from Old Change.—The Meat and Poultry Market Act 1860 (23 & 24 Vic. cap. 193) set apart a portion of Smithfield for the Hay and Straw Market, and provided that this should for ever be reserved as an open public space.

1861.

COHEN, the blind fiddler, who had been a familiar figure for thirty years in the neighbourhood of the Royal Exchange, died in the London Hospital at the opening of the year 1861.—On 10 Jan., the Common Council voted £1,000 to a general fund for the relief of the suffering poor of the City of London, inclusive of coal whippers and Fellowship porters.   At the same time a Bill was passed into law and became an Act of Common Council, for reducing the number of Rulers of the Fellowship of Corn and Salt Porters of the City of London (commonly known as Billingsgate porters) from seven to six, and for regulating their admission into the office.—A system of overhead telegraphs was established for the City police, each of the six stations being put into direct communication with the head office, Old Jewry.—It was announced that the total receipts of the Indian Relief (Mutiny) Fund, inaugurated by Lord Mayor Finnis in 1857, was £466,422, of which there remained a balance of upwards of £229,000.—The three surviving compurgators claimed compensation for the loss of fees on the admission of persons to the freedom of the City by redemption, but the claim was not allowed by the Corporation (7 Mar.).   The practice of employing six individuals to stand bail for such freemen as might present themselves (a purely formal office), had been abolished by the Corporation, which gave rise to the above application.—The Court of Common Council resolved to present to the London Rifle Brigade a set of camp colours, with the arms and crest of the City emblazoned thereon, at a cost not exceeding £100.—The Common Council also voted (21st) an address of condolence to the Queen on the death of the Duchess of Kent, which took place on the 16th.—It was ascertained that the missing portion of the volume known by the name of the *Liber Custumarum*, belonging to the City Records in the custody of the Town Clerk, had been found among the Cottonian MSS. at the British Museum; the Common Council on the 21st instructed the Library Committee to inquire how it became transferred and what steps should be taken to secure its restoration.—The Court further resolved to petition

Parliament to provide special facilities for the working classes by any trains which might come into the City.—On 26 Mar., it was referred to the Bridge House Estates Committee to obtain designs for the construction of a new bridge at Blackfriars.—An Indian Famine Relief Fund was started at the Mansion House (28 Mar.). At first there was no response to the Lord Mayor's appeal, but after His Lordship had announced that he had written to Calcutta to say that he would not be able to meet the wishes of the Relief Fund Committee, contributions flowed in. The Corporation contributed to the three Famine Funds of 1861, 1874, and 1877, £2,500.—The Stationers' Company opened a Middle Class School in Bolt Court, Fleet Street (8 Ap.).—The Library of Doctors' Commons was sold.—The Earl of Elgin, on his return to this country after the completion of his mission to China, was entertained at the Mansion House, the Lord Mayor giving a banquet in his honour (8 May).—Mr. George Stacy, Fruit Meter, and secretary to the City of London Literary and Scientific Institution, died 13 May, in his 75th year. The Corporation decided that henceforth the duties of Fruit Shifter should be performed by the Fruit Meter.—On 4 June a Court of Husting, the oldest Court of Record within the City, was held at Guildhall, to enrol certain endowments for the City of London School.—The Home Secretary approved the Corporation plans for a Pauper Lunatic Asylum for the City of London (6 June).—The decennial census showed a marked decrease in the resident population of the City, but failed to record the marvellous extent of the day population. These facts were fully brought to light by Mr. Scott, the Chamberlain, in his "Statistical vindication of the City of London."

The progress of City improvements, coupled with the increasing tendency of the trading classes to occupy suburban dwellings, had caused a great decline in the number of resident citizens. In the central district the decrease since 1851 was 19 per cent.; in the East London Union 7½ per cent., and in the West London Union 5½ per cent, or about 10 70 per cent. in the whole of the City.

The old East India House, Leadenhall Street, was sold by tender for £155,000 (20 June). The building was shortly afterwards taken down.—The Act to abolish and dismantle Newgate Market, and for the removal of shambles, slaughter-houses, and other nuisances in the vicinity, was laid before the Common Council (20th).— Numerous meetings were held in different parts of the City for the promotion of a free library for the City, culminating in a meeting of the ratepayers at Guildhall on 11 July. A motion in favour of establishing a free library under the Public Libraries and Museums Act, 1855, was however rejected.—Mr Braidwood, Superintendent of the London Fire Brigade, met with a sad death, while in the act of encouraging his men in their perilous labour, at the great fire at Cotton's Wharf and other buildings in Tooley Street (22nd).

The fire burned fiercely for four days and lasted altogether fifteen days. Besides Mr. Braidwood, two other persons perished, and an unknown number lost their lives in the river while endeavouring to recover salvage from the blazing warehouses. This was regarded as the greatest fire since the Fire of London. Cotton's Wharf alone contained merchandise estimated to be worth a million, the whole of which was destroyed. Braidwood's funeral procession from Watling Street Station to Abney Park Cemetery was witnessed by an immense concourse of people, the Rifle Brigade and police attending

East India House, 1829.

in strong force. A Braidwood Testimonial Fund was started at the Mansion House, and a tablet was erected to Braidwood's memory by the M Division of Metropolitan Police, near the spot where the gallant Fire Brigade Superintendent met his death.

On 17 July, Mr. Cobden and Mr. Bright were entertained at a banquet at the Mansion House, in special recognition of Mr. Cobden's services in negotiating the French Commercial Treaty.—Lord John Russell, on being raised to the peerage, took leave of his constituents, at the Guildhall, after twenty years' service (24th).—An Act to continue the duties levied by the Corporation on coal and wine was laid before the Court of Common Council (25th).—The Lord Mayor (Conservative) gave up his seat at Andover and offered himself as a candidate for the City, his opponent being Mr. Western Wood (Liberal). Mr. Wood was returned (31st) with 4,442 votes, against 3,011 given to the Lord Mayor.— A great fire broke out in Paternoster Row (5 Sept.). It originated in a corn warehouse in London House Yard, and embraced the tallow warehouse of

Messrs. Knight & Son. The publishing warehouses on both sides of the Row suffered severely.—The three City Gas Companies having announced that the price of gas would be increased to 4s. 6d. per thousand feet, the Common Council wished on the 19th to take action, but was advised that the Act left the matter in the hands of the Commissioners of Sewers.—A Common Hall was held on Saturday, 28 Sept., for the election of Lord Mayor. The retiring Lord Mayor (Alderman William Cubitt) having rendered conspicuous service in opposing the Government attempts to destroy the privileges of the City, he was again returned by the Livery, together with Alderman Sir Henry Muggeridge. A poll was demanded, when the Lord Mayor came out first, Sir Peter Laurie being second, and Sir H. Muggeridge third. The Court of Aldermen re-elected Alderman Cubitt to be Lord Mayor for the year ensuing.—A meeting to establish the City of London College was held (2 Oct.), the Bishop of London presiding.—Orders were given to pull down the Almshouses in Coopers' Row, Crutched Friars, which were founded by Sir John Milborne in the middle of the 16th century. The ground was the property of the Drapers' Company, who built new Almshouses at Twickenham.—The Prince of Wales (31 Oct.) opened the new Library for the Benchers of the Middle Temple, which had been erected at a cost of £14,000.—The first trip was taken on the Metropolitan Railway from Paddington to King's Cross, the only part then completed.—Alderman Sir Peter Laurie, knight, died (3 Dec.) at his residence, 7, Park Square, Regent's Park, in his 83rd year. He was Lord Mayor in 1832.—Just after midnight on Sunday morning, 15 Dec., the booming of the great bell of St. Paul's announced to the citizens the death of the Prince Consort, which took place at Windsor Castle, shortly before 11 o'clock on Saturday night (14th).

The news came as a terrible surprise, the public only having been warned by the *Court Circular* on the 8th that Prince Albert had been confined to his apartments by a feverish cold and pains in the limbs. The Common Council met on the 16th, and passed a vote of condolence with the Queen ; a few days later (21st) the Court of Aldermen did the same. Another address to the Queen, expressing the grief and sympathy of the citizens of London, was carried in Common Hall on the 24th. On the day of the funeral (23rd) the City was wrapped in gloom. Nearly all the wholesale houses suspended business during the day, and many large retail establishments were entirely closed. There was no postal delivery in the afternoon. Omnibus and carriage drivers had rosettes of crape attached to their whips. The bells of the City churches tolled in the morning, the booming of the great bell of St. Paul's being heard for nearly two hours. A funeral service was held at the Cathedral in the afternoon. The fact was recalled that it was Prince Albert who had suggested the inscription on the front of the Royal Exchange, "The Earth is the Lord's and the fulness thereof."

The presentation of the Corporation colours to the London Rifle Brigade took place on the 20th.

1862.

SIR CHAPMAN MARSHALL, knight, late Alderman, and Lord Mayor 1839-40, died on 9 Jan., 1862, at Pembridge Crescent.— At a meeting at the Mansion House, on the 14th, it was resolved that a memorial should be erected, of a monumental and national character, to the memory of Prince Consort, and that its design and mode of execution should be approved by Her Majesty. A letter was afterwards read from the Queen to the Lord Mayor, dated Osborne, 19 Feb., in which Her Majesty expressed a desire that an obelisk should be erected in Hyde Park, on the site of the Great Exhibition of 1851, and that at the base of the obelisk there should be groups of statuary. In a second letter the Queen expressed a desire, not as wife, but as Sovereign, to contribute to the Memorial Fund. The Common Council subscribed £500 to this object (23 Jan.)—Mr. John Masterman, who represented the City for several years in the Conservative interest, died (23rd) in his 81st year.—The Common Council subscribed £105 for the relief of the widows and families of those who had perished in the Hartley Coal Mine Disaster, near North Shields, when upwards of 200 men and boys were buried alive (23rd). —The death was announced (1 Feb.) of the Rev. Thomas Hartwell Horne, D.D., rector for twenty-nine years of the united parishes of St. Edmund the King and St. Nicholas Acons. He was in his 85th year and had held for many years an appointment in the British Museum.—The Common Council (20 Feb.) decided to place a bust of the Prince Consort in the Council Chamber. The Court also resolved to contribute £100 in aid of the subscription being raised by the surrounding inhabitants, to prevent the rebuilding of the fat-melting house in London House Yard, St. Paul's.—Sir Henry Muggeridge resigned his aldermanic gown. It was announced (8 Mar.) that the firm of Sir H. & E. Muggeridge had suspended payment, with liabilities amounting to from £150,000 to £200,000.—Mr. George Peabody, an American merchant in London, announced, on the 12th, his gift to the London poor, irrespective of religion or party politics, of £150,000. This was afterwards increased by other donations to £500,000.—Rev. A. McAuslane, of Newport, having accepted the pastorate of the late Dr. Fletcher's congregation, at Finsbury Chapel, preached his first sermon there on the 16th.—The International Exhibition was opened on 1 May. The Lord Mayor, Sheriffs, Aldermen, and forty Commoners went to the Exhibition in state, and took part in the official proceedings.—The Common Council (22nd) voted 250 guineas towards the relief of the operatives in Lancashire and Cheshire, who were bravely facing the cotton famine which arose through the Civil War in America. Subsequent grants were made, the Corporation contributing altogether £1,262 10s. House-to-house collections were made in the City, and several of the leading firms gave £500 each. Gifts in kind were also received in great abundance at the depôt of the Mansion House Committee. The total subscriptions up to 22 Nov. amounted to £219,416 and were remitted to the local Committees for distribution.— The Common Council resolved to bestow the freedom of the City, in a gold box, upon Mr. George Peabody, in recognition of his "princely munificence" to

the poor of London (22nd). The presentation took place on 10 July, Mr. Peabody being afterwards enter-tained at a banquet at the Mansion House.—The free-dom of the City was voted (5 June) to Earl Canning for his eminent services as Governor-General of India during the mutiny. He was the first Viceroy, and did not live to receive the honour which the citizens desired to bestow upon him. The Corporation ordered a bust of Lord Canning to be placed in the Guildhall (26 June). — The National Association for the Pro-motion of Social Science opened its Congress at the Guildhall (7 June), the courts and chambers having been placed at the disposal of the Council by the Cor-

Great St. Helen's, Bishopsgate, 1870. From the West.

poration.—A portion of the Fleet Sewer, about 20 feet in length, near Raymond Street, Clerkenwell, fell in (15th), flooding the houses and doing considerable damage to the Metropolitan Railway works.—On 3 July the Common Council consented to the London, Chatham, and Dover Railway Company commencing the construction of a bridge across the Thames to correspond with the new bridge which the Corporation was about to build at Blackfriars. [The plan was agreed to 18 Sept.] At the same Court it was decided to accept the plan of Joseph Cubitt for the construction of Blackfriars Bridge.—A banquet was given at the Mansion House in honour of the Viceroy of Egypt (5th) — On the 17th the Corporation gave a grand entertainment at the Guildhall to the distinguished foreigners and other eminent persons visiting London upon the occasion of the International Exhibition —An Act was passed to continue the duties levied on coal and wine by the Corporation of London (22nd).—The Common Council approved of plans for removing the Guildhall roof and replacing it by an open roof, orders being given for the execution of the work —The Metropolitan Railway Company (6 Aug) obtained power to raise £300,000 more capital. A trial trip on the new line was made from Edgware Road to Farringdon Street, viâ King's Cross.—The Thames Embankment Bill received the Royal assent (7th).—The removal was announced (16th) of some old and extensive premises at the back of 17, Fenchurch Street. Here, during the last century, was the noted tavern, called Langbourn Coffee House. It afterwards became the birth-place of Young, the tragedian, a contemporary of Charles Kemble —A Sunday School Convention, in connection with the International Exhibition, was held at the rooms of the Sunday School Union, Old Bailey (1 to 4 Sept) Mr. Charles Pearson, the City Solicitor, died (14th).

He was born in Clement's Lane, Lombard Street (4 Oct., 1793), had filled the office of City Solicitor for twenty-three years, and was for three years M P for the borough of Lambeth He was also solicitor to the Commissioners of Sewers and to the Irish Society His speech in defence of the Corporation, printed in 1844, is an admirable exposition of its subject. His wife, née Dutton, painted the portraits of Lord Denman and Sir J. Shaw now in the Guildhall, and his only daughter became the wife of Alderman Sir Thomas Gabriel.

Cripplegate Church was re-opened after considerable alterations, including the removal of the north and south galleries (5 Oct.).—Alderman William Anderson Rose was elected Mayor.—At the Lord Mayor's banquet (10 Nov.) Mr. Alderman Cubitt announced his resignation of the Aldermanic gown. He died on 28 Oct in the following year, at Andover.—The entire fabric of Doctors' Commons was sold (25th).—Baron Bramwell, by the severity of his sentences at the Old Bailey Sessions (commencing 26 Nov.), put a check on the brutal garotte crimes which for months past had been the terror of London. An Act authorising the flogging of such criminals was passed shortly afterwards —The Lord Mayor was elected M.P. for Southampton (5 Dec.).—The Common Council instructed the Bridge House

Committee to consider what steps should be taken to remedy the evils arising from the great increase of traffic over London Bridge (11th).—On the 18th the Police Committee presented a draft Bill for regulating the traffic in the streets of the City, and to prevent obstruction therein. The Bill was approved by the Council and in the next Session became an Act of Parliament. [The Act was reported to the Common Council, 6 Sept., 1863].—Thomas James Nelson was elected City Solicitor (18th).

Formerly the City Solicitor had been paid entirely by fees. That system of payment was now abolished and a fixed salary was attached to the office, clear of all office expenses, and to include all emoluments whatsoever. At the same time the clerks in the City Solicitor's office were precluded from practising as solicitors.

A statue to General Sir W. F. P. Napier was unveiled at St. Paul's Cathedral.—The Drapers' Company's Almshouses were removed from Beech Street, Barbican, to Tottenham.

1863.

THE Metropolitan Railway was opened to the public from Farringdon Street to Paddington (10 Jan., 1863).—The Common Council agreed (22nd) to enlarge the Freemen's Orphan School, so as to provide for 150 instead of 100 children.—The Rev. C. H. Spurgeon, whose Tabernacle had recently been completed, preached at Broad Street Chapel (11 Feb.).—The Prince of Wales was admitted to the freedom of the Fishmongers' Company (12th).—The Common Council instructed the Finance Committee to dispose of the 2,000 shares which the Corporation held in the Metropolitan Railway Company (19th).—Mr. Daniel Whittle Harvey, first Commissioner of the City Police, died on 24 Feb. in his 80th year.—The Corporation made elaborate preparations for the reception of the Princess Alexandra on her arrival in England, inviting the co-operation of the Commissioners of Lieutenancy, the Livery Companies, the Honourable Artillery Company, and the commanding officers of the Royal London Militia and the several volunteer regiments of the City.

Princess Alexandra arrived at Gravesend on 7 Mar., being met by the Prince of Wales, who escorted the Princess from the Royal yacht, "Victoria and Albert." On the arrival of the Royal train at Bricklayers' Arms Station, the Lord Mayor and Sheriffs were introduced to the Prince and Princess, and thenceforward they became responsible for their safe conduct as far as Temple Bar. A long and imposing procession was formed in which the principal City Companies took part. The civic procession, headed by the Lord Mayor and Sheriffs, was followed by six Royal carriages containing the Royal party and their suite, escorted by detachments of Horse and Life Guards. The streets were densely crowded with spectators, and the route was festooned with flags and other decorations, the most elaborate display being reserved for London Bridge. Here, in addition to the Venetian masts surmounted by the Danish emblems, castellated elephants and ravens, medallions of the ancient kings of Denmark, and a hundred tripods stored with incense, was the towering triumphal arch, seventy feet high, near Fishmongers' Hall. This arch spanned the entire roadway and was resplendent with numerous allegorical devices, statues, and other ornaments ; its enormous centre-piece in gold and colours, displayed Britannia and various gods and goddesses, and a colossal equestrian group in plaster formed its finial ornament. The numerous craft in the river were gaily decked out and crowded with spectators. The greatest crush in the streets was at the Mansion House, where a bouquet was presented to the Princess by the Lady Mayoress, who was attended by eight young ladies. A series of galleries had been erected in St. Paul's Churchyard, accommodating 10,000 persons, and Temple Bar was converted into a triumphal arch, the upper part representing a tent of cloth of gold Here the City Deputation took leave of the Royal procession. A medal was afterwards struck by the Corporation in commemoration of the event.

At night the City was brilliantly illuminated Unfortunately, the occasion did not pass without some serious accidents, and the procession was more than once broken up by the crowd. On the night of the illuminations several persons were crushed to death. This led to a warm controversy between the Home Office and the City. Returns of the accidents were moved for in the House of Commons, and Sir George Grey introduced a Bill for amalgamating the City and Metropolitan police, which was strongly opposed by the City A great meeting was held at the Guildhall, and in the end the Home Secretary's Bill was thrown out on the ground of non-compliance with standing orders. On the Monday following the Reception (9 Mar.) the Lord Mayor, accompanied by the Royal Reception Committee, waited upon the Princess Alexandra at Windsor, and, on behalf of the Corporation, presented Her Royal Highness with a diamond necklace and ear-rings, of the value of £10,000.—The Common Council (12 Mar.) voted an address of congratulation to the Queen and "compliments of congratulation" to the Prince and Princess of Wales. The Prince and Princess of Wales were entertained by the Corporation at the Guildhall on 8 June.

The Prince having been presented with the freedom of the City, in a gold box, the Lord Mayor led off the ball with Her Royal Highness Princess Alexandra, immediately in front of the *haut pas* in the great Hall, and the Prince of Wales with the Lady Mayoress Prince Alfred, the Duke of Cambridge, the Prince of Orange, the Duke of Manchester, Lord Granville, the Princess Mary of Cambridge, and other distinguished personages, joined in the dance. Supper was laid for sixty in the Council Chamber. Upon the Royal table was a silver-gilt plateau and service, which formerly belonged to Louis Phillipe, King of the French, and a number of gold plates and dishes made for the Queen of Spain. The dessert plates had in the centre the Prince's plume and the City Arms. The City Companies lent their cups and salvers, scarcely anything but gold appearing in the Royal buffet ; almost the only exception was the Pepys' cup, with its exquisite chasing The whole entertainment was carried out on the most lavish scale, at a cost of about £15,000. The Royal visitors left the Guildhall with an escort of Life Guardsmen, the route from Marlborough House to the City being brilliantly illuminated.

The foundation stone of the London, Chatham and Dover Railway Bridge, Blackfriars, was laid by Lord Sondes, chairman of the Company (2 May). Much excitement was caused by the proposal of this Company to throw a bridge across Ludgate Hill, which would shut out the west view of St. Paul's, and be otherwise a great disfigurement from an architectural and æsthetic point of view. The Common Council (7 May) instructed the Improvement Committee to continue its opposition to the proposed viaduct Unfortunately, the opposition was unavailing, and the engineering atrocity was perpetrated.

Punch, in an article headed "Surgery in the City," said the London, Chatham and Dover Railway Company will, unless restrained by Parliament from accomplishing their design, adorn the Metropolis of England with a structure which will be interesting to surgeons. The tunnel which they were going to build over Ludgate Hill would be a greater eye-sore than any case in the Ophthalmic Hospital.

On the 21st, Col. James Fraser, Chief Constable of Berkshire, was elected Commissioner of the City Police.—The British Orphan Asylum held a bazaar, which was opened by the Prince of Wales, at the Guildhall (11, 12, and 13 June). —Rev. William Rogers, M.A., late incumbent of St. Thomas, Charterhouse, was inducted to the Rectory of St Botolph, Bishopsgate (26th).—The Lord Mayor gave a banquet at the Mansion House to Earl Derby and his political supporters (1 July). Lord Derby referred to "the scandalous monopoly by which the Liberal party monopolised the whole of the four seats of the City."— Mr. Edward Tyrrell resigned the office of Remembrancer on the ground of ill-health (2 July).—The Prince of Wales received the freedom of the Mercers' Company (8th). The *Times* tells an amusing story about the Prince being put down at the side entrance in Ironmonger Lane, and received by an old lady who was looking out for some one else, instead of by the Master and Wardens who were waiting in state at the front door in Cheapside.— A national subscription was opened at the Mansion House in co-operation with the Dean and Chapter of St. Paul's, with a view to embellishing the Cathedral according to the original design of Sir Christopher Wren.—The long-pending dispute between Mr. Kay Dimsdale and the Saddlers' Company was settled in the House of Lords (28th).

The Saddlers' Company had ejected Mr. Dimsdale on the ground that he was actually insolvent before he was admitted to the Court of Assistants. Their lordships issued a mandamus directing the wardens to restore Mr. Dimsdale to his office

The Fishmongers presented the freedom of their Company to the Duke of Cambridge (1 Aug.).—The first pile of the temporary wooden bridge at Blackfriars was driven on 7th Aug —About this time the City police adopted the helmet in place of the old-fashioned civilian's tall hat —Mr. Richard Lambert Jones died at Lowestoft (16th).   He had been for thirty-one years a member of the Common Council, and had been prominently associated with the building of London Bridge and the Royal Exchange, and the establishment of the Guildhall Library.   The following letter was addressed by the Duke of Wellington to Mr. Jones :

"London, Aug. 19, 1839.—The Duke of Wellington presents his compliments to Mr. Jones, and regrets that he should have taken the trouble to write to him, for he has not been able to read his handwriting "

The Irish Society was present at the opening of the new Derry Bridge by the Lord-Lieutenant of Ireland (26th).—Alderman William Lawrence was elected Lord Mayor (29th).—On 1 Oct. a letter was read from Mr. James Bunstone Bunning, resigning the office of Architect and Surveyor, after twenty years' service.   His death was announced shortly afterwards (5 Nov.).   Mr. Bunning had designed the Freemen's Orphan School, Billingsgate Market, the Coal Exchange, the new Cattle Market (Islington), the City Prison at Holloway, the City of London Lunatic Asylum (Stone), and other important buildings, of the aggregate cost of about £750,000.—The death of Mr. George Hitchcock, head of the firm in St. Paul's Churchyard, and a zealous supporter of the Young Men's Christian Association, and the Early Closing Association, occurred on the 3rd Oct —William Anthony, supposed to be the last of the "Charlies," died on the 13th — About this time the Salters' Almshouses, in Monkwell Street, established under the will of Sir Ambrose Nicholas, Kt. (1641), and re-built after the Fire in 1666, were taken down for warehouses.—The Post Office Savings Bank was removed from St. Martin's-le-Grand to 27, St. Paul's Churchyard (29th).—The Common Council instructed the General Purposes Committee to apply for a mandamus to compel St. Bartholomew's Hospital to allow the Lord Mayor to take his seat as President (5 Nov.).—The Corporation were ordered to pay £31,715 to the Guardians of the West London Union, for the removal of the Workhouse grounds in West Street, Smithfield, to make way for the western approach to the new Meat and Poultry Markets (6th).—The Common Council agreed to the erection of artizans' dwellings on a portion of their ground in Victoria Street (afterwards called Farringdon Road), at an estimated cost of £20,000, to be provided out of the Finsbury Estate Surplus Fund (19th).—St. Bride's Church was re-opened after extensive alterations (29th).— A great fire occurred in Wood Street and Milk Street (20 and 21 Dec.).   The estimated losses were upwards of £100,000.—During this year the Blackfriars Bridge Act was passed, authorising the Corporation to raise on the credit of the Bridge House Estates, a sum of £300,000 for rebuilding the Bridge.

1864.

IT was announced (2 Jan., 1864) that the site of the old Fleet Prison, Farringdon Road, latterly used as the City stone-yard, had been given up to the London, Chatham and Dover Railway Company, the stone-yard being removed to the "Finsbury Estate," in the neighbourhood of Worship Street. An agreement was sealed by the Corporation (21 Ap.), the Railway Company paying £60,000 for the site.—The Princess of Wales was delivered of a son (8 Jan.). The Common Council, on the 12th, voted an address to the Queen congratulating Her Majesty on the happy event, and "compliments of congratulation" were passed to the Prince and Princess of Wales.—On the 14th, Mr. William Corrie, magistrate at Bow Street Police Court, was elected Remembrancer.—Early in Feb. Messrs. Edwin Fox & Bousfield sold the premises occupied by the Colonial Life Office, at the western end of Lombard Street, at the rate of one million and three-quarters sterling per acre.—Five of the seven pirates convicted of the murder of the Captain of the "Flowery Land" were executed in front of Newgate (22nd), amid the usual scenes of disgraceful levity on the part of the crowd.—The Prince of Wales attended the public supping of the Bluecoat boys at Christ's Hospital (25th).—Mr. Horace Jones was elected architect, surveyor and clerk of the City's works (26th).—Barbican Chapel, an old-established Nonconformist place of worship, held its closing services (28th), the site being required for the Metropolitan Railway.—At least 250 persons lost their lives by an inundation in the neighbourhood of Sheffield. The Common Council voted 400 guineas in aid of the sufferers (17 Mar.).—A marble bust of the late Earl Canning, by Mr. Noble, was placed in the Loggia at Guildhall (17th).—On 1 Ap. Smithfield was hoarded in, prior to the sale of the pens, and the excavations for the goods station underneath the proposed Meat and Poultry Market.—A vote of thanks was passed by the Common Council (7th) to Sir Moses Montefiore for the signal services rendered by him to the cause of humanity.—Petitions were presented from a number of wards and parishes praying the Corporation to sanction the erection of baths and washhouses in the City.—Garibaldi, having made a public entry into London amidst an extraordinary demonstration of popular enthusiasm, was presented with the freedom of the City, in a gold box, on the 20th. An immense crowd assembled in the streets around the Guildhall, and the press was so great that Menotti, the

son of the Italian patriot, was unable to gain admission. Menotti was to have received the gold box, on behalf of his father, who had previously said that as he had always refused any gifts he could not make an exception. Garibaldi was entertained at a banquet at the Fishmongers' Hall on the following day. The Lord Mayor received several letters from Italian municipalities, including those of Santa Maria and Capua, expressing the thanks of the inhabitants for the warm and generous reception accorded to Garibaldi.—The Emperor of Russia presented the Corporation with a copy of the "Bibliorum Codex Sinaiticus" (recently published, at his expense, at Constantinople), which was placed in the Guildhall Library.— Amongst the many houses undergoing demolition at this time (14 May), for the purposes of the new Markets and Metropolitan Railway extension at Smithfield, was that in which once resided, and where died, Richard Baxter, author of the "Saint's Everlasting Rest." This was on the eastern side of Charterhouse Lane, near the Charterhouse.—The Common Council resolved to assist the Commissioners of Sewers (the rating body for the City) in carrying out important street improvements. The Improvement Committee was instructed (19th) to confer with the Commissioners and report from time to time as to the amounts which they recommended should be paid out of the City's cash towards such objects. This was continuing an old practice of the Court, and it is only necessary to mention that from the year 1780 a sum of £186,031 had been expended in this way.— The new Almshouses of the Salters' Company, at Watford, erected at a cost of about £8,000, were opened on the 18th.—On the 26th, Mr. Tyrrell, late Remembrancer, offered to the Corporation a collection of transcripts of records relating to the City from the British Museum and Public Record Office, which was subsequently purchased.—Extensive alterations were in progress (28th) in the church of St. Mary the Virgin, Aldermanbury, during the course of which the vaults were filled in.

In closing the vault of the notorious Judge Jeffreys the workmen discovered a small brass plate affixed to the wall, inscribed as follows: "The Honourable Mrs. Mary Dive, oldest daughter of the Right Honourable George Lord Jeffrey, Baron of Wern and Lord High Chancellor of England by Ann his lady, daughter of Thomas Bludworth, sometime Lord Mayor of the City of London, died 4 Oct, 1711, in the 31st year of her age." The brass was inserted in the wall of the north aisle.

A temporary foot-bridge at Blackfriars, erected at a cost of £42,125, was opened for traffic on 1 June.—On the 12th a funeral service was held at South Place Chapel in memory of the late Mr. W. J. Fox, who had been for upwards of forty years its minister.—The Bishop of London divided the City into two urban or rural deaneries, eastern and western.—The Holborn Valley Improvement Act received the Royal assent on the 23rd.

The scheme comprised a high level street to be carried on a viaduct, commencing at Ely Court, Holborn Hill, and extending to the Old Bailey, with streets branching from it at either end into Farringdon Road ; the widening of Shoe Lane , and the altering of the levels of the streets over which the Viaduct was to pass.

The freedom of the City was voted to Sir Jamsetjee Jeejeebhoy, a Bombay merchant, in recognition of his munificent gifts to various charitable institutions of the City and the Metropolis at large. —Omnibus fares between the Angel and the Post Office and London Bridge were reduced from fourpence to threepence (2 July).—The foundation stone of the Thames Embankment was laid on the 8th. —The Prince of Wales was presented with the freedom of the Clothworkers' Company (11 July).—The Corporation, at the invitation of the Metropolitan Board of Works, inspected the works for the main drainage of the Metropolis (25th) —Milton's house in Barbican was removed for the Metropolitan Railway. —A great fire occurred in Gresham Street, destroying the ancient and stately hall of the Haberdashers' Company and many valuable carvings and paintings. Some costly pictures and oak carvings were however saved.   The adjoining premises of Tapling and Co and Hellaby and Son were burned down, the loss being estimated at from £150,000 to £200,000 (19th).—The church of St. Giles, Cripplegate, was re-opened, after restoration, as a national monument to the poet Milton (17th).—Deputy Fenning (Cheap), the oldest member of the Corporation, died (27th).—The trial train, containing a number of the directors of the London, Chatham, and Dover Railway and others, passed over the new Blackfriars Bridge to Ludgate Station (6 Oct.).   This was the first railway train which had come within the bounds of the City proper.   The line was opened for traffic 20 Dec.—The Common Council decided to accept a proposal of the Southwark Bridge Company to open the bridge to the public, free of toll, for six months for the sum of £1,834, and with the option of continuing the opening for twelve months for a further sum of £2,750.   The bridge was opened, free of toll, on 8 Nov.—Alderman Warren Stormes Hale was elected Lord Mayor.—Mr. F. O. Martin, one of Her Majesty's Inspectors of Charities, opened an official inquiry into the foundation, endowments, and objects of Bridewell Hospital and King Edward's Schools, and the present circumstances of these charities. —During the year one of Dr. Salviati's mosaics was set up in St. Paul's Cathedral.   It was a representation of Isaiah writing his prophecies.   The design was by Mr A. Stevens.

1865.

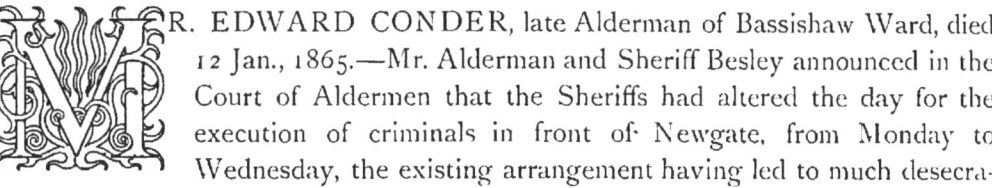R. EDWARD CONDER, late Alderman of Bassishaw Ward, died 12 Jan., 1865.—Mr. Alderman and Sheriff Besley announced in the Court of Aldermen that the Sheriffs had altered the day for the execution of criminals in front of Newgate, from Monday to Wednesday, the existing arrangement having led to much desecration of the Sabbath (7 Feb.).—A great watch and jewel robbery took place at Mr. Walker's, 63, Cornhill (5th), the loss amounting to £6,000. £1,400 worth of the stolen jewellery was recovered. A number of Mr. Walker's gold watches were afterwards fished up from the Thames, near Blackfriars Bridge. This and a number of other burglaries gave rise to considerable alarm as to the insecurity of property in the City, and at a special meeting of the Court of Aldermen held on the 14th, it was decided to increase the pay of the police.—At the meeting of the Common Council on 9 Feb., the death of Mr. William Turner Alchin, the City Librarian, was announced, and shortly afterwards Mr. W. H. Overall was appointed to succeed him in the office.—On 18 Mar. two official reports on the gas supply of the City were published. This subject had for some time excited a considerable amount of interest in the City, and meetings were held to denounce the action of the gas companies in raising the price of this commodity. The Special Gas Committee of the Commissioners of Sewers issued one of the reports and the other had been jointly prepared by Mr. Haywood, Engineer to the Commission, and Dr. Letheby, the Medical Officer of Health, and Gas Analyst to the City.

From these reports it appeared that three companies were now supplying gas in the City :—1. The Chartered Company, incorporated 1810 ; 2 The City of London Company, incorporated 1817, 3 The Great Central Company, incorporated 1851. In 1823 the price of gas was 15s per thousand and in 1848 it was 6s. In the latter year the Commission endeavoured in vain to persuade the companies to lower the price to 4s In 1849 a Bill was brought into Parliament for the incorporation of the Great Central Gas Consumers' Company, but the Bill was lost The same year, however, the companies then supplying the City reduced the price to 4s The Great Central Company obtained leave of the Commission (7 Dec, 1849), to lay pipes in the City, the company having entered into an undertaking never to charge more than 4s. per thousand cubic feet for gas, the agreement being ratified by an indenture on 12 Feb, 1850. For ten years the maximum price was 4s., and the illuminating power of the gas had been raised from twelve to fourteen wax candles. After considerable agitation in 1859 and 1860, the Metropolis Gas Act (1860) was passed, which made an end of competition. This Act enabled the company to raise the price, and on 31 Jan, 1861, the charge was 4s. 6d, while the quality of the gas was inferior.

Mr. Philip Cazenove presented the Corporation with a full-length portrait of Mr. Geo. Peabody, by H. W. Pickersgill, R.A. (23rd).—The Rev. Dr. Mortimer resigned his position as Head Master of the City of London School (6 Ap.)—The

Court agreed to purchase a private collection of Roman and other antiquities found within the City during the last fifteen years, at a cost not exceeding £200.—It was decided that Southwark Bridge should continue open free of toll for another period of six months on the terms already stated.—News was received (26th) of the assassination of President Lincoln.   There was great excitement on the

Stock Exchange and throughout the City. On the following day the Common Council passed a resolution expressing its profound sympathy with the people of the United States, and recording its detestation of the atrocious crime. —The Prince of Wales dined at Fishmongers' Hall (10 June).—At a special Court of Common Council (15 June) it was announced that the Princess of Wales had given birth to a prince (3 June). The usual address to the Queen and "compliments" to the Prince and Princess of Wales were voted and presented.— The Court granted £500 for restoring the foundations of the Mansion

View from St. Paul's Pier, Southwark Bridge in distance.

House, the cost of which operation up to May, 1866, was £7,500.—The Corporation resolved to place a bust of the late Mr. Cobden, in the Council Chamber, at a cost not exceeding £200 (15th).—The Remembrancer announced the appointment of a Commission for building the Courts of Justice, and Mr. Alderman James Clarke Lawrence, M.P., was selected as the nominee of the Corporation for appointment on the Commission.—On the 24th it was reported that, since the recent jewel robberies in the City, fifteen of the principal firms in Cornhill had jointly availed themselves of the services of members of the Corps of Commissionaires, for the protection of their shops and houses at night and on Sundays. —The City Parliamentary election resulted in the return (11 July) of G. J. Goschen, 7,102 ; R. W. Crawford, 7,086 ; Alderman W. Lawrence, 6,637 ; and Baron Lionel de Rothschild, 6,525.   The unsuccessful candidates were Mr. George Lyall, who polled 4,197 votes, and Mr. R. N. Fowler who received 4,086 votes.— On the 20th the Lord Mayor laid the first stone of the new Blackfriars Bridge, the ceremony being followed by a banquet at

Old Blackfriars Bridge, about 1800.

the Mansion House.—The Rev. Edwin Abbott Abbott, M.A., Second Master at Clifton College, was elected Head Master of the City of London School (25th).— A new workhouse for the poor chargeable to the West London Union, was opened at Holloway (29th).   The aged paupers were removed to the new house from the old building in Smithfield.—About this time the cattle disease was making extensive ravages throughout the Metropolis, and a meeting of medical officers of health, veterinary surgeons, cattle salesmen and others, convened by the Markets Committee of the Corporation, was held at the Mansion House, at which a Committee was appointed to take whatever steps might be deemed necessary.   The Metropolitan Cattle Plague Committee held numerous meetings, and a special meeting of the Common Council was convened.   A Compensation Fund was started, which, on 5 Oct., amounted to nearly £1,600.   The Lord Mayor, accompanied by the members of the Markets Committee, had an interview with the Lords of the Council at Whitehall, and was informed that a Royal Commission for the purpose of inquiring into the question of the Cattle Plague was being organised (18 Sept.).—On 2 Sept. there died in the Debtors' Prison, Whitecross Street, George Middleton Ball, an octogenarian, who had been confined there nearly twenty-two years.—The death was recorded (23rd) of Alderman Thomas Farncomb, Lord Mayor in 1849, at the age of eighty-seven.—The Dutch Church, Austin Friars, was opened after undergoing complete restoration (1 Oct.).—The Lord Mayor and Lady Mayoress gave a banquet in honour of the Dowager Queen Emma of Hawaii (23rd).— The Guildhall and Royal Exchange were closed, and business in the City was largely suspended on the day of the public funeral of Lord Palmerston, which was attended by the Lord Mayor and Sheriffs and a small deputation from the Corporation (27th).—The formal opening of the City extension of the North London Railway, from Dalston to the new Broad Street terminus, took place on the 31st.—A public meeting was held at the Mansion House to consider a proposal by the Rev. William Rogers for a scheme of middle-class education in the City. A Committee was appointed and a charter was eventually obtained for the establishment of the Cowper Street School.—Alderman Benjamin Samuel Phillips was elected Lord Mayor.—The Guildhall Banquet on 9 Nov. was regarded as the formal uncovering of the new open oak roof, which was much admired.

Amongst other alterations in the Guildhall were the following : The original windows on the north and south sides of the hall, which about the beginning of the century had been built up, were opened and restored , one on the south side was filled with stained glass   The statues of Chatham, Pitt, Beckford, and Wellington, were lowered, and the hall was for the first time lighted with sixteen chandeliers, designed in accordance with the architecture of the hall. The alterations were carried out under the direction of Mr. Horace Jones.

The Common Council expressed regret that the Ecclesiastical Commissioners had not shown any disposition to concur in an arrangement for the preservation of Bunhill Fields Burial Ground, except upon terms of sale and purchase, and protested against the ground being used for secular purposes. In view of the high historic interest attaching to this celebrated Nonconformist cemetery, the Court expressed itself willing to accept the care and preservation of the ground on behalf of the public.—The Corporation decided to lend the Guildhall for six weeks to the Committee of the City of London Working Classes Industrial Exhibition (7 Dec.).— The Lord Mayor announced to the Court of Aldermen that the Government desired Mr. Russell Gurney, the Recorder, to act as Commissioner for inquiring into the recent lamentable occurrences in Jamaica. The Recorder shortly afterwards sailed for that island, and conducted an inquiry into the conduct of Governor Eyre.

1866.

R. GOSCHEN was appointed Chancellor of the Duchy of Lancaster, with a seat in the Cabinet of Earl Russell's Administration (11 Jan., 1866). The new Minister was re-elected for the City (27 Feb.).—At a public meeting at the Mansion House, it was resolved to urge Parliament to take immediate steps with a view to preserve the commons and open spaces around the Metropolis for the use of the public (24 Jan.).—The Commissioners of Sewers decided to widen and improve the public thoroughfare at the south-west corner of St. Paul's Churchyard (30th).—The Lord Mayor laid before the Common Council an extract from the presentment of the Leet Jury of the Great Liberty Manor, Southwark, to the Court of Aldermen, as Lords of the Manor, regretting that there was no Town Hall in the borough, and that the only available place for holding the Court of Record, public meetings and the like was an hotel (8 Feb.).—In consequence of the increased cost of provisions the Court resolved to distribute among the aged and infirm inmates of the London Almshouses and Rogers' Almshouses at Brixton a sum of £100.—The Corporation voted £1,000 in aid of the fund for the promotion of Middle Class Education in the City (22nd).—Mr. Crawford moved the second reading of the Corporation Gas Bill in the House of Commons (6 Mar.). It was agreed to by a majority of twenty-six and referred to a Select Committee. The object of the Bill was to empower the Corporation to undertake the manufacture and sale of gas within the City.—On 8 Mar. the Corporation resolved to erect a Meat and Poultry Market at Smithfield at the cost of £200,820. —Several scholars at the City of London School had been debarred from acquiring honours and endowments to which they were entitled at Oxford and Cambridge owing to the declaration required by the Act of Uniformity. The Corporation therefore decided to petition Parliament to repeal the clauses of the disqualifying Act.—The 20th was appointed by the Bishop of London as a day of humiliation on account of the Cattle Plague. The Lord Mayor and Sheriffs attended a special service at St. Paul's.—The Corporation resolved, by sixty-three votes to thirty-six, to petition Parliament in favour of the legalization of marriage with a deceased wife's sister (22nd).—It was decided to obtain for the Guildhall a bust of Lord Palmerston at a cost not exceeding £250.— Mr. Haywood, Engineer and Surveyor to the Commissioners of Sewers, prepared an elaborate plan for the reconstruction of the City, especially with a view to relieving the increased traffic.—An enthusiastic meeting was held at the Mansion House in support of the Government Reform Bill (12 Ap.). The Common Council agreed to petition Parliament in favour of the Bill (19th).—The City of London Lunatic Asylum, Stone, near Dartford, Kent, was opened on the 16th.

The building was erected at the Corporation's expense and not by means of a county rate, at a cost of about £77,000, including the purchase of the freehold. Provision was made for 125 patients of either sex. The Asylum was afterwards enlarged to accommodate 456 patients, the total cost to the Corporation being £126,898, while the total amount paid out of the City's cash (in the absence of a county rate) for the maintenance of pauper lunatics without settlement, up to 31 Dec., 1892, has been £39,833 17s. 6d.

Mr. Peabody distributed the prizes at the close of the City of London Working Classes Exhibition at Guildhall (opened on 6 Mar.) and was received with great applause (17th).—The Corporation resolved to convert the two vacant hotels at the Metropolitan Cattle Market into improved dwellings for the labouring poor, at an estimated cost of £10,000 (3 May). It was decided (4 Oct.) that preference should be given to persons displaced by the Holborn Valley improvements. —On the 8th Mr. Kennedy moved in the House of Commons for returns relating to the affairs of the Irish Society, the motion being substantially agreed to.—On the 10th a fountain was opened on the north side of the Church of St. Lawrence Jewry, to commemorate the pious gifts of parochial benefactors. This day was known as Black Friday in the City, the failure of Messrs. Overend, Gurney & Co., which had recently been made a joint-stock limited liability company, causing a commercial panic. The Bank rate went up from 8 to 9 per cent. and numerous failures, including that of the great railway contractors, Peto & Betts, ensued. Mr. Gladstone, after conferences with bank directors and others, announced the suspension of the Bank Charter Act, which had the effect of allaying the panic.— The Commissioners of Sewers signed an agreement with the London, Chatham and Dover Railway Company for the purchase of land at the foot of Ludgate Hill for the proposed circus (15th).—A terrible state of overcrowding in the City was revealed at a meeting of the City of London Union on the 22nd.

One of the relieving officers found in a house of nine rooms in Three Herring Court, St. Katherine's Cree, forty-five persons, or an average of five to a room. In one of the apartments nine persons were living. In another house in the court, containing eight rooms, forty persons resided Scarlet fever had attacked the inmates.

The Duke of Edinburgh, K.G. (Prince Alfred), received the freedom of the Grocers' Company, in a gold box (28th).—In consequence of the valuable services rendered to the City by Deputy Henry De Jersey, the Common Council decided to present him with a piece of plate, subscribed for by members of the Court (31st).—At the same meeting it was resolved to purchase Southwark Bridge for

£200,000.—The Duke of Edinburgh received the freedom of the Merchant Taylors' Company on 5 June, and on the 7th took up the freedom of the City, to which he was entitled by patrimony.   His Royal Highness was afterwards entertained at a déjeuner at the Guildhall.—The Mercers' Company gave a banquet to the Prince of Wales and a number of distinguished guests on the 9th, and on the 11th H.R.H. laid the first stone of the British and Foreign Bible Society's building in the new thoroughfare, Queen Victoria Street.   The Prince afterwards lunched with the Lord Mayor.—Several workmen having been injured by the fall of some scaffolding in Guildhall Yard, the Common Council voted £100 towards the relief of the sufferers and their families (21st).—The Court resolved to insure the Guildhall, Mansion House, Sessions House, the City Mews, and Rogers' Almshouses for £200,000.—The King and Queen of the Belgians were entertained at the Mansion House (6 July).   The Prince and Princess of Wales and the Duke of Edinburgh were also present.—Upwards of a hundred Belgian riflemen, who had come over to the National Rifle Meeting, at Wimbledon, presented an address of thanks to the Lord Mayor for the hospitality which had been extended to them (11th).—The long struggle between the Corporation and the West London Guardians over the Smithfield Workhouse came to an end. Legal proceedings were taken, and eventually the house was cleared on the 12th. —The Archæological Institute of Great Britain and Ireland held its annual congress at the Guildhall (17th).—It was decided to pull down the parish church of St. Benet Gracechurch and St. Leonard Eastcheap, under the powers of the Union of Benefices Act, the site being thrown into the public way.—On the 19th the workmen making excavations for the Holborn Viaduct came into contact, at the bottom of Holborn Hill, with a solid body of masonry, which was supposed to be one of the abutments of the ancient Holborn Bridge.— An alteration was made in the railings and steps in front of the Mansion House, which afforded increased accommodation for pedestrian traffic.   The cost was £305.—The Atlantic cable between Europe and America was completed on the 28th.   The event was celebrated by a banquet at the Mansion House (30 Oct.). —During the summer and autumn the cholera was raging in London; 5,548 persons died of cholera, and 2,692 of diarrhœa and other similar ailments.   The Lord Mayor started a fund to relieve the sufferers at the East End, the Queen subscribing on 2 Aug. £500.   By 3 Sept. £17,000 had been raised and applied to the relief of poor cholera patients and the maintenance of orphans whose parents had died during the epidemic.—A great meeting of working men was held at the Guildhall in favour of the Reform Bill, the Lord Mayor presiding.

The great hall was crowded with from five to six thousand persons, who arrived in processional order, accompanied by bands and banners. The speakers included Mr. E. Beales, president of the Reform League; Mr. George Potter; Mr. Connolly (stonemason); Mr. Odger (cordwainer); Mr. Upshall (joiner); Mr. Coffey (bootmaker); and Mr. Bradlaugh. The Lord Mayor, who replied to the criticisms which had been made upon him for allowing the use of the Guildhall for such a purpose, was enthusiastically cheered at the close of the proceedings. Overflow meetings were held in the Guildhall Yard. Placards were freely posted about with the inscriptions "Long live Gladstone, Bright, Beales, and the Lord Mayor;" "We working men are for peace and order and a vote in Parliament."

The new Cannon Street terminus, of the South Eastern Railway, was opened for passenger traffic (1 Sept.). The whole of the Steel-yard, rich in historic memories, was covered by the terminus and its connected works. It was pointed out that the fine view from London Bridge of St. Paul's and the spires

Cannon Street Station from River.

of Wren's City churches was utterly destroyed by the huge and hideous roof of the South Eastern Railway terminus.—The Corporation resolved to construct additional bullock lairs at the Metropolitan Cattle Market at an estimated cost of £6,000.—Mr. James Levick, Governor of the Crédit Foncier et Mobilier of England, laid the corner stone of an extensive suite of offices at the southern corner of Lombard Street and Gracechurch Street (20th).—On the 28th a meeting was held at the Mansion House to relieve the famishing natives of Orissa.—It was announced (6 Oct.) that extensive alterations were about to be made at Drapers' Hall at a cost of £28,000.—On the 12th a stormy meeting of the London, Chatham and Dover Railway Company was held at St. James's Hall.—On the 20th some workmen engaged in excavations in London Wall, at a depth of about 30 feet, came upon a quantity of bones of horses, oxen, and deer, the horns of the latter being in a fine state of preservation. There were also goats' horns, and parts of the jaw of the wild boar, together with partially decayed spear handles.

Altogether about twenty cart-loads of bones were taken out.—Dr. Conquest, a celebrated City medical practitioner, died at Plumstead (24th).—Attention was called in the Court of Common Council to the enormous increase in the City assessments, which had gone up £996,469 in ten years. This was attributed chiefly to the passing of the Union Assessment Act, which gave to another body the power to re-value the City (1 Nov.).—Alderman Thomas Gabriel was elected Lord Mayor.—The Local Government and Taxation Committee was instructed to introduce an Election Act Amendment Bill, with a view to enabling all persons on the Parliamentary register to vote at ward elections (12th). This would increase the electorate from about 6,700 to 15,000.—A bazaar and flower and fruit show was held at Guildhall on the 13th, in aid of the Albert Orphan Asylum, the Duke of Edinburgh attending.—The Corporation voted £500 for the relief of sufferers by the lamentable and extensive fire in Quebec (15th).—Mr. C. Buxton presided at a meeting, at St. James's Hall, of the Metropolitan Municipal Association, recently formed for promoting the better local government of the Metropolis (11 Dec.).—A day census of the City was taken and submitted to the Common Council on the 13th.

According to this interesting return the night population was found to be 113,387, while the residents in the day-time numbered 283,520. The number of persons resorting to the City, not included in the above, was 509,611. The night population, as taken by the Government, only accounted for 356 merchants out of nearly 6,000, 9 bankers out of 263 ; and 33 brokers out of 3,297.

Four persons were killed in an accident outside Aldersgate Station, caused by the fall of a girder upon the end carriages of a passing train during the construction of the new Meat Market (19th).

1867.

 MEETING was held at the Mansion House, to devise measures for alleviating the distress at the East End (21 Jan., 1867).—The last service was performed in the church of St. Mary Somerset and St. Mary Mounthaw.

This was the first of the City churches to be removed under the provisions of the Bishop of London's Union of Benefices Act, 1859. It was one of Wren's churches, the former church of St. Mary Somershythe having been destroyed in the Great Fire. A new church bearing the same name was to be built in the populous district of St. Mary's, Hoxton, and the parishes of St. Mary Somerset and St. Mary Mounthaw would be in future united with the joint benefice of St. Nicholas Cole Abbey and St. Nicholas Olave.

It was announced that the Old Cock Tavern, Fleet Street, was about to be taken down for the approach to the Law Courts.—The Common Council voted the usual address and compliments of congratulation, on the birth of a princess to the Princess of Wales (25 Feb.).—The great western window at St. Paul's Cathedral was unveiled (4 Mar.).—The Roman hexagonal column inscribed by Anencletus to his "conjux pientissima Claudia Martina," discovered beneath the wall of Ludgate, in 1806, and since lost, was now found in the open yard of the London Coffee House, on Ludgate Hill. The Library Committee was instructed (7th) to take immediate steps for its preservation in the Guildhall Museum.—Mr. Benjamin Scott's *Statistical Vindication of the City of London* was published by the Corporation.—A great meeting was held at the Guildhall to oppose the Metropolitan Improvement Rate Bill then before Parliament (20th).

The object of this Bill was to empower the Metropolitan Board of Works to levy a charge of fourpence in the pound upon property situated within the Metropolis, including the City. As the citizens would thus be taxed without having adequate representation on the Board which would spend the money, the Bill was opposed as tyrannical at meetings held in the Guildhall, and in various wards throughout the City.

Mr. Henry Thomas Riley, M.A., was engaged by the Common Council, to compile a volume of extracts from the earliest Corporation records, published as *Memorials of London and London Life* (21st).—A deputation from the Common Council and others waited upon Sir Stafford Northcote, to urge the necessity of obtaining an amendment of the Metropolitan Gas Act 1860 (27th). —A stained-glass window was placed in the north-west corner of the Guildhall by Mr. Cornelius Lea Wilson, a warden of the Goldsmiths' Company, the subject being the presentation of the four principal charters of the City (4 May).—On the 16th, the Local Government and Taxation Committee reported on the second report of the Select Committee of the House of Commons on Metropolitan Government, which proposed to extinguish the County of the City of London, and convert the Metropolitan Board of Works into a Municipal Council for the whole area.—A sum of £30,000 was voted by the Corporation towards the cost of the improvement effected by the Commissioners of Sewers in Mansion House Street (16th).—The Court of Aldermen gave instructions to enforce the bond of £1,500 against a stockbroker, who was alleged to have been guilty of defrauding a client of £350, which had been paid for investment in consols (27th).—The chief stone of the Holborn Valley Viaduct was laid (3 June). This important work was to put an end to the great evils which had hitherto attended the traffic up and down Holborn Hill and Snow Hill, where an enormous number of casualties and many deaths had occurred owing to the steep declivities.

—The Metropolitan Municipal Association had its first annual meeting (5th) It was resolved. to support the Bill introduced by Mr. John Stuart Mill, to establish Municipal Corporations conterminous with each Parliamentary borough. —The chief corner stone of the new Metropolitan Meat and Poultry Market was laid at Smithfield.—On the 18th, at a meeting of the Court of Aldermen, Mr. Alderman Wilson, Colonel of the Royal City of London Militia, called attention to the passage of the Militia through the streets the previous Monday week, and to the assaults and robberies committed on the occasion, at various parts of the route.

> The Alderman said the question was one of very great importance to the City, for according to the ancient custom of London no troops had a right to pass through the City with colours flying or bayonets fixed, except the 3rd Regiment, usually called the Buffs, which, in consequence of its having been originally formed from the Trained Bands of London, had the privilege of marching through the City with bayonets fixed and colours flying It was an important question whether troops should be allowed to pass through the City without the consent of the Lord Mayor.

A communication of General Sir Hope Grant on the above subject was referred to the Privileges Committee for consideration.—The Common Council resolved to present an address to the Emperor of Russia, expressing horror and indignation at the recent attempt upon his life made at Paris, whither His Majesty had gone to attend the Great Exhibition, and congratulating him upon his providential escape (20th). An address was also resolved upon to the Emperor of the French, whose life had been endangered.—The Lord Mayor and Sheriffs, accompanied by other members of the Corporation, went in state to visit the Paris Exhibition, and were received by the Emperor of the French at the Tuileries, where the Corporation address was presented, and a verbal answer given by Napoleon III.—On 11 July, 2,400 Belgian Volunteers arrived in London, on an invitation from a Committee of English Riflemen. On the following day, they were entertained at a déjeuner in the Guildhall.—The Lord Mayor gave banquets at the Mansion House to the Viceroy of Egypt on the 11th, and on the 20th to the Belgian officers.—The Haberdashers' Company presented the Corporation with a stained glass window for the Guildhall (13th).—About this time the Rev. Leycester Lyne, better known as Brother Ignatius, attracted large numbers of merchants, bankers and others, to his special Friday mid-day services, in the church of St. Edmund the King, Lombard Street. Not only the church, but the porch itself was crowded to overflowing.—The Sultan Abdul Aziz visited the Guildhall on the 18th, and was presented with an address, which was handed to His Majesty in a gold casket. The Sultan shortly afterwards sent to the Lord Mayor a sum of £2,500, to be distributed amongst the poor. The Corporation likewise presented an address to the Viceroy of Egypt, which was also contained in a gold casket. The Viceroy returned the compliment by offering to the Lady Mayoress a brooch of exquisite beauty and great value.—On the 23rd, a public meeting was held at the London Tavern to protest against the spread of ritualism.—It was announced (2 Aug.) that a baronetcy would be conferred upon Lord Mayor Gabriel, and that the honour of knighthood would be bestowed upon the Sheriffs (Mr. Alderman Waterlow and Mr. Lycett).—After much negotiation with the Ecclesiastical Commissioners, an Act was passed (30 & 31 Vic. cap. 38) for the preservation of the Bunhill Fields Burial Ground as an open space, and it was referred to a Committee of the Corporation to carry it into execution (2nd). A resolution of thanks to the Corporation for its zealous efforts in the promotion of this object was passed at a meeting, presided over by Mr. Samuel Morley.

> This ancient burial ground of nearly four acres was laid out by the Corporation two centuries ago. It formed part of the Finsbury Estate, held by the Corporation on lease from the Ecclesiastical Commissioners, and when the lease of the estate expired, the above mentioned negotiations took place. Under the Act the Corporation was to maintain and keep the ground in repair at its own cost and charges, and a sum of £3,015 was expended at the outset. The Ecclesiastical Commissioners reserved to themselves the right to assume the management of the ground as an open space by giving six months' notice.

A public meeting was held at Guildhall, to consider the Lords' amendments to the Government Reform Bill (8th).—During the month an emblazoned and framed address was presented to Mr. George Peabody, in the name of the working class exhibitors at the Industrial Exhibition at Guildhall, the ceremony taking place at the Guildhall Tavern. Mr. Peabody in reply said that when he first started in life his prospects were more gloomy than were those perhaps of any working man on the Committee, but God had prospered him, and he felt great pleasure in spreading that which had been so mercifully and profusely showered on him.—The scheme for the management of the property belonging to the French Protestant church of St. Martin-le-Grand was settled by the Master of the Rolls. —The North London Railway Company, in making the approaches to the terminus in Liverpool Street, removed a brick wall, in which was found a stone with the following inscription :

> "Thomas Rowe miles cum prætor esset Londinensis hunc locum reipublicæ in usum publicæ sepulturæ communem suo sumptu dedicavit. Anno Domini 1569" Sir Thomas Rowe was Lord Mayor of London in 1568, settled in Shacklewell, and died in 1570. He was buried in old Hackney Church.

Dean Milman died at Dean's Court, St. Paul's (24 Sep.).—There was considerable opposition in the City to the proposal of the Government to annex the parishes of St. Luke and Clerkenwell to the East and West London Unions, and the Common Council voted against it.   A deputation waited upon the Poor Law Board and protested against the proposed annexation, which was never carried into effect (3 Oct.).—Mr. Anthony Trollope was entertained at dinner, at the Albion Tavern, by a large number of his colleagues in the General Post Office, on the occasion of his leaving the establishment (31st).   The chair was taken by Mr. Scudamore, and the vice-chairs by Mr. Edmund Yates and Mr. George Chetwynd.

Mr. Trollope drew a picture of a large square room, looking out upon Goldsmiths' Hall, in which chamber he had begun his official life thirty-three years before "as a junior assistant, probationary, temporary extra clerk," condemned to eleven years' preliminary service without any pay, the twelfth year rewarding him with the sum of £9 2s. 6d

The Corporation resolved to erect slaughter-houses at the Metropolitan Cattle Market, with a boiling-house and other conveniences, at an estimated cost of £36,550.—Alderman William Ferneley Allen was elected Lord Mayor.   The Lord Mayor's procession this year was altogether devoid of pageantry.   There was only one band, that of the Royal Horse Guards, and an escort of the 3rd King's Own Hussars.   The Lord Mayor and Sheriffs' Committee having decided not to use the old State Coach, the Common Council passed the following resolution (24 Oct.):—

"That, in accordance with the resolution of this Court of the 25 Sept, 1777, the Lord Mayor elect be requested to use the State Coach on the occasion of his going to Westminster, to be sworn into office on the 9th November next"

Notwithstanding this resolution, the Lord Mayor rode in his semi-state carriage, and it was arranged that the civic procession should move at a brisk pace to avoid the necessity of closing the streets.   This innovation gave rise to much comment and dissatisfaction.—A sum of £250 was voted towards the relief of the sufferers from the hurricane in the West Indies.—The Egyptian Hall and Saloon, at the Mansion House, were ordered to be repaired and re-decorated, at a cost not exceeding £2,800 (2 Dec.).—£200 was voted in aid of the sufferers from the Ferndale Colliery Disaster.—Mr. T. Cave, M.P., ex-sheriff, was sued in the Court of Exchequer, Guildhall, for £105, for services alleged to have been rendered at the shrievalty election, in 1863.   The jury found a verdict for the defendant.—A terrible Fenian explosion took place on the 13th outside the House of Detention, Clerkenwell, by which seven persons were killed and about fifty wounded, and on the 20th the Lord Mayor and Alderman Sir R. W. Carden were occupied several hours at the Guildhall, swearing in special constables to act in case of need for the City.   The enrolling of people from all classes of society continued for a fortnight, when the number of special constables in the City amounted to 6,532.—General Pitt Rivers discovered the remains of Roman pile-buildings near London Wall.—Doctors' Commons was pulled down.—The City of London Municipal Elections (Amendment) Act was passed, fixing the qualifications of voters.—The County Courts Act, 1867 (31 & 32 Vic. cap. 71), effected a change in the title of the Sheriffs' Court, which from 1 Jan., 1868. was known as the City of London Court.

1868.

THE Corporation having agreed to the purchase of the London Coffee House, Ludgate Hill, for £38,500, the agreement was carried into effect on 18 Jan., 1868. The building was afterwards taken down.—For the first time in six years a Court of Husting was held in the Guildhall (21st) This is a Court of Record and only meets occasionally for the enrolment of deeds.—On the 23rd the Common Council passed the following resolution.—

"That an address be presented to Her Majesty, expressing the indignation and sorrow with which the Court has heard of crimes of violence and outrage committed by certain desperate and abandoned men, who, in the prosecution of their base designs, have ruthlessly sacrificed the lives and property of Her Majesty's loyal subjects; and declaring their determination to support the constituted authorities in their efforts to suppress the secret, disloyal and seditious organization of men banded together for revolutionary purposes under the name of Fenians."

The address was presented to the Queen at Windsor on 10 Mar. The Court also voted £100 towards the relief of the sufferers by the Clerkenwell Explosion. —It was announced on 25 Jan. that the Weavers' Company had presented a stained glass window to the Guildhall It represented Henry Fitz Ailwyn, the first Mayor of London.—The old posting house, the "Saracen's Head," Snow Hill, from which long-distance coaches used to run, especially to the Midland Counties, was taken down for the Holborn Valley improvement.—The controversy as to the seal to be used in the City of London Court was brought to a close. Mr. Kerr on 1 Jan., when the name of the Court was changed from the Sheriffs' to the City of London Court, had directed a new seal to be used, containing the Royal arms, in lieu of the former seal. Mr. Justice Willes decided against the Commissioner, and the Common Council undertook (20 Mar.) to prepare a new seal, adopting the City arms as in the old one, but with the altered legend "City of London Court." —The whole question of the future government of the Metropolis was referred on the 26th to a special Committee of the Common Council, and the reference was afterwards transferred to the Local Government and Taxation Committee (20 Ap.).—

Alderman William Taylor Copeland died (12 Ap.)—Extraordinary precautions were taken while the Fenian prisoners were in Newgate awaiting their trial for the Clerkenwell explosion.   The gaol was guarded outside night and day by a picked body of police, armed with cutlasses and revolvers.   Barrett was condemned to death and executed (26 May).   Casey was acquitted, Burke was sentenced to fifteen years' and Shaw to seven years' penal servitude.—The governors of Bridewell refused to receive an apprentice, committed by the Chamberlain for refractory conduct, as there were three already under detention.   Mr. Benjamin Scott reported the matter to the Common Council (1 May).—On the same day the Corporation adopted an address to the Queen, expressing the horror and indignation felt by the Court at the recent attempt upon the life of the Duke of Edinburgh, and congratulating Her Majesty upon his providential escape.   The address was presented at Buckingham Palace on the 13th.—Alexander Mackay, aged eighteen, who was sentenced to death for the murder of his mistress, Emma Grossmith, of Artillery Passage, Norton Folgate, was the first person executed within the precincts of Newgate, under an Act passed this session (8th).—The Queen laid the foundation stone of the new St. Thomas's Hospital, near Lambeth Palace (13th).—Mr. Effingham Wilson, of the Royal Exchange, and one of the oldest members of the publishing trade, died (9 June).

It was stated at the time that Mr. Wilson was the first publisher of Tennyson.   This, however, appears to be a mistake.   The *Poems by Two Brothers* (Alfred and Charles Tennyson) were published in 1827 by Mr. Jackson, of Louth.   It was in 1830 that Mr. Effingham Wilson received Tennyson's MS. from Cambridge, together with the MS. of some poems by Mr Arthur H. Hallam, the subject of *In Memoriam*.   Hallam's poems were apparently not printed, but Alfred Tennyson's name was prefixed to a thin duodecimo of 154 pages, published by Effingham Wilson, Royal Exchange, and entitled *Poems, Chiefly Lyrical*   This little volume is now exceedingly rare   Effingham Wilson was also the first publisher of the works of Thomas Campbell, in a complete form, and of Robert Browning's *Paracelsus*, which was printed in 1835   He published some of the earlier works of Jeremy Bentham.   Mr. Wilson visited his friend Hone in Newgate the night before his celebrated trial began in 1817.

Mr. Disraeli delivered a manifesto on the union of the Church and State at a banquet at Merchant Taylors' Hall, where the first toast is always "Church and Queen" (17th).—The Corporation voted the freedom of the City, with a sword of the value of 200 guineas, to Major General Sir Robert Napier, G.C.B., G.C.S.I., Commander of the forces in Bombay, in recognition of his services in bringing the Abyssinian war to a successful and brilliant close (18th).— The old church of St. Benet, Gracechurch Street, was razed to the ground. —A disorderly meeting of citizens, presided over by the Lord Mayor, was held at the Guildhall. The meeting was convened for the purpose of discussing Mr. Gladstone's Irish Disestablishment Bill, and was addressed by Mr. Vernon Harcourt and others (25th).—The Princess of Wales was delivered of a daughter (Victoria Alexandra Olga Mary) on 6 July, and the customary addresses were voted by the Corporation (15th)'—The gratitude of the Cotton Districts for the help extended to them in their time of distress was remarkably demonstrated at the Guildhall on the 15th, when a deputation attended to present to the Corporation of London the Memorial Window, at the east end of the Guildhall, subscribed for by the operatives of the Cotton District. The Court voted a sum of £750 for the necessary repairs to be made for the reception of the window.— The Corporation ordered a bust of Lord Brougham and Vaux at a cost not exceeding £250 (23 July).—Orders were given by the Common Council to continue the streets on the northern side of the Meat and Poultry Market through Charterhouse Square to Aldersgate Street (17 Sept.).—A medal was ordered to be struck commemorating the visit of the Sultan of Turkey.—The Rev. Henry Langueville Mansel, D.D., was appointed Dean of St. Paul's as successor to Dr. Milman.— Considerable alterations were made in the arrangements for the Guildhall banquet, especially as to the invitation of guests. The bar which hitherto had been erected in the Guildhall on these occasions was ordered to be removed (1 Oct.).— Robert Triphook died at the Charterhouse in his 87th year (4th). His book shops in St. James's Street and Old Bond Street had been the rendezvous of celebrated men. Sir Walter Scott employed Mr. Triphook to collect the books of information on which he founded the *Pirate*. Byron, Shelley and Coleridge were among his customers.—A public meeting was held at the Guildhall on behalf of the sufferers from the terrible earthquakes in Peru and Ecuador (13th), and the Corporation voted £500 towards the fund which was then inaugurated (22nd).—It was reported (17th) that a memorial tomb and window had been erected in the south aisle of St. Paul's Cathedral to the memory of the late Dr. Blomfield, Bishop of London.— Field Marshal Sir John Fox Burgoyne, Bart, G.C.B., Constable of the Tower of London, was admitted to the freedom of the City (22nd).—Alderman James Clarke Lawrence was elected Lord Mayor.—At the Guildhall banquet on the 9th the principal interest centred in the speeches of Mr. Reverdy Johnson, United States Minister, and Mr. Disraeli, the Premier. The former referred to the happy conclusion of the differences which had existed between England and America, and the latter expressed a hope that Lord Stanley, who had so successfully terminated the differences referred to, would be able, with the other Powers, to mediate as successfully between France and Prussia and settle their misunderstandings.—The General Election took place, and on 18 Nov. Mr. Goschen, Mr. Crawford, Mr. Alderman Lawrence, and Mr. Bell were returned for the City, the last-named (a Conservative) taking the place of Baron Rothschild, who was at the bottom of the poll. At the same election Mr. John Stuart Mill lost his seat for Westminster.—The Lord Mayor opened the Metropolitan Meat and Poultry Market at Smithfield (24th).

New Smithfield Market.

Old Smithfield Market was founded in 1614 for live stock, the sale of which was removed to the Islington Market in 1854. The Dead Meat Market had hitherto been carried on in the neighbourhood of Newgate Street. The Act of 1860 authorized the utilization of part of the site of old Smithfield Market for the establishment of the new Market, and also conferred powers of purchasing additional land. Although a portion of the site of this Market was outside the City, it was by the Act (Sec. 11) declared to be within the City, and to form a part of the ward of Farringdon Without. The Market was designed and planned by the City Architect, Mr. Horace Jones, the contractors being Messrs. Browne and Robinson. The building covers an area of 620 feet by 240 feet, and has extensive subways. It is believed to be the largest Dead Meat Market in the world. The cost of the building was less than £200,000, the amount estimated, while a sum of £420,000 was borrowed for the purchase of additional land and the making of the necessary approaches. The construction of the Market had been completed in less than eighteen months   The opening ceremony was followed by a banquet, to which 1,200 persons sat down, in the covered roadway of the Market.   The Market was opened for business on 1 Dec.   The Western Approach street to the Holborn Valley Viaduct was also declared open.

There was a panic on the Stock Exchange caused by rumours of the sudden death of the Emperor Napoleon (5 Dec.).—On the same day Mr. Peabody gave another donation of £100,000 for the poor of London, making a total of £350,000—The Lord Mayor laid the memorial stone of the Central Middle Class Schools in Cowper Street, Finsbury (15th).—Mr. Goschen, having accepted the Presidency of the Poor Law Board, was re-elected for the City on the 21st.—Coopers' Hall, in Basinghall Street, having been taken down, a new building was erected on part of the site.—Most of the houses in the parish of St. Mary Mounthaw were removed about this time.—Crosby Hall, Bishopsgate Street, was opened as a restaurant.

1869.

THE six directors in Overend, Gurney and Co., who had appeared several times at the Mansion House Police Court, on a charge of conspiracy, were committed for trial by the Lord Mayor on 27 Jan., 1869.   The firm was in liquidation, the costs of which up to this time had been £70,000.   It was stated that the losses of the new company during nine months' trading, irrespective of what they had lost by the old firm, were £1,400,000.   During that period they had discounted £56,000,000 worth of bills.   The trial did not come on till 13 Dec., when it lasted nine days in the Court of Queen's Bench, and resulted in a verdict of acquittal.—The Court of Aldermen decided on the 9th, that prisoners of all denominations confined in the City Prison, Holloway, should be allowed equal privileges of seeing their respective ministers, when desirous of so doing, according to the custom existing in all the City gaols for many years past.—A painted window, representing the "Crucifixion," the gift of the Drapers' Company, was unveiled at St. Paul's Cathedral (10 Feb.).—Baron Rothschild was elected, without opposition, to fill the vacancy in the City representation, caused by the death of Mr. Bell (22nd).—The Common Council adopted a rule that no extraordinary work should be undertaken, and no public or charitable grant made, involving a sum exceeding £100, until the Finance Committee had considered and reported upon the question (25th).—The Queen, accompanied by Princess Louise, paid a visit to St. Bartholomew's Hospital (6 Ap.).   Her Majesty having expressed a desire to see the new Meat

Market, she was driven very slowly through the Central Avenue.—Dr. Jackson was enthroned as Bishop of London at St. Paul's (8th).—Mr. Maguire moved in the House of Commons for a Royal Commission to inquire into the manner in which the Irish Society administered their property in the north of Ireland. The Government having after a four hours' debate, promised to consider the matter, the motion was withdrawn (13th).—The Lord Mayor read a letter to the Common Council from Mr. Bacon, the sculptor, containing an offer of a statue of the Prince Consort, for the Holborn Valley Viaduct (29th). The offer was accepted,

Portion of Roman Pavement found in Bucklersbury.

and it was decided to place the statue at the western end of the Viaduct (27 May).—The Court also resolved that the west window of the Guildhall should be filled with stained glass in the highest . style of art, in commemoration of the many virtues of the Prince Consort, and of his "high and spotless character." The necessary preparations for the reception of the window were made at a cost of £800 (17 June).—A letter from the Poor Law Board was read at the West London Union, proposing to amalgamate the West and East London Unions with the City of London Union for all Poor Law purposes. This arrangement, it was thought, would enable the City Guardians to utilize the existing workhouses to a greater extent than if each remained under separate management (1 May).—The Town Clerk was instructed to apply to the Metropolitan Board of Works requesting that the tessellated Roman pavement, recently discovered during the excavations at Bucklersbury, might be deposited, with other interesting antiquities, in the Guildhall Museum (13th).—Mr. Goschen moved the second reading of the Metropolis Poor Act (1867) Amendment Bill, which included the amalgamation of the City Unions and was ultimately carried (28th).—It was announced (5 June) that the Merchant Taylors' Company had paid £90,000 out of their corporate funds to the Governors of the Charterhouse, for 5½ acres of land lately occupied by the Charterhouse Schools, and that they intended to remove the Merchant Taylors' School from Suffolk Lane to that locality.   They· had let a portion of the land for building purposes but retained 3½ acres for the school and its playground.   The Charterhouse School was being removed to Godalming.—Mr. John Bennett bought the freehold of his premises in Cheapside, at auction, for £14,000 (23rd).—During the six months ending 30 June, 20,087,000 passengers were stated to have been carried over the Metropolitan Railway system. —At a banquet given to Her Majesty's Ministers at the Mansion House, on the · 30th, Mr. Gladstone said :—

" He was enabled, from past associations, to speak of the great efforts which the Corporation of the City had made in developing principles of liberty combined with order, and he was sure however great changes the progress of time might effect in the municipal arrangements of this vast Metropolis, none could in the least degree impair the consequence, dignity or importance of the honoured office of the Lord Mayor."

The Executive Committee of the Thomas Wright Memorial Fund presented to the Corporation Mr. Mercier's picture, " The Condemned Cell," which represents Mr. Wright in the act of ministering to a condemned criminal.· For a great number of years Mr. Wright, a working man, had alleviated the misery of the working classes and of condemned convicts, after his usual hours of labour (1 July). —Sir Moses Montefiore offered to place a stained-glass window in the Guildhall (22nd).—Dr. William Sedgwick Saunders, who was this year chairman of the Library Committee, issued a pamphlet entitled, " The Guildhall Library : Its origin and progress," being an appeal to the Corporation of London for its reconstruction.

The writer pointed out the inconvenience, danger and discredit of the existing accommodation, and at last recognising the great importance of establishing a Library and Museum worthy of the City of London, the Common Council agreed on the 22nd to erect a new building at an expense not exceeding £25,000.   It was afterwards decided (16 Sept.) that the building should be at the eastern end of the Guildhall, on a plot of land belonging to the Corporation, and that the Library should be freely open to the public, without ticket or any other formality.

The Prince of Wales unveiled the statue of Mr. Peabody, at the eastern side of the Royal Exchange, and on the site of the burial-ground formerly attached to the church of St. Benet Fink, towards which the Corporation had contributed 100 guineas (23rd).—A proposal having been made to re-elect Alderman Lawrence as Lord Mayor for a second year, a vigorous canvass was got up on behalf of Alderman Besley, the alderman next in rotation for the mayoralty. A poll was demanded on 29 Sep., the result being that Alderman Besley was elected by 1,501 votes, as against 644 for the Lord Mayor, and 580 for Alderman Wilson.—At the Common Council on 7 Oct., a letter was read from the Clerk of the Metropolitan

Board of Works, enclosing a proposal by the Metropolitan District Railway Company to carry the railway under the entire length of the new street from Blackfriars to the Mansion House. The communications were referred to the Commissioners of Sewers.—Bunhill Fields Burial Ground, an old Nonconformist cemetery, just outside the borders of the City, was opened by the Corporation as a public recreation ground (14th).

Mr. Deputy Charles Reed, M.P., Chairman of the Bunhill Fields Preservation Committee, addressing the Lord Mayor, said: "Five centuries have passed since this manor was granted by the Prebend of Halliwell and Finsbury to the citizens of London in return for services rendered to the Church, and it was by virtue of this grant that your predecessors in olden times bore the title of Lords of Finsbury as well as Lord Mayor of London." In 1549, more than a thousand cartloads of human remains were removed from the Charnel House of St. Paul's Cathedral and deposited here. The Lord Mayor declared the ground open, and the Earl of Shaftesbury and Mr. Samuel Morley were amongst those who addressed the very large number of persons who had assembled to witness this interesting ceremony.

Bunyan's Monument, Bunhill Fields.

The Corporation on the 28th passed a vote of sympathy and condolence on the occasion of the death of the Earl of Derby, K.G., the late Prime Minister, and a marble bust of the deceased earl was ordered to be executed (16 Dec.)—An Act of Common Council was passed abolishing the custom by which the Sheriffs had hitherto taken the forfeited recognisances, etc., at the Sessions (28th).—The 6th of November was a great day in the annals of the City of London, it being the day on which Her Majesty the Queen opened two of the greatest works undertaken and carried out by the Corporation, viz.: Blackfriars Bridge and Holborn Viaduct.

The bridge, which cost £401,131, took five years and five months to build. It consists of five iron arches surmounted by an ornamental cornice and parapet. The steepest gradient is 1 in 40, whereas the gradient in the old bridge was 1 in 24, and originally 1 in 16. The central arch is 185 feet clear between the piers, those on either side 175 feet each, and the end arches give a span of 155 feet. The total length of the bridge, clear of the shore abutments, is 923 feet. On each of the stone piers are two columns of polished red granite, one on either side of the bridge. Each column weighs over

30 tons and is 11 feet high   They are the largest used until then in any bridge, and cost £800 each. The bridge was designed by Mr Joseph Cubitt, and the birds and marine plants ornamenting the stone capitals were carved by Mr. J. B. Philip

     Holborn Viaduct was a much more costly undertaking, involving as it did the purchase of valuable property. The total cost of the Viaduct and approaches, including the purchase of ground, premises, goodwill, &c , was £2,552,406, a considerable portion of which has since fallen upon the City revenues owing to the refusal of Parliament to grant a renewal of the coal dues. The actual work of construction was only commenced in June, 1867, so that the Viaduct took less than two years and a-half to complete. Mr. Haywood, Engineer to the Commissioners of Sewers, superintended the work, which was carried out by Messrs Hill & Keddell, contractors, for £99,837. The height of the level of the viaduct above the former roadways, as they existed in 1863, is 32 feet at Farringdon Street Bridge, which spans the deepest portion of the Fleet Valley. From the circus at its western end to Giltspur Street at its eastern end, the viaduct is 1,285 feet long and 80 feet wide. The bridge over Farringdon Street consists of three spans, the arches being supported on granite pillars. On each side of the bridge are granite piers and pedestals, surmounted by bronze statues, representing the Fine Arts, Science, Agriculture, and Commerce. Public staircases, on which are statues of celebrated citizens, afford communication between the Viaduct and Farringdon Street It was pointed out by the Lord Mayor (Jan 24, 1870), that the Holborn Viaduct Improvement Committee had had to settle between 600 and 700 claims for compensation, and that if the ground had been cleared by a staff of surveyors and valuers, the commission on the amount paid, £1,565,000, would have formed one of the largest items in the cost of the improvement.

Galleries had been erected on Blackfriars Bridge, draped with scarlet and white cloth, from which hundreds of spectators witnessed the opening ceremony. The Queen was received by the Lord Mayor, the Sheriffs, and other representatives of the Corporation. The Recorder read an address, and the Home Secretary handed to the Lord Mayor a copy of the Queen's reply. After formally declaring the bridge open for traffic, the Queen, preceded by the Lord Mayor and Corporation, passed under the Viaduct and through Smithfield and Giltspur Street to the east end of the structure, where two colossal plaster statues, representing "Victory" and "Peace," had been erected. A beautiful volume, containing a description of the Viaduct, was handed to the Queen, who declared the second great work of the Corporation open for the use and enjoyment of the public. The Common Council ordered a medal to be struck in honour of the occasion. On the 18th it was announced that a baronetcy would be conferred upon the Lord Mayor, that the Sheriffs would be knighted, and that Colonel Fraser, Commissioner of the City Police, would be made a Companion of the Bath.—On the occasion of the visit of the King of the Belgians to the Queen (25th), the Lord Mayor presented His Majesty with an address, signed by upwards of 300 Mayors, Lord-Lieutenants, High-Sheriffs of counties, and other representative men, welcoming him to this country, and thanking him and the Belgian people for their hospitality, especially to the English volunteers. In the evening the Lord Mayor entertained His Majesty at the Mansion House.—The Princess of Wales gave birth to a daughter (Maud

Charlotte Mary Victoria) on the 26th, and the Corporation voted the usual address and compliments of congratulation.—The Court recorded its deep sorrow for the death of " that distinguished citizen and universal philanthropist," George Peabody, which took place at Eaton Square (4 Dec.).—With a view to the prevention of the introduction into Great Britain of contagious diseases among animals, an Act was passed (32 and 33 Vic. cap., 70), under which the Corporation was made a Local Authority, with power to appoint inspectors, provide wharves, lairs, sheds, markets, &c., for the landing, reception, slaughter, and sale of foreign animals, and for this last purpose the Corporation was appointed the exclusive Local Authority in and for the Metropolis ; subject to its providing and opening for public use a market before 1 Jan., 1872.—The houses on the east side of Bath Street, Newgate Street, were swept away to make room for the new General Post Office.—The Inner Temple Hall was demolished.—The site of Newgate Market was sold by auction.

1870.

THE first commitment to Whitecross Street Prison under the Debtors' Act of last session, was made on 8 Jan., 1870 — The Common Council decided to erect a fountain in Smithfield, in the vicinity of the new markets, at a cost of £1,200 (24th).— Sir James Vallentin, one of the Sheriffs of London and Middlesex died, and Mr. John Paterson was elected in his place, on 2 Mar.—A Martyrs' Memorial was unveiled in Smithfield by the Earl of Shaftesbury under the auspices of the Protestant Alliance (11th).

The memorial, which occupies a space in the wall of St. Bartholomew's Hospital, bears the following inscription " Blessed are the dead which die in the Lord," and (underneath) the words " The noble army of Martyrs praise thee." In the centre of the monument are the following words : " Near to this spot John Rogers, John Bradford, Archdeacon Philpot and other servants of God suffered death by fire for the faith of Christ, in the years 1555, 1556 and 1557." The memorial cost about £230.

The Prince of Wales, accompanied by the Princess, visited the Middle Class Schools in Cowper Street, the Revs. W. Rogers and W. Jowett acting as guides, and the work of the School being carried on without interruption. At the conclusion of the Royal visit, a march-past of nearly 1,000 boys took place in the playground (30 Mar.).—A scheme of amalgamation between the Gas Light and Coke Company and the City of London Gas Light and Coke Company, was confirmed by Her Majesty by an Order in Council (31st), and on 6 July a scheme of amalgamation between the companies so amalgamated and the Great Central Gas Company was also approved.—The Tower Subway, a circular iron tube extending from Great Tower Hill, on the north side, to near Pickle Herring Stairs, on the south side of the Thames, constructed by a Joint Stock Company, was opened about this time for foot passengers, who were charged a toll of a halfpenny each.— The Common Council accepted an offer from the inhabitants of Farringdon

Martyrs' Memorial, Smithfield.

Without Ward to place in the Guildhall a stained-glass window, to commemorate the great improvements which had recently been carried out in the ward by the Corporation at an expense of £3,500,000 (7 Ap.).—The Remembrancer reported that three bills were before Parliament, viz.: the Municipal Boroughs (Metropolis) Bill, the County of London Bill and the Corporation of London Bill, which if carried into effect would destroy the Corporation and transfer all its property, charters, privileges, honours and rights to a new Corporation, and abolish the Court of Aldermen (14th).—Another stained-glass window was placed in the Guildhall, by Alderman Sir David Salomons, M.P., to commemorate the removal of Jewish disabilities.—Under the Union of Benefices Act, the church of Allhallows Staining, Mark Lane, which for a long time had been almost deserted, was finally closed (10 May).— The Local Government and Taxation Committee suggested that the best form of government for the Metropolis would be the establishment of municipalities in the different parliamentary boroughs, and this principle was adopted by the Common Council, who instructed the Committee to oppose the Bills relating to the subject then before Parliament (12th).—Mr. Buxton moved the second reading of the Municipal Boroughs (Metropolis) Bill, in the House of Commons (17th). It was carried by 130 to 66, and referred to a Select Committee.—Princess Louise, who was accompanied by Prince Christian, opened the new hall at the Inner Temple (14th).—The foundation stone was laid of a new hall for the Coach and Coach Harness Makers' Company, in Noble Street, Gresham Street (16 June); the old hall was erected in 1841.—The Merchant Taylors' Company opened a Convalescent Home at Bognor (5 July).

> This home was founded mainly " for the reception and maintenance of patients in indigent circumstances recently or about to be discharged from any hospitals in or near the Metropolis , and for such other cases among the poor of the Metropolis, as the Committee may consider fit and proper objects for admission, but principally for those recovering from injuries and surgical operations."

The Corporation voted the Freedom of the City to M. Ferdinand de Lesseps for his skill in designing and his indomitable energy and perseverance in carrying to a successful completion the Suez Canal (11th).   The presentation was made at the Guildhall, on the 30th.—The Prince of Wales inaugurated the northern Thames Embankment, which the Metropolitan Board of Works named the Victoria Embankment.—On the same day a meeting was held at the Mansion House to further the movement for the completion of Wren's greatest work, St. Paul's Cathedral.   Mr. Gladstone said :—

> " If they wanted to see the monument of Sir Christopher Wren, they might look to the fabric of St. Paul's ; but if they looked to the state in which it remained, if they looked to its cold dark columns, and its almost repulsive general condition, he asked them whether the inscription did not carry with it a burning reproach to Englishmen.   St. Paul's was a noble church, and he knew of only one to compete with it in that respect, and that was the church of St Peter, at Rome, the interior of which at least had been treated with the fullest justice by those who designed and carried it into execution."

The Corporation authorised the Gas Committee to confer with the New River Company with a view to obtaining a constant supply of water for the consumers (21st).—The Corporation voted £500 towards the fund in aid of the sufferers by the recent calamitous fire at Constantinople.   In this terrible conflagration 20,000 houses were destroyed and 1,000 lives were lost (29th).—A Joint Committee of the Corporation of London and the Metropolitan Board of Works had been appointed under the provisions of the Act of 1869, for freeing the Thames bridges from toll. Kingston Bridge had already been freed, and on 1 Aug., a similar boon was conferred upon Walton, the little town being *en fête*.—The Elementary Education Act was passed on the 9th.—The Drapers' Company gave a banquet to M. de Lesseps, on the 11th.—The Elcho Shield won in the Wimbledon contest was brought in triumph to the Guildhall, a procession of volunteers having been formed on the Victoria Embankment. The Lord Mayor received the shield on behalf of the citizens (20th).—A monument to Daniel Defoe was unveiled in Bunhill Fields Burial Ground (16 Sept.).—The Corporation subscribed the sum of £1,000 in aid of the sick and wounded in the Franco-German War. Paris was now besieged.—A Mansion House Fund was opened for the widows and orphans of the officers and crew of Her Majesty's ironclad ship "Captain," which went down in a gale off Finisterre with all hands on board (about 500 men) except a few sailors who managed to escape in a boat (12 Oct.).—A letter was received by the Corporation from the Metropolitan Board of Works presenting, for preservation in the Guildhall Museum, several coins, a silver medal, and a massive plate found in the foundation stone of old Blackfriars Bridge during the course of excavation for sewage works (20th).—Imprisonment for debt having been virtually abolished, orders were given to pull down Whitecross Street Prison, the last of the debtors' prisons in London, and to dispose of the materials of the building by public auction. The building was actually closed at the end of July, when the remaining twenty-seven prisoners were transferred to Holloway Gaol. Among the gifts to poor prisoners continued to the last and "carried forward" to Holloway was that of Nell Gwynn, viz., thirty-two penny loaves every month (18 Oct.).—The foundation stone of the New Guildhall Library and Museum was laid by Dr. W. Sedgwick Saunders, Chairman of the Library Committee (27th).—Prince Arthur, on behalf of the Queen, was present at the unveiling of the Prince Consort Memorial Window, at the west end of the Guildhall, and made his first speech in public (3 Nov.). —Alderman Thomas Dakin was elected Lord Mayor.—In the Court of Aldermen, Sir S. H. Waterlow brought up a report on the London Brokers' Relief Act, 1870, which abolished the supervision exercised by the Court over brokers for nearly six centuries. In future there would be no sworn brokers, and London brokers would stand in the same position as the brokers in any other part of the Kingdom (14th).—The Lord Mayor's procession went for the first time to Westminster by way of the Thames Embankment (9th).—The offer of Alderman Cotton to place a stained-glass window in the Guildhall was accepted (17th).—The Venerable William Hale Hale, Archdeacon of London, died at the Charterhouse (27th).—The Corporation, in accordance with the recent Act of Parliament, decided to construct a Foreign Cattle Market at Deptford, by a resolution containing the following provision :—

"That this Court in undertaking the responsibilities involved in providing a new Foreign Cattle Market, do affirm that they do so in the fullest confidence that the bye-laws of the said market shall provide for such wharf and other charges as shall not only defray the necessary expenses and the interest on loans, but also discharge within a reasonable period the debts incurred in relation to the sale of cattle in the Metropolis" (17th).

General Post Office, 1893.

The Corporation at the same time instructed the Markets Committee to prepare plans for the enlargement and improvement of Billingsgate and Leadenhall Markets.— A special Committee was appointed to consider the best way of dealing with the large amount of unproductive land, owned by the Corporation (24th).—The first election of the London School Board took place (29th); the Rev. W. Rogers, Mr. S. Morley, Mr. Alderman Cotton and Mr. W. Sutton Gover were returned for the City.—Mr. Ayrton, M.P., in the absence of Lord Hartington, laid the foundation stone of the new General Post Office, in St. Martin's le Grand (16 Dec.).—Dr. Hessey, Head Master for twenty-five years at Merchant Taylors' School, took formal leave of the pupils (20th). He was succeeded in the head mastership by the Rev. W. Baker, of St. John's College, Oxford.—Allhallows Church, Lombard Street, was re-opened after thorough restoration, which cost £4,000 (30th).—The District Railway Company, having failed in their application to Parliament to make the Mansion House their terminus, continued the railway to Cannon Street.

The Church of Allhallows Barking was restored and the gallery removed.

1871.

THE Rev. Dr. Currey was elected Master of the Charterhouse in the place of the late Archdeacon Hale (17 Jan., 1871).—The Corporation received a letter from Lord Lawrence, chairman of the London School Board, conveying the thanks of the Board for the prompt and courteous manner in which the Council Chamber at Guildhall had been placed temporarily at its service (19th).—The Rev. Thomas Binney, LL.D., preached his farewell sermon at the King's Weighhouse Chapel, Fish Street Hill, after forty years' ministry (29th).—A meeting was held at the Mansion House to consider the best means of relieving the inhabitants of Paris from the great distress they were suffering in consequence of the siege, which had lasted four months (8 Feb.). On the following day the Corporation voted £2,000 in aid of the fund, which, by the 17th, had reached a total of about £100,000.—Asphalte was first adopted for road-paving by the Commissioners of Sewers (21st). The experiment was tried in Lombard Street.—An agreement was arrived at between the Common Council and the Commissioners of Sewers with regard to the question of Local Authority in relation to the tramway companies, full power being reserved to the Lord Mayor and Commissioner of Police to stop up streets and regulate the traffic (30 Mar.).—Sir William Magnay, Bart., who was Lord Mayor in 1843–4, died at the age of 74 (3 Ap.). —The Corporation resolved to construct a poultry market upon the site of the Meat Market at Leadenhall, at a cost of £25,000, and to obtain parliamentary powers for dismarketing the existing hide and poultry Markets (5th).—Closing services were held at Devonshire Square Chapel (9th). The pastor reminded the congregation that, when their forefathers first gathered there, the Long Parliament was sitting. A new chapel to replace the old one was being erected in Stoke Newington Road.—Mr. Haywood, the Engineer, in his report of works executed by the Commissioners of Sewers during the year 1870, gave a table showing what improvements had been carried out during the previous twenty years, from which it appeared that almost every important thoroughfare had been dealt with, and that improvements had been effected in twenty-three out of the twenty-six wards of the City (15th).—On the 17th the band of the Garde de Paris gave a selection of music at the Mansion House, in complimentary acknowledgment of the valuable gifts sent to the beleaguered inhabitants of Paris by the Lord Mayor.— The Corporation resolved to enlarge and improve Billingsgate Market at a cost not exceeding £150,000 (20th).—An influential meeting to protest against the Endowed School Commissioners' scheme for Emanuel Hospital was held at the Mansion House on the 21st.

Emanuel Hospital first came under the control of the Lord Mayor and Aldermen of the City of London in 1623, having been founded in the year 1600, under the will of Anne Lady Dacre, who directed her executor to purchase certain lands in Tothill Fields, Westminster, and build thereon a hospital for twenty poor folk and twenty poor children, for which purpose she bequeathed £300. Under the fostering care of the Corporation the funds of Emanuel Hospital had increased to £4,000 a year. The Endowed Schools Commissioners prepared a scheme for the diversion of these funds, against which the Aldermen decided to petition Parliament.

The Right Hon. W. Cowper-Temple submitted a resolution in the House of Commons to secure the preservation of the unenclosed portions of Epping Forest as an open space for the enjoyment of the people of the Metropolis (28th). Mr. Gladstone (the Premier) and Mr. Lowe opposed the motion on the ground that the land was the property of the Crown The Prime Minister stated that the Government had secured 1,000 acres of the Forest as a recreation ground for the people, but the House was not satisfied, and the resolution was carried by a large majority. On May 25th the Common Council resolved to approach the Government with a view to ascertaining on what terms and conditions the Corporation could secure the unenclosed parts of the Forest for the benefit of the people. The conference took place on 6 June, when the Corporation submitted an offer to the First Commissioner of Works, viz., to abandon its right to compulsory metage, and to devote the revenue arising from a fixed duty, which it was proposed should be levied in lieu thereof, to the preservation of Epping Forest.— Mr. Secondary Potter died after a long and painful illness (14 May).

Mr. Potter was the last who acceded to this office by purchase. He stated in evidence before the Royal Commissioners, who investigated the affairs of the Corporation in 1854, that he gave £5,000 for the office under an arrangement with his immediate predecessor, who sold it to the Corporation for £8,000, the Corporation finding £3,000 of the money and the witness £5,000

The Bank Holiday Act was passed (25th).—Alderman Sir Joseph Causton died at Champion Hill (27th).—The charity children of the Metropolitan schools, to the number of about 4,300, assembled at St. Paul's, presenting a curious spectacle in their varied garbs and uniforms (8 June). One hundred and sixty-seven years had elapsed since the first anniversary, which was held at St. Andrew's Church, Holborn. The Corporation attended in state.—It was announced on the 24th that a scheme for the regulation of the charity founded by Mary Datchelor, in the parish of St. Andrew Undershaft, had been approved by the Charity Commissioners. The scheme provided for pensions and the middle-class education of girls.—On the 21st the Queen opened the new St. Thomas's Hospital, a magnificent pile of buildings at Stangate, opposite the Houses of Parliament. The cost, exclusive of the site, was about £400,000. —The Marquis of Salisbury moved an address to Her Majesty in the House of Lords against the scheme of the Endowed Schools Commission for the management of Emanuel Hospital, which was looked upon as the beginning of a crusade against endowments in general (20th). The motion was carried, and the proposal was eventually dropped.—A Bill having been brought into Parliament by the Government for the preservation of Epping Forest, the Corporation decided to petition Parliament to insert a clause prohibiting further enclosures of land, or the felling of any trees in the enclosed portions of the Forest, until the Commissioners to be appointed by the Act had made their report (20 July). This Act was called the Epping Forest Act, 1871 (34 and 35 Vic. cap., 93).—Mr. Ex-Sheriff Nissen, through Mr. Alderman David Salomons, presented the Corporation with a collection of drawings of old London Bridge by E. W. Cooke, R.A. (20th).—Prince Arthur, who had been invited to take up the freedom of the City by patrimony, was entertained at a déjeuner at the Guildhall, (25 July).—The Emperor and Empress of Brazil arrived in London in the course of an extended European tour, and the Corporation presented the Emperor through the Brazilian Legation, with an address of congratulation (29th).—Dr. Mansel, Dean of St. Paul's, died at Cosgrove Hall, Northampton (29th).—The City Solicitor, by direction of the Corporation, began a suit in the Court of Chancery, before the Master of the Rolls (14 Aug.), in the name of the Commissioners of Sewers, as owners of Ilford Cemetery, on behalf of themselves, and all other owners and occupiers of lands and tenements, against Lords of Manors in the Forest, for the purpose of staying any further illegal enclosures, and also for the purpose of obtaining a declaration that all owners and occupiers of lands and tenements within the Forest were entitled to rights of common pasture and pannage over the whole of the waste lands of Epping Forest. The proceedings were eventually successful.—In Sept. cholera was raging in the Metropolis, and the Sanitary Committee of the Commissioners of Sewers was empowered to take such measures and incur such expense as might be deemed necessary (5 Sept.).—The Rev. Dr. Mortimer, late Head Master of the City of London School, died on the 7th.—The Endowed Schools Commission issued an amended scheme for the reconstruction of Emanuel Hospital (16th).—The Corporation voted 1,000 guineas for the relief of sufferers from the disastrous fire at Chicago (13 Oct.).—Alderman Sir Francis Graham

Moon, Bart., a fine art publisher, and Lord Mayor 1854–5, died on the 13th.
—Mr. Sheriff Young died, and Mr. John Bennett, who had several times come
forward as a candidate for the shrievalty, was elected to fill the vacancy (15th).
—The Very Rev. Richard William Church, M.A., was installed Dean of St.
Paul's (17th).—On 19 Oct. a very pleasing exchange of municipal amenities
took place between London and Paris.   M. Léon Say, Prefect of the Seine,
and M. Vautrain, President of the Municipal Council of Paris, attended at
the Guildhall, and presented to the Corporation an address, a bronze model of
the Hôtel de Ville (which was destroyed by the Commune), and a gold medal,
in recognition of the help afforded by the Corporation and citizens of London
in revictualling Paris after the siege of 1870–1.   The address and gifts were
deposited in the Guildhall Library and Museum.   M. Léon Say and M. Vautrain
were entertained by the Lord Mayor to a banquet at the Mansion House (18th).
The President of the Municipal Council of Paris, in replying to a toast, said
the City of London had done more for the alliance of the two peoples by
its one spontaneous act, than the most formal treaties could ever have
accomplished, thereby cementing a lasting alliance between the two countries.
—Columbia Market, Bethnal Green, was formally transferred to the Corporation
(3 Nov.).

This market was opened by the Baroness (then Miss) Burdett-Coutts as a general market 28 Ap,
1868, and as a fish market 21 Feb, 1870.   The market had cost the Baroness a quarter of a million,
and she proposed to spend £60,000 more on improving the approaches.

Queen Victoria Street was opened (4th).   This was one of the several great
improvements which had been, during the past few years, transforming the
outward aspect of the City.   Queen Victoria Street completed the new and
spacious thoroughfare from the Houses of Parliament to the Mansion House,
thus connecting the centres of legislation and commerce   The total length of
the thoroughfare was two miles, while the distance along the Strand route was
one-third of a mile greater.   The formation of Queen Victoria Street cost £52,000,
and the purchase-price of property along the line of route reached over two millions
sterling.   Colonel Hogg, M.P., chairman of the Metropolitan Board of Works,
declared the street open, and the Lord Mayor expressed the great satisfaction
which the Corporation had experienced in working hand in hand with the Metropolitan Board, in carrying out these great public improvements.   A piece of ground
at the Mansion House corner of Queen Victoria Street was let by the Metropolitan
Board of Works for £5,500 a year, which was equal to about a sovereign per
square foot.—Alderman Sills John Gibbons was elected Lord Mayor.—The

verderers of Epping Forest held a Court of Attachments at the Town Hall, Stratford (11th), and subsequently the ancient procedure of summoning the "Swain mote" was revived, for the first time since the period of Charles I. This was a jury of "Swains," or dwellers in the district about the Forest.

The City Solicitor (Mr. T. J. Nelson) addressing the Swain mote said the last Court was held on the 11th of June, in the 16th year of the reign of Charles I, that is 1640, or 231 years ago. At that time a perambulation was made of the Forest of Waltham, and it was found by the Commissioners that

A bit of Epping Forest.

the Forest consisted of 60,000 acres, of which 48,000 were enclosed land belonging to private persons, over which the Crown had the right of hunting, and there were 12,000 acres of open land, of which 3,000 were in the Forest of Hainault. There was no other record of the state of the Forest till 1793, and in that year there were still 12,000 acres left for the enjoyment of the Sovereign and the recreation of the public. In 1851 the 3,000 acres in Hainault Forest were disafforested, but 9,000 acres still remained open to the public. In that year the management of the Forest was given to the Commissioners of Woods and Forests, and shortly afterwards the Commissioners reported that between 1793 and 1851, 2,000 acres had been lost to the public, and there were therefore only 7,000 left. Since that time, up to 1863, some 4,000 acres had been enclosed, some by the right of encroachment and simply by placing fences around the land, and the rest by the sale of the forestal rights to the Crown, which had produced £16,795 16s. 6d., or the paltry sum of £4 an acre. There remained 3,000 acres, which had already been marked for slaughter, as it might be called, by the Commissioners of Woods and Forests, who were willing to accept £12,187, or about £4 an acre, for the Crown rights over this open place of recreation, and that at a time when hundreds of pounds an acre were being given elsewhere for the purpose of creating parks for the people. The Corporation of London had instituted a suit in Chancery to prevent further enclosures, and the Court of Queen's Bench had issued a prohibition staying all the proceedings of the verderers accordingly. He could say on behalf of the Corporation that, as that body had taken up the matter on behalf of the people of the east end of the Metropolis, although the Government had abandoned them, and the Metropolitan Board of Works would have nothing to do with them, the Corporation, having put their hand to the plough, would not look back.

Mr. Henry de Jersey was elected Secondary (16th)   An Act of Common Council was passed repealing former Acts and regulations, and enacting that the same person should fill the offices of Secondary of the Poultry and Giltspur Street Compters, under the title of Secondary of the City of London.—The new thoroughfare, connecting Ludgate Hill with Holborn Circus, was opened (20th).—The Bishop of London ratified a scheme for the union of the benefices of St. Mildred, Poultry, and St. Olave, Jewry (30th).   The scheme provided that St. Mildred's Church should be closed, and that the funds obtained for the site should be devoted to the erection of a church in the district of St. Paul's, Clerkenwell.--The Prince of Wales was dangerously ill, and the Corporation passed a resolution of sympathy with the Queen, the Princess of Wales, and the other members of the Royal family, and expressed a hope for the Prince's speedy recovery (15 Dec.).—The Foreign Cattle Market at Deptford was opened by the Lord Mayor on the 30th without ceremonial.   The total sum expended by the Corporation in acquiring the site and constructing the market was £379,500.—During the year Tallow Chandlers' Hall, Dowgate Hill, was re-built, and Bridewell Chapel was demolished.

1872.

 MEETING was held at the Mansion House to consider how the City Guilds could revert to their old function of directing the arts and manufactures of the country (10 Jan., 1872).— The Prince of Wales having recovered from his dangerous illness, the Common Council decided to present an address of congratulation to the Queen, and "compliments" to the Prince and Princess of Wales (1 Feb.).—The Corporation purchased for the Guildhall Library from Mr. Tyrrell, the late Remembrancer, some valuable MSS., relating to the rights and affairs of the City, for £850.—The new ranges of the City of London Rifle Volunteers were inaugurated (10th).—The 27th was Thanksgiving Day for the Prince's recovery, when the Queen with the Prince and Princess of Wales and other members of the Royal family, accompanied by all the High Officers of the Crown, proceeded in state to St. Paul's Cathedral.

The whole line of route from Buckingham Palace was decorated, and the day being a general holiday, the streets were crowded with spectators.   The procession started shortly after twelve o'clock. First came the carriages of the Speaker, the Lord Chancellor and the Commander-in-Chief, followed by nine Royal carriages, six of them occupied by ladies and gentlemen of the Court, the seventh by the younger brothers of the Prince, another by the Master of the Horse, and the last by the Queen, the Prince and Princess of Wales, Prince Albert Victor and Princess Beatrice.   In the park, as the *cortège* passed along, a band of 30,000 children sang the National Anthem. At Temple Bar the Royal party was received by the Lord Mayor, and by the Sheriffs, six Aldermen and eight members of the Common Council, all of whom were mounted. The City Trumpeters, the City Marshal and the Sword and Mace Bearers were in attendance. Advancing uncovered, the Lord Mayor handed the City Sword to the Queen, who thanked him and said, she had much pleasure in returning it to his keeping. The Lord Mayor then bearing the Sword, resumed his place at the head of the Civic Deputation, who escorted the Royal party to St. Paul's, the cheers along the route being almost deafening. In the Cathedral was assembled a vast company of 13,000, comprising members of

Parliament, representatives of the Army and Navy, the Corporation, the Masters and Wardens of the City Companies, and civic dignitaries from all parts of the Kingdom. Two or three hundred tickets were given to the working classes by desire, it was stated, of the Queen. The arrangements were perfect and there was not the slightest confusion. At one o'clock the procession arrived at the great western entrance to the Cathedral and passed through

Queen Victoria at Temple Bar. Thanksgiving Day, 1872.

the vestibule erected on the steps, which bore the inscription "I was glad when they said unto me, we will go into the House of the Lord." The Queen was received by the Dean and Chapter of St. Paul's and conducted to the Royal pew. The service began with the Te Deum and concluded with a special thanksgiving hymn, the Archbishop of Canterbury delivering a short discourse. The Royal party returned by way of Ludgate Hill, Old Bailey, Holborn Viaduct and Oxford Street. At night the City was splendidly illuminated.

The Queen conferred a baronetcy upon the Lord Mayor, and the Sheriffs and the Deputy-Recorder (Mr. T. Chambers, Q.C., M.P.) were knighted. Thanksgiving Day was commemorated by a medal struck by order of the Corporation.—A boy named Arthur O'Connor, living in Church Row, Houndsditch, was charged at Bow Street with having presented an unloaded pistol at the Queen (1 Mar.).—A meeting was held at the Mansion House in aid of the Fund for the completion and decoration of the interior of St. Paul's Cathedral.—The Corporation resolved to contribute £1,000 towards the City of London Industrial School, which was being erected at Bisley, on the understanding that it should be used exclusively for boys brought before the Lord Mayor and City Magistrates

(11 Ap.).—The freedom of the Grocers' Company was presented to Prince Arthur, (12th).—The old Cock and Woolpack Tavern, Finch Lane, Cornhill, was sold (25th).—The foundation stone of the Memorial Hall was laid on the site of the old Fleet Prison, Farringdon Street, (10 May).—It was announced on the 25th that the site of the Poultry Chapel, had been knocked down for £50,200 or nearly £7 per foot. The sale was made with the authority of the Charity Commissioners.—The new offices of the City of London Union in Bartholomew Close were completed (28th).

Interior of St. Paul's Cathedral, during Thanksgiving Service.

For over twenty-one years the work of the City of London Union had been transacted in most inconvenient premises in St. Mary Axe. The offices had been removed thither in 1851 from the neighbourhood of Cannon Street, where they had been established at the formation of the Union in 1837. The Bartholomew Close freehold site of 5,000 feet cost £11,000. The building, which was designed by Mr. W. Hudson, was to cost £5,894.

As a permanent memorial of the great worth and public services of the late Rev. Dr. Mortimer, the Common Council resolved that an annual grant of £20 should be made in order to provide prizes for the special encouragement of the study of English in the City of London School, and that such prizes should be called the Mortimer Memorial prizes (6 June). The proposal to remove the slaughter houses in Aldgate aroused strenuous opposition on the part of the Jewish inhabitants and others in the ward of Portsoken, and two petitions on the subject were presented to the Commissioners of Sewers (11th). The Jewish community desired the slaughter houses to be retained, as, according to the memorial, slaughtering was carried on there in a way "consistent with their laws and the dictates of their consciences." The other memorial reminded the Commissioners that when cholera was raging all around, Aldgate High Street was free from the contagion. The Commissioners, nevertheless, resolved to petition Parliament with a view to getting the slaughter houses suppressed.—The closing services at the Poultry Chapel took place on the 16th and 20th.

The congregation traced its descent from Dr. Thomas Goodwin, who on his return from Holland, about the beginning of the Long Parliament, collected a body of fellow disciples at the meeting houses somewhere in Thames Street. The Church then formed had successively occupied buildings in Paved Alley, Lime Street, Miles's Lane and Camomile Street. Dr. Goodwin, was greatly favoured by Cromwell, whom he visited on his dying bed.

The City Solicitor informed the Common Council that Mr. Alex. Melville, the artist, had commenced proceedings to recover the sum of £4,950 for his picture, representing the presentation of the Freedom of the City to the Prince of Wales in 1863. The subject was referred to a Committee (27th).—Mr. Alderman Owden laid the foundation stone of the new ward schools for Bishopsgate, on a plot of ground between Skinner Street and Primrose Street (4 July). The schools were established in 1702.—The freedom of the Turners' Company was presented to the Baroness Burdett-Coutts (10th), and her ladyship received the Honorary Freedom of the City on the 18th. She was the first lady upon whom such a distinction had been conferred.—The Corporation authorised the purchase of a steam launch for £750 to secure a more efficient system of inspection of ships coal-laden in the Thames.—The Fox and Knot Schools and Mission, founded about 1840, held their first meeting at the new premises in King Street, Snow Hill, under the presidency of the Lord Mayor (12 Aug.)—The failure of Gledstanes and Co., an East India firm, for nearly two millions, was announced (22nd).—Mr. Alderman Hale died at West Hill, Hampstead, on the 23rd.—A Committee of investigation was appointed by the shareholders of the Metropolitan Railway Company, in consequence of the mismanagement of the line (28th), and on 19 Oct. a new Board was formed.—Sir Moses Montefiore offered up thanksgiving at the Synagogue of the Sephardim congregation in Bevis Marks for his prosperous journey to Russia and safe return (24th).—A special Court of Common Council was convened to receive the resignation of Mr. Brooke, who was elected sheriff on Midsummer Day. A Common Hall was held on 16 Sept., when Mr. F. Perkins was chosen to fill the vacancy.—The Corporation decided to provide a suitable pedestal for the Prince Consort's statue in Holborn Circus, at a cost of £2,000 (19th).—The church of St. Andrew's, Holborn, was re-opened after undergoing material alteration.   A stained-glass window, the gift of a parishioner, was placed at the west end, and the brickwork removed from an old arch, which dates back to the 15th century.   A fine new organ was also introduced (13 Oct.).— A draft scheme of the Endowed Schools Commissioners for the future management of Dulwich College was issued (2 Nov.).

Guildhall Library.

The College was founded by Edward Alleyne in 1619, and was a Corporation consisting of Master, Warden, six Fellows, six poor Brothers, five poor Sisters, and twelve Scholars.   It stands in the parish of St. Giles, Camberwell, and Alleyne associated with this parish the three London parishes of St. Botolph Bishopsgate, St. Luke's Finsbury, and St. Saviour's Southwark.   The value of its property had increased from £1,400 in 1738, and £8,000 in 1835, to £17,000 in 1866.

A meeting was held at the Mansion House in connection with Sir Bartle Frere's mission for the suppression of the slave trade on the east coast of Africa (4 Nov.).—The new Library and Museum, erected by the Corporation at the Guildhall, was opened, on the 5th, by the Lord Chancellor (Lord Selborne), in the unavoidable absence of the Prince of Wales.   The Corporation had voted £1,500 (6 June) for the entertainment of the guests, who numbered about 2,000.   A notable collection of engravings, gems, and other works of art, and of archæological drawings and prints of old London, was exhibited on the occasion. The Lord Chancellor complimented the Corporation upon adding the finishing touch to an educational work which had been going on for ages.

The new building, designed by Mr. Horace Jones, the City Architect, consists of a Library, which will accommodate 150 readers, a Newspaper Room for journals and handy books of reference, and a Committee Room on the upper floor, with a Museum and strong-rooms in the basement. The old building occupied the site of the corridor, which now forms the approach to the present library from the Guildhall porch. The Library, which is exceedingly light and pleasant, is a hall 100 feet in length, 65 feet wide, and 50 feet in height, divided like the Museum, into nave and aisles. The latter are fitted with handsome oak bookcases, and form twelve bays, into which the furniture can be moved, when the nave is required on state occasions as a reception hall. The roof is of oak, and the general style of architecture is perpendicular Gothic in agreement with that of the Guildhall. The total cost of the buildings, including the estimated value of the site, was about £100,000.

Alderman Sidney Hedley Waterlow was elected Lord Mayor.—Earl Granville attended the Lord Mayor's Banquet on the 9th, in place of Mr. Gladstone, the Prime Minister, who was indisposed.—A great fire occurred at Hadley's City Flour Mills, Upper Thames Street, in which a fireman, named Guernsey, lost his life (11th).—The City of Boston, U.S., having been devastated by fire, the Lord Mayor was requested by the Common Council to telegraph to the Mayor of Boston an expression of its profound regret and deepest sympathy with the inhabitants and the whole American people (14th).—The Court resolved to construct a tramway connecting Columbia Market, which had not hitherto been a success, with the Great Eastern Railway.—The first step was taken towards the establishment of a London Tribunal of Commerce, a committee being instructed to give the necessary parliamentary notice (14th).—The Earl of Kimberley presided at a banquet at the Cannon Street Hotel, to celebrate the inauguration of the British Australian Telegraph. Connecting wires were carried into the great hall of the hotel, and compliments were exchanged between the company present and those at the Antipodes (15th).—A resolution, expressing the Corporation's appreciation of the eminent services of Mr. Henry M. Stanley, in his endeavours to discover and relieve Dr. Livingstone, was ordered to be written on vellum, emblazoned and framed, and presented to the American explorer. The Court also instructed a committee to ascertain upon what terms Cæsar's Camp at Wimbledon might be preserved as an open space for the people (21st).—A meeting of treasurers and other representatives of London Hospitals was held at the London Tavern, with a view to establishing a Hospital Sunday in London. Mr. R. B. Martin, in the absence of the Lord Mayor, presided (21st).—The house in Plough Court, Lombard Street, where Pope was believed to have been born, was pulled down during this month.—St. Peter's Church, Cornhill, was re-opened after extensive alterations and repairs (1 Dec.).—The Common Council voted a sum of 500 guineas for the relief of sufferers from the recent floods in Italy (12th). —A public meeting of liverymen, merchants, and traders of the City, presided over by the Lord Mayor, was held at the Guildhall to protest against the income-tax, as inquisitorial in its character, unjust in its operation, and demoralizing to the national character (13th).—The ward of Aldersgate presented a stained-glass window to the new Guildhall Library ; the two principal lights represent Caxton presenting his first English printed book to Edward IV, and Richard of Bury buying books for his library (20th).—A voluntary offer was made to the first Commissioner of Works, on behalf of the Corporation, to abandon its right to compulsory Metage, and to devote the revenue arising from a fixed duty, which it was proposed should be levied in lieu thereof, to the preservation of Epping Forest This offer resulted in the passing of the Metage on Grain Act, 1872.   In the same session the Corporation promoted a Bill in Parliament for the permissive sale to the City, by the various Lords of Manors, of their interests in the Forest ; but this failed to pass owing to the strength of private opposition.—The Corporation of London was legally constituted the Port of London Sanitary Authority this year by the 20th section of the Public Health Act, 1872, which states : " The Mayor, Aldermen, and Commons of the City of London, shall be deemed to be the Sanitary Authority of the Port of London, and shall pay out of their Corporate funds all their expenses, as such Port Sanitary Authority."—During the year the church of St. Mildred the Virgin, Poultry, was taken down

1873.

THE new Post Office building in St. Martin's-le-Grand was opened without ceremony, Jan., 1873, and the telegraph department was removed thither from Telegraph Street.

The building faces the old Post Office. The principal front towards St. Martin's-le-Grand and that towards Bath Street are each 286 feet long, the ends fronting Newgate Street and Angel Street are each 142 feet, the height from the pavement is 84 feet ; there is in addition a light basement and an additional attic available for a large number of clerks. The great room which was to have been a stately public hall has had to be appropriated to clerks, owing to the growth of the Post Office work. The telegraph instrument room is 125 feet by eighty feet. The total cost of the building was about half-a-million, of which more than half was paid for the site and as compensation to outgoing tenants

The suspension was announced of Messrs. Pawson and Co., St. Paul's Church-yard, with liabilities estimated at upwards of £600,000 (4th).   A limited company was afterwards formed to take over the business.   About the same time Anselmo Vivanti, a silk merchant in St. Mary Axe, failed for a similar amount.—The Lord Mayor and Mr. Sheriff Perkins attended the funeral of Napoleon III at Chislehurst.   The " Dead March" in *Saul* was played at St. Paul's and reference

to the event was made at many of the City churches (15th).—A letter of thanks was received from the Italian Government for the 500 guineas contributed by the Corporation to the Italian Inundation Relief Fund (16th). —The Endowed Schools Commission issued a draft scheme for the management of Sir John Cass's Charity in the parish of St. Botolph, Aldgate (16th).— It was decided that the Gas Committee of the Corporation should henceforth be called the Gas and Water Committee, this Committee having now to deal with the two great monopolies which controlled the lighting and water supply of the City. —It was reported that another old City land-mark was about to be removed, viz.: Garraway's Coffee House, Change Alley, Cornhill, which was required for a firm of bankers.

Back of Martin's Bank on the site of Garraway's— designed by Norman Shaw.

Garraway's was for a long period one of the most noted coffee houses in the City.   Here it was that the first step towards popularising the use of tea in England was taken by the original proprietor, Thomas Garway, "tobacconist and coffee-man," about the year 1600.   He issued a handbill offering tea at from 16*s.* to 50*s.* per pound.   Hitherto, he said, it had been sold for £6 and sometimes £10 the pound weight, and had been only used in "high treatments and entertainments," and as presents to "Princes and grandees."   Dr. John Radcliffe, the celebrated physician, according to his biographer, was generally to be found about the time that the merchants went on 'Change seated at a table in Garraway's Coffee House, with apothecaries and surgeons flocking around him.

A Mansion House Fund was opened for the relief of the survivors from the wreck of the emigrant ship, "Northfleet," which was sunk off Dungeness. Amidst a scene of wild confusion Captain Knowles did his best to save the women and children, and himself went bravely down with the ship. The Corporation contributed £200 to the Northfleet Fund.—A resolution, which gave rise to

" Baker's," an 18th century Coffee House, still in Change Alley.

much controversy in the religious world, was passed by the Common Council on the 30th, in the following terms :—

> "That the church and congregation, connected with the Poultry Chapel, having purchased of the City a freehold site on the Holborn Viaduct, at a cost of £25,000, upon which they are now erecting a church to be known as the City Temple, designed (exclusive of large provision for Day and Sunday Schools) to accommodate 2,500 persons, and involving an expenditure of more than £31,000, thus making a total minimum outlay of £56,000 ; this Court being desirous of evincing its interest in so great a movement, and in recognition of the public spirit displayed in the determination to perpetuate a long-existing connection with the City, do present to them a pulpit, to be for ever held as the commemorative gift of the Corporation of London."

The Coachmakers' Company presented its honorary freedom to the Duke of Edinburgh (7 Feb.).—Kew Bridge was opened, free of toll, by the Corporation and Metropolitan Board of Works, the Lord Mayor and Sheriffs passing over it at the head of a procession (8th).—It was decided that the new Guildhall Library should henceforth be devoted to the free use of the public, and it was referred to the Library Committee to consider the desirability of an extension of hours and the establishment of a free circulating library for the use of the citizens generally (13th). The library and reading room were opened to the public, free, on 10 Mar., but the proposal for a free circulating library has not, up to the present, borne fruit.—The Clockmakers' Company deposited in the Guildhall Library a valuable collection of ancient clocks, watches, watch movements, etc., belonging to the Company, together with their library of works on horology and watch-making (13 Feb.).—The question of allowing tramways to enter the City came before the Corporation and the Commissioners of Sewers. The latter body resolved, subject to the sanction of the Common Council, to allow tramways to be laid down in Aldgate as far as Church Row, and in Finsbury Place as far as the north side of Fore Street. The Police Commissioner, however, considered that to allow tramways to come into the City would be in the highest degree objectionable, and the Common Council adopted this view (27th). The Commissioners, as the subordinate body, had therefore to give way and the limit was fixed at the City boundary.—The question of the removal of Temple Bar was now being agitated, and the City Lands Committee was instructed to confer with the Government as to the extent to which the old City gate would be affected by the construction of the Law Courts (6 Mar.).—Another discussion took place in the Common Council with regard to contributions for religious purposes on Holborn Viaduct, this time the Established Church being in question (6th). By the casting vote of the Lord Mayor it was decided that 500 guineas should be paid towards the restoration of St. Sepulchre's Church, the parish having purchased of the City a freehold site on the Holborn Viaduct at a cost of £4,200, for the purpose of throwing the same into the public way, and proposing to expend a further sum of £6,000 in restoring and decorating the fine tower and interior of the church. This resolution, however, was rescinded on the 27th.—Mr. William Harvey, surgeon, died at Lonsdale Square, Islington, aged 77 (18th).

> Mr. Harvey was well-known to readers of the *City Press* as "Aleph," over whose signature for thirteen years had appeared nearly 700 articles relating to the history of the City of London, many of them of great antiquarian interest A selection of these was published in two volumes, entitled, *London Scenes and London People*, and *The Old City*.

Her Majesty's Ministers were invited to meet the Lord Provost of Edinburgh, the Lord Mayors of Dublin and York, and about 200 mayors of the principal boroughs of England and Wales, at a banquet at the Mansion House (26th).

—The Baroness Burdett-Coutts made a free gift to the Corporation of two pieces of land in the neighbourhood of Columbia Market (3 Ap.).—The Lord Mayor, on behalf of the Corporation, presented Mr. Benjamin Bower with a silver salver, bearing a suitable inscription, on his retirement, after thirty-six years' services as a member of the Court.

Mr. Bower was Chairman of the Improvement Committee from 1857 to 1861, when the Clerkenwell Improvement was carried out, and it was on his advice and in the teeth of much opposition that the Corporation voted over £200,000 to assist in the construction of the Metropolitan Railway. That recommendation resulted not only in the carrying out of a great public work, but in the repayment of the whole of the money advanced by the Corporation, augmented by a large profit beyond the sum expended.

The Common Council ordered a bas relief to be placed on each side of the pedestal of the Prince Consort statue at a cost of 500 guineas (3rd).—The memorial stone of the new hall of the Curriers' Company was laid (17th), the old hall on the same site having been pulled down.—Sir William Tite, C. B., M.P., architect of the Royal Exchange, died at Torquay (20th) —The Commissioners, appointed by the Board of Trade to consider the application of the Gas Light and Coke Company for an increase in the price of gas, announced their decision (24th), viz.: an addition of 7d. for the ordinary common gas (16-candles) making the price 4s. 2d., and for cannel gas, none of which was used in the City, an increase of 10d, raising the price to 6s. 9d. Under the terms of the scheme for the amalgamation of the City of London with the Chartered Gas Company the manufacture of gas at Blackfriars was to cease within two years after the completion of the works at Beckton, which would be within eighteen months of the present time. —The Clothworkers' Company held a conference at their hall in Mincing Lane to consider the best means to be adopted for promoting technical education in connection with the cloth trade at the principal centres of that industry (8 May). It was decided to found a professorship of textile fabrics in connection with the College of Science at Leeds, four scholarships for districts in Yorkshire connected with the clothing industry, and four scholarships in relation to that industry in other parts of the country —Mr. Crawford moved in the House of Commons for an address to the Queen, praying Her Majesty to withhold her assent from another scheme of the Endowed Schools Commissioners for the future management of Emanuel Hospital. Mr. Gladstone made a powerful speech in support of the scheme and the motion was defeated by 286 votes against 238 (13th). Under this scheme, the School branch of Emanuel Hospital was separated from the Almshouse branch of that foundation, and the United Westminster Schools were placed under the control of a new governing body of twenty-one persons, including the

Lord Mayor, the Recorder, nine governors nominated by the Lord Mayor and Aldermen, and ten nominated by the Westminster members of the London School Board.—Mr. Frederick Woodthorpe, the Town Clerk, tendered his resignation on the ground of ill-health (15th). He was afterwards (3 July) granted a retiring allowance of £1,000 per annum, which, however, he did not long live to enjoy.—The Corporation resolved to widen the roadway at the western end of the Metropolitan Meat and Poultry Market at a cost of £2,150 (15 May).—A public meeting, convened by the Lord Mayor at the Guildhall, resolved that it was desirable to establish tribunals of Commerce and Courts of Reconcilement and Arbitration (20th). — Alderman Sir Jas. Duke died at Laughton Lodge, Sussex (28th).

Sir James was born at Montrose in 1792 In 1819 he began his commercial career in the City, then became a Common Councilman, and in 1840 on the resignation of Alderman Harmer was elected Alderman of Farringdon Without He was Sheriff in 1836, and Lord Mayor in 1848. From 1837 to 1849 he represented Boston in Parliament in the Liberal interest ; and from the latter date to July, 1865, he was one of the members for the City.

The Lord Mayor was appointed governor of the Irish Society on the resignation of that office by Alderman Sir W. A. Rose (29th).—The Corporation decided to enlarge the City of London Lunatic Asylum at an expense of £4,000 (29th).—The Recorder (Mr. Russell Gurney) wrote from New York on the 30th, regretting his prolonged absence, and stating that, under the Washington Treaty, the investigation of claims could not last beyond the 26 Sept., when his powers would expire.—The Corporation voted 100 guineas to the Hospital Sunday Fund (12 June) The first Hospital Sunday was held in London on 15 June, the amount collected being £27,700 8s. 1d.—It was resolved to dispose of the portion of the Synagogue in Duke Street, Aldgate, which belonged to the Corporation. —The Shah, Nasser-el-Din, was presented with an address by the Corporation, and entertained at the Guildhall at a magnificent reception (20th). Upwards of 3,000 guests were invited, and the presentation of the address was followed by a ball ; supper being served in the Old Council Chamber. The Corporation afterwards received a letter of thanks from the Lord Chamberlain for its hospitality, and the excellent arrangements made for the reception of the Persian monarch. —In view of the large attendance at the Guildhall Library, an increased staff was ordered to be appointed, and the annual allowance for the purchase of books was raised from £300 to £500 (26th).—Prince Arthur was presented with the honorary freedom of the Haberdashers' Company, and was afterwards entertained at a banquet in their Hall (2 July).—The Corporation resolved to present the freedom of the City to Sir Albert David Sassoon, K.C.S.I., in recognition of his munificent and philanthropic exertions in the cause of charity, and the promotion of education ; more especially, though not exclusively, in our Indian Empire (3rd). [The presentation was made 6 Nov.]—The first step towards the establishment of a School of Music was taken on the 3rd, when the Common Council instructed the General Purposes Committee to consider and report upon the best means of providing approved musical performances and other intellectual entertainments in the Guildhall, or in any other way to encourage the study of music in the City of London for the public benefit.—The first Board School in London was opened in Old Castle Street, Whitechapel (12th).—It was announced that a baronetcy had been conferred upon the lord mayor, and the dignity of knighthood upon the sheriffs.—Mr. John Braddick Monckton was elected Town Clerk on the 17th. He polled 85 votes as against 72 for Mr. E. T. E. Besley.—Alderman Sir David Salomons, M.P., died at Great Cumberland Place, Hyde Park, on the 18th.

Sir David was second son of Mr. Levy Salomons, a retired merchant and underwriter of London, and his wife, Matilda Detnetz, of Leyden He was born in 1797, and married Jeannette, daughter of Mr. Solomon Cohen in 1825. He was Sheriff of London and Middlesex 1835-6, and High Sheriff of Kent 1839-40. He was elected Alderman 1847, and was Lord Mayor in 1855-6 He was M P for Greenwich in 1851-2, and from 1859 till his death.

The Prince of Wales held a conference at Marlborough House of representatives of the principal City Companies, with a view to discussing how technical instruction might be promoted by the Livery Companies acting in concert with the International Exhibition. A scheme was submitted and approved (21st).—The new hall at the Middle-Class Schools in Cowper Street was opened by Earl Russell (24th).—Sir Albert David Sassoon presented two scholarships of the value of £50 each to the City of London School (24th).—The foundation stone of a church in Prebend Square, Islington was laid (25th). This was to be erected by the Clothworkers' Company, in accordance with the Act providing for the removal of William Lambe's Chapel in Monkwell Street. Free sittings were to be set apart for 500 people. The ancient crypt of Lambe's Chapel was reconstructed on the south side of the church of Allhallows Staining, to receive the remains found beneath it on its demolition.—The trial commenced on 18 Aug., at the Central Criminal Court, of Austin Biron Bidwell, Geo. Macdonnell, Geo. Bidwell and Edward Moyes, for forging foreign bills of exchange, and thereby defrauding the Bank of England of over £100,000. The whole of the prisoners were found guilty and sentenced to transportation for life. An attempt was made to rescue the prisoners during their incarceration in Newgate. Warders were found to be in communication with the prisoners' friends and to have received

large sums of money.   They were dismissed the service, and the prisoners while
awaiting trial were removed from Newgate to Pentonville.—Weigh House Chapel
was re-opened after undergoing considerable alteration at a cost of between £6,000
and £7,000 (6 Sept.).—At the Common Council on the 18th a letter was read from
Messrs. Roy and Cartwright, announcing bequests to the Corporation by the late
Alderman Sir David Salomons, of the presentation plate given to him by the Jews
(on attaining the honour of the shrievalty), for his exertions in the advancement
of religious liberty, and of £1,000 as an acknowledgment of the influence of the
Corporation throughout the civilised world in favour of religious toleration.   This
sum was to be expended in some useful memorial of the donor in connection with
the Library and Museum.—The Lord Mayor and Lady Mayoress, the Sheriffs,

members of the Corpora-
tion and its chief officers,
were entertained by the
Lord Mayor of York and
the Mayors of England
and Wales, at a banquet
at York, on the 25th.
The Lord Mayor and
Sheriffs went in full state,
the procession traversing
the main streets of the City
to the Mansion House.
Dinner was served in the
Guildhall, one of the oldest
gothic rooms in the king-
dom, and was followed by
a ball in the Assembly
Rooms. — Sir Edwin
Landseer was buried in
the crypt of St. Paul's
(11 Oct.).—The Corpora-
tion ordered a medal to be
struck in commemoration

Crypt of Gerard's Hall, Basing Lane, removed for widening Cannon Street.

of the reception of the Shah (23rd).—The Lord Mayor laid the foundation stone
of the building of the new Safe Deposit Company at the eastern end of Queen
Victoria Street. In digging the foundations, the builders laid bare a portion of the

course of the old Wall Brook, which brought to light a remarkable collection of Roman antiquities, now preserved in the Guildhall Museum.—The Common Council passed a resolution, congratulating the Right Hon. Russell Gurney, Q.C., Recorder, on his return to this country and upon the termination of his labours in connection with the settlement of the Alabama claims (6 Nov.).—The Court voted £2,000 a year, for five years, out of the Metage on Grain Fund, in aid of the fund that was being raised for the purchase of West Ham Park.— The Corporation appointed one of the fifteen managers of Aske's Charity, Hoxton, the scheme for which had been approved by Her Majesty in Council on 9 Aug.—A controversy arose between the Churchwardens of St. Vedast *alias* Foster, and the rector, the Rev. T. Pelham Dale, on account of the ritualistic views of that clergyman and certain alterations which he had made in the church (6 Nov.).—Alderman Andrew Lusk was elected Lord Mayor.—The Lord Chief Baron, addressing the new Lord Mayor on the 9th, referred to the changes in the constitution of the High Courts of Justice, and said this might be the last time that the Chief Baron of the Exchequer would have an opportunity of welcoming the Lord Mayor of London on such an auspicious occasion.—The Epping Forest Commissioners opened their sittings at the Sessions House, Westminster (11th).—The City and Spitalfields School of Art was opened in Skinner Street, Bishopsgate (20th). This was an amalgamation with an old school started in Spitalfields in 1841.—The School Board election in the City (28th) gave the following result:

Alderman Cotton, 5819 ; Rev. Canon Gregory, 5703 , F. Peek, 5648 , S Morley, M P , 4851 , Sir John Bennett, 3522 ; W S Gover, 3432 , Mrs. Burbury, 2136   The first four were elected

The case of Melville *v.* the Corporation of London came on in the Court of Queen's Bench (1 Dec.). This was a claim by the painter of the picture, representing the presentation of the freedom of the City to the Prince of Wales, for £4,950 The artist urged that he had been led to believe the Corporation would accept his picture, that the work had occupied him for five years, and that a room had been set apart for his use at the Guildhall. He had painted upwards of 450 portraits Mr. Justice Blackburn pointed out that there was no contract, and the plaintiff was non-suited.— Sir Charles Reed was elected chairman of the London School Board (10th).—Compensation was paid to certain meters, whose services were dispensed with owing to the abolition of compulsory metage, the money being paid out of the City of London Grain Duty (11th) —The death was announced of Mr. Frederick Woodthorpe, late Town Clerk (19th). The deceased's grand-father had filled the office of Town Clerk from 1801 to 1825, and his father held the office from 1825 to 1842.

During this year the parish of St. Martin Outwich was united with that of St. Helen, Bishopsgate; a railing was put round St. Paul's Cathedral; and the Bell Savage, or Belle Sauvage, Ludgate Hill, which in the *London Gazette* of 1676 was termed an " antient inn," was pulled down.

1874.

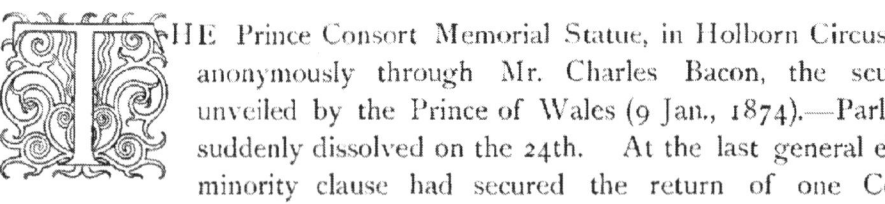

THE Prince Consort Memorial Statue, in Holborn Circus, presented anonymously through Mr. Charles Bacon, the sculptor, was unveiled by the Prince of Wales (9 Jan., 1874).—Parliament was suddenly dissolved on the 24th. At the last general election, the minority clause had secured the return of one Conservative candidate, Mr. Bell, who, however, was replaced on his decease by a Liberal, Baron Rothschild. There were, therefore, four Liberal members sitting for the City at this time. From 1857 to 1867 none but Liberals had represented the City. Now there was a great revulsion of feeling, and when the poll was declared on 6 Feb., it was found that three Conservatives headed the list, viz., Mr. Alderman Cotton, Mr. P. Twells, and Mr. Hubbard, and that only the minority seat was held by a Liberal, Mr. Goschen, the other two candidates, Mr. Alderman Lawrence and Baron Rothschild, being defeated.—The Corporation voted £1,000 towards the Bengal Famine Relief Fund (12th), which was opened at the Mansion House (16th) and in nine days reached the sum of £25,000. The Queen sent £1,000 direct to Calcutta in aid of the sufferers.—Mr. William Haywood, the Engineer, having presented to the Commissioners of Sewers an elaborate report on different kinds of paving, it was agreed that, under proper conditions, asphalte, granite, and wood might continue to be laid as pavements in the City (17th).—Dr. Letheby, Medical Officer of Health for the City of London, resigned on account of ill-health.—The Rev. Thomas Binney, late minister of the King's Weigh House Chapel, on Fish Street Hill, near the Monument, died on the 24th, aged seventy-five.

Mr. Binney, who was one of the leading nonconformists of his time, was called to Weigh House in 1829, and continued there till Jan., 1871, being succeeded by the Rev. W. Braden, of Huddersfield. He received from the University of Aberdeen the degree of LL.D., and that of D.D. from the United States. He introduced chanting into the service of Independent congregations, and gave a great impulse to congregational psalmody by his Service of Song. One of his best known works was a book entitled, *Is it possible to make the best of both Worlds?* As a preacher he was especially attractive to young men. At his funeral, in Abney Park Cemetery, Dean Stanley performed part of the service.

The Saddlers' Company gave two scholarships for Oxford and Cambridge to the City of London School (26th).—The freedom of the City was voted to Sir Bartle Frere in testimony of his long and honourable career in India, and of his successful mission to the east coast of Africa which resulted in a treaty with the Sultan of Zanzibar for the total abolition of the slave trade on that coast (26th). The presentation was made on July 16th.—It was announced on the 7 Mar. that the Peabody Trustees had received from Mr. Peabody's executors, in accordance with the terms of the will, a sum of £150,000, so that the whole amount given and bequeathed by this eminent philanthropist, for the poor of London, was half-a-million sterling.— The Corporation resolved to present the Duke and Duchess of Edinburgh with plate to the value of 3,000 guineas, as a marriage gift (16 Mar.). [The presentation was made privately to their Royal Highnesses at the Mansion House, on 11 May, 1875.] On the 18th an address was presented to the Queen at Windsor, and compliments of congratulation were tendered to the Duke and Duchess at Buckingham Palace. A ball was given in honour of their Royal Highnesses at the Mansion House on 29 Ap.—The Corporation resolved (Ap.) to present Sir Garnet Wolseley with the freedom of the City and a sword of the value of 100 guineas, in recognition of the ability and gallantry displayed by him in his command of the expedition to the Gold Coast. The presentation was made at the Guildhall on 22 Oct. The Emperor of Russia having visited this country shortly after his daughter's marriage with the Duke of Edinburgh, the Corporation entertained His Majesty at the Guildhall and presented him with an address on 18 May. Reference was made in the address to the great boon which the Czar Alexander II had conferred upon his people by the abolition of serfdom throughout his vast dominions. The Queen, through the Home Secretary and the Lord Chamberlain, and the Emperor, through the Russian Ambassador, expressed their great satisfaction with the magnificent hospitality of the City. The Czar gave £1,000 to the Bishop of London and the Lord Mayor for the London poor. A medal was struck in commemoration of the visit.—The City Temple, a Congregational place of worship, was opened on the Holborn Viaduct (19th).

Externally and internally the building has a light and elegant appearance. It is in the classic Italian style of architecture, with a tower at one end. The length of the building is 160 feet, and its width 63 feet within, with a height of 54 feet. It affords seating accommodation for 2,500 people, but room can be found for 500 more. The pulpit (the gift of the Corporation) is of white marble. The site cost £25,000, and the building £30,000.

A licence in mortmain was obtained on the 22nd, enabling the Corporation to hold West Ham Park (consisting of 77 acres), as an open space, and thereupon the

Corporation paid the first instalment of £2,000 to Mr. Gurney, the vendor. The conveyance was executed on 20 July. Altogether, the Corporation expended on the park £18,544, exclusive of the cost of annual maintenance, which, in 1892, was £1,012 5s. 4d. paid out of the City's Cash.—The Commissioners of Sewers resolved to contribute £130,000 towards the street improvements in connection with the Inner Circle Railway in the neighbourhood of Fenchurch Street (26th).—The Corporation voted £600 as premiums for designs for a new Fruit and Vegetable Market (2 June).—Dr. W. Sedgwick Saunders was elected Medical Officer of Health for the City of London (9th).—The Broderers' Company presented the Corporation with a scholarship of the value of 50 guineas per annum for the City of London School (18th).—It was announced that a baronetcy would be conferred upon the Lord Mayor, and that the Sheriffs would be knighted in connection with the visit of the Emperor of All the Russias (21st).—The Right Hon. Benjamin Disraeli, Lord Derby, and the Marquis of Salisbury, were enrolled as honorary members of the Merchant Taylors' Company (24th).—The Corporation resolved to erect a new Fruit and Vegetable Market on the site adjoining the new Meat and Poultry Market extension at Smithfield (29th). A Select Committee of twelve was appointed on 22 Oct. to prepare plans and estimates.—Notwithstanding every effort made by the Corporation, Columbia Market still proved a failure; and it was decided (2 June) to offer to re-transfer the property to the Baroness Burdett-Coutts. The offer was accepted, and on 2 July instructions were given for the transfer to be effected.—The new low-level station of the London, Chatham and Dover Railway, at Snow Hill, was opened (1 Aug.).—Mr. Alderman Challis died at Enfield at the age of eighty (20th). From 1852 to 1858 the alderman was M.P. for Finsbury. He was also chairman of the Sunday School Union.—Two of the masters of the City of London School met with sudden deaths by accident, Mr. Frederick Wilton on the top of Snowdon, and Mr. J. L. Clowes, who was drowned while bathing at Whitby.—Mr. John Henry Foley, the sculptor, was buried in St. Paul's Cathedral, close to the graves of Wren, Landseer, and Sir Joshua Reynolds (4 Sept.).—Various proposals were made to the Corporation for the removal of Temple Bar, and the whole subject was referred to a committee for consideration.—The Congress of Orientalists, who had been sitting at the Royal Institution, were invited to a banquet at the Mansion House (19th).—The first Hospital Saturday collection was made (Oct. 13).—A deputation of the School Board for London, headed by Sir Charles Reed, the chairman, presented to the Corporation a resolution of thanks for the use of the Council Chamber and the Committee Rooms of the Guildhall during the last four years (22nd). The first meeting of the Board in its new premises on the

Embankment was held on 30 Sept.—The Patriarch of Syria and the Bishop of Jerusalem, who were visiting the educational institutions of the country, were received at Christ's Hospital (26 Oct.).—The foundation stone of the new Billingsgate Market was laid on the 27th.—While the Corporation was endeavouring to secure open spaces for the public beyond its borders, it was not unmindful of the need of utilizing, as far as possible, the little breathing spaces within the "one square mile."   On 22 Oct. it passed the following resolution :—

"That the health of the immense population of London imperatively demanding that every available open space in the City should be preserved and utilized for purposes of recreation, it be referred to the Coal and Corn and Finance Committee to enquire as to the existing open spaces, and what steps (if any) should be taken to preserve them for the public ; and especially to enquire if access, during the day-time, be obtainable by the public to the gardens of Trinity Square, Finsbury Circus, and the enclosed ground around St. Paul's Cathedral, and to report thereon to this Court."

Alderman David Henry Stone was elected Lord Mayor.—Mr. Deputy Harris presented a stained-glass window to the Guildhall (14th).—The Master of the Rolls delivered judgment in the long-pending Chancery suits in regard to Epping Forest (10 Nov.).   He decided in favour of the Corporation, holding that the right of common pasture throughout the entire forest was established, and he ordered all the Lords of the Manors (with the exception of the Lord of the Manor of West Ham, who had practically parted with all the wastes of that manor), to pay the costs of the suit.   By this decision all the enclosures made subsequent to Aug., 1851, were declared to be illegal.   The decision had the effect of keeping open and unenclosed for ever the large space of 5,000 acres of land in Epping Forest.   The Town Clerk on 3 Dec. laid before the Common Council resolutions and letters from various public bodies, thanking the Corporation for its action in regard to the preservation of Epping Forest. —An application was made by the Solicitor to the Treasury for £6,000 forfeited by John Hegan, Esq., one of the sureties for the appearance of J. J. de Lizardi. By an arrangement between the Solicitor and the Corporation, the question at issue was referred to the Court of Exchequer (19th).—Sir William Harcourt presided at a public meeting in the Town Hall, Shoreditch, at which gratitude to the Corporation was expressed for its efforts to preserve Epping Forest (9 Dec.).

"Happily," said Sir William, "at last they found a champion, a happy deliverer, in the body which had always taken a conspicuous part in the liberties of the country—the Corporation of the City. When he contrasted the public spirit of the Corporation with the rather narrow ideas which had been entertained by those centralising departments, who were unquestionably supposed to have a monopoly of political success, he must say that, for his part, he preferred the policy of the Corporation.   They had been entrusted with great revenues and they had expended them well."

The attendance for the first complete year of the new Guildhall Library showed an aggregate of 173,559, as against 14,316 in 1868, the last year of the old Library.—Several City churches were taken down during the year, viz., St. Martin's Outwich, St. James's Duke's Place, and St. Antholin's Watling Street.—The Wool Exchange in Coleman Street, and the Midland Railway Goods Station, Whitecross Street, were erected, and the Prerogative Will Office was removed from Doctors Commons to Somerset House.

1875.

THE Lord Mayor and Sheriffs paid a state visit to Paris (5 Jan., 1875), with a view especially to the opening of the new Opera House

The civic party, who stayed at the Hôtel Bristol, were met, on their arrival in Paris, by the Prefect of the Seine and the Prefect of Police. On the morning of the 5th the Lord Mayor and Sheriffs in their State carriages, and escorted by a squadron of Dragoons, proceeded to the Elysée, where they were received by the President of the Republic, Marshal MacMahon The civic party, both going and returning, were much cheered by the people who thronged the streets At night the Opera House was opened with great ceremony and a grand performance. The Marshal-President came in full state, being preceded by an escort of Cuirassiers bearing torches. The Lord Mayor arrived in the Place de l'Opéra also in full state. A squadron of the mounted Republican Guard, three hundred strong, escorted the Lord Mayor (who rode in his carriage and four) and the Sheriffs from the Place Vendôme. The Rue de la Paix was densely crowded with spectators, who were again very demonstrative and enthusiastic. The place in the Opera House assigned to the Lord Mayor and his colleagues was one of the proscenium boxes next to that occupied by President MacMahon, and immediately opposite one set apart for the President of the National Assembly. Amongst those who witnessed the performance were Queen Isabella of Spain, King Alphonso XII, the Count and the Countess of Paris. Wednesday was taken up with ceremonial visits, and the following evening the Lord Mayor entertained a party at the Hôtel Bristol A breakfast was given at the Grand Hotel by the British Chamber of Commerce, in honour of the Lord Mayor and Sheriffs. The President invited the Lord Mayor to dinner, and Madame MacMahon paid a visit to the Lady Mayoress. His lordship was also entertained by Lord Lyons at the British Embassy, and the Lord Mayor and Sheriffs attended a banquet given by the Prefect of the Seine, at the Palais du Luxembourg, at which the Ministers and high government functionaries were present. During the Lord Mayor's stay in Paris the President placed an escort of 200 horse soldiers at his lordship's disposal On the return journey the civic party were entertained at a banquet and ball by the municipality of Boulogne, many of the buildings being decorated and illuminated at night.

The Memorial Hall, Farringdon Street, was formally opened by a dedication service, at which most of the leading nonconformists were present (19th).— The Corporation resolved to erect a new Council Chamber at a cost of about £50,000, exclusive of fittings, and to re-arrange and re-construct the Committee rooms and offices on the north side of the Guildhall at an estimated cost of

£56,000 (28th).—The case of Thorn v. the Lord Mayor and Corporation, which was a claim in connection with the removal of old Blackfriars Bridge, was decided by the Court of Exchequer in favor of the Corporation, who, it was held, were not responsible for the delay which involved additional expense on the part of the contractors (8 Feb.).—Lord Elcho introduced into the House of Commons his Bill for creating a County and Municipality of London, and the Common Council instructed the Local Government and Taxation Committee to watch the progress of the measure (11th).—Judgment was given in the Consistory Court by Dr. Tristram, Chancellor of the Diocese of London, in the suit of Sergeant and others v. Dale, clerk (15th).

The petitioners were the churchwardens, and the defendant the Rev Thomas Pelham Dale the rector, of the united parishes of St. Vedast otherwise Foster, and St. Michael-le-Querne, in the City. The petitioners complained that the rector, after the month of Nov., 1873, without a faculty or even the sanction of the vestries or churchwardens of the united parishes, made certain alterations in their parish church, which were subsequently condemned by votes of the vestries. The alterations were, the removal of the Reading Desk and Clerk's Desk, minor alterations in certain pews, and the placing of two rows of benches or platforms for choristers in the east end of the church. The rector pleaded ignorance of the law. The Court ordered that a faculty be issued to the churchwardens, authorising them to replace the articles removed and to remove the seats for the choristers.

In view of the displacement of the working and poorer classes by large public improvements, the Corporation resolved that it was desirable that Parliamentary sanction should be necessary for such works, and the obligation imposed of providing improved dwellings for the industrial poor (25th).—A few days later (18 Mar.) Mr. Cross's Artisans' Dwellings' Bill was before Parliament, and Mr. Fawcett moved that the Corporation be not constituted a Local Authority under the Act, but that it be placed, like the Vestries of London, under the Metropolitan Board of Works. The House, however, decided by 222 to 84 votes that the Corporation should not be deprived of its right to administer the Act within its own jurisdiction. The Bill was shortly afterwards passed as the Artisans' and Labourers' Dwellings' Improvement Act, 1875, and was referred by the Common Council to the Commissioners of Sewers to carry into execution (1 July).—£500 was voted by the Corporation in aid of the sufferers by the famine in Asia Minor (4 Mar.).—Messrs. J. C. Thurm and Co., merchants, Leadenhall St., suspended payment, with liabilities of over £3,000,000 (13th). Several joint-stock companies shortly afterwards failed.—The Tower of London was opened free to the public (3 Ap.).—The new Merchant Taylors' School, Charterhouse Square, was opened by the Prince and Princess of Wales on the 6th. The Company had spent £30,000 out of their Corporate funds on the new buildings and alterations, and the accommodation provided was twice as large as at the old school in Suffolk Lane.—At a banquet to the London School Board at the Mansion House (24th), Sir Charles Reed, the chairman, said the School Board had been the means of adding 100,000 children to the school roll of London, and 40,000 of these had gone to other than Board Schools.—The Common Council resolved

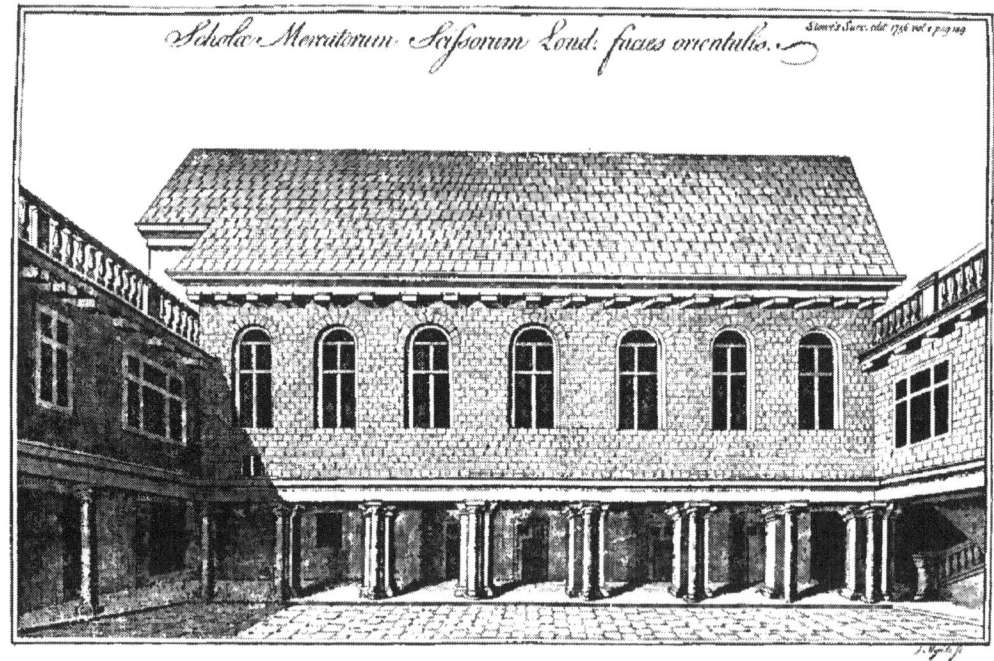

Old Merchant Taylors' School, Suffolk Lane.—Designed by Christopher Wren.

to support the memorial of the Association of Municipal Corporations to the Home Secretary, praying Her Majesty's Government to introduce a Bill giving Municipal Corporations permissive power to superannuate officers whose whole time is devoted to the service (29th).—It was decided to present the freedom of the City, in a gold box, to Sir George Biddell Airy, K.C.B., etc., Astronomer Royal, in recognition of his indefatigable labours in astronomy and of his services in the advancement of practical science.   The presentation took place in the Guildhall on 4 Nov., and in acknowledging the address of the Chamberlain Sir George related an interesting reminiscence.   He said :—

"When I was a young man, a student at Cambridge, and rather poor than otherwise, I received a small exhibition from one of the London Companies (the Fishmongers).   It came to me through the hands of persons whom I did not know, but it was forwarded to me in some way at Trinity College.

It was the first money I ever possessed of my own, but that money gave me independence at the time. How much it may have contributed to what some persons may consider my success in life, I cannot say, but that it did contribute much I have no doubt."

The Lord Mayor and Sheriffs proceeded in state to open the Alexandra Palace, Muswell Hill, which had been rebuilt after the fire in 1873. A large number of provincial mayors were also present (1 May).—A statue to the Rev.

Crypt, Laurence Pountney Hill—destroyed 1894-5.   The property of the Merchant Taylors' Company.

Joshua Hughes, first Secretary to the Bible and Religious Tract Societies, was unveiled in Bunhill Fields (4th).—The new church of St. James the Apostle, which had been erected on the Packington Estate, in Prebend Square, Islington, by the Clothworkers' Company, was consecrated by the Bishop of London (4th). The church was erected, in accordance with the terms of an Act of Parliament obtained by the Company, in place of Lambe's Chapel in Monkwell Street.—The hospitable and enthusiastic reception accorded to the Lord Mayor and Sheriffs by the Municipal authorities of Paris led the Corporation on the 27th to pass a resolution, inviting the Prefect of the Seine and the Municipal authorities of various cities of France and other parts of the Continent to meet the Mayors, etc., of the Corporations of the United Kingdom at a banquet in the Guildhall ; to this was afterwards added an evening entertainment, and a special Ward Committee was appointed to make the necessary arrangements.—A roadway, connecting

Charterhouse Street with King Street, Smithfield, at the western end of the Markets, was ordered by the Corporation to be made at a cost of £5,000.—A Bill for the regulation of the Gas Companies, introduced by the Corporation and the Metropolitan Board of Works, was, notwithstanding a vigorous opposition on the part of the Companies, read a second time in the House of Commons by an overwhelming majority (13 May). It was referred to a Select Committee, and the preamble of the Bill was passed, but owing to the state of business nothing further could be done with it that session.—The Lord Mayor laid before the Common Council (3 June) a letter from H.R.H. the Prince of Wales, with reference to the establishment of a National Training School for Music. The Court thereupon proceeded to appoint a deputation, consisting of the Lord Mayor, the Sheriffs, four Aldermen, and eight Commoners, to attend the conference called by H.R.H. at Marlborough House—The new Schools of the Haberdashers' Company, at Hoxton, were opened by the Duke of Connaught (5th). These schools were the result of a reconstruction of the Aske Charity under a scheme of the Endowed Schools' Commission.—The Corporation voted £1,000 for placing stand-pipes for the supply of hydrants in the City as a protection against fire, and a further sum of £50,000 for the new Billingsgate Market.—The Corporation voted 500 guineas for the relief of the sufferers by the inundations in the south of France. At Toulouse as many as 3,000 persons were reported to have been drowned.—A sum of 500 guineas was also voted to the British and Foreign School Society.—It was resolved that the bequest by Sir David Salomons of £1,000 should be expended on the purchase of books, and the preparation of a catalogue of the Hebrew books in the Guildhall Library (1 July).—The Corporation presented an address to the Sultan of Zanzibar, reference being made to the conclusion of the Treaty for the suppression of the Slave Trade within His Majesty's jurisdiction (12th). The Sultan was afterwards entertained at a déjeuner in the Mansion House and a banquet at Fishmongers' Hall. The Sultan presented the Lord Mayor with a very handsome scimitar, shield, dagger and belt, of African workmanship—The International Municipal entertainment took place at the Guildhall on the 29th. At the banquet the Lord Mayor had on his right and left the Prefect of the Seine and the French Ambassador, and amongst the after-dinner speakers were the Mayor of Quebec, the Syndic of Rome, the Lord Mayor of Dublin, the Lord Provost of Edinburgh, the Lord Mayor of York, and the Burgomaster of Brussels. The French Ambassador referred to the two recent occasions on which London, renowned for its splendid hospitalities, had come to the assistance of France, once during the siege of Paris, and again when the cities of France were destroyed by water and their inhabitants were without food or shelter.   On the following night a grand ball was given at the Guildhall to the Municipal guests, a large quantity of valuable plate being lent by the City companies.   The Lord Mayor and Lady Mayoress met the visitors at Alexandra Palace on the 31st, and afterwards received them at the Mansion House.   The gathering at the Mansion House took the form of an International fête for the benefit of the sufferers by the inundations in France On Sunday afternoon (1 Aug) many of the Municipal representatives attended a service at St. Paul's Cathedral.—Mr. Thomas Nelson, City Solicitor, urged before the Epping Forest Commissioners the right of the Corporation to hunt in the Forest, and to receive out of the Forest every year certain bucks, etc.   He quoted a number of charters and other documents, showing that from time immemorial the citizens, had, by the Lord Mayor and other officers, exercised this right.   In 1807 the Corporation abolished the office of Common Hunt and broke up the establishment of hounds, but that was their own act, and the City by its officers had not hunted since (27th).—At a public meeting, held at the Mansion House, a draft scheme was approved for the London Society for the extension of University Teaching.   Mr. Goschen, one of the chief promoters of the movement, appealed to the City companies for help (28th).—It was reported that the Charity Commissioners had approved of a scheme for the future management of St. Bride's Parochial Charities, which had been framed by the Vestry of that parish (28 Aug.). —The Corporation voted 100 guineas towards the erection of a statue in the Metropolis to Lord Byron (16 Sept.).—A new scheme was issued by the Endowed Schools' Commissioners for the future regulation of Lady Owen's Charity.   The charity, consisting of a free school and almshouses, was founded in Islington by Lady Owen in 1613, its management being left to the Brewers' Company (18th).— A special thanksgiving service was held at the great Synagogue, Aldgate, for the safe return of Sir Moses Montefiore (then over ninety years of age) from Jerusalem, where he had gone to inquire into the condition of the Jews in that city (18th).— The first pile of the Steam Ferry landing-place, at Wapping, was struck by the Lord Mayor (11 Oct.).—The Corporation paid a ceremonial visit to Epping Forest in celebration of the victory obtained last year (14th).—The Lord Mayor and Lady Mayoress celebrated their silver wedding at the Mansion House, a presentation being made to them by the inhabitants of Bassishaw Ward (19th).— Prince Leopold took up his freedom at the Guildhall, the Chamberlain remarking that the circumstance was interesting and unique as being the only instance in the history of the City of all the sons of the reigning Sovereign recording their names on the Municipal Roll (25th).—Sir Charles Reed opened the new Aske's

School at Hatcham, New Cross, for 300 boys and 200 girls, in connection with the Hoxton scheme already noticed. This is also under the management of the Haberdashers' Company (6 Nov.).—Alderman William J. Richmond Cotton was elected Lord Mayor.—A Mansion House Fund was opened for the relief of sufferers from the disastrous floods on the banks of the Thames and in other localities (17th). The Queen contributed 100 guineas and the Corporation subscribed £500.—The Lord Mayor formally opened the new Poultry and Provision Market, Smithfield (30th).

The buildings are 264 feet long and 248 wide, covering a superficial area of 65,472 feet. The style is Italian, the market consisting of an avenue in the figure of a parallelogram, with two additional avenues intersecting it north and south, and two east and west, containing from two to four shops each. Beneath the whole is a lofty, well-lighted range of vaults. The exterior is of red brick and Portland stone, with towers at four corners. The building, which was designed by Mr. Horace Jones, cost £50,000, apart from the site and approaches.

Liverpool Street Station.

About this time a new school for the St. Paul's Cathedral choir was erected in Carter Lane from designs of Mr. F. C. Penrose. The building is an elegant 17th century Renaissance structure of two stories.—Between the Old Bailey and Fleet Lane a great range of buildings had been constructed for Messrs. Cassell, Petter and Galpin, from the designs of Mr. F. Chambers. This was one of the largest printing offices yet built. The machine room had an area of 12,600 feet, and there were five floors above the basement.—The new terminus of the Great Eastern Railway, Liverpool Street, was completed and opened in Oct. of this year.

This was the largest station in London, having an area of ten acres, and a length of 2,000 feet. The building, which was designed by the Company's engineer, Mr. Edward Wilson, is of white brick and stone, the style being Early Domestic Gothic. The leading feature of the front is the arcade of twenty-four lofty arches. The Station area, containing ten platforms, is covered by a roof of two bays. The new building was intended not only for traffic, but to serve as the Company's headquarters.

A house in Ship Court, Old Bailey, where Hogarth's father kept a school, was pulled down, and Ludgate Circus was completed.—The Commissioners of

Sewers purchased Letts's Wharf, Commercial Road, Lambeth, at a cost of £24,525, where stabling, sheds, and appliances for dealing with the City refuse, etc., were constructed at a further cost of £25,530.

1876.

THE Common Council agreed to a report of the Library Committee recommending that a Records Clerk should be appointed to act under the Town Clerk. Mr Reginald Robinson Sharpe, B.C.L., was appointed to this office on June 8th.

This recommendation was the outcome of references to the Library Committee to consider the question of the preservation of the City records, and the best means of making them available for historical studies. Further results of their deliberations took shape in the publication of the "Analytical Index to the Remembrancia," 1878; "London's Roll of Fame," 1884, "Calendar of Letters, 1350-70," 1885; "A Descriptive Account of the Guildhall," 1886; "Calendar of Husting Wills, 1889-90," etc.

It was referred to the Bridge House Estates Committee to consider the question of erecting a bridge over or subway under the Thames, east of London Bridge, with a view to relieving the continuously increasing traffic of the City (3 Feb.). This reference was afterwards transferred to a special Committee, known as the Special Bridge or Subway Committee, who were authorised to employ professional assistance.—A report having been submitted to the Common Council with reference to the National Training School for Music, the Court resolved to establish ten free scholarships of the value of £40 per annum each for five years (10th).—Mr. C. E. Lewis, M.P., gave notice of a motion in the House of Commons for the disestablishment of the Irish Society, and the Local Government and Taxation Committee of the Corporation were instructed to take whatever steps might be thought expedient for the maintenance of the rights and privileges of the Corporation and of the Livery Companies (10th).—Mr. Gladstone was presented with the freedom and livery of the Turners' Company (16th).— A draft scheme for the administration of Colfe's Charity (originally established under the will of Abraham Colfe in 1656) was issued by the Charity Commissioners, the Leathersellers' Company being the governing body of the foundation (19th). —The Lord Mayor and Lady Mayoress were present at the launching of the first ferry boat over the Thames, which was to ply between the tunnel and Rotherhithe (26th).—The Queen visited the London Hospital, and opened the new wing erected by the Grocers' Company. This wing was the latest development of an institution dating from 1740, and incorporated by a charter granted by King George II. The Grocers' Company voted £20,000 for the wing, and large sums were added by other City Companies, notably the Skinners' and Clothworkers', and by the Corporation which subscribed £1,000 (7 Mar.).—The freedom of the City was presented to Sir Alex. J. E. Cockburn, Bart., G.C.B., the Lord Chief Justice of England (9th).—The Jubilee of Finsbury Chapel was celebrated on the 22nd.—The Clothworkers' Company offered 500 guineas per annum for five years for the chemical department of the proposed University College, Bristol, with a special view to the trade education of youths engaged in the dyeing and clothworking industries of the neighbourhood (22nd).—Dr. Henry Letheby, late Analyst and Medical Officer of Health for the City of London, died on the 28th, aged fifty-nine. —In compliance with a petition presented to the Corporation by warehousemen, traders, and their employés in the City, it was resolved to keep the Guildhall Library open till 9 o'clock every evening, except Saturday, for twelve months, as an experiment (6 Ap.).—Mr. John Ruskin lectured to the Bluecoat boys at Christ's Hospital on " Stones."—Hydrants were ordered to be laid down in the City for the extinction of fire and for street cleansing, at an expense to the Corporation of £2,800 (27th). The Corporation had expended on hydrants up to the year 1886 £25,531.—Proclamation was made at the Mansion House of the Queen's new title " Indiæ Imperatrix," or Empress of India (1 May).—A splendid entertainment was given by the Corporation to the Prince of Wales on his return from India (19th). An address, referring to the " dignity, urbanity, and courtesy," which had effected so much among the varied populations and nationalities of the East, was presented to His Royal Highness. The Prince was then entertained at a banquet, which was followed by a ball on a grand scale.

A large ball-room had been erected in Guildhall Yard, the front of the building being battlemented and ornamented with the Prince of Wales's plume, between two shields. It extended from the solid masonry of the Guildhall, nearly to Gresham Street, and was 160 feet long and 60 feet wide. There were nine bays on either side of the room, formed by square pillars of looking-glass, and arched with a kind of Watteau-trellis, on which slender plants were lightly trailed. Above the arch of every bay was a rich Indian carpet, like a tapestried panel, with trophies of flags. Rich furniture and beautiful floral decorations completed the picture. The architectural beauty of the great hall, where the banquet was held, was enhanced by a profusion of palms, ferns, azaleas, orchids, and exotics of various kinds There was also a magnificent display of ancient and curious plate lent by the City companies. The Exchequer chamber was set apart as a Royal Supper room, and the Members' Reading Room which was turned into a drawing room for the Princess of Wales, had a most pleasing appearance with its light blue hangings, its profusion of lace and choice ornamental china. The Aldermen's Room, Council Chamber, and other apartments, were transformed into drawing rooms. One of the ball rooms was erected on the vacant ground at the back of the Museum, and was called the Indian Room; its special ornamentation was adapted to remind the Prince of Wales of the scenes he had recently visited, and included the representation of a Hindoo temple, seen through a grove of palms and tropical plants.—The Corporation presented to the Queen at Osborne (24 July), an address of congratulation on the Prince's safe return.

Mr. James in the House of Commons moved for a return of the real and personal property of the City companies, of their charities, and of their expenditure and receipts for the last three years. After some discussion, however, the motion was withdrawn (23rd).—Earl Granville laid the first stone of the new City Liberal Club House in Walbrook (29th). To get a foundation for the club, the builders had to go down to a depth of forty feet, and many coins and bones of animals were brought to light.—The freedom of the Fishmongers' Company was presented to the Duke of Connaught (7 June).—The once celebrated London Tavern in Bishopsgate Street Within was closed, the property having been purchased by the Royal Bank of Scotland for £80,000, or about £13 per superficial foot.—Lord Elcho moved a resolution in the House of Commons (which was

Church of Allhallows, Bread Street—destroyed 1877.

afterwards withdrawn) in favour of one municipality for London (13th).—A great fire occurred at Brooks's wharf, Upper Thames Street, causing damage to the estimated amount of £150,000 (15th).—A deputation from the Courts of Aldermen and Common Council waited upon the Home Secretary (Mr. Cross) and protested against the clauses of the Prisons Bill, which under the guise of uniformity of administration would destroy the authority of the magistrates (26th). One object of the Bill was to transfer the maintenance of prisons from the rates to the Imperial Exchequer.—The Rev. R. Lee, M.A., the First Assistant Upper Grammar Master at Christ's Hospital, was elected head master of the school in the place of the Rev. G. C. Bell, M.A., who had been appointed to the head mastership of Marlborough College (21 July).—The freedom of the City was presented to

Sir Salar Jung, G.C.S.I., Prime Minister of the Nizam of Hyderabad, who had been faithful to the British during the dark days of the Indian Mutiny (25th).— About this time the Epping Forest Commissioners issued a draft scheme in favour of placing the management and control of the Forest in the hands of the Corporation.—The foundation stone was laid of the new hall of the Carpenters' Company in London Wall (1 Aug.). By the demolition of much property a new thoroughfare, now called Throgmorton Avenue, was opened up between London Wall and Throgmorton Street.—The Marquis of Salisbury at a banquet to Her Majesty's Ministers at the Mansion House (5th) warned the Turkish Government to put a stop to the Bulgarian atrocities.—Previous to removal, the church of Allhallows, Bread Street, where Milton was christened, and which contained an inscription to the poet, was deconsecrated by Bishop Claughton (19th). A bust of Milton was subsequently placed on the site.—The old inscribed stone, set up shortly after the Great Fire in front of the house in Pudding Lane where the fire is said to have originated, was found in the back yard of the premises, 25, Pudding Lane, which were in course of demolition (20th). This relic is preserved in the Guildhall Museum.—A great meeting presided over by the Lord Mayor was held at the Guildhall for the purpose of denouncing

Milton's Bust, Bread Street, on site of Allhallows Church.

the Bulgarian atrocities (18 Sept.). The meeting was called in consequence of a numerously signed requisition, the first signature being that of Mr. Gladstone, followed by that of the Duke of Westminster, who described himself as a Liveryman. Resolutions condemning the Turks were enthusiastically passed, and the meeting broke up with cheers for the Queen and the Lord Mayor.— The Commissioners of Sewers gave orders for the footways in Cheapside to be asphalted (23rd).—New middle-class schools, erected by the Grocers' Company at Hackney Downs, under a scheme by which a number of non-educational charities were amalgamated for the purpose, were opened by the Master. The schools, providing accommodation for from 500 to 600 boys, cost about £15,000 (27th).—With a view to the public convenience the Corporation ordered that Temple Bar should be removed.—The Commissioners of Sewers approved and authorised an important scheme, under the Artizans' and Labourers' Dwellings Improvement Act, 1875, in respect of areas in Holiday Yard, Blewitt's Buildings, Golden Lane, and Petticoat Square.   The last two sites were cleared at a cost of £236,604 (24 Oct.).—The Corporation voted 100 guineas to the Mansion House Fund in aid of the sufferers from the wreck of Her Majesty's ship *Thunderer.*—Rev. Thomas Pelham Dale, rector of St. Vedast, Foster Lane, was suspended by the Court of Arches for not refraining from ritualistic practices as ordered by the Court, under the Public Worship Regulation Act (3 Nov.).— Alderman Thomas White was elected Lord Mayor.—Lord Beaconsfield, speaking at the Guildhall Banquet on the 9th, said·—

"We have nothing to gain by war * * * but if the struggle comes, it should also be recollected there is no country so prepared for war as England, because there is no country whose resources are so great.   In a righteous cause, and I trust that England will never embark in war except in a righteous cause, a cause that concerns her liberty, her independence or her empire,— England is not a country that will have to enquire whether she can enter into a second or third campaign.   In a righteous cause England will commence a fight that will not end until right is done."

This historical speech at the Guildhall was followed by a warlike note from the Czar, at Moscow, the next day.—Mr. George Moore, senior partner in the firm of Copestake, Moore, Crampton and Co., Bow Churchyard, and well-known for his religious and philanthropic work, died suddenly on the 21st.

On the previous day Mr. Moore had been knocked down and trampled upon by a frightened horse in the streets of Carlisle   He was conveyed to a neighbouring hotel and Sir William Gull was summoned from London, but he was unfortunately past the aid of surgical skill.   At his funeral, at Carlisle, on the 25th, the pall was borne by, among others, the Archbishop of York.   At a crowded and enthusiastic meeting, presided over by the Archbishop of Canterbury, at the Cannon Street Hotel, on 14 Dec., it was resolved to raise a fund for a memorial to the deceased philanthropist

The Corporation purchased the waste lands in the manor of Chingford (the first Epping Forest negotiation), consisting of 275 acres, for £4,000 (27th).— A large meeting of Egyptian bondholders was held at Cannon Street Hotel to receive from Mr. Goschen, M.P., an announcement of the results of his mission to the Khedive (28th).—At the third election of the School Board for London, Sir John Bennett (who headed the poll), Mr. W. S. Gover, Mr. F. Peek, and Mr. Alderman Cotton were returned for the City, Mr. G. A. Spottiswoode being defeated (30th).—Some Roman architectural antiquities, recently discovered in a bastion of the London Wall, in Camomile Street, Bishopsgate, were deposited in the Guildhall Museum (7 Dec.).—The officers of the ships *Alert* and *Discovery* recently engaged in the Arctic Expedition under Captain G. Nares, were entertained at a banquet at the Mansion House (8th).—A third "Saddlers' Guild" scholarship was presented to the City of London School (14th).—Some interesting historical discoveries were made at the Tower on the 18th. Whilst restoring the church of St. Peter ad Vincula, coffins containing the remains of persons executed for state offences were found, and by an examination of contemporary chronicles one body was identified as that of the Countess of Salisbury, the last of the Plantagenets, executed by Henry VII, and another as that of Robert Dudley, Earl of Northumberland, the father of Lady Jane Grey. — The church of Allhallows the Great was partially taken down in connection with the widening of Upper Thames Street.— Queen Victoria Street was fast becoming a double line of tall and costly structures, mostly stone-faced, with an abundance of bold carving. —The London, Chatham and Dover terminus was carried to Holborn Viaduct, the station and hotel having a frontage of 235 feet. The double building, which is in the Italian style, cost £120,000.—The Finsbury printing and stationery works of Messrs. Waterlow & Sons

Roman statue from Camomile Street.

were erected on the site of old Finsbury Market. The building comprises a basement and five upper stories, and provides working room for 2,000 people.

1877.

 FUND for the relief of sufferers from the inundation of the Thames was opened at the Mansion House (13 Jan., 1877). A sum of £8,904 was obtained. Lord Beaconsfield ordered £250 to be issued from the Royal Bounty Fund especially for the benefit of people whose dwellings had been swamped at the East End. —A resolution was passed by the Common Council in favour of a bridge or subway

east of London Bridge, and it was referred to the Committee to obtain estimates (25th).—The Shipwrights' Company presented its honorary freedom to Captain Sir G. S. Nares, R.N., K.C.B., the Arctic explorer. The casket accompanying it was a model of a sledge as fully equipped on the ice at the extreme latitude attained by the Arctic Expedition of 1875-6 (27th).—The second reading of Mr. Cross's Prisons' Bill was carried in the House of Commons by 279 to 69 (15 Feb.). This Bill afterwards became law, since which time Newgate has ceased to be a gaol for the confinement of prisoners before and during trial, and has been used only for the temporary detention of persons awaiting trial, and for the confinement of persons convicted of a capital charge and awaiting execution.—A meeting, attended by representatives of the Mercers', Drapers', Goldsmiths', Merchant Taylors', Haberdashers', Ironmongers', Vintners', Clothworkers', Dyers', and Armourers and Brasiers' Companies, was held at Drapers' Hall in furtherance of a proposal to establish a Central Technical University, with affiliated schools of technical instruction, in connection with the various industries carried on in the suburbs of London and the manufacturing districts of the United Kingdom (21st). Alderman Sir S. H. Waterlow, M.P., who was acting as Chairman of the Joint Committee of the Drapers' and Clothworkers' Companies, gave an outline of the proposed scheme, and stated that each of the Companies he represented had promised £2,000 a year, with such further assistance as might be necessary. It was resolved to invite the assistance of the Corporation and to convene a meeting of the representatives of such Companies as were willing to participate in the work.—A summons, issued at the instance of the City Guardians, was heard at a special Sessions at Guildhall against the overseers of the parish of St. Martin, Ludgate, for non-payment of a contribution of £818. An immediate distress warrant was ordered to be issued (17th).—Mr. C. E. Lewis's motion in the House of Commons for a Select Committee to inquire into the affairs of the Irish Society was rejected by 108 to 53 votes (28th).—The Directors of the Royal Bank of Scotland assembled on the site of the old London Tavern, Bishopsgate, on the occasion of laying the foundation stone of the new Bank (5 Mar.).—The Home Secretary (Mr. Cross) was waited upon by a deputation, representing fifty-five Livery Companies of the City, with reference to the motion of which Mr. James had given notice, empowering the Crown to make full investigation into the condition and revenues of the Guilds. The motion was introduced on 10 Ap. and rejected by 168 to 72.—Mr. Samuel Morley, M.P., moved for a return showing the income of the Parochial Charities of the Cities of London and Westminster (5th).—During the gales in the North Sea thirty-six vessels and smacks belonging to Yarmouth, Lowestoft, Grimsby, Hull, and Ramsgate had been lost. No fewer than 215 men and boys had been drowned; and 88 widows, 164 children and 15 aged relatives had been left entirely destitute. A fund for the relief of the sufferers which was inaugurated at the Mansion House realised £7,491, and the Corporation contributed to it 300 guineas (22nd).

—The Government reluctantly agreed to a motion, by Mr. R. Yorke, for a Royal Commission to enquire into the constitution and customs of the Stock Exchange (20th). — The Lord Mayor presided at a meeting at the Mansion House to consider a proposal to establish, in a central position in London, an Imperial Museum for the Colonies and India (20th).—In furtherance of a project for celebrating the 400th anniversary of the introduction of the Art of Printing into England a meeting was held at the Mansion House, presided over by the Lord Mayor and addressed by Mr. Anthony Trollope, Count

Interior of the Stock Exchange.

Münster, German Ambassador, Sir Charles Dilke, Sir Charles Reed, and others. It was resolved that a loan collection of the works of Caxton, and of appliances connected with printing, should be held in London in the month of June, and that a Caxton Celebration Fund should be opened for the purpose of establishing permanent pensions for decayed and aged printers and their widows (26 Mar.). The Exhibition was opened by Mr. Gladstone at South Kensington (30 June). —Mr. C. Nichols, representing the Home Secretary, completed the enquiry, at the Guildhall, concerning the Artizans' Dwellings' Scheme in Golden Lane.—

The second reading of the North Metropolitan Tramways Extension Bill, which would have enabled the Company to bring their lines into the City, was defeated in the House of Commons by 203 to 103 votes (17 Ap.).—A Sub-Committee of the Royal Institute of British Architects was appointed to visit the City Churches, in view of the proposed demolition of some of them; and elaborate reports on the subject were made by Messrs. W. M. Teulon, E. B. Ferrey and R. Phéné Spiers.—Another stage in the preservation of Epping Forest was reached, the Corporation having obtained legal sanction for the removal of the remaining enclosures found to be within the scope of the decree (23rd).—The Corporation voted 100 guineas to the Mansion House Fund (£4,674), for recognition of the heroism displayed in rescuing, under circumstances of great danger, the unfortunate miners who were entombed for several days in the Colliery at Pontypridd, and also for the relief of the survivors of those who lost their lives by the inundation (26th).—A deputation of the Municipal Council of Paris, headed by the President, M. Bonnet-Duverdier, having visited the Metropolis for the purpose of examining the Underground Railway and certain Municipal institutions, were entertained at a banquet at the Mansion House (2 May).—The Epping Forest Commissioners presented their final report to Parliament on the 8th, which was printed by order of the House of Commons.— The Lord Mayor and Sheriffs went in state to the Alexandra Palace to assist at the festival on its re-opening (10th).—A Committee of the House of Commons threw out Mr. Torrens's Bill dealing with the charities of St. Giles's, Cripplegate, and St. Luke's parishes (11th).—Lord Chief Justice Cockburn wrote to the Lord Mayor, with reference to the attendance of judges at St. Paul's. He said the judges did not desire to give up attending altogether, but they wished their visits to be once a year instead of three times, and according to an established rota. As Serjeants' Inn, the place at which the judges were accustomed to assemble and to be met by the City Marshal before proceeding to St. Paul's, was no longer at their disposal, the judges attending would go separately straight to the Cathedral and there meet the City authorities as heretofore. The letter was referred to the privileges committee of the Court of Aldermen (18th) —Mr. Alderman Allen died suddenly at his office, 13, Waterloo Place (22nd)

The late Alderman of Cheap Ward, who was in his 61st year, had spent some years of his life in India. He was a publisher of high standing, and proprietor of *Allen's Indian Mail*, and formerly carried on business in Leadenhall Street. He published, during his shrievalty, a little book, entitled *The Corporation of London, its rights and privileges.* During his Mayoralty he insisted (as did Sir Robert Fowler at a later date), on the whole of his officers and servants having a complete rest on Sunday. The Alderman's remains were interred at Sevenoaks.

The Shipwrights' Company exhibited a large number of ship models and drawings at Fishmongers' Hall (28th).—After a keen contest for the Aldermanic gown of Cheap Ward, Sir John Bennett was declared elected having polled 234 votes against 233 for Mr. Waddell (4 June). A scrutiny was demanded, but was afterwards withdrawn.—The Holborn Viaduct Hotel was inaugurated by a banquet, given to the directors of the London, Chatham and Dover Railway Company, by Mr. Lewis H. Isaacs, the architect (5th).—A meeting of the associated Livery Companies was held at Mercers' Hall to initiate a national scheme of technical education. The Corporation sent three delegates and most of the City Companies were represented. A committee was appointed to prepare a draft scheme, Lord Selborne being chairman, and Mr. F. J. Bramwell, Prime Warden of the Goldsmiths' Company, vice-chairman (7th).—The Marquis of Salisbury and the Earl of Derby attended a banquet, given in their honour, at Merchant Taylors' Hall, the latter observing, in reference to the rumours of war, that the greatest British interest was peace (11th).—The honorary freedom of the City was presented to General Grant, late President of the United States, in recognition of the distinguished ability with which he had governed his country, and the eminent services he had rendered to the cause of civilisation, by maintaining amicable relations with Foreign Powers (15th).—A school, erected at the cost of the Clothworkers' Company, was opened, at Peel, in the Isle of Man (15th).—The enormous increase which had taken place in the value of City property was strikingly illustrated, in connection with the sale of some property belonging to the Drapers' Company, in Lombard Street. A house there was let in 1668 for £25 a year. This year (1877) the site let for £2,600 a year ground rent, and the lessee having expended £10,000 on the building got a return of £7,000 a year rent (4 July).—A Bluecoat boy named William A. Gibbs, committed suicide by hanging himself in Christ's Hospital, after stating that he had been unduly punished for insubordination (6th). A Coroner's jury returned a verdict of " Suicide while under temporary insanity."

A Royal Commission was afterwards appointed to inquire into the circumstances attending the death of Gibbs and into the management of Christ's Hospital. The Commissioners were Mr. Russell Gurney, M.P. (chairman), Mr. Walpole, M.P., Mr. W. E. Forster, M P., Mr. Walter, M.P., and the Dean of Christ Church. The first meeting of the Commissioners was held in the Hospital Library on the 16th. Mr Allcroft, the treasurer, and Mr. Gibbs, the father of the deceased being under examination, but the proceedings throughout were private The governors held a separate enquiry the same day and it was decided that "Speech Day" should not be observed this year.

Four lives were lost in a fire at 42, Little Britain (9th).—A special meeting of the Court of Aldermen was held to receive the return of the Aldermanic election for the ward of Cheap (10th).

Petitions were presented against the return, the consideration of which the Aldermen decided to postpone, disregarding Sir John Bennett's protest. Another special Court was held on the 13th, the Solicitor-General appearing for Sir John Bennett, and Mr. Winch for the petitioners. A large and demonstrative crowd assembled in the Court and its vicinity, it being understood that the Aldermen would not receive Sir John as a member of their body. The Court was again broken up without any decision having been come to. Sir John was cheered by the crowd as he left the Aldermen's Chamber, and some of the Aldermen were hissed. Mr. Goschen took the chair at a complimentary banquet to Sir John Bennett, at Cannon Street Hotel, on the 17th. On the 27th the Aldermen were addressed by Mr. Winch for the petitioners and by the Solicitor-General for Sir John Bennett, after which they retired for about twenty minutes and discussed the matter *in camera*. On their return to the Court Room the Recorder said the following motion had been adopted, Mr Alderman Sidney alone dissenting: "That having heard the petitioners by their counsel and witnesses, and Sir John Bennett by his counsel, this Court doth judge and determine according to the discretion and sound conscience of the members of this Court, Sir John Bennett, Knight, is not a person fit and proper to support the dignity and discharge the duties of the said place and office of an Alderman of this City." The announcement of this decision was received by the crowd, beyond the bar, with hisses and groans. It was understood that the Lord Mayor would issue a precept for a new election.

The Corporation voted 300 guineas to the Mansion House Fund (£7,062), for the relief of sufferers by a great fire at St. John's, New Brunswick (12th).—The Royal Society House, in Crane Court, Fleet Street, purchased on the motion of Sir Isaac Newton in 1710, was destroyed by fire on the 14th. At the time of its destruction the house belonged to the Scottish Corporation, and had previously been rented by the Philosophical Society, during whose tenancy, Mr. Coleridge delivered in the hall his course of twelve lectures on Shakespeare.—On the 18th the Common Council decided to widen London Bridge. This project, however, met with considerable opposition and was never carried out. It was considered that the effect of widening would be to mar the artistic beauty of the bridge.—The church of St. Mary Aldermary, was re-opened after having been closed for restoration during sixteen months (17th).—The new Billingsgate Fish Market was opened on the 20 July.

This Market stands on the site of the Old Fish Market, but occupies a somewhat larger area, in all about 40,000 feet. The basement groined and vaulted and well lighted, with a clear height of 24 feet, and reached by stone staircases from the river and Thames Street fronts, is appropriated to the Shell Fish Market. Above this is a General Fish Market on the Thames Street level, 43 feet high, and carried on lattice girders of 60 feet span, supported by iron columns, 31 feet high. A gallery, about 30 feet wide, with an area of 4,000 superficial feet, runs north and south above the General Market. The building is Italian in character, of Portland stone, with red granite plinth. The river front presents a handsome arcade of eleven bays with a central pediment The Thames Street front, with differences in detail, is similar in character. The building, which was designed by Mr. Horace Jones, cost £272,000.

Mr. Alderman Knight laid the foundation stone of the new middle class school for girls, erected in Mare Street, Hackney, by the trustees of the Lady

Holles's trust in the parish of St. Giles, Cripplegate, under a scheme of the Endowed Schools Commission (23rd.)—The Marquis of Hartington received the freedom of the Fishmongers' Company, and was entertained at a banquet at which Earl Granville, Mr. Lowe, and Lord Shaftesbury were present (25th). —The Corporation declined to undertake the control of the Cannon Street foot bridge, which Mr. J. Willing, lessee of the tolls of the South Eastern Railway Company's Bridges, stated that he was about to throw open free to the public, for six months, as an experiment (26th).—The Library Committee reported to the Common Council upon the experimental opening of the Guildhall Library in the evenings during the past year, and recommended that the arrangement should be permanently continued at an annual cost not exceeding £1,060, exclusive of the charge for warming and lighting. This was agreed to, and as an evidence of public appreciation, a letter of cordial thanks was presented to the Court (13 Sep.), by "young men from the various mercantile and banking establishments of the City."—The Corporation increased the allowance to inmates of the London and Rogers' Almshouses to 16s. per week for married couples, and 12s. for single inmates.—It was decided that the rights of twelve Deputy Day Oyster Meters who had purchased their offices should be re-purchased by the Corporation for the sum of £2,500, fresh arrangements being made with respect to oyster metage for the future (26th).—Miss Ada Louisa White (the Lady Mayoress) was married by the Archbishop of Canterbury at St. Paul's, to Mr. Cecil Herbert Thornton Price, this being the first wedding celebrated within the Cathedral for 120 years. The wedding breakfast was served in the Egyptian Hall, at the Mansion House, and a most extensive and valuable collection of presents was displayed in the State drawing room (9 Aug.). About fifty officers of the Corporation presented the Lady Mayoress with a handsome gold bracelet, set with diamonds.—Sir John Bennett was again returned for the ward of Cheap, his opponent, this time, being Mr. Deputy Breffit. Sir John polled 217 votes to the Deputy's 99 (11th). — The Lord Mayor called attention to the famine raging in Southern India and offered to open a fund for the relief of the sufferers. Within a week £24,000 had been subscribed, and the Corporation at its first meeting after the recess (13 Sep.), voted £1,000 to the fund, which eventually reached a total of £515,200. Help was indeed urgent, ·for the mortality during July was 80,052 above the average, and nearly two millions and a half of famine-stricken people were being gratuitously fed by the government.—The report of the Commissioners appointed to inquire into the circumstances attending the suicide of the boy Gibbs, at Christ's Hospital was issued.

It was addressed to the Home Secretary, and signed by the Right Hon Spencer H. Walpole, the Right Hon. Russell Gurney, the Right Hon. W. E. Forster, the Very Rev. H G Liddell and Mr. John Walter.   The report stated that Gibbs was a boy of indifferent character and that the Commissioners could not rely upon his unsupported statements   No blame was attaching to the authorities, and though Copeland, the monitor complained of, had struck Gibbs against the rules, custom had sanctioned this practice.   Whatever defects there were in the management and discipline were not due to the shortcomings of individuals, but to evils inherent in the system which expected that 700 boys should, except when at lessons, be kept in order by the head-master and warden, assisted by the matron, beadles, and some of the boys.   The relations between the head-master and warden were not clearly defined, and both were subordinate to the treasurer   As far as they could judge petty tyranny or "bullying" had greatly diminished during the last ten years, and Old Blues had the pleasantest recollections of their school life

The Court of Aldermen confirmed its previous decision with regard to Sir John Bennett's election as Alderman, the proceedings being again marked by considerable uproar (25th).   A third election took place in the ward of Cheap on 3 Oct., Sir John Bennett and Mr. Deputy Breffit again contesting the Aldermanic gown   On the poll being announced it was found that Sir John Bennett had received 210 votes and the Deputy 107   There was great excitement in the vicinity of the wardmote, and Sir John addressed about 2,000 people, who had assembled in Guildhall Yard, from a window of the Guildhall Tavern.—The Aldermen who assembled on the 16th declined to give way.   Mr. Mason, solicitor on behalf of Sir John Bennett, admitted that the Aldermen's right of veto was unquestionable, but, he said, it should be clearly understood that Sir John shrank from no charges, and if made he would be prepared to meet them.   Mr. Hughes said as Sir John Bennett did not intend to appeal to a Court of Law the petitioners left the matter in the hands of the Court, who thereupon decided to adjourn for a week in order that they might consider whom to appoint to fill the vacancy.   On the 23rd three names were proposed by different Aldermen, and the Court having been cleared a scrutiny was held as in the case of the election of Lord Mayor, the result being that Deputy Breffit was declared to be duly elected Alderman of Cheap.   This gentleman was admitted forthwith and invested with the Aldermanic gown, and thus closed one of the most exciting municipal contests of modern times.

Mr. H. Homewood Crawford, in a letter to the *City Press*, dated 27 Oct., pointed out the precedent of Michael Scales, who was thrice rejected by the Court of Aldermen in 1831, after being three times elected as Alderman for the ward of Portsoken, by which it would be seen that the Lord Mayor and Aldermen had a complete precedent and ample authority for not making public the grounds of their recent decision in connection with the ward of Cheap.   The case of Scales was heard by the Queen's Bench, the Court of Exchequer, and afterwards by the House of Lords.

The Corporation sanctioned the making of a pathway across the portion of the churchyard of St. Giles Without, Cripplegate, held by the parish, on lease, from the Corporation, and through the "Woolpack" public-house in Hart Street (25th).—The Lord Mayor opened the Thames Steam Ferry, at Rotherhithe (31st).—The Corporation voted £2,850 for a detached Hospital, in the grounds of the City of London Lunatic Asylum, for the isolation of patients suffering from infectious diseases (1 Nov.).—Alderman Thomas Scambler Owden was elected Lord Mayor.—The City Lands Committee were instructed to remove Temple Bar forthwith, and to see whether a site could not be found where "the time-honoured memorial of the City might be preserved for the respect and admiration of future generations" (29th).—In response to an appeal from the National Artillery Association, the Corporation decided to make an annual grant of twenty-five guineas for a prize to be called the "Corporation of London Prize" and to be contended for yearly at Shoeburyness (13 Dec.).—The Corporation also resolved to erect a new Council Chamber at an estimated expense of £50,000, exclusive of fittings.—A suitable steam launch was ordered for the Port of London Sanitary Committee at a cost of £836 (20th).—An agreement was entered into by the Corporation with the Dean and Chapter of St. Paul's for effecting certain improvements in the enclosed ground around the Cathedral at an estimated expense of £5,000, and £400 per annum for maintenance (20th).—The Rev. Dr. Moffat was presented with the freedom of the Turners' Company, in recognition of his work in South Africa (20th).—There being a sum of £40,000 in hand for the decoration of the interior of St. Paul's the Executive Committee passed a resolution to "carry into effect, as far as possible, the wishes of Sir Christopher Wren by decorating the dome with mosaic, in a similar style to the dome of St. Peter's at Rome." The work has since been carried out by Dr. Salviati.—The City of London was rapidly undergoing a process of re-construction, the prevailing style of architecture being some kind of Renaissance, but there were many Gothic buildings some Elizabethan, as the large Inn in Fenchurch Street, and some Queen Anne's, as in Aldersgate Street and Farringdon Road. On the south side of Fleet Street, next to Salisbury Court, ten houses, erected in 1665, were pulled down this year and replaced by a handsome pile of buildings in the Renaissance style.—It had long been a complaint that St. Paul's Cathedral was without a peal of bells, and during the year several of the City Companies, in conjunction with the Baroness Burdett-Coutts, determined to provide it with a complete peal of twelve bells. They were cast by Messrs. Taylor, of Loughborough, weighed about 11 tons, and cost £6,000. The first and second bells were presented by the Drapers' Company, the third, fourth, fifth, and sixth by the Baroness and the Turners' Company jointly, the seventh by the Salters, the eighth by the Merchant Taylors, the ninth by the Fishmongers, the tenth by the Clothworkers, the eleventh by the Grocers, and the twelfth and largest, by the Corporation.—The Dyers' and Vintners' Companies had for a long time enjoyed the privilege of keeping swans on the Thames. The total number of these birds permitted by the Crown, as settled this year, was about 510, of which 400 belonged to the Crown, 65 to the Dyers' and 45 to the Vintners'. The number of swans afterwards became smaller.—Founders' Hall, St. Swithin's Lane, was rebuilt.—St. James's Church, Garlickhithe, Upper Thames Street, and St. Luke's Church, Old Street, were restored, the latter at a cost of over £7,000, the churchyard being converted into a public recreation ground.—The Canal Boats' Act (1877) imposed a large amount of additional work upon the Port Sanitary Committee, in regard to supervision and inspection.

1878.

THE Corporation decided to construct a new police station in Bow Lane, on the site of the existing one, costing £16,500 (17 Jan., 1878). —Mr. W. H. Smith, M.P., First Lord of the Admiralty, and Sir Charles Adderley, M.P., President of the Board of Trade, were admitted to the honorary freedom of the Shipwrights' Company, at Grocers' Hall (23rd).—The Corporation voted £200 for the relief of the distress in South Wales, which was principally due to the stoppage of a number of great ironworks.—The Police Force was ordered to be increased by twenty-eight men, for the purpose of regulating the vehicular traffic of the City.—About this time, owing to the Russo-Turkish war and the attitude of the Government towards Russia, there was great excitement, especially in the City. The Russian troops were within a short distance of Constantinople, and on 25 Jan., the British Fleet entered the Dardanelles. It was afterwards withdrawn, but on 7 Feb. it was again ordered to Constantinople. The Chancellor of the Exchequer had, meantime, moved for a credit of six millions in the House of Commons, and the Opposition, under the nominal leadership of Lord Hartington, was offering a divided resistance. The Government at this critical moment found its chief support in the City, where some remarkable incidents occurred. A meeting to denounce the threatening attitude of Lord Beaconsfield was convened at the Cannon Street Hotel for 31 Jan. A few members of the City Liberal Club were holding a preliminary conference in one of the rooms of the hotel, when a mob burst into the room and dispersed the occupants. The hotel and its approaches were, in fact, in possession of the Government supporters. The police were sent for and eventually the hotel was cleared. The "peace party," however, found it necessary to abandon their public meeting. Meantime, a large and excited crowd which had assembled outside the hotel, was addressed by Alderman Sir Robert Carden, Captain Ritchie, M.P., Mr. R. N. Fowler, chairman of the City Conservative Association, Mr. E. Hughes, and others, from the steps of the hotel. The excitement extended to Lloyd's and the Stock Exchange, where lively demonstrations in support of the Government policy were made. A large crowd also assembled outside the Mansion House, and having given three cheers for the Lord Mayor proceeded to the Guildhall, which was speedily filled, the contingent from Cannon Street Hotel having apparently met there also. Lord Mayor Owden, who had been presiding at the Common Council, was persuaded to take the chair, and after the singing of patriotic airs and the waving of the British flag, which caused considerable excitement, resolutions were carried amid great enthusiasm. These resolutions were presented to the Prime Minister, through Lord John Manners, and the following reply was received from the Earl of Beaconsfield:

"Such a decided and spontaneous expression of opinion in favour of the Foreign policy of Her Majesty's Government by so important an assemblage, will strengthen Her Majesty's Government in their endeavours to preserve peace, to support the honour of our Sovereign, and to secure the interests of our country."

On the day of the Guildhall demonstration, a largely attended meeting of Nonconformists was held at the Memorial Hall, to protest against the vote of six millions, "or any other measure calculated to embroil this country at the present crisis." On the following day (1 Feb), the merchants at the Corn Exchange passed a resolution of confidence in the Government by a large majority. On the 8th, the Credit vote was carried in the House of Commons by 328 to 124. —The Right Hon. Russell Gurney, Q.C., M.P., the Recorder, tendered his resignation to the Court of Aldermen, on account of ill-health (5 Feb.). The Common Council was "deeply moved" on receiving the news and passed a resolution referring to Mr. Russell Gurney's twenty years of service, during which time he had obtained "the confidence of Parliament, the approbation of the public, and the esteem and respect of every member of the Corporation."— The Common Council resolved to make a new road to Chingford railway station to open up Epping Forest, at a cost of £600 (14th).—At the same Court the Recorder's salary was fixed at £3,000 a year. — A remarkable gathering of clergy in "retreat" took place at St. Paul's Cathedral,

At 7.15, the Dean of St. Paul's celebrated the Holy Communion in the Crypt Chapel, Canon Gregory assisting him. At 8 o'clock there was a second celebration in the choir, the Bishop of London being the celebrant, assisted by the Archdeacon of London (Bishop Piers Claughton) when some hundred clergymen communicated   Many were present at the 10 o'clock ordinary matins, and from the hour when the service was concluded till 11 30, a large number of clergymen remained on their knees   The leading London clergy of all shades of opinion listened to a sermon by the Bishop of London (26th).

Sir Thomas Chambers, Q.C., M.P., Common Serjeant, was elected Recorder by the Court of Aldermen (5 Mar.).—At a public meeting at the Mansion House, it was resolved to promote the holding of a great Agricultural Exhibition in London, the following year, under the auspices of the Royal Agricultural Society of England (13th).—The site of the church of Allhallows Bread Street was sold for £32,254 (20th).—The quincentenary of Wycliffe was celebrated in the City.   There was an early service at St Anne's, Blackfriars, where Dr. Vaughan, Master of the Temple delivered an address, another service at the City Temple, and a meeting at the Mansion House, presided over by the Lord Mayor (22nd).—Two new schemes, one relating to Sir Andrew Judd's School at Tonbridge, and the other to a new school to be established there, had been prepared by arrangement between the Skinners' Company and the Charity Commissioners (30th). —The Right Hon. R. A. Cross, M.P., Home Secretary, was admitted to the honorary freedom and livery of the Clothworkers' Company (3 Ap.).—Sir U. Kay Shuttleworth's resolution, in favour of London Municipal Reform was defeated in the House of Commons by 116 votes to 73.   Mr. Goschen spoke in support of the resolution (5th).—Mr. William Thomas Charley, M.P., D.C.L., was elected Common Serjeant, at a salary of £2,000 a year (11th).—The church of St. Botolph, Bishopsgate, was re-opened, after undergoing considerable alterations and repairs (21st).—The City made its first experiments in electric lighting at the Mansion House and Royal Exchange.   The result was not considered to be very satisfactory (8 May).—Mr. Alderman Carter died at his residence, Stamford Hill —The members of the Bar practising at the Central Criminal Court presented Mr. Russell Gurney with an illuminated photographic album, containing a valedictory address (8th).— The memorial stone of the Welsh Calvinistic Methodist Chapel in Bridgewater Gardens, Barbican was laid (15th).   This chapel was founded in 1774 in Smithfield, and was afterwards removed to Wilderness Row, and thence to Jewin Crescent, where it remained fifty-four years.—The Right Hon. Russell Gurney, Q.C., M.P. (late Recorder), died at Palace Gardens, Kensington (31st).   Dean Stanley con-ducted the funeral service at Kensal Green Cemetery.—An attempt having been made to assassinate the Emperor William of Germany, the Court of Aldermen passed a resolution expressing sympathy with His Majesty (3 June).—The Clothworkers' Company presented its honorary freedom to the Right Hon. W. E. Forster, M.P. (5th).—The Court of Arbitration appointed to hear appeals in respect to the Golden Lane and Petticoat Square scheme, under the Artizans and Labourers' Dwellings Act, concluded its sittings in the Aldermen's Chamber at Guildhall (5th).—Mr. William Corrie, the Remembrancer, sent in his resignation to the Common Council (6th).—The Court resolved to take down the upper portion of the wall of Bunhill Fields Burial Ground, next to Bunhill Row, leaving the lower portion, and adding an iron coping and palisading, with a pair of gates, at a cost of £430.—The Corporation subscribed 100 guineas to the Mansion House Fund for the relief of sufferers from the Haydock Colliery Explosion, which reached a total of £1,128 (20th).—The King of Bonny was present at a meeting at the Mansion House to hear a statement from Mr. Donald Mackenzie on the opening up of Central Africa to commerce and civilization (27th).—The Lady Mayoress opened a very successful exhibition of the Fanmakers' Company at Drapers' Hall (2 July).—The Tithe Question at Christ Church, Newgate Street (St. Bartholomew's Hospital v. Phillips), was settled by the Master of the Rolls.—The Common Council voted £500 to the Mansion House Fund for the London International Agricultural Exhibition (4th). This fund amounted to £8,580.—The Library Committee obtained authority to print and publish extracts from the records relating to the possession of Richmond Park by the Corporation at the time of the Commonwealth, and its subsequent surrender by them to King Charles II.—It was reported that a marble relievo " Peace, or the Soldier's return " had been completed for the Corporation, by Mr. Bell. It represented the return of Wellington and his army after the declaration of Peace following the Battle of Waterloo.—The Epping Forest Act, 1878, was read a third time in the House of Commons and passed. The forest was by this Act placed under the regulation and management of the Corporation of London, acting by the Court of Common Council as the conservators of the forest, a proposal by Mr. Fawcett to give the Metropolitan Board of Works representation on the Committee of Management having been rejected by the decisive vote of 209 to 49. The Corporation were empowered by the Act to appoint a Committee of twelve, to be styled the Epping Forest Committee, and the four verderers who are elected by the commoners in pursuance of the Act are also members of the Committee. — About this time the Tin-plate Workers' alias Wire Workers' Company opened an exhibition at the Crystal Palace.—Mr. Goschen's resignation as one of the representatives of the City was tendered at a meeting of the City

Liberal Club (15th). Mr. Goschen afterwards addressed a letter to the Liberal electors and the Livery, explaining that he was retiring in consequence of his views on the extension of the County Franchise.—Mr. Alderman Fowler, in the absence of the Duke of Richmond, laid the foundation stone of the City Carlton Club, St. Swithin's Lane.—The Earl of Beaconsfield and the Marquis of Salisbury, having returned from the Berlin Congress, bringing "peace with honour," the Corporation decided to confer upon them the freedom of the City, and to entertain them at a déjeuner in the Guildhall. The ceremony took place on 3 Aug., in the great hall, where some 2,000 persons had assembled. The Chamberlain (Mr. B. Scott) in addressing Lord Salisbury referred to the fact that Lord Salisbury could claim descent from no less than three Aldermen of this City, the last of whom, Sir Crisp Gascoyne, was the first Lord Mayor to occupy (in 1752) the present Mansion House. —The Christ Church, Newgate Street, Tithes Commutation Bill was rejected in

St. Dionis Backchurch.

the House of Commons by 78 votes to 71 (8 Aug.).—The City Solicitor laid before the Common Council the Act for "the dis-afforestation of Epping Forest, and the preservation and manage-ment of the enclosed parts as an open space for the recreation and enjoyment of the public and for other purposes" (9th). — The church of St. Dionis Backchurch, Fenchurch Street, one of Wren's churches, was demolished, the benefice being united with that of Allhallows, Lombard Street. —Medallions of Temple Bar were ordered to be struck out of the lead from the roof of that struc-ture. — A fire occurred at Castle Baynard Wharf, Blackfriars (Messrs. Price), the damage being estimated at £35,000 (3 Sep.).—One of the most terrible river disasters occurred the same day on the Thames. The "Princess Alice," crowded with excursionists from Southend and Gravesend, was run into by the steamer "Bywell Castle," off Woolwich, and foundered. A Mansion House Fund was immediately opened, and the Queen telegraphed to the Lord Mayor, asking his lordship to assist Her Majesty in making known her deep sympathy with the friends of the sufferers. The Mansion House Fund reached a total of £38,246.— On 14 Sept. another fund was opened at the Mansion House for the relief of sufferers from the dreadful explosion at the Abercarne Colliery, near Newport, South Wales, when 257 lives were lost. This fund amounted to £33,007. —-The last sermons were preached in Jewin Street Wesleyan Chapel prior to its demolition (22nd). — Waterloo and Charing Cross Bridges were opened, free of toll, by the Metropolitan Board of Works (5 Oct.).—The Church of St. Augustine, Old Change, was re-opened, after being closed for re-decoration (10th).—-Rev. W. H. Aitken conducted a series of special services for young men at the Guildhall, beginning on the 22nd.—Centenary services commenced at the City Road Wesleyan Chapel (27th).—-Mr. Charles Henry Robarts was elected Remembrancer (31st). — The new bells of St. Paul's were dedicated (1 Nov.). The Corporation bell cost £639 18s.—The Common Council agreed to the construction of a low level bascule bridge across the Thames, east of London Bridge, and resolved to approach Parliament for the necessary powers to raise £500,000 on the credit of the Bridge House Estates, and for a continuance of the Coal Dues, which were to provide the balance of £250,000 (7th).—Alderman Charles Whetham was elected Lord Mayor.—Lord Beaconsfield, speaking at the Guildhall banquet, where there was "a chance of hearing the voice of sense and truth," said, what we needed was a "scientific frontier" in Afghanistan. He expressed his belief that Russia would carry out with integrity the Berlin Treaty, and added that the Government were determined it should be complied with both in spirit and in letter (9th).—The Common Council decided to remove the City of London School from Honey Lane Market to the Victoria Embankment (14th).—The Corporation also resolved to go to Parliament for authority to dis-market the Meat and Poultry Markets at Leadenhall, with a view to the construction of a new Meat, Fish and Poultry Market, on or near the existing site.—St. Botolph's Church, Aldersgate, was re-opened after extensive alterations and repairs (17th).— A large deputation, headed by Mr. Alderman Figgins, and representing the vestry of St. Bride's, Fleet Street, the City United Wards' Club, the City of London Tradesmen's Club, and the Bartholomew Club, had an interview with the Home Secretary, on the subject of the unprotected state of the City, in case of fire, owing to the withdrawal of fire stations from the City (19th).

It was pointed out that the districts in question (the western districts) were little better off than they were fifty years ago when they depended, in case of an outbreak of fire, on the small parish engines. Down to the year 1866 each parish in the City had its own fire engine, and was aided by the several fire offices, who provided twenty effective fire engine stations, with all the men and appliances necessary, eight stations with 131 men being available for immediate use in the City. Now only two stations, Watling Street and Bishopsgate, with fewer men, were available. Mr. Cross (the Home Secretary) promised to communicate with the Metropolitan Board of Works, and at the next meeting of the Board (29 Nov.) the Fire Brigade Committee was authorised to place additional men at the fire stations in the City, and to make other provisions for the protection of the City from fire.

Dr. Tristram, Vicar-General of the Bishop of London, held a Consistory Court in St. Paul's Cathedral, for the purpose of hearing an application on behalf of the Churchwardens of St. Sepulchre, Middlesex, for an order to restrain any deviation from the terms of the faculty granted by the Bishop for the restoration of the parish church (25th). The subject had created a considerable amount of feeling in the parish.—A mass meeting of watermen and lightermen of the river Thames was held at Cannon Street Hotel, and the report of the Board of Trade on the " Princess Alice " disaster was condemned as a grave impeachment of nearly 9,000 public servants.—About this time several important experiments with electric lighting were made in the City. Billingsgate Market was illuminated by the Jablochkoff system on the 25th, and the same system was tried on Holborn Viaduct on 14 Dec. The Thames Embankment was also lighted experimentally on the 13th, and about the same time the Prince of Wales and other distinguished visitors witnessed the experiments at the *Times* office.—The bell of St. Paul's was tolled for the death of Princess Alice, whose loss was universally regretted (18th). The Corporation passed a vote of condolence with the Queen and Royal family, and referred to the Princess as one " whose virtues had rendered her universally beloved."—On the 19th the Lord Mayor, six Aldermen, the Recorder, and twelve members of the Common Council were appointed to serve on the Board of Governors of the Livery Companies, for the advancement of Technical Education.—Leathersellers' Hall was re-built on a large scale, and in the Elizabethan style, from designs by the Company's Surveyor, Mr. G. A. Wilson. The Livery hall is 32 feet by 26. One of the most noteworthy features of this building are the hand-wrought iron gates at the entrance. — Cannon Street Railway Bridge was permanently closed with the consent of the Metropolitan Board of Works. —The removal of Temple Bar was commenced towards the close of the year. The stones of the grim old edifice (about a thousand in number) lay exposed to the weather for nearly ten years. Upon the request of Sir H. B. Meux, Bart., the Common Council presented the stones to him in June, 1887, for the purpose of re-erecting Temple Bar at the entrance to Theobald's Park, Cheshunt.—By Act of Common

Council all orders relating to the nomination and election of Sheriffs were repealed, and fresh regulations substituted.—In the course of some repairs at St. Paul's Cathedral a discovery was made of the basement walls, in the cloister and chapter house of the former cathedral, relics of a building every trace of which was supposed to have disappeared. — The Wellington Monument, upon which Mr. Stevens had been at work for twenty years, was at last completed, but it was placed in the south-west chapel of the cathedral where it could not be seen to any advantage. [The removal of this monument to its present position in the north side of the nave was successfully completed in Jan., 1894.]

1879.

THE Charity Commissioners issued a draft scheme for the future administration of Alleyn's College, Dulwich (4 Jan., 1879).—Lord Penzance, the Dean of Arches, heard in a Committee Room of the House of Lords the case of Sergeant and others v. Dale (10th). On a former occasion the Rev. T. Pelham Dale was prosecuted for ritualistic practices in St. Vedast Church, Foster Lane, and condemned by the Court of Arches. The proceedings, however, were subsequently set aside by the Court of Queen's Bench. The present suit was authorised by the Bishop of London, and on 10 Feb. judgment was given against Mr. Dale who was condemned with costs. The ritualistic practices were, however, continued.—The Charity Commissioners issued a scheme dealing with Dean Clarke's Charity for St. Paul's Cathedral and the augmentation of Benefices (15th).—Sir Arthur Hobhouse, Q.C., K.C.S.I., having been appointed Arbitrator in matters of dispute between the Conservators of Epping Forest and parties claiming an interest in the Forest, the first case, that of Mr. Mills, was heard at 6, Old Palace Yard, Westminster (16th).—The new Jewin Welsh Chapel in Fann Street, Aldersgate, a Gothic structure, costing £10,000, was opened on the 17th.—The freedom of the City, in a gold box, was voted to Sir Rowland Hill, K.C.B., in acknowledgment of the great social and commercial benefits this country has derived from the adoption in 1840 of his system of uniform penny postage in the United Kingdom (30th). In consequence of the state of Sir Rowland's health and his advanced age (83) the presentation was made by a small deputation, accompanied by the Chamberlain and Town Clerk, at the residence of Sir Rowland Hill, at Hampstead, on 6 June.

Sir Rowland having signed the Roll of Honorary Citizens, the Chamberlain pointed out to him that he was the third of the name and family connected with the City of London. The first was Sir Rowland Hill, citizen and mercer, who was Lord Mayor in 1549, and the second, General Sir Rowland Hill, who received the freedom in 1814 for his services at the Battle of Vittoria.

The result of several years' litigation between the parish of St. Michael's, Cornhill, and the City of London Real Property Company, as to a right of way in St. Michael's Alley, having been to finally affirm the title of the parish as owners of the space formerly covered by the Churchyard wall, the parish authorities gave effect to the decision by re-building the wall across the footpath (5 Feb.).—The Fanmakers' Company petitioned the Court of Aldermen for permission to increase the number of the Livery of that Guild from 60 to 200. It was intimated that the fine payable on admission to the freedom and Livery would be raised and that ladies would be received as members. The Aldermen after some discussion granted the application. A question was asked by Mr. James, in the House of Commons (28th), as to whether a City Company could be allowed, in this way, to create parliamentary votes, and the Home Secretary replied that he supposed they were within their rights. Mr. James, not satisfied with the answer, moved (13 Mar.).

MONVMENT TO THE DVKE of WELLINGTON IN ST· PAVL'S CATHEDRAL

Wellington Memorial, St. Paul's Cathedral.

That the sale of the Parliamentary franchise by the City Guilds, with the consent of the Court of Aldermen, is an abuse and should be abolished.

Sir Charles Dilke and Mr. Herschell supported the motion, which was opposed by Alderman Cotton, Mr. Charley, and Sir Trevor Lawrence, who said at least two-thirds of the Court of the Fanmakers' Company were good Liberals. The motion was defeated by 153 votes to 114. The Aldermen resolved (25 Mar.) that in future such applications should be referred to a Committee of the Court.—The rapidly increasing charges made by the London School Board gave rise to a long discussion in the Commission of Sewers, extending over three sittings. A condemnatory motion was carried by 29 votes to 19 (25 Feb.).—Rev. F. G. Blomfield, M.A., Prebendary of St. Paul's and Rector of St. Andrew Undershaft (son of the late Bishop of London), died at Ilfracombe (28th). — Under the auspices of a Committee of Clergymen, formed to consider the relation of the Church to Trades Unions, the first meeting of a series was held at the Chapter House, St. Paul's Churchyard, to discuss the question "How far is over-production the cause of the present commercial depression?" Rev. J. Oakley, Vicar of St. Saviour's, Hoxton, presided, and the meeting was addressed by Messrs. Brassey, Geo. Potter, E. J. Watherston, Mundella, M.P., Broadhurst, and others (1 Mar.).—Weston, the pedestrian, reached the Royal Exchange at 11.54 on the 1st, having walked 2,000 miles in 1,000 consecutive hours and lectured in fifty towns.—Colonel Haywood (Engineer to the Commissioners of Sewers), reporting on the Electric Lighting Experiment on Holborn Viaduct, said "The principal results appeared to be that the light was about seven and a-half times the cost of gas, and that, subject to the conditions under which it is given off, the illuminating power was about seven times that of gas" (11th).—Mr. P. Wyndham moved in the House of Commons for a return of the number of churches in the City pulled down or now condemned under "The Union of Benefices Act, 1860;" stating how much had been realised by the sale of the site; what new churches had been built out of the proceeds in lieu of the churches pulled down; their situation and cost, and what had been done with the parochial endowments. This was agreed to (12th).—Mr. Douglas Straight, who had been engaged in extensive practice at the Central Criminal Court, was appointed to the Judgeship of the High Court of the North-west Provinces of India, at a salary of £4,500 a year.—The King of the Belgians, who was presented with the honorary freedom of the Turners' Company, said "The late King, my father, felt great pride and satisfaction in belonging to one of the great commercial fraternities of this City" (18th).—The Drapers' Company offered three new scholarships to the London School Board, two to be competed for by boys and one by girls (26th).—The Corporation resolved to present an address to the Queen on the occasion of the marriage of the Duke of Connaught with Princess Louise Margaret, third daughter of Prince Frederick Charles of Prussia (27th). The address was presented at Windsor (13 May).—A proposal, made by the Conservators of Epping Forest, for an assessment of 1s. per cent. upon land illegally held and enclosed came before Sir Arthur (now Lord) Hobhouse for arbitration at Guildhall (1 Ap.). The Arbitrator awarded £24 an acre in a test case as to the value of the rights of fuel possessed by some 24 owners and occupiers of lands in the manors of Waltham Holy Cross and Sewardstone, and on this basis all the owners of "Fuel Assignments" were compensated at an expenditure of about £15,000.—Dr Vaughan, Master of the Temple, was consecrated Dean of Llandaff.—The Corporation voted 100 guineas to the Mansion House Fund for the relief of sufferers from the terrible floods in Hungary (3rd). This fund reached a total of £11,265. The Corporation also voted 100 guineas to the Zulu War Sufferers' Relief Fund (Mansion House), which amounted to £15,709.—The Remembrancer (Mr. C. H. Robarts) having complained of the unsatisfactory state of the internal organization of his office, the Common Council resolved that while regretting the differences which had arisen between the Remembrancer and his Clerks it declined to dismiss Mr. Howkins, the Chief Clerk, whose apology should have been accepted (3rd).—A Library, Museum, and other rooms and offices were added to St. Bartholomew's Hospital, and opened by the Prince of Wales.—The eastern block of the new Palace of Justice, was opened on the 21st.—A special Musical Military Service was held at St. Paul's, a sermon being preached on behalf of the Royal Society for Daughters of Officers of the Army (29th).—The Cutlers' Company's exhibition was opened by the Earl of Carnarvon at the Hall in Cloak Lane (1 May). This old Hall was pulled down shortly afterwards (1883).—The Church of St. Katherine Cree, Leadenhall Street, was re-opened after having been thoroughly repaired and re-decorated (4th).—Mr James Grant, author and journalist, and editor of the *Morning Advertiser*, from 1850–71, died at the age of seventy-seven (23rd).—It having been proposed to remove the Fish trade of Billingsgate to a more central and easily approached position, the Common Council resolved that having recently expended £300,000 on the enlargement and improvement of the Market, which was appreciated by the trade and was a great financial success, they did not consider it desirable to remove it from the present site (29th).—The Coach Makers and Coach Harness Makers' Company opened an interesting exhibition at the Mansion House (2 June).—Baron Lionel Nathan de Rothschild, for many years member of Parliament for the City, and head of the great mercantile house of N. M. Rothschild & Sons, New Court, St. Swithin's Lane, died on the 3rd at his residence in Piccadilly.

The deceased baron, who had been partially an invalid for some years, was the grandson and English representative of Meyer Anselm, the founder of the House of Rothschild and of its fortunes at Frankfort. Lionel was born in New Court, St. Swithin's Lane, in 1808, and succeeded to the title of Baron on the death of his father in 1836. His persistent and successful struggle for the admission of Jews to Parliament has been already recorded. One of his most noteworthy transactions was the advance to the Government, of which Lord Beaconsfield was premier, of £4,000,000, to purchase the Khedive's shares in the Suez Canal. This turned out a very good investment for the country as well as for the Rothschilds, whose commission amounted to £99,414 11s. 1d.

The Clothworkers' Company voted £13,500 for a building for the textile industries and dyeing instruction departments at Yorkshire College, Leeds, and agreed to maintain the building in operation for five years (6th). The College was opened 3 Dec., 1880. About the same time the Company presented a number of scholarships to various educational institutions.—The first Board School in the City was opened by Sir Charles Reed, Chairman of the London School Board, in Greystoke Place, Fetter Lane (10th). The total cost of the building and site was £15,558 or £35 13s. 8d. per head.—It was referred to the Music

Portion of Frieze, new Cutlers' Hall, Warwick Lane.

Deputation to ascertain if there were any demand for musical education in the City, such as was supplied at the West End of London, and the best mode of supplying the same (19th).—The Corporation offered its condolence to the ex-Empress Eugénie on the irreparable loss which had befallen her in the untimely death of her only son, who had fallen a victim to "an impulsive instinct of chivalry, characteristic of the nation to which he belonged." The Prince Imperial, whose untimely fate was lamented, was killed by natives in South Africa.—The Corporation instructed the Finance Committee to consider the desirability of purchasing Burnham Beeches (26th). A fortnight later a provisional agreement was entered into with Sir Henry Peek, Bart., the then owner, for the purchase of 374 acres, 2 roods, 23 poles of the waste lands of the Manor of Allerds, in East Burnham, in the county of Bucks, comprising an open space known as East Burnham Common and Burnham Beeches, the latter famed for its magnificent beech trees.—On the same day Mr. John Alexander Brand was elected Comptroller.—The Lord Mayor and Sheriffs attended the opening of the International Agricultural Exhibition (30th). His Lordship, as Chairman of the Mansion House Committee, entertained the

Prince of Wales (its President) and the Council of the Royal Agricultural Society of England to a banquet at the Mansion House (1 July).—Lord Beaconsfield on the same day was presented with the honorary freedom of the Grocers' Company; this compliment had been voted more than four years before, but his Lordship's onerous functions had, hitherto, prevented his attendance at the Hall to receive it.—Owing to the agricultural depression, the Haberdashers' Company, who owned some 1,200 acres, tried the experiment of farming their own land (2nd).—Rev. W. Walsham How, rector of Whittington, Salop, was nominated Bishop of Bedford, under the

Portion of Frieze, new Cutlers' Hall, Warwick Lane.

Act of Henry VIII, as Suffragan to the Bishop of London with charge of the eastern and northern divisions of the Diocese. The living of St. Andrew Undershaft (£2,000 per annum), was attached to the Bishopric as an endowment (7th). Dr. How was consecrated at St. Paul's on the 25th.—An Act had been passed enabling the Corporation to carry out their scheme for the erection of a new City of London School, on the Thames Embankment, on land belonging to them of the value of £100,000. The school buildings were to cost another £100,000 (10th).—The Common Council agreed to erect a new fruit and vegetable market at a cost of £115,000, and an additional sum of £2,100 was voted for the vehicular approach to the vaults beneath the Poultry and Provision Markets (10th). —The church of St. Mary Abchurch with St. Laurence Pountney was re-opened after renovation and re-decoration (13th).—A meeting of representatives from City Charities was held at St. Bartholomew's Hospital to protest against the Government proposal for a tax of one per cent. on the gross income of all charities for the expenses of the Charity Commissioners (14th).—The scheme of the Ecclesiastical Commissioners for uniting the benefices of St. Nicholas Cole Abbey with St. Nicholas Olave, and St. Mary Somerset with St. Mary Mounthaw, into a united benefice with St. Benet, Paul's Wharf, and St. Peter's, Paul's Wharf, was approved by Her Majesty in Council.—An additional slaughter house and other improvements were ordered at the Foreign Cattle Market, Deptford, at an expense of £25,000 (18th).—A Select Committee of the House of Commons, appointed to enquire into the merits of the Tower (High Level) Bridge Bill, decided that the preamble of the Bill had not been proved (21st).—A new church built by the Goldsmiths' Company, at East Acton, was consecrated by the Bishop of London (22nd).—The Salters' Company established two exhibitions of the value of £80 per annum each, for the encouragement of the study of natural science, at one of the Universities, being open to competition by scholars of the City of London and King's College Schools (24th).—The Corporation decided to restore the East window of the beautiful Lady Chapel of St. Albans Abbey at a cost of £350 (24th).—The City Lands Committee was authorised to co-operate with the Society of Arts in the erection of memorial tablets in the City. —The Common Council ordered the construction of sewers and vaults in connection with their vacant land on the Victoria Embankment at an expense of £12,500.— It was decided to complete the Corporation Buildings, Farringdon Road, by erecting an additional block at a cost of £4,500.—A sum of £6,520 was voted for the repaving of Blackfriars Bridge (24th).—The church of St. Peter, Cornhill, celebrated its 17th centenary (27th).—At the Mansion House banquet to Her Majesty's Ministers, Lord Beaconsfield defended his foreign policy and said it was the patriotism of the City of London that had supported the Government during the recent crisis. He was sorry he could not congratulate them on the termination of the commercial depression which had lasted over four years (6 Aug.).—The annual conference of the Association for the reform and codification of the Law of Nations was opened at the Guildhall, the Lord Mayor presiding. Sir Robert Phillimore delivered the inaugural address (11th).—At a special sitting of the Consistory Court of London at St. Paul's Cathedral, Dr. Tristram, the Vicar-General, gave his decision in regard to the restoration of St. Sepulchre's Church, situated partly in the City of London and partly in the County of Middlesex. The decision was in favour of the Middlesex Churchwardens who objected to some of the proposed alterations (9th).—" Tower Chambers " was completed at the corner of London Wall, facing the Old Moorgate.

The site of this building was formerly occupied by the Albion Presbyterian Chapel. The soil, 30 feet below, was perfectly black and in some places putrid, probably from the number of bodies deposited here during the Plague.

St. Paul's Churchyard, laid out as a garden.

St. Mary-le-Bow Church, Cheapside, was re-opened, the interior having been thoroughly restored by Mr. A W. Blomfield (14 Sept).—The enclosed space round the north-eastern part of St. Paul's, having been converted by the Corporation into a pleasant garden, was publicly opened by the Lord Mayor on the 22nd. Here the weary may sit amidst flowers and shrubs, beneath the shadow of the great Cathedral, and enjoy rest and seclusion from the turmoil of City life; flocks of pigeons may be seen here daily, so tame that they will feed out of children's hands. It is a small garden, but it is a great boon to many of the workers round about and to the children of the neighbourhood, as well as to visitors from a distance.—At the beginning of Oct. the new Manchester Hotel, Aldersgate Street, was opened for business. Some famous taverns had occupied the site on which this hotel now stands at the corner of Long Lane. Here, in succession, were the "Sun," the "Half Moon," and the "Magpie."—Mr. Deputy Hartridge presented the Guildhall Library with a collection of cuttings and engravings, descriptive of London and the various changes which have taken place in the City and its suburbs.—A printed catalogue of the books and manuscripts forming the library of the Dutch Church in Austin Friars, also deposited in the Guildhall Library, was printed at this time.—An Act having been passed empowering the Corporation to improve the Surrey side approaches to London Bridge, the matter was referred to Committee (16 Oct.).—A petition presented to the Common Council to open the Guildhall Library on Sundays from two o'clock was, after discussion, rejected by 104 votes to 34 (16th).—The church of St. Margaret Pattens with St. Gabriel Fenchurch was re-opened after renovation and alteration (19th).—The foundations were laid of a new building for the Jerusalem Coffee House, in Cowper's Court, Cornhill. The Jerusalem, which was one of the first Coffee houses established in the City, is used largely by merchants, shipowners and ship captains.—The first lecture in connection with the City and Guilds of London Institute for the advancement of Technical Education was delivered in Cowper Street Schools, Finsbury, by Professor W. E. Ayrton, who chose for his subject "The improvements science can effect in our trades, and in the condition of our workmen" (1 Nov.). At the close of the lecture Mr. F. J. Bramwell, who presided, explained the object which the Institute had in view. He said:—

"Many of them had for a long time earnestly desired to see an improvement in the technical knowledge of the workmen of England. They had seen the apprenticeship system dying out, as mechanical appliances were substituted for handicraft labour, and they felt that there was no provision made in this country to enable a workman to follow intelligently the principles which guided him in the peculiar manufacture in which he was engaged. The City and Guilds of London Institute did not propose to establish a workshop where actual handicrafts were to be taught, but to suggest such practical teaching as should always form an adjunct to the training of the workshop, and to show the application of science and art to the ordinary industries."

The London School Board resolved to close the recently opened school in Greystoke Place, Fetter Lane, on account of its insanitary condition (4th).— Sir Francis Wyatt Truscott was chosen Lord Mayor.—The City Carlton Club's new premises in St. Swithin's Lane were opened (12th). The club was established in 1867 at 83, King William Street, where it had hitherto remained. The new club house was designed by Mr. R. Roberts, architect, and cost about £40,000, including the sums paid for unexpired leases.—A fund was started about this time at the Mansion House for a national memorial to the late Sir Rowland Hill, the objects being to establish a Benevolent Institution for aged and distressed Post Office servants and those dependent on them, and to erect a statue or other monument of the deceased. The Corporation voted 100 guineas to this fund. —The School Board election in the City resulted in the return of Mr. H Spicer (who headed the list), Miss Davenport Hill, Mr. W. H. Bonnewell, and Mr. W. S. Gover (28th).—The Old Bailey dinners to the Judges and the Bar, which had been suspended owing to a fire which took place in 1877, were revived during the present Mayoralty.—The Common Council resolved to appoint a curator of the works of Art belonging to the Corporation at a salary of 100 guineas (1 Dec.). —The City Road Wesleyan Chapel was destroyed by fire (7th).—The Corporation leased a piece of land on the Victoria Embankment to Sion College at £1,265 per annum, with the option of acquiring the freehold at twenty-five years' purchase (11th) —The Lord Mayor opened Holborn Town Hall, the foundation stone of which had been laid eighteen months before by Sir James McGarel-Hogg, Chairman of the Metropolitan Board of Works. This building, situated in the Gray's Inn Road, forms a notable addition to the municipal halls of the Metropolis (18th).—Telegraphic communication was established between London and the Cape, the connection having been completed between Aden and Zanzibar, reducing the time occupied in the transmission of a message by a fortnight (29th).—The Leadenhall Market Act, 1871, was repealed by the Leadenhall Market Act of this year (1879). The last named Act abolished the then existing Market and conferred powers upon the Corporation for the improvement of the land occupied by the Market, the laying out and formation of new streets, and the construction of a new Market for the sale of "Meat, Fish, and Poultry and other Provisions," with authority to borrow £99,000 for the purpose.—Her Majesty, in accordance with the Epping Forest Act, appointed the Duke of Connaught as Ranger of the Forest.—About this time a new chancel and vestry were added to St. Swithin's Church, London Stone; a drinking fountain was erected at the back of the Royal Exchange at a cost of £1,500; a house popularly, but erroneously, known as "Shakespeare's London house," in Aldersgate Street, was pulled down; Girdlers' Hall, Basinghall Street, was restored; and a number of old houses in Fore Street, from Wood Street to Aldermanbury Postern, were demolished —Mr. Penrose discovered the foundations of St. Paul's Cross at the north-east angle of the Cathedral Churchyard, and the spot is marked in the public garden. The crypt of the Cathedral was also cleared of lumber, and thrown open to the public; the eastern portion, on the site of the ancient church of St. Faith, was arranged as a small church for daily early morning service, and some of the old monuments rescued from the original Cathedral were arranged here.

1880.

SHORTLY before the execution of a man named Shurety at the Old Bailey (5 Jan., 1880), a letter was handed to Mr. Sydney Smith, governor of Newgate, purporting to come from the Home Office and countermanding the order for execution. A close examination of the envelope and seal convinced the governor that the letter was a forgery and the execution was proceeded with.—The Metropolitan Board of Works voted £500,000 towards street improvements in connection with the Metropolitan and District Railways (City Lines and Extensions) Act, 1879. A further sum of £250,000 was voted by the Commissioners of Sewers on the 13th, to widen Eastcheap and practically make a new street from King William Street to the Tower. About the same time great improvements were taking place in Cheapside. A spacious block of buildings had been erected between 23 and 29, Cheapside, and "Sweeting's," at the western corner, was almost entirely rebuilt.—The Duchess of Marlborough wrote to the Lord Mayor, on the 14th, thanking his Lordship for the third generous donation of £2,000 towards her Irish Relief Fund. The Mansion House branch of this fund eventually reached a total of £35,431. — Sir Arthur Hobhouse held a Court at Guildhall, under the Epping Forest Act (14th) The Arbitrator's decision was given on the 26th confirming to those householders in the manor and parish of Loughton who occupied houses built before 1851, the right to lop in the Forest. This privilege, it appears, had existed for 160 years.—It was announced on the 17th that the Rev. W. H. Lyall, rector of St. Dionis Backchurch, had gone over to the Church of Rome.—St. Sepulchre's Church, at the eastern end of Holborn Viaduct, was opened after extensive alterations.

The body of the Church was restored under Mr. Robert Billing, architect, new windows, filled with tracery, being inserted, new buttresses, battlements and pinnacles added, and the interior made to harmonise. A prominent feature, in the structural alterations of the interior, consisted of a new organ chamber; this was provided in the recess on the north side of the Church called St. Stephen's Chapel. The old oak pews were removed and open benches substituted. The new clergy and choir stalls are all in oak, and a lofty oak screen was erected across the church at the west end

The Church of Allhallows, Lombard Street, was re-opened (26th).—It was ordered that the Guildhall Library should remain open on Saturdays until the same time as on other evenings of the week (29th).—The Lord Mayor opened the inaugural exhibition of the City of London Society of Artists at Skinners' Hall (1 Mar.)—The Home Secretary (Mr. R. A. Cross) moved in the House of Commons for leave to bring in a Bill to make further provision for the supply of water to the Metropolis.

The Bill was opposed on the ground that the compensation proposed to be given to the Water Companies was excessive, and would impose an unjust and unnecessary burden on the ratepayers of the Metropolis. It was contended that, by the Bill, twenty-two millions was to be paid for twelve millions of capital, and that a bonus of nine millions was to be added, making a total of thirty-one millions. The introduction of the Bill gave rise to much excitement on the Stock Exchange Notwithstanding the enormous advance previously realized in Water Companies' stocks, another extraordinary bound took place, representing in one case about thirty-five per cent.

At the General Election, the Conservative candidates, Alderman Cotton, the Right Hon. J. G. Hubbard and Alderman Fowler were elected, the Liberal minority seat falling to Mr. Alderman Lawrence (1 Apr.). The City, however, did not reflect the feeling of the country, which returned Mr. Gladstone to power with a large majority. The Lord Mayor was defeated at Gravesend.—After a pastorate of eighteen years, the Rev. D. M'Auslane preached his farewell sermons at Finsbury Chapel, having accepted an invitation to become the minister of Victoria Park Chapel (14th).—The foundation stone of the New Fruit and Vegetable Market, Smithfield, was laid on the 17th.—A notice of inhibition was affixed to the door of St. Vedast's Church, precluding Mr. Dale from performing any service in the Church or otherwise exercising the cure of souls within the diocese (21st).—According to an ancient custom on Good Friday, sixty younger boys from Christ's Hospital attended the Church of Allhallows, Lombard Street, where in pursuance of the will of Peter Symonds, made in 1593, they each received, at the hands of the church-wardens, a new penny and a packet of raisins (26th).—The report of the Royal Commissioners appointed to enquire into the City Parochial Charities was issued (7 Ap.). The Commissioners were the Duke of Northumberland, the Rev. Canon Gregory, the Rev. William Rogers, Mr. Farrer Herschell, Q.C., M.P., Mr. Cubitt, Mr. Albert Pell and Mr. Henry Hucks Gibbs.

The report recommended the appointment, for a certain time, of an Executive Commission, paid from the funds of the City Charities, to consist of three persons with power to examine into the trusts, charters, deeds and documents relating to the origin as well as the administration of the City Charities, into the leases granted by the trustees and the employment of the revenue and to examine into their accounts for the last seven years. The dole system was generally condemned, and the Commissioners expressed themselves decidedly against the practice of applying, except as regards certain endowments, sums of money, bequeathed for charitable purposes, in payment of poor rates, to which the parishes are liable. The income of the charities, at the last return to Parliament in 1876, was £104,904, of which £81,014 was still under the uncontrolled administration of the local authorities

The Commissioners of the Exhibition of 1851 having offered the City and Guilds of London Institute a site at South Kensington for a Central Technical College, the Council of the Institute applied to the Corporation for substantial assistance towards the building fund (15 Ap). After full consideration, the Corporation sub-sequently resolved (2 Dec.) to contribute an annual sum of £2,000 for a period not exceeding five years. The Institute was about this time registered under the Limited Liability Companies Act.—It was reported in the *Daily News* that the last fragments of the river face of old Whitefriars were doomed to speedy demolition.

Clinging to the Temple the little knot of lanes had hitherto escaped destruction, "but Watermen's Alley and the dwellings clustered round New Wharf must," said the writer, "soon undergo their fate and leave available the whole of the great square, of about eighty acres in extent, lying south-west of the site of the ancient palace of Bridewell, and bounded on the north by Temple Street and Tudor Street, on the south by the Thames Embankment, and stretching from De Keyser's Hotel on the east, to the Temple on the west. The eastern half, or thereabouts, of this valuable space was formerly occupied by the City of London Gas Works, removed some time since to Barking " The writer proceeds "the old 'Rose and Crown' presents the oddest figure now that it is high and dry. It was evidently one of the genuine old-fashioned water-side inns, like the Watermen's Arms at Limehouse, a type of a class almost vanished from the banks of the Thames. There is yet the projecting wooden structure like the stern galley of a ship, as well as the open leads on which many a squire of Alsatia took his ease, his tobacco and strong waters, in the interval of predatory excursions into the neighbourhood."

The writer goes on to say that the *Daily News* office now stands on part of what was once the Carmelite Monastery.—Lord Cranbrook and Sir Stafford Northcote were admitted to the honorary freedom of the Merchant Taylors' Company (28 Ap.).—A great fire took place in Aldersgate Street in which two lives were lost. It originated at Messrs. Hodgkinson, Stead and Treacher's, wholesale druggists, Nos. 125 and 127, whose premises, together with the printing works of Messrs. W. H and L. Collingridge, and the old White Bear tavern were almost entirely destroyed (30th).—The Corporation after full enquiry resolved to establish a high class School of Music in the City of London, which was to be temporarily located in some large warehouses, belonging to the Corporation, in Aldermanbury (30th).— Sir John Goss, many years organist at St. Paul's, died at the age of eighty (10 May). —The Corporation voted 100 guineas for the sufferers from the famine in Kurdistan,

Armenia and Persia.—A deputation from the Commissioners of Sewers had an interview with the Home Secretary (Sir William Harcourt), as to the course which would be pursued by the Government, with respect to the water supply of London. Sir William Harcourt expressed a desire to hear the views of the City authorities as to the desirability of purchasing the Water Companies' interests, the proposed terms of transfer, and the formation of a water trust (13th).

The Commissioners of Sewers adopted a report, suggesting that the provisional agreements entered into for the purchase of the Water Companies' properties should be carefully considered by a Select Committee of the House of Commons, with a view to ascertaining whether all or any of them were beneficial to the inhabitants of the Metropolis, and should be carried into effect, or whether the expenditure contemplated under the agreements for acquiring the existing supply might not be more judiciously spent in procuring a new and better supply of water for London. It was also suggested that the Corporation should take part in the enquiry, and particular attention was called to the basis of charge as requiring consideration (25th).

The Corporation voted an address to the King of the Hellenes (9 June). The address was presented in a gold box on the 16th. King George and their Royal Highnesses the Prince and Princess of Wales (the latter being sister to the king), the Duke of Cambridge, and other distinguished guests being afterwards entertained to a déjeuner in the Guildhall. Mr. Gladstone, Prime Minister, proposed the toast of "the Lord Mayor and Corporation."—The Right Hon. W. H. Smith, M.P., received the honorary freedom of the Stationers' Company (10th).—Mr. J. F. B. Firth introduced a Municipality of London Bill into the House of Commons, providing that the Metropolis should be a county by itself—the County of London, and that all the powers and jurisdiction of the Corporation should cease. The Bill was down for second reading on the 29th, but on that occasion the House was counted out.—The celebration of the Sunday School Centenary, which was attended by delegates from all parts of the world, commenced in the City and Metropolis on the 27th. An inaugural meeting of churchmen and nonconformists was held at the Guildhall under the presidency of the Lord Mayor, the first resolution being moved by the Archbishop of Canterbury. The great hall was packed to the doors. A special commemoration service, attended by the Lord Mayor, was held at St. Paul's, and during the week numerous conferences took place. There were great gatherings at the Crystal Palace and Lambeth Palace, the latter being attended by the Prince and Princess of Wales, and the Lord Mayor and Sheriffs in state ; a statue to Robert Raikes, the founder of Sunday Schools, was unveiled by Lord Shaftesbury on the Thames Embankment.—The deed for the conveyance to the Corporation of Burnham Beeches was sealed (1 July), and on the following day this charming piece of woodland was opened to the public. The

Burnham Beeches—Winter.

purchase money was fixed at £6,000 and £1,624 16s. for timber, but the total cost to the Corporation, including conveyancing costs and road improvements, to the end of 1888, was £10,241.—A Select Committee of the House of Commons approved of a Bill for enabling the Metropolitan and District Railway Companies to complete the Inner Circle between Aldgate and Mansion House Stations, a duty imposed upon the Companies by Parliament sixteen years before. The Bill, however, was afterwards thrown out.—The new Scottish Hall, in Crane Court, Fleet Street, was opened by the Duke of Argyll, K.T., Vice-President of the Scottish Corporation (21st). The building, which includes a spacious chapel, was erected upon the site of the old hall (destroyed by fire) at a cost of over £6,000.—By invitation of the Governors of Bridewell and Bethlem Hospitals, the Lord Mayor paid a state visit to the King Edward Schools at Witney (22nd).—The Charity Commissioners issued a new scheme for the administration of Christ's Hospital, requiring the Council of Almoners, within three years, to provide a suitable site within a convenient distance of the City for a boarding school for 1,000 boys. The scheme also included the establishment of a school for girls, at Hertford, where the preparatory work of Christ's Hospital had hitherto been carried on (3 Aug.).—The Savings Bank department of the General Post Office was transferred from St. Paul's Churchyard to the great building, newly erected for its occupation in Queen Victoria Street, next to the depository of the British and Foreign Bible Society. The building was erected from the designs and under the superintendence of Mr. Jas. Williams, of Her Majesty's Office of Works and Public Buildings.—The Select Committee of the House of Commons, on the water question, reported recommending that a water authority for the Metropolis should be created, with statutory powers which would enable such body to acquire and utilize, so far as may be deemed expedient, existing sources of supply and to have recourse to such other sources of supply as, upon investigation, may prove to be available and desirable (6th).—The Epping Forest Continuance Bill received the Royal assent (7th). This Bill enabled the Conservators (the Corporation), with the approval of the Arbitrators, to make exchanges of land in the Forest and to acquire the charming pleasure grounds of Wanstead House, covering 100 acres.—The first meeting of the Royal Commissioners on the City Guilds was held at Lord Derby's House, St. James's Square (9th).—The foundation stone of the Temple Bar Memorial, on the site of old Temple Bar was laid (10th).—The Lord Mayor and Lady Mayoress left London for Brussels (14th) on the invitation of the Municipality, to attend the fêtes in commemoration of the 50th anniversary of Belgian Independence.—The death was announced of the Rev. Edward Auriol, for many years rector of St. Dunstan-in-the-West and Prebendary of St. Paul's (18th).—The electric light was introduced at Liverpool Street Station.—The re-building of Mercers' Hall, Cheapside, was completed (25th).—The annual banquet to Her Majesty's Ministers, at the Mansion House, had to be abandoned in consequence of the illness of Mr. Gladstone.—The Committee of the House of Commons on the Census Bill proposed to insert a clause enabling the Corporation, at their own expense and with the consent of the Local Government Board, to take a census of the City, between 10 and 4 in the day-time, within a week of the general census. The proposal was rejected by 69 to 24 (2 Sept.).—The Churches of St. Giles, Cripplegate, and St. Matthew, Friday Street, were re-opened after restoration (5th).—Christ Church, Newgate Street, was re-opened after being extensively repaired (21st).—The Corporation voted 100 guineas to the Mansion House Fund (£9,897) for the relief of the widows and orphans of the officers, seamen, and marines of Her Majesty's ship "Atalanta" (23rd). The Corporation also subscribed 100 guineas for the sufferers from the colliery accident at Risca. The Mansion House fund amounted to £7,677.—The Lord Mayor entertained, at the Mansion House, the team of Australian Cricketers whose brilliant performances on English ground had excited great interest (4 Oct.).—The freedom of the City was presented to Sir Henry Bessemer, F.R.S., M.I.C.E., in recognition of his valuable discoveries which had so largely benefited the iron industries of the country, and of his scientific attainments (6th).—The foundation stone of the new City of London School buildings on the Victoria Embankment was laid (14th).— At the invitation of the Lord Mayor, the Verderers, and the Epping Forest Committee, the Duke and Duchess of Connaught paid a visit to Chingford, and assisted in planting memorial trees in celebration of the successful termination of the efforts to secure a great part of the Forest as a place of recreation for the people for ever. A déjeuner was served at the newly erected Forest Hotel (16th).—The Lord Mayor gave a banquet to the representatives of the Municipal Councils of Paris and Brussels, together with members of the City Corporation and other Municipal bodies in this country (19th)—The Hall of the Painters' Company, Little Trinity Lane, which was built in 1668, was greatly improved by the addition of a new wing, the inauguration taking place on St. Luke's Day.—The Lord Mayor, as Junior Grand Warden of Freemasons in England, entertained a very distinguished company at a Masonic banquet at the Mansion House to meet the Prince of Wales, the Most Worshipful Grand Master (25th).—The Churchyard garden and recreation ground of St. Botolph, Aldersgate, was opened to the public with a religious service conducted by the vicar, the Rev. S. Flood Jones, M.A. (28th).—The

Topographical Society of London held its first meeting at the Mansion House.—A writ of imprisonment was issued by Lord Penzance against the Rev. T. Pelham Dale, rector of St. Vedast, Foster Lane, who, up to this time, had obstinately resisted all processes issued by the Court of Arches ordering him to abstain from ritualistic practices.   Mr. Dale was committed to Holloway Prison.—A remarkable floral offering was made to the Lord Mayor by the President and members of the Municipal Council of Paris in acknowledgment of the "magnificent and cordial reception" given to its deputation at the Mansion House.

It was in the form of a magnificent bouquet, measuring $8\frac{1}{2}$ feet in circumference, and representing the arms of the City of Paris with its motto *Fluctuat nec mergitur* in proper heraldic colours.   The ship in the City's Arms was composed of white lilac on a ground of red carnations, and was surmounted by three Fleurs-de-Lys on a ground of blue corn-flowers, with a coronet of gold-coloured chrysanthemums. The motto was in damask rosebuds with a wreath of oak leaves and laurels.   The ground-work of the bouquet was white lilac and white carnations, with wreaths six inches deep of corn-flowers, Souvenir de Malmaison roses, white chrysanthemums, orchids and ferns.   The bouquet, which was so large that it had to be unpacked in the street before it could enter any door at the Mansion House, was hung with tri-coloured ribands with the inscription : "Au Lord Maire, Oct 26, 1880."

The French floral tribute was afterwards exhibited at the Crystal Palace.— Baroness Burdett-Coutts, who was wearing the Turners' Company's badge, was presented with the freedom and livery of the Haberdashers' Company (1 Nov.), it being the first time that a lady was admitted to the Livery of this Guild. —The Corporation voted 100 guineas for the widows and children who suffered from a terrible fatality at the Seaham Colliery.—Prince Leopold distributed, at Guildhall, the prizes to the successful students of the Metropolitan Drawing Classes.   A guard of honour was formed by a detachment of the London Rifle Brigade.—The Prince was admitted to the honorary freedom, livery, and Court of Assistants of the Vintners' Company on the 6th.—Prince Leopold unveiled the Temple Bar Memorial (8th).   Sir Thomas Chambers, the Recorder, read an address in which he stated that the building recently removed was erected by Sir Christopher Wren in the year 1670 to mark the western boundary of the City.

The memorial is 31 feet 6 inches high, 5 feet wide, and 7 feet 8 inches long, and is surmounted by a bronze dragon (commonly styled "the Griffin") by C. B. Birch, A.R.A.   The memorial was designed by Sir Horace Jones, the City Architect, and the marble statues of the Queen and the Prince of Wales are the work of Sir E. Boehm.   The portrait medallions on the east and west sides represent the Prince of Wales and Sir Francis Wyatt Truscott, Lord Mayor.   The decorations upon the pedestal of the memorial consist of four basso-relievos, in bronze.   That on the north represents the Queen with the Prince and Princess of Wales, passing through the City to St. Paul's Cathedral on Thanksgiving Day, 1872.   The western tablet, upheld by Gog and Magog, contains the City insignia, while upon the eastern side old Temple Bar is portrayed.   The last of the four reliefs representing the procession of the Queen to the Guildhall banquet, 9 Nov., 1837, was not inserted till Dec., 1882.   The total cost was £10,960 6s 5d.

Alderman William McArthur was elected Lord Mayor.—At the Guildhall banquet, on the 9th, Mr. Gladstone, the Premier, dwelt chiefly upon the state of Ireland, and observed that Her Majesty's Ministers recognised the paramount duty of maintaining order.—Sir Arthur Hobhouse delivered judgment, at Old Palace Yard, in the arbitration between the inhabitants of Loughton and the Conservators of Epping Forest as to the amount of compensation to be paid for lopping rights. The award was that the Conservators should deposit a sum sufficient to secure £210 a year in consols. Sir Thomas Nelson, City Solicitor, said he had a blank cheque in his pocket and would fill it up for £7,000 so that the matter might be settled forthwith (11th).—The Commissioners of Sewers resolved to adopt the electric light in the following thoroughfares New Bridge Street, Ludgate Circus, Ludgate Hill, St. Paul's Churchyard (north side), Cheapside, Poultry, Mansion House Street, Royal Exchange, King William Street, Adelaide Place, Queen Street, Queen Street Place, Queen Victoria Street, King Street, Guildhall Yard, London Bridge, Southwark Bridge and Blackfriars Bridge.— Canon Gregory made a public appeal for £2,500 to purchase a great bell, of about twelve tons, for St. Paul's (16th).—The Corporation voted 200 guineas to the Mansion House Fund for the sufferers from the earthquake at Agram, in Austro-Hungary (18th). The fund amounted to £1,312.—Field Marshal Sir Charles Yorke, K.C.B., Constable of the Tower, died at the age of ninety (20th) He was the last Field Officer in the Army, and had fought in the Peninsula and at Waterloo. —The Carpenters' Company gave a banquet to celebrate the opening of their new hall in the newly constructed thoroughfare known as Throgmorton Avenue (25th). A notable feature of the banqueting hall is the ceiling, a close imitation of the ceiling of the original hall, the work of Inigo Jones. Much of the oak used in the construction of the hall was preserved from the old building.—The Bridge House Committee were authorised to make arrangements with the Commissioners of Sewers for the experimental lighting of London, Southwark and Blackfriars Bridges by electric light (2 Dec.).—Lieutenant-General Sir Frederick Roberts, V.C, G.C.B., C.I E , late Commander of Her Majesty's Forces in Southern Afghanistan, was, after the celebrated march to Candahar, admitted to the freedom of the Fishmongers' Company (3rd).—Judgment was given in the Queen's Bench Division against the Rev. T. Pelham Dale (13 Dec.). Mr. Dale finally severed his connection with the City, 30 Ap., 1881, on being appointed to the rectory of Sansthorp, Lincolnshire.—Sir Frederick Roberts was presented with the honorary freedom of the Merchant Taylors' Company (14th).—Additional lairage accommodation at the Foreign Cattle Market was ordered at a cost of £12,000

(16th).—The Corporation voted 200 guineas to the Mansion House Fund for the relief of sufferers from the Colliery Explosion at Pen-y-Craig, which reached a total of £2,245.—John Joseph Mechi, ex-Sheriff, and widely known for his connection with agriculture and cutlery, died at his farm, Tiptree Hall, Essex, at the age of seventy-eight.—A memorial of St. Antholin's Church, Budge Row, was unveiled on the site of the old church (29th).

The memorial, of Portland stone, stands about 16 feet high with a marble panel in the centre containing an engraved outline of the original church tower and spire. This is flanked on both sides by Corinthian columns of dark marble supporting an entablature of the Corinthian order and terminating with a circular pediment which bears a stone representation of the Bible and Cross, and the words "I am the Resurrection and the Life." Below the central panel is inscribed the legend "Here stood the Parish Church of St. Antholin, destroyed in the Great Fire, A.D. 1666, rebuilt A.D., 1677, by Sir Christopher Wren, Architect." On the base is the following historical reminiscence: "The changed population in the City, during two centuries, rendering the Church no longer necessary, it was taken down, A.D. 1875, under an Act of Parliament for uniting City benefices. The funds derived from the sale of the site were devoted, in part, to the restoration of the neighbouring church of St. Mary Aldermary, where are also re-erected the monumental tablets removed from St. Antholin's, and the erection at Nunhead of another church, dedicated to St. Antholin, greatly needed in a thickly populated district."

The inner quadrangle, or Merchants' area of the Royal Exchange, which was formerly open to the sky, was covered in about this time by a glass and iron roof from the designs of Mr. Charles Barry, architect.—Anderton's Hotel, successor to the Horn Tavern, Fleet Street, was re-built in the Queen Anne style.—The Three Nuns Inn, Aldgate High Street, was also re-built.—A new building was erected for the Royal General Dispensary, at 25, Bartholomew Close.—Child's Bank, and Child's Place, near Temple Bar, were pulled down early in the year.

The old ledgers of the Bank, weighing many tons, were stored in the room over Temple Bar until the arch of the structure gave way in 1874. In them are the accounts of Oliver Cromwell, Nell Gwynne, John Dryden, the Duke of Marlborough, William III, etc. Child's was the first banking house established in London, and dates from the Seventeenth century. It was re-built on the site of Child's Place.

1881.

OME portions of the old Roman wall were found within the precincts of the Tower of London, 16 feet below the surface, early in Jan., 1881. Other portions of the wall were discovered, about the same time, during the excavations for Fenchurch Street Station and Messrs. Samuels' premises in Houndsditch.—The Grocers' Company presented Lieut.-General Sir Frederick Roberts with the freedom of their Guild and entertained him to a banquet in the old Hall (7th).—Owing to the want of harmony which existed between the majority of the Common Council and Mr. C. H. Robarts, it was resolved to declare the office of Remembrancer vacant and the City Solicitor was authorised to act as Remembrancer until the vacancy was filled (3 Feb.).—Lieut.-General Sir Frederick Roberts, G.C.B., V.C., was admitted to the freedom of the City and presented with a sword of the value of 100 guineas, in recognition of his brilliant services in Afghanistan (14th).—The Medical Officer of Health of the Port of London reported to the Port Sanitary Committee of the Corporation (18th) that during the previous summer the insanitary condition of the Thames had attracted general attention, owing principally to the discharge of enormous quantities of sewage into the river. Letters which were afterwards addressed by the Corporation to the riparian authorities on the subject produced some important changes of a beneficial character.—The Town Clerk informed the Common Council that a writ in Chancery had been served upon him officially in a suit between Charles Henry Robarts, plaintiff; and the Mayor, and Commonalty, and citizens of the City of London, defendants. The City Solicitor was authorised to enter an appearance on behalf of the Corporation, and defend any action that might be taken.—Mr. Spencer Walpole, Inspector of Fisheries, issued a report on the enquiry opened by him at Fishmongers' Hall, 14 Dec., 1880, as to the destruction of fish at Billingsgate.

> The report showed that in the seventeen months ending 30 Nov., 1880, 777 tons of fish were condemned in Billingsgate. This quantity represented the $\frac{1}{222}$ part of all the fish received during this period at Billingsgate. The condemned fish was to all the fish very much as a penny is to a pound. More than half the condemned fish was shell fish, and 300 out of 427 tons represented shells. Of the 350 tons of fish other than shell fish 69 tons reached Billingsgate by water and 281 by land. The story that fish was condemned to keep up the price was unfounded. The insufficiency of the market approaches led to delay, and this would, no doubt, in many cases cause the fish to go bad.

Mrs. Twells offered the Commissioners of Sewers, through the Metropolitan Drinking Fountain and Cattle Trough Association, a granite drinking fountain, as a memorial to her husband, the late Mr. Philip Twells, for some time M.P. for the City (8 Mar.).—A building in Serjeants' Inn, formerly occupied by the Registrar of Joint Stock Companies, was purchased by the Church of England Sunday School Institute, with a view to make it in future the centre of their operations. The lecture hall was to be used for conferences, etc. (16 Mar.).—The Drapers' Company resolved to increase their contribution to the City and Guilds of London Technical Institute from £2,000 to £4,000 a year. The Company had already promised a donation of £10,000 to Finsbury College, the City branch of the Institute.—The Common Council on the 17th was occupied with two matters

of startling interest.   The first was an attempt to blow up the Mansion House.
Various proposals were made, but it was resolved for the time being to leave the
matter in the hands of the police, who were making strict enquiries.   No clue was
obtained to the perpetrator of the outrage.   Meantime, a terrible tragedy had taken
place in St. Petersburg, where the Emperor Alexander II had been assassinated
by means of a bomb, which was thrown at him after he had descended from his

The Mansion House.—A wet Sunday morning.

carriage.   The Court passed a resolution expressing its indignation and horror,
and its sentiments of deep-felt sympathy and sincere condolence with the Imperial
Family in their sorrow and affliction.   Copies of the resolution were ordered to
be forwarded to the Russian Ambassador and the Duchess of Edinburgh.—The
Corporation ordered the Local Government and Taxation Committee to prepare a
day census of the City, at a cost not exceeding £1,200.—The Music Deputation
was authorised to arrange for concerts by the Guildhall Orchestral Society, at
the Guildhall and Mansion House.—William Corrie, late Remembrancer, died in
his seventy-fifth year (24th). — Sir Chas. Reed, M.P., Deputy, and Chairman
of the London School Board, died on the 25th, in his sixty-second year.
The Corporation, of which Sir Charles was a much respected member, passed
a resolution of condolence with the widow and family.

Sir Charles Reed was educated at the Hackney Grammar School and University College, London, and was, at the time of his death, the head of the Fann Street Letter Foundry, Aldersgate Street. He represented the Borough of Hackney in the House of Commons in the Liberal interest from 1868 to 1874, and St. Ives, Cornwall, from 1880 up to the time of his death. He was first elected to the Common Council in 1861. He was the author of several works, including " A Plea for a Free Library for the City of London," and "The Life and Philanthropic Labours of Andrew Reed, D.D." (father of the author) He was buried at Abney Park Cemetery on the 30th, the funeral being attended by deputations from a large number of representative bodies. The Lord Mayor sent his carriage, and the Board Schools throughout London were closed.

The Lord Mayor presided at the Mansion House at a meeting for the erection of a statue on the Thames Embankment to William Tyndale, "who first translated the New Testament from Greek into English, and who died as a martyr of the faith " (25th).—The Corporation voted 100 guineas to the Mansion House Fund for the relief of sufferers from the Ohio Earthquake (12 Ap.).—Dr. Tristram, Chancellor for the Bishop of London, gave judgment in the Consistory Court, St. Paul's Cathedral, in favour of the rector and churchwardens of St. Mary-at-Hill, Eastcheap, on the application for a faculty to execute certain alterations in the interior of the church (14th).—A great meeting was held at Guildhall, under the presidency of the Lord Mayor, to celebrate the eightieth birthday of the Earl of Shaftesbury, whose religious and philanthropic work had won for him universal esteem. All classes of society were represented, from the humble costermonger, to the Cabinet Minister. An address was presented by Mr. H. R. Williams, on behalf of the children and teachers of the Ragged Schools of London (28th).— The executors of the late Mr. E. J. Esdaile, lay rector and impropriator of the tithes of St. Botolph Without Aldgate, claimed £90,000 as a capitalised value of the tithes of property which the Metropolitan and Metropolitan District Railway Companies were taking for their City extension railway. The arbitration, which occupied nine days, was concluded 4 May, when it was agreed that a schedule of the property to be taken should be supplied to the arbitrator.—The Corporation expressed its great regret at the death of the Earl of Beaconsfield, K.G., which took place at Curzon Street, Mayfair, on 19 Ap., the resolution referring to him as " a statesman, who for so many years exercised his great abilities and talents in his country's service, and whose decease is regarded by men of all shades of political opinion as the nation's loss." The Court gave directions for a marble bust of the ex-Premier to be executed at an expense of £250. A marble bust of Earl Russell, K.G., was also ordered by the Corporation (5 May).—The Lord Mayor gave a banquet to the Rev. Dr. Moffat, the venerable African traveller, and other distinguished visitors at the Mansion House (7th).—Prince Leopold laid the foundation stone of the Technical College, Cowper Street, Finsbury, in the presence of the Lord Mayor and Sheriffs, the Council of the City and Guilds of London Institute, and many members of the Corporation (10th).—The Burgomaster of Vienna offered for the acceptance of the Corporation a copy of an artistically executed representation of the great festival held on the 27 Ap., 1879, in lasting memory of the patriotic celebration of the silver wedding of the Emperor and Empress. The work was deposited in the Guildhall Library (2 June).—A sub-committee of the churchwardens of City parishes issued a draft scheme for a Bill for the management of the City Parochial Charities.—Alderman Sir William Anderson Rose died at the age of seventy (9th). He represented Southampton as a Conservative in the House of Commons from 1862 to 1865.—A census of

Leadenhall Market.

the congregations of City churches and chapels taken on the morning of Sunday, 1 May, 1881, was issued by the *St. James's Gazette*, and re-published in the *City Press* (15th). Afterwards (20 July) a return was issued showing the attendance on all the Sundays of May at a group of four City churches.—The church of St. Margaret, Lothbury, was re-opened after undergoing restoration. The screen erected by Sir Christopher Wren was replaced and the galleries removed. The west window, which had been blocked up by the organ gallery, was opened out and the entire flooring was repaired. In the course of the repairs some interesting relics of the old church of St. Margaret, destroyed by the Great Fire, were found (20 June).—The corner stone of the new Leadenhall Market was laid (28th).—The window erected in memory of the late Rev. E. Auriol, M.A., Rector of St. Dunstan-in-the-West, Fleet Street, was unveiled in the church (29th).—The Corporation resolved to invite the International Medical Congress to a conversazione at Guildhall, at an expense of £2,000 (30th).—The Court also passed a resolution recognising "with utmost satisfaction the spirit of true liberality and religious toleration which has prompted His Majesty King Alphonso XII to invite the Jewish subjects, whether fugitive or otherwise, of foreign countries to establish for themselves a home in the Spanish peninsula, where in the Middle Ages their co-religionists attained such great prosperity" (30th).—Mr. Spencer Walpole's report having been referred to the Fish Supply Committee, the Corporation resolved that the latter's functions should be so extended as to enquire into the question of the food supply generally of the Metropolis, and especially as to the high price of meat. The Committee, however, devoted itself almost exclusively to the question of fish, and on 5 July opened a public enquiry into "the present unsatisfactory state of the fish supply of the Metropolis" in the Exchequer Court at Guildhall.—The Corporation expressed sympathy with the people of the United States in the dastardly attack which had been made upon the life of President Garfield (14 July). The President, after lingering for some time, died of his wounds, and the Corporation again (22 Sept.) expressed its utmost sorrow and regret.—Owing to the remarkable success of the Guildhall School of Music and the large and rapid increase of its membership, it was referred to the City Lands Committee to enquire as to the terms and conditions on which it could be permanently established on some vacant land on the Thames Embankment.—The Lord Mayor gave a banquet at the Mansion House to the King of the Sandwich Islands and to various representatives of the Colonies (16th).—The Prince of Wales laid the foundation stone of the Central College of the City and Guilds of London Institute for the Advancement of Technical Education, at South Kensington (18th).

The Lord Chancellor, in an address to His Royal Highness, said that in consenting to become President of the Institute the Prince had shown in the most marked manner his approval of the endeavour to establish a system of Technical Education for artisans and manufacturers, intimately associated with the purposes for which some of the City Guilds were originally founded. The Institution had grown up by the united efforts of a few of those ancient Guilds, other Livery Companies later on coming to their support. The number of candidates recently examined in various branches of Technology was 1,563, as compared with 816 the previous year. £31,000 had been already subscribed by four Guilds towards the building fund.

At a meeting at the Mansion House a Committee was appointed to take preliminary steps to establish a Chamber of Commerce for London, the Lord Mayor being elected chairman (25th).—The Corporation Fish Enquiry was brought to a close on the 27th, some serious allegations being made by a Yarmouth witness, a consignor of fish, with regard to the alleged "Ring" at Billingsgate. Altogether fifty-eight witnesses had been examined. The Fish Supply Committee presented its report to the Common Council (11 Aug.)

The examination of witnesses had occupied fourteen days and the whole of the evidence had been printed and circulated day by day. The report stated that the evidence proved conclusively that large quantities of immature fish are uselessly destroyed, also that many of the ancient fishing grounds had been and are greatly deteriorated and had ceased to be productive. Legislation, it urged, was necessary to stop this evil. On the question of the carriage of fish the report recommended that the Corporation should seek to obtain the right to representation before the Railway Commissioners. In the opinion of the Committee one wholesale market was calculated to meet the requirements of the trade and the interests of the public. Such market should be at the water-side, and there should be ample approaches, those at Billingsgate being absolutely insufficient. They suggested as a site for a new market the north-east side of Blackfriars Bridge. Billingsgate would be desirable if the adjoining Custom House, or wharves, could be obtained. An inland market in the neighbourhood of Smithfield, for the reception and sale of railway-borne fish, was also required, and an official salesman should be appointed.

City Green Yard.

The Fish Market question having been debated at several meetings of the Common Council it was resolved (15 Sept.) that the Fish Market should be based upon the same system as is at present in existence in Paris, viz., a wholesale, a semi-wholesale, and a retail market, all under one roof, and that an official salesman should be appointed, acting under the control of the Markets Committee.—The City Liberal Club gave a complimentary banquet to Mr. Goschen on his return from Constantinople, where he had been to insist upon the fulfilment of the Berlin Treaty, as regards the Government of Armenia.—The Corporation decided upon the removal of the Gresham Almshouses from the City Mews (or Green Yard),

Whitecross Street, to Brixton, at an expense of £4,000 (28 July).—The Commissioners of Sewers received a letter dated 1 Aug. from Sir E. W. Watkin and Mr. J. S. Forbes, stating they would recommend their constituents to make the proposed street from King William Street to Tower Hill, in connection with the Inner Circle Railway if the contribution from the public bodies were increased from £750,000 to £850,000, and in the hope that the contribution might be payable in sections. It was agreed on the 4th that the contribution of the Commission of Sewers should be increased from £250,000 to £300,000, payable in sections, the new street to be 60 feet wide. The Metropolitan Board of Works, however, declined to depart from the original agreement, which was to contribute £500,000. —The reception given by the Corporation to the International Medical Congress at Guildhall took place on 5 Aug.—A very destructive fire took place at Messrs. Foster and Co.'s premises at the corner of Bread Street, Cheapside (1 Sept.).—The extension of the Metropolitan Railway from Aldgate to Trinity Square, Tower Hill, was formally inaugurated by the Lord Mayor in Chequer House Yard (5th).— At a luncheon, which was given on the same day to celebrate the event, Sir Edward Watkin stated that of the 110,000,000 passengers carried annually by the Metropolitan Railway, 20,000,000 were carried at a penny fare.—The Lord Mayor and Lady Mayoress held a reception of delegates to the Trades Union Congress and their wives at the Mansion House (14th).—The Corporation subscribed 100 guineas to the Mansion House Fund for the sufferers from the disaster to the Mail Steamer, "Teuton" (15th). The fund reached a total of £1,588.— The non-political character of the Corporation and its recognition of great ability and devoted service, in whatever political party they may be found, were remarkably illustrated when a motion for an address to Mr. Gladstone was carried in the Common Council by 104 votes to 14; some uncomplimentary references to the Premier by one of the minority being vigorously repressed and reprobated. The resolution was in the following terms:

That an address, in a suitable gold box, be presented to the Right Hon. William Ewart Gladstone, Prime Minister of England, who for fifty years has occupied a distinguished position and now fills a foremost place in the great Council of the Nation, as a token of the estimation in which he is held by the citizens of London, and of their appreciation of his high character, rare genius, and varied gifts, which have been devoted for so long a period to the service of his country; and that the right hon. gentleman be respectfully invited to sit for a marble bust to be placed in the Guildhall.

A remarkable demonstration took place at the Guildhall, on the occasion of presentation (13 Oct.). The freedom of the City of London having been already presented, the good wishes of the Corporation necessarily took the form of an address, which was signed by the Town Clerk, and read by the Recorder. In the course of his reply, Mr. Gladstone said :

"I desire to express the hope that the day may come when, in consequence of judicious measures, enabling us to deal with this arrear of public business, the great question of Local Government in this vast Metropolis may likewise be entertained by Parliament. Making the declaration on the spot on which I now stand in this noble hall, and in the fresh and vivid recollection of its traditions, I feel I am not disloyal, but loyal, to those traditions in cherishing the hope that the day may not be very far distant when that work shall be taken in hand. But of one thing I feel the most perfect and absolute confidence. Nothing that will ever be sanctioned by the Parliament of this Country will tend to degrade your great Corporation or to impair its efficiency, but only new dignity, new energy, and a further enlargement of public confidence, fresh records of good work done and of great services rendered to the country, will be the unfailing consequence of any such measure as Parliament will adopt for the purpose of dealing with the Municipal institutions of London."

A most dramatic point of the speech was reached when Mr. Gladstone came to speak of the difficulties of Government in Ireland. A few minutes after the commencement of the speech a note bearing an official seal was brought into the hall, and a whisper circulated that it was marked "immediate" and "important," and was from one of the Premier's private secretaries. Earl Spencer opened and read the letter, and passed it on to the Prime Minister, who, without pausing for a moment in his speech, glanced over the contents, and laid the document on the table before him. Then, when he came to announce the determination of the Government to discharge their duties in Ireland, he took it up again and pointing to it, said :

"Even within these few moments I have received the tidings that towards the vindication of law, order, and the rights of property, of the freedom of the land, of the first elements of political life and civilization, the first step has been taken in the arrest of the man who unhappily, from motives which I do not challenge, which I cannot examine, and with which I have nothing to do, has made himself beyond all others prominent in the attempt to destroy the authority of the law, and to substitute what would end in being nothing more nor less than an anarchical oppression exercised upon the people of Ireland."

This allusion to the arrest of Mr. C. S. Parnell, M.P., who was that day lodged in Kilmainham Gaol under the Irish Coercion Act, 1881, was received by the audience with tumultuous applause.—The Lord Mayor, accompanied by the Sheriffs, opened a Leather Trades Exhibition at the Agricultural Hall (26 Sep.).— Sir John Musgrove, Bart. (Lord Mayor in 1850), died at Rusthall House, near Tunbridge Wells, in his eighty-ninth year (5 Oct.). He was the only son of Mr. John Musgrove, a merchant of Austin Friars, residing at Hackney.— The Corporation voted £200 per annum to the Music Deputation for exhibitions, and the Deputation were authorised to apply to the Livery Companies and other sources for donations.—The Common Council discussed the question of Municipal Government, and resolved by 81 votes to 22 that " it would be unwise, if not uncalled for, for the Corporation of the City of London to take the initiative in drafting a scheme affecting representative bodies outside the City."—It was referred to the Port of London Sanitary Committee to enquire into the sanitary condition of the River Thames, in the neighbourhood of Crossness and other outfalls, and to report what steps should be taken to remedy any existing evils thereat, with authority to confer with Her Majesty's Government.—The "Great Eastern" steamship was put up for auction at Lloyd's (19th). The first bid of £20,000 by slow degrees rose to £30,000. No further advance being obtained, the ship was withdrawn.—As an experiment the Egyptian Hall and Saloon at the Mansion House were ordered to be lighted by electricity for twelve months (20th).—Medals were ordered to be struck to commemorate Temple Bar (removed in 1878), and the visit of the King of the Hellenes.—The death of George Russell French (78), for many years architect and surveyor to the Ironmongers' Company and author of several works on Shakespeare, was announced (2 Nov.).—On the recommendation of the Fish Supply Committee it was decided to open the Central Fruit and Vegetable Market, at Smithfield, now approaching completion, as an Inland Fish Market, and Parliamentary powers were obtained for the purpose (3rd).—Alderman John Whittaker Ellis was elected Lord Mayor.—The Corporation voted 200 guineas to the Mansion House Fund for the relief of fishermen, in Eyemouth and the adjacent villages, who had suffered from the recent fishing disaster. The fund amounted to £3,884. The Corporation also subscribed 200 guineas to the Fish Trade Association, for the relief of the widows and orphans of the 200 English coast fishermen who perished about the same time.—The new schools of the Brewers' Company, founded by Dame Alice Owen in 1609, and situated near the Angel at Islington, were opened on the 15th. The new scheme provided for the establishment of a middle-class school of the modern type for the inhabitants of Islington and the neighbourhood.—Sir Henry W. Peek having appealed to the Court of Arches, with respect to the granting of a faculty for certain alterations in the Church of St. Mary-at-Hill, Eastcheap, Lord Penzance reversed the decision of the Court below and the faculty was refused (16th).—The Church of St. Dunstan-in-the-West was re-opened after restoration (24th).—The Court of Aldermen received a letter from the Home Secretary stating that, after 1 Jan. next, prisoners on remand from Guildhall, or the Mansion House, should be sent to the prison at Clerkenwell and not to Newgate, as heretofore (26th)—The Lord Mayor opened the International Exhibition of Smoke-Preventing Appliances at South Kensington

(30th).—The Markets Committee were authorised to expend out of the revenues of the Foreign Cattle Market £8,000, in purchasing a suitable vessel for the trans-shipment of cattle to the Market (1 Dec.).—The church of St. Mary-le-Bow, Cheapside, was re-opened (15th), the service being announced by the famous peal of bells, increased from ten to twelve in number.—The new Leadenhall Market was opened by the Lord Mayor (15th).

Cheapside and the Church of St. Mary-le-Bow.

This market occupies part of the site of the ancient manor of Leadenhall, which in 1309 was owned by Sir Hugh Neville, and in 1408 was purchased by Sir Richard Whittington. In the hall of the old manor house were kept the military arms and accoutrements for the protection of the City. So far back as 1309 a market of some description existed on the manor of Leadenhall, and in 1357 poultry was ordered to be sold there. About 1662, when Leadenhall was the great Meat Market, the Spanish Ambassador, after visiting it, told King Charles II that he believed more meat was sold in that market alone than in the whole of Spain. The new market has a light and cheerful appearance, with a principal entrance from Gracechurch Street. Intersecting the main arcade is another running from the main gateway on the Leadenhall Street side to the southern extremity of the building. The cost of re-building was £99,000, and the cost of the approaches and avenues came to £148,800 more, the latter amount having been borrowed on the credit of the general revenues of the Corporation. The whole sum, £247,800, remains as a debt upon the market.

The Local Government and Taxation Committee presented its report on the Day Census of the City of London, which had been taken by order of the Corporation, and which was afterwards published as a volume. This little work contains a large amount of valuable statistical information not otherwise obtainable, and shows the relative importance of the City in a way which Dr. Farr, Statistical Superintendent in the Registrar-General's Office, admitted was not shown in the Imperial Census.—The Port Sanitary Committee prepared an elaborate report on the condition of the Thames, which was communicated to the Home Secretary. —The Corporation voted 500 guineas in aid of the new building for the City of London College, and £5,000 out of the grain duty towards the expenses of the proposed park and recreation ground at Paddington.—The Guildhall Orchestral Society gave a very successful performance of the "Messiah" at Guildhall, under the direction of Mr. Weist Hill, the Principal (17th).—A fund for the defence of property in Ireland was started at the Mansion House, and reached a total of £21,422, but the subject gave rise to some controversy (28th).—The City of London Commissioners of Sewers (Artizans' Dwellings) Act was passed this year to enable the Commissioners to raise money at a cheaper rate of interest.—The late Mr. William Ward, of Brixton Hill, by his will dated 3 June, 1881, bequeathed £20,000 to the Mayor and Commonalty and Citizens of the City of London, for the building and maintenance, on lands belonging to them, of a High School for Girls to be called "The City of London School for Girls, founded by William Ward." Chancery proceedings delayed the carrying out of this scheme.

1882.

IN the enlarged and renovated saloon at the Mansion House the Lord Mayor, as president of the City of London Society of Artists, presented a marble bust to Alderman Sir F. W. Truscott in recognition of the services which he had rendered to the Society as its first president (5 Jan., 1882).—On the recommendation of the Port of London Sanitary Committee the Corporation communicated with the Home Secretary with a view to action being taken under the provisions of the 21st and 22nd Vic. Cap. 104 Sec. 31 to improve the sanitary condition of the Thames in the neighbourhood of Crossness and other outfalls (19th).—

The first general meeting of the London Chamber of Commerce was held in the Egyptian Hall, Mansion House, the Lord Mayor presiding (26th).— An interesting ceremony took place at Christ's Hospital, the occasion being the presentation to the Governors of the Institution of a bust of the late Major Sir P. Louis Cavagnari, a former scholar who had ended a brilliant career in a most tragical manner at Cabul, during the recent campaign in Afghanistan. The Duke of Cambridge presided (31st).—The Corporation voted £500 to the Mansion House Fund, for the relief of Jews suffering from persecution in Russia (2 Feb.). On the same day a large and influential meeting was held at the Mansion House, and the Earl of Shaftesbury, Cardinal Manning, and others, strongly denounced the Russian persecutions. The resolutions passed were forwarded to the Prime Minister and Foreign Secretary. The fund reached a total of £108,809.—A meeting was held in the Egyptian Hall, Mansion House (14 Mar.) for the encouragement of the British Woollen Industries.

> The Lord Mayor presided, and the Marquis of Salisbury moved a resolution "that under present circumstances it is a matter of national interest that the purchasers of textile fabrics should as far as possible give the preference to goods of British origin"

It was referred to a Special Committee to consider the announcement in the Queen's speech having reference to the reform of the Corporation of London, and the extension of Municipal Government to the Metropolis, with instructions to do therein as they might deem expedient (16th).—The Lord Mayor opened St. Bride's Youths' Institute, Shoe Lane, Fleet Street, intended especially for the hundreds of lads employed in the numerous printing establishments in the neighbourhood (20th).—The following resolutions were passed by the Corporation and forwarded to Her Majesty's Government and the Postmaster-General.

> 1. That an Inland Parcels Post, a reduction in the price of Telegrams and the introduction of the Telephone into the Postal Service should be established. 2. That the Head Office of the General Post Office be retained in the City (2 Mar.)

A special meeting of the Common Council resolved upon an address, expressing deep indignation at the late "dastardly and traitorous attack" on the Queen at Windsor (3 Mar.).—The Prince of Wales, who had accepted the presidency of the City and Guilds of London Technical Institute, took the chair at the annual meeting of the Institute in Mercers' Hall (13th).

> It was stated, that since the last annual report the funds had been augmented by contributions from eight additional companies, viz. the Grocers, Skinners, Vintners, Tallowchandlers, Plumbers, Wheelwrights, Bowyers and Curriers. The classes of the City School of Art had been transferred to the Finsbury Technical College.

The Duke of Connaught, Prince Christian, and others attended a conference at the Mansion House with a view to the permanent establishment and endowment of a Royal College of Music (20th).—A select committee of the House of Commons passed the preamble of the Bill for establishing a river-side fish market, at Shadwell, of which Mr. Hewett was the chief promoter (24th).   The Corporation opposed the Bill.—The Corporation passed an address of congratulation to the Queen, on the occasion of the marriage of H.R.H. Prince Leopold, Duke of Albany, K.G., with Her Serene Highness Princess Helen of Waldeck (19 Ap.).—The Bishop of London introduced a Bill in the House of Lords for the appointment of seven "City Benefices Commissioners" to effect the union of City livings.—The Duke of Edinburgh presided at a public meeting in the Mansion House, in support of the proposal to hold an International Fisheries Exhibition in London next year (20th).—The Queen formally declared Epping Forest open to the use and enjoyment of the public for ever (6 May).

Her Majesty, accompanied by Princess Beatrice went in state from Windsor to the Forest, where they were received by the Lord Mayor and Sheriffs, the Duke of Connaught, Ranger of the Forest, the Epping Forest Committee, etc   The general public assembled in large numbers to witness the interesting ceremonial   The address which was presented to Her Majesty contained the following expressions :—"The Royal Forest was for many centuries a hunting ground for the Sovereigns of this Kingdom.   It has been reserved for your Majesty in the gracious exercise of Royal prerogative, with the consent of Parliament, for Royal privilege to substitute popular right, and to dedicate these beautiful scenes to the enjoyment of your people for ever.   Many difficulties which had to be overcome in bringing about this happy result are at length terminated, and an open space of nearly 6,000 acres of almost unbroken forest scenery, extending from the confines of the Metropolis for a distance of thirteen miles, is now available for public health and recreation."   The total area of the forest (including Wanstead Park, but not Highams Park) is 5,529 acres. For the 1,842 acres, purchased under the orders of the arbitrator, £77,506 was paid for purchase-money and £17,032 for costs   The price per acre varied from £25 to £300 and averaged £70. There was also compensation for lopping rights, etc., the total sum paid being £109,505.   Of the 3,000 acres of illegal enclosures existing in 1876 only about 500 acres remained enclosed at the end of the arbitration, 2,500 acres having been restored to the Forest, in addition to the 3,000 acres of then existing open forest land.

Shortly after the Phœnix Park murders, the Common Council expressed "the feelings of horror and indignation" with which its members had heard of the assassinations, and conveyed to Lady Frederick Cavendish and Miss Burke their deep sympathy.   Lord Frederick Cavendish was a Liveryman of the Cloth-workers' Company.—A canister, containing explosives, was found attached to the rails at the back of the Mansion House.—On Ascension day the ancient custom of "beating the bounds" was observed in several of the City parishes (18th).— The return of Mr. Polydore De Keyser, as Alderman, was petitioned against on the ground that he was an innkeeper and an alien born, and was therefore disqualified (22nd).   A special meeting of the Aldermen was called to hear counsel argue the question (20 June), and they ultimately gave their decision in favour of Mr. De Keyser, a result which met with general approval.—The new bell for St. Paul's Cathedral, "Great Paul," weighing 17 tons, which was cast at Lough-borough, arrived at its destination after having been eleven days on the journey of 112 miles by road; it was dedicated at the Cathedral (22 May).   On the bell is the Latin inscription: *Væ mihi si non evangelisavero (Woe unto me if I preach not the gospel).*—A baronetcy was announced for the Lord Mayor and knighthood for the Sheriffs (Mr. Alderman Hanson and Mr. W. A. Ogg).—The Corporation offered to the Italian nation its deep sympathy on the loss of its most illustrious citizen, Giuseppe Garibaldi, "whose courage and disinterested patriotism had so largely conduced to make Italy united and free" (8 June).—A sum of £5,000 was voted by the Corporation, in aid of the Royal College of Music, in annual sums of £1,000 for five years.—The Court resolved to oppose the Bishop of London's Bill for the further destruction of City churches.—A Parliamentary return (issued 13 June) showed that within the five years, 1877–81, sixty-eight bodies (sixty male and eight female) were found in the Thames within the precincts of the City of London district.   Twenty-five were cases of accidental death, two of murder, and nine of suicide, while in thirty-two cases no opinion was expressed as to the cause of death.—The Prince of Wales unveiled the statue to Sir Rowland Hill (Onslow Ford, sculptor), erected by public subscription at the Royal Exchange.   The statue is of bronze, on a granite pedestal, bearing the inscription, "Rowland Hill—he founded uniform penny postage" (17th).—It was announced that a Royal Commission had been appointed, with reference to the pollution of the Thames (22nd).

The first meeting of the Commission was held on the 25th when the Corporation, the Thames Conservancy, and several other bodies appeared as complainants and the Metropolitan Board of Works as respondents.   The amount disbursed by the Corporation, in connection with the London Water Supply, from 1876 to 1892, was £51,067 4s. 2d.

The Prince and Princess of Wales opened the Technical School at Bradford (the gift of the Clothworkers' Company), in the presence of the Lord Mayor and Lady Mayoress, the members of the Technical Commission, and representatives of the Guild of Clothworkers (23rd).—Mr. Deputy Shephard, Chairman of the Gresham Committee (City side) laid the foundation stone of the new Gresham Almshouses, Brixton (26th).—The Corporation subscribed 100 guineas to the Egyptian Refugees Relief Fund at the Mansion House; the total subscriptions reached £8,152.—Mr. James Abbiss, J.P., for twenty-five years Chairman of the City of London Union, died in his seventy-first year (7 July).

Mr. Abbiss was formerly a Sheriff, and Alderman for the Ward of Bridge, having resigned the latter office in 1867.   He was also treasurer of the Earlswood Asylum for Idiots.

The church of St. Peter, Cornhill, was re-opened after renovation.—The Cooks' Company celebrated its fourth centenary at the Crystal Palace (11th).— This being the 300th anniversary of the completion of Sir Francis Drake's circum-navigation of the globe, a meeting was held at the Mansion House to raise a fund for the erection at Plymouth Hoe of a national memorial to the Elizabethan hero (19th).—An Act was obtained empowering the Corporation to convert their London Central Fruit, Vegetable and Flower Market, then approaching completion, into an Inland Fish Market and to continue the use of Farringdon Market for the sale of fruit and vegetables (20th).—The Lord Mayor and others passed over the completed portion of the Inner Circle Railway, from Aldgate Station to Trinity Square, Tower Hill.—The final award in connection with the Epping Forest Arbitration was signed at Old Palace Yard, Westminster, and an historical statement was made by the City Solicitor (24th); the work of the Corporation in connection with the Forest was further developed by the opening of Wanstead Park, a charming old pleasure ground (1 Aug.)—A scheme for effecting the union of the parishes of St. Vedast alias Foster and St. Michael-le-Querne with those of St. Matthew, Friday Street and St. Peter Cheap, having been approved by Her Majesty, the church of St. Vedast was re-opened on the 14th.   The Rev. W. Sparrow Simpson, D.D., F.S.A., rector of St. Matthew, Friday Street, and St. Peter Cheap, was inducted to the living of St. Vedast, Foster Lane.— The Common Council sanctioned an arrangement with the Commissioners of Sewers for the widening of Temple Street, Tudor Street and Bouverie Street, the Corporation giving up land in Temple Street and Tudor Street to be thrown into the public way; the Corporation also contributed a sum of £1,000 towards the improvement, and the cost of setting back the Value House, in Tudor Street, belonging to the Gas Light and Coke Company, estimated at £5,000.—The Lord Mayor and Sheriffs left London on a State visit to Holland, where they were most hospitably entertained by the King of the Netherlands and the civic authorities at the Hague.   The Lord Mayor took occasion to present the King with the Corporation address in a gold box.—During the work of demolition in Fleet Street, between Chancery Lane and the new Law Courts, the houses fronting the "Cock Tavern" were pulled down.—The Horners' Company held an interesting exhibi-tion at the Mansion House (25th Oct.).—An interesting double ceremony took place at the Guildhall, when the Lord Mayor unveiled the busts of the two great political rivals—Mr. Gladstone and Lord Beaconsfield.

The bust of Mr. Gladstone, by his own wish, had been classically treated in Greek form by Mr. T. Woolner, R.A , the pure white marble, called Pentelicon, having been quarried near Athens and sent as a present from the Greeks. The bust of Earl Beaconsfield, in the robes of the Garter, was of Carrara marble and was executed by Mr. Richard Belt.

The Corporation contributed 200 guineas to the Egyptian War Fund, in aid of the families of our wounded soldiers, sailors, and marines (26th).— Alderman Henry Edmund Knight was elected Lord Mayor.--Owing to the approaching completion of the Law Courts, the Civic procession to Westminster, for the purpose of presenting the Lord Mayor to the Judges, took place for the last time on the 9th Nov. At the Guildhall banquet in the evening Mr. Gladstone made an important reference to the London Government Bill, in the course of which he said ·

"You will still meet in this ancient Hall from year to year as the representatives of the first Municipal Community in the world, strengthened as I hope and invigorated by whatever changes may come upon you, and associated as you have ever been with the history of the country ; able as you have ever been found to meet the demands of public duty"

The Commissioners of Sewers affirmed by resolution that it was desirable to allow the electric lighting experiments to be conducted at the expense of the Companies instead of at the cost of the ratepayers (21st).—The dignity of K.C.M.G. was conferred upon Alderman Sir William M'Arthur, M.P. (late Lord Mayor).—At the triennial election of the London School Board Alderman Sir Reginald Hanson, Mr. H. C. Richards, Mr. H. Spicer, and Miss Davenport Hill were returned for the City, Sir John Bennett and Mr. Bonnewell being unsuccessful candidates.—The Corporation ordered from the artist, Mr. Hamilton P. McCarthy, a replica of his bust (at Fishmongers' Hall) of the Right Hon. Russell Gurney, for twenty-two years Recorder of the City (30th).—The Corporation agreed to purchase from Mr. Edmond Byron, Lord of the Manor, his interest in 347 acres of unenclosed portions of the four commons known as Riddlesdown, Kenley, Farthing Downs, and Coulsdon for the sum of £7,000, to be paid out of the City of London Grain Duty.—The Queen, accompanied by Princess Christian and Princess Beatrice, opened the new Law Courts, erected after the designs of G. E. Street, R.A., the ceremonial being attended by the Lord Mayor and other representatives of the Corporation (4 Dec.).—A great fire devastated a portion of Wood Street on the 8th.

The block of buildings where the fire broke out, and which was almost entirely gutted, was bounded on the north by London Wall, on the south by Addle Street, on the east by Philip Lane, and on the west by Wood Street, and was occupied by Messrs. Rylands and Company,

Limited, warehousemen ; Messrs Foster, Porter and Company, Limited , Messrs Silber and Fleming ; Messrs. Sargood, Butler and Nichol, and others. The fire originated in Messrs. Foster, Porter and Company's premises and destroyed an enormous amount of property, the claims upon the insurance companies being upwards of a million sterling   Brewers' Hall and the Library of Sion College had a narrow escape

In view of this disastrous fire in Wood Street, the Corporation referred it to the Gas and Water Committee to consider the advisability of applying to Parliament for better protection from fire in the City of London. The Commissioners of Sewers at the same time decided to widen the thoroughfare and to secure the necessary ground in Wood Street for that purpose (19th).—The Prince of Wales, who was accompanied by the Princess of Wales, opened the City of London School on the Victoria Embankment (12th)

The boys and their friends assembled in the commodious playground at the back of the building, and nearly a thousand persons were accommodated with seats in the large hall. The Lord Mayor (an old City of London School boy) and the Lady Mayoress, accompanied by the Sheriffs (Mr. Alderman De Keyser and Mr. Savory), came in state from the Mansion House ; the Town Clerk read an address briefly relating the history of the school, which was supplemented by some remarks from the Lord Mayor, after which the Prince of Wales declared the building opened   It was announced that through the beneficence of a lady (Miss Alston) who wished to erect a memorial to her father, late of the City, the two large windows at the east end of the hall were to be filled with stained glass containing life-size figures of Greek and English poets and philosophers   All the foundations of the school building are carried to an average depth of 28 feet below the level of the school playground, and large rectangular holes were sunk through the made ground down to a bed of Thames ballast, which was met with at that level over the whole site, and which doubtless formed at one time the bottom of the river. The hat and coat room, dining-room, and covered playground are on the basement, the administration rooms and library are on the ground floor, the great hall on the first floor, natural science school and lecture hall on the second floor, and twenty class rooms are distributed over the building   The gymnasium is a detached building in the playground   The exterior, facing the Embankment, is constructed entirely of Portland stone, but the columns of the windows have polished red granite shafts   The style is that of the Renaissance enriched with carving and sculpture. The Embankment front of the building is 120 feet long and a wide flight of steps leads up to the porch. The tympana beneath the arched heads of the first floor windows are filled in with allegorical seated figures representing various arts and sciences, and the wall spaces between these have square-headed niches containing portrait statues of Bacon, Sir Thomas More, Shakespeare, Milton, and Newton   The great hall is 100 feet by 45 feet with a handsome open-timbered roof 38 feet high. The floor is of oak and the walls are faced with Portland stone. The building, which was designed by Messrs Davis and Emanuel, architects, cost about £100,000, and the ground upon which it was erected, and which was a free gift of the Corporation, was estimated to be worth £100,000 more

The Corporation voted 100 guineas for the relief of sufferers by the destruction of the Alhambra Theatre by fire (14th).—During the year, Shaftesbury House, Aldersgate Street, was pulled down.—The Chios Earthquake Relief Fund at the Mansion House amounted to £24,750. The other Mansion House Funds were for Irish Ladies in Distress £16,464 ; Emigration £196 ; Sir Rowland Hill Memorial £18,507

1883.

THE Corporation subscribed 200 guineas to the Mansion House Fund for sufferers from the great fire at Kingston, Jamaica (18 Jan., 1883). The fund reached a total of £7,867.—The Corporation offered their condolence and sympathy to the French people, on the loss of their great statesman, M. Léon Gambetta.—The first annual meeting of the London Chamber of Commerce, was held in the Egyptian Hall, Mansion House, the Lord Mayor presiding. It was reported that there were 1,386 members, of whom 117 were life members (24th).—The Markets Committee were instructed by the Corporation to appoint an official salesman for the Central Fish Market (1 Feb.).—A design by Mr. Charles Barry for covering over the area of the Royal Exchange having been accepted, the Coal and Corn and Finance Committee were instructed to pay £6,000 as the City's half of the cost (15th.)—Mr. Philip Magnus, Director of the City and Guilds of London Institute, delivered an inaugural address at the opening of the new Finsbury Technical College (19th).—A letter was received by the Corporation from the Home Office, dated 19 Feb., asking that the Secretary, Sir William Harcourt, might be supplied with copies of all accounts relating to the income and expenditure of the City of London, including the amounts raised by rates and the amounts received from the property of the City, together with copies of reports made by sanitary and other officers. Sir John Monckton (Town Clerk) forwarded the documents required (21st). On 1 Mar. the Common Council resolved to refer this correspondence to the Special Committee to take such further action thereon as might be deemed expedient, with a view to afford any additional information that the Home Secretary might require.—The Corporation subscribed £1,000 to the International Fisheries Exhibition, in view of the great benefits accruing from the fisheries industry, not only as supplying a staple commodity of food, but as the nursery for the sailors of our mercantile marine.—A quaint ceremony was observed at the church of St. Mary-le-Bow, Cheapside, in confirmation of the election of Dr. Benson to the See of Canterbury (3rd).

The proceedings were opened in the large vestry room, in which until so recently as the reign of George IV the Archbishop's Court of Peculiars was held. Here Dr. Deane, Q C., the Vicar-General of the Province, presented to the Archbishop-elect Dr Tristram, Q C., Commissary-General to the City and Diocese of Canterbury, and other officers. Dr. Tristram then asked the Archbishop-elect to give his consent to the election, which having been duly signed by Dr. Benson, morning prayers were read, and the legal business was proceeded with. At one time the Archbishop's Court of Arches was held at Bow Church,

In the appeal case of Mr. C. H. Robarts (late Remembrancer) and the Corporation, the Master of the Rolls and Lords Justices Baggallay and Lindley, without hearing the Counsel for the Corporation, gave judgment for the respondents (9th).—A resolution viewing with alarm the enormous increase in the School Board rate was carried at a meeting of the Commissioners of Sewers (20th).—The Grocers' Company issued a scheme for the encouragement of original research in sanitary science, establishing three research scholarships, each of £250 a year, and a discovery prize of £1,000, to be given once every

King's Weigh House Chapel, 1830.

four years.—Divine service was celebrated in the King's Weigh-house Chapel, Fish Street Hill, for the last time, on Sunday 1 Ap. The church had existed more than 200 years, the first pastor, Samuel Slater, having died in 1670. The site of the chapel was needed for the completion of the Inner Circle Railway.—The Cutlers' Company presented the freedom of their guild to Lord Alcester (3rd).— The Corporation resolved that the sums hitherto paid to the sheriffs should be commuted for a fixed annual sum of £814 15s. 8d., to be paid out of the City's cash, being the same amount as was then paid under various ancient charters (5th).—Lord Wolseley, G.C.B., and Lord Alcester, G.C.B., having returned from Egypt were presented, the former with an address, and the latter with the Freedom (11th).—The Lord Mayor opened a fund at the Mansion House for the sufferers from the terrible gales on the north-east coast (12th). The Corporation subscribed 300 guineas, and the fund altogether amounted to £1,796.—The Duke of Albany laid the foundation stone of the new buildings for the Birkbeck Institution, in Bream's Buildings, Fetter Lane, His Royal Highness being received there by the Lord Mayor and Sheriffs and the Building Committee (23rd).—The foundation stone of the New Council Chamber at Guildhall, was laid (30th). In connection with this work many ancient portions of the Guildhall were removed, including the old Exchequer Chamber. For the first time for many years the windows of the crypt were exposed, and the illustration gives a view of the old west doorway. — The Royal College of Music, to which the Corporation and City Companies had largely contributed, was opened by the Prince of Wales on the 7th May.—The Lord Mayor, accompanied by the Sheriffs, opened the new Central Fish Market in Farringdon Street (10th). The building, which was originally intended as a market for fruit and vegetables, cost about £160,000, and, together with the site, was valued at £436,000, the expense of converting it into a fish market being £5,000.

Doorway of Western Crypt, Guildhall.

The plan of the market gave an area of nearly 44,000 feet, devoted to wholesale market purposes, surrounded by forty-one shops without dwellings, fronting the several streets, which could be used for retail or other purposes; these occupied an additional area of 16,800 feet. The market area was approached by three main or vehicular entrances and two for foot passengers, and consisted of a series of shops or stalls, thirty-three in number, having in front stands for barrows, etc. It was stated that in a little over thirty years the Corporation had spent nearly three millions of money on the erection of markets, which had conferred great benefits on the people of London.

The Prince of Wales opened the International Fisheries Exhibition at South Kensington, the Corporation sending twenty-five representatives (12th).

In the evening the occasion was celebrated by a banquet at Fishmongers' Hall, the company including the Prince of Wales, the Duke of Edinburgh, the Duke of Connaught, the Duke of Albany, the Duke of Cambridge, the Duke of Teck, etc.

The Duke of Connaught took up his freedom at Merchant Taylors' Hall (18th).—Coulsdon Commons, which had been acquired by the Corporation under the Corporation of London (Open Spaces) Act, 1878, were opened by Mr. Shaw Lefevre, First Commissioner of Works, in the presence of the Lord Mayor and Sheriffs and members of the Corporation.

The commons included Farthing Downs, 121 a. 1 r. 39 p.; Riddlesdown, 78 a. 3 r. 5 p.; Coulsdon Common, 76 a. 3 r. 38 p., Kenley Common, 70 a. 0 r. 20 p., in all a total acreage of 347 acres 1 rood and 22 perches. The subject was first brought under the notice of the Corporation in July, 1878, by two gentlemen named Hall, of Kenley, near Croydon, who the previous year had taken legal proceedings in Chancery, with some success, to prevent the enclosure of the commons by the Lord of the Manor. The unenclosed portions of the commons were eventually purchased for a sum of £7,000, the purchase being completed on 5 Feb., 1883. The cost of maintenance in 1892 was £331 4s. 1d, charged to the Grain Duty account.

At a special Quarter Sessions at Guildhall, a jury awarded £19,698 as compensation for the freehold and goodwill of the "Cock Tavern," Fleet Street.—In pursuance of a petition from the Corporation, it was ordered by Her Majesty in Council that all issues or enquiries at Nisi Prius which would otherwise be tried and executed in the Court of the City of London should for ever hereafter be tried and executed at the new Courts of Justice (22nd).—The Law and City Courts' Committee reported on the bequest for charitable purposes affecting the City of London, by the late Thomas Alexander Mitchell, M.P., and four members of the Corporation were elected as representatives on the Board of Trustees (24th).

The fund in 1879 amounted to about £60,000, and under the will another £40,000 would under certain conditions be eventually added to it. The scheme settled by the Court of Chancery and confirmed by an order of the 20 Jan., 1883, directs that the trustees shall be fifteen in number, nine representative and six co-optative. Of the former, four were to be appointed by the Corporation, three by the London School Board and two by the governing body of Christ's Hospital. One third of the income of the charity is to be applied for the relief of the poor of the City of London by monetary assistance, grants to dispensaries, workmen's clubs, and pensions to deserving and necessitous persons, and the remaining two-thirds for the advanced education and benefit of the children of poor parents connected with the City of London, by apprenticeship premiums, weekly payments to encourage attendance at school, the granting of scholarship exhibitions, rewards and prizes, the maintenance of orphans, etc.

In accordance with a recommendation of the Port Sanitary Committee, a hospital was ordered to be built on the Kentish shore, in the immediate neighbourhood of the hospital ship "Rhin."—It was decided to offer for sale the site of the City of London School, in Milk Street. The freehold building was sold privately (10 Aug.) and fetched the sum of £65,000.—Mr. Gladstone announced that the London Municipal Reform Bill would not be proceeded with this session (29 May).—The Lord Mayor presided at a meeting at the Mansion House, in aid of a fund for providing a new diocese of Southwell, in accordance with the Act passed in 1878 (1 June).—The Commissioners of Sewers gave instructions to acquire property for the widening of Queen Street, Cheapside, at a cost of about £105,000 (5th).— An exhibition of Irish lace, with a view to creating an interest in this industry, was opened at the Mansion House by the Duke of Connaught, who was accompanied by the Duchess. Some very fine specimens of work were contributed by Her Majesty and the Princess of Wales.—Dr. William Spottiswoode, F.R.S., died at the age of fifty-eight.

He succeeded his father as manager of the business of the Queen's Printers, was President of the British Association in 1878, and was elected President of the Royal Society in 1879. The remains were deposited in Westminster Abbey on 5 July.

The Corporation agreed to pay the Commissioners of Sewers £4,100 for the purpose of widening Fenchurch Street.—The Prince of Wales, accompanied by the Princess, opened the new buildings of the City of London College, White Street, Moorfields (7 July).

This excellent institution was originated by the Rev. Prebendary Mackenzie, M.A. (rector of Allhallows, Lombard Street), and the Rev. Prebendary Whittington, M.A (rector of St. Peter-upon-Cornhill) in 1848; it was then known as the Metropolitan Evening Classes, which met at Crosby Hall, Bishopsgate Street. In 1860 these classes were transferred to Sussex Hall, Leadenhall Street, and constituted the City of London College. The growth of the work and the increasing number of students had rendered a new building absolutely essential. The site in White Street was granted by the Charity Commissioners, and the cost of the building, which is of red brick, with dressings of Portland stone, was about £16,000. The large Hall is capable of seating 1,000 persons.

Deputy Henry Lowman Taylor, J.P., a very active member of the Corporation, died at Anerley.—An Embroidery Exhibition, in connection with the Royal School of Art Needlework, South Kensington, was opened by Princess Christian at the Mansion House (11th).—The new Parcels Post came into operation, and during the first four days nearly 30,000 parcels were delivered in London (1 Aug.).—On the same day the limits of the Port of London Sanitary Authority were defined by a Treasury Minute. These limits extend down both sides of the river Thames, from high water mark at Teddington Lock to an imaginary line drawn from the Pilot mark, at the entrance of Havengore Creek, to the Land's End at Warden Point, in the Island of Sheppey.—The City of London Parochial Charities Act was passed on the 20th.—The Lord Mayor opened a fund at the Mansion House for the relief of sufferers by the recent earthquake in the Island of Ischia, outside the Bay of Naples, when more than 5,000 lives were lost. The fund reached a total of £2,933, the Corporation contributing 200 guineas (21st).—The Lord Mayor laid the foundation stone of a new public hall at Loughton, provided out of the funds (£2,780), awarded by the arbitrator as compensation by the Corporation for the loss by the inhabitants of Epping Forest of their rights of lopping (18 Sep.).—A fire broke out at the Foreign Cattle Market, Deptford, resulting in the destruction of £10,000 worth of property.—The Corporation voted 200 guineas to the Mansion House Fund for the sufferers from cholera in Egypt. The fund reached a total of £2,910.—The election of Lord Mayor on 29 Sept. was the occasion of a sharp conflict between the Livery and the Aldermen.

Mr. Simeon Charles Hadley was the next Alderman in rotation for the Civic chair, and his supporters assembled in large numbers at the Common Hall. It was understood that the Aldermen would refuse to accept his nomination if returned by the Livery. The latter voted almost unanimously in his favor. The Sheriffs declared that the choice of the Livery had fallen upon Simeon Charles Hadley and Robert Nicholas Fowler, M.P. This decision was loudly and repeatedly challenged, but the Aldermen retired to their chamber and after the lapse of half-an-hour returned to the hustings, when it was at once seen that the selection had not fallen upon Mr. Hadley. A stormy scene immediately followed. The Livery hooted, and hissed, and shouted "Hadley," and it was some time before the Recorder could be heard making the announcement that the election had fallen upon Mr Alderman Fowler. The Lord Mayor could not for a considerable time obtain a hearing, and the Lord Mayor elect said he had come there that morning without the smallest idea that this honour would be conferred upon him. Mr. Alderman Hadley thanked the Livery for their sympathy and support, and said he could not imagine why the usual course had not been taken by his brethren the Aldermen. The storm having somewhat abated the customary votes of thanks were passed, together with the following resolution —"That the Liverymen of the City of London assembled in Common Hall view with alarm the interference with the rights, liberty and freedom of the Livery to elect their Lord Mayor, and call upon the Common Council to take such steps as they may in their judgment deem expedient to abolish the selection of an Alderman in opposition to the rights and privileges of this Livery."

Subsequent events fully justified the course taken by the Court of Aldermen on this occasion.—Burnham Beeches, which had been purchased by the Corporation, were dedicated to the use and enjoyment of the public by the Duke of Buckingham and Chandos, Lord Lieutenant of the County, in the presence of the Lord Mayor and Corporation (4 Oct.).

The story of Burnham Beeches, one of the most beautiful stretches of woodland scenery within easy access of London, may be told in a few words. On 24 June, 1879, Messrs. Driver and Co put up to auction at the Mart, Tokenhouse Yard, the property described as portions of the Dropmore Estate, which included in one lot 374 acres of open wood and common, and 175 acres of enclosed woodlands, farmhouse and orchards. The sale was not effected, but as the result of some correspondence between Mr F G Heath and the Corporation, the latter resolved to purchase the wood and common for the use and enjoyment of the public. It being thought that someone might try to make money out of the business, Sir H. W. Peek bought up the whole at the reserve price of £12,000, and the Corporation agreed to purchase the 374 acres of open land for £6,000, Sir H. W. Peek retaining the enclosed land and paying the difference. The Corporation also agreed to pay £3,000 as the value of the timber, and to make the necessary roads. The Duke of Buckingham on the day of dedication referred to the Beeches as a valued remnant of the old Chiltern Wood. The principal road through the

Old Sion College, London Wall.

Beeches was named the Duke's Drive, the other main paths receiving the names of the Lord Mayor's Drive, Bedford Road, and Halse Drive. The Mayor and Corporation of Wycombe took occasion to present an address of thanks to the Lord Mayor for the great boon which had been conferred upon the town by the preservation of the wood and common.

The Bridge House Estates Committee were authorised to obtain Parliamentary powers to establish or maintain one or more steam ferries across the Thames, east of London Bridge (18th).—The Corporation granted the governors of Sion College the lease of a plot of land on the Victoria Embankment for eighty years at £1,265 per annum, with the option of purchasing the freehold for £31,625.—The Commissioners of Sewers resolved to widen Old Broad Street to 39 feet, and decided that it was desirable to proceed with the diagonal street from Monument Yard to the Coal Exchange (23rd). — On the occasion of his entering upon the 100th year of his age, the Common Council offered its sincere and hearty congratulations to Sir Moses Montefiore, Bart., who in 1837 filled the office of Sheriff of London and Middlesex.—The Common Council passed a resolution sympathising with the poorer classes of the Metropolis who had been turned out of their homes to make way for public improvements, and instructed the Finance Committee to see what funds were available for providing artizans' dwellings in districts where they might be specially needed.—M. De Lesseps, constructor of the Suez Canal, was present at the Lord Mayor's banquet (9 Nov.). — The Corporation voted £6,000, half the cost of removing the projecting houses in Long Lane, which were an obstruction to the traffic.— The Lord Mayor presided at a crowded and enthusiastic meeting at the Mansion House to protest against the proposed alteration of the Bechuanaland frontier in favour of the Transvaal. The Earl of Shaftesbury and Mr. W. E. Forster, M.P., were among those who spoke in the interest of the natives (27th).—The Corporation resolved to co-operate with the Prince of Wales and the Livery Committees in promoting the forthcoming International Health Exhibition, and contributed £5,000, with a guarantee of £10,000 in furtherance of the object (29th).—Mr. Alderman Finnis, senior member of the Court of Aldermen and Father of the Corporation, died in his eighty-third year (30th).— The reconstruction of the Fenchurch Street terminus of the Great Eastern Railway Company was completed (5 Dec.).—Lady Ellis was presented at the Mansion House with a marble bust of Alderman Sir John Whittaker Ellis, by inhabitants of Broad Street Ward, as a mark of their appreciation of her genial courtesy and of the distinguished services of her husband during his mayoralty.—The Commissioners of Sewers voted a sum of £2,050 towards the widening of New Broad Street (20th).—Mansion House Funds were raised in connection with the Irish Famine, £5,571; Destitution in the Western Islands of Scotland, £5,539; Clay Cross Colliery disaster, £1,681; Anatolia Earthquake, £295.— Dolly's Chop House, Queen's Head Passage, Paternoster Row, was pulled down. — The Gresham Almshouses having been removed from the City Mews or Green-yard, Lower Whitecross Street, the old buildings were used as dwellings for married constables of the City police. The new Almshouses, erected at Brixton, cost £4,250, the amount being paid out of the City's cash.

1884.

THE Commissioners of Sewers decided to take property for the new diagonal street from Monument Yard to the Coal Exchange in Thames Street (4 Jan., 1884)

So far back as 1862 a deputation of owners and occupiers of property in the Ward of Billingsgate presented a petition to the Common Council for a street improvement in this neighbourhood   The plan adopted was to make a street from Monument Yard to the south-west corner of the Coal Exchange, crossing diagonally Pudding Lane, Botolph Lane and Love Lane, and taking in several houses opposite Billingsgate Market.   The removal of the houses in Thames Street it was thought would afford an excellent lay-bye and give a wide entrance to the new street   The width of the new street was to be 50 feet and the length 465 feet

Sir Moses Montefiore sent £99 to the Mansion House Poor Box, which was one pound for every completed year of his life.—A new and splendid thoroughfare, known by its old name of Eastcheap, was inaugurated by Sir Edward Watkin, Alderman Sir W. McArthur, K.C.M.G., M.P., and several other members of Parliament, Mr. George Shaw (Chairman of the Commissioners of Sewers) and other members of the Corporation.   The improvement was due to the joint efforts of the Metropolitan and Metropolitan District Railway Companies, the Metropolitan Board of Works and the Commissioners of Sewers (25th).— The case of the Queen on the prosecution of Kerr v. Scott, came on for argument in the Court of Appeal, before the Master of the Rolls and Lord Justice Bowen (5 Feb.).

This was an appeal from a decision of the Divisional Court, which refused to grant, at the instance of Mr. Commissioner Kerr, the Judge of the City of London Court, a mandamus to Mr. Benjamin Scott, the Chamberlain, directing him to pay to Mr. Kerr 19-40ths of the fees received in the City of London Court.   Their lordships dismissed the appeal.

A great meeting took place at the Guildhall to consider the Government policy in the Soudan.   The Lord Mayor presided, and an overflow meeting was held in Guildhall Yard (15th).—It was announced that the total sum contributed by the City Companies to the City and Guilds of London Technical Institute from 1878 to 1883 was £152,127 10s., including £44,562 10s. by way of donations to the building fund (23rd).—The Lord Mayor, accompanied by the Sheriffs, unveiled a memorial window to Shakespeare, presented by an anonymous donor, in the church of St. Helen, Bishopsgate (29th).—The Lord Mayor entertained representatives of the great religious and philanthropic societies to meet the Earl of Shaftesbury.   The company included the Archbishop of Canterbury, the

President of the Wesleyan Conference, and the Rev. Dr. Allon, who was looked upon as the father of Congregationalism (5 Mar.).—A large and enthusiastic meeting of City ratepayers was held at the Mansion House, to protest against the growing expenditure of the London School Board (17th).—A memorial bust of Samuel Pepys was unveiled in St. Olave's, Hart Street (19th).—At a meeting of the Mansion House Council on the Dwellings of the Poor, held at the Mansion House, the report, the adoption of which was moved by the Marquis of Salisbury and seconded by the Archbishop of Canterbury, showed that special attention had been directed to sanitary questions, such as overcrowding, ventilation, water-supply, drainage, etc. (24th).—Viscount Cranbrook presided at a dinner, to celebrate the opening of the City Conservative Club, Lombard Street, Lord Randolph Churchill being one of the speakers (25th).—The Prince of Wales appealed, in a letter to the Lord Mayor, to the Corporation and Livery Companies for further aid to the City and Guilds of London Technical Institute (27th). The Common Council (3 Ap.) voted £1,000 towards the £20,000 required for the equipment of the Central Institute, conditionally upon the Livery Companies subscribing a further sum of £19,000 to that object. Upwards of £17,000 having been obtained the Corporation's condition was afterwards withdrawn.—The Common Council passed a resolution affirming that the London School Board rate was excessive, and its incidence unjust, and that Parliament should limit its amount —On the announcement of the death of H.R.H. Prince Leopold, Duke of Albany, K.G., at Cannes, the great bell of St. Paul's, and the bells of many of the City churches were tolled, and flags were floated at half-mast from the various public buildings (28 Mar.). The Corporation on the 31st passed a resolution of condolence with Her Majesty and another expressing sympathy with the Duchess of Albany.—The Earl of Carnarvon opened the City Constitutional Club, Milk Street, the old City of London School having been adapted for the purpose (29th).—A great fire took place in Paternoster Row, originating in Lovell's Court, on the premises of Messrs. Pardon and Sons, Printers. It extended from Newgate Street almost to St. Paul's Churchyard, and embraced forty houses and establishments, the damage being estimated at £250,000 (2 Ap.).— Sir William Harcourt's London Government Bill, which proposed the practical abolition of the Corporation, and the creation of one municipality for the whole of London, was read a first time in the House of Commons (8th).—The new hospital for infectious diseases, near Gravesend, was opened by the Lord Mayor (17th).

The Hospital was built by order of the Corporation from designs of Mr. Horace Jones, assisted by Dr. Collingridge, Medical Officer of Health for the Port of London. For twelve years the Port

Sanitary Committee had carried on its useful work of protecting London from the infection of diseases imported from foreign parts, in the old French warship the *Rhin* lent for the purpose by the Admiralty. The inconvenience of transferring patients to a floating vessel in an advanced stage of decay had long been apparent, the result being that a hospital was built about a mile beyond Gravesend.

On the following day (18th) the Corporation Special Committee brought up a report on the London Government Bill, and submitted the following resolutions, which were adopted by the Common Council, viz. :

1. That in the deliberate opinion of this committee the London Government Bill is opposed to the interests, not only of the citizens of London, but of the Metropolitan Ratepayers generally. 2. That by its provisions the principle of Local Self Government, so far from being encouraged or supported, is practically destroyed. 3. That judging from past and present experience at home and abroad, the result of the proposed monster Municipality must inevitably be a great increase in public rates and expenditure, and decrease in personal care and supervision on the part of those who had hitherto, as local authorities, occupied themselves in the local government of the Metropolis. 4. That the Bill, while performing its extension and enlargement, practically extinguishes the ancient Corporation of the City of London, with its charters, liberties and traditions. 5. That for the foregoing, amongst other reasons, the Bill should be strenuously opposed and the Committee authorised to act accordingly, with all possible vigour and dispatch.

The Common Council decided to petition against the Bill and a similar course was adopted by the Commissioners of Sewers (22nd). Resolutions in opposition to the Bill poured into the Guildhall from local bodies in all parts of the Metropolis, only two or three memorials being in favour of the measure. Upwards of 200 petitions, containing more than 20,000 signatures, were presented to the House of Commons against the London Government Bill. A great meeting of City electors was held at Guildhall under the presidency of the Lord Mayor in protest, the proceedings being marked with great enthusiasm (9 May).—In the course of excavations, in Seething Lane, for the Metropolitan Extension, the remains of a bronze Roman statue of heroic size were found. Two coins, one bearing the superscription of Nero and the other that of Vespasian, were also discovered (23 Ap.).—The chief attraction of the Health Exhibition, at South Kensington, was the representation of "Old London," suggested by Mr. George Shaw, who presided over a Committee appointed to carry out the idea. The street was designed by Mr. G. H. Birch, and consisted of shops of the Elizabethan period, fitted up by some of the City Companies to represent the exercise of various handicrafts of that time.—The freedom of the Salters' Company was presented to the Earl of Shaftesbury, K.G., D.C.L. (14 May).—The Corporation subscribed 100 guineas to the Mansion House Fund ($£10,535$) for the sufferers from the recent earthquake in Essex (15th).—The City of London Society of Artists opened an Exhibition of Pictures and Sculpture at the Guildhall (20th).—An Exhibition of works in wood was opened by the Lord Mayor at Carpenters' Hall, the Exhibition being free to the public (23rd).— The Port of London Sanitary Committee were authorised to pay £10,096 7s. 6d. which had been expended in connection with the Royal Commission on the pollution of the Thames by sewage (29th).—The Earl of Shaftesbury, K.G., D.C.L.,

St. Paul's School, St. Paul's Churchyard, 1827.

was presented with the freedom of the City in testimony of the esteem and admiration of the Corporation, and "in recognition of his Lordship's life-long and successful labours on behalf of the young, the suffering, the degraded, and the oppressed ; and the devotion by him of high position, wealth, time, and influence to the alleviation of human suffering both at home and abroad" (20 June).—The Royal Commission of Enquiry into the Livery Committees of the City of London issued their report recommending certain reforms (26th). A separate minority report was prepared by Sir R. Cross's directions and signed by him, Sir N. de Rothschild, Bart., M.P., and Mr. Alderman Cotton, M.P., the latter also adding a separate protest. —The City and Guilds of London Technical Institute at South Kensington was opened by the Prince of Wales on the same day.

His Royal Highness was received by Lord Selborne, Lord Chancellor; Sir F. Bramwell and Sir Sydney H Waterlow, Bart., Vice-Presidents of the Institute; Mr. J. Watney and Mr. (afterwards Sir) Owen Roberts, M.A , Hon. Secretaries, and Mr. (afterwards Sir) P. Magnus, Director and Secretary of the Institute; the Right Hon Lord Carlingford and the Right Hon. A. J. Mundella on the part of Her

Majesty's Government, the Lord Major and Sheriffs; M. Waddington, French Ambassador, Professor Huxley, President of the Royal Society, and many others distinguished in the world of science. The Lord Chancellor said it was estimated that the building when fully equipped would cost nearly £100,000. His lordship mentioned incidentally that the number of students recently examined at the Technological Examinations was 3,628, a large increase on previous years. The Prince of Wales expressed a hope that the Livery Companies would continue to subscribe liberally to this great National School of Technical Science and Art, which would help to promote the development of our leading industries. The Corporation on the same day voted, in connection with the opening of the Central Institution, a scholarship of £50 a year for three years, to be called the Royal Albany Scholarship.

The new building erected at Hammersmith for St. Paul's School, in place of that which existed for so long a period in St. Paul's Churchyard, was opened by the Lord Chancellor (19 July).

> The building and grounds occupy a site of about 16 acres. The former has a frontage of 350 feet and is constructed of red brick and terra-cotta. The school was built from designs of Mr. Waterhouse, A.R.A., at a cost of about £90,000, the total outlay being about £100,000, exclusive of the site, for which £41,000 was paid. The top story contains an immense dining room and kitchens for the scholars' mid-day meals, besides two large lecture rooms and two physical and chemical laboratories. The ground floor and first floor are occupied by twenty-four class-rooms, drawing-class rooms, a large library and the masters' common rooms. At the western end is a large hall, 80 feet by 40 feet, and covered playgrounds and workshops occupy the lower story. To the left of the school are eight fives-courts, and beyond them and immediately behind the school a fine open garden of about 10 acres, turfed in the middle for cricket and other games. The school is capable of accommodating 1,000 boys. It was founded in the year 1510, by Dr. John Colet, Dean of St. Paul's. The total income of the foundation in 1879 was about £12,000 a year. According to the new scheme of the Endowed Schools Commissioners of 1876 (amended in 1879) provision was to be made for 500 boys on the classical and 500 on the modern side, and a school was to be established for the accommodation of not less than 400 girls. There are 153 foundation scholars.

Mr. John Derby Allcroft, Treasurer of Christ's Hospital, was presented by the Duke of Cambridge (President), in the name of the governors and subscribers, with his portrait by Mr. Herkomer, A.R.A., and a group in silver, in recognition of his services to the school (24th).—The Common Council resolved that a selection from the early wills preserved among the archives of the Corporation should be prepared for printing, together with a calendar and index (28th).—The new street from King William statue to Tower Hill was completed (31st).—The jubilee of the abolition of slavery in the British Colonies was celebrated by a great meeting at Guildhall. The Prince of Wales presided, supported by the Lord Mayor and Sheriffs, the Archbishop of Canterbury, and Cardinal Manning (1 Aug.).— The City Constitutional Club having acquired and adapted the buildings formerly belonging to the City of London School, in Milk Street, the Lord Mayor presided at an inaugural banquet (15th).—The church of St. Olave,

Old Jewry, was condemned under the Union of Benefices Act.—The foundation stone of the new hall of the Butchers' Company was laid in Bartholomew Close (1 Sept.).—The Inner Circle Railway was completed (17th).

A numerous company, including the Lord Mayor and Sheriffs who attended in state, assembled at Cannon Street Station and proceeded by special train over the new line, stopping at each station *en route*. A déjeuner was afterwards served at the Cannon Street Hotel, at which Sir Edward Watkin said that for

Interior of Monument Station.

the undertaking just completed the two Companies (the Metropolitan and the Metropolitan District) were practically liable for two millions of money, after deducting the £500,000 subsidy from the Metropolitan Board of Works and the £300,000 from the Commissioners of Sewers. These bodies had availed themselves of the opportunity offered by the construction of the line to effect a great public improvement in the widening of Eastcheap. The cost of the section just completed was £1,043,000, and the whole length only 1,200 yards, so that it had cost £854 a yard. Between the King William statue and Trinity Square the outlay was 1,000 guineas per yard. The Inner Circle Railway was opened to the public on 6 Oct.

The Corporation voted 100 guineas to the Mansion House fund in aid of the sufferers from cholera at Naples (25 Sept.). The fund realised £1,531.—The Markets Committee presented a report to the Common Council showing a deficiency on the London Central Fish Market of £5,303 13s. 1d. per annum. If, however, all the shops had been let the deficiency would have been covered.

Mr. F. P. Alliston, Chairman of the Markets Committee, in the course of his explanatory statement said: "Against 4,294 tons delivered at the Central Fish Market in the course of the year he had to place 123,421 delivered at Billingsgate in the same period. A year's trade at the Inland Fish Market was, in fact, equal to about ten days' trade at Billingsgate."

It was thereupon referred to the Markets Committee to consider the question of the future of the Market.—The new Council Chamber at Guildhall was formally opened (2 Oct.).

The building, which was designed by the late Sir Horace Jones, stands on the north side of the Guildhall and on the site originally occupied by the Court of Exchequer, a portion of the Chamberlain's office, and the offices of the Town Clerk and Architect. It is duodecagonal in plan, and in style it harmonises with the Guildhall and Library. The interior of the Chamber is 54 feet in diameter and is surrounded by a corridor 9 feet wide. Sitting accommodation is provided for the 206 members of the Common Council, the seats being arranged concentrically to the Lord Mayor's chair and on rising platforms. Seats for twenty-five Aldermen, the Recorder and Sheriffs, are provided on the dais on either side of the Lord Mayor, the officers sitting immediately below and in front of his Lordship. Accommodation is found for the press and public in the gallery which surrounds the building. The dome, which is 61 feet 6 inches above the floor of the Chamber, is surmounted by an oaken lantern. The acoustic properties of this splendid Chamber were at first somewhat defective, but they have since been improved. The cost of the building, exclusive of the value of the site, was nearly £45,000. Before taking possession of the new Council Chamber a meeting was held in the old one, which had been erected about the year 1777 by the then City Architect, Mr George Dance. The Council then proceeded to the new Chamber, where prayer was offered by the Rev Prebendary Whittington, M.A., chaplain to the Lord Mayor, and an address was delivered by his lordship. A medal was ordered to be struck to commemorate the occasion.

The Corporation resolved to continue the London Central Fish Market, but to discontinue the appointment of an official salesman. — It was announced that the order for the second reading of the London Government Bill had been discharged (19 Oct.).—The Lord Mayor opened a handsome drinking fountain in Adelaide Place, London Bridge. The fountain was modelled by Mr. Charles Barry, and was a replica of one in Cincinnati (28 Oct.).—The Bridge House Committee submitted two designs for the new bridge across the Thames, one a swing bridge and the other a bascule bridge. The latter was adopted by the Corporation (28th) — *London's Roll of Fame* was published (1 Nov.). This work was prepared by the Chamberlain (Mr. B. Scott) by direction of the Common Council, and included the addresses of the Chamberlains of the City to those on whom its honorary freedom had been conferred, from the accession of George III, together with the replies of the recipients; also the addresses presented by the Common Council to foreign sovereigns and other distinguished persons.—The Lord Mayor (Mr. Alderman Fowler, M.P.) was presented with the honorary freedom of the Grocers' Company (7th).—Alderman George Swan Nottage was elected Lord Mayor.—For some years the condition of the Queen Anne statue in front of St. Paul's Cathedral, with its mutilated face, had been a disgrace to the City. The Corporation now ordered a replica of the entire group in Sicilian marble, at a cost of £1,800 (6 Dec.).—Sermons commemorating the 100th anniversary of the death of Dr. Johnson were preached in the City, especially in the neighbourhood of Fleet Street (14th).—The Commissioners of

Sewers agreed to widen Cloak Lane, making it 25 feet between Dowgate Hill and College Hill, at an expense of £6,000 (16th).—A dynamite explosion occurred on London Bridge (13 Dec.).

A charge of dynamite had been attached to one of the buttresses and exploded, shattering many windows in the neighbourhood and severely shaking some of the foot passengers, but doing no damage

Staple Inn and Holborn Bars.

to the masonry of the bridge. The Corporation offered a reward of £5,000 for the discovery of the perpetrator or perpetrators of the outrage.

The Corporation voted 200 guineas to the funds of the Marine Biological Association of the United Kingdom for scientific observation or culture of sea fish and the improvement and regulation of the British Sea Fisheries.—A memorial stone of the Freemen's Almshouses at Brixton was laid (24th).—A Mansion House Fund was opened for the captive crew of the *Nisero*, and a sum of £1,237 was collected.—The Hospital Sunday Fund amounted to £41,124.

An addition was made to the Stock Exchange.—Staple Inn, Holborn was sold.—An apparatus, termed a Destructor, for burning refuse, was erected at Lett's Wharf by the Commissioners of Sewers, at a cost of about £12,100. The smoke and vapour passes through superheated furnaces and then to a clearing shaft 150 feet high. The quantity of house and trade refuse consumed in the Destructor is about 25,000 loads annually, or more than half the total quantity of refuse removed from the City.

1885.

THE Right Rev. John Jackson, the Bishop of London, died at Fulham Palace (6 Jan. 1885), the great bell of St. Paul's being tolled.—The Corporation voted addresses of compliment and congratulation to the Queen, the Prince and Princess of Wales, and Prince Albert Victor of Wales, K.G., on the occasion of the coming of age of the latter, the young Prince being invited to take upon himself the freedom of the City, to which he was entitled by patrimony (8th).—Two large and imposing blocks of labourers' and artizans' dwellings, erected by the Commissioners of Sewers in Petticoat Square, were opened (26th). The two blocks are known as King's and South Blocks. The cost of clearing the Golden Lane and Petticoat Square sites was £120,526, and the cost of the buildings £80,389.—A resolution of the Hon Artillery Company was forwarded to the Corporation, conveying the assurance of the readiness of the members of the Company to assist the civil authorities in protecting the public buildings of the City from attack by dynamiters (29th).—Sir T. J. Nelson, City Solicitor, died suddenly (7 Feb).

Thomas James Nelson was the eldest son of Mr Thomas Nelson, for over seventy years a ship-broker, carrying on business in the City He was born on 18 Oct, 1826, at Walthamstow He was appointed City Solicitor at the age of thirty-six, and in 1864 as Acting Remembrancer he helped to pass the Holborn Valley Improvement Bill. The two important subjects, gas and water, had also engaged his attention, but his great work was connected with the preservation of Epping Forest. It was at Sir Thomas Nelson's suggestion that the Livery Franchise, which had been fixed at a seven-mile residence from the City, was extended by the Reform Bill of 1867 to 25 miles.

The Ecclesiastical Commissioners offered the Corporation, for the use and enjoyment of the people, Gravel Pit Wood, Highgate (69 acres), and some land at Kilburn (30 acres), on condition that the Corporation would lay out the sites and maintain them in perpetuity (12th). In May the offer was accepted so far as it related to Highgate Wood.—A sum of 100 guineas was voted by the Common Council to the Essex Agricultural Society, for Corporation prizes at the forthcoming show at Waltham Abbey, under the presidency of the Duke of Connaught, Ranger of Epping Forest.—The Tower of St. Magnus the Martyr Church, near the foot of London Bridge, was restored under the direction of Mr. A. Billing, (14th).—A public meeting was held at Cannon Street Hotel (16th), to protest against the proposal contained in the Re-distribution of Seats Bill, to reduce the City representation from four to two. Mr. Alderman Fowler vigorously opposed the Bill in Committee of the House of Commons but his amendment to substitute four for two was negatived.—It was announced that the Fishmongers' Company had decided to dispose of their Irish Estates, the rent roll of which amounted to about £9,000 per annum (18th).—Mr. Robarts, the late Remembrancer, by persistent application to the Corporation, was eventually successful. On the 18th, it was resolved, after considerable discussion, that his appeal to the generosity of the Court should be complied with, that the payment of £1,000 should be made to him out of the City's cash, and that the taxed costs payable by him to the Corporation should not be enforced against him. — The Corporation voted 500 guineas for the relief of sufferers from the recent earthquakes in Spain, and 100 guineas in aid of the fund for the relief of widows and orphans of the crew of the wrecked steamship *Pochard*, which was engaged in connection with the Foreign Cattle Market, Deptford.—The honorary freedom of the Tinplate Workers'

Bird's-eye view of Christ's Hospital.—From an old print.

Company, was conferred upon the Marquis of Lorne at the Mansion House.— The first piles of the London Riverside Fish Market, Lower Shadwell, were driven by the Duke of Westminster and the Baroness Burdett-Coutts. The site had been under consideration since 1868, when a petition was presented by the Limehouse District Board of Works to the Common Council, urging them to use the site for a fish market, instead of obtaining powers to enlarge Billingsgate. The first attempt to float a company was a failure, but another essay was more successful (24 Feb.).—The Charity Commissioners published a draft scheme for the re-organisation of Christ's Hospital.—With a view to relieve the finances and the City ratepayers, the Finance Committee of the Commissioners of Sewers suggested the raising of a loan of a million by means of 3½ per cent. debentures, repayable by the appropriation of a fixed annual sum. The Committee also recommended that a fixed annual sum of £70,362 should be appropriated to the discharge of such debentures and interest within a period of twenty years, as provided by the Local Loans Act, 1875. By this arrangement the rates would be relieved to the extent of a penny and a fraction in the £. The report was adopted (4 Mar.).—During the excavations for Messrs. Waterlow's new premises in London

Wall, a large portion of the ancient City wall was unearthed.—Mr. H. H. Crawford was elected City Solicitor (12th).—The Lord Mayor presided at a meeting of the Gordon Memorial Committee at the Mansion House (14th), General Gordon having been betrayed and killed in the defence of Khartoum on 24 Jan. The Corporation voted 100 guineas to the Mansion House Fund and 250 guineas for a bust of General Gordon to be placed in the Guildhall.—The Common Council agreed to erect a building for the Guildhall School of Music on the Victoria Embankment, at a cost of £20,000, an additional £2,600 being afterwards voted for Portland stone (26th).—The Servian Minister informed the Lord Mayor at the Mansion House that the King had nominated him Grand Officer of the Royal Order of Takovo, in appreciation of his services to the cause of progress and his sympathy with Servia (1 Ap.). — London was startled by the announcement that the Lord Mayor had died at the Mansion House after a short illness (11th).

Statuette of Bluecoat Boy, Christ's Hospital.

Lord Mayor Nottage, who was sixty-one years of age, was the founder of the London Stereoscopic and Photographic Company; while at Brighton he was well known for the great improvements he had made in the King's Road by the erection of handsome blocks of buildings. He was elected Alderman in 1875 and Sheriff in 1877. More than 100 years had passed since the death of a Lord Mayor during his year of office, the last occasion being that of Lord Mayor Beckford, who died in 1770.

Extensive preparations were made for the burial of the late Lord Mayor at St. Paul's on the 18th.

On that day dense crowds gathered along the line of route from the Mansion House to St. Paul's, business being temporarily suspended. The road was kept by detachments of the London Rifle Brigade and the 1st City of London Artillery, while the Hon. Artillery Company took up a position in St. Paul's Church-yard. Three thousand persons received tickets of admission to the Cathedral, the northern side of the dome being reserved for members of the Common Council in mazarine gowns and their ladies, while facing them were some fifty provincial Mayors in scarlet gowns and gold chains. The Duke of Edinburgh and the Duke of Cambridge were also present. Close to Nelson's famous tomb in the crypt were laid the ashes of Lord Mayor Nottage, the spot being marked by a brass plate which was afterwards placed there by order of the Corporation.

Alderman Fowler was elected Lord Mayor for the remainder of the term of the Mayoralty.—A meeting presided over by the Lord Mayor was held at the Cannon Street Hotel, to give expression to the anxiety felt by the commercial world at the condition of the navy. A resolution urging the Government to take immediate steps to improve the navy, was moved by Mr. H. Hucks Gibbs and seconded by the Right Hon. W. H. Smith.—The foundation stone of Sion College, was laid on the Victoria Embankment, by the Rev. A. Povah, M.A., President of the College (21st). —It was referred to the Library Committee to consider the desirability of establishing an Art Gallery, for the reception and exhibition of works of art belonging to the Corporation. The vacant Court of Queen's Bench in the Guildhall Yard was appropriated for the purpose. — The Corporation having passed a congratulatory address to the King of the Belgians, on the recognition by the Powers of the Congo Free State, of which the King was named Protector, the Lord Mayor, the Sheriffs, and a deputation of members of the Corporation proceeded to Brussels (4 May). After visiting the Palace, where they were received by the King, to whom the Corporation address was presented, the Civic party went to the Hotel de Ville, where they were welcomed

Staircase of House, Botolph Lane, used since 1859 for Tower and Billingsgate Ward School.

by the Burgomaster and Municipal Council. His Majesty conferred upon his visitors various grades of the Royal Order of Leopold, the Lord Mayor being designated a Knight Commander of the Order. — With a view to a more efficient control over expenditure, the 47th standing order of the Common Council was amended as follows (7th):—

> No street improvement, public work or entertainment shall be undertaken or extraordinary work performed, and no grant for any public, charitable or other purpose shall be made, whereby the funds belonging to or under the control of the Corporation may be given in any manner, charged or affected, beyond the sum of 100 guineas, until the expense or an estimate thereof shall have been first submitted to the Coal and Corn and Finance Committee and that Committee shall have reported to the Court.

The boundaries of the parish of St. John the Baptist upon Walbrook were beaten, and the memorial on the site of the ancient parish church and churchyard was unveiled in Cloak Lane (15th).—James Gilbert *alias* Cunningham, and Harry Burton, were sentenced at the Old Bailey to penal servitude for life, in connection with the dynamite explosions at the Tower of London, the Houses of Parliament and elsewhere (18th).—A testimonial subscribed for by citizens of all ranks, in recognition of the services rendered by the Lord Mayor during his last mayoralty,

Interior of Allhallows-the-Great.—Recently demolished.

was presented at the Mansion House.   Nearly a thousand citizens contributed to the fund.   The testimonial consisted of a solid silver centre piece, and a portrait by Frank Holl, for the Lord Mayor, and a diamond necklace for the Lady Mayoress (28th).—Rev Edwin Paxton Hood, minister of Falcon Square Chapel, died in Paris, (12 June).

Mr. Hood was the son of one of Nelson's old sailors who fought on the "Téméraire," and was born at Westminster in 1820.   He was for some years editor of the *Eclectic Review* and was the author of many works, including biographies of Swedenborg, Wordsworth, Oliver Cromwell, Carlyle, and Thomas Binney.   His hymns are widely known, especially in Nonconformist Chapels and Sunday Schools.

The draft scheme of the Ecclesiastical Commissioners for effecting the union of the two benefices of St. Margaret Lothbury with St. Christopher-le-Stocks and St. Bartholomew Exchange, and St. Olave Jewry with St. Martin Pomeroy, St. Mildred Poultry and St. Mary Colechurch, was signed at a meeting of the joint vestries (18th).—The ward of Farringdon Within presented the Corporation with a marble bust of their Alderman, Sir Benjamin Phillips.—Prince Albert Victor of Wales, K.G., was presented with the honorary freedom of the Fishmongers' Company (24th).—Canon Elwyn, Vicar of East Fairleigh, at one time Head Master of the Charterhouse School, was elected to the Mastership of the Charterhouse.—The Prince and Princess of Wales, accompanied by Princess Louise of Wales, Prince George, and the Duke of Cambridge attended at the Guildhall, on the occasion of H.R.H. Prince Albert Victor of Wales, their eldest son, taking upon himself the freedom of the City by patrimony (29th). Addresses of congratulation were presented to the Prince of Wales, the Princess of Wales and Prince Albert Victor of Wales; the Prince of Wales briefly replied. A medal to commemorate the occasion was ordered to be struck (16 July).—The foundation stone was laid of a block of artizans' dwellings on the site of an old rookery called Chatham Gardens, Nile Street, Hoxton, the funds having been provided by a charity known as Bleyton's trust, originally bequeathed in 1585 for the benefit of the poor of the joint parishes of St. Giles, Cripplegate and St. Luke's. Bleyton was a Cripplegate butcher. The cost of the buildings, which were to accommodate 700 people, was estimated at £52,000 (1 July).—The Prince of Wales, accompanied by the Princess of Wales, Prince Albert Victor and Princess Victoria, opened the new building of the Birkbeck Literary and Scientific Institution, towards the cost of which the Corporation and several of the City Companies had generously contributed.

The building, which cost over £20,000, is situated on a plot of land having frontages to Bream's Buildings and Rolls Buildings, and provides accommodation for 6,000 students The large lecture hall is 66 feet by 50 feet, with circular galleries, and is capable of seating 1,200 persons. In addition to class rooms, etc., there are thoroughly fitted-up laboratories for practical scientific instruction. The style of architecture is a modern adaptation of the Elizabethan, Fareham red bricks and Portland stone being used for both fronts.

The Lord Mayor laid the foundation stone of the new artizans' dwellings belonging to the City and Central Dwellings Company, Limited, in Seward Street, Goswell Road (11th).—The honour of a baronetcy was conferred upon the Lord Mayor (16th).—In response to a letter from the Prince of Wales as President of the Royal Windsor Tapestry Works, the Corporation agreed to expend £1,000 in the purchase of tapestry of approved design from the works at Windsor.—The foundation stone of the new building for the Guildhall School of Music on the Victoria Embankment was laid (21st).—Ex-Sheriff Sir Moses Montefiore, Bart., died at Ramsgate on the 28th, having nearly reached his one-hundred-and-first year.—A marble bust of Alderman Sir Robert Walter Carden, Knight, M.P., was ordered to

Pulpit of Church of Allhallows-the-Great.

be executed at a cost of £250 and placed in the Guildhall as a mark of esteem.—At a meeting summoned by the Plumbers' Company at Guildhall, at the instance of Mr. George Shaw and presided over by Earl Fortescue, it was announced that the Court of the Company had decided to recommend the establishment of a system of registration of plumbers within the City of London and a circuit of seven miles thereof; the register to include master plumbers and journeymen, and to be open to the admission of those who satisfy the Court of their qualification. Registered plumbers were to be entitled to use "R. P." after their names. These and other recommendations were agreed to (31st).—The Tower Bridge Bill was passed on 14 Aug.; it empowered the Corporation to construct within four years a bridge over the Thames, near the Tower of London, with all the necessary approaches. The Corporation were also empowered by the Act to borrow on the credit of the Bridge House Estates a sum of £750,000 for the above purpose.—The Lord Mayor opened the new building for the St. Anne's Society at Red Hill, which had been appropriately erected in the Queen Anne style at a cost of nearly £40,000 (14 Aug.).

The school was established in the first year of the reign of Queen Anne in a house in Aldersgate Street, where twelve boys were clothed and educated. The Institution remained practically unchanged till 1790, when thirteen girls were added. In 1820 thirty girls and thirty boys were clothed and educated at the school. Buildings were afterwards taken at Streatham, from which place the scholars (excepting those educated in the City) were now removing to Red Hill, the number of children for whom accommodation was provided being 400.

Alderman Sir Charles Whetham, Knight, died (4 Sept.).—The new hall of the Butchers' Company in Bartholomew Close was opened (7th).

The building was designed by Mr. Alex. Peebles and cost about £12,000. The banqueting hall is 46 feet by 30 feet and about 18 feet high.

The Special Committee reported to the Common Council on the subject of London Government, re-affirming as a principle the policy of separate municipalities (17th) which they afterwards (5 Nov.) recommended should be ten in number, including the City.—The Corporation voted 200 guineas to the Mansion House Fund for sufferers from the cholera in Spain. The fund amounted to £4,243.— The system of sixpenny telegrams came into operation (1 Oct.).—The Lord Mayor, who had frequently accepted invitations to preach at Missions and Music Halls, occupied the City Temple pulpit (4th).—The Common Council ordered a bust of the late Earl of Shaftesbury to be executed at a cost of 200 guineas. —The City Solicitor was instructed to appear by Counsel in support of the petition in favour of the incorporation of West Ham.—Mr. Horace Jones, City Architect, was appointed architect for the erection and construction of Tower Bridge ; Mr. John Wolfe Barry, civil engineer, was associated with him in carrying out the work, the sum of £30,000 being paid to them jointly, including the expenses of all superintendents and clerks of works (15th).—At a meeting at the Mansion House, presided over by the Lord Mayor, it was resolved, on the motion of Earl Granville, that a fund should be opened for a national memorial to the late Lord Shaftesbury (16th).—The Special Committee of the Commissioners of Sewers presented a report showing that the amount required from the City by the School Board had gone up from £5,069, or a rate of ½d. in the £ in 1871, to £128,983, or a rate equal to 8¾d. in the £ in 1885. The Committee recommended that London should be divided into districts with a School Board for each district and that the system of cumulative voting should be abolished (20th). The report was ultimately adopted by the Commissioners.— At the London School Board Election (3 Nov.) Mr. Spicer, Miss Davenport Hill, Alderman Savory and Sir R. Temple, Bart., were returned for the City.— The new London Almshouses, for the accommodation of decayed freemen and their widows, or the daughters of freemen householders, were opened at Shepherd Lane,

Brixton.   The cost of the buildings was £11,437.—A meeting of the parishioners of St. Olave Old Jewry was held for the appointment of a divinity lecturer.   Ninety-four clergymen offered themselves as candidates for the lectureship, the value of which was £300 per annum, a fund for the purpose having been bequeathed by Dame Mary Wild in 1622.   The Rev. G. Davenport was elected (6 Nov.).—Alderman John Staples was elected Lord Mayor. — The Streets Committee reported to the Commissioners of Sewers that they were legally advised that

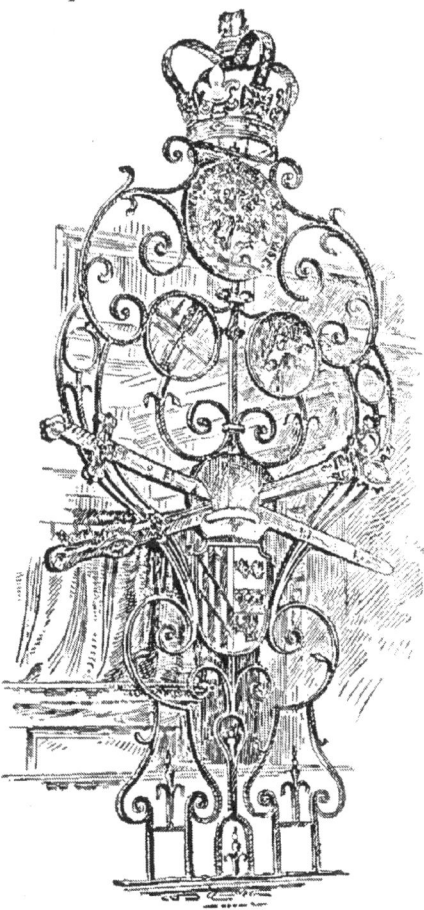

Sword Rest, Church of Allhallows-the-Great.

the Commissioners had no power to construct subways in the vicinity of the Mansion House. The Commissioners had contemplated making subways with the view to diminish the dangers of the crossing at this spot (17th).—The new tax of 5 per cent. upon the corporate property of the City Guilds (after allowing for expenses of management) was estimated to produce at least £10,000.—Three stone statues, supposed to represent Charles I and his Queen, and Edward VI, were removed from the cellars under the Law Courts, and placed in the Guildhall Museum.

They were executed in stone and originally occupied three niches in front of Guildhall Chapel, which formerly stood in Guildhall Yard. Upon the demolition of the Chapel, to make room for the Law Courts, in 1822, they were removed to the stone screen at the east end of Guildhall where they remained until 1866, when the present oak screen was erected. The statues are in a good state of preservation.

On the recommendation of the Markets Committee, and in response to numerous petitions, the Common Council resolved to construct upon the vacant triangular site abutting on Snow Hill, a market for the sale of fish and other provisions, the existing Inland Fish Market reverting to its originally contemplated purposes of a Fruit and Vegetable Market (19th). — The Remembrancer (Mr. Gabriel Goldney) presented the Corporation with his law library.—The first Parliamentary Election for the City, under the new Re-distribution of Seats Act took place on 25 Nov.   There were four candidates for the two seats.   Sir Robert Fowler (Conservative) headed the poll with 12,827 votes; Mr. Hubbard

(Conservative), who came next, polling 8,802 votes. The numbers recorded for Mr. Low (Liberal) were 5,817, and for Mr. Alderman Cotton, 5,563.—Extensive alterations were made in the internal arrangements of the Chapter House, on the north side of St. Paul's Churchyard, to provide a residence for the Archdeacon of London (12 Dec.).—Arrangements were made by the Commissioners of Sewers with the Anglo-American Brush Electric Light Corporation, to light the area bounded on the north by Fleet Street, Ludgate Hill, St. Paul's Churchyard and Poultry, extending east as far as the Royal Exchange and bounded on the south by Queen Victoria Street and Victoria Embankment.—Sir J. A. Macdonald, G.C.B., D.C.L., Prime Minister of the Dominion of Canada, was presented with the honorary freedom of the Turners' Company (17th).—The Corporation resolved to erect a new building for the City of London Court, at a cost of £16,000.—The right of the Corporation to control the Fellowship Porters of the City of London by Act of Common Council was upheld by a judgment of the High Court (21st).—The last of the six City Police Stations was built in Cloak Lane.

1886.

A a meeting of the Common Council, on the 21st Jan., 1886, a letter was read from the President of the Royal Institute of British Architects (Mr. Edwin Christian), on the subject of the proposed enlargement of the area of St. Paul's Churchyard, pointing out that a valuable opportunity offered not only to open up the eastern end of the Cathedral but to effect a great improvement in the roadway which skirted it. This had reference to the site of St. Paul's School which was in course of removal. The subject was referred to the Commissioners of Sewers, who decided that as the proposed improvement in St. Paul's Churchyard was rather for the purpose of opening up a view of the Cathedral, than for any necessities of the traffic at that spot, they were not called upon to undertake the work (20 Ap.).—Colonel Fraser, C.B., Commissioner of the City Police, was made a Knight Commander of the Bath (4 Feb.).—A deputation of working men having appealed to the Lord Mayor to open a fund for the unemployed of the Metropolis, the first meeting of the Committee of the Fund was held on the 10th. The Corporation subscribed 500 guineas (11 Mar.), and instructed the Epping Forest Committee to expend a sum not exceeding £800 in draining and levelling Wanstead Flats. The distress owing to the lack of employment was at this time both wide-spread and acute, and the appeal from the Mansion House to the generosity of the public resulted in a sum of £78,629 being collected and distributed amongst the deserving poor.—The Corporation

resolved to co-operate with the Prince of Wales and the Livery Companies in promoting the forthcoming Colonial and Indian Exhibition, and guaranteed a sum of £10,000 in furtherance of the object (18 Feb.). At the same time a special Ward Committee was appointed to make arrangements for the reception of "Our Colonial

Interior of Cock Tavern, Fleet Street.

and Indian Brethren." It was agreed to have a state service at St. Paul's Cathedral, and a reception and ball at the Guildhall (11 Mar.).—Mr. W. P. Treloar urged the Commissioners of Sewers to complete the widening of Ludgate Hill without further delay (22nd).—In the course of a discussion in the Commission of Sewers, on the water supply of the City, an important statement was made by Dr. Sedgwick Saunders, the Medical Officer, as to fresh sources of supply (8 Mar.).

He said that for the last twelve years no well had been closed of a greater depth than thirty feet. These wells had been practically closed by basements and the Underground Railway. A number of wells known to him had been sunk some hundreds of feet. One near Blackfriars Bridge, 580 feet deep, produced a most beautiful and unique supply of soft and pure water. At Blackfriars the supply of water was so enormous, that they had to run away over a million gallons a day. If they sunk wells at 1,500 or 2,000 feet they would get water as organically pure as, and infinitely better than, the New River supply.

Prince Albert Victor was presented with the freedom and livery of the Goldsmiths' Company (30th). —A meeting was held at Guildhall to protest against Home Rule for Ireland (2 Ap.).—About this time the site of the Cock Tavern, in Fleet Street, was acquired by the authorities of the Bank of England, for the erection of a branch establishment.

> The "Cock Tavern" was originally known as the "Cock and Bottle," perhaps meaning that liquors were to be obtained either on draught or in bottle, the word "cock" signifying the tap of a barrel. The "Cock" was a celebrated old tavern, which enjoyed the patronage of barristers and journalists, Tennyson, Dickens and Thackeray being amongst those who frequented it.

Mr. Edward Waller, Master of the Stationers' Company, placed a handsome stained-glass window in Stationers' Hall, the subject being St. Cecilia, the patron saint of music, whose festival, then called the Music Feast, was held in this Hall in 1684 and several subsequent years.—The new Parcels Post rates came into force (1 May).—Prince Albert Victor took up the freedom of the Mercers' Company to which he was entitled by patrimony.—The Queen opened the Colonial and Indian Exhibition, at South Kensington, the Corporation and City Companies being represented.—The Commissioners of Sewers accepted the tender of the Stock Exchange, of £36,750, for a freehold building site in Old Broad Street, having an area of 1,285 superficial feet and a frontage of 42 feet 3 inches.—An arrangement having been come to by the Corporation with regard to taking over, from the Ecclesiastical Commissioners, the lands at Highgate and Kilburn, an Act was passed this session vesting such open spaces in the Corporation, in mortmain in perpetuity, as public parks or open spaces for the perpetual use and recreation of the public, adding with regard to Highgate Wood, that the natural aspect of the Wood was, as far as possible, to be preserved. The Common Council now ordered that a keeper should be appointed for Highgate Wood. The Court also voted £3,500 for the drainage, laying out, and enclosing of Kilburn Park.—Lord Salisbury's name was added to the roll of honorary freemen of the Grocers' Company, on the occasion of the annual Restoration Feast, which the Company continue to hold, in commemoration of the return of Charles II from exile (29th).—The Churchill "Home," for working women in the City, at the corner of Finsbury Street, in Chiswell Street, was opened by the Lord Mayor (5 June).—The Glovers' Company having been resuscitated, the first Court since its revival was held at the Guildhall, Mr. Benjamin Scott (the Chamberlain) presiding (8th).— The Queen on the 20th entered upon the fiftieth year of her reign, and the 1,500 Colonial and Indian representatives in London attended a service at St. Paul's

Cathedral to which the Lord Mayor and Corporation went in State. Handel's Coronation Anthem was given.—The Prince of Wales, on behalf of the Queen laid the memorial stone of the Tower Bridge (21st).

His Royal Highness was received at the Tower by Field-Marshal Sir Richard Dacres (Constable of the Tower), and other officers, who conducted the Royal party to a pavilion, where the Lord Mayor, the Sheriffs, the Bridge House Estates Committee, and the high officers of the Corporation were waiting to greet them. The Recorder read an address relating briefly the story of the Bridge House Estates, and the steps which led up to the decision of the Corporation to construct a new bridge at a cost of £750,000. The Prince briefly replied, and the stone having been laid, the Tower guns fired a salute The Chairman of the Bridge House Estates Committee presented to the Princess of Wales an emblem of the Bridge House Estates set in diamonds, as a souvenir of the occasion

The new Corporation Art Gallery was opened by the Lord Mayor. The exhibition included a selection of the City's works of art (oil paintings, sculpture, engravings and miniatures), and it has since been greatly enriched by gifts and bequests. The Corporation were indebted for the gift of nearly half their oil paintings to Alderman Boydell, the celebrated engraver, Lord Mayor in 1790 (24th).—Our Colonial and Indian visitors were entertained at a grand reception and ball in the Guildhall (25th). A medal was struck to commemorate the occasion —The Prince of Wales, accompanied by the Princess of Wales, laid the foundation stone of the People's Palace, in the Mile End Road, to which the Corporation and some of the Livery Companies had liberally subscribed (28th).

The idea had its root in the Beaumont Trust scheme of 1841, Mr. J. T. Barber Beaumont having bequeathed a sum of £12,500 to provide for the intellectual improvement and rational recreation and amusement of the inhabitants of East London Mr. Walter Besant had shown what might be done to elevate and brighten the lives of East Londoners, and Sir Edmund H. Currie, Chairman of the Beaumont Trustees, set industriously to work to carry out the idea. Something like £100,000 was needed. The Drapers' Company gave £20,000 for technical schools, and up to the present time they have generously expended upon this work not much less than £100,000 Amongst other companies who contributed were the Clothworkers, £1,000; the Carpenters and Grocers, £500 each; the Skinners, £300; the Mercers, 250 guineas; the Fishmongers, 200 guineas, and the Merchant Taylors, 100 guineas.

Mr. Deputy Fry, for thirty-three years an active member of the Corporation, died on the 30th.—Shed works at Deptford Market were ordered to be carried out at an expense of £42,000.—It having been ascertained, by circular, that a very large majority of the citizens appealed to were in favour of the ballot, the Common Council ordered that it should be adopted instead of open voting at municipal elections.—M. Léon Say and a number of distinguished journalists were entertained at the Mansion House (2 July).—The freedom of the Fishmongers' Company was presented to Sir Charles Tupper (9th).—The Corporation voted

£5,000 for furniture, etc., for the Guildhall School of Music (15th).—The Commissioners of Sewers decided to widen Lime Street at its south-east corner (20th).—Samuel Morley died at 34, Grosvenor Street (5 Sept.).

He was born at Hackney in 1809, being the youngest son of Mr. John Morley, of Wells Street. The house in Wood Street was founded by Samuel's father, but it was owing especially to the energy of the son that it attained to eminence. Samuel Morley sat in Parliament as a Liberal for a number of years, but his chief work was of a religious and social character. He was an ardent nonconformist, and gave £6,000 towards the erection of the Memorial Hall, in Farringdon Street

It was announced that Her Majesty intended to confer the honour of knighthood upon Mr. Horace Jones, City Architect (16th).—A preliminary meeting was held at the Mansion House (the Lord Mayor presiding), to consider the Prince of Wales's proposal for an Imperial Institute as a memorial by her subjects of Her Majesty's Jubilee (24th). It was decided to open a fund for the purpose.—The Corporation resolved to amend the rules of the Fellowship Porters of the City of London (30th).—The Lord Mayor dedicated Gravel Pit Wood, Highgate, which had been taken over by the Corporation, to the public use and enjoyment for ever (30 Oct.). An attempt had been made to secure the remainder of Highgate Woods, but without success. Gravel Pit Wood, which is situated on the north side of Muswell Hill Road, contains 69a. 1r. 13p.—A meeting was held at the Mansion House in furtherance of the Beaumont Trust scheme for the establishment of a People's Palace for East London, the Lord Mayor presiding. Sir E. H. Currie announced that £77,000 had been already secured.—Sir Reginald Hanson, Kt., was elected Lord Mayor.

Col Sir James Fraser, Commissioner of the City Police, issued a notice (2 Nov) proclaiming the Socialist procession announced for Lord Mayor's Day, and notifying that no other procession but that of the Lord Mayor's would be allowed on that day within the City precincts. Although considerable excitement prevailed, owing to the Socialists' threats, everything went off quietly on the 9th, extraordinary precautions having been taken by the police. The Lord Mayor's procession passed through the streets unmolested, but the number of spectators was smaller than usual.

It was announced that Her Majesty had conferred upon the retiring Lord Mayor the dignity of K.C.M.G.—A deputation representing the Metropolitan Board of Works and the Corporation, waited upon the Chancellor of the Exchequer to ask the Government to support the renewal of the coal and wine dues (18th). Lord Randolph Churchill said the Government had decided not to do so, and supported their decision in an argumentative speech of considerable length. In reply to a question, the City Chamberlain said that the dues last year produced £450,000 net, which was equivalent to a sum of fourpence in the £ on the rateable value of London. — The Corporation resolved to commemorate the Jubilee of Her Majesty's Reign, the arrangements being entrusted to a

Committee of the whole Court.—The churches of St. Bride, Fleet Street, and St. Mary Woolnoth were re-opened, after undergoing restoration, and in the latter case the sealing of the vaults (21st). — Staple Inn, Holborn, one of the remnants of Old London, was sold at auction by the Antients of the Inn to the Prudential Assurance Company, for £68,000 (26th).—The ancient and historical church of St. Bartholomew-the-Great, Smithfield, was re-opened, after having undergone restoration.

The factory building, which used to cover all the apsidal end of the church, was bought by subscription, and the intruding part cleared away. The Norman triforium was continued so as to complete the apse, the lower portion of which was rebuilt in 1866. The alterations were carried out under the direction of Mr. Ashton Webb, architect. In pulling down the end wall numerous very interesting remains of the ancient work were found embedded in it

Alfred James Waterlow, C.C., senior partner in the firm of Waterlow Brothers and Layton, died, aged seventy-one (30th).—A great fire broke out on the premises of a wholesale paper dealer, Knightrider Street, Doctors' Commons, and resulted in the complete destruction of the church of St. Mary Magdalen, one of the plainest of Wren's structures, but solidly built. Damage was done to the extent of upwards of £100,000 (2 Dec.).—A meeting was held at the Mansion House to inaugurate the building of a Church House, as the Church of England Memorial of the Queen's Jubilee (8th). (The opening of the building took place in Feb., 1896)—The new building for the Guildhall School of Music was opened by the Lord Mayor, on the Victoria Embankment (9th).

The ceremony took place in the large hall of the City of London School close by, which was connected with the new building by a temporarily covered way. The building, which is in the Italian Renaissance style, occupies 8,000 square feet, and has three frontages to new roads It consists of four floors and 42 class rooms, on the second floor is the Orchestral Practice room, 70 feet by 28 feet. The elevations are of Portland stone. The building, which was erected from the designs of Sir Horace Jones, cost about £26,000. Hitherto the school had occupied a large warehouse, belonging to the Corporation, in Aldermanbury. The Institution, however, had grown rapidly, and there are now (1896) about 3,500 scholars taught by 100 professors.

Extensive alterations were completed at Innholders' Hall (10th). — The foundation stone of the new Central Fish Market was laid (13th). — The new building for Sion College was opened by the Prince of Wales, on the Victoria Embankment (16th).

An address was presented to His Royal Highness by the President of the College (the Rev. Prebendary Whittington, M.A.), who pointed out that the clergy of the City of London, with its suburbs, were incorporated under the style and title of the President and Fellows of Sion College, and that this College was established by Dr. Thomas White, Rector of St. Dunstan-in-the-West, in the year 1630 for "the maintenance of truth in doctrine, love in conversing together, and for the repression of such sins as do follow us men." With a view to combine "sound learning" there had been added to the foundation a library which contained nearly 80,000 books. The building is of red brick in

New Sion College and the City of London School, Victoria Embankment.

the Gothic style.   On the ground floor is the large hall, wainscoted with fine old oak panelling from the former College, and at the top is a splendid library with galleries and bays, 96 feet by 45 feet. The freehold site cost £32,000, and the building about £25,000.

The Lord Mayor unveiled the replica of the Queen Anne Statue, ordered by the Corporation, in front of St. Paul's Cathedral. The original statue, which had fallen into a very dilapidated condition, was erected in 1712 to commemorate the completion of the Cathedral (20th).—Field-Marshal Lord Napier of Magdala was appointed Constable of the Tower in the place of Sir R. J. Dacres (21st).

Careful drawings of the old Court of Exchequer and other buildings surrounding the Guildhall, removed to clear the site of the new Council Chamber, were prepared. These formed the basis of a handsome volume entitled "A descriptive account of the Guildhall, its history and associations, by John Edward Price, F.S.A.," which was issued under the direction of the Library Committee.—Mansion House Funds were raised during the year for sufferers from earthquakes in Charleston and in Greece, £7,308; for sufferers from the hurricane in St. Vincent, £1,359; and for the defence of property in Ireland, £21,422.

1887.

ANOTHER great fire broke out in Wood Street, nearly opposite the church of St. Alban, and destroyed a number of warehouses, the damage being estimated at £240,000 (1 Jan., 1887).—Mr. Henry Morton Stanley was presented, at the Guildhall, with the freedom of the City, in appreciation of his many services to the cause of science and humanity, and of his successful endeavours to discover and relieve Dr. Livingstone, the uncertainty of whose fate had caused deep anxiety. Mr. Stanley was about to set out through "Darkest Africa" in search of Emin Pasha, the lieutenant of General Gordon (13th).—The Court of Common Council expressed itself deeply moved by the sudden death of the Earl of Iddesleigh, and ordered a marble bust of the genial Conservative statesman to be executed for the Guildhall

(20th).—The Lord Mayor received at the Mansion House an influential deputation from the Irish Defence Union in aid of persons suffering from illegal coercion in Ireland. The Duke of Abercorn introduced the deputation and appealed to the public for help. The Lord Mayor said this was not a party question and he should be glad to recommend their cause to the citizens of London, and the whole English people irrespective of creed and party (8 Feb.).—Mr. Lewis H. Isaacs, M.P. for Walworth, introduced a Bill, backed by eight other Metropolitan members, for the better Government of London. The Bill provided for twelve distinct Municipalities (9th).—On the occasion of the Queen's Jubilee the Common Council resolved to present a loyal and dutiful address to Her Majesty, and to contribute £5,000 towards the Imperial Institute (14th).—The London Coal and Wine Duties Continuance Bill was introduced into the House of Commons, but was ultimately rejected.—A number of Socialists attended afternoon service at St. Paul's Cathedral, having previously given notice of their intention. Beyond occasional interruptions during the sermon, preached by Archdeacon Gifford, there was no disturbance (27th).—The tithe question gave rise about this time to considerable agitation in the parish of St. Botolph Without Aldgate (Mar.).—The Select Committee of the House of Commons, appointed at the instance of Mr. Howell, to enquire into the alleged malversation of funds by the Corporation, held its first sitting in a Committee room of the House of Commons (19th). Their report was issued on 21 May.—The year 1889 being the 700th anniversary of the institution of the mayoralty, it was referred to the Library Committee, on the motion of Mr. George Shaw, to examine such records of the Corporation as bore upon the history of London from the earliest times, with a view to the preparation of a work showing the pre-eminent position occupied by the City of London, and the important function it exercised in the shaping and making of England. The distinctive feature of the work was to be a record of the lives and deeds of those who had filled the highest civic office (24 Mar.).—The death was announced of Mr. Woodthorpe Brandon, assistant judge of the Mayor's Court.— The Corporation granted 1,000 guineas in aid of the funds of the City and Guilds of London Technical Institute, and £500 to the fund for Guy's Hospital (21 Ap.).— In order further to commemorate the Jubilee of the Queen's reign, it was resolved to hold a Reception and Ball in the Guildhall, at an expense not exceeding £6,000. A Jubilee Medal was also ordered to be struck, entertainments to be provided for the children of the Freemen's Orphan School, and for the inmates of the London Almshouses and the City of London Union (4 May).—The Committee of Lloyd's presented to the Corporation a gun recently salved from

H.M.S. "Lutine," wrecked off the coast of Holland in the year 1799 (5th).—
The Lord Mayor and Corporation attended Her Majesty The Queen, at
Buckingham Palace, and presented the Corporation's address rejoicing at the
forthcoming completion of the fiftieth year of Her Majesty's beneficent and
enlightened reign (9th).—The Queen opened in person the Queen's Hall (the
great Central Hall, which was the only part of the building then completed) of
the People's Palace, Mile End Road (14th).

Her Majesty, accompanied by Princess Beatrice and Prince Henry of Battenberg, drove in an
open carriage from Paddington to Mile End, being throughout received with great enthusiasm by vast
crowds of people.   The main streets of the City through which Her Majesty had to pass were gaily
decorated   In accordance with ancient custom, the Queen was received at the City boundary by the
Lord Mayor, who preceded Her Majesty over the Viaduct, and along Newgate Street and Cheapside, to
the Eastern boundary of the City, at Aldgate.   Here the civic carriages drew aside, the mace being
reversed and the sword lowered as the Queen passed.   Her Majesty amidst great enthusiasm declared the
Hall open.   Before proceeding to lay the foundation stone of the Technical and Handicraft Schools,
for which the Drapers' Company had subscribed £20,000, Her Majesty conferred the honour of
Knighthood upon Mr. John Rogers Jennings, Master of the Company.—An intimation having been
conveyed to the Lord Mayor that the Queen would be pleased to break the return journey at the
Mansion House, the most elaborate preparations were made for Her Majesty's reception.   The Mansion
House itself was gaily adorned on the outside with flags and trophies, while the balconies were draped
with crimson cloth, and the pillars hung with wreaths of primroses and violets   Inside was a picture of
floral beauty, everywhere being stately palms, flowering plants, roses, orchids, and other sweet-scented
flowers, the Egyptian Hall being decorated with flags and banners, Royal, Civic, and personal   The Royal
party included Princesses Helena and Beatrice, the Princess of Wales and her Daughters, the Princesses
Louise and Victoria, the Duke of Cambridge, Prince Christian, Prince Henry of Battenberg, the Duchess
of Teck, the Crown Prince of Denmark, and lastly the Prince of Wales   A service of solid gold was
provided specially for the Queen, who expressed great satisfaction with the proceedings of the day   Her
Majesty also, before leaving, shook hands with the veteran Alderman, Sir Robert Carden, and said, "I
am pleased, Sir Robert, to see you looking so well."   The 4th Battalion Royal Fusiliers furnished a
guard of honour at the Mansion House   It was announced on the 18th that Her Majesty had conferred
a baronetcy upon the Lord Mayor, and that the Sheriffs were to be knighted

Sir Horace Jones, City Architect, died on the 21st May.

He was born in Sise Lane, Bucklersbury, 20 May, 1819, and during the twenty-three years he
had held office under the Corporation a large number of important works had been carried out
He did not live to see the completion of his latest design, that of Tower Bridge.

It was announced that Her Majesty had conferred a baronetcy upon
Sir Robert Walter Carden, Knight, the senior Alderman and Father of
the City (9 June).—The Select Committee of the House of Commons on
the London City Tithes (St. Botolph Without Aldgate) Bill decided that
it should not be proceeded with (15th).—At the Jubilee service, held in Westminster Abbey, the City deputation included the Lord Mayor and Lady Mayoress,
the Sheriffs, and nearly one hundred Aldermen and members of the Common
Council, who proceeded to the Abbey in state.

In the evening the City was brilliantly illuminated. The Drapers' Company treated 20,000 children to a day's holiday at the People's Palace, and 4,000 adults were afterwards entertained in a similar manner. Most of the other City Companies did something to commemorate the Jubilee of Her Majesty's reign, which was celebrated in all parts of the world. A special thanksgiving service was held at St. Paul's Cathedral on the 23rd and was attended in state by the Corporation, the Livery Companies, and the Court of Lieutenancy. Several Indian princes and other Jubilee guests were entertained to dinner at Fishmongers' Hall (24th).

The Jubilee Ball, at the Guildhall, was the civic event of the year (28th). Several crowned heads and many representatives of the Royal families of Europe, including nearly every member of our own Royal House, honoured the City with their company.

The Guildhall was magnificently upholstered and decorated, and fragrant with sweet scented flowers with a background of palms and ferns A bridge had been specially constructed over the library staircase and a communication made into the old Bankruptcy Court or Annexe, where a splendid suite of apartments had been extemporised for the use of the guests. A dais was erected at the northern side of the Hall, and behind this all the apartments were reserved for royalty. The old Council Chamber and the Aldermen's Court Room were converted into royal supper rooms. After two quadrilles had been danced, the Royal guests, with the Lord Mayor and Lady Mayoress, proceeded thither in the following order :—

The Lord Mayor
H M the King of Denmark
H.M. the King of the Hellenes
H.M the King of the Belgians.
H.M. the King of Saxony.
H.R.H the Prince of Wales.
H.R H. the Crown Prince of Portugal.
H.R H. the Grand Duke of Mecklenburg-Strelitz.
H.R.H. the Crown Prince of Sweden.

H R H. the Grand Duke of Hesse
H.I.H. the Grand Duke Serge
H.R.H. the Duke of Edinburgh
H.R.H. the Duke of Connaught.
H.R.H. the Duke of Cambridge

H.R H Prince William of Prussia.

H R H the Duke of Sparta
H R H. Prince Louis of Bavaria.
H.R.H the Infante Antonio d'Orléans

H.M. the Queen of the Belgians.
The Lady Mayoress
H.R H. the Princess of Wales.
H I. & R H. the Crown Princess of Germany.
H.R.H the Crown Princess of Portugal.
H.M. the Queen of Hawaii.
H.R.H the Infanta Eulalia of Spain.
H I.H the Grand Duchess Elizabeth of Russia.
H.R.H. the Grand Duchess of Mecklenburg-Strelitz
H.R H the Princess William of Prussia.
H.R.H. the Duchess of Edinburgh
H.R.H. the Duchess of Connaught.
H R.H the Princess of Saxe-Meiningen.
II.R.H. the Hereditary Grand Duchess of Mecklenburg-Strelitz.
H.R.H. the Princess Christian of Schleswig-Holstein
H.R H the Princess Beatrice.
H R H the Duchess of Teck.
H R.H. the Princess Philip of Saxe-Coburg and Gotha

The Common Council resolved that the stones and other portions of old Temple Bar should be given to Sir Henry Bruce Meux, Bart., upon the understanding that the Bar was to be re-erected at the entrance to Theobalds Park, Cheshunt, at the cost of Sir Henry (23rd).—The Lord Mayor opened the new thoroughfare from Monument Yard to the Coal Exchange, in Lower Thames Street, made by the Commissioners of Sewers, with the object of relieving the congestion of traffic at Billingsgate (6 July).—The Honourable Artillery Company celebrated the 350th anniversary of its incorporation by a regimental parade and banquet, at their headquarters, Finsbury (11th).

A deputation attended from the Ancient and Honourable Artillery Company of Boston, U.S.A. This corps is itself nearly 250 years old, and was founded by Robert Keane, a member of the Honourable Artillery Company of London, who left the old country for conscience' sake.

The Common Council agreed to a design for the erection of a new City of London Court, at a cost of £16,000, including fittings. — The foundation stone of Bancroft's School, at Woodford, which was to be erected at a cost of £50,000 by the Drapers' Company, who

View of the Monument, and the Roadway of Old London Bridge, 1809.
From an Old Print, preserved in the Guildhall Library.

also gave the site, was laid by Prince Albert Victor. The school was intended to board, clothe and educate 100 boys, one-half of whom were to be selected by public examination from the elementary schools of London. This was the first experiment of the kind (16th). — Mr. T. C. Baring was returned unopposed as a representative of the City in Parliament, in succession to the Hon. J. G. Hubbard, who had been raised to the peerage (20th).—The members of the Association for the Reform and Codification of the Law of Nations met in conference at Guildhall (25th).—A memorial medallion portrait of Charles Reade, the novelist, was unveiled in the Crypt of St. Paul's (2 Aug.).—A range of new buildings, known as St. Dunstan's House, Fetter Lane, were opened by Messrs. Sampson Low & Co. (23rd).—The Common Council decided to appoint a City Surveyor, at a salary of £800 per annum, instead of an Architect, in place of the late Sir Horace Jones (20 Sept.). This resolution, however, was rescinded, and it was resolved (3 Nov.) to appoint an Architect and Surveyor at a salary of £1,500 per annum. Mr. Alexander Marshall Peebles was elected to the office (15 Dec.). — The Lord Mayor opened Kilburn Park, which had been taken over from the Ecclesiastical Commissioners, and laid out by the Corporation at an expense of about £3,000 (5 Nov.).—Lord Mayor Polydore De Keyser arranged for an in-

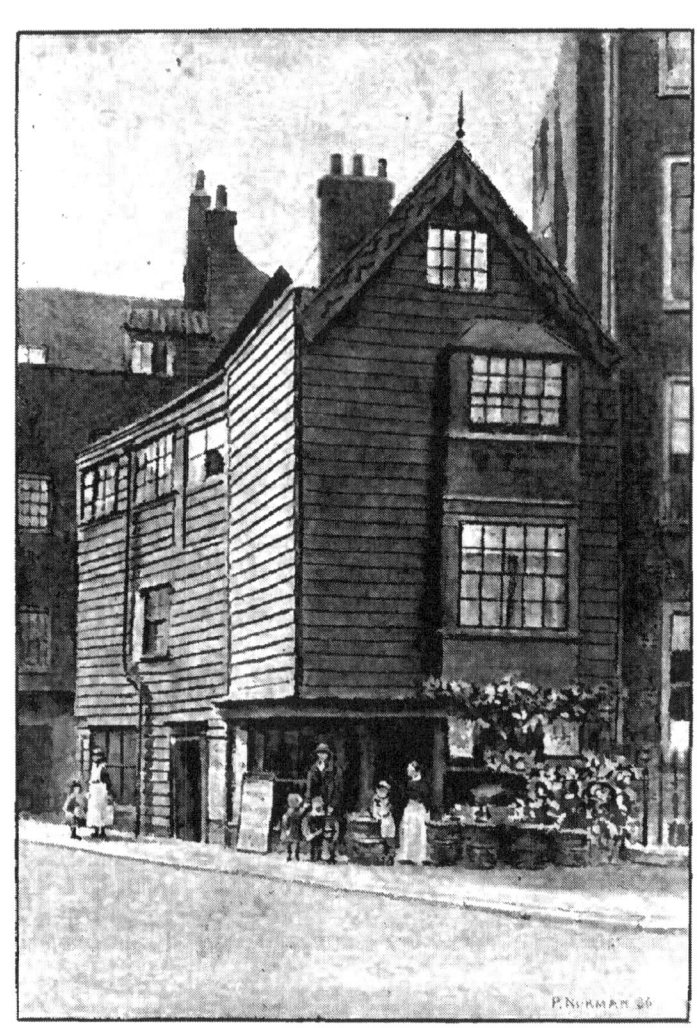

Old House, Bartholomew Close—destroyed 1887.

teresting procession on 9 Nov., but the effect was marred by the weather. At the Guildhall Banquet in the evening, Lord Salisbury announced that Ayoob Khan, the pretender to the throne of Afghanistan, had surrendered himself to the Indian Government.—The Lord Mayor received at the Mansion House the Burgomasters of Brussels, Liège, and Termonde (his native town), who presented him with addresses of congratulation (10th).—Alderman Sir William McArthur, K.C.M.G., died suddenly on the Underground Railway (16th).—The Lord Chancellor laid the foundation stone of the new building for the City of London Court (23rd). —A special Committee was appointed by the Common Council to inquire fully into the finances of the Corporation, with a view to extending its usefulness (8 Dec.).—During the year (1887) Mr. John Morley delivered an address at the Mansion House, on the Study of Literature, in connection with the London Society for the extension of University Teaching.—The Lord Mayor gave a banquet to the International Congress which met to celebrate the Tercentenary of Shorthand.—The City of London Ballot Act, promoted by the Corporation, was passed.—By orders of the Local Government Board, 7 June and 26 July, 1887, the Port of London Sanitary Authority was made the registration authority under the Canal Boats' Act, 1877, in respect of the Grand Surrey Canal, the Regent's Canal, and the Thames River.—Mansion House funds were raised in connection with the fire at Exeter, £1,621; and the cholera at Malta, £149.

1888.

THE *Times* newspaper completed its 100th year of publication under that title (1 Jan., 1888).—The honour of knighthood was conferred upon Mr. Owen Roberts, M.A., F.S.A., clerk of the Clothworkers' Company, in order to mark Her Majesty's sense of the important public services he had rendered in connection with technical education (7th).—A letter was read to the Court of Aldermen addressed to the Chamberlain by the clerk of the Stationers' Company, repeating a suggestion, made by the Company in 1858, with regard to apprenticeship. It expressed the hope that the Aldermen would take the necessary steps to revive, within the City, the ancient and honourable custom of apprenticeship, by revising the terms of the indentures so as to make them more in accord with the custom of printers in the City. It was pointed out that the indentures had long become obsolete owing to the discontinuance of the practice of taking indoor apprentices. The proposal was favourably commented upon and referred to a committee for consideration.— Alderman Sir John Staples, K.C.M.G., died (19th).

Mr. John Staples entered the Common Council in 1865. He was the author of " Notes on the Church of St. Botolph, Aldersgate," and took much interest in antiquarian subjects, and in the welfare of the Guildhall Library.

The Rev. H. C. Shuttleworth headed a deputation to the Common Council in support of a petition of the National Sunday League praying that the Guildhall

Library and Museum, and the Art Gallery might be opened on some part of Sundays. A proposal to refer the subject to committee was rejected by 54 votes to 50 (19th). —Sir Robert Walter Carden, Bart., Senior Alderman, died at 64, Wimpole Street.

> Robert Walter Carden was born 7 Oct., 1801, his mother being a daughter of Mr. John Walter, founder of the *Times.* He obtained a commission in the 82nd Foot in 1816, and remained in that regiment until 1822, when he was admitted a member of the Stock Exchange. He died "father of the House" after 65 years of membership He entered the Corporation as Alderman of Dowgate Ward, in 1849, and was afterwards transferred to Bridge Without. Sir Robert was a thorough-going Tory, and an excellent magistrate He interested himself greatly in the work of Ragged Schools, and his generosity and geniality made him a universal favourite

A reredos of marble, in many varieties and colours, was erected in St. Paul's Cathedral at a cost of some £25,000.

> Messrs. Bodley and Garner were the architects, and the latter the designer of this further effort to complete St Paul's according to the intentions of Sir Christopher Wren. In one compartment was a representation of the crucifixion in bas relief, and above this was a statue of the Virgin and Child. The reredos, which was publicly dedicated on the 25th, gave great offence to the Evangelical party in the church, who petitioned the Privy Council against it Four persons at once commenced proceedings with a view to having the erection declared illegal, on the ground that "such sculptures tended to encourage superstitious ideas and devotions, and were unlawful," according to the Public Worship Regulation Act. The Bishop of London refused to allow the case to proceed, but the High Court of Justice decided that the Bishop had no absolute discretion to stop the case, and ordered him to withdraw his veto (1 June, 1889). After further litigation, on 17 June, 1890, a rule *nisi* for a mandamus was granted by the Queen's Bench

The Lord Mayor visited Brussels and was the guest of the King and Queen of the Belgians at a Court dinner given in his honour at the Palace (7 Feb.).—The Right Hon. G. J. Goschen, M.P., D.C.L., was presented with the freedom of the Fishmongers' Company.—The Special Committee presented a report to the Common Council on London Government, and recommended for adoption the principle of nine separate Municipalities as affording the best guarantee for the good government of the Metropolis, and the municipal welfare of its inhabitants. The report was agreed to (9th).—The Corporation also subscribed 200 guineas towards the fund for securing the holding of the centenary meetings of the Royal Agricultural Society, at Windsor in 1889 (16th). The Mansion House Fund for this object reached a total of £5,919.—The Corporation voted 100 guineas to the Mansion House Fund to meet the expenses of the British section of the Paris Universal Exhibition, 1889, and at the same time gave a guarantee of £1,000.—A memorial to the late Sir Bartle Frere was dedicated in the Crypt of St. Paul's (3 Mar.).— The Lord Mayor announced to the Common Council the death of the Emperor of Germany, and a resolution of condolence with the Imperial family was passed (9th).—The Lord Mayor and a deputation from the Corporation attended the

Prince and Princess of Wales, at Marlborough House (in accordance with a resolution of 15 Dec., 1887), to present the City's congratulations on the occasion of their silver wedding, and presented the Princess with a silver model of the Imperial Institute (10th).—The Corporation resolved to appear by counsel, if

The last private garden in the City—No. 4, Crosby Square.

necessary, against the London City Tithes (St. Botolph Without Aldgate) Bill, for the purpose of obtaining some reduction in the terms of the Act of 1881 (15th).—By the demolition of the house, 21, Austin Friars, an interesting relic of Old London passed away.

This was one of the last of the old mercantile residences of the City, and stood on what was formerly part of the garden of the Priory of the St. Augustine monks. The house in question was probably built between the years 1660 and 1670, and appears on the Map of London prepared by John Ogilby and William Morgan who were appointed to make a survey of the City after the Great Fire. It was a large and substantial building, lined throughout with solid wainscoting, its apartments roomy, and its staircases broad and carved with curious antique designs. The garden and all the original offices were preserved, and the counting-house, the yard, the coach-house and stables, the bakehouse, even the old well and pump, remained as they were at the time when the house was built.

Mr. Ritchie, President of the Local Government Board, introduced the Local Government Bill in the House of Commons, a Bill which created the London County Council and deprived the City of some of its privileges (19th).—The

Common Council decided to construct chill rooms at the Foreign Cattle Market, Deptford, at a cost of £13,000.—Mr. John Stoneham, a member of the Common Council, who started the discount book trade in the City, at his shop in Cheapside, died (8 Ap.).—The Corporation voted 100 guineas to the Mansion House Fund for the relief of sufferers from the inundations at Posen, in Germany. The fund reached a total of £5,766.—The Marquis of Hartington was presented with the freedom of the City as a mark of the Corporation's high appreciation of the wise and patriotic spirit evinced by his Lordship during his parliamentary career, and especially in connection with the events of recent times affecting the welfare of the United Kingdom (18th). — The Local Government Bill was read a second time in the House of Commons without a division (20th).—A portion of old London Wall was laid bare by the removal of the Bull and Mouth Hotel and the French Protestant Church, which were taken down to make room for the new buildings for the General Post Office.

> The length of wall exposed to view was about 100 feet, the lower portion of it being composed of stones and bricks laid in alternate strata after the manner of the Romans. It was arranged that, as far as possible, the wall should remain undisturbed by the new building.

Mr. Firth, in the House of Commons, moved :

> " That in the opinion of this House it is necessary, without delay, to place the expenditure of the Corporation of London under similar statutory restrictions to those to which other Corporations in the Kingdom are subject "

The resolution was rejected by 156 votes to 133 (8 May).—An order was issued to the City of London Volunteers stating that the country was in danger and that all leave of absence was cancelled until further notice (11th).—Representatives of the Burgomasters and other members of the Civic Corporations of Belgium accepted the invitation of the Lord Mayor to visit London for a few days, and were entertained at the Mansion House.—Dr. Stainer, organist of St. Paul's Cathedral, was Knighted (2 June).—The Corporation voted 200 guineas towards the expenses of the Irish Exhibition (7th).—A meeting in support of a scheme to establish a Polytechnic in South London was held at the Mansion House (8th). Amongst those who supported the Lord Mayor were the Marquis of Salisbury and the Earl of Rosebery.—It was announced that the Prince of Wales had sent a command to the Hon. Artillery Company to place itself at once under the Volunteer or Mutiny Acts (13th).

> The trouble which gave rise to this order began soon after the change in the appointment of Lieutenant-Colonel of the Company. Almost autocratic power gradually fell into the hands of the Adjutant, which occasioned much ill-feeling, only increased by the references to insubordination which appeared in a short history of the Company, written by Captain Woolmer Williams. Resolutions

were passed in accordance with the "proposal" of the Prince of Wales, and the Secretary of State for War promised, in the House of Commons, that an enquiry should be made into the charge of insubordination.

A tablet to the memory of the War Correspondents, who were killed during the Soudan Campaign, was unveiled in St. Paul's Cathedral (16th) —The Common Council passed a resolution expressing deep regret at the intelligence of the death of the Emperor of Germany, son-in-law of Her Majesty the Queen (21st).—The Commissioners of Sewers instructed the Remembrancer to oppose the Technical Instruction Bill, then before Parliament, it being stated that under the Bill the School Board would be entitled to levy an additional rate of one penny in the pound for technical education (26th).—Mr. W. H. Overall, F.S.A., Librarian of the Guildhall Library, died on the 28th.

He was born in 1829, and entered the service of the Corporation in 1847 as an assistant in the Town Clerk's Office. He had been connected with the Library since 1857.

The Duchess of Albany laid the foundation stone of the new schools for the parish of St. Bartholomew-the-Great, Smithfield, on some vacant land, south of the buildings which up to the time of Henry VIII formed the Lady Chapel of the Priory Church (5 July).—The Lord Mayor and Lady Mayoress gave a banquet to celebrate the fiftieth anniversary of Her Majesty's Coronation —On the 18th the Library Committee appointed Mr Charles Welch to the office of City Librarian — The freedom of the Grocers' Company was presented to Mr A. J. Balfour, M.P., and Sir Frederick Leighton (25th).— In connection with a fire in La Belle Sauvage Yard, Mr. Langham, City Coroner, held the first fire inquest under the Act, recently passed, for holding inquests on all fires occurring within the City. The Coroner pointed out that this was really the revival of an old custom (26th).—The Corporation voted 100 guineas to the Mansion House Fund for the sufferers from floods at Poplar and the Isle of Dogs (2 Aug.). The total sum raised was £4,547. —Lord Salisbury, speaking at the Ministerial banquet at the Mansion House (8th), complimented Mr. Ritchie on having carried the Local Government Bill through the House of Commons, and remarked :

"I may be allowed, though I touch on delicate subjects, to say that not the least among the pleasures which his success has given me is the feeling that if this settlement is final, as I believe it will be, we have solved the problem, the difficult problem, of the Government of this Metropolis without any substantial injury to the long descended and valuable privileges which you, my Lord, and the Corporation which you so worthily rule over, have so long exercised and enjoyed. On the contrary, I venture to prophesy that under the new state of things the Lord Mayor and the Corporation of London will be, if it is possible, even a greater factor in our political affairs, a more splendid figure in the eyes of all foreign nations, than they have been up to this time."

In the House of Commons the Lords' amendments to the Local Government Bill were considered (10th).

An amendment which proposed to retain the appointment of the Recorder in the hands of the Corporation of the City of London, with a proviso that after the next vacancy no Recorder should exercise any judicial functions unless appointed by Her Majesty to exercise such functions, was agreed to in the Commons by a majority of 33. The Common Serjeant and the Judge of the City of London Court, who were formerly appointed by the Common Council, are, under the Local Government Act, 1888, appointed by the Crown, but their salaries are fixed and paid by the Corporation. Under the same Act the citizens were deprived of the right of electing a Sheriff of Middlesex, which had been granted by Charter of Henry I. A number of minor changes affecting the City were also made by the Local Government Act

The Mansion House Conference on the unemployed reported that relief works were an injury to the community and calculated to intensify rather than remedy the evil (9th).

Of the 456 men to whom work was offered 14 per cent. put in no appearance, 30 per cent. were dismissed for incapacity or misconduct, 4 per cent. left for better employment, 6 per cent. emigrated, 12 per cent. were effectually assisted in various ways, and 36 per cent. the Committee were unable to raise from their low social status

Mr. Edward Stanhope, Secretary for War, wrote to the Lord Mayor with reference to the willingness of the Corporation to grant a site for military purposes on Coulsdon Common, and expressing the thanks of the Government for the patriotic consideration the Corporation had given to the matter (10th).—The Lord Mayor, accompanied by the Sheriffs, made a state visit to his native town, Termonde or Dendermonde, in Belgium (26th). The house where the Lord Mayor was born bears a commemorative tablet which tells how its former occupant became Chief Magistrate of the City of London.—The Common Council adopted a report of the City of London School Committee in favor of greater attention being given to the teaching of modern languages (20 Sept.).

Dr Abbott (the headmaster) expressed the opinion that the teaching of German should be made compulsory, and that French should be taught by the class masters as well as by the French master. A proposal to establish two distinct branches of education, 1 a Classical School 2 a Commercial School, was rejected.

Mr. Alderman and Sheriff Gray opened St. Dunstan's College, the funds of which were derived from the charities of St. Dunstan's-in-the-East (21st).— Alderman James Whitehead was elected Lord Mayor.—About this time a number of horrible murders were committed, the victims being women of the "unfortunate" class ; no trace whatever could be found of the perpetrator of these atrocities, who was known by the name of Jack-the-Ripper.

Most of the murders and mutilations took place in the East of London, but in the early morning of the 30th the body of Kate Conway was found within the City precincts, in Mitre Square, and about the same hour the body of another woman, named Stride, was discovered in Bradford Street. The Lord Mayor at once offered a reward of £500 for the discovery and conviction of the Mitre Square murderer or murderers, an action which was approved by the Common Council (4 Oct.). All attempts to find the assassin were however ineffectual, and the crimes remained a mystery.

The new technical schools, provided by the Drapers' Company, at the People's Palace, at a cost of £20,000, were opened by the Master of the Company (5 Oct.)— It was announced that the Goldsmiths' Company intended to erect and endow an Institute at New Cross at a cost of £85,000 (9th).—The Lord Mayor, accompanied by the Sheriffs, opened the new Fish Market, erected by the Corporation, on Snow Hill, replacing the market opposite, which it was intended should revert to its original purpose of a Fruit and Vegetable Market, but which was actually converted into an annexe of the Meat and Poultry Market. The new market, designed by Sir Horace Jones, occupies a space of 14,000 square feet and cost about £25,000 (7 Nov.).— The "Show" on Lord Mayor's day was devoid of the spectacular element, an innovation which was regarded by some with favour and by others with disapproval.

Lord Mayor Whitehead and Mr. Alderman and Sheriff Newton, by way of compensation, gave a substantial meal and entertainment to 10,000 poor people in East London, and also arranged for special gifts to the pauper children at Hanwell, and the sick inmates of the City of London Union at Margate

Miss Davenport Hill, Mr. Albert Rutson (Progressives), Rev. W. Martin and Sir R. Temple, Bart., M.P. (Moderates) were elected for the City on the London School Board (27th).—It was decided to erect a Fruit and Vegetable Market on a portion of the vacant land north of Charterhouse Street at a cost of £15,500, also to build on the vacant land opposite Billingsgate Market, which the Corporation were about to acquire from the Commissioners of Sewers, a structure of three floors of offices, the ground floor being used for the purpose of shops and stalls for the fish trade.—The new building for the City of London Court was opened by the Lord Mayor (6 Dec.).

The new Court building is situated on the south side of Guildhall Buildings and on the west side of Basinghall Street, and occupies the site of the old Court Buildings, the old Land Tax Offices, and the "tap" of the Guildhall Tavern. On the ground floor are offices for the clerks and bailiffs, and above are the Judges' Court and the Registrar's Court. The building is in the Gothic style and harmonises with the Guildhall. Mr. Andrew Murray, A R.I.B.A., was the architect.

The Cheapside end of Queen Street was widened, and considerable alterations were made at the north-west corner of St Paul's Churchyard.—Lady Holles' School for Girls, in Redcross Street, was re-built.—The union of St. Margaret's Lothbury with St Olave's Old Jewry was effected.

1889.

LORD ROSEBERY came forward as a candidate for the City in the new London County Council (7 Jan., 1889). Addressing a City meeting under the presidency of the Rev. Prebendary Rogers, he explained the motives of his candidature. He said :—

"I am glad that my first appearance as a candidate should be under the auspices of one of the best and largest-hearted men I know. As he says, it is not personal ambition that brings me forward I do not think the work will be of that brilliant or attractive sort that it will cause those who wish to make a show in the world to be anxious to take a part in it. My point of view is more simple. I received an invitation from more than 1,100 citizens, of all shades of politics, asking me to come forward, and I thought it a clear case of duty to comply with that request, for it seemed to me that the experiment you are about to make is so vast a one that it needs the co-operation and energy of every inhabitant of London, however humble, to bring the undertaking to a successful issue." Speaking later on at the Memorial Hall, Lord Rosebery said he did not come before them as the owner of two houses in the City of London, or as being connected with any commercial firm, but on the broad ground of a United London. A United London was the great principle laid down by the Local Government Bill, as far as it affected London, and for the first time it brought London into a harmonious whole, with the City as its centre, and he hoped as its leader.

The first elections to the London County Council took place on the 17th. The following were returned for the City:—Sir John Lubbock, Bart., 8,976 ; Lord Rosebery, 8,032 ; Mr. Benjamin L. Cohen, 3,925 ; Mr. Henry Clarke, 3,022.   The unsuccessful candidates were Mr George Shaw, 2,752 ; Mr. G. N. Johnson, 729 Lord Rosebery was elected Chairman of the Council, Sir John Lubbock, Vice-Chairman, and Mr. Firth, Deputy-Chairman.—The Lord Mayor accompanied by Mr. Sheriff Newton paid a state visit to Kendal (8th).— Alderman Sir Thomas Scambler Owden died at Sutton (8th)

He had been connected with the Corporation for 41 years, having been returned as a member of the Common Council for Bishopsgate Ward in 1847 He was Chairman of the East London Union until it was united with the West London Union, under the title of the City of London Union.

A conference on vagrancy was held in the Board Room of the City of London Union, delegates attending from nearly all the Metropolitan Unions (14th).—A farewell banquet was given at the Mansion House to the American Minister (Hon. E. J. Phelps).   The company included leading statesmen, bankers and merchants, distinguished representatives of art, science, literature and law, ministers of religion, journalists and dramatists.

The American Minister recalled how, nearly four years ago, in that hall, at a dinner given by Lord Mayor Fowler, he made his first appearance on any public occasion in England, and addressed his first words to an English company, and now his last public words were being spoken under the same hospitable roof Alluding to the fallibility of public men he made use of a happy epigram : "The man who never makes a mistake never makes anything." This Mansion House festivity had more than usual significance, the relations between this country and the United States being somewhat strained, owing to a letter having been written by the British Ambassador at Washington to some news-paper correspondent just before the Presidential Election, which led the United States Government to demand his recall Mr Phelps afterwards wrote to the Lord Mayor to say that such felicitous amenities as the welcome he had received at the Mansion House were stronger than treaties.

The first meeting of the London County Council was held in the Board Room of the Metropolitan Board of Works, Spring Gardens (31st).—In response to a letter from Sir John Lubbock, Bart., M.P., provisional chairman of the London County Council, the Corporation agreed to lend the Council Chamber at Guildhall for the purposes of the London County Council, for a period of three months (7 Feb.).—The Common Council passed a resolution of regret and condolence on the occasion of the sudden death of the Crown Prince Rudolph of Austria-Hungary.—The Commissioners of Sewers decided to advertise for tenders to light the whole City by electricity, reserving to themselves the right to acquire the undertaking by purchase at the end of twenty-one years (26th). For the purposes of lighting, the City was divided into three districts western, central, and eastern. Special provision was made for the supply of electricity to any owner or occupier within 25 yards of the mains.—The Lord Mayor and Lady Mayoress gave a reception and conversazione to London and provincial journalists at the Mansion House in connection with the inauguration of the Institute of Journalists (9 Mar.).—The Rev. Dr. Abbott tendered his resignation as Head Master of the City of London School (14th).—A Bill in relation to the binding of apprentices according to the custom of the City of London, and the form of indenture of City apprenticeship, was read a third time and became an Act of the Court of Common Council.—The Corporation voted £105 to the Mansion House Fund for the purpose of sending a representative body of London workmen to the Paris Exhibition with a view of supplying industrial reports on the various exhibits of arts and manufactures. The fund amounted to £1,361.—The Blacksmiths' Company opened an Exhibition at Ironmongers' Hall (25th).—The Common Council passed a resolution of regret at the death of the Right Hon. John Bright, "a good man and a distinguished statesman" (28th).—The Court resolved to celebrate in a suitable manner the 700th anniversary of the mayoralty of the City of London.—The Library Association of the United Kingdom visited the Guildhall Library and Museum. The Librarian read a paper on the "Guildhall Library and its work," which was afterwards issued as a pamphlet with additions and an appendix (10 Ap.).—The Common Council expressed sympathy with the Queen and the Duke of Cambridge on the death of Her Royal Highness the Duchess of Cambridge.—The Engineer to the Commissioners of Sewers (Col. Haywood) in a report issued on 20 Ap. gave an account of improvements effected by the Commissioners during the last thirty-eight years. He said ·

"In the year 1879 I found that, counting every street, court and place which was public way, however small, the Commissioners had improved, in a greater or less degree, since the year 1843, upwards of 400 of them. The total number of public ways of all classes now existing in the City is 731, and the Commissioners had effected improvements in 262 of them. With the exception of King William Street, Moorgate Street, Holborn Viaduct and approaches, and Cannon Street improvement, carried out by the Corporation, and also Queen Victoria Street, which, although constructed by the Metropolitan Board of Works, was designed by the Corporation, there is not a main thoroughfare in

FFF 2

the City which the Commissioners have not, to some extent, and in many cases to a large extent, improved, and every ward of the City has had its share of expenditure for that purpose. During the past thirty-eight years the Commissioners have expended out of the consolidated rate of the City a gross sum of upwards of £3,900,000 for improvements. Towards these the Metropolitan Board has contributed something like £591,000, which amount, together with that received by the Commissioners for the sale of surplus lands, etc., amounting to £1,121,000, leaves a sum approaching £2,188,000 spent by the Commissioners for improvements in the City since the year 1850. In addition to this large expenditure it must be borne in mind that the City of London pays annually about one-eighth of the entire cost of all the improvements in the Metropolis effected by the Metropolitan Board of Works."

With a great gathering in Holloway Hall, the Lord Mayor brought to a successful close the four mass meetings which he had addressed in aid of a new hospital scheme. The object of the movement was to organize in every factory, workshop, warehouse, club, and all centres of labour a contribution of a penny a week towards the support of hospitals, dispensaries, and convalescent homes (27th).—The Lord Mayor and Sheriffs, at the invitation of the President of the French Republic, visited Paris and attended the Universal Exhibition in commemoration of the commencement of the Revolution of 1789 (9 May). Special significance was attached to this visit owing to the fact that the British Ambassador in Paris was not allowed to attend the festivities.

The Lord Mayor was received by the President of the French Republic (M. Carnot), the Prime Minister (M. Tirard), the President of the Paris Municipality (Dr. Emile Chautemps), and the people of Paris, with many signs of appreciation and esteem. The Lord Mayor made a visit to the Pasteur Institute for the treatment of hydrophobia, for which he afterwards raised funds amounting to £2,839. His lordship dined with President Carnot at the Elysée, and was entertained at a splendid banquet at the Hotel de Ville, afterwards receiving the ministers as his guests at the Grand Hotel. A deputation from the British Chamber of Commerce in Paris waited upon the Lord Mayor.

The Corporation, at the request of Lord Rosebery, agreed to allow the London County Council the further use of the Guildhall Council Chamber for a period of three months (16th).—A Bill to repeal the rights possessed by the City and the late Metropolitan Board of Works with regard to the coal dues was debated in the House of Commons (22nd). The London County Council supported the measure, which was read a second time, and subsequently passed into law.

A duty of 1s. 1d. had been levied on all coal coming into the police area, which extended over 700 square miles. The money thus raised was applied exclusively to Metropolitan and City improvements, the City share of the tax being 4d.

Alderman Sir Thomas Dakin, the "father" of the Corporation, died in his 82nd year (24th).

In early life he was an active promoter of mechanics' institutions, and himself lectured on chemistry and electricity. He entered the Corporation in 1842 as a representative of the Ward of Candlewick.

Sir Thomas Fowell Buxton, Bart , and Mr. Edward North Buxton presented the Corporation with fifteen acres of land at Theydon Bois, called "Oak Hall Enclosure," as an addition to the area of Epping Forest (23rd).—It was resolved to improve the external lobby of the Council Chamber in the Guildhall at a cost of £2,146.—The Lord Mayor organized a scheme for the thorough equipment of the volunteer force within the Metropolitan area.   In an article, which he contributed to the June number of the *Contemporary Review*, entitled "A Patriotic Volunteer Fund" he said :

"Within the Metropolitan area there are forty-three volunteer regiments, numbering about 31,000 men Out of these 31,000 men there are, according to the returns furnished me, 26,000 who have no great coats, 6,000 without water bottles, 6,000 without haversacks, 25,000 without mess tins, 29,600 without undress tunics, 31,000 (the whole number) without extra trousers, 23,600 without either kit-bags or valises, 31,000 (the whole number) without a pair of strong military boots, and 31,000 (the whole number again) without knife and lanyard."

The Lord Mayor appealed to the City Companies and others for a sum of £85,000, the Corporation voting £5,000 in five annual instalments.   A sum of about £42,000 was raised.—The freedom of the City was presented to the Marquis of Dufferin and Ava, late Viceroy and Governor-General of India, and formerly Governor-General of Canada, in recognition of his distinguished and valuable services to his country as a statesman and diplomatist throughout a long public career (29th).—Prince George of Wales was admitted to the freedom of the City by patrimony (1 June).—The Select Committee of the House of Commons threw out the London Central Subway Railway Bill (7th).—On the motion of Mr. Treloar it was referred to the Finance and Improvement Committee of the Commissioners of Sewers to take immediate steps to complete the improvement of Ludgate Hill (18th).—The Sheriffs were elected for the first time for the City of London only, the right to elect a Sheriff of Middlesex having been taken away by the Local Government Act of 1888 (24th).—An attack was made in the House of Commons upon the Irish Society and the City Companies who had estates in Ireland, and a Committee was appointed to enquire into the allegations (28th).

The Committee reported to Parliament that, from the evidence of the witnesses examined, it appeared that there was no complaint as to the manner in which the Irish Society had performed its duties ; and with regard to the different City Companies it was admitted that till recently they had acted with liberality   They had built churches and schools throughout their respective districts, and had subscribed with great liberality to the local charities.

The Foreign and Colonial Delegates who were attending the World's Sunday School Convention in the City were received by the Lord Mayor at the Mansion House (1 July).—The Corporation presented an address to the Shah at Guildhall. His Imperial Majesty, who was a second time welcomed to the City of London, was entertained to a déjeuner in the Guildhall, the Lord Mayor presiding, amongst the guests being the Prince of Wales and the Marquis of Salisbury.—The Common Council agreed to a report of the Library Committee upon the reference to prepare, at an expense not exceeding £1,000, a work showing the pre-eminent position occupied by the City of London and the important function it exercised in the shaping and making of England ; illustrating, as far as possible from the City's archives, the various points in the reference of the 24 Mar., 1887. This work was placed in the hands of Dr. R. R. Sharpe, the Records' Clerk, and has since been completed. A medal was at the same time ordered to be struck to commemorate the 700th anniversary of the Mayoralty (11th) — The further use of the Council Chamber was granted to the London County Council until the enlarged chamber at Spring Gardens should be ready for occupation —At a large meeting of London and provincial merchants and traders at the Mansion House, an association was formed to oppose the revised classification and schedule of railway rates which enabled the Railway Companies greatly to increase their charges on various classes of goods. A fund was opened at the Mansion House to provide the necessary means for opposing the Railway Companies in Parliament and before the Board of Trade (26th).—The "Magdalena," having on board the Lord Mayor and Corporation, was the only merchant vessel entitled to go in the Royal procession to witness the Naval Review at Spithead (3 Aug.).—Mr. R. W. Crawford, a director of the Bank of England and formerly M.P. for the City, died.—The Charity Commissioners issued a draft scheme for dealing with the Parochial Charities of the City of London (4 Sept.).—The Mansion House Committee of Conciliation, presided over by the Lord Mayor, succeeded in bringing to a close the Great Dock Strike which had paralysed the trade of London for five weeks.

The Lord Mayor was assisted in the work of conciliation by Cardinal Manning and Mr. Sydney Buxton, M.P., advice also being given from time to time by the Bishop of London, Lord Brassey, and others. At one time the negotiations threatened to break down, but on the evening of 14 Sept. the strike leaders assembled at the Mansion House and formally signed the agreement which ended the labour war.

The Common Council decided to present compliments of congratulation to the Duke and Duchess of Fife on the occasion of their marriage (26 Sept.).—The Corporation voted a further sum of 1,000 guineas to the City and Guilds of London Institute (3 Oct.).—Sir Benjamin Samuel Phillips, late Alderman, died on the 9th.

Born in 1811, he established in partnership with his brother-in-law, Mr. Faudel, the business carried on under the title of Faudel, Phillips and Sons. For thirty-six years he was an active member of the Corporation,

The Remembrancer was instructed to retain counsel on behalf of the Corporation in the Railway Rates Enquiry which was opened by the Board of Trade (15 Oct.).—The working-men delegates, who, at the instance of the Mansion House Committee had visited the Paris Exhibition, presented the Lord Mayor with a specially bound volume of their reports, which were of an interesting character (26th).—Sir Henry Aaron Isaacs, Knight, was elected Lord Mayor. The Lord Mayor's Show, arranged by the Hon. Lewis Wingfield, included groups illustrating the sports and pastimes of Old England and of English worthies connected with the City (9 Nov.).—Sir Sydney Waterlow, late Alderman, offered the London County Council 29 acres of land, at Highgate, now known as Waterlow Park, to be used as a place of public recreation (12th).—A letter from Lord Salisbury announced that the late Lord Mayor had been made a baronet (14th).— Arthur Tempest Pollard, M.A., Vice-Master of the Manchester Grammar School, was elected Head-Master of the City of London School.—A scheme for the establishment of a City Polytechnic, in which were to be amalgamated the City of London College and the Birkbeck Institute, was issued by the Charity Commissioners (11 Dec.).—The building lately by the Inland Fish Market in Farringdon Road was re-opened by the Lord Mayor as a Poultry and Provision Market, the necessary alterations having been made at a cost of about £12,000 (13th).—About this time the Company of Paviors was reconstituted, Mr. Ex-Sheriff Burt, being the first Master.—The London County Council practically declined to make the usual contribution towards the cost of City improvements, by imposing restrictions which it was impossible for the City to comply with (28th).

The Commissioners of Sewers pointed out that in the early days of the Metropolitan Board of Works it was the practice of the latter body to contribute one half the cost of City improvements, but the Treasury afterwards restricted the Board to an expenditure of £100,000 a year for improvements for the whole Metropolis, and the Board offered to give the City £30,000 out of that £100,000. The annual contribution of the Metropolitan Board of Works to City improvements had since been limited to that sum.

It was arranged, owing to the increase of business, that the City of London Court should sit continuously throughout the year without any vacation.—The China Famine Relief Fund at the Mansion House amounted to £32,654, and the Gardens and Pleasure Grounds Fund to £5,303.—The new Law Courts branch of the Bank of England, a building of bold Italian design, was erected by Mr. (afterwards Sir A. W.) Blomfield.—Between Moorgate Street, Lothbury, and London Wall an improvement was carried out by the demolition of Bell Alley and its surroundings, the space thus obtained being covered by new buildings. In Austin Friars and Drapers' Gardens blocks of offices were erected.—During the latter part of this year specifications were prepared and tenders invited by the Commissioners of Sewers for lighting the City by electricity. Eventually contracts were entered into with two Companies, afterwards merged in the City of London Electric Lighting Company, and the whole of the main thoroughfares in the City were lighted by arc lamps at a cost of about £12,272 per annum.

1890.

FIELD MARSHAL LORD NAPIER OF MAGDALA, G.C.B., G.C.S.I., Constable of the Tower, died in his eightieth year from influenza (14 Jan., 1890). The burial took place at St. Paul's Cathedral on the 21st, thirty members of the Corporation attending in their gowns. A fund for raising a memorial to Lord Napier was opened at the Mansion House on the 27th, the Corporation contributing 100 guineas. The fund reached a total of £5,446.— Alderman Sir Polydore De Keyser entertained the French Ambassador, the Executive Council of the British Section of the Paris Exhibition, and those to whom special awards had been made by the French Government, to a banquet at the Mansion House (27th).—A meeting was held at the Mansion House to consider a scheme of commercial education, drawn up by the Committee appointed by the London Chamber of Commerce, and afterwards modified by the advice of the Oxford and Cambridge School Examination Board. The scheme, which proposed to enable English youths to meet the better educated German clerk upon his own ground, was adopted by the meeting. In the junior course, Latin was entirely omitted (5 Feb.).—The Corporation resolved to support the Inhabited House Duty Repeal Association in its endeavours to remove certain anomalies incidental to the said duty (13th).—The Llanerch Colliery Explosion Fund opened at the Mansion House reached a total of £7,625, the Corporation subscribing 200 guineas.—Alderman David Henry Stone died on the 26th.

> He was born in 1812; the family from which he claimed descent having been for upwards of three centuries large landed proprietors near Lewes Early in life he practised as a solicitor and first became associated with the Corporation in 1840, when he was appointed Under-Sheriff. He was elected Alderman of Bassishaw in 1865.

At a meeting of the Commissioners of Sewers attention was drawn to the extraordinary increase in the value of City property. In twenty years, (1870 to 1890) the assessable value of City property had risen 150 per cent. (4 Mar.).

—The Common Council finally adopted, as a site for Ward's City of London School for Girls, a plot of land on the Victoria Embankment at the rear of the Guildhall School of Music.—The Corporation contributed 100 guineas towards the expense of converting the old burial ground in Seward Street, Goswell Road, into a public recreation ground.—It was also resolved to hold a Loan Exhibition of Works of Art at the Guildhall Art Gallery.—The Mansion House Fund for the sufferers from the Morfa Colliery Disaster amounted to £2,973, the Corporation contributing 200 guineas.—A letter was received by the Lord Mayor from Lord Rosebery, enclosing a resolution from the London County Council expressing its warm appreciation of the generous hospitality of the Corporation in having granted the use of their chamber for the weekly meetings of the Council during fourteen months.—Mr. William Blades, printer, bibliophilist and antiquary, a man of much learning and taste, died at the age of sixty-six (27 Ap.).

His fame rests chiefly upon his monumental work, "The life and typography of William Caxton," published in 1861-3　His library of books on printing is preserved, *in memoriam*, in St. Bride's Institute, and the larger part of his collection of printers' medals was purchased for the Guildhall Museum. His latest works were the "Pentateuch of Printing," and some valuable bibliographical monographs.

A conversazione was given at Guildhall to welcome Mr. H. M. Stanley on his return from his long and arduous journey in search of Emin Pasha (13 May).—Ex-Alderman Hadley who was rejected by the Court of Aldermen as a candidate for the civic chair, died at Kensington (15th).—The Jubilee Anniversary of the introduction of Inland Penny Postage was celebrated at Guildhall (16th).

The reception of about 3,000 guests, including the Prince of Wales, took place in the Library, most of the exhibits being in the great Hall, which had somewhat the appearance of a huge postal and telegraph office combined. There were examples of the development of pillar boxes, from the original square ones of 1855, through the tall elaborate edifice, with crown and cushion, which formerly stood on London Bridge, to the modern pillar with its wire interior. On the east side of the Guildhall was the telegraph department, where every system, from Cooke and Wheatstone's 4-needle machine requiring four wires, to the present single wire and almost instantaneous machine, was exhibited. Several offices at the Guildhall were in direct communication with posts at Aberdeen, Bristol, Penzance, and other distant towns with which telegrams were exchanged in the space of a few minutes. There was a fully equipped mail coach and numerous reminiscences of the old coach days　The work of sorting and dispatching letters was also illustrated. Speeches were delivered in the course of the evening by the Lord Mayor, the Postmaster-General, Sir James Whitehead, and others.

Mr. H. M. Stanley was presented with the freedom of the Fishmongers' Company (2 June).—A scheme was adopted at the Mansion House, under the auspices of the Farriers' Company, the Royal Agricultural Society of England, and the Royal College of Veterinary Surgeons, for the National Registration of Farriers or Shoeing Smiths.—An enquiry into the water supply of the Metropolis, conducted by the County Purposes Committee of the Corporation at a cost of £2,178, was opened at Guildhall, Sir W. Guyer Hunter, K.C.M.G., M.P., presiding (4th).

Thirteen sittings were held, during which thirty-seven witnesses were examined. The result of the examination showed that there was a consensus of opinion that the water supply should be in the hands of a Public Authority. It was clear from the evidence that wealthy consumers were able to obtain advantages from the Water Companies which were not shared by the general public. The Committee visited Manchester and Glasgow, and the officials there gave evidence showing the benefits accruing to the consumers and to the Cities themselves from the supply being in the hands of a Public Authority. The Committee recommended the creation by Parliament of a Water Authority, with representatives of the areas affected, as the most effectual way of governing the watershed and managing the supply, with power to confer with the Conservators of the Thames and Lea; and that such representatives should be chosen from the various Municipal Corporations, County Councils and Sanitary Authorities, over whose areas the Water Authority would have control.

Mr. John Morley presided at the first meeting of the Select Committee of the House of Commons, appointed to inquire into the terms under which the Irish Society and the London Companies held their estates in Ulster, and as to the administration of the funds derived from such estates. A mass of evidence was taken, but the Committee reported on 24 July that it was out of their power to conclude the investigation that session, and suggested the appointment of another Committee next session.—The first Loan Exhibition of Pictures was opened by the Lord Mayor in the Guildhall Art Gallery (10 June)

The exhibition was open free to the public for three months, and was visited by 109,000 persons.

It was resolved on the recommendation of the Special Finance Committee of the Corporation to increase the fee for obtaining the freedom of the City from 5s. to one guinea (18th)—Sir James Fraser, K.C.B, Commissioner of City Police, resigned his appointment after a service of twenty-seven years. Lieut.-Colonel Henry Smith, the Chief Superintendent, was appointed to the vacant post (26th)—On the death of Thomas Woodward, Keeper of the Monument, it was resolved to abolish the office and to appoint a third assistant to take charge in conjunction with the two assistants already appointed.—The London County Council informed the Commissioners of Sewers that for various reasons it had been decided that it was not expedient for the Council to contribute any proportion of the cost of City street improvements (30th).

The two reasons given were that the City (not the Commissioners) would be in receipt of the proceeds of the Coal duty until the following month, and that City improvements had been proceeded with before the views of the Council could be ascertained.

Wardmotes were held throughout the City to consider the Police Bill before Parliament. The citizens expressed themselves almost unanimously against the proposed interference with the City Police (4 July).—The duty on coal, which in one form or another had existed for centuries, and was one of the most fertile sources of revenue by which the Metropolis had been rebuilt, was abolished by Parliament (5th).—The Corporation agreed to pay £1,000 towards the expenses incurred by the plaintiffs (the Banstead Commons Preservation Committee) in the action

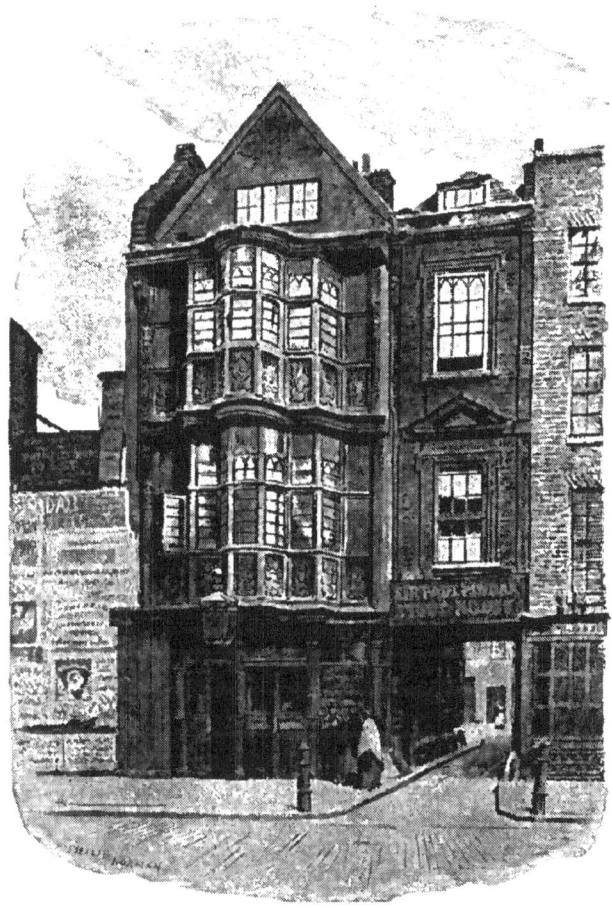

Sir Paul Pindar's House, Bishopsgate Street.

brought against Sir John Hartopp and others for illegally enclosing a portion of Banstead Downs and Commons, and the Coal, and Corn, and Finance Committee was authorised to obtain, if possible, such a holding of property in the neighbourhood as would secure to the Corporation in future a *locus standi* in the event of any further attempt at encroachment on the rights of the Commoners (10th).— Mr. Alderman and Sheriff Knill offered to decorate the outer lobby of the Council Chamber as a memorial of his year of shrievalty. The offer was accepted by the Common Council, and the decorations (which have since been carried out) took the form of a series of mural paintings, having allegorical reference to the City of London and the Livery Companies.—Earl Granville distributed at the Mansion House the prizes and certificates awarded by the London Chamber of Commerce, in connection with the first examination under the recently approved Commercial Education Scheme (24th).— The Common Council voted 100 guineas to a fund on behalf of the survivors of the Light Brigade who took part in the charge of Balaclava.—The remains of Canon Liddon were interred in the crypt of St. Paul's Cathedral (16 Sept.).—Attention was drawn in the press to the approaching demolition of Sir Paul Pindar's mansion, long used as a public-house, in Bishopsgate Street.

From the first floor upwards the front consisted of two oriel windows, one being imposed upon the other, the oak timbers of which were of great antiquity and beauty. Sir Paul Pindar erected the building as a residence towards the end of Elizabeth's reign.

The Mansion House Fund in aid of the sufferers from the fire at Salonica reached a total of £3,740, the Corporation contributing 100 guineas (25th).—A man named Easton shot himself in St. Paul's Cathedral during morning service (28th) A "service of reconciliation" or "act of reparation to Almighty God for dishonour done to his sanctuary" was held, to purge the Cathedral from the guilt of the suicide. The Bishop of London conducted the service (13 Oct.)—The Common Council resolved to provide additional chill-room accommodation at the Foreign Cattle Market, Deptford, at a cost of £5,756 (2 Oct.).—An exhibition of hardy fruit, under the auspices of the Fruiterers' Company, was opened by the Lord Mayor at the Guildhall (6th).—A fire occurred at a hat factory in Cloth Fair. Women and girls in a state of panic threw themselves from the windows of the burning building, five being killed and ten injured; three of the latter afterwards died (13th).—Mr. E. Onslow Ford, A.R.A., presented to the Corporation his statue of Mr. Henry Irving as "Hamlet" (21st).—The London County Council who had obtained Parliamentary powers to expend a sum of £5,000 on Water enquiries approached the Corporation, and several conferences between the two bodies took place without practical result.—The City and South London Electric Railway was opened by the Prince of Wales (4 Nov.).—The Corporation guaranteed £1,000 in furtherance of a Naval Exhibition to be held in 1891.—Sir John Gordon Sprigg, K.C.M.G., late premier of the Cape, was presented with the freedom of the Turners' Company (6th).—Alderman Joseph Savory was elected Lord Mayor.—The City of London passed through a grave financial crisis (14th).

The firm of Baring Brothers became embarrassed through the Argentine collapse, and was on the verge of ruin After some days of uncertainty, the Bank of England and other large banks came to the rescue and a guarantee fund of £17,000,000 was secured, thus preventing a very serious disaster

A resolution of condolence was passed by the Common Council on the occasion of the death of the King of the Netherlands (27th).—A new statue of the Queen was ordered for the Royal Exchange at a cost of £2,000, the Corporation and the Mercers' Company jointly contributing to its cost.—The Very Rev. R. W. Church, dean of St. Paul's, died at the age of seventy-five (9 Dec.).—A large meeting, presided over by the Lord Mayor, was held at Guildhall to protest against "the renewed persecutions to which millions of the Jewish race are subjected in Russia under the yoke of severe and exceptional edicts and disabilities" (10th).

The meeting was addressed by the Duke of Westminster, the Bishop of Ripon and others, and a memorial, signed by the Lord Mayor, in the name of the citizens of London, was sent to St. Petersburg Early in the following Feb. it was returned to the Lord Mayor through the Foreign Office.

Sir Edgar Boehm, R.A., the eminent sculptor, was buried in St. Paul's Cathedral by special desire of the Queen (12th).—A presentation was made to Mr. John Derby Allcroft on his retirement from the Treasurership of Christ's Hospital in consequence of the passing of a scheme for the reconstruction of the school which greatly alienated the support of the important class of donation governors (18th).

Up to this time Christ's Hospital had been governed in exactly the same way as the other Royal Hospitals, but, under the new scheme of the Charity Commissioners, the Aldermen, while remaining *ex-officio* governors were, with the exception of the Lord Mayor, deprived of their rights of presentation.

During the severe frost a great fire took place in Queen Victoria Street, a large block of buildings being destroyed (30th).

The intense cold, combined with the heat of the fire produced some curious effects The showers of water from the hose almost froze as they fell and every fireman became rapidly coated from head to foot in ice (30th)

1891.

THE new scheme for the management of Christ's Hospital came into operation (1 Jan, 1891).

The new Council of Almoners numbered forty-three, of whom the Duke of Cambridge was appointed President for life. The Lord Mayor was to be an ex-officio member, and the remaining members were to be chosen by different public bodies or nominated by the present governors. The governors were to consist of four classes, viz., ex-officio governors, Common Council governors, donation governors, six governors by special vote, and governors by right of Almonership. The Council of Almoners were under the scheme to provide hospital schools within a convenient distance of London, for 700 boy boarders and 350 girl boarders, with a preparatory school for 120 boarders There was also to be a science school for 600 scholars, and a girls' day school for 400 scholars. Amongst other objects of the scheme was the removal of the school from London Owing to the rapid diminution of donation governors, there has been a considerable falling off in the revenues of the Institution.

The Executive Committee of the first Italian Exhibition of Architecture, at Turin, granted a diploma of honour to the Corporation for their exhibits (29th). —The Court of Common Council voted 200 guineas for the relief of distress in the West of Ireland.—The Corporation passed a resolution of regret on hearing of the death of H.R.H. Prince Baldwin, heir presumptive to the throne of Belgium — The Lord Mayor inaugurated the permanent lighting of the City by electricity by laying the foundation stone at the main junction, connecting the conductors to be laid down in Walbrook, outside the Mansion House (3 Feb.).

Experiments had been in progress for several years, and a definite scheme was at last agreed to

Mr. James Rowlands introduced in the House of Commons a motion for the abolition of the Livery Franchise in accordance with the recommendation of the City of London Livery Companies Commission.   The resolution was rejected by 148 votes to 120 (6th).—On the motion of Mr. Treloar, the Commissioners of Sewers resolved to acquire Messrs. Dakin's premises in St. Paul's Churchyard, to complete the widening of Ludgate Hill (10th).   The purchase was effected on the 24th for £22,500.—The Local Government and Taxation Committee were instructed to take a Day Census of the City (19th).—The London Water Commission Bill of the Corporation for the purpose of creating a public body to control the water supply of London, or to acquire other sources of supply, was read a second time in the House of Commons, and referred to a Select Committee of nine members (20th).   This Committee sat for the first time on 28 Ap. (Sir Matthew White Ridley, Bart., in the Chair) and considered the Corporation Bill and several other Water Bills which had been submitted to it.

Upon the conclusion of the case for the Corporation Bill, the Committee intimated that the proposal to constitute a new Water Authority with powers of enquiry and negotiation should not be proceeded with, but that there was no objection to that part of the Bill which allowed applications to Parliament by the London County Council, and their expending moneys on enquiries.

Alderman Sir Thomas Gabriel, Bart., died at Wimbledon, at the age of eighty (23 Feb.).   He was a successful timber merchant, and was elected Alderman of the Ward of Vintry in 1857.—The Restoration Committee of St. Bartholomew-the-Great viewed the finished south transept, the great arch of which had for years been concealed by a canvas-covered vestry room (28th).

The Norman arch on the east side of the transept (date 1123) had served as a fire-place to the vestry. A corresponding arch on the west side (date about 1180) had been for centuries concealed in plaster.   The opening out of this transept was a great improvement to this ancient London church.   The Bishop of London formally inaugurated the restoration, 14 Mar.

A telephone system between London and Paris was inaugurated (18 Mar.). —In response to a letter from the Lord Chancellor, it was agreed that the old Council Chamber should be appropriated for the hearing of special jury cases before Her Majesty's Judges (19th).—The City of London Union and other local bodies successfully appealed at the Clerkenwell Sessions House against the revised assessments of the London County Council, which would have enormously increased the rates of the City (26th).—Mr. Joseph Beck, Chairman of the City Lands Committee, and a man of considerable scientific attainments, died in his 63rd year (18 Ap.)—The City Parochial Foundation under the City Parochial Charities Act came into operation.

The " City Parochial Foundation " was the official title of the funds to be administered by the new governing body of the central scheme of the City parish charities. These funds were handed over to the care of twenty-one gentlemen selected by the Crown, the Corporation, the London County Council, the Ecclesiastical Commissioners, the University of London, University and King's Colleges, the Wards of Bishopsgate and Cripplegate, and the City and Guilds Institute. The income was under £100,000 per annum, and of this one-third was ecclesiastical income, which had been devoted to City church purposes, and which was to be still devoted to such purposes under the scheme. The £35,000 a year of the City Church Fund was to be wholly separated from the control of the new governing body as rapidly as possible, and handed over to the rectors and churchwardens of each of the parishes concerned, to the extent specified in the central scheme, and the surplus was to be transferred bodily to the Ecclesiastical Commissioners, whose two representatives on the new governing body should thenceforward cease to belong to it. On the £56,000, which was general charity income, the Charity Commissioners were to raise £335,000 for open spaces, poly-technics, etc., which at 4 per cent. they calculated would reduce the income to be administered by the new governing body to about £40,000 yearly. The first meeting of the governors was held at the Mansion House (1 May) when the Lord Mayor was elected chairman.

The Select Committee of the House of Commons on the Irish Society and City Companies possessing property in Ireland was reappointed, and after due enquiry presented their report (4 May).—Mr. William Lidderdale, Governor of the Bank of England was admitted to the freedom of the City, in recognition of the services rendered by him during the monetary crisis of the previous November, whereby (to quote the resolution of the Court) " disastrous and far-reaching panic was averted, and commercial and fiscal confidence was restored."

The Chamberlain in making the presentation referred to the Chamber at the Guildhall as the oldest bank in the country, dating from at least the 12th century, when it was farmed of the Crown.

A drinking fountain, presented to St. Mary Aldermary, by Mr. Deputy Rogers, was inaugurated in the parish churchyard, which had been thrown open to the public (11th).—Alderman Sir Robert Nicholas Fowler, Bart., M.P., died on the 22nd.

Sir Robert, born in 1828, was one of the best known men in the City. He was essentially a fighting politican, but his sterling qualities and genial character won for him a host of friends, even in the camps of his political opponents. He was a man of literary tastes, and a distinguished graduate of the University of London. He was greatly interested in religious and philanthropic work, and preached many times to large congregations during his mayoralty. A bust of Sir Robert Fowler was ordered to be placed in the Art Gallery.

The annual allowance for the purchase of books for the Guildhall Library, and the purchase of antiquities, etc., for the Museum, was increased from £800 to £1,000 per annum (28th).—A controversy took place with regard to the sanitary condition of St. Bartholomew's Hospital, and the Medical Officer of Health (Dr. Sedgwick Saunders) advised the removal of the antiquated brick drains then in use, and the substitution of a safer system. This was eventually adopted.— Alderman Sir Reginald Hanson, Bart., was elected to fill the vacancy in the parliamentary representation of the City, caused by the death of Sir Robert Fowler

(3 June).—The Duke of Connaught visited Epping Forest as Ranger, and in the presence of the Lord Mayor and Sheriffs and other members of the Corporation opened the latest addition to the Forest, viz., some 30 acres of Highams Park, which had been acquired at a cost of £6,000 (16th).

> This property connected the part of the forest known as the "Lops," near Woodford, with the extensive thicket near Hale End, and comprised beautiful timbered land and a lake a quarter of a mile in length. One half of the purchase money was found by the Corporation, the other half being provided by various local bodies and private subscriptions.

Sir Henry Aaron Isaacs tendered his resignation as Alderman of the Ward of Portsoken (16th).—A distinguished company, including the Prince and Princess of Wales and other members of the Royal Family, assembled at Guildhall to meet the Emperor and Empress of Germany, when an address of welcome was presented by the Corporation (10 July). The occasion was remarkable, as no German Emperor had visited England since the Middle Ages. The preparations at the Guildhall were on a very elaborate scale.

> The Kaiser in returning thanks for the address, said :—
>
> "I thank you with many thanks, and I hope that the Mayor and Corporation of London will always enjoy all the progress and prosperity it can have under the glorious and peaceful reign of Queen Victoria, my beloved grandmother."
>
> At a déjeuner served in the Guildhall, at which the Prime Minister (Lord Salisbury) was also present, the Emperor in reply to the toast of his health, said :—
>
> "I have always felt at home in this lovely country, being the grandson of a Queen whose name will ever be remembered as a noble character, and a lady great in the wisdom of her counsels, and whose reign has conferred lasting blessings on England. Moreover, the same blood runs in English and German veins. Following the examples of my grandfather, and of my ever lamented father I shall always, as far as it is in my power, maintain the historical friendship between these our two nations, which as your lordship mentioned have so often been seen side by side in defence of liberty and justice . . . My aim is above all the maintenance of peace, for peace alone can give the confidence which is necessary to the healthy development of science, art and trade."
>
> The Lord Mayor received a baronetcy and the Sheriffs knighthood, in connection with the Emperor's visit.

The House of Lords confirmed the refusal of the Court of Appeal to issue a mandamus to the Bishop of London, to compel him to allow action to be taken with regard to the reredos in St. Paul's Cathedral, the judgment of Lord Coleridge in the Queen's Bench Division being reversed (20 Aug.).—The foundation stone of the new Free Library and Museum, Whitechapel, was laid by the Lord Mayor (27th).—Rev. W. Carlile, known as the founder of the Church Army, was inducted into the church and parish of St. Mary-at-Hill, Love Lane (28th).— The Prince of Naples dined with the Lord Mayor and Lady Mayoress at the Mansion House.—The Technical Institute, established by the Goldsmiths' Company at New Cross, was opened by the Prince of Wales.—One of the chief attractions of the Naval Exhibition at South Kensington, was a collection of relics of the Nelson period, partly lent by the Corporation. Amongst the swords was that presented by the Corporation to Lord Nelson after the battle of the Nile (Sep.).—The Corporation voted 200 guineas for the sufferers from the calamitous inundations in Spain.—The Lord Chief Justice and Mr. Justice Wills opened the Guildhall sittings of the Queen's Bench Division, for the trial of City *nisi prius* actions, thus reviving a custom which had been discontinued since May, 1883 (28 Oct.).

Member of Metropolitan Fire Brigade.

The Lord Mayor welcomed Her Majesty's Judges to the City, remarking that the Corporation had been from time immemorial the representative of justice in the City. Lord Coleridge having expressed his thanks, said: "It was supposed that the trial of mercantile issues, especially those arising between citizens of London, had diminished out of all proportion to their importance, in consequence of their removal from that place to the Royal Courts of Justice in the Strand. He expressed no opinion as to whether that belief was well or ill-founded, but it seemed to him that, occupying the great position of Lord Chief Justice of England, it would have been most unbecoming if he had attempted to interpose the slightest obstacle, nay if he had not done his best to forward in every way a change of practice which it was supposed at least would restore these causes to their ancient and legitimate tribunals." The Lord Chancellor speaking at the Guildhall banquet (9 Nov.) said he had observed that instead of the great commercial causes which he had expected to find decided in the City of London, a great many people had come from such remote places as Northumberland, Cornwall and Somersetshire, instead of taking their questions for adjudication to their own native courts. He intimated that if this were not put a stop to, the commercial interests of the City of London might be seriously imperilled.

Alderman David Evans was elected Lord Mayor.—The Medical Officer of Health reported that the well at the Artizans' Dwellings had reached a depth of 450 feet, of which 218 were bored into the chalk. The water as it issued from the well was odourless and pleasant to the taste. It was decided to continue the boring about 100 feet (17 Nov.).—A draft scheme for the establishment of a High School for Girls under the Ward bequest was agreed to by the Common Council (3 Dec.).—The Corporation ordered a marble bust to be executed of the late Right Hon. W. H. Smith, M.P., First Lord of the Treasury.—The results of the City Day Census were embodied by Mr. James Salmon, F.S.S., in an interesting narrative entitled, "Ten Years' Growth of the City of London."—A sum of 50 guineas was voted by the Corporation to a fund being raised by the Master of the Haberdashers' Company, for the relief of two girls who were severely injured in Cannon Street during the progress of the Lord Mayor's procession on 9 Nov.—The freedom and livery of the Coachmakers' Company was conferred upon Captain Sir Eyre Massey Shaw, who was for twenty-six years Chief of the Metropolitan Fire Brigade, and had recently retired (10th).—Lady

Charlotte Schreiber, who had in various ways done much to promote the cause of technical education, was presented with the honorary freedom of the Fanmakers' Company at Drapers' Hall (17th).—The Corporation expressed its gratification at the announcement of the engagement of H.R H. The Duke of Clarence and Avondale, K.G., to Her Serene Highness The Princess Victoria Mary of Teck, and voted the sum of 2,500 guineas for the purchase of a suitable wedding present (17th).—Sir Thomas Chambers, Q.C., the Recorder, died on the 24th.

Sir Thomas was born in 1814, at Hertford, which town he afterwards represented in Parliament, being subsequently a member for the borough of Marylebone.

A fund amounting to £3,231 was raised at the Mansion House for the sufferers from the loss of H.M.S. "Serpent."—The final report of the Royal Commission on Market Rights and Tolls was issued, the history of the London markets, and of the rights and policy of the Corporation in relation thereto, being fully discussed.—Shiplake Island, in the Thames (County of Oxford) was purchased by the Corporation, to preserve it from being built upon.

Being beyond the 25 miles limit, a licence in mortmain was necessary, and the total cost of the acquisition was £836 12s. 8d. The island is largely used by camping-out parties, and is open to bathers.

1892.

HE Engineer reported to the Commissioners of Sewers that the boring of the artesian well had been stopped at a depth of 513 feet, the character of the chalk having changed. By means of the present pumps a daily supply of 70,000 gallons of water could be raised, which was more than three times the quantity required for the Artizans' Dwellings, and in the opinion of the Engineer the well was capable of raising 100,000 gallons in twenty-four hours (12 Jan., 1892).— Prince Albert Victor, Duke of Clarence and Avondale, K.G., K.P., died on the 14th, on the eve of his marriage with Princess May.

A memorial service, simultaneously with the funeral service at St George's Chapel, Windsor, was held at St. Paul's Cathedral on the 20th, the Lord Mayor and Sheriffs and other members of the Corporation, with the Masters of the Livery Companies, attending in state. The Corporation passed resolutions of condolence and regret, and referred it to a Committee to consider the desirability of erecting a stained-glass window in the Guildhall, in memory of the late prince (21st).

At the same time (21st) the Court of Common Council learned with deep regret of the death of the City Chamberlain (Mr. Benjamin Scott) "who in the course of an unusually prolonged service had so performed the important duties of his ancient and dignified office as to earn the esteem of the Court, the love of his friends, and the respect of all men." It was decided to place a bust of the late Chamberlain in the Guildhall.—The Corporation voted 300 guineas to the fishermen of Lowestoft and Yarmouth for the relief of sufferers from the disastrous gale in Nov., 1891 (28th).—Alderman Cotton was elected Chamberlain (5 Feb.).— The representatives of St. Saviour's, Southwark, attended the Court of Aldermen praying the Court to recognise the right of the inhabitants of Southwark, under a Charter of King Richard II, to vote in the election of an Alderman to fill the vacancy in the ward of Bridge Without, caused by the appointment of Alderman Cotton as Chamberlain. The petition was referred to a Committee (12th)

The Lord Mayor said this subject was before the Court fifty years ago, but the petition would he referred to Committee. Meanwhile, the Court elected Sir Andrew Lusk to the Aldermanry of Bridge Without. A deputation from Southwark afterwards waited upon the Committee of Aldermen, and contended that the action which had been taken by the Aldermen since the year 1725 with regard to Bridge Without was illegal. This application produced no result, but recently another deputation attended from the parishes of St. Saviour, St. Olave, St. John, and St. Thomas Southwark, with a petition for incorporation with the City, which is now under consideration.

Sir Charles Hall, K.C.M.G., Q.C., M.P., was appointed Recorder (5th), and on the 12th he attended the Court of Aldermen and took the customary oath.— The City coal porters struck work (10th).—The Common Council voted 150 guineas for a Corporation prize to be competed for by the Colonial and Indian Volunteers at the forthcoming Bisley meeting (18th).—Rev. Joseph Harris, M.A., resigned his position as a master at the City of London School after 51 years' service (17 Mar.).—The site of Farringdon Market (1½ acres) was sold by auction (18th), and a fine block of buildings has since been erected thereon.

Old Farringdon Market, which was built in 1829 after the removal of Fleet Market, was always a commercial failure. Twenty years before its sale the entire revenue of the market which cost the Corporation £280,000 was £225, but the receipts had since increased to £2,000. The fruit market in earlier times occupied the site of the Mansion House, and was known as Stocks Market.

The second Loan Exhibition of pictures, at the Guildhall Art Gallery, was opened by the Lord Mayor (28th).

The attendance was much larger than on the first occasion, and the pictures, numbering 178, included many works of great value, some of which had never before been publicly exhibited, and nearly all them hitherto inaccessible to the general public. The exhibition was open free for three months; a catalogue was prepared by Mr. A. G. Temple, the Director.

Mr. Joseph Barnby was elected Principal of the Guildhall School of Music in succession to the late Mr. Weist Hill (31st).—The Merchant Taylors' Company presented its honorary freedom to Mr. A. J. Balfour, M.P., in recognition of his eminent public services as Chief Secretary for Ireland and Leader of the House of Commons (9 Ap.).—The death was announced of Col. Sir James Fraser, K.C.B., Commissioner of the City Police (28th).—A sum of 100 guineas was voted by the Corporation for the relief of distress among the unemployed drovers in the Metropolitan Cattle Market.—The Corporation sent hearty congratulations to the King and Queen of Denmark on the occasion of their golden wedding (26 May).—Sir Polydore De Keyser resigned his position as Alderman of Farringdon Without on account of increasing deafness (30th).

> The announcement was received with much regret by the Court of Aldermen, who expressed their high appreciation of Sir Polydore's services to the City. The retiring Alderman had occupied a unique position in the Corporation, having been, it is believed, the first Roman Catholic to fill the civic chair, since the Reformation period

The Central London Railway Bill was considered by the Commission of Sewers, and the proposed scheme for an underground station beneath the public way in front of the Mansion House, with the suggested approaches, was generally approved.

> It was decided that clauses should be introduced to compensate those persons whose property might be injured by the vibration of trains, though the engineers assured the Joint Committee of the Houses of Lords and Commons that there would be absolutely no vibration.

A motion in the Common Council to open the Loan Exhibition of pictures on the last three Sundays in June was defeated by 95 votes to 70 (2 June).—The Mansion House Fund for the sufferers from the terrible hurricane in Mauritius amounted to £12,118 2s. 4d., the Corporation subscribing 100 guineas.—The Prince of Bulgaria lunched with the Lord Mayor and Lady Mayoress at the Mansion House (10th).—An exhibition of saddlery, harness and other horse furniture, ancient and modern, was opened by the Saddlers' Company at their Hall (13th).—The new Fruit and Vegetable Market, in Farringdon Road, to the north of Charterhouse Street, was opened by the Lord Mayor.

> This building, which is admirably adapted for its purpose, cost (in addition to the value of the site) about £70,000, of which £41,000 was spent in the substructure and the extensive basement works required in accordance with the terms of an agreement entered into with the Great Northern Railway Company, who now lease the substructure The railway company has altogether an area of about 100,000 feet under the Central Markets, with large hydraulic lifts and inclined roadways.

Mr. Henry Hucks Gibbs resigned his position as M.P. for the City.—It was resolved to fit the Guildhall Library and Council Chamber with installations of electric lighting (16th).—The London Water Bill (No. 1), promoted jointly by the Corporation and the London County Council, chiefly for the purpose of enabling the latter body to pay the costs and expenses of Bills and Enquiries, passed both houses of Parliament and received the Royal Assent (27th). The consent of

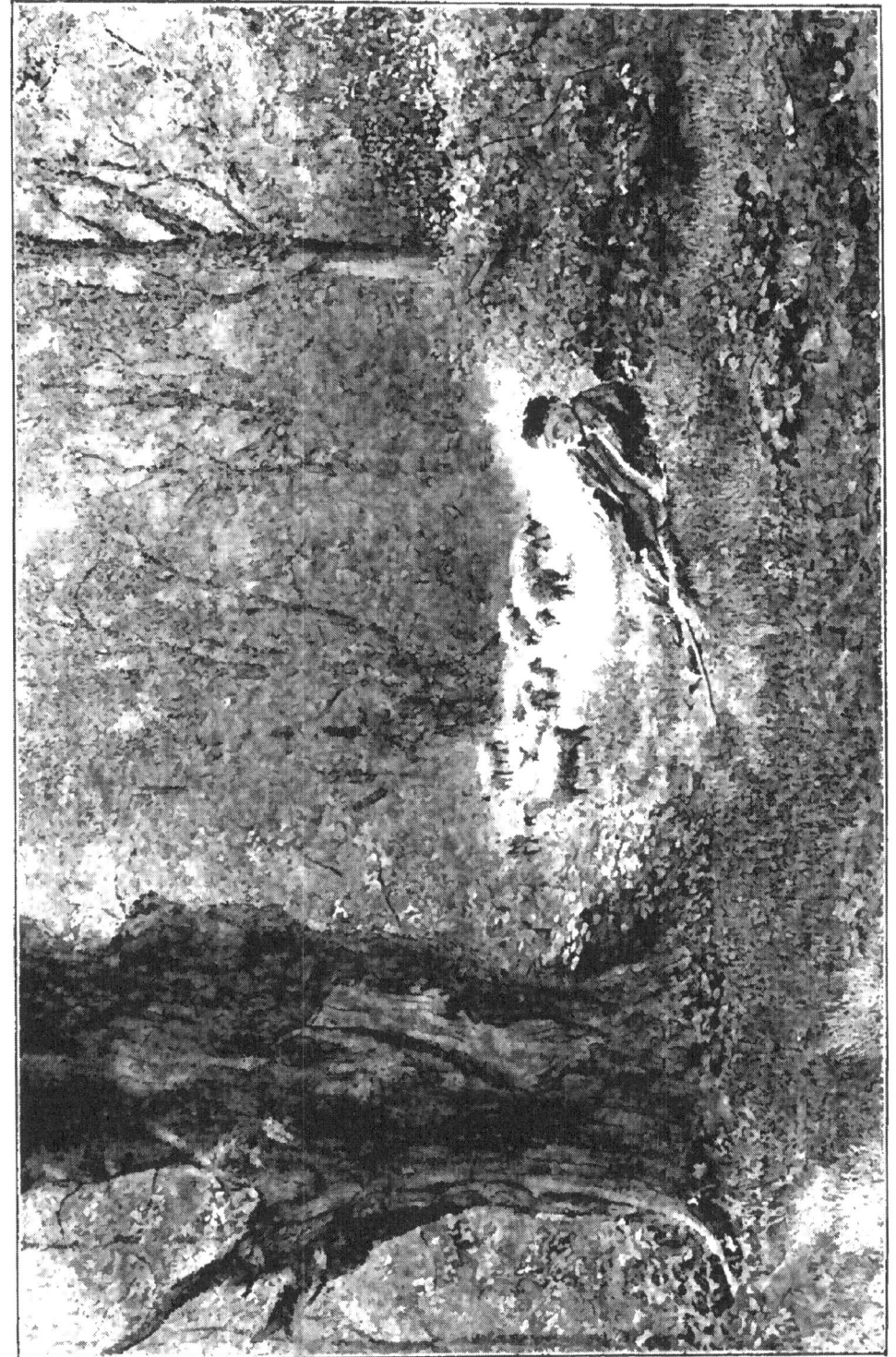

West Wickham Common, now in charge of the Corporation of London.

the Corporation Committee to the Bill proceeding was given on the distinct understanding that the position of the Corporation with reference to the promotion of Bills relating to the water question, under the Agreement of 13 May, 1891, was to be upheld. — The Corporation agreed to complete the purchase of West Wickham Common, at a cost of £500 (the purchase money being £2,000), and maintain the same as an open space (30th).

This now forms a beautiful addition to Hayes Common, and is much appreciated by South Londoners. It comprises twenty-five acres of well-wooded common land, and was publicly opened by the Lord Mayor and Sheriffs (12 Nov.).

The Hon. George R. Dibbs, Premier of New South Wales, was made an Honorary Freeman of the Turners' Company (13 July). — The Mansion House Fund, in aid of the sufferers from the disastrous fire at St. John's, Newfoundland, amounted to £24,635 0s. 2d., the Corporation contributing two hundred guineas (14th).—The foundation stone of the Mercers' Company's new Grammar School, at Horsham, originally founded in 1540, by Richard Collier, a Citizen and Mercer of London, was laid by the Master of the Company. Under the new scheme of the Charity Commissioners the Mercers' Company would contribute an endowment of £3,000 and a grant of £700 per annum — Sir William Thomas Charley, Q.C., resigned the office of Common Serjeant (28th).— Mr. Sims Reeves was appointed Professor of Solo Singing at the Guildhall School of Music. —The Corporation resolved to continue the annual grant of 100 guineas to the London Society for the Extension of University Teaching for another period of five years. —A sum of £500 was voted towards the fund for preserving Mitcham Common, conditionally on the necessary balance being found within twelve months. — The Corporation also subscribed £105 in aid of the removal of the Wellington Monument from the Consistory Court to a better position in St. Paul's Cathedral (29 July). — The Commissioners of Sewers resolved to widen Gresham Street, by taking portions of Nos. 34 and 36 (12 Aug.). —A large block of buildings was destroyed by fire in Jewin Street (29th).— The Welsh National Eisteddfod was opened by the Lord Mayor, at Rhyl (6 Sept.). His lordship visited a number of other places in Wales, and was presented with numerous addresses of welcome, being everywhere received with great enthusiasm. It was announced that the Lord Mayor had had the honour of a K.C.M.G. conferred upon him by Her Majesty (22nd).— There was a great run on the Birkbeck Bank through the failure of certain building societies; the Bank, however, came safely through the crisis, and all claims were met (12 Sept.). — James Forrest Fulton, Esq., Q.C., was appointed Common Serjeant, and the honour of knighthood was conferred upon him (22nd).—Alderman Stuart Knill was elected Lord Mayor (29 Sept.).

The proceedings were of a very disorderly character, owing to the religious views of the Alderman, who was a Roman Catholic, and declined to attend the customary services at the church of St. Lawrence, Jewry. He, however, undertook to be represented at Protestant churches by a *locum tenens*.

The Public Baths and Wash-houses at Camberwell were opened by the Lord Mayor (1 Oct.). — The Town Clerk laid before the Common Council a letter from the Willesden Local Board expressing high appreciation of the work of the Corporation at Queen's Park, Kilburn, and of the liberal provision made for the convenience of the public (6th).—It was decided to erect a small pavilion for the isolation of small-pox patients on land belonging to the Corporation adjoining the Hospital, at Denton. — The Bridgend Colliery Explosion Fund, at the Mansion House, amounted to £4,902 5s. 8d., the Corporation contributing three hundred guineas. — The last services were held at Emanuel Hospital, Westminster, which had been under the control of the Lord Mayor and Aldermen of the City since 1623 (9th)   The site and buildings were shortly afterwards sold for £37,500.   A new scheme was drawn up for the regulation of the charity.—The Guildhall underwent complete renovation.

The roof, which was built only twenty-seven years before, was found to need thorough repair, great fissures having been made by the gas in the oaken beams   At the same time the gaseliers were exchanged for electroliers.

Mr. Deputy Walter, Father of the Court of Common Council, died at the age of 88, having represented the Ward of Farringdon Without since 1846 (13th).—On the occasion of the death of Lord Tennyson, the Corporation expressed its great admiration for the genius of the Poet Laureate, and ordered a marble bust of him to be executed and placed in the Art Gallery (27th)—Two thousand children of the ward schools of the City were entertained by the Lord Mayor, at Guildhall (11 Nov.)—The new London Chamber of Arbitration having been formed, Mr. F. A. Philbrick, Q.C., was appointed Legal Assessor.—The new offices for the City officers at Guildhall were approaching completion, and those of the surveyor were occupied by his staff at Christmas.—The Monument was visited this year by 63,455 persons.—The Bank of Messrs. Prescott, Dimsdale, Cave, Tugwell & Co., Limited, in Threadneedle Street was pulled down, and removed to new premises in Cornhill.   The original site of Dimsdale, Fowler, Barnard & Co.'s Bank prior to the amalgamation.   A view of the interior of the new buildings is given.

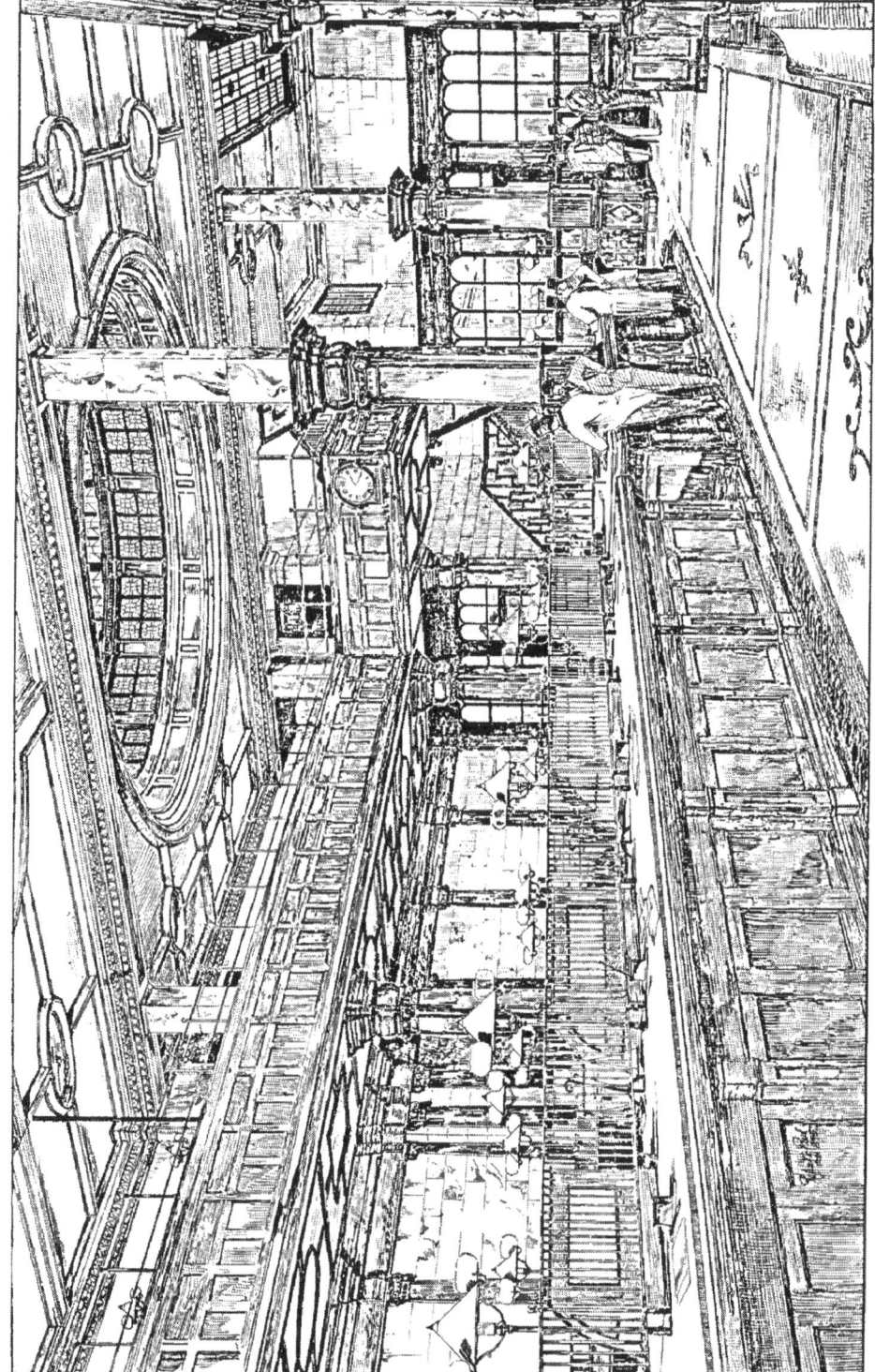

The Bank of Messrs. Prescott, Dimsdale, Cave, Tugwell & Co., Limited, Cornhill.

1893.

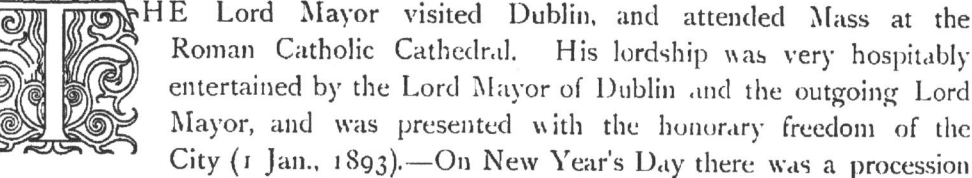

THE Lord Mayor visited Dublin, and attended Mass at the Roman Catholic Cathedral. His lordship was very hospitably entertained by the Lord Mayor of Dublin and the outgoing Lord Mayor, and was presented with the honorary freedom of the City (1 Jan., 1893).—On New Year's Day there was a procession of the unemployed to St. Paul's, where a sermon was preached by the Rev. Canon Scott-Holland.—The new Technical Schools at Nottingham, to which the Drapers' Company had largely contributed, were opened (12th).—The widening of Ludgate Hill, from 47 to 60 feet, was completed, at a net cost to the City of about £200,000 (24th).—Resolutions passed at the different wardmotes against the proposed Unification of London under one Municipality were presented to the Court of Common Council, which resolved that, in view of the continuous attacks made upon the constitution, rights, and privileges of the Corporation, in and out of Parliament, a Special Committee should be appointed to deal therewith. The Court also resolved—

That the suggested Unification of London is an unworkable scheme, and would be injurious to the interests of the whole body of ratepayers.

A Special Committee was appointed forthwith, and the outstanding references to the old Special Committee were transferred to it.—Delegates from all parts of the United Kingdom attended a conference at the Mansion House to protest against the increase of the railway rates and the increased powers accorded to the Railway Companies.—With a view to economy the Court of Common Council abolished the annual summer water excursions, for which purpose a sum of £750 had been allocated since 1837 (2 Feb.).—The Duke of York was admitted an honorary member of the Merchant Taylors' Company (7th).—The second reading of the Plumbers' Registration Bill, embodying a scheme of the Plumbers' Company for the protection of the public, was passed in the House of Commons (17th).

The Bill did not make registration compulsory, but it legalised the work of the guild and gave the public additional security. There were at this time 7,000 plumbers on the Company's register, meetings having been held in all parts of the country with a view to popularise the work of registration.

The Corporation voted 250 guineas to the London Trades Council towards a prize fund, in connection with the approaching Workmen's National Exhibition, at the Agricultural Hall, Islington (2 Mar.). For the same object a fund was raised at the Mansion House, amounting to £1,235 3s.—The Lord Mayor gave a farewell banquet to M. Waddington, the French Ambassador, at the Mansion House (4th).

M. Waddington in responding to the toast of his health, said : "The Lord Mayor of London was always regarded as a great man in the City, but he was a still greater man in Paris. In the eyes of the population of Paris—he had witnessed it himself—the Lord Mayor formed a very considerable proportion of the power and the prestige of England. They were evidently passing through a time when the old landmarks were rapidly disappearing If he might be allowed as a stranger and a foreigner to have an opinion on such a subject—it was as a student of England's history— he would express his admiration for the historical career of the City and its Lord Mayors. The City for many years had been a stronghold of political and religious liberty The freedom of opinion which was enjoyed here was not often found in other parts of Europe. He could not forget that during the ten years he had been there as Ambassador he had seen two Roman Catholics and one Jew occupying the Civic chair, and he did not think they would find any capital in Europe where such absolute religious freedom had been practised. The City might be looked upon as an example by many modern great cities. The gratitude of the French residents in London towards the City Corporation was deep-seated "

The Lord Mayor presided at a crowded meeting in the Egyptian Hall, Mansion House, in favor of the opening of Museums and Art Galleries on Sunday (8th)—A Royal Commission was appointed to consider the proper conditions under which an amalgamation of the City and County of London could be effected, and to make specific and practical proposals for that purpose.

The Corporation accepted the nomination by the Government of Mr. Henry Homewood Crawford (the City Solicitor) as its representative on the Royal Commission, the other members being the Right Hon L. H. Courtney, M P (Chairman), Sir Thomas Farrer (representing the London County Council), Mr R. D. Holt, Mayor of Liverpool, and Mr E. Orford Smith, Town Clerk of Birmingham

A sum of £400 was voted by the Corporation for the purchase, as an addition to the Guildhall Museum, of a unique collection of Roman and Mediæval antiquities found in the City (16th).—Owing to the increase of cholera abroad, the Corporation placed £2,000 at the disposal of the Port of London Sanitary Committee to be used, if necessary, for the transportation and isolation of cholera cases in the Thames (23rd). At the instance of the Committee, and with a view to promote unity of action among Sanitary Authorities, a conference of Port Sanitary Authorities of England and Wales, presided over by the Lord Mayor, was held.—It was resolved, in future, to pay the Sheriffs an annual sum of £750, in lieu of the existing allowances.—In consequence of the distress caused by the disastrous landslip at Sandgate a fund was opened at the Mansion House, realising £734 3s. 5d., the Corporation contributing 200 guineas. The Corporation also subscribed 100 guineas to the Queensland Floods Relief Fund.—Sir John Gilbert, R.A., offered his valuable art collection as a gift to the Galleries of London, Liverpool and Manchester (5 Ap.). The Lord Mayor laid before the Common Council a letter from Sir John Gilbert presenting fourteen paintings to the Guildhall Art Gallery. The Court subsequently (27th) resolved that the freedom of the City should be presented to the donor in recognition of his long and honourable career in the world of art, and more especially of his generous gift to the Art Gallery of the Corporation.—The Lord Mayor gave a banquet to Cardinal Vaughan and the Roman Catholic Bishops who assembled in their pontifical robes at the Mansion House. The Lord Mayor gave as the first toast:—

"The Holy Father and our most beloved Queen, Empress of our country and our hearts," and alluded to the Pope as "the vice-gerent of the King of Kings, seated on Rome's heights in incense-laden atmosphere." It was understood that no dinner had ever before been given in the Mansion House (which was built in 1753) exclusively to Roman Catholics, and the remarks of the Lord Mayor gave rise to controversy both within and outside the Corporation.

New Offices of the Institute of Chartered Accountants.

The Egyptian Hall, Mansion House, presented an unwonted appearance on the 29th, being crowded with factory girls who, as members of the Factory Helpers' Union, had come to receive prizes from the Duchess of Teck or witness their distribution.—The Governors of Christ's Hospital invited competitive designs for the new boarding school which it was proposed to erect at Horsham, Sussex. The award was given to Messrs. Aston Webb and Ingress Bell.

The design shows the majority of the buildings grouped round a flat semi-ellipse. The central feature is the school hall, and round it are thirty class rooms, connected by covered arcades. To the north-west stand the dining hall, chapel and library, while east and west of these are the residences, each consisting of two houses for boys, connected by one for the masters. Other blocks contain the infirmary, science schools, and laboratories. Considerable opposition has been made to the site on sanitary and other grounds, and the commencement of the buildings has been long delayed.

The new and beautiful building of the Institute of Chartered Accountants in Moorgate-place was opened on 10 May. The architect was Mr. John Belcher, and the sculptures were executed by Mr. Hamo Thornycroft, R.A., and Mr. H. Bates, A.R.A.—The foundation stone of Bishopsgate Institute was laid by the Rev. Prebendary Rogers, in the presence of the Earl of Rosebery, who delivered an address (13 May).—The Corporation voted a sum of 2,500 guineas for the purpose of a wedding present on the occasion of the marriage of H.R.H. the Duke of York, K.G., and H.S.H. the Princess Victoria Mary of Teck; an additional £1,500 being voted for a suitable entertainment to their Royal Highnesses (18th).

A fund was opened at the Mansion House, to present a suitable wedding gift from London. The amount subscribed, £2,790 6s. 6d., was devoted to the purchase of tapestry for the decoration of York House. The Corporation gifts took the form of a silver dinner service and a diamond and pearl necklace.

Frieze by Thornycroft.—Offices of the Institute of Chartered Accountants.

The Lord Mayor of Dublin attended the Common Council and was presented with an address of thanks for the kindness he had shown to the Lord Mayor of London during his visit to the capital of Ireland.—The Corporation resolved to sell to the London County Council a site in John Carpenter Street, at the rear of Sion College, for the erection of a new fire station, for a sum of £16,000.—In the presence of the Prince of Wales, the Archbishop of Canterbury, and the Bishops of London and Bedford, the north transept of the ancient priory church of St. Bartholomew-the-Great, West Smithfield, was re-opened (5 June). The work of restoration up to this time had cost £28,000.—The Duke of Connaught was presented with the honorary freedom of the Saddlers' Company (12th).—A sum of 250 guineas was voted by the Corporation towards the erection of head-quarters and a drill-hall for the London Rifle Brigade (22nd).—The loss by collision during some naval manœuvres of H.M.S. "Victoria," with many of those on board, caused widespread sympathy, and a fund opened at the Mansion House realised £68,883 16s. 11d., the Corporation contributing 500 guineas (30th).—The wedding of the Duke of York and Princess May, as she was popularly called, took place on 6 July.

Great preparations were made in the City for their Royal Highnesses' reception. The main streets were profusely decorated, and a tier of seats, suitably draped, was erected in St. Paul's Churchyard for the accommodation of the members of the Corporation and their ladies. The children of the Freemen's Orphan School witnessed the procession from the premises of Mr. Alderman Treloar, on Ludgate Hill. Crowds of enthusiastic spectators lined the route. The Lord Mayor, Sheriffs, Under Sheriffs, and a few members of the City Lands Committee, with their ladies, met the Royal procession in St. Paul's Churchyard, and conducted the Duke and Duchess of York to the Mansion House, which was almost concealed by flowers and crimson cloth. Detachments of the 1st Life Guards and of the Grenadiers kept an open space around the building. As the Royal carriage drove up amidst a deafening volley of cheers and the strains of martial music, little children sprinkled flowers over the carpeted footway in front of the Mansion House, and the Lady Mayoress stepped forward and handed a bouquet to the Princess. The Lord Mayor presented the Duke of York with the address voted by the Corporation, in a red scroll, and His Royal Highness handed the Lord Mayor a written reply. His lordship then placed in the hands of the Prince a beautifully designed address from himself and the Lady Mayoress, and, after a few words of acknowledgment, the carriage drove off amidst a renewed outburst of cheering. In the evening the City was brilliantly illuminated. The Lord Mayor accompanied by about sixty-five members of the Corporation proceeded to Windsor Castle on the 14th, and offered an address to Her Majesty, compliments of congratulation being also presented to the Duke and Duchess of York. The Lord Mayor received a baronetcy, and the Sheriffs knighthood, in connection with the Royal wedding, and a medal was ordered to be struck in honour of the occasion.

The King and Queen of Denmark were invited to the Guildhall and presented with an address by the Corporation (8 July).

The King in the course of his reply said: "It was my privilege, as a young man, to be present at the Coronation of the Queen, and my thoughts have never been absent from this country since we brought our beloved daughter

OFFICES·OF·MESSRS·BARING BROTHERS·BISHOPSGATE· STREET·WITHIN:1894:

Specimen of Modern Architecture, designed by Norman Shaw.

to her English home." Their Majesties and a distinguished company were afterwards entertained at a déjeuner in the Guildhall. A medal, designed by Mr. Frank Bowcher, was struck by the Corporation in commemoration of the event.

A great fire, involving the ward schools, occurred in St. Mary Axe (18 July).—
The Corporation voted 100 guineas for the relief of the families who suffered from
the boat accident at Skegness, and 50 guineas in connection with the Pontypridd
colliery disaster. For the latter object a sum of £543 13s. 3d. was collected at
the Mansion House (20th).—A scheme for establishing a Pension fund for the
official staff of the Corporation, largely at the expense of the officials themselves,
was adopted (27th).—The Fellowship Porters took forcible possession of the Hall
of their Corporation in Rose Court, Great Tower Street, to emphasise their
protest against an alleged misappropriation of their funds (20 Sept.).—The Institute
of Journalists held its first congress in London. Mr. W. L. Thomas, founder of the
Graphic and *Daily Graphic*, read a paper on "Illustrated Journalism" at the Mansion
House, and in the evening the members of the Institute were entertained at Guildhall
(22nd).—Sir John Gilbert, R.A., was presented with the freedom of the City (26th).
—It was resolved that the approaches to the Tower Bridge should be maintained
and repaired by the Corporation, through the Commissioners of Sewers —A statement as to the origin, position, powers, duties, and finances of the Corporation of
London, on the preparation of which the Town Clerk and the City Solicitor had
been for some time engaged, was presented to the Royal Commission (27th).

This was a comprehensive and detailed document, practically covering the essential features in
the history of the Corporation from the earliest times It was prefaced by a "protest," the chief
points of which were that the Corporation was no party to the inception of the present enquiry,
that there was uncertainty as to the terms of the reference, that the enquiry emanated from the London
County Council and was not the result of a general demand on the part of the inhabitants of London,
and that "amalgamation" in the minds of those who were instrumental in procuring the appointment of the Royal Commission meant "absorption and destruction of the City of London as it had
for centuries existed, and abolition and annulment of its rights and privileges, thereby involving
confiscation of its property and deprivation of that which lawfully belongs to its citizen." The
Commissioners of Sewers also presented a statement of the powers and duties of that body, together
with a brief history of the origin and progress of the Commission since the year 1667. Corporation
witnesses having given evidence before the Royal Commission, the Special Committee reviewed the
situation, and submitted to the Common Council a resolution recommending "That the Corporation,
whilst ready and anxious to continue to tender evidence, can only proceed upon the assumption and
on assurance that the Royal Commissioners will be ready to hear evidence when tendered upon the
question of desirability as well as of the convenient practicability of an amalgamation of the City
and County of London" (16 Nov.). A deputation from the Corporation waited upon the President
of the Local Government Board, and in consequence of his assurances and at his request, the
Special Committee was authorised to prepare and tender to the Royal Commissioners the fullest
amount of evidence procurable on the problem submitted to their consideration (5 Dec). Alderman
Sir David Evans, the Chairman of the Special Committee and a minority of its members were
in favour of at once withdrawing from the enquiry

Alderman George Robert Tyler was elected Lord Mayor.—The Prince
of Wales, accompanied by the Princess Louise, laid the memorial stone of the

St. Bride Foundation Institute, Bride Lane, in the presence of the Lord Mayor and Sheriffs (20 Nov.).—The Medical Officer of Health presented a report to the Commissioners of Sewers on the insanitary condition of Christ's Hospital,

Old House, over entrance to Dean's Court—Destroyed, 1895.

and an order was issued for the reconstruction of the drainage (21st). As a result of this order the school was broken up and the building remained closed for several months.—The memorial stone of the new City Greenyard, in Whitecross Street, was laid (12 Dec.). —Mr. Deputy Snowden having offered a picture for one of the panels at the Royal Exchange, Mr. R. W. Macbeth, R.A., was commissioned to produce a painting illustrative of the opening of the Exchange by Her Majesty. Sir Frederic Leighton was also preparing a painting for another panel.

The Mansion House Fund for a national memorial of the Jubilee of Queen Victoria, which was closed this year, amounted to £28,626 8s. 1d. The fund for the unemployed came to £1,403 16s. 8d., and that on behalf of the sufferers from the Thorn Hill colliery disaster to £749 3s. 10d.

A new clock, by Messrs. Smith, of Derby, was placed in position at St. Paul's Cathedral, the old clock made by Langley Bradley, in 1708, having been removed some time before (21st).

A dedication service was held in the Clock Tower conducted by the Dean and Canon Newbolt, and, during a short pause, the clock was set in motion by one of the Dean's daughters. The service was so timed as to finish when the clock began striking twelve. [The old house over the entrance to Dean's Court (Doctors' Commons), of which a view is given, was pulled down in 1895.]

1894.

SOME fifteen hundred poor children, from different parts of London, were entertained at the Guildhall, the funds being provided mainly by the readers of two magazines (2 Jan., 1894).—Mr. E. Armitage, R.A., presented to the Guildhall Art Gallery his picture entitled "Herod's Birthday Feast" (10 Feb.).—In consequence of the attitude of the Royal Commission towards the City witnesses the Common Council decided not to tender further evidence (12th). The City

Solicitor at the same time obtained Her Majesty's permission to withdraw from the Royal Commission, a step which was fully endorsed by the Corporation.— A sum of £1,700 was voted by the Corporation for structural improvements at the Old Bailey (15th).—Alfred Cohen, "the City harpist," a talented street musician, and a familiar figure in the neighbourhood of the Stock Exchange, was found dead in his house at Stepney (16th).—One of the oldest of the labour guilds in the country, the Fellowship of Porters, was disbanded by the Corporation at the request of the porters themselves (15 Mar.).

Originally the carrying work, both at Billingsgate and from the wharves to the warehouses of the City within a certain radius, was performed by the Fellowship Porters, but of late years they had had to compete with outside labour, and the Act of 1872 dealing with the metage of grain had contributed largely to their decay. Thirty years before there were about 2,000 Fellowship Porters, and it was a common spectacle, in the early morning, to see hundreds of the porters "turning out" for their labour on Tower Hill, when, after counting themselves into teams of seven, along with their respective meters, they would break up for an early breakfast, after which they would again meet at their various jobs on the river or at the docks. They made up a notable picture of old London life, but for the last twenty years they had been a source of trouble to the Corporation.

A little row of almshouses founded by a merchant named Christopher Eyre, under his will dated 29 July, 1617, had existed for over 200 years at the back of Moorgate Street, the recipients of the charity being the aged poor of St. Stephen, Coleman Street. Under an order of the Charity Commissioners the inmates were dispersed with a liberal allowance, and the almshouses were pulled down.—The third Art Loan Exhibition was opened at the Guildhall Gallery by the Lord Mayor and Sheriffs (3 Ap.).

The value of the pictures exceeded £300,000, one of the most notable exhibits being Landseer's "Monarch of the Glen." Upwards of 300,000 visitors passed the turnstile, and the exhibition was for the first time open for some hours on alternate Sundays.

An exhibition of blacksmiths' work, under the auspices of the Blacksmiths' Company, was opened by the Lord Mayor at Ironmongers' Hall. The exhibits came chiefly from the provinces (11th).—Col. William Haywood, who a short time previously had retired from the position of Engineer and Surveyor to the Commissioners of Sewers and was appointed Consulting Engineer to that body, died on the 13th after a long illness.

Col. Haywood, who was a man of singular ability and sound judgment, entered the service of the Commissioners as Assistant Surveyor in 1845, and a year later was unanimously appointed Surveyor, to which post the title of Engineer was afterwards added. His chief work was the building of Holborn Viaduct.

The Salters' Company celebrated its 500th anniversary, the charter of the guild having been granted by Richard II.—Mr. Ex-Sheriff Burt died at Swanage at the age of seventy-seven (18th). He had helped to resuscitate several of the City Guilds and had been a liberal supporter of City Charities.—The Italian Ambassador (Count Tornielli), accompanied by a deputation of his countrymen, attended the Court of Common Council and presented the Corporation with a painting, by Signor Michele Tedesco (representing an invasion of a garden of Pythagoreans by Sybarites), in recognition of the kindly feeling shown to the Italian Exhibitors at the Italian Exhibition of Arts and Industries which was opened by the Lord Mayor in 1888 (3 May).—The City Solicitor informed the Court of Aldermen that the new scheme for the management of Emanuel Hospital had recently received the sanction of Mr. Justice Chitty, and under it, notwithstanding great opposition, the Lord Mayor and Aldermen would be continued as the governing body.

Under this scheme out-pensions only would be granted, and the number was increased from ten to forty, to be called the Lady Dacre pensions   The amount of the out-pensions was increased from £10 to £25 per annum (8th)

Dr. Samuel Johnson's house, in Gough Square, Fleet Street, was threatened with destruction, but although one side of the Square has been rebuilt, the abode of the famous lexicographer still remains standing.

It was here that Johnson lived for ten years from 1748, and a tablet notifying the fact was affixed to the building by the Royal Society. Here, too, the Doctor began the publication of the *Rambler*, and completed his Dictionary. His wife died in the house in 1752.

The first volume of "London and the Kingdom," by Dr. Sharpe, was issued under the direction of the Library Committee of the Corporation (28th). — In celebration of the Jubilee of the Young Men's Christian Association, about 3,000 invitations were issued to a conversazione at the Guildhall, and the freedom of the City was presented to Mr. (now Sir) George Williams (4 June).

The Corporation thus testified their appreciation of Sir George Williams' life-long services in the cause of philanthropy, and his special efforts for the welfare of the young men of the City, which, commencing in 1844, resulted in the permanent establishment of the Young Men's Christian Association. This flourishing institution had begun in a humble room, and then numbered in the United Kingdom 843 branches, with a membership of 87,464 persons; while throughout the world there were over 5,158 branches and a membership of half-a-million.

Christ's Hospital was re-opened after the completion of the drainage works.— Miss Alice Eliza Blagrave was elected headmistress of the new City of London School for girls (14th).—The Guardians of the City of London Union were desired by the London County Council to reduce the number of guardians to thirty, the number proposed by the Union being seventy-five (16th).—The crypt in Laurence Pountney Lane, which once formed part of the Manor of the Rose, built by Sir John Pountney in the fourteenth century, was threatened with destruction.   An unsuccessful attempt was made to preserve this interesting relic (20th).—The Court of Common Council passed a resolution expressing the utmost indignation at the dastardly outrage which had deprived France of its head by the assassination of President Carnot (28th).—Tower Bridge was opened by the Prince of Wales, who was accompanied by the Princess of Wales and other members of the Royal family (30th).

Royal Cortége crossing Tower Bridge at the opening, June 30th, 1894.

Covered seats were erected to accommodate about 5,000 spectators, and the neighbouring streets were adorned with flags and bunting, and crowded with people ; while the river presented a scene of great animation. The Royal party, having been received by the Lord Mayor and Sheriffs, and the Members of the Bridge House Estates Committee, at the City end of the Bridge, drove across to the southern approach, and returned to the pavilion amidst the cheers of the spectators. The address, presented by the Recorder, stated that the Tower Bridge was estimated to be completed in four years, and to cost £750,000. The time had to be extended, and the cost would reach the sum of £1,184,000, the whole of which would be provided by the Bridge House Estates Committee, without any cost whatever to the ratepayers. The Prince of Wales replied, and then, in the name of the Queen, declared the Bridge open for "land traffic," and putting his hand on a lever in connection with the bascules, announced the Bridge open for "river traffic." This was the most novel and interesting feature of the ceremony. The enormous leaves rose gradually from a horizontal to a perpendicular position amidst the deafening boom of guns, the screaming of whistles and syrens, and the plaudits of the people.

The bridge has two side spans of 270 feet in the clear, and a central opening span of 200 feet clear width, with a height of 135 feet above Trinity high water when open, and a height of 29½ feet when closed. While the leaves of the central span are raised, and the vehicular traffic is stopped, foot passengers are conveyed by hydraulic lifts to a gallery above, so that their progress is never impeded. The towers form a fine architectural feature of the bridge, harmonising with the Tower of London at the western end.

In connection with this important event the Lord Mayor received a baronetcy, and the Sheriffs with the Chairman of the Bridge House Estates Committee (Mr Albert Joseph Altman) the honour of knighthood. An illustrated history of the Tower Bridge, and of the Bridge House Trust from very early times, was prepared by the City Librarian under the directions of the Committee, and a copy was presented by the Lord Mayor to the Prince of Wales. A medal was also ordered to be struck to commemorate the occasion. A sum of £300 was voted by the Corporation for the entertainment of the workpeople employed on Tower Bridge and their wives.

The Duke of York laid the memorial stone of the new Cripplegate Institute in Golden Lane (3 July).—A meeting was held at the Mansion House for the purpose of considering the position of Christ's Hospital (11th).

The Duke of Cambridge (the President) said : " He saw nothing in the future for the school but absolute ruin. He considered it a great mistake to take the school out of London, and owing to the abolition of donation governors they had had to draw heavily upon their capital." A resolution was adopted to the effect that the new boarding schools should not be proceeded with until it was known that the available funds were sufficient for the purpose. Sir Henry Peek strongly opposed the Horsham site as utterly unsuitable, and supported an alternative site at Wimbledon.

In view of the great and increasing quantities of fish which were being sold at the Shadwell Riverside Market, where no tolls were charged, the Corporation resolved that only half tolls should in future be collected at Billingsgate (12th).—The usual loyal addresses were voted by the Corporation on the occasion of the birth of Prince Edward, son of their Royal Highnesses the Duke and Duchess of York (13th).—A Mansion House Fund was opened on behalf of the sufferers from the Albion Colliery accident, South Wales, when 300 lives were lost. The sum received was £5,972 16s. 7d., of which the Corporation subscribed 250 guineas.—The freehold hall at 17 St. Mary-at-Hill, occupied by the Fellowship Porters for upwards of one hundred years, but disused of late, was sold by auction (20th).—West India House was opened by Alderman and Sheriff Sir Joseph Dimsdale (23rd).—By order of the Ecclesiastical Commissioners the site and fabric of Allhallows-the-Great-and-Less, Upper Thames Street, were offered for sale.

The property was eventually knocked down for £13,100 to a Brewery Company, whose premises occupied the block of buildings next to the church. The earliest mention of the church is in 1361, but it was destroyed in the Great Fire and rebuilt by Sir Christopher Wren. The beautifully-carved screen and pulpit which it possessed have been re-erected in the church of St. Margaret Lothbury.

A Mansion House Fund, for sufferers from the earthquakes in Turkey, amounted to £1,314 11s. 6d., the Corporation contributing 100 guineas.—The

Common Council also voted £500 a year for three years to the City and Guilds of London Institute (26th).—A novel recreation ground was formed on the roof of some premises in Bucklersbury for the benefit of the employés, the space being provided with tables and garden seats, and adorned with shrubs.—An interesting old London Inn, the "Goose and Gridiron," in London House Yard, St. Paul's Churchyard, was about to be pulled down (29 Aug.).

Here, in 1717, Masonry was revived and the first Grand Lodge of the world founded. Before the Great Fire the house was known as the "Mitre." The sign is in the Guildhall Museum.

A unique collection of clocks and watches, illustrating the progress made in the art of horology during the past three centuries, was presented to the Clockmakers' Company, by the Rev. H. L. Nelthropp, M.A., F.S.A., the Master, and deposited in the Guildhall Library.—The Mercers' School was removed from College Hill, Cannon Street, to the new buildings in Barnard's Inn, Holborn (11 Sept.).

In 1892 the Mercers' Company purchased the site of Barnard's Inn, which gave them a superficial area of 27,000 feet, including the buildings standing thereon. Among these buildings was the Hall of the old Inn which the Company decided to retain and make part and parcel of the school premises. The new school, which was opened by the Earl of Selborne (a former master of the Company), will accommodate 300 boys. The site cost £43,000, and the new buildings were estimated to cost between £20,000 and £30,000.

A conversazione, attended by the Lord Mayor and Sheriffs, marked the formal opening of the City of London School for Girls (Ward's Bequest) on the Victoria Embankment (13th).—There was a contest for the mayoralty on the 29th, and for the first time in the history of the Corporation a one-day poll was taken, in accordance with the City of London Ballot Act, 1888,

Decorations in St. Paul's Cathedral, designed by W. B. Richmond, R.A.

which also abolished open voting. Alderman Sir Joseph Renals, the senior Alderman below the Chair, headed the poll with 1,462 votes; Mr. Alderman

Faudel Phillips coming next with 1,360 votes.   An adjourned Common Hall was held (3 Oct.), when the election of Sir Joseph Renals was endorsed by the Court of Aldermen. — The Royal Commission issued their report proposing the creation of a new central body for London, and the practical extinction of the "old Corporation," most of its powers and privileges, including its financial resources, being transferred to a new Corporation.

Decorations in St. Paul's Cathedral, designed
by W. B. Richmond, R.A.

The Commissioners stated that they regarded the existence of local bodies throughout the Metropolis as essential. In consideration of the fact that the rateable value of the City is about one-eighth of the whole rateable value of the Metropolis it was proposed that the City should have eight representatives on the new Council, which would consist of about 118 Councillors and 19 Aldermen. The new Corporation was to have a Lord Mayor who was to be titular Chairman of the Council.

The Special Committee of the Common Council, referring to the Report, said: "It is silent as to the reasons which have induced the Commissioners to consider it just and reasonable, or (to use their own expression) 'natural' to suggest the confiscation of the ancient rights and privileges of the Corporation, and the transfer of its property and possessions, including even its Guildhall, its Mansion House, its Library and Museum, its School of Music, its City of London Schools for Boys and Girls, and even its plate and public records, in exchange for an annual allowance of 10,000 guineas, clothed with conditions as to the continued maintenance of the Freemen's Orphan School and other Institutions which render the consideration worse than valueless. Nor is any justification attempted for depriving the Liverymen of London of the privileges which they have enjoyed for many centuries." In the judgment of the Special Committee the Corporation had a right to take its stand upon the Parliamentary compact entered into at the passing of the Local Government Bill of 1888. It always had been favourable to the formation of Municipal Councils, and had even expressed its readiness to loyally assist in carrying out such a plan as was proposed in the Bill of 1888, by allocating a portion of its funds to such Municipal Councils, for the purpose of assisting in defraying such corporate expenditure as could not be properly chargeable upon the Local Rate. This report was adopted by the Common Council.

The Corporation resolved to subscribe £500 per annum for four years to assist in completing the internal decorations of St. Paul's Cathedral (4 Oct.).

The eight spandrels of the Dome of St Paul's were filled with mosaic by Dr. Salviati, of Venice, from designs by Mr. G. F. Watts, R.A., Mr. A Stevens, and Mr. Brittan, during the years 1863-1892 ; the subjects being the four Evangelists and the four greater Prophets.   Since 1891, the work of decorating the choir with mosaic has been carried on under the direction of Mr. W. B. Richmond, R.A., and from his designs.

Prince Ademuyiwa Haastrup, of the, Independent State of Jebu Remo, on the West Coast of Africa, attended the Common Council (1 Nov.)

At the close of the proceedings he expressed his thanks to the Lord Mayor and said he should advise his cousin, who occupied the Throne, to place his country under Her Majesty the Queen's protection, as he felt that he was dealing with those who were truly Christians

Lord Rosebery, as Prime Minister, was the chief guest at the Guildhall Banquet (9th).—The Common Council passed a resolution of sympathy with the Russian people on the occasion of the death of the Emperor Alexander III.— St. Bride Foundation Institute was opened by the Lord Mayor (20th).

The building was erected on a piece of freehold land in Bride Lane, with an area of 7,500 square feet, which had been purchased by the Governors for £11,300; the building and equipment costing £20,000 more.   The Institute embraces a swimming bath and washing baths, lending library and reading rooms, gymnasium, lithographic school, printing museum with the Blades typographical Library adjoining, printing school, students' gallery, etc

The Duke of Newcastle, Mr. W. H. Key. Mr. Patrick H. White, and Mr. Claude J. Montefiore were elected as representatives of the City on the London School Board (22 Nov.). — The new Bishopsgate Institute was opened by Lord Rosebery (24th).

The building was erected out of money granted by the Charity Commissioners for the Bishops-gate Charities, supplemented by grants from the City Parochial Foundation.   The trusts of the old charities were abrogated, and a Board of Governors was appointed, of which the Rev. William Rogers, M.A., was the Chairman.   The Institute, which was built and equipped at a cost of £70,000, is of original design, and contains a large hall 50 feet long, 48 feet wide and 42 feet high   The reference library and reading rooms are open to the general public, and there is a lending library for the use of persons resident or employed in the eastern half of the City.   Prior to the opening of the Institute a meeting was held at the Mansion House, at which the Rev. William Rogers, M A, was presented with a portrait in oils of himself and a service of plate, on the occasion of his 75th birthday   The presentation was made on behalf of the subscribers by Lord Rosebery

The Corporation made a further grant of 200 guineas towards the costs incurred in the preservation of Banstead Downs.—A sum of £250 was voted out of the City's cash in aid of the unemployed, and to continue the drainage (as a relief work) of Wanstead Flats.—A fund was also raised at the Mansion House for the unemployed amounting to £1,314 11s. 6d. — Another Mansion House Fund, in aid of the sufferers from the earthquake in Greece, realised £5,455 10s. 8d.—The Hospital Sunday Fund amounted to £43,679 11s. 8d.—

Cooling rooms and further chill-room accommodation at the Foreign Cattle Market, Deptford, were ordered to be provided at a cost of £41,500 (13 Dec.).—The *History of the Tower Bridge* was revised, and published towards the close of the year. Two other works were issued under the auspices of the Corporation during 1894, viz.: the second volume of *London and the Kingdom*, by Dr. R. R. Sharpe (the appearance of the first volume has been noted under 28th May), and *Numismata Londinensia : Medals struck by the Corporation of London to commemorate important municipal events, 1831 to 1893.*

Guildhall Yard on Michaelmas Day, during Common Hall for the
election of Lord Mayor.

Michaelmas Day at Guildhall, with the wicket gates to admit the
Liverymen of the various Companies.

INDEX.

By HERBERT C. WELCH.

ABBREVIATIONS·—Ald , *Alderman* ; App , *Appointed* , Arch , *Architect* ; C of l , *City of London* ; Co Co., *Common Council*, Co Hall, *Common Hall*, el , *elected*, House of C , *House of Commons*, House of L., House of Lords , L C C., *London County Council* L M , *Lord Mayor* , L S B , *London School Board* , Parl., *Parliament* , Sher , *Sheriff*

LIST OF SUBSCRIBERS.

LARGE PAPER COPIES.

H. J. Adams, Esq., 58, Cannon Street, E.C.

The Most Hon. The Marquis of Ailsa, Culzean Castle, Maybole, N.B. (Per Mr. R. J. Bush.)

T. W. Aldwinckle, Esq., 1, Victoria Street, S.W.

Count Albert Armand, 11, Lafon Street, Marseilles.

Mrs. T. R. Armitage, 34, Cambridge Square, Hyde Park, W. (Per Messrs. Truslove & Hanson.)

W. H. Ash, Esq., 51, Hamilton Terrace, N.W.

C. Austen-Leigh, Esq., 35, Cadogan Square, S.W.

S. P. Avery, Esq., New York. (Per Mr. G. E. Stechert.)

Messrs. Baring Bros. & Co., Ltd., 8, Bishopsgate Street Within, E.C.

Thomas J. Barratt, Esq., 71, New Oxford Street, W.C. (Per Messrs. Truslove & Hanson.)

G. R. Barrett, Esq., Drakesleigh, Plymouth. (Per Messrs. Bazley & Co.)

Right Rev. J. C. Beardwood, Abbot of Mount St. Joseph, Roscrea, Ireland (Per Mr. Henry Gray.)

E. C. Beedell, Esq., C.C., 14, Throgmorton Street, E.C.

C. Bennett, Esq., 2, Capel Court, E.C.

A. T. Bevan, Esq., Bessels Green, Chevening, Kent.

Paul Bevan, Esq., M.A., F.C.A., Tryfan, Hardwick Road, Eastbourne (Per Messrs. Ellis & Elvey.)

A. F. Blades, Esq., 23, Newlands Park, Sydenham.

G. R. Blades, Esq., The Firs, Worcester Road, Sutton, Surrey.

R. H. Blades, Esq., F.S.S., F.R.G.S., The Firs, Worcester Road, Sutton, Surrey.

Mr. W. Blair, *Free Press*, Tonbridge.

T. Bliss, Esq., M.N.L.S., Coningsburgh, Bethune Road, Stamford Hill, N.

Rev. J. B. Bolton, Badsworth Rectory, Pontefract.

W. E. Bools, Esq., 7, Cornhill, E.C.

H. H. P. Bouverie, Esq., 32, Hill Street, W.

F. Braby, Esq., F.C.S., F.G.S., M.I.A., etc., Bushey Lodge, Teddington.

Mr. William Brown, 26, Princes Street, Edinburgh.

W. P. Brown, Esq., 3, Austin Friars, E.C.

A. Giraud Browning, Esq., F.S.A., 16, Victoria Street, Westminster, S.W.

Sir Harry Bullard, M.P., Hellesdon House, Norwich.

G. Burt, Esq., 19, Grosvenor Road, S.W.

G. Burt, Esq., 37, Grosvenor Road, Westminster, S.W.

G. Burt, Esq., Purbeck House, Swanage.

Messrs. Butterworth & Co., 7, Fleet Street, E.C.

C. W. Cattell, Esq., 13, Hartfield Square, Eastbourne.

R. K. Causton, Esq., 12, Devonshire Place, W.

C. E. H. Chadwyck-Healey, Esq., 119, Harley Street, W.

W. H. Chaplin, Esq., M.A., 13, Pen-y-wern Road, S.W.

J. J. Chapman, Esq., Whitby, Yorkshire. (Per Mr. T. B. Bumpus.)

G. Christie, Esq., Southfield House, Stirling, N.B.

W. Church, Esq., Kobe, Japan. (Per Mr. R. J. Bush.)

D. Clarke, Esq., Glenthorne, Cheam Road, Sutton, Surrey.

Sir Edward Clarke, Q.C., M.P., 37, Russell Square, W.C.

E. Clarke, Esq., 31, Threadneedle Street, E.C.

Percy Clarke, Esq., 13, Fleet Street, E.C.

C. Clay, Esq., Manor House, Dewsbury.

John Clayton, Esq., Town Clerk, Melbourne. (Per Messrs. G. Robertson & Co.)

R. Clout, Esq., Brome House, West Malling, Kent.

J. Colman, Esq., Gatton Park, Surrey.

J. W. Colmer, Esq., 7, King William Street, E.C.

J. M. Cook, Esq. (Messrs. T. Cook & Son), Ludgate Circus.

Mr. A. Cooper, Charing Cross Road, W.C.

Lieut.-Col. A. J. Copeland, F.S.A., High Beach, Westgate-on-Sea.

Nathaniel Cork, Esq., F.R.G.S., F.S.S., The Grennell, Sutton, Surrey.

The Right Hon. The Earl of Cranbrook, P.C., G.C.S.I., 17, Grosvenor Crescent, S.W.

William Creasey, Esq., London Wall, E.C.

W. D. Cronin, Esq., F.R.G.S., M.R.I., Woodcote, Cleve Road, West Hampstead, N.W.

W. T. Crosweller, Esq., F.I.Inst., M.S.A., F.Z.S., Kent Lodge, Sidcup.

E. Curwen, Esq., Withdeane Court, Brighton. (Per Mr. H. Gray.)

The Worshipful Company of Cutlers, The Hall, Warwick Lane, E.C.

Augustin Daly, Esq., Daly's Theatre, Leicester Square, W.C.

Stephen Darby, Esq., 140, Leadenhall Street, E.C.

C. Y. Dean, Esq., 1, Wickham Road, S.E. (Per Mr. J. D. Smith.)

J. T. Denniston, Esq., 45, New Broad Street, E.C.

F. D. Dew, Esq., 138, King's Road, Chelsea, S.W.

Alderman Sir J. C. Dimsdale, 3, Lancaster Street, Hyde Park, W.

The Worshipful Company of Drapers, The Hall, Throgmorton Street, E.C. (Per W. P. Sawyer, Esq.)

W. T. Dunlin, Esq., F.R.G.S., 7, Albion Terrace, Cartergate, Grimsby.

Miss S. R. Dunn, Sutton Hall, Thirsk. (Per Messrs. J. Cornish & Sons.)

J. Elin, Esq., 33, Upper Hamilton Terrace, N.W.

H. J. Evans, Esq., Greenhill, Whitchurch, Cardiff.

J. K. Farlow, Esq., Junr., 118, Cannon Street, E.C.

C. Farris, Esq., 81, Bishopsgate Street Within, E.C.

Thomas Fenn, Esq., 44, Coleman Street, E.C.

T. J. Fisher, Esq., 6 and 7, Clement's Lane, E.C.

F. A. C. Fletcher, Esq., L.R.C.P., L.R.C.S., Holly Bank, Cross Hills, via Keighley.

Edwin Fox, Esq., 99, Gresham Street, E.C.

W. L. T. Foy, Esq., 104, Bishopsgate Street Within, E.C.

Miss G. Franklin, 3, Park Villas, Winchmore Hill, N. (Per Mr. W. H. Batho.)

T. F. Franklin, Esq., F.S.I., 25, Ludgate Hill, E.C.

W. D. Freshfield, Esq., 5, Bank Buildings, E.C.

Rev. E. H. Gifford, Arlington House, Oxford.

Messrs. Gilbert & Field, 67, Moorgate Street, E.C.

Sir Alfred Sherlock Gooch, Bart., D.L., J.P., Benacre Hall, Wrentham. (Per Mr. W. Downing.)

James F. Goodhart, Esq., 25, Weymouth Street, W. (Per Messrs. Truslove & Hanson.)

The Right Hon. The Earl of Gosford, 22, Mansfield Street, W. (Per Messrs. Truslove & Hanson.)

Baron Albert Grant, D.L., 2, Tokenhouse Buildings, Lothbury, E.C.

P. H. Griffin, Esq., Combe Wood, Bonchurch, Isle of Wight.

Joseph Grimshire, Esq., 27, Warwick Road, Upper Clapton. (Per Mr. Elliot Stock.)

The Worshipful Company of Haberdashers, The Hall, Gresham Street, E.C. (Per Mr. W. H. Batho.)

Mrs. A. Hamilton, 27, Bolton Gardens, South Kensington.

A. C. Harper, Esq., F.C.A., 10, Trinity Square, E.C.

Messrs. Harris & Co., 21, Birchin Lane, E.C.

C. W. Harrison, Esq., 66, Mark Lane, E.C.

Miss Hartshorne, Ashbourne, Derbyshire.

R. H. Hawes, Esq., 89, Oxford Terrace, W.

Rev. J. J. Hazell, 41, Brook Green, Hammersmith, W.

G. H. Herring, Esq., 31, Walbrook, E.C.

Mr. John Heywood, Shoe Lane, E C.

Mr. F. Hockliffe, Bedford.

T. A. Hodgkinson, Esq., 3, Queenhithe, E C.

W. R. Horncastle, Esq., C C., Taymouth House, Hackney, N.E.

R. Hovenden, Esq., F.S.A , F. R H S., Heathcote, Park Hill Road, Croydon.

W. G. Howard, Esq, C C , 53, Isledon Road Finsbury Park, N.

H. S. Howlett, Esq , 26 and 27, Bush Lane, E.C

H. Hoxby, Esq., 17, Richmond Road, Walthamstow.

Rev. Canon Ingram, M.A , St. Margaret's Rectory, 20, Finsbury Square, E.C.

Institute of Chartered Accountants in England and Wales (Reginald B. Fellows, Esq., B.A , Librarian), Moorgate Place, E.C.

The Rt. Hon. Lord Iveagh, Elveden, Thetford. (Per Messrs. Ellis & Elvey.)

T. E. Jacobson, Esq , Surgeon, Sleaford, Lincolnshire.

A. A. James, Esq., 66, Coleman Street, E.C.

Francis James, Esq., F.S.A., 190, Cromwell Road, Earls Court, S.W.

J James, Esq , J.P., St. Martin's Crescent, Haverfordwest.

John Jamieson, Esq., 27, Duddingston Park, Portobello, N.B.

Richard Jehu, Esq , 33, Mark Lane, E.C.

Edgar F. Jenkins, Esq., 16, Godliman Street, E.C.

R. Johnson, Esq , The Hope House, Little Burstead, Billericay.

W. Jordan, Esq., 55, Highbury Park, N.

Arthur L. Josephs, Esq., Roseneath, Broxbourne, Herts.

C. A. C. Keeson, Esq., 9, Loudoun Road, St. John's Wood, N.W.

H. Kendrick, Esq., F.C.A., 10, Pancras Lane, E.C.

D. W. Kettle, Esq., F.R.G.S., Hayes Common, Kent. (Per Mr. R. H. Laurie.)

Alderman Sir Stuart Knill, Bart., LL.D., Fresh Wharf, London Bridge (2 copies.)

J. Lakeman, Esq., C.A., 5, St. Peter's Alley, E.C.

Lt.-Col. Lambert, 10, 11 and 12, Coventry Street, Piccadilly, London, W.

H. J. Lardner, Esq., 24, Hosier Lane, E.C.

H. Lescher, Esq., 6, Clement's Lane, E.C.

R. B M. Lingard-Monk, Esq., Fulshaw Hall, Wilmslow, Cheshire (Per Mr. Henry Gray.)

G. Hamilton Lloyd, Esq., A.M I.C.E., M.I.M.M. 7, St. Mildred's Court, E C.

Edward J. Lowther, Esq., A R.I.B.A., Finsbury House, Blomfield Street, E.C.

N Lubbock, Esq., 65, Earl's Court Square, S.W.

William Lynch, Esq , 113, William Street, Melbourne, Victoria. (Per Messrs G Robertson & Co.)

W. O. Lyon, Esq., Glamis, Nicoll Road, Harlesden, N W

A. W. Mackenzie, Esq., 2, Gloucester Road, Brownswood Park, London, N.

J. H. Mallard, Esq , 119, Wood Street, E C

Mr W B Martin, 2, High Street, Sandown, Isle of Wight.

Robt Mason Mills, Esq., Bourne, Lincolnshire. (Per Mr J. T. Morris)

Charles Maw, Esq., 7, Aldersgate Street, E C.

John D Mayne, Esq (Per Messrs. H. Sotheran & Co.)

The Worshipful Company of Merchant Taylors, The Hall, Threadneedle St., E C (2 copies) (Per Edward Nash, Esq., M A , LL.B.)

J. H. Membrey, Esq , 28, Mincing Lane, E C

R. Milne-Redhead, Esq , F.L.S., Holdenclough, Clitheroe.

Minet Public Library, Camberwell, S.E. (C. J. Courtney, Esq., Librarian.)

W. E. Morden, Esq., Tooting Graveney.

W. F. Morice, Esq., 23, Old Broad Street, E.C

C. G. Mott, Esq , Harrow Weald, Middlesex.

K. R. Murchison, Esq., 116, Park Street, Park Lane, W. (Per Messrs. Truslove & Hanson.)

E. Montague Nelson, Esq , 15, Dowgate Hill, E.C.

A. H. Newton, Esq., Pury Lodge, Northamptonshire.

Mr Alderman A. J. Newton, The Wood, Sydenham Hill, Kent.

John Norbury, Esq., 32, Gordon Square. (Per Mr. T. B. Bumpus)

W. Oatley, Esq , 57, Amhurst Park, Stamford Hill.

Major F. F. Parkinson, Eppleton, Streatham Park, Surrey.

Owen Parry, Esq., Eweland Hall, Ingatestone, Essex.

Alfred Patchett, Esq. (Per Messrs. H. Sotheran & Co.)

T. F. Peacock, Esq., F.S.A , Fernlea, Sidcup, Kent.

Andrew Pears, Esq., J.P., Spring Grove House, Isleworth. (Per Messrs. J. Cornish & Sons.)

Rev. E. B. Penny, Christ's Hospital, E.C. (Per Mr. W. H. Batho.)

W. F. Perowne, Esq., Stock Exchange.

H. Phillips, Esq., 145, Walworth Road, S.E.

G. A. Pickering, Esq., Chamberlain's Office, Guildhall, E.C.

The Right Hon Lord Pirbright.

Francis W. Pixley, Esq., F.S.A., 23, Linden Gardens, W.

The Hon. Gerald Ponsonby, 3, Stratford Place, W. (Per Messrs. Truslove & Hanson.)

John Pound, Esq, Alderman and Sheriff of London, India House, 84, Leadenhall Street

Rev A. Povah, D.D., 8, The Boltons, South Kensington.

Campbell Praed, Esq., 39, Norfolk Square, W.

F. G. Hilton Price, Esq., Director S A., 17, Collingham Gardens, South Kensington. (Per Messrs. Truslove & Hanson.)

W. Pritchard, Esq., M.R.C.V.S , 5, Regent's Park Road, Gloucester Gate.

F. Pullman, Esq., J.P , Nottingham. (Per Mr Geo. Evans.)

J. J Purnell, Esq., Woodlands, Streatham Hill, S.W.

A. Pye-Smith, Esq. (Per Messrs. H. Sotheran & Co)

Mr. Bernard Quaritch, 15, Piccadilly, W.

C. J W. Rabbits, Esq., J.P., 8, Palace Gate, W.

W. T. Rabbits, Esq. (Per Messrs. H. Sotheran & Co.)

Francis Ravenscroft, Esq., 64, Springfield Road, St. John's Wood, N.W.

C. Rees-Price, Esq., 163, Bath Street, Glasgow. (Per Mr. Elliot Stock.)

Rittenhouse Club, Philadelphia. (Per Mr. B. F Stevens.)

J. Rock, Esq., 56, Friday Street, E C.

M. T. Roe, Esq , 80, Lexham Gdns., Kensington.

Sir Albert K. Rollit, LL.D., F.R.A.S., M.P., Dunster House, Mark Lane, E.C

A. Romano, Esq., 399, Strand, W.C.

E. L. Rowcliffe, Esq., Cumberland Gate, Regent's Park. (Per Messrs. J. Cornish & Sons)

Mrs Rylands, Longford Hall, Stretford, Manchester. (Per Mr. Elliot Stock)

The Worshipful Company of Saddlers, The Hall, Cheapside, E.C. (Per Mr. W. H. Batho)

R. H. Salmon, Esq., 28, Fenchurch Street, E.C.

The Worshipful Company of Salters, St. Swithin's Lane, E.C. (Per E. Lionel Scott, Esq.)

A. G. Sandeman, Esq., 20, St. Swithin's Lane, E.C.

Hermann R. Schmettau, Esq., 31, Abchurch Lane, E.C.

A. J. Scrutton, Esq., 75, Old Broad Street, E.C.

Mrs Mariame Sharp, Addison Villas, Nottingham. (Per Mr. Geo. Evans.)

A. Siemens, Esq., F.R.G.S., 7, Airlie Gardens, Campden Hill, W.

Messrs. Simpkin, Marshall, Hamilton, Kent & Co., Limited, Stationers' Hall Court, E.C.

George T. Skilbeck, Esq., 205, Upper Thames Street, E.C.

H. F. Slattery, Esq., 13, Old Broad Street, E.C.

J. Challenor Smith, Esq , F S.A , Kyngeshene, Guildford.

Percy Smith, Esq., Bardon Lodge, Wimbledon Common, S W.

J. Snelgrove, Esq., Torquay. (Per Mr. Andrew Iredale)

R. V. Somers-Smith, Esq., Grocers' Hall, Princes Street, E.C.

J. T. Spalding, Esq. (Per Messrs. H. Sotheran & Co.)

W. H. Stanger, Esq., M.I.C.E., F.C.S , Broadway, Westminster, S.W.

T. P. Staley, Esq., F.S.A., F.Z.S., 120, Sinclair Road, Kensington.

Richard Stanley, Esq., Durban, Natal.

J. Stedman, Esq., The Bank, Nottingham. (Per Mr. Geo. Evans.)

Mr. B. F. Stevens, 4, Trafalgar Square, W.C.

Mr. Elliot Stock, 62, Paternoster Row, E.C.

W. Teetgen, Esq., Bishopsgate Street Within, E.C. (Per Mr. W. H. Batho.)

W. Curtis Thomson, Esq., F.C.A., 15, George Street, Mansion House, E.C.

H. W. Tinné, Esq., Union Club, Trafalgar Square.

J. Wrench Towse, Esq., Fishmongers' Hall, London Bridge, E.C.

George Turner, Esq., 78, Leadenhall Street, E.C.

Sir John Turney, Alexandra Park, Nottingham (Per Mr Geo Evans.)

Gerárd Van de Linde, Esq., Glebe Knoll, Bromley, Kent.

T. C. Venables, Esq., C.C., 17, Queenhithe, E.C.

Robert Vigers, Esq. (Per Messrs. H. Sotheran & Co.)

James G. Wainwright, Esq., Treasurer's House, St. Thomas's Hospital

Hubert Waldron, Esq., 14, Old Jewry Chambers, E.C.

John Warren, Esq., 95, Lancaster Gate, W. (Per Messrs. Truslove & Hanson.)

E. Waterhouse, Esq., 44, Gresham Street, E.C.

John Watney, Esq., F.S.A., Mercers' Hall, E.C.

W. H. Watson, Esq., 104, Rectory Road, Stoke Newington.

Matthew Righton Webb, Esq., J.P., Kensington Court, W. (Per Mr W. H Batho.)

Isaac Webster, Esq., Rainsford. (Per Messrs. H. Young & Sons.)

Messrs. W. Wesley & Sons, 28, Essex Street, Strand, W.C.

W. H. Westwood, Esq., Oatlands Park, Weybridge, Surrey.

Lynch White, Esq., Homefield, Bickley, Kent.

W. W. White, Esq., Lindum House, Anerley, S E

Sir James Whitehead, Bart., D.L., J.P., F.S.A., Wilmington Manor, near Dartford, Kent.

W. E Whittingham, Esq., Comely Bank, Walthamstow.

Sir F. Wigan, Clare Lawn, East Sheen.

J Wigan, Esq., Cromwell House, Mortlake, Surrey.

H. R. Williams, Esq., J.P., The Priory, Hornsey.

W. Woodward, Esq., A.R.I.B.A., F S I, 13, Southampton Street, Strand, W.C

John W. Woodthorpe, Esq., F.C.A., Oakfield, Park Avenue, Wood Green, N. (Per Messrs. Ellis & Elvey.)

E. M. Wright, Esq., Lancarfe, Albemarle Road, Beckenham

F. Youle, Esq., 2, Vicarage Gardens, Montpellier Road, Brighton

Mr. J. Zaehnsdorf, Cambridge Circus, Shaftesbury Avenue, W C

Sir A. W Zeal, President, Legislative Council of Victoria. (Per Messrs G. Robertson & Co)

SMALL PAPER COPIES.

Aberdeen University Library, Aberdeen. (Per Messrs. D. Wyllie & Son.)

Lord Addington, 24, Prince's Gate, S.W. (Per Messrs. Truslove & Hanson.)

Stanworth Adey, Esq., Liverpool

H. M. Aldridge, Esq., Westover, Bournemouth.

Dr. Allchin, 5, Chandos Street, Cavendish Square, W.

C. H. Allen, Esq., 17, Well Walk, Hampstead, N.W.

Mr. E. G. Allen, 28, Henrietta Street, Covent Garden, W.C (6 copies.)

J. Allen, Esq., Nantes Villa, Caroline Road, Moseley, Birmingham

J. R. Allen, Esq., Mapperley Road, Nottingham (Per Mr. Geo. Evans.)

E. Almack, Esq., 99, Gresham Street, E.C.

T F. Althaus, Esq., 21, Adamson Road, N.W

Eustace Anderson, Esq., 17, Ironmonger Lane, Cheapside, E.C.

John Eustace Anderson, Esq., Acton House, Mortlake.

Mrs. T. R. Armitage, 34, Cambridge Square, Hyde Park, W (Per Messrs. Truslove & Hanson.)

Army and Navy Club, Pall Mall, S W.

Capt. C. E. Arundel, 24, Albion Street, Leeds.

Messrs. Asher & Co , Berlin.

Astor Library, New York. (Per Mr. B. F. Stevens.)

J. J. Baddeley, Esq., Moor Lane, E.C.

Herren J. Baer & Co., Frankfort A M.

R Baker, Esq , Ballingdon, 141, Green Lanes, N.

A. Baldwin, Esq , Wilden House, nr. Stourport.

Messrs. Ball, Baker, Deed, Cornish & Co., 1, Gresham Buildings, E.C.

C. L. Barber, Esq., 7, Portugal Street, W.C.

E. E. Barclay, Esq., 54, Lombard Street, E.C. (Per Mr. Henry Gray.)

Lieut.-Col. J. R. Barnes, The Quinta, Chirk, near Ruabon.

Mr W. H. Batho, 7, Gresham Street, E.C.

Mr. B. T. Batsford, High Holborn, W.C. (2 copies.)

Battersea Public Library, Lavender Hill, S.W. (Lawrence Inkster, Esq, Librarian).

W. W. Baynes, Esq., Pickhurst Wood, Bromley, Kent.

W. Beck, Esq., 3, Glebe Place, Stoke Newington, N.

The Hon. Sir James Bell, Bart., Lord Lieutenant of the County of the City of Glasgow, and Lord Provost of the City (Per F. T. Barrett, Esq.)

P. W. Bell, Esq., 36, Lynette Avenue, Clapham Common.

Rev Canon Benham, 32, Finsbury Square, E.C.

W. Bethell, Esq, Derwent Bank, Malton (Per Messrs. W. H. Smith & Son.)

A. T. Bevan, Esq., Bessels Green, Chevening, Kent.

B. Biggs, Esq., Laurence Pountney Hill, E.C.

A. G. Billinge, Esq., Guardian Assurance Company, 11, Lombard Street, E.C.

Free Public Library, Birkenhead. (William May, Esq., Librarian.)

W. G. Blackie, Esq., Ph.D, LL.D. (Principal of St. Mungo's College). 1, Belhaven Terrace, Glasgow.

Mr. W. Blair, *Free Press*. Tonbridge.

Thomas Blashill, Esq, 29, Tavistock Sq., W.C.

Major-General Bond, Dullerton, Londonderry.

F. Bowker, Esq., Lankhills, Winchester.

Mrs. G. P. Boyce, West House, 35, Glebe Place, Chelsea, S.W. (2 copies.)

Public Library, Bridgeport, Conn. (Per Mr. B. F. Stevens.)

F. M. Bridgewater, Esq, Thirlstaine, 25, Conyers Road, Manor Park, Streatham.

Joseph Bright, Esq., Lincoln Villa, Park, Nottingham. (Per Mr. Geo. Evans.)

J. Potter Briscoe, Esq., Free Public Libraries, Nottingham. (Per Messrs. H. Sotheran & Co.)

J Britten, Esq., 18, West Square, S.E.

Rev. J. M. S. Brooke, Rector of St. Mary Woolnoth, Lombard Street, E.C.

C. Brown, Esq., 40, Carleton Road, Holloway.

D. Buckney, Esq, 51, Highbury Park, N.

Buffalo Library, Buffalo, New York. (Per Mr. B. F. Stevens.)

Mr. T. B. Bumpus, 2, George Yard, Lombard Street, E.C

Henry C. Burdett, Esq, The Lodge, Porchester Square, W.

Miss Burstall, B.A. (Per Messrs. H. Sotheran & Co.)

C. W. Burt, Esq., 25, Aberdare Gardens, Hampstead, N.W. (6 copies.)

A. J. Butler, Esq., 5, Groombridge Rd., Hackney

Mr. E. Capdeville, Madrid. (Per Mr. B. F. Stevens.)

Cardiff Free Libraries (John Ballinger, Esq., Librarian).

J. Carey, Esq., G.P.O. (Per Mr. W. H. Batho.)

E. Carlile, Esq., Kingsbury, Richmond Hill. (Per Mr. Henry Gray.)

The Earl of Carlisle, 1, Palace Green, Kensington, W.

Rev. F. C. Cass, M.A., V.-P. London and Middlesex Archæological Society, 9, Heene Terrace, Worthing

James Castello, Esq., 7, Compayne Gardens, South Hampstead, N.W.

Robert Catchpole, Esq., 5, Ave Maria Lane, E.C.

Arthur Cates, Esq., 12, York Terrace, Regent's Park, N.W.

A. Chancellor, Esq., M.S.A., Norfolk House, Kew Road, Richmond, Surrey.

W. H. Chaplin, Esq., M.A., 13, Pen-y-wern Road, S.W.

G. Chater, Esq, F.R.G.S., 68, Cannon Street, E.C.

Public Library, Chicago, Ill. (Per Mr. B. F. Stevens.)

R. Clark, Esq., 13, Stanhope Road, Walthamstow.

James G. Clarke, Esq., J.P., 13, Fleet Street, E.C.

R. Clarke, Esq, 49, Moorgate Street, E.C.

S. Clarke, Esq., F.S.A., 3, Whitehall Court, S.W.

T. Clarke, Esq., Clarendon House, Brentford

Messrs. Clarke & Hodgson, 3, St. Martin's, Leicester.

C. J. Clay, Esq., M.A., West House, Cambridge.

T E. H. Clay, Esq., Chingford. (Per Mr. W. H. Batho.)

Mr W. E. Clegg, 30, Market Place, Oldham.

Walter H. Clements, Esq., Wood Street, E.C. (Per Mr. W. H. Batho.)

E. Payton Clench, Esq., 16, Hanover Square, W.

C. Cobham, Esq., F.S.I., The Shrubbery, Gravesend. (Per Mr. Henry Gray.)

G. R. Cobham, Esq., F.S.I., 1, Edwin Street, Gravesend.

T. B. Cockerton, Esq., 7, Egerton Place, S.W.

G. E. Cokayne, Esq., F.S.A. (Per Messrs. H. Sotheran & Co.)

Hugh Collingridge, Esq. City Press, Aldersgate Street, E.C. (Per Mr. W. H. Batho.)

E. J. Collins, Esq., Mere Road, Leicester. (Per Mr. W. H. Holyoak)

J. H. Colls, Esq., 5, Coleman Street, E.C.

Mr. J. G. Commin, 230, High Street, Exeter.

E. Conder, Esq., Terry Bank, Kirkby Lonsdale, and New Court, Colwall, Malvern. (Per Mr. Henry Gray.)

E. E. Cook, Esq., Francesco, Upper Norwood.

Frank S. Cook, Esq, 151, Willesden Lane, Brondesbury, N.W.

J. Earley Cook, Esq., Knowle Hill, Cobham, Surrey.

Messrs. Thomas Cook & Sons, Ludgate Circus, E.C.

Mr. A. Cooper, Charing Cross Road, W.C.

F. G. Coote, Esq., Guardian Fire and Life Office, Lombard Street, E.C

J. Corbett, Esq., Impney, Droitwich. (2 copies.)

T. C. S. Corry, Esq., M.D., 1, Glenfield Place, Belfast.

W. Costeker, Esq., 46, Evelyn Gardens, South Kensington.

Dr. Coupland, 16, Queen Anne Street, W. (Per Messrs. Truslove & Hanson.)

T. W. Courtenay, Esq., 33, Orsett Terrace, Hyde Park, N.W.

The Right Hon. Leonard Courtney, M.P., 15, Cheyne Walk, Chelsea.

N. L. Cowan, Esq., Stanley Crescent, W. (Per Mr. G. E. Waters.)

Rev. J. H. Coward, M.A., 86, St. George's Square, Pimlico.

Edwin W. Cox, Esq., Meadowbank, 8, Ellerdale Road, Hampstead, N.W.

G. B. Craig, Esq., Rosehill, Wellington-on-Tyne.

G. P. Craven, Esq , 3, Great St. Helens, E C.

J A. Crawford, Esq., 42, Clarendon Road, Notting Hill, W. (Per Mr. Andrew Elliot.)

Cripplegate Institute, E.C.

Col. Crosse, Shaw Villa, Chorley, Lancashire.

F. Crowley, Esq., Ashdell, Alton, Hants.

W. H. Cullingford, Esq., Kensington, W. (Per Mr. G. E. Waters.)

L. Culver, Esq., 20, Tufnell Park Road, Holloway, N.

J. Curtis, Esq., F.S.A., F.R.S.L., 179, Marylebone Road, N.W.

G. S. Dare, Esq , 5, Creed Lane, E.C.

A. Day, Esq , Clifton Lodge, St. John's Road, Blackheath, S E.

Mr. C. Day, 96, Mount Street, W.

F. De Buriatte, Esq., 169, Fleet Street, E.C.

R. De Coverley, Esq., St. Martin's Court, W.C. (Per Mr. Henry Gray.)

L. De Jonquières, Esq., 29, Lambton Road, Hornsey Rise, N.

Messrs. Deighton, Bell & Co., Cambridge.

Department of Science and Art, S. Kensington

Public Library, Detroit. (Per Mr. B. F. Stevens)

J. Dixon, Esq , Circulation Office, General Post Office, E.C.

F. T. Doe, Esq., 6, Clarence Road, Windsor. (Per Messrs. W. H Smith & Son.)

Jonathan Downes, Esq,, Controller, Returned Letter Office, General Post Office, E.C.

Mr. W. Downing, Chaucer's Head Library, Birmingham.

H. M. Draper, Esq (Per Messrs H Sotheran & Co.)

A. G. Dryhurst, Esq., 6, John Street, Hampstead, N.W

Augustus Durant, Esq , 32, Gresham Street, E.C.

T. G. Dyson, Esq , 1, Rothesay Villas, Windsor.

R. East, Esq., Connemara, Victoria Grove, Southsea.

Mr. Eennug, London, E.C. (Per Mr. W. H. Batho.)

J. Eisenmann, Esq., 41, Tavistock Square, W.C.

Mr. A. Elliot, 17, Princes Street, Edinburgh.

Messrs. Ellis & Elvey, 29, New Bond Street, W.

C. W. Empson, Esq, 11, Palace Court, W. (Per Messrs. Truslove & Hanson.)

James Johnson Evans, Esq, 5, Ave Maria Lane, E.C.

Miss Ewart, 68, Albert Hall Mansions, S.W.

E. A. R. Ewen, Esq., Percy House, West End, Esher.

W. D. Fane, Esq , J.P., Fulbeck Hall, Grantham.

Messrs. Farmer & Sons, Booksellers, 1, Edwardes Terrace, Kensington

Messrs. Farmer & Sons, Booksellers, 36, Kensington High Street, W.

A. J. Fentiman, Esq., 2, Upper East Smithfield, E.C.

Messrs. Field & Sons, F.S.I., 54, Borough High Street, S.E., and 52, Chancery Lane, W.C.

F. Filliter, Esq., St. Martin's House, Wareham, Dorsetshire.

S. T. Fisher, Esq., F.S.A., The Grove, Streatham.

C. H. Fison, Esq, J.P., Ford Place, Thetford, Norfolk. (Per Mr. H. Green.)

F. Fitch, Esq, F.R.G.S., F.R.I., Hadleigh House, 40, Highbury New Park.

Mrs. W. A. Forbes, 36, Kensington Park Gardens.

Edward Foskett, Esq (Per Messrs. H. Sotheran & Co.)

J. Foster, Esq, 21, Creechurch Lane. E.C.

C. G. Fothergill, Esq., 20, Esplanade, Waterloo, Lancashire.

T. Kyffin Freeman, Esq., F.G.S., F.S.S., Master of the Worshipful Company of Shipwrights, Blairgowrie, Whitehall Park, N.

H. Frowde, Esq., Oxford Press, Amen Corner, E.C.

Mr. A. Gait, 13, Market Place, Grimsby. (2 copies.)

S. Gardner, Esq., 13, Copthall Court, E.C.

J. R. Garstin, Esq., J.P., D.L., F.S.A., Braganstown, Castle Bellingham, co. Louth.

J. Gay, Esq., M.R.C.S, F.R.C.P., D.P.H., 119, Upper Richmond Road, Putney.

R. Gibson, Esq., Portobello, N.B. (Per Messrs. T. Murray & Son, Limited.)

Rev. T. W. Gibson, M.A., St. Sepulchre's Vicarage, 5, Charterhouse Square, E.C.

Mr. H. M. Gilbert, 26, Above Bar, Southampton.

Messrs. Gilbert & Field, 67, Moorgate Street, E.C. (3 copies.)

J. T. Glazier, Esq., Mavis Bank, Park Hill Rise, Croydon.

J. Barber Glenn, Esq , 7, Poultry, E.C.

Miss Emily Godber, 10, Third Avenue, Sherwood Rise, Nottingham.

Rev. John H. Godber, M.A., Mount Vernon House, Waverley Street, Nottingham. (Per Mr. Geo. Evans.)

R. Goff, Esq , Summers, Billinghurst, Sussex.

G. T. Goodinge, Esq , Harden Court, Polworth Road, Streatham, S.W.

Rev. A. W. Gough, M.A., St. John's Vicarage, 111, Highbury Quadrant, N.

Henry Gough, Esq. (Per Messrs. H. Sotheran & Co.)

A. W. Gould, Esq., 10, Cleve Road, West Hampstead. (Per Mr. Henry Gray.)

Bailie Robert Graham, D.L., J.P., 108, Eglinton Street, Glasgow. (Per F. T. Barrett, Esq.)

Mr. Henry Gray, 47, Leicester Square, W.C.

Mr. Alderman Green, 193, Upper Thames Street, E.C.

Everard Green, Esq., Rouge Dragon Pursuivant, College of Heralds.

J. Greenfield, Esq., 37, Queen Victoria Street, E.C.

H. J. Griffin, Esq , 10, Corn Exchange Chambers, Seething Lane, E.C.

Robert Griffin, Esq. (Per Messrs. H. Sotheran & Co.)

T. P. Griffin, Esq , F.R.G.S., 3, Philpot Lane, E.C.

F. Griffiths, Esq., 210, Elms Road, Clapham Park.

Haileybury College Library, Haileybury College, Herts.

Prof. John W. Hales, M.A., 1, Oppidans Road, Primrose Hill, N.W. (Per Messrs. Truslove & Hanson.)

A. E. Hall, Esq , Hammet Street, E.C.

W. H. Hall, Esq., Summerleigh, Birkenhead Avenue, Kingston-on-Thames. (Per Mr. Elliot Stock.)

Public Library, Priory Road, Hampstead, N.W.

Alderman Sir Reginald Hanson, Bart., M.P., 47, Botolph Lane, E.C.

G. H. Harmer, Esq., Apsley Villa, Cirencester.

W. Harrison, Esq, 29, Hamsell Street, Jewin Street, E.C.

G. A. Harvey, Esq., 43, Buckland Crescent, Belsize Park, N.W.

Rev. Canon Harvey, M.A., Vicar's Court, Lincoln.

G. C. A. Hasloch, Esq., 5, Red Lion Passage, Fleet Street, E.C.

Dr. Hastings, 566, Mile End Road, E. (Per Messrs. Jones & Evans.)

G. W. L. Hazard, Esq., Dewhurst, Merton Park, Surrey.

Ronald W. Heaton, Esq., M.A., Director, Bishopsgate Institute, E.C.

W. C. Heaton-Armstrong, Esq., 4, Portland Place, W.

Rev. Prebendary Hedgeland, M.A., Penzance.

H. G. Henderson, Esq. (Per Messrs. H. Sotheran & Co.)

R. C. Henderson, Esq., Oakleigh, Brunswick Road, Sutton, Surrey.

Mr. John Heywood, Shoe Lane, E.C. (2 copies.)

J. S. C. Heywood, Esq., 19, Inverness Terrace, W.

C. Hill, Esq., F.S.A., Rockhurst, West Hoathly, Sussex.

T. B. Hill, Esq., 29, Threadneedle Street, E.C.

T. F. Hobson, Esq., M.A., Fountain Court, Temple, E.C.

Mr. F. Hockliffe, Bedford. (2 copies.)

J. S. Hodson, Esq., F.R.S.L., 20, High Holborn, W.C.

Mrs. M. C. Holt, Sutton, Surrey.

W. H. Hopewell, Esq., Quarndon House, Sherwood Rise, Nottingham. (Per Mr. Geo. Evans.)

O. Tatton Hopwood, Esq., Public Library, Southampton.

G. Horlock, Esq., 175, Pelham Street, Mile End New Town.

E. J. Hoskins, Esq., Hammam Chambers, 76, Jermyn Street, S.W.

W. Hounsell, Esq., J.P., Mountfield, Bridport.

W. E. Hughes, Esq., 89, Alexandra Road, South Hampstead.

W. Hughes-Hughes, Esq., 5, Highbury Quadrant, N.

Rev. J. R. Humble, 2, Dean's Yard, Westminster.

W. J. Humfrys, Esq., Hereford. (Per Messrs. Jakeman & Carver.)

Lieut.-Col. Gould Hunter-Weston, F.S.A.. Hunterston, West Kilbride, Ayrshire. (Per Messrs. Mitchell & Hughes.)

Rev. T. S. Hutchinson, M.A., 3, Bridewell Place, E.C.

J. E. Ingpen, Esq., 7, The Hill, Putney.

W. C. Jackson, Esq., 2, Vicarage Gate, Kensington, W.

J. H. Jacoby, Esq., The Ropewalk, No. 32, The Park, Nottingham. (Per Mr. Geo. Evans.)

John Jaques, Esq., Hillside, Duppas Hill, Croydon.

F. L. Jermyn, Esq., The Wilderness, Holly Hill, Hampstead, N.W.

Andrew Johnston, Esq., J.P., M.C.C., 5, Digby Road, Brownswood Park, N.

J. Johnston, Esq., 38, Botolph Lane, E.C.

Edward Jones, Esq., Brooklands, Leyton. (Per Mr. T. B. Bumpus.)

Messrs. Jones & Evans, 77, Queen Street, Cheapside, E.C.

H. E. Kearley, Esq., Woburnhurst Park, Addlestone, Surrey.

Kimberley Public Library. (Per Messrs. H. Sotheran & Co.)

Sir H. Seymour King, K.C.I.E., M.P., 25, Cornwall Gardens, South Kensington

Messrs. H. S. King & Co., 65, Cornhill, E.C.

J. E. S. King, Esq., 16, Finsbury Circus, E.C.

J. B. Knapp, Esq., 6, Sutton Street, Commercial Road, E.

B. Koppel, Esq., 9, Wetherby Gardens, S.W.

The Ladies' Reading Club, Copenhagen.

Major John L'Aker, F.I.L., F.R.G.S., F.H.S., etc., Stourwood House, Southbourne, Hants.

Lt.-Col. Lambert, V.D., F.S.A, 10, 11 and 12, Coventry Street, Piccadilly, London, W. (6 copies.)

J. Lane, Esq., F.C.A., Bannercross, Torquay.

P. H. Lawrence, Esq., 21, Carlyle Mansions, Cheyne Walk, Chelsea.

Free Public Library, Leamington.

Leeds Public Library. (James Yates, Esq., Librarian.)

Rev. H. G. B. Lemoine, High Street, Long Buckby, near Rugby.

J. W. Leng, Esq., The Oaks, Gleneagle Road, Streatham. (Per Mr. Henry Gray.)

Mrs. Lennon, Algoa House, Sherwood, Nottingham. (Per Mr. Geo. Evans.)

F. T. Lewin, Esq., D.L., J.P., Castle Grove, Tuam, Co. Galway.

Library of Congress, Washington, U.S.A. (Per Mr. E. G. Allen.)

Library of Parliament, Ottawa, Canada. (Per Mr. E. G. Allen.)

S. G Lidstone, Esq., 35 and 36, Hosier Lane, West Smithfield, E C.

Liverpool Free Public Library, William Brown Street, Liverpool.

E. O. V. Lloyd, Esq., Berth, Ruthin, and Rhagatt, Corwen, North Wales.

H. C. Lloyd, Esq., J.P., Bryntirion, Exeter.

John Henry Lloyd, Esq., Merton Lane, Highgate.

T. H. Lloyd, Esq., 205, Mary Street, Balsall Heath, Birmingham.

Lewis Loan, Esq., Walhalla, Victoria. (Per Messrs G Robertson & Co.)

H. W. Lock, Esq., 19, Harringay Park, Crouch End.

The London Municipal Society, 16, George Street, Westminster.

Lopping Hall Library, Loughton, Essex.

Messrs. Sampson Low & Co., St. Dunstan's House, Fetter Lane, E.C.

City Library, Lowell, Mass. (Per Mr. B. F Stevens)

Rev. J. H. Lupton, D.D, St. Paul's School, West Kensington. (Per Mr. Henry Gray.)

C. Lynam, Esq., F.S.A , Stoke-on-Trent. (Per Mr. Henry Gray.)

J. J. Macdonald, Esq., Armadale, Howard Road, South Norwood.

R. B. Martin, Esq., M.P., Chislehurst, Kent (Per Messrs. Jones & Evans.)

Mr. W. B Martin, 2, High Street, Sandown, Isle of Wight.

The Supreme Council 33° of the Ancient and Accepted Rite of Masonry. (Per Hugh D. Sandeman, Esq., Grand Secretary General, 33, Golden Square, W.)

J. Douglass Mathews, Esq., F.R.I.B.A., C.C., 11, Dowgate Hill, E.C.

W. Matthew, Esq., Senr., 62, Goldhurst Terrace, South Hampstead

W E Matthiessen, Esq , 1, Furnival's Inn.

W. J. Mercer, Esq., 12, Marine Terrace, Margate.

E. B. Merriman, Esq , 11, Clarges Street, W.

T. J. Merritt, Esq., Chester Lodge, Tyrwhitt Road, S.E.

G. Mills, Esq., 3, Old Jewry, E.C.

Lieut.-Gen. B. Milman, C.B., Queen's House, Tower, E.C.

Rev. Canon W. H. Milman, M.A., Minor Canon of St. Paul's. (Per Mr. Elliot Stock.)

Edward Milner, Esq., Hartford Manor, Northwich. (Per Messrs. Truslove & Hanson)

Mitchell Library, Glasgow.

Mr. Alderman W. Vaughan Morgan, Christ's Hospital, E.C (2 copies.)

John Morison, Esq., 11, Burnbank Gardens, Glasgow

H. C. Morris, Esq., C.C., 2, Walbrook, E.C.

S. D. Morris, Esq., 48, Christchurch Road, Streatham Hill.

Hew Morrison, Esq , Public Library, Edinburgh. (Per Mr. Andrew Elliot.)

C. T. Murdoch, Esq , Buckhurst, Wokingham.

F. J. Murphy, Esq. (Per Mr. W. H. Batho.)

G. Muskett, Esq., 33, Throgmorton Avenue, E.C.

Rev. R. S. Mylne, M.A., B.C.L., F.S.A., Great Amwell, Herts.

E. Montague Nelson, Esq , Hanger Hill House, Ealing, W. (Per Messrs. H. T. Cooke & Son.)

Rev. H. L. Nelthropp, M.A., F.S.A., 124, Church Road, Upper Norwood.

Edward Newbigen, Esq., Stella, Punt Road, Prahran, Victoria. (Per Messrs. G. Robertson & Co.)

Newcastle-on-Tyne Public Libraries (W. J. Haggerston, Esq., Librarian). (Per Mr. Henry Gray.)

Francis Nicholls, Esq., 14, Old Jewry Chambers, E.C.

J. O. Nicholson, Esq., Upton, near Macclesfield.

E. Norman, Esq., 68, Lombard Street, E.C.

T. Notthafft, Esq., St. Petersburgh. (Per Messrs. P. S. King & Son.)

Oldham Free Public Library (T. W. Hand, Esq., Librarian). (Per Messrs. Truslove & Hanson.)

Cary Palmer, Esq., 36, Warkworth Street, Cambridge.

Miss Pattison, 7, Cornwall Terrace, Regent's Park, N.W (Per Messrs. Truslove & Hanson.)

W. Payne, Esq., 350, Kennington Road, S.E.

Sir Henry Peek, Bart., Rousdon, Devon,

Geo. P. A. Pembroke, Esq., 11, King's Bench Walk, Inner Temple, E.C.

People's Palace Library, Mile End Road, E. (2 copies.)

J Perkins, Esq., C.C., F.R G.S , 90, Lower Thames Street, E.C.

W. F. Perowne, Esq., Stock Exchange, E.C.

W. Petley, Esq., Sutton, Surrey.

Henry Pfungst, Esq , F.S.A., 23, Crutched Friars, E.C.

E Phillips, Esq., 14, Ellerker Gardens, Richmond Hill.

H. M. Phillips, Esq., 11, Bolton Street, Piccadilly, W.

Henry Laverock Phillips, Esq , 18, Kennington Park Road, S.E.

W. D. Pink, Esq., Leigh, Lancashire.

G. Pitt, Esq., Grove Road, Sutton, Surrey.

Public Library, Plymouth. (Per W. H. K. Wright, Esq., F.R.H.S)

A. Gordon Pollock, Esq , 95, Cornwall Gardens, South Kensington.

J. Lulham Pound, Esq , 81, Leadenhall Street, E.C.

E. Powell, Esq., Constitutional Club, W.C. (Per Mr. Henry Gray.)

Henry Power, Esq., 37A, Great Cumberland Terrace, Hyde Park, W. (Per Messrs. Truslove & Hanson.)

B. Pratt, Esq., 1, Wood Street, E.C.

Mr. Price, Brixton. (Per Mr. W. H. Batho.)

H. Rokeby Price, Esq , 1, Cowper's Court, Cornhill, E.C.

Sir Walter S. Prideaux, Goldsmiths' Hall, E.C. (Per Mr. W. H. Batho.)

A. Purssell, Esq., 9, Belsize Grove, N.W.

John Putley, Esq., 15, Apsley Road, South Norwood Junction.

Eben. Putnam, Esq. (Per Messrs. H. Sotheran & Co.)

F. W. Quanbrough, Esq , 35, Nicholas Lane, E.C.

Mr. B. Quaritch, Piccadilly, W. (2 copies.)

W. H. Quarrell, Esq. (Per Messrs. H. Sotheran & Co.)

H. G. Quartermain, Esq., The Oriels, Merton Park.

E. T. Ratcliff, Esq., 13, Gray's Inn Square, W.C.

Walter Ravaison, Esq., 31, Greville Road, Kilburn. (Per Messrs. Truslove & Hanson.)

Dr. W. Rawes, St. Luke's Hospital. (Per Mr. W. H. Batho.)

A. Rawlings, Esq., Reading.

H. Rawlings, Esq , Thornhill Park, Sunderland.

Reform Club, Pall Mall, S.W.

John Reid, Esq , Vernon House, 27, Gwendwr Road, West Kensington.

The Religious Tract Society, 56, Paternoster Row, E.C.

Mrs. Rendle, Irvine, Balham Park Road, S.W. (2 copies.)

J. P. Renowden, Esq., 243, Burdett Road, E

Rev Prebendary Bernard Reynolds, M.A., Archbishop's Inspector of Training Colleges, 5, Amen Court, St. Paul's, E C. (Per Mr. Elliot Stock.)

H C Richards, M P , 2, Mitre Court Buildings, Temple.

Mr. W. C. Rigby, 74, King William Street, Adelaide, South Australia.

C. R. Rivington, Esq., F.S.A , 74, Elm Park Gardens, Chelsea.

Herr J G. Robbers, Amsterdam (3 copies.)

W. B. Roberts, Esq., The Manor House, Hampton-on-Thames.

C. E Robinson, Esq , 36, Coleman Street, E.C.

G. H. Robinson, Esq., G.P.O. (Per Mr. W. H. Batho.)

N. Robinson, Esq., 26, Gaisford Street, Kentish Town, N.W.

J. J. Roddy, Esq , 10, Rahere Street, E.C (Per Mr. Henry Gray.)

Mr. Roe, New Broad Street, E.C. (Per Mr. W. H. Batho.)

J. T. Rogers, Esq , River Hill, Sevenoaks.

William Rome, Esq., F.S.A., F.L.S , Oxford Lodge, Wimbledon Common.

W. H. Burch Rosher, Esq., Wigmore, Walmer, Kent. (Per Mr Henry Gray.)

George Routledge, Junr., Esq , Broadway, Ludgate Hill, E.C.

Messrs. George Routledge & Sons, Limited, Broadway, Ludgate Hill, E.C.

A J. Rowson, Esq., 35, Tooley Street, S.E

H. L. Rutter, Esq., 41, Lothbury, E.C.

H Sadler, Esq., Sub-Librarian, Freemasons' Hall, W.C.

His Grace The Duke of St. Albans, Bestwood Lodge, Arnold, Notts.

Public Library, St. Louis, Mo. (Per Mr. B. F. Stevens.)

St. Martin-in-the-Fields Public Library.

St Paul's Cathedral Library.

Miss S. J. Salisbury, Myerscough Hall, Preston, Lancs. (Per Mr. E. C. Vincent.)

James Salmon, Esq., C C , 46, Tower Chambers, Finsbury Pavement, E.C. (3 copies.)

Latimer H. Saunders, Esq., Trevone House, Trevone, near Padstow, Cornwall.

W. Sedgwick Saunders, Esq., M.D., F.S.A., 13, Queen Street, Cheapside, E.C.

J. B. Sedgwick, Esq., J.P , 1, St. Andrew's Place, Regent's Park, W.

J. Seear, Esq., Cheam, Surrey.

P. Selby, Esq., Bank of Australasia, 4, Threadneedle Street, E.C.

Col. T. Davies Sewell, Chamberlain's Court, Guildhall, E.C.

J. E. Shearman, Esq , 10, Idol Lane, E.C. (2 copies.)

Ernest Sheppard, Esq., 81, Elizabeth Street, Eaton Square, S.W. (Per Messrs. Truslove & Hanson.)

Alfred Spencer Silva, Esq. (Per Mr. W. H. Batho.)

H. Simmons, Esq., Seaford, Sussex. (Per Mr. G. E. Waters.)

Messrs. Simpkin, Marshall, Hamilton, Kent & Co., Ltd., Stationers' Hall Court, E.C.

A. F. Simpson, Esq , 14, Putney Hill, S.W.

G. Simpson, Esq., Kingston Villa, Newmarket, Cambs.

Rev. Dr. W. Sparrow Simpson, F S A , 9, Amen Court, E.C.

Sion College, Victoria Embankment, E.C.

Martin S. Skeffington, Esq., 43, Compayne Gardens, West Hampstead, N.W.

W. E. Skeffington, Esq , 24, Sheffield Terrace, Kensington, W.

D W. Skilton, Esq., Hartford, Conn.

Francis A. Smith, Esq., Bank, Nottingham (Per Mr. Geo. Evans.)

G. E. Smith, Esq., 58, Mapperley Road, Nottingham. (Per Mr. Geo Evans.)

Geo. Poole Smith, Esq., Ashurst, Thurlow Park Road, West Dulwich.

Henry Smith, Esq., Sherborne, Thurlow Park Road, West Dulwich.

Rev. S. A. Smith, The Vicarage, Chatteris

Samuel Smith, Esq., Central Free Library, Sheffield

W. J. Smith, Esq., 3, Pancras Lane, E.C.

Mr. W. J Smith, 41, 42 and 43, North Street, Brighton. (2 copies.)

W. M. Smith, Esq., 18, Cedars Road, Clapham Common.

Major F. Smythe, 35, Mattock Lane, Ealing, W.

W. W. Snelling, Esq., 3, Cornwall Road, Stroud Green, N.

Messrs. Swan Sonnenschein & Co , Paternoster Square, E.C.

Messrs. Henry Sotheran & Co , 140, Strand, W.C.

W. J. Soulsby, Esq , C.B., Mansion House, E.C.

Arthur N. Spencer, Esq., 20, Ely Place, E.C. (Per Mr. W. H. Batho.)

S. Spencer, Esq , C C , A.C.I.E., 14, Great St. Thomas Apostle, E.C.

J. F. Spriggs, Esq , 1, De Crespigny Terrace, Denmark Hill, S.E.

W. J. J. Spry, Esq., R.N., F.R G.S., Therapia, St. Andrew's Road, Southsea.

Stadtbibliothek, Frankfort A.M. (Per Herren Jos. Baer & Co)

Richard Stanley, Esq., Durban, Natal.

C. H. Stanton, Esq., 65, Redcliffe Gardens, S.W.

J. W. B. Steggall, Esq., 3, Queen Square, Bloomsbury, W.C.

E. S. Stidolph, Esq., Langdale House, Greenwich.

J. Stiff, Esq., High Street, Lambeth.

J. Russell Stilwell, Esq., Killinghurst, Haslemere.

D Stock, Esq., 171, Queen Victoria Street, E C., and Haslemere, 3, Christchurch Road, Streatham Hill, S.W.

Captain J. H. Story, 17, Bryanston Square, W.

C. Strudwick, Esq., 57, Upper Marylebone Street, W. (Per Messrs. Truslove & Hanson.)

C. W. Sutton, Esq., Free Public Library, Manchester.

W. Sweetland, Esq., 23, Fenchurch Street, E.C. (Per Mr. A. Wilson.)

G. E. Swithinbank, Esq., LL.D., 1, New Square, Lincoln's Inn, W.C.

A. Syer, Esq., 32, Highbury Grove, N.

Mrs. Sophia Sykes, 52, Ropewalk, The Park, Nottingham. (Per Mr. Geo. Evans.)

A. F. Tait, Esq., 34, Woodlands Road, Ilford, Essex.

J. G. Talbot, Esq., 10, Great George Street, S.W.

James Taylor, Esq., J.P., Essendon, Victoria. (Per Messrs. G. Robertson & Co.)

N. Taylor, Esq., J.P., 3, Clarendon Place, Hyde Park Gardens.

H. R. Tedder, Esq., F.S.A., Secretary and Librarian, The Athenæum, Pall Mall, S.W.

C. J. Thomas, Esq., F.I.I., C.C., 202, Bishopsgate Street, E.C.

Y. Thomason, Esq., 9, Observatory Gardens, Kensington.

W. Thompson, Esq., Market Place, Saffron Walden.

Henry E. Thornton, Esq., J.P., Bank, Nottingham. (Per Mr. Geo. Evans.)

Mr. C. J. Thynne, 6, Great Queen Street, W.C. (2 copies.)

J. Tickle, Esq., 63, Cheapside, E.C.

C. J. Todd, Esq., Wentworth House, Richmond, Surrey.

Toronto Public Library. (Per Messrs. H. Sotheran & Co.)

Andrew Tuer, Esq., F.S.A., Leadenhall Press, E.C.

T. Tully, Esq., *The Review*, 20, Bucklersbury, E.C.

R. T. Turnbull, Esq., 5, East India Avenue, E.C.

T. Turpin, Esq., Wellesley Villa, Sutton, Surrey.

W. H. Tylden-Pattenson, Esq., Dashmonden, Biddenden, Staplehurst. (Per Mr. Henry Gray.)

Messrs. Unwin Brothers, 15, Queen Victoria Street, E.C.

E. D. Vaisey, Esq., Stratton Lodge, Hermitage Road, Upper Norwood.

H. W. Vanderpart, Esq., Stockwell Lodge, Worple Road, Wimbledon.

Mr. E. C. Vincent, 7, Paternoster Square, E.C.

W. G. Vizard, Esq., Guardian Fire and Life Assurance Office, Lombard Street, E.C. (2 copies.)

J. F. Wadmore, Esq., Dry Hill, Tonbridge, Kent.

H. Wagner, Esq., M.A., 13, Half Moon Street, Piccadilly, W.

John Waite, Esq., Headingley, Leeds.

N. H. Walker, Esq., 17, Cockspur Street, S.W.

A. Wallis, Esq., Stainforth House, Letherhead.

The Library, Department of State, Washington. (Per Mr. B. F. Stevens.)

William Henry Wayland, Esq., 3, Groombridge Road, South Hackney.

T. Webber, Esq., 136, Stockwell Park Road, S.W.

Isaac Webster, Esq., Rainsford. (Per Messrs. H. Young & Sons.)

Mrs. Welby, Mapperley House, Sherwood, Nottingham. (Per Mr. Geo. Evans.)

Dr. Samuel Welch, Knight's Hill Lodge, West Norwood.

Charles E. Wells, Esq., Highfield, Woodside.

W. Wellsman, Esq., F.R.S.L., 12 & 13, Red Lion Court, Fleet Street, E.C.

H. B. Wheatley, Esq., F.S.A., 2, Oppidans Road, Primrose Hill, N.W.

J. G. White, Esq., Deputy, 91, Cannon Street, E.C.

Whitechapel Public Library (W. E. Williams, Esq., Librarian.) (Per Mr. Henry Gray.)

S. Wightman, Esq., Rosemont, Queen's Road, Leytonstone.

W. D. Wilkes, Esq., 27, New Canal, Salisbury.

H. Wilkins, Esq., 24, Christchurch Road, Streatham, S.W.

H. R. Williams, Esq., J.P., The Priory, Hornsey.

H. J. Wilson, Esq., Osgathorpe Hills, Sheffield.

Rev. W. Windle, M.A., 17, Breakspear Road, Brockley, S.E.

F. J. Winkley, Esq., 4, Southwark Street, S.E.

B. Winstone, Esq., M.D., 53, Russell Square, W.C.

Mrs. G. B. Wollaston, Bishop's Well, Chislehurst.

G. H. Wood, Esq., Williams Deacon, and Manchester and Salford Bank, Manchester.

J. Woodhead, Esq., Longdenholme, Huddersfield.

J. E. Woodley, Esq., 95, Fore Street, E.C.

T. J. Woodrow, Esq., C.C., 22A, Finsbury Circus, E.C.

T. M. Wright, Esq., 10, Billingsgate Market.

W. Wright, Esq., The Grange, Denmark Hill, S.E.

Free Library, Middlegate Street, Great Yarmouth (William Carter, Esq., Librarian).

F. Youle, Esq., 2, Vicarage Gardens, Montpellier Road, Brighton.

F. J. E. Young, Esq., 8, New Street Square, E.C.

Sidney Young, Esq., F.S.A., 15, Alwyne Road, Canonbury, N.

T. Pallister Young, Esq., B.A., LL.B., 29, Mark Lane, E.C.

J. W. Zambra, Esq., 80, Fitzjohn's Avenue, N.W.

Sir W. A. Zeal, President Legislative Council of Victoria. (Per Messrs. G. Robertson & Co.)

BIBLIOLIFE

Old Books Deserve a New Life
www.bibliolife.com

Did you know that you can get most of our titles in our trademark **EasyScript**™ print format? **EasyScript**™ provides readers with a larger than average typeface, for a reading experience that's easier on the eyes.

Did you know that we have an ever-growing collection of books in many languages?

Order online:
www.bibliolife.com/store

Or to exclusively browse our **EasyScript**™ collection:
www.bibliogrande.com

At BiblioLife, we aim to make knowledge more accessible by making thousands of titles available to you – quickly and affordably.

Contact us:
BiblioLife
PO Box 21206
Charleston, SC 29413

Lightning Source UK Ltd.
Milton Keynes UK
UKOW07n0835131015

260439UK00010B/161/P